**Fodor's**

# SCOTLAND

21st Edition

Where to Stay and Eat
for All Budgets

Must-See Sights
and Local Secrets

Ratings You Can Trust

Fodor's Travel Publications   New York, Toronto, London, Sydney, Auckland
**www.fodors.com**

914. 11 / Fodor's

## FODOR'S SCOTLAND

**Editors:** Linda Cabasin, Mark Sullivan

**Editorial Production:** Tom Holton
**Editorial Contributors:** Nick Bruno, Shona Main, Fiona G. Parrott
**Maps & Illustrations:** David Lindroth, *cartographer*; Bob Blake and Rebecca Baer, *map editors*
**Design:** Fabrizio LaRocca, *creative director*; Guido Caroti, Siobhan O'Hare, *art directors*; Tina Malaney, Chie Ushio, Ann McBride, *designers*; Melanie Marin, *senior picture editor*; Moon Sun Kim, *cover designer*
**Cover Photo** (Sweetheart Abbey, Dumfries and Galloway): Wysocki Pawel/Hemis/age fotostock
**Production/Manufacturing:** Angela McLean

## SPECIAL SALES

This book is available at special discounts for bulk purchases for sales promotions or premiums. Special editions, including personalized covers, excerpts of existing books, and corporate imprints, can be created in large quantities for special needs. For more information, write to Special Markets/Premium Sales, 1745 Broadway, MD 6-2, New York, New York 10019, or e-mail specialmarkets@randomhouse.com.

## AN IMPORTANT TIP & AN INVITATION

Although all prices, opening times, and other details in this book are based on information supplied to us at press time, changes occur all the time in the travel world, and Fodor's cannot accept responsibility for facts that become outdated or for inadvertent errors or omissions. So **always confirm information when it matters,** especially if you're making a detour to visit a specific place. Your experiences—positive and negative—matter to us. If we have missed or misstated something, **please write to us.** We follow up on all suggestions. Contact the Scotland editor at editors@fodors.com or c/o Fodor's at 1745 Broadway, New York, NY 10019.

PRINTED IN THE UNITED STATES OF AMERICA
10 9 8 7 6 5 4 3 2 1

# Be a Fodor's Correspondent

Your opinion matters. It matters to us. It matters to your fellow Fodor's travelers, too. And we'd like to hear it. In fact, we need to hear it.

When you share your experiences and opinions, you become an active member of the Fodor's community. That means we'll not only use your feedback to make our books better, but we'll publish your names and comments whenever possible. Throughout our guides, look for "Word of Mouth," excerpts of your unvarnished feedback.

Here's how you can help improve Fodor's for all of us.

Tell us when we're right. We rely on local writers to give you an insider's perspective. But our writers and staff editors—who are the best in the business—depend on you. Your positive feedback is a vote to renew our recommendations for the next edition.

Tell us when we're wrong. We're proud that we update most of our guides every year. But we're not perfect. Things change. Hotels cut services. Museums change hours. Charming cafés lose charm. If our writer didn't quite capture the essence of a place, tell us how you'd do it differently. If any of our descriptions are inaccurate or inadequate, we'll incorporate your changes in the next edition and will correct factual errors at fodors.com immediately.

Tell us what to include. You probably have had fantastic travel experiences that aren't yet in Fodor's. Why not share them with a community of like-minded travelers? Maybe you chanced upon a beach or bistro or B&B that you don't want to keep to yourself. Tell us why we should include it. And share your discoveries and experiences with everyone directly at fodors.com. Your input may lead us to add a new listing or highlight a place we cover with a "Highly Recommended" star or with our highest rating, "Fodor's Choice."

Give us your opinion instantly at our feedback center at www.fodors.com/feedback. You may also e-mail editors@fodors.com with the subject line "Scotland Editor." Or send your nominations, comments, and complaints by mail to Scotland Editor, Fodor's, 1745 Broadway, New York, NY 10019.

You and travelers like you are the heart of the Fodor's community. Make our community richer by sharing your experiences. Be a Fodor's correspondent.

Happy Traveling!

Tim Jarrell, Publisher

# CONTENTS

# CONTENTS

# ABOUT THIS BOOK

## Our Ratings

Sometimes you find terrific travel experiences and sometimes they just find you. But usually the burden is on you to select. That's where our ratings come in.

As travelers we've all discovered a place so wonderful that its worthiness is obvious. And sometimes that place is so unique that superlatives don't do it justice. These sights, properties, and experiences get our highest rating, **Fodor's Choice** indicated by orange stars throughout this book. Black stars highlight sights and properties we deem **Highly Recommended** places that our writers, editors, and readers praise again and again for consistency and excellence.

By default, there's another category: any place we include in this book is by definition worth your time, unless we say otherwise. And we will.

Disagree with any of our choices? Care to nominate a place or suggest that we rate one more highly? Visit our feedback center at www.fodors.com/feedback.

## Budget Well

Hotel and restaurant price categories from £ to £££££ are defined in the opening pages of each chapter or in Where to Stay and Where to Eat sections in city chapters. For attractions, we always give standard adult admission fees; reductions are usually available for children, students, and senior citizens. Want to pay with plastic? **AE, DC, MC, V** following restaurant and hotel listings indicate whether American Express, Diner's Club, MasterCard, and Visa are accepted.

## Restaurants

Unless we state otherwise, restaurants are open for lunch and dinner daily. We mention dress only when there's a specific requirement and reservations only when they're essential or not accepted—it's always best to book ahead.

## Hotels

Hotels have private bath, phone, TV, and air-conditioning and operate on the European Plan (aka EP, meaning without meals), unless we specify that they use the Continental Plan (CP, with a continental breakfast), Breakfast Plan (BP, with a full breakfast), or Modified American Plan (MAP, with breakfast and dinner). We always list facilities but not whether you'll be charged an extra fee to use them.

### Many Listings

| | |
|---|---|
| ★ | Fodor's Choice |
| ★ | Highly recommended |
| ⌧ | Physical address |
| ✛ | Directions |
| ⌂ | Mailing address |
| ☎ | Telephone |
| 🖷 | Fax |
| ⊕ | On the Web |
| ✇ | E-mail |
| 🏷 | Admission fee |
| ☉ | Open/closed times |
| Ⓜ | Metro stations |
| 🖃 | Credit cards |

### Hotels & Restaurants

| | |
|---|---|
| ☍ | Hotel |
| ↳ | Number of rooms |
| ♨ | Facilities |
| ¶⊖¶ | Meal plans |
| ✗ | Restaurant |
| ⌕ | Reservations |
| ⊠ | Smoking |
| ℘ | BYOB |
| ✗☍ | Hotel with restaurant that warrants a visit |

### Outdoors

| | |
|---|---|
| ⚐ | Golf |
| ⛺ | Camping |

### Other

| | |
|---|---|
| ℭ | Family-friendly |
| ⇨ | See also |
| ⌧ | Branch address |
| ☞ | Take note |

# WHAT'S WHERE

| | |
|---|---|
| **EDINBURGH & THE LOTHIANS**  | Scotland's capital captivates many people at first sight, with Edinburgh Castle looming from the crags of an ancient volcano, and Georgian and Victorian architecture forming a skyline that looks locked in the past. But this is a modern, cosmopolitan city, and the new Scottish Parliament Building says so loud and clear. Edinburgh should not be missed: iconic sights (even more than Glasgow, its rival 50 mi to the west, offers), the ancient Old Town and 18th-century New Town, and first-class restaurants. However, as with any major city there are tradeoffs: lodging, food, and pub prices are high; there's a lot of traffic and too many tourists, particularly in August during the Edinburgh International Festival. Avoid the throngs and head for the museums (the Royal Museum, Museum of Scotland, and National Gallery of Scotland are impressive), the Royal Botanical Gardens, or Arthur's Seat, the small mountain with spectacular views. These free sites are all within the city center or within walking distance of it. Another option for escaping the crowds is to leave the city altogether. The Lothians—West Lothian, East Lothian, and Midlothian—beckon with quick getaways to coastal towns, quiet beaches, ancient chapels (including Rosslyn Chapel, mentioned in *The Da Vinci Code*) and castles. |
| **GLASGOW**  | In Gaelic, Glasgow means "the Dear Green Place," a fitting title for the city with more parks per square mile than any other in Europe. The city has changed dramatically over the years, from prosperous Victorian hub to world shipbuilding center to depressed urban area. Today a reenergized Glasgow is thriving, famous for its passion for football (soccer) and fabulous shops that beat those in Edinburgh hands-down. Its distinguished university is more than 500 years old and worth a visit, as is the Kelvingrove Art Gallery and Kelvingrove Park. Glasgow is proud of its buildings by two great homegrown architects, Charles Rennie Mackintosh (Arts and Crafts) and Alexander Thomson (Victorian). Cafés and pubs, some with live music, are a refuge for those interested in more local, thirst-quenching activities. Most impressive, though, are the Glaswegians, so genuine that their warmth and lyrical way of speech stay with you long after you leave Scotland. Yes, the city has some rough patches; drugs and poverty tie areas like the Gorbals and East End together, but major cleanup efforts have been made. True, you're guaranteed rain, but you don't have to worry about armies of tourists in Scotland's largest and friendliest city. |

| | |
|---|---|
| **THE BORDERS & THE SOUTHWEST**<br> | Gateway to Scotland from England, the Borders and Southwest are rustic; not a lot happens here, and they aren't the top tourist destinations—but that's not necessarily a bad thing. The Borders, site of past conflict between Scotland and England, is known for being the home of Sir Walter Scott, the 19th-century author of *Ivanhoe*. It's also Scotland's main woolen-goods district; if you want a warm sweater or scarf, this is the place. The countryside is made up of great rolling fields, wooded river valleys, and farmland running south from Lothian to England. People interested in walking, stately homes, and magnificent, ruined abbeys tend to spend their vacations here. The Southwest, or Dumfries and Galloway region, is perfect for scenic drives and castles. It's on the shores of the Solway Firth where palm trees and other exotic fauna thrive due to the North Atlantic Drift (Scotland's Gulf Stream). Inland the landscape transforms to a darker scene, with moorlands blanketed in thick forests. |
| **FIFE & ANGUS**<br> | The "kingdom" of Fife, northeast of Edinburgh, is considered the sunniest and driest part of Scotland. Plenty of sandy beaches, appealing fishing villages, and stone cottages are scattered along narrow, twisting roads. Also here is St. Andrews, the exclusive town that is not only a famous golf center but also home to the oldest university in the country. It attracts plenty of students and tourists in search of something more than just the Edinburgh–Glasgow experience. Several dozen golf courses grace Fife, many of them seaside links. Farther north, in Angus, is the reviving city of Dundee, not a major tourist destination—though the Dundee Contemporary Arts center is renowned for its performances. Another worthwhile site in Angus is Glamis Castle, the magnificent landmark that connects more than 1,000 years of British royalty and is the legendary setting of Shakespeare's *Macbeth*. |
| **THE CENTRAL HIGHLANDS**<br> | A favorite vacation destination for Edinburghers and Glaswegians because it's an easy trip north from those cities, this area encompasses some of Scotland's most beautiful terrain. Perth and Stirling are the main metropolitan hubs. Perth has a prominent past with attractions to match, including Scone Palace, although sights are spread out and can be difficult to get to. On the other hand, many attractions in Stirling are within walking distance of Stirling Castle, the landmark with epic views that stretch from coast to coast. Beyond the built-up areas are the Central Highlands themselves: rugged, |

# WHAT'S WHERE

dark landscapes broken up by lochs and fields. Here you can find Loch Lomond and the Trossachs, Scotland's first national park and one of Wordsworth's favorite places, enticing nature enthusiasts, hikers, and picnickers when the weather permits. The winding banks of Loch Lomond can be easily followed on foot, by car, or even by boat.

**ABERDEEN & THE NORTHEAST**

Its predominantly granite buildings give the port city of Aberdeen a silvery tint in the sunshine but an inescapable gray hue in the rain. The region's primary industry, North Sea oil, has created an international mix of city dwellers and an excellent restaurant scene here. Malt-whisky buffs use Aberdeen as a base for visiting the area south of Elgin and Banff, which has Scotland's greatest concentration of malt-whisky distilleries; this is the popular Malt Whisky Trail. The city is also a good starting point for touring Royal Deeside, where the Castle Trail links 11 of the more notable landmarks. The Grampian Mountains and the Cairngorms (site of Britain's largest national park) rise majestically to the west, covered in heather and forest groves, with sharp granite peaks and deep glens; both are ideal terrain for hill walking and skiing.

**ARGYLL & THE ISLES**

Although this fractured southwestern coastline is one of Scotland's less-visited areas, it has an excellent selection of gardens, religious sites, and even distilleries to choose from. To experience the region in full, you need to catch a ferry to Mull and the southern isles; the adorable town of Oban, a great place for a fish-and-chips supper, is where you catch these ferries. If you like whisky, go to Islay; if it's mountains you're after, then Jura is a better bet; if the most important Christian site in the country strikes a chord, make Iona your destination. If you want to see all of Scotland's diversity shrunk down to a smaller, more manageable size, Arran is the place to go. The area does catch rain from Atlantic weather systems, but its beauty makes the wetness worthwhile.

**AROUND THE GREAT GLEN**

An awe-inspiring valley laced with rivers and streams defines this part of rural Scotland. The glen is ringed by Scotland's tallest mountains; it also contains, depending on what you believe, the monster Nessie, who resides in Loch Ness. Nearby Inverness—a town useful mostly as a base for exploring the area—encourages the hype by selling Nessie paraphernalia. There are prettier lochs in Scotland, but Loch Ness draws the crowds. Mountaineers and naturalists are drawn to the

Great Glen because of Ben Nevis, Britain's tallest mountain. It's an astonishing sight and deserves some time, even if you don't plan on climbing it. At its base is Fort William, a town worth stopping in only for supplies. Those interested in Scottish history should head to haunting Glencoe, where in 1692 MacDonald clan members were shamelessly massacred by the Campbell clan, or to Culloden, where Bonnie Prince Charlie's forces were destroyed in 1746.

## THE NORTHERN HIGHLANDS & THE WESTERN ISLES

To many Scots, the Northern Highlands are the real Scotland—the land of the lore of clans, big moody skies, and wild rolling moors. The far northern part of the country is linked together by narrow roads, tranquility, and dramatic, changing landscapes. It's also home to one of Scotland's most picturesque castles, Eilean Donan, which you pass on the way to the Isle of Skye. Don't let the tour buses stop you; the castle deserves a visit. Skye is ideal for moderate walks and has remote beaches and misty mountains. In its coastal villages you'll still hear Gaelic (Scotland's native language). The stark, remote Outer Hebrides, or Western Isles, offer the ultimate peace-and-quiet experience. Ruined forts and chapels are the main attractions, and Harris tweed is on sale in just about every shop. This is possibly the most rugged part of Scotland, with frequent wind and rain, so pack your bag accordingly.

## ORKNEY & SHETLAND

Way up north, the days are incredibly long in summer and equally short in winter. If you want to feel as if you've reached the end of the world, go to Orkney and Shetland. These isles (200 in all, many uninhabited) require tenacity in getting to; once here, you may marvel at the abundance of prehistoric sites. Orkney has the greatest concentration in Scotland, including well-preserved standing circles, *borchs* (circular towers), and tombs. Orkney is also a destination for sea fishing and loch angling. The Shetland isles, with their barren moors and vertical cliffs, are well-known for seabirds and diving opportunities; oil money has brought prosperity here. Both Orkney and Shetland host numerous festivals throughout the year, making this region popular with music fans and people who just want to get away.

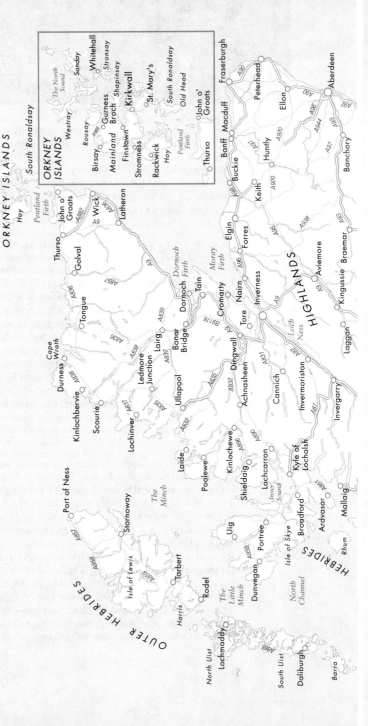

Scotland

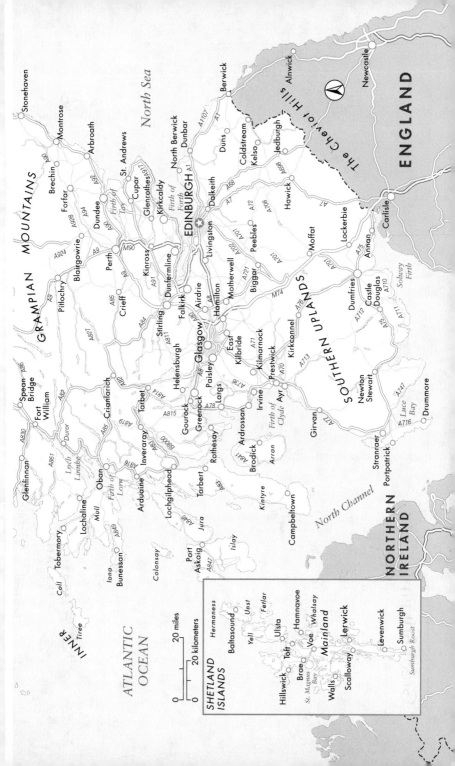

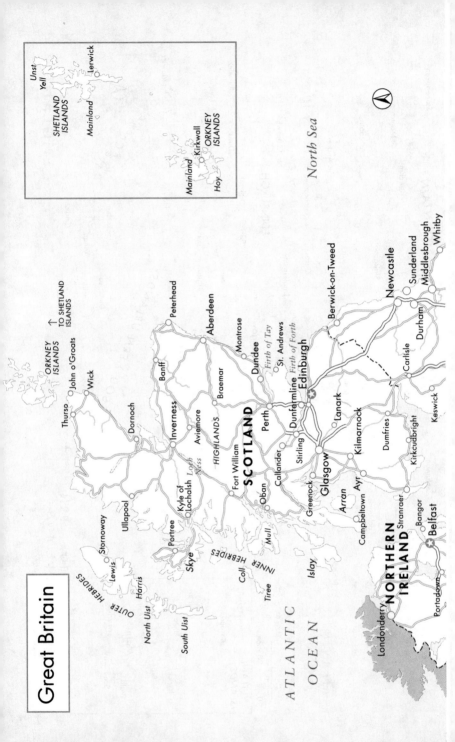

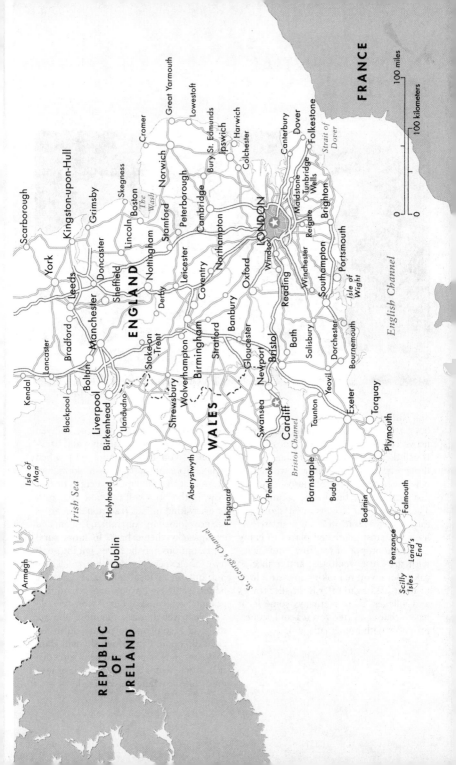

# QUINTESSENTIAL SCOTLAND

### The Kettle's On

Scots are always eager to stop for a cup of tea and catch up with the local gossip. Tea is still the most popular refreshment, but the spread of café culture has introduced a new generation of coffeehouses—and not just in the cities but in the countryside. The Willow Tea Rooms in Glasgow and the Balmoral Hotel in Edinburgh are perhaps the most gentrified places to enjoy an afternoon pot of tea, tiny sandwiches with the crusts removed, and a slice of cake. But if you're looking to taste a little of what life has to offer in smaller towns and villages, there is always some local haven that can offer you tea and scones, probably with homemade jam.

### It's Your Round

Going to the pub is a pastime enjoyed by men and women of all ages and backgrounds; you can find out why when you explore a few. The no-smoking laws mean that the pub environment is fresher now. In the cities you can take your pick of every kind of bar; traditional favorites are now joined by Australian, Cuban, and even wacky theme bars. In more rural areas, options may be fewer, but the quality of the experience, which may include pub quizzes or local folk bands, may be better. There isn't a pub in Scotland that doesn't sell whisky, but if you seek to sample a wee dram of the more obscure malts, ask someone to point you in the right direction. Fans of whisky will want to go beyond the pubs and head for a distillery or two for a tour and a tasting—on or off the Malt Whisky Trail.

If you want to get a sense of contemporary Scottish culture, and indulge in some of its pleasures, start by familiarizing yourself with the rituals of daily life. These are a few highlights—things you can take part in with relative ease.

## It's Only a Game

Listening to Scots talk about football—please don't call it soccer—gives a fine insight into the national temperament. "Win, lose, or draw, you go home to your bed just the same," sang Scottish singer Michael Marra, and the Scots will try to make you believe it's only a game. But go to a match or be in a pub when a game is on the TV, and you can see plenty of grown men (and women) having a vigorous emotional workout. The main league, the Scottish Premiership, is dominated by the Rangers and Celtics. However, other teams, such as Aberdeen, delight in slaying, these giants. The state of the national team is debated everywhere from newspaper shops to the Scottish Parliament, but although Scotland loses out in collecting trophies, the Tartan Army (those who loyally follow the national team) are consistently applauded as the most agreeable and entertaining traveling fans.

## Who Ate All the Pies?

Although the treats may not perhaps be as elegant as those produced in an Italian *panificio* or a French patisserie, Scots love their bakeries. Go beyond shortbread and oatcakes and sample local favorites during your travels. From the Aberdeen buttery (a melting, salty *bap*, or soft morning roll) to the Selkirk bannock (a sweet, raisin-strewn scone, perfect when buttered and served with tea) to Forfar bridies (an Angus specialty, similar to a meat pasty), regional specialties are abundant. Most areas have their own interpretations of the popular Scotch pie (with beef mince, mutton, bean, and macaroni among the varieties available). There's even a Scotch Pie Championship each year. The rise of large supermarkets is putting many establishments out of business, but it's worth seeking out an independent bakery and trying the delicacies.

# IF YOU LIKE

## Castles

Whether a jumble of stones atop a hill, or still in private ownership, or under the care of a preservation society—such as Historic Scotland (a government agency) or the National Trust for Scotland (a private, charitable organization)—Scotland's castles powerfully demonstrate the country's lavish past and its once-uneasy relationship with its southern neighbor. Scotland has every type of castle imaginable, from triangular 13th-century fortresses complete with gory tales, such as **Caerlaverock**, to picturesque stereotypes like **Eilean Donan**, stuffed with artifacts and surrounded by lochs. Royal Deeside, west of Aberdeen, has an eclectic group strung together along a series of roadways called the **Castle Trail**. Here you can find Drum, Crathes, Balmoral, Braemar, Corgarff, Glenbuchat, Kildrummy, and Dunnottar, all within a 100-mi radius. **Glamis Castle**, northeast of Dundee, is one of Scotland's most beautiful castles, connecting Britain's royalty from Macbeth to the late Princess Margaret. Farther south, in the Borders, are several stunning castles—all good representations of medieval architecture and lifestyle. Among these, the **Hermitage Castle**, where Mary, Queen of Scots, traveled to visit her lover, the earl of Bothwell, is dark and foreboding; **Floors Castle** is extraordinary, with grand turrets and towers; and **Neidpath Castle** has dungeons carved out of solid rock. Keep in mind that Scottish castles are not restricted to country roads or seaside cliffs; most are, however, on the mainland. If time permits you to visit only urban areas, there are castles here, too. Majestic **Edinburgh Castle** has dramatic views of Fife, and **Stirling Castle** is a must for anyone interested in Scottish history.

## Mountains & Lochs

For the snowcapped mountains and glassy lochs (lakes) for which Scotland is famous, you have to leave the south and the cities behind you—though some Lowland lakes are beautiful. Among these is **Loch Lomond**, 20 minutes from Glasgow, which has shimmering shores and plenty of water-sport options. **Loch Leven**, in Fife, is famed for its bird life and fighting trout. It was also where Mary, Queen of Scots, signed the deed of abdication in her island prison. **Loch Katrine**, in the heart of the Trossachs in the Central Highlands, was the setting of Walter Scott's narrative poem *The Lady of the Lake*. In summer you can take the steamer *SS Sir Walter Scott* across it. From the parking lot of **Loch Achray** you begin the climb to **Ben An**, the sheer-faced mountain with fabulous views of the Trossachs. Half of Scotland's munros (highest mountains) are in **Cairngorms National Park**, east of the Great Glen, an excellent place for hiking, skiing, and reindeer sightings. In the Great Glen, monumental **Ben Nevis** hovers over Fort William; no matter when you visit, you'll probably see snow on the summit plateau. **Glen Torridon**, east of Shieldaig in the Northern Highlands, has the finest mountain scenery in the country. **Loch Maree**, also in the Northern Highlands and one of Scotland's most scenic lochs, is framed by Scots pines and Slioch Mountain. If birds are your thing, **Loch Gruinart**, on Islay, is the winter nesting ground for thousands of white-fronted and barnacle geese. Wherever you go in Scotland, nature is at your fingertips.

## Fabulous Festivals

The **Edinburgh International Festival** is the spectacular flagship of Scotland's cultural events, with everything from orchestral music to comedy skits. Indeed, the capital suffers from festival overkill in late August, partly because of the size of the **Fringe**, the official festival's less formal, rowdier offshoot. This huge grab bag of performances spreads out onto the streets of Edinburgh. Adding to the August pileup are the **Military Tattoo, International Film Festival, Book Festival,** and **International Jazz Festival.** But if crowds and famous faces aren't your thing, plenty of other (more low-key) festivals take place year-round, predominantly in and around the major cities and islands. In the last two weeks of January Glasgow presents **Celtic Connections,** during which musicians from all over the world gather to play Celtic-inspired music. During the first two weeks of November Glasgow also hosts **Glasgay,** a cultural festival focusing on gay and lesbian themes. Another popular festival is **Up Helly Aa,** held in Shetland at the end of January; food, drink, and dressing up come to a spectacular end with the burning of a replica Viking ship. April's **Shetland Folk Festival** and October's **Shetland Accordion and Fiddle Festival** draw large numbers of visitors at times of year when the weather is a bit more temperate. Orkney hosts music festivals in spring and summer, including the **St. Magnus Festival** in June, the **Jazz Festival** in April, and the **Folk Festival** in May. Cultural festivals thrive in Scotland; no matter where you are, you can probably find one to suit you.

## Perfect Links

Some of the most scenic, established, and challenging courses in the world are in Scotland, the home of 550 golf courses and, arguably, the game itself. A few clubs are exclusive, but most are affordable and accessible, even to beginners; the cost of a round can go from £30 on a good course to well over £100. Many golf pilgrimages to Scotland begin with a visit to the legendary **St. Andrews,** now so popular that reservations for summer play are required a year in advance. **Nairn,** on the Moray Coast, is the regular home of Scotland's Northern Open and has breathtaking views across the Moray Firth; **Rosemount, Blairgowrie Golf Club,** in Perthshire, is laid out on rolling land with wide fairways and large greens; and **Western Gailies,** in Ayrshire, is the finest natural links course in the country. But don't limit yourself to the expensive, well-known greens. Off the beaten track are some good-value classic courses with striking views, particularly in the Stewartry, at **Powfoot** and **Southerness.** The Northeast has more than 50 courses, many with exceptional reputations, such as the reasonably priced **Boat of Garten,** at Speyside, Scotland's greatest "undiscovered" course. Western Scotland has nearly two dozen golf courses; **Machrihanish,** near Campbeltown, and **Machrie,** on Islay, are the most popular. Keep in mind that attractive courses can be found in or near the urban centers; there are 30 in or close to Edinburgh and 7 courses in Glasgow. Just make reservations in advance, and you won't be disappointed.

# IF YOU LIKE

## Island Havens

A remote, windswept world of white-sand beaches, forgotten castles, and crisp, clear rivers awaits you in the Scottish isles. Out of the hundreds of isles (islands), only a handful are actually inhabited, and here ancient culture and tradition remain alive and well. Each island has its own distinct fingerprint; getting to some might be awkward and costly, but the time and expense are worth your while. Near Glasgow, the **Isle of Bute** is one of the more affordable and accessible isles, drawing celebrities to its estates for lavish weddings and Glaswegians to its rocky shores for summer holidays. Like Bute, **Arran** is not too costly and mirrors the mainland, with activities from golf to hiking, but on a smaller, more intimate scale. **Islay**, on the Kintyre Peninsula, is where you go to watch rare birds, buy woolen goods, and taste the smoothest malt whiskies. Spiritual and spectacular **Iona** was the burial place of Scottish kings until the 11th century. Smaller isles like Rum, Eigg, Muck, and Canna are isolated and atmospheric but offer nothing in the way of lodgings or eateries. Although more populated and touristy, **Skye**, with its legends, hazy mountains, hidden beaches, and glens, is unsurpassed. It also has good hotels, B&Bs, and restaurants. **Orkney** and **Shetland**, two remote island groups collectively known as the Northern Isles, have a Scandinavian heritage that adds color to their severe landscapes. If you're after remarkable prehistoric artifacts and festivals, go to Orkney; if you prefer something with more sophistication, Shetland is your isle.

## Hiking

People who have hiked in Scotland often return again and again to explore the country's rural landscape of loch-dotted glens and forested hills. From Edinburgh's **Arthur's Seat** to **Ben Nevis**, Britain's tallest peak, the country holds unsurpassed hiking possibilities, no matter what your ambitions. The best time for hiking is from May to September, the same time the country's native insect, the midge, makes an unfavorable appearance (no amount of repellent will deter it). More moderate hikes can be found in places like **Glen Nevis**, with footpaths leading past waterfalls, croft ruins, and forested gorges. Even parts of the **Southern Upland Way**, the famous 212-mi coast-to-coast journey from Portpatrick to Cockburnspath, can be comfortably walked in sections. A local's favorite, the **West Highland Way**, from Milngavie to Fort William, is a well-marked 95-mi trek with various hotels to stay in along the way. Other popular Highland trails are on **Ben Lawers, Ben Ledi**, and **Ben Lomond**. Scotland has two national parks, **Loch Lomond and the Trossachs National Park** in the Central Highlands, and **Cairngorms National Park** east of the Great Glen. Some park trails are unmarked, so check with area tourist information centers before you set out. In the **Great Glen** area, some of the best routes can be found near **Glen Nevis, Glencoe**, and on the mighty **Ben Nevis**. As with all outdoor activities, be sure you're properly equipped with appropriate shoes and clothing. Keep in mind that weather conditions can and do change rapidly in the Scottish hills, even at low altitude.

## Megalithic Monuments

Scattered throughout the Scottish landscape are prehistoric standing stones, stone circles, tombs, and even stone houses that provide a tantalizing glimpse into the country's remarkable past and people. If you're interested in ancient remains, leave the mainland and head for the isles, where the most impressive and important are found. Arran's **Machrie Moor Stone Circles,** a mixture of granite boulders and tall redsandstone circles, are in the middle of an isolated moor 11 mi north of Lagg. **Calanais Standing Stones,** on the Isle of Lewis in the Outer Hebrides, are reminiscent of those at Stonehenge; it's believed they were used in astronomical observations. Tiny Colonsay in the western isles has the standing stones at Kilchattan Farm, called **Fingal's Limpet Hammers** after Fingal MacCoul, the larger-than-life warrior in Celtic mythology. Orkney, however, has the greatest concentration of these types of prehistoric structures. Between Loch Harray and Loch Stennes is the **Ring of Brogar,** a magnificent circle made up of 36 Neolithic stones. **Maes Howe** (circa 2,500 BC) is an enormous burial mound measuring 115 feet in diameter, with an imposing burial chamber. The Vikings raided the site in the 12th century and Norse crusaders used the area for shelter; you can still see the runic inscriptions they left behind. Orkney's Neolithic village of **Skara Brae,** first occupied around 3,000 BC, was well preserved in sand until it was discovered in 1850. Here the houses are joined by covered passages, with stone beds, fireplaces, and cupboards—more intriguing remnants from the distant past.

## Retail Therapy

No longer is Scotland simply the land of whisky and wool. International names from Louis Vuitton to Versace have all set up shop here, and top British department stores like John Lewis, Harvey Nichols, and Debenhams are peppered throughout the major cities. Prices aren't cheap at these locations, but quality is first class and products are fashionable and longlasting. **Glasgow** claims the best shopping in Britain, outside of London's Oxford Street; **Buchanan Street** is the best place to start. **Edinburgh** is popular for crystal and clusters of antique shops, especially on St. Stephen and Dundas streets. Just outside of **Perth** is Caithness Glass, a factory renowned for its attractive glassware. **Aberdeen** and the **Northeast** are good places for trying and buying malt whisky. If your shopping agenda favors the traditional, head to the islands of **Shetland, Skye,** and **Arran** for tweeds, knitwear, woolens (including knits), tartan blankets, Celtic silver, and pebble jewelry; these items can often be found in urban specialty shops as well. The **Scottish Highlands** bristle with old bothies (farm buildings) that have been turned into small crafts workshops selling attractive handmade pottery and wood, leather, and glass items. Rich chocolates (often with whisky fillings), marmalades, heather honeys, and the traditional petticoat-tail shortbread are tasty and easily portable gifts. So, too, are the boiled sweets (hard candies) in jars from particular localities—**Berwick** cockles, **Jethart** snails, **Edinburgh** rock, and more. **Dundee** cake, a rich fruit mixture with almonds on top, is among the other prize edibles on sale in the city they're named after.

# GREAT ITINERARY

## BEAUTIFUL SCOTLAND: CASTLES, LOCHS, GOLF &WHISKY
10 days
Edinburgh

**Days 1 and 2.** The capital of Scotland is loaded with iconic sights in its Old Town and New Town. Visit Edinburgh Castle and the National Gallery of Scotland, and take tours of the Museum of Scotland and the modern Scottish Parliament building. Walk along Old Town's Royal Mile and New Town's Princes Street for some fresh air and retail therapy. When the sun goes down, feast on the food of your choice and seek out a traditional pub with live music that will keep your toes tapping.

**Logistics:** Fly into Edinburgh Airport if you're flying via London and take a taxi or bus to the city center. If you're flying directly into Glasgow from overseas, make your way from Glasgow Airport to Queen Street Station (if traveling by train) or Buchanan Bus Station (if traveling by bus) via taxi or bus. It takes an hour to travel from Glasgow to Edinburgh by car or bus, about 45 minutes by train. Once in the city, explore by foot, public transportation, or taxi. There's no need to rent a car.

### Stirling to St. Andrews
**Day 3.** Rent a car in Edinburgh and drive to the historic city of Stirling. Spend the day visiting Stirling Castle and the National Wallace Monument. If you're eager to tour a distillery, make time for a stop at the Famous Grouse Experience in Crieff. Then drive to the legendary seaside town of St. Andrews, famous for golf. Have dinner at one of the city's exceptional seafood restaurants.

**Logistics:** Leave Edinburgh after 9 AM to miss the worst rush-hour traffic. It's 35 mi or a one-hour drive to Stirling from Edinburgh, and 50 mi and 90 minutes from Stirling to St. Andrews. You can easily take a train or bus to these destinations.

### St. Andrews to Inverness
**Day 4.** Spend the morning exploring St. Andrews, known for its castle and the country's oldest university as well as its famous golf courses. The British Golf Museum is here, too. If you've booked well in advance (the time varies by season), play a round of golf. After lunch, drive to Inverness. Along the way, stretch your legs at one of Scotland's notable sights, Blair Castle (just off the A9 and 10 mi north of Pitlochry), a turreted white treasure with a war-torn past. Head to Inverness in the Highlands for the night.

**Logistics:** It's 150 mi from St. Andrews to Inverness via the A9, a drive that will take 3½ hours. This is a scenic journey, so do stop along the way. You can also take a train or bus.

### Around Inverness & Castle Country
**Day 5.** Use Inverness as a base for exploring the Northeast, a region known for tempting castles and whisky distilleries. Don't visit too many or your day may become a forced march; two to three castles or distilleries is a good number. Some of the region's most interesting castles are Kildrummy, a 13th-century architectural masterpiece, and Balmoral, popular because of its royal connection to Queen Elizabeth. Castle Fraser has beautiful gardens. End your day with a visit to Culloden Moor, where Bonnie Prince Charlie's forces were destroyed by the duke of Cumberland's army. Keep Inverness as your base because

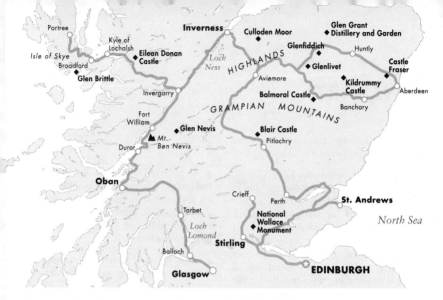

of the number of restaurants and entertainment venues.

**Alternatives:** Prefer whisky to castles? Explore the Malt Whisky Trail in Speyside, near Inverness. Glenfiddich, Glenlivet, and Glen Grant are good choices. Another option for the day is to visit Loch Ness, though it's not one of Scotland's prettiest lakes; still, perhaps you'll spot Nessie. It's just a 20-minute drive from Inverness.

**Logistics:** A car is best for this part of your journey. Rent one in Inverness or sign up for an organized tour, as public transportation is not viable. Castles are open seasonally; check in advance. It's about 2 hours from Inverness to Kildrummy. Some sample distances are 30 mi (1 hour) from Balmoral Castle to Kildrummy Castle; 20 mi (30 minutes) from Kildrummy Castle to Castle Fraser; and Castle Fraser to Balmoral, 40 mi (90 minutes). The distilleries are about 90 minutes from Inverness. Some distances between distilleries are 18 mi (50 minutes) from Glenfiddich to Glenlivet; 17 mi (30 minutes) from Glenlivet to Glen Grant; and 13 mi (30 minutes) from Glen Grant to Glenfiddich.

## The Isle of Skye

**Day 6.** Leave Inverness early and head south to Skye. The drive to the island is peaceful, full of raw landscapes and big, open horizons. Stop at Eilean Donan Castle on the way; go in, walk around, and take a few photos. The castle is the stuff postcards are made of. Explore Skye; Glen Brittle is the perfect place to enjoy mountain scenery, and Armadale is a good place to go craft shopping. End up in Portree for dinner and the night.

**Logistics:** It's 80 mi (a 2-hour drive) from Inverness to Skye. You can take public transportation, but it's best to have the freedom of a car.

## Oban via Ben Nevis

**Day 7.** Leave Skye no later than 9 AM and head for Fort William. The town isn't worth stopping for, but the view of Britain's highest mountain, the 4,406-foot Ben Nevis, is. If time permits, take a hike in Glen Nevis. Continue on to Oban, a traditional Scottish resort town on the water. Outside Oban, stop by the Scottish Sealife Sanctuary. At night, feast on fish-and-chips in a local pub.

**Logistics:** It's nearly 100 mi from Skye to Oban; the drive is 3½ hours without stop-

# GREAT ITINERARY

ping. Public transportation is an option but a challenging one.

## Loch Lomond to Glasgow

**Days 8 and 9.** Enjoy a leisurely morning in Oban and take a waterfront stroll. Mid-morning, set off for Glasgow via Loch Lomond. Stop in Balloch on the loch for fresh oysters and a walk along the bonnie banks. Arrive in Glasgow in time for dinner; take in a play or concert. Spend the next day and night visiting the sights: Kelvingrove Art Gallery, Charles Rennie Mackintosh's Glasgow School of Art, and the city's imposing cathedral are a few highlights.

**Logistics:** It's 127 mi (a 3-hour drive) from Oban to Glasgow via Balloch. Traveling by train is a possibility, but you won't be able to go via Balloch. Return your rental car in Glasgow; it's easy to travel around the city by foot, subway, or train.

## Glasgow

**Day 10.** On your final day, leave your suitcases at your hotel and hit Buchanan and Sauchiehall Streets for some of Britain's best shopping. Clothes, whisky, and tartan items are good things to look for.

**Logistics:** It's less than 10 mi (15 minutes) by taxi to Glasgow's international airport in Paisley but over 30 mi (40 minutes) to the international airport in Prestwick. Be sure you have the correct airport information.

## TIPS

■ You can begin this itinerary in Glasgow and finish in Edinburgh, or adjust the timing to your interests. For example, if you enjoy castles, you might stay in Inverness longer; if you like golf, St. Andrews may deserve more time.

■ August is festival season in Edinburgh; make reservations there well in advance during that month.

■ Remember to drive on the left side of the road and keep alert, especially on small, narrow country roads. Travel will take longer on smaller roads.

■ Weather is unpredictable; always dress in layers. Hikers should carry a cell phone and tell someone where they're going. Golfers and everyone else should carry rain gear.

■ Pack bug repellent for the midges, small, biting insects that travel in swarms. These insects breed in stagnant water; their season is April through October.

■ When visiting distilleries, choose a designated driver or take a bus tour. Drunken drivers aren't tolerated.

# WHEN TO GO

The best months for a visit to Scotland are May, June, September, and October, when all visitor attractions are open and less crowded, lodging is easy to find, and the weather is often dry, sunny, and warm (for Scotland, that is). Try to avoid July and August, when British schools are on holiday and everything is much more crowded. That said, Edinburgh festival time in August, when up to six major arts festivals are under way, is absolutely thrilling—the highlight of many a trip. Just book ahead. City museums stay open year-round, but some tourist sites, such as historic homes, close from November to Easter; check in advance.

## Climate

The Scottish climate has been much maligned, sometimes with justification. You can be unlucky and spend a summer week under low clouds and drizzle. But on the other hand, you may enjoy calm Mediterranean-like weather even in early spring and late fall. Generally Scotland is three or four degrees cooler than southern England, and the east is drier and colder than the west. Dawn in Orkney and Shetland in June is around 1 AM, no more than an hour or so after sunset. Winter days in Scotland are very short; they can be cold and dreary or filled with brilliant light. The country has few thunderstorms and little fog, except for local mists near the coasts. However, there are often variable winds that reach gale force even in summer. Winds blow away the hordes of gnats and midges, the biting insects that are the curse of the country, especially the western Highlands and islands, from late May to mid-September.

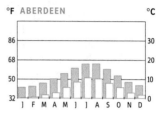

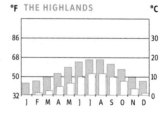

# ON THE CALENDAR

| | |
|---|---|
| | **Homecoming Scotland** (⊕ *www.homecomingscotland.com*) is a yearlong celebration of Scotland and its heritage throughout 2009, the 250th anniversary of the birth of Robert Burns, the country's national poet and icon. Festivities will also celebrate Scotland's contributions to the world, from golf and whisky to scientific innovation. **The Gathering** (⊕ *www.the gathering2009.com*), a celebration of clans, will be held in Edinburgh in July of that year. At the time of this writing, other events and exhibitions were being planned. |
| **WINTER** <br> Dec. 30–Jan. 1 | **Hogmanay** is Scotland's ancient, still-thriving New Year's celebration. Edinburgh's celebration lasts four days. In rural areas, neighbors bring gifts to each other's houses—thereby ensuring the good luck of the household—and receive presents in return. |
| Jan. 25 | **Burns Night** dinners and other events are held in memory of poet Robert Burns on his birthday. |
| Mid-Jan.–Early Feb. | **Celtic Connections** (☎ *0141/353–8000* ⊕ *www.celticconnections.com*), Glasgow's annual homage to Celtic music, hosts hands-on workshops and international musicians. |
| Last Tues. in Jan. | During **Up Helly Aa** (☎ *01595/693434* ⊕ *www.shetlandtourism.com*), Shetlanders celebrate their Viking heritage and torch a replica Viking longship. |
| Mar. | The **Borders Banquet** (☎ *01896/758991* ⊕ *www.borders banquet.co.uk*) is a two-week culinary festival highlighting delicacies of the Borders region, including samples of prize-winning haggis and ales. |
| **SPRING** <br> Late Apr.–Early May | **Shetland Folk Festival** (☎ *01595/694757* ⊕ *www.shetlandfolk festival.com*) is one of the biggest folk gatherings in Scotland, set in the heart of fiddle-playing country. |
| Apr. 30 | The **Beltane Fire Festival** (☎ *0131/228–5353* ⊕ *www.beltane. org*) celebrates the rites of spring according to the traditional Celtic calendar. You can witness displays of pyrotechnics and elaborately costumed mythological creatures at Calton Hill in Edinburgh. |
| Late May | **Orkney Folk Festival** (☎ *01856/ 851635* ⊕ *www.orkneyfolk festival.com*) brings the folkies back up to the remote far north by the hundreds. |

| | |
|---|---|
| **SUMMER**<br><br>June–Aug. | **Highland Games,** held annually in many Highland towns, include athletic and cultural events such as hammer throwing and caber tossing. |
| Third wk in June | The **St. Magnus Festival** (☎*01856/871445* ⊕*www.stmagnus festival.com*) on Orkney is a feast of classical and modern music, often showcasing new vocal or orchestral compositions. |
| Early Aug.–Early Sept. | The **Edinburgh International Festival** (☎*0131/473–2000* ⊕*www.eif.co.uk*) is the world's largest festival of the arts. The **Edinburgh Festival Fringe** (☎*0131/226–0026* ⊕*www.edfringe.com*) is the rowdy, unofficial escort of the Edinburgh International Festival. The **Edinburgh International Film Festival** (☎*0131/228–4051* ⊕*www.edfilmfest.org.uk*) concentrates on the best new films from all over the world. The **Edinburgh Military Tattoo** (☎*0131/225–1188* ⊕*www.edin tattoo.co.uk*) is a show of marching bands and military regiments. |
| Early Sept. | The **Braemar Royal Highland Gathering** (☎*013397/55377* ⊕*www.braemargathering.org*) hosts kilted clansmen from all over Scotland. |
| **FALL**<br><br>Mid-Oct. | The **Royal National Mod** (☎*01463/709705* ⊕*www.the-mod.co.uk*) is a Gaelic festival with speech competitions and plays (in Gaelic), in addition to piping, choir, and highland dancing performances. The location changes each year. **Shetland Accordion and Fiddle Festival** (☎*01595/693162* ⊕*www.shetlandaccordionandfiddle.com*) concentrates on two of the most popular instruments of folk musicians in Scotland. |
| Early Nov. | **Glasgay** (☎*0141/552–7575* ⊕*www.glasgay.co.uk*) is a celebration of gay comedy, music, film, theater, visual art, performance art, and literature taking place in Glasgow. |
| Late Nov.–Dec. 24 | During **Winterfest** (⊕*www.winterfestglasgow.com*) in Glasgow, George Square is transformed into a winter wonderland: sparkling Christmas ornaments and an impressive palace facade tower over a gigantic ice rink. Festive markets and other seasonal events are part of the program, too. |

# Edinburgh & the Lothians

**WORD OF MOUTH**

"In Edinburgh the teens enjoyed seeing the street performers on the Royal Mile, and of course the castle was a big hit. Hiking up to Arthur's Seat was a highlight of our time. This takes a couple of hours but gives an amazing view of the city below. The Scott Monument in Edinburgh was also fun for my family to climb. I didn't go up, but apparently it gets a bit tight towards the top."

—noe847

"A short train ride from Edinburgh is Linlithgow, a historic town with beautiful old buildings and Linlithgow Palace, the birthplace of Mary, Queen of Scots and her father, James V. The palace is on the shore of Linlithgow Loch and is spectacular."

—Rosemary M

Updated by
Shona Main
and Nick
Bruno

**EDINBURGH IS TO LONDON AS POETRY IS TO PROSE**, as Charlotte Brontë once wrote. One of the world's stateliest cities and proudest capitals, it's built—like Rome—on seven hills, making it a striking backdrop for the ancient pageant of history. In a skyline of sheer drama, Edinburgh Castle watches over the capital city, frowning down on Princes Street as if disapproving of its modern razzmatazz. Its ramparts still echo with gunfire each day when the traditional one-o'clock gun booms out over the city, startling unwary shoppers.

Nearly everywhere in Edinburgh (the *burgh* is always pronounced *burra* in Scotland) there are spectacular buildings, whose Doric, Ionic, and Corinthian pillars add touches of neoclassical grandeur to the largely Presbyterian backdrop. The most notable examples perch amid the greenery of Calton Hill, which overlooks the city center from the east. Large gardens and greenery are a strong feature of central Edinburgh, where the city council is one of the most stridently conservationist in Europe. Conspicuous from Princes Street is Arthur's Seat, a mountain of bright green and yellow furze rearing up behind the spires of the Old Town. This child-size mountain jutting 822 feet above its surroundings has steep slopes and little crags, like a miniature Highlands set down in the middle of the busy city. Appropriately, these theatrical elements match Edinburgh's character—after all, the city has been a stage that has seen its fair share of romance, violence, tragedy, and triumph.

## PARLIAMENT & POWER

Three centuries after the Union of Parliaments with England in 1707, Edinburgh is once again the seat of a Scottish parliament. A new parliament building, designed by the late Spanish architect Enric Miralles, stands adjacent to the Palace of Holyroodhouse, at the foot of the Royal Mile. The first-time visitor to Scotland may be surprised that the country still has a capital city at all; perhaps believing the seat of government was drained of its resources and power after the union with England, but far from it. The Union of Parliaments brought with it a set of political partnerships—such as separate legal, ecclesiastical, and educational systems—that Edinburgh assimilated and integrated with its own surviving institutions.

Scotland now has significantly more control over its own affairs than at any time since 1707, and the 129 Members of the Scottish Parliament (MSPs), of whom 40% are women, have extensive powers in Scotland over education, health, housing, transportation, training, economic development, the environment, and agriculture. Foreign policy, defense, and economic policy, however, remain under the jurisdiction of the U.K. government in London.

## BUILDING THE CITY

Towering over the city, Edinburgh Castle was actually built over the plug of an ancient volcano. Many thousands of years ago, an eastward-grinding glacier encountered the tough basalt core of the volcano and swept around it, scouring steep cliffs and leaving a trail of matter, like the tail of a comet. This material formed a ramp gently leading down from the rocky summit. On this *crag* and *tail* would grow the city of Edinburgh and its castle.

The lands that rolled down to the sea were for centuries open country, sitting between Castle Rock and the tiny community clustered by the shore that grew into Leith, Edinburgh's seaport. By the 12th century Edinburgh had become a walled town, still perched on the hill. Its shape was becoming clearer: like a fish with its head at the castle, its backbone running down the ridge, and its ribs leading briefly off on either side. The backbone gradually became the continuous thoroughfare now known as the Royal Mile, and the ribs became the closes (alleyways), some still surviving, that were the scene of many historic incidents.

By the early 15th century Edinburgh had become the undisputed capital of Scotland. The bitter defeat of Scotland at Flodden in 1513, when Scotland aligned itself with France against England, caused a new defensive city wall to be built. Though the castle escaped destruction, the city was burned by the English earl of Hertford under orders from King Henry VIII (1491–1547) of England. This was during a time known as the "Rough Wooing," when Henry was trying to coerce the Scots into allowing the young Mary, Queen of Scots (1542–87) to marry his son Edward. The plan failed and Mary married Francis, the Dauphin of France. By 1561, when Mary returned from France already widowed, the guesthouse of the Abbey of Holyrood had grown to become the Palace of Holyroodhouse, replacing Edinburgh Castle as the main royal residence. Mary's legacy to the city included the destruction of most of the earliest buildings of Edinburgh Castle, held by her supporters after she was forced to flee to England, where she was eventually executed by Elizabeth I.

In the trying decades after the union with England in 1707, many influential Scots, both in Edinburgh and elsewhere, went through an identity crisis, characterized by people like the writer James Boswell (1740–95), who, though he lived with his family in Edinburgh, preferred to spend most of his time in London. Out of the 18th-century difficulties, however, grew the Scottish Enlightenment, during which educated Scots made great strides in medicine, economics, and science.

Changes came to the cityscape, too. By the mid-18th century it had become the custom for wealthy Scottish landowners to spend the winter in the Old Town of Edinburgh, in town houses huddled between the high Castle Rock and the Royal Palace below. Cross-fertilized in coffeehouses and taverns, intellectual notions flourished among a people determined to remain Scottish despite their parliament's having voted to dissolve itself. One result was a campaign to expand and beautify the city, to give it a look worthy of its future nickname, the Athens of the North. Thus was the New Town of Edinburgh built, with broad streets and gracious buildings creating a harmony that even today's throbbing traffic cannot obscure.

## EDINBURGH TODAY

Today the city is the second-most important financial center in the United Kingdom, and the fifth most important in Europe. This is one of the many reasons that people from all over Britain come to live here. Not the least of the other reasons is that the city regularly is ranked near the top in quality-of-life surveys. Accordingly, New Town apartments on fashionable streets sell for considerable sums. In some senses the city is showy and materialistic, but Edinburgh still supports learned societies, some of which have their roots in the Scottish Enlightenment. The Royal Society of Edinburgh, for example, established in 1783 "for the advancement of learning and useful knowledge," remains an important forum for interdisciplinary activities, both in Edinburgh and in Scotland as a whole. Hand in hand with the city's academic and scientific pursuits is a rich cultural life. In October 2004 Edinburgh became UNESCO's first City of Literature, and the city is known worldwide for the Edinburgh International Festival, which attracts lovers of all the arts in August and September.

Even as Edinburgh moves through the 21st century, its tall guardian castle remains the focal point of the city and its venerable history. Take time to explore the streets—peopled by the spirits of Mary, Queen of Scots, Sir Walter Scott, and Robert Louis Stevenson—and pay your respects to the world's best-loved terrier, Greyfriars Bobby. In the evenings you can enjoy candlelighted restaurants or a folk *ceilidh (a traditional Scottish dance with music [pronounced kay-lee]),* though you should remember that you haven't earned your porridge until you've climbed Arthur's Seat. Should you wander around a corner, say, on George Street, you might see not an endless cityscape, but blue sea and a patchwork of fields. This is the county of Fife, beyond the inlet of the North Sea called the Firth of Forth—a reminder, like the mountains to the northwest, which can be glimpsed from Edinburgh's highest points, that the rest of Scotland lies within easy reach.

# EXPLORING EDINBURGH & THE LOTHIANS

Edinburgh's Old Town, which bears a great measure of symbolic weight as the "heart of Scotland's capital," is a boon for lovers of atmosphere and history. In contrast, if you appreciate the unique architectural heritage of the city's Enlightenment, then the New Town's for you. If you belong to both categories, don't worry—the Old and the New towns are only yards apart. The Princes Street Gardens roughly divide Edinburgh into two areas: the winding, congested streets of Old Town, to the south, and the orderly, Georgian architecture of New Town, to the north. Princes Street runs east–west along the north edge of the Princes Street Gardens. Explore the main thoroughfares but also don't forget to get lost among the tiny *wynds* and *closes*: old medieval alleys that connect the winding streets.

Like most cities, Edinburgh incorporates small communities within its boundaries, and many of these are as rewarding to explore as Old Town and New Town. Dean Village, for instance, even though it's close

## TOP REASONS TO GO

**Kaleidoscope of culture:** From floor-stomping ceilidhs to avant-garde modern dance, from traditional painting and sculpture to cutting-edge installations, from folksy fiddlers to the latest rock bands, Edinburgh covers it all.

**The power and the glory:** History plays out before your eyes in this centuries-old capital. Edinburgh Castle and the Palace of Holyroodhouse were the locations for some of the most important struggles between Scotland and England.

**Awe-inspiring architecture:** From the Old Town's labyrinthine medieval streets to the neoclassical orderliness of the New Town to imagina-

tive modern developments like the Scottish Parliament, Auld Reekie has awe-inspiring architecture.

**Food, glorious food:** Edinburgh has sophisticated restaurants serving cuisines from around the world. Perhaps the most exotic, however, is genuine Scottish cuisine, with its classic dishes like Cullen skink, haggis, and neeps and tatties.

**Retail therapy:** Scotland has a strong tradition of distinctive furniture makers, silversmiths, and artists. Look to the "villages" of Edinburgh—such as Stockbridge—for exclusive designer clothing, edgy knitwear, and other high-end items.

to the New Town, has a character all of its own. Duddingston, just southeast of Arthur's Seat, has all the feel of a country village. Then there's Corstorphine, to the west of the city center, famous for being the site of Murrayfield, Scotland's international rugby stadium. Edinburgh's port, Leith, sits on the shore of the Firth of Forth, and throbs with smart bars and restaurants. Between the city and Leith are areas like Pilrig and Inverleith, and to the south there's Sciennes (pronounced "Skeens"), with its prosperous Victorian villas and terraces.

The hills, green fields, beaches, and historic houses and castles in the countryside outside Edinburgh—Midlothian, West Lothian, and East Lothian, collectively called the Lothians—can be reached quickly by bus or car, welcome day-trip escapes from the festival crush at the height of summer.

## OLD TOWN

East of Edinburgh Castle, the historic castle esplanade becomes the street known as the Royal Mile, leading from the castle down through Old Town to the Palace of Holyroodhouse. The Mile, as it's called, is actually made up of one thoroughfare that bears, in consecutive sequence, different names—Castlehill, Lawnmarket, Parliament Square, High Street, and Canongate. The streets and passages winding into their tenements, or "lands," and crammed onto the ridge in back of the Mile really *were* Edinburgh until the 18th century saw expansions to the south and north. Everybody lived here, the richer folk on the lower floors of houses, with less well-to-do families on the middle floors—the higher up, the poorer. Time and progress (of a sort) have

# GREAT ITINERARIES

Edinburgh's spectacular setting makes a good first impression. You can be here for a day and think you know the place, as even a cursory open-top bus tour enables you to grasp the layout of the castle, Royal Mile, Old Town, and New Town. If your taste is more for leisurely strolling through the nooks and crannies of the Old Town closes, however, then allow three or four days for exploring.

## IF YOU HAVE 2 DAYS

To start off, make your way to Edinburgh Castle—not just the battlements—and spend some time here, if only to revel in its sense of history. Take a city bus tour for an overview of Edinburgh, and while you ride, consider your must-sees: the National Gallery of Scotland, the Royal Museum, and, unless it's January or February, the Georgian House for an idea of life in the New Town.

## IF YOU HAVE 5 DAYS

Five days allow plenty of time for Old Town exploration, including the important museums of Edinburgh and the People's Story (in the Canongate Tolbooth), and for a walk around the New Town, including a visit to the Scottish National Portrait Gallery and the Scottish National Gallery of Modern Art. You'll also have time for shopping, not only in

areas close to the city center, such as Rose Street and Victoria Street, but also in some of the less touristy areas, such as Bruntsfield. Head to Leith to visit the former royal yacht *Britannia* and to have a meal on the waterfront. You could also get out of town: hop on a bus out to Midlothian to see the magnificent Rosslyn Chapel at Roslin (it's of interest to more than *Da Vinci Code* fans), and visit Crichton Castle, parts of which date back to the 14th century. Consider spending another half day traveling out to South Queensferry to admire the Forth rail and road bridges; then visit palatial Hopetoun House, with its wealth of portraits and fine furniture.

## IF YOU HAVE 8 DAYS

In eight days, in addition to a thorough exploration of Edinburgh's Old Town and New Town, including a few museums and a shopping trip or two, you will not only have time to explore Leith, Roslin, and South Queensferry but you may also be able to take a couple of side trips from the city. Allow at least a day for each trip so you have time to enjoy stately homes, historic ruins, beaches, and museums. If it's festival time, however, you might want to take in shows, concerts, and exhibitions for eight solid days and hardly stray from the city center.

swept away some of the narrow closes and tall tenements of the Old Town, but enough survive for you to be able to imagine the original profile of Scotland's capital. There are many guided tours of the area or you can walk around on your own. The latter is often a better choice in summer when tourists pack the area and large guided groups have trouble making their way through the crowds.

TIMING  An exploration of the Old Town could be accomplished in a day, but to give the major sights—Edinburgh Castle, the Palace of Holyroodhouse, and the Royal Museum—the time they deserve and also to see at least some of the other attractions properly, you should allow two

CLOSE UP

# Edinburgh's Castle Fit for a King

1

Archaeological investigations have established that the rock on which Edinburgh Castle stands was inhabited as far back as 1000 BC, in the latter part of the Bronze Age. There have been fortifications here since the mysterious people called the Picts first used it as a stronghold in the 3rd and 4th centuries AD. Anglian invaders from northern England dislodged the Picts in AD 452, and for the next 1,300 years the site saw countless battles and skirmishes. In the castle you'll hear the story of how Randolph, earl of Moray, nephew of freedom-fighter Robert the Bruce, scaled the heights one dark night in 1313, surprised the English guard, and recaptured the

castle for the Scots. At the same time he destroyed every one of its buildings except for St. Margaret's Chapel, dating from around 1076, so that successive Stewart kings had to rebuild the castle bit by bit.

The castle has been held over time by Scots and Englishmen, Catholics and Protestants, soldiers and royalty. In the 16th century Mary, Queen of Scots, gave birth here to the future James VI of Scotland (1566–1625), who was also to rule England as James I. In 1573 it was the last fortress to support Mary's claim as the rightful Catholic queen of Britain, causing the castle to be virtually destroyed by English artillery fire.

days. ■TIP→ **Don't forget that some attractions have special hours during the Edinburgh International Festival. If you want to see something special, check the hours ahead of time.**

### MAIN ATTRACTIONS

**1** **Edinburgh Castle.** The crowning glory of the Scottish capital, Edinburgh Castle is popular not only because it's the symbolic heart of Scotland but also because of the views from its battlements: on a clear day the vistas—stretching to the "kingdom" of Fife—are breathtaking. ■TIP→ **Don't plan on rushing through Edinburgh Castle. There's so much to see that you need at least three hours to do the site justice.**

Fodor's Choice ★

You enter across the **Esplanade,** the huge forecourt built in the 18th century as a parade ground; it now serves as the castle parking lot. The area comes alive with color and music each August when it's used for the Military Tattoo, a festival of magnificently outfitted marching bands and regiments. Heading over the drawbridge and through the gatehouse, past the guards, you can find the rough stone walls of the **Half-Moon Battery,** where the one-o'clock gun is fired every day in an impressively anachronistic ceremony; these curving ramparts give Edinburgh Castle its distinctive appearance from miles away. Climb up through a second gateway and you come to the oldest surviving building in the complex, the tiny 11th-century **St. Margaret's Chapel,** named in honor of Saxon queen Margaret (1046–93), who had persuaded her husband, King Malcolm III (circa 1031–93), to move his court from Dunfermline to Edinburgh. Edinburgh's environs—the Lothians— were occupied by Anglian settlers with whom the queen felt more at home, or so the story goes (Dunfermline was surrounded by Celts). The **Crown Room,** a must-see, contains the "Honours of Scotland"—

the crown, scepter, and sword that once graced the Scottish monarch. Upon the **Stone of Scone**, also in the Crown Room, Scottish monarchs once sat to be crowned. In the section now called **Queen Mary's Apartments,** Mary, Queen of Scots, gave birth to James VI of Scotland. The **Great Hall** displays arms and armor under an impressive vaulted, beamed ceiling. Scottish parliament meetings were conducted here until 1840. During the Napoleonic Wars in the early 19th century, the castle held French prisoners of war, whose carvings can still be seen on the vaults under the Great Hall.

> ## SAVE ON SIGHTS
>
> The money-saving **Edinburgh Pass** (☎0131/473-3600 ⊕www.edinburghpass.org) gives you city bus transport (including a return ticket on the airport bus), access to more than 30 attractions, and other exclusive offers. A one-day pass costs £24; two-day pass £36, and three-day pass £48. Passes are available from the tourist information centers in Princes Street, at Edinburgh Airport, or online.

Military features of interest include the **Scottish National War Memorial,** the **Scottish United Services Museum,** and the famous 15th-century Belgian-made cannon *Mons Meg.* This enormous piece of artillery has been silent since 1682, when it exploded while firing a salute for the duke of York; it now stands in an ancient hall behind the Half-Moon Battery. Contrary to what you may hear from locals, it's not *Mons Meg* but the battery's time gun that goes off with a bang every weekday at 1 PM, frightening visitors and reminding Edinburghers to check their watches. ✉ *Off Castle Esplanade and Castlehill, Old Town* ☎*0131/225–9846 Edinburgh Castle, 0131/226–7393 War Memorial* ⊕*www.historic-scotland.gov.uk* ✉*£11* ☉*Apr.–Oct., daily 9:30–6; Nov.–Mar., daily 9:30–5; last entry 45 min before closing.*

**NEED A BREAK?** You can have lunch or afternoon tea overlooking panoramic views of the city at the Edinburgh Castle Café ( ✉ *Edinburgh Castle, Old Town* ☎*0131/225–9746).* Baked sweets, sandwiches, soup, tea, and Starbucks coffee are all available at reasonable prices.

🕒 **High Kirk of St. Giles.** Sometimes called St. Giles's Cathedral, this is one of the city's principal churches. However, anyone expecting a rival to Paris's Notre Dame or London's Westminster Abbey will be disappointed: St. Giles is more like a large parish church than a great European cathedral. There has been a church here since AD 854, although most of the present structure dates from either 1120 or 1829, when the church was restored. The tower, with its stone crown towering 161 feet above the ground, was completed between 1495 and 1500. The most elaborate feature is the **Chapel of the Order of the Thistle,** built onto the southeast corner of the church in 1911 for the exclusive use of Scotland's only chivalric order, the Most Ancient and Noble Order of the Thistle. It bears the belligerent national motto NEMO ME IMPUNE LACESSIT ("No one provokes me with impunity"). Inside the church stands a life-size statue of the Scot whose spirit still dominates the place—the great religious reformer and preacher John Knox, before whose zeal all of Scotland once trembled. The church lies about one-third of the way along the Royal Mile from Edinburgh Castle. ⊠*High St., Old Town* 🕾*0131/225–9442* ⊕*www.stgiles.net* 🖃*£3 suggested donation* ☉*May–Sept., weekdays 9–7, Sat. 9–5, Sun. 1–5; Oct.–Apr., Mon.–Sat. 9–5, Sun. 1–5.*

🔞 **High Street (Royal Mile).** Some of Old Town's most impressive buildings and sights are on High Street, one of the five streets making up the Royal Mile. Also here are other, less obvious historic relics. Near Parliament Square, look on the west side for a **heart** set in cobbles. This marks the site of the vanished Tolbooth, the center of city life from the 15th century until the building's demolition in 1817. The ancient civic edifice housed the Scottish parliament and was used as a prison—it also inspired Sir Walter Scott's novel *The Heart of Midlothian.*

Just outside Parliament House is the **Mercat Cross** (*mercat* means "market"), a great landmark of Old Town life. It was an old mercantile center, where in the early days executions were held, and where royal proclamations were—and are still—read. Most of the present cross is comparatively modern, dating from the time of William Ewart Gladstone (1809–98), the great Victorian prime minister and rival of Benjamin Disraeli (1804–81). Across High Street from the High Kirk of St. Giles stands the **City Chambers,** now the seat of local government. Built by John Fergus, who adapted a design of John Adam in 1753, the chambers were originally known as the Royal Exchange and intended to be where merchants and lawyers could conduct business. Note how the building drops 11 stories to Cockburn Street on its north side.

A *tron* is a weigh beam used in public weigh houses, and the **Tron Kirk** was named after a salt tron that used to stand nearby. The kirk itself was built after 1633, when St. Giles's became an Episcopal cathedral for a brief time. In this church in 1693, a minister offered an often-quoted prayer for the local government: "Lord, hae mercy on a' [all] fools and idiots, and particularly on the Magistrates of Edinburgh."

You would once have passed out of the safety of the town walls through a gate called the **Netherbow Port.** Look for the brass studs in the street cobbles that mark its location. A plaque outside the Scottish Storytelling Centre at 43 High Street depicts the gate. ⊠*Between Lawnmarket and Canongate, Old Town.*

🔞 **John Knox House.** It's not certain that Scotland's severe religious reformer John Knox ever lived here, but there's evidence to show that he died here in 1572. Mementos of his life are on view inside, and the distinctive dwelling gives you a glimpse of what Old Town life was like in the 16th century. The projecting upper stories were once commonplace along the Royal Mile, darkening and further closing in the already narrow passage. Look for the initials of former owner James Mossman and his wife, carved into the stonework on the marriage lintel. Mossman was goldsmith to Mary, Queen of Scots, and was hanged in 1573 for his allegiance to her. ⊠*45 High St., Old Town* 🕾*0131/556–2647* ⊕*www.scottishstorytellingcentre.co.uk* 🖃*£3* ☉*Mon.–Sat. 10–6; last admission half hr before closing.*

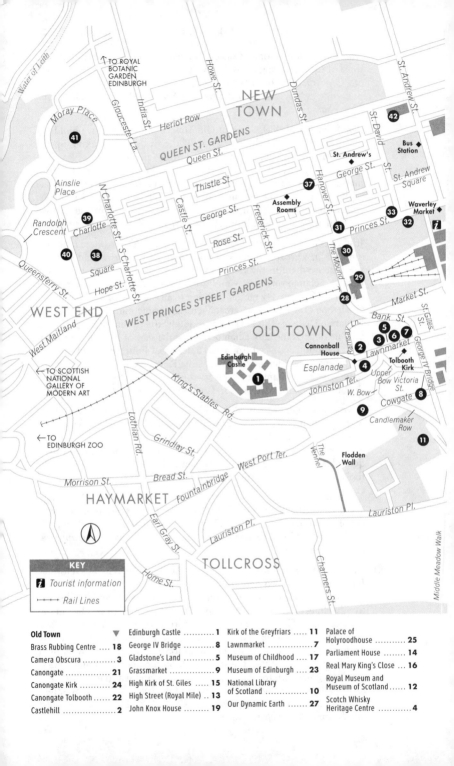

**KEY**

🛈 Tourist information

＋—＋ Rail Lines

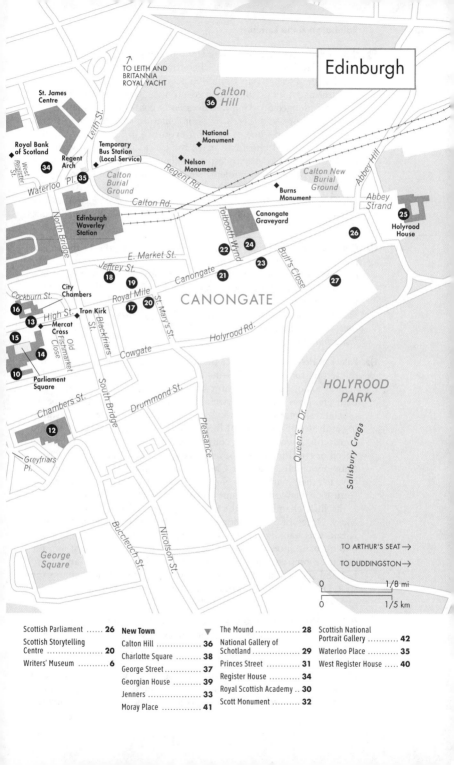

# Edinburgh

TO LEITH AND
BRITANNIA
ROYAL YACHT

St. James
Centre

Calton Hill **36**

National
Monument

Royal Bank
of Scotland

Regent
Arch

West Register St.

**34** Waterloo Pl. **35**

Temporary
Bus Station
(Local Service)

Nelson
Monument

Regent Rd.

Calton New
Burial
Ground

Abbey Hill

Calton
Burial
Ground

Calton Rd.

Burns
Monument

Abbey
Strand

North Bridge

Edinburgh
Waverley
Station

Canongate
Graveyard

**25**

Holyrood
House

E. Market St.

Tolbooth Wynd

**22** **24**

**26**

Jeffrey St.

**18** **19**

**21** **23**

Butt's Close

Cockburn St.

City
Chambers

Royal Mile

Canongate

**27**

**16**

High St.

**17** **20**

CANONGATE

**13** Tron Kirk

Mercat
Cross

St. Mary's St.

Blackfriars St.

Holyrood Rd.

**15**

Old Fishmarket Close

Cowgate

**14**

Holyrood Rd.

**10**

Parliament
Square

HOLYROOD
PARK

Chambers St.

South Bridge

Drummond St.

**12**

Pleasance

Queen's Dr.

Salisbury Crags

Greyfriars
Pl.

George
Square

Buccleuch St.

Nicolson St.

TO ARTHUR'S SEAT →

TO DUDDINGSTON →

0          1/8 mi

0          1/5 km

**⑪ Kirk of the Greyfriars.** Greyfriars Church, built circa 1620 on the site of a medieval monastery, was where the National Covenant, declaring that the Presbyterian Church in Scotland was independent of the monarch and not Episcopalian in government, was signed in 1638. The covenant plunged Scotland into decades of civil war. Informative panels tell the story, and there's a visitor center on-site. Be sure to search out the graveyard—one of the most evocative in Europe. Its old, tottering, elaborate tombstones mark the graves of some of Scotland's most respected heroes and despised villains. Nearby, at the corner of George IV Bridge and Candlemaker Row, stands one of the most photographed sites in Scotland, the Greyfriars Bobby statue. ⊠ *Greyfriars Pl., Old Town* ☎ *0131/225–1900* ⊕ *www.greyfriarskirk.com* ⊡ *Free* ⊙ *Easter–Oct., weekdays 10:30–4:30, Sat. 10:30–2:30; Nov.–Easter, Thurs. 1:30–3:30.*

**㉗ Our Dynamic Earth.** Using state-of-the-art technology, the 11 theme galleries at this interactive science gallery educate and entertain as they explore the wonders of the planet, from polar regions to tropical rain forests. Geological history, from the big bang to the unknown future, is also examined. ⊠ *Holyrood Rd., Holyrood* ☎ *0131/550–7800* ⊕ *www.dynamicearth.co.uk* ⊡ *£8.95* ⊙ *Apr.–June, Sept., and Oct., daily 10–5; July and Aug., daily 10–6; Nov.–Mar., Wed.–Sun. 10–5; last admission 1 hr before closing.*

**㉕ Palace of Holyroodhouse.** Once the haunt of Mary, Queen of Scots, and ★ the setting for high drama—including at least one notorious murder, several major fires, and centuries of the colorful lifestyles of larger-than-life, power-hungry personalities—this is now Queen Elizabeth's official residence in Scotland. A doughty and impressive palace standing at the foot of the Royal Mile in a hilly public park, it's built around a graceful, lawned central court at the end of Canongate. When the queen or royal family is not in residence, you can take a guided tour. Many monarchs, including Charles II, Queen Victoria, and George V, have left their mark on its rooms, but it's Mary, Queen of Scots, whose spirit looms largest. For some visitors the most memorable room here is the little chamber in which David Rizzio (1533–66), secretary to Mary, Queen of Scots, met an unhappy end in 1566. In part because Rizzio was hated at court for his social-climbing ways, Mary's second husband, Lord Darnley (Henry Stewart, 1545–65), burst into the queen's rooms with his henchmen, dragged Rizzio into an antechamber, and stabbed him more than 50 times; a bronze plaque marks the spot. Darnley himself was murdered the next year to make way for the queen's marriage to her lover, Bothwell.

■ TIP➡ There's plenty to see here, so make sure you have at least two hours to tour the palace. The **King James Tower** is the oldest surviving section, containing the rooms of Mary, Queen of Scots, on the 2nd floor, and Lord Darnley's rooms below. Though much has been altered, there are fine fireplaces, paneling, plasterwork, tapestries, and 18th- and 19th-century furnishings throughout. At the south end of the palace front you can find the **Royal Dining Room,** and along the south side are the **Throne Room** and other drawing rooms now used for social and ceremonial occasions.

At the back of the palace is the **King's Bedchamber.** The 150-foot-long **Great Picture Gallery,** on the north side, displays the portraits of 110 Scottish monarchs. These were commissioned by Charles II, who was eager to demonstrate his Scottish ancestry—some of the royal figures here are fictional and the likenesses of others imaginary. All the portraits were painted by a Dutch artist, Jacob de Witt, who signed a contract in 1684 with the queen's cash keeper, Hugh Wallace. The contract bound him to deliver 110 pictures within two years, for which he received an annual stipend of £120. Surely one of the more desperate scenes in the palace's history is that of the artist feverishly turning out potboiler portraits at the rate of one a week for two years.

**Queen's Gallery,** in a former church and school at the entrance to the palace, holds rotating exhibits from the Royal Collection. From the top of Edinburgh's minimountain, **Arthur's Seat** (822 feet), views are breathtaking.

Holyroodhouse has its origins in an Augustinian monastery founded by David I (1084–1153) in 1128. In the 15th and 16th centuries, Scottish royalty, preferring the comforts of the abbey to the drafty rooms of Edinburgh Castle, settled into Holyroodhouse, expanding and altering the buildings until the palace eventually eclipsed the monastery. Look for the brass letters SSS set into the road at the beginning of Abbey Strand (the continuation of the Royal Mile). The letters stand for "sanctuary" and recall the days when the Palace of Holyroodhouse served as a retreat for debtors. This role lasted until 1880, when the government stopped imprisoning people for debt. The poet Thomas de Quincey (1785–1859) and the comte d'Artois (known as Charles X, 1757–1836), brother of the deposed king of France, Louis XVIII (1755–1824), were two of the more famous of Holyrood's denizens.

After the Union of the Crowns in 1603, when the Scottish royal court packed its bags and decamped for England, the building fell into decline. Oliver Cromwell (1599–1658), the Protestant Lord Protector of England who had conquered Scotland, ordered the palace rebuilt after a fire in 1650, but the work was poorly carried out. When the monarchy was restored with the ascension of Charles II (1630–85) to the British throne in 1660, Holyrood was rebuilt in the architectural style of Louis XIV (1638–1715), and this is the style you see today.

In 1688 an anti-Catholic faction ran riot within the palace, and in 1745, during the last Jacobite campaign, Charles Edward Stuart occupied the palace, followed a short while later by the duke of Cumberland, who defeated Charles at Culloden. After the 1822 visit of King George IV (1762–1830), at a more peaceable time, the palace sank into decline once again. But Queen Victoria (1819–1901) and her grandson King George V (1865–1936) renewed interest in the palace: the buildings were once more refurbished and made suitable for royal residence. Behind the palace lie the open grounds and looming crags of Holyrood Park, the hunting ground of early Scottish kings. ⊠*Abbey Strand, Holyrood,*

*Old Town* ☎0131/556–1096 🖷0131/557–5256 ⊕*www.royal.gov.uk* ✉*£9.50* ⊙*Apr.–Oct., daily 9:30–6; Nov.–Mar., daily 9:30–4:30; last admission 1 hr before closing. Closed during royal visits.*

**⑯** **Real Mary King's Close.** Hidden beneath the City Chambers, this narrow, cobbled *close*, or lane, named after a former landowner, is said to be one of Edinburgh's most haunted sites. The close was sealed off in 1645 to quarantine residents who became sick when the bubonic plague swept through the city, and many victims were herded there to die. After the plague passed, the bodies were removed and buried, and the street was reopened. A few people returned, but they soon reported ghostly goings-on and departed, leaving the close empty for decades. In 1753 city authorities built the Royal Exchange (later the City Chambers) directly over the close, sealing it off and, unwittingly, ensuring it remained intact, except for the buildings' upper stories, which were destroyed. Today you can walk among the remains of the shops and houses. People still report ghostly visions and eerie sounds, such as the crying of a young girl. Over the years visitors have left small offerings for her, such as dolls, pieces of ribbon, or candy. ■ **TIP**➔ **Although kids like the spookiness of this attraction, it's not for the youngest ones. In fact, children under 5 are not admitted.** ✉*Writers' Court, Old Town* ☎0870/243–0160 ⊕*www. realmarykingsclose.com* ✉*£9.50* ⊙*Apr.–July, Sept., and Oct., daily 10–9; Aug., daily 9–9; Nov.–Mar., daily 10–4.*

**⑫** **Royal Museum and Museum of Scotland.** In an imposing Victorian building on Chambers Street, the Royal Museum houses an internationally **Fodor's**Choice renowned collection of art and artifacts relating to natural, scientific, ★ and industrial history. Its treasures include the Lewis Chessmen, 11 intricately carved ivory chessmen found on one of the Western Isles in the 19th century. The museum's main hall, with its soaring roof and bird-cage design, is architecturally interesting in its own right. The striking, contemporary building next door houses the Museum of Scotland, with modern displays concentrating on Scotland's own heritage. This state-of-the-art, no-expense-spared museum is full of playful models, complex reconstructions, and paraphernalia ranging from ancient Pictish articles to 21st-century cultural artifacts. ✉*Chambers St., Old Town* ☎0131/225–7534 ⊕*www.nms.ac.uk* ✉*Free* ⊙*Daily 10–5.*

**NEED A BREAK?** Café Delos ( ✉*Chambers St., Old Town* ☎0131/225–7534) in the Royal Museum's main hall serves tea, coffee, cookies, cakes, and savory snacks from 10 to 4. The Soupson Tearoom ( ✉*Chambers St., Old Town* ☎0131/225–7534), also in the museum, adds soups and salads to its offerings.

**㉖** **Scottish Parliament.** Scotland's somewhat controversial Parliament building is dramatically modern, with irregular curves and angles that mirror the twisting shapes of the surrounding landscape. The structure's artistry is most apparent when you step inside, where the gentle slopes, (sustainable) forest's worth of oak, polished concrete and granite, walls of glass, water features, and subtle imagery create an understated magnificence appropriate to the modest but proud Scots. It's worth taking the 45-minute tour to see the main hall and debating chamber, a com-

# A GOOD WALK

A perfect place to start your stroll through the Old Town is Edinburgh Castle. After exploring its extensive complex of buildings and admiring the view from the battlements, set off down the first part of the Royal Mile. The Outlook Tower affords more splendid views of the city. The six-story tenement known as Gladstone's Land, a survivor of 16th-century domestic life, is on the left as you head east. Near Gladstone's Land, down another close, stands the Writers' Museum, in a fine example of 17th-century urban architecture called Lady Stair's House. Farther down on the right are the Tolbooth Kirk (a *tolbooth* was a town hall or prison, and *kirk* means "church") and Upper Bow.

Turn right down George IV Bridge to reach the historic Grassmarket, where parts of the old city walls still stand. Turn left up Candlemaker row and you can see the Kirk of the Greyfriars, and the little statue of faithful Greyfriars Bobby. On Chambers Street, at the foot of George IV Bridge, are the impressive galleries of the Royal Museum and Museum of Scotland, the former housed in a lavish Victorian building, the latter in an attached late-20th-century structure.

Returning to the junction of George IV Bridge with the Royal Mile, turn right (east) down High Street to visit the old Parliament House; the High Kirk of St. Giles; the Mercat Cross; and the elegant City Chambers, bringing a flavor of the New Town's neoclassicism to the Old Town's severity. Beneath the chambers is the eerie Real Mary King's Close, a lane that was closed off in the 17th century when the bubonic plague struck the city.

A short distance down Canongate on the left is Canongate Tolbooth. The Museum of Edinburgh stands opposite, and the Canongate Kirk and Acheson House are nearby. This walk draws to a close, as it started, on a high note: the Palace of Holyroodhouse, full of historic and architectural interest and some fine paintings, tapestries, and furnishings to admire, in Holyrood Park.

mittee room, and other areas. Another option is to call well in advance to get a free ticket to view Parliament in action. Originally conceived by the late Catalan architect Enric Mirales, who often said the building was "growing out of the ground," the design was completed by his widow, Bernadette Tagliabue, in August 2004. ⊠ *Horse Wynd, Old Town* ☎ *0131/348–5200* ⊕ *www.scottish.parliament.uk* ⊠ *Free; £5 for tour* ⊙ *Tours Nov.–Mar., daily 10–4; Apr.–Oct., daily 10–6; no tours when Parliament is sitting, generally Tues.–Thurs.*

## ALSO WORTH SEEING

**⑱ Brass Rubbing Centre.** No experience is necessary for you to make your own souvenirs of Scotland at this center. You can explore the past by creating do-it-yourself replicas from original Pictish stones and markers, rare Scottish brasses, and medieval church brasses, or you can buy them in the shop for anywhere between, £1.50 and £30. All the materials are here, and children find the pastime quite absorbing. The center occupies the surviving piece of a Gothic church down a close opposite the Museum of Childhood. ⊠ *Trinity Apse, Chalmers Close, Old Town* ☎ *0131/556–4364* ⊕ *www.cac.org.uk* ☒ *Free* ☉ *Apr.–Sept., Mon.–Sat. 10–5, Sun. during festival noon–5.*

❸ **Camera Obscura.** Want to view Edinburgh as Victorian travelers once
☽ did? Then head for the 17th-century Outlook Tower's camera obscura, where an optical instrument—a sort of projecting telescope—affords bird's-eye views of the whole city (on a clear day, that is) illuminated onto a concave table. The tower was significantly altered in the 1840s and 1850s with the installation of the telescopic "magic lantern."
■ TIP→ The site is not in the best of shape, but if you're interested in this type of thing it's still worth a visit. ⊠ *Castlehill, Old Town* ☎ *0131/226–3709* ⊕ *www.camera-obscura.co.uk* ☒ *£7.50* ☉ *Apr.–Oct., daily 9:30–6; Nov.–Mar., daily 10–5.*

㉑ **Canongate.** This section of the Royal Mile takes its name from the canons who once ran the abbey at Holyrood. Canongate—in Scots, *gate* means "street"—was originally an independent town, or *burgh,* another Scottish term used to refer to a community with trading rights granted by the monarch. Here you'll find ⇨ **Canongate Kirk** and its graveyard, ⇨ **Canongate Tolbooth,** and the ⇨ **Museum of Edinburgh.** ⊠ *Section of Royal Mile from end of High St. to Abbey Strand at entrance to Palace of Holyroodhouse, Old Town.*

㉔ **Canongate Kirk.** This unadorned building, built in 1688, is run by the Church of Scotland and has an interesting graveyard. Although you can find information about the graveyard in the church, local authorities actually oversee it. This is the final resting place of some notable Scots, including economist Adam Smith (1723–90), author of *The Wealth of Nations* (1776), who once lived in the nearby 17th-century Panmure House. Also buried here are Dugald Stewart (1753–1828), the leading European philosopher of his time, and the undervalued Scots poet Robert Fergusson (1750–74). That Fergusson's grave is even marked is the result of efforts by the much more famous Robert Burns (1759–96). On a visit to the city Burns was dismayed to find the grave had no headstone, so he commissioned an architect—by the name of Robert Burn—to design one. (Burn reportedly took two years to complete the commission, so Burns, in turn, took two years to pay.) Burn also designed the Nelson Monument, the tall column on Calton Hill to the north, which you can see from the graveyard.

Against the eastern wall of the graveyard is a bronze sculpture of the head of Mrs. Agnes McLehose, the "Clarinda" of the copious correspondence in which Robert Burns engaged while confined to his lodgings with an injured leg in 1788. Burns and McLehose—a high born, talented woman who had been abandoned by her husband—exchanged passionate letters for some six weeks that year. The missives were dispatched across town by a postal service that delivered them within the hour for one penny. The curiously literary affair ended when Burns left Edinburgh in 1788 to take up a farm tenancy and to marry Jean Armour. ⊠ *Canongate, Old Town* ☎ *0131/556–3515* ⊕ *www.canongatekirk.com* ☒ *Free* ☉ *Daily.*

㉒ **Canongate Tolbooth.** Nearly every city and town in Scotland once had a tolbooth. Originally a customhouse where tolls were gathered, a tolbooth came to mean town hall and later prison because detention cells were in the basement. The building where Canongate's town council once met now has a museum, the **People's Story,** which focuses on the lives of "ordinary" people from the 18th century to today. Exhibits describe how Canongate once bustled with the activities of the tradespeople needed to supply life's essentials in the days before superstores. Special displays include a reconstruction of a cooper's workshop and a 1940s kitchen. ⊠*163 Canongate, Old Town* ☎*0131/529–4057* ⊕*www.cac. org.uk* 🎫*Free* ⊙*Mon.–Sat. 10–5, Sun. during festival 2–5.*

**NEED A BREAK?**

You can get a good cup of tea and a scone, a quintessentially Scottish indulgence, at Clarinda's (⊠*69 Canongate, Old Town* ☎*0131/557–1888*). Like most tearooms, Clarinda's doesn't accept reservations. You may have to wait a short while for a table, but the experience is well worth it.

❷ **Castlehill.** In the late 16th century, alleged witches were brought to what is now a street in the Royal Mile to be burned at the stake, as a bronze plaque here recalls. The cannonball embedded in the west gable of Castlehill's **Cannonball House** was, according to legend, fired from the castle during the Jacobite Rebellion of 1745, led by Charles Edward Stuart (also known as Bonnie Prince Charlie, 1720–88), the most romantic of the Stuart pretenders to the British throne. Most authorities agree on a more prosaic explanation, however; they say it was a height marker for Edinburgh's first piped-water-supply system, installed in 1681. Atop the Gothic **Tolbooth Kirk,** built in 1842–44 for the General Assembly of the Church of Scotland, is, at 240 feet, the tallest spire in the city. The church houses the Edinburgh Festival offices, the **Festival Centre.**

The **Upper Bow,** running from Lawnmarket to Victoria Street, was once the main route westward from the town and castle. Before Victoria Street was built in the late 19th century, the Upper Bow led down into a narrow dark thoroughfare coursing between a canyon of tenements. All traffic struggled up and down this steep slope from the Grassmarket, which joins the now-truncated West Bow at its lower end. ⊠*East of the Esplanade and west of Lawnmarket, Old Town.*

**OFF THE BEATEN PATH**

**Duddingston.** Tucked behind Arthur's Seat, and about a 1-hour walk from Princes Street via Holyrood Park, this little community, formerly of brewers and weavers, still seems like a country village. The Duddingston Kirk has a Norman doorway and a watchtower that was built to keep body snatchers out of the graveyard. The church overlooks Duddingston Loch, popular with bird-watchers, and moments away is an old-style pub called the Sheep's Heid Inn, which serves a wide selection of beers and has the oldest skittle (bowling) alley in Scotland. ⊠*Duddingston* ⊹*Take Lothian Bus 42.*

❽ **George IV Bridge.** It's not immediately obvious that this is in fact a bridge, as buildings are closely packed most of the way along both sides. At the corner of the bridge stands one of the most photographed sculptures in Scotland, *Greyfriars Bobby.* This statue pays tribute to the famous Skye terrier who kept vigil beside his master John Gray's grave in the Greyfriar's churchyard for 14 years after Gray died in 1858. Bobby left only for a short time each day to be fed at a nearby coffee house. The 1961 Walt Disney film *Greyfriars Bobby* tells the story, though liberties were taken with the historical details. ⊠*Between Bank St. and intersection with Candlemaker Row, Old Town.*

❺ **Gladstone's Land.** This narrow, six-story tenement, next to the Assembly Hall on Lawnmarket, is a survivor from the 17th century. Typical Scottish architectural features are evident on two floors, including an arcaded ground floor (even in the city center, livestock sometimes inhabited the ground floor). The house has magnificent painted ceilings and is furnished in the style of a 17th-century merchant's home. ⊠*477B Lawnmarket, Old Town* ☎*0131/226–5856* ⊕*www.nts.org.uk* 🎫*£5* ☉*Apr.–June, Sept., and Oct., daily 10–5; July and Aug., daily 10–7; last admission 30 min before closing.*

❾ **Grassmarket.** For centuries an agricultural marketplace, Grassmarket now is the site of numerous shops, bars, and restaurants, making it a hive of activity at night. Sections of the Old Town wall can be traced on the north (castle) side by a series of steps that run steeply up from Grassmarket to Johnston Terrace above. The best-preserved section of the wall can be found by crossing to the south side and climbing the steps of the lane called the Vennel. Here the 16th-century **Flodden Wall** comes in from the east and turns south at Telfer's Wall, a 17th-century extension.

From the northeast corner of the Grassmarket, **Victoria Street,** a 19th-century addition to the Old Town, leads up to George IV Bridge. Shops here sell antiques, designer clothing, and high-quality gifts.

❼ **Lawnmarket.** The name "Lawnmarket" is a corruption of "land market," and is the second of the streets that make up the Royal Mile. It was formerly the site of the produce market for the city, with a once-a-week special sale of wool and linen. Now it's home to ⇨**Gladstone's Land** and the ⇨**Writers' Museum.** At different times the Lawnmarket Courts housed James Boswell, David Hume, and Robert Burns. In nearby Brodie's Close in the 1770s lived the infamous Deacon Brodie, pillar of society by day and a murdering gang leader by night. Robert Louis Stevenson (1850–94) may well have used Brodie as the inspira-

---

**ON THE GALLOWS**

Grassmarket's history is long and fabulous. Nineteenth-century body snatchers William Burke and William Hare lived close to here, and the cobbled cross at the east end marks the site of the town gallows. Among those hanged here were many 17th-century Covenanters, members of the Church of Scotland who rose up against Charles I's efforts to enforce Anglican or "English" ideologies on the Scottish people. Judges were known to issue the death sentence for these religious reformers with the words, "Let them glorify God in the Grassmarket."

tion for his *Strange Case of Dr. Jekyll and Mr. Hyde,* though the book isn't set in Edinburgh. ⊠*Between Castlehill and High St., Old Town.*

**NEED A BREAK?** Several atmospheric pubs and restaurants bustle on this section of the Royal Mile. Try the friendly Jolly Judge ( ⊠*7 James Ct., Old Town* 🕾*0131/225–2669*), where firelight brightens the dark-wood beams and a mixed crowd of university professors and students sip ale and eat light lunches of soup, pasta, quiche, or baked potatoes.

**⑰ Museum of Childhood.** Even adults tend to enjoy this cheerfully noisy museum—a cacophony of childhood memorabilia, vintage toys, and dolls, as well as a reconstructed schoolroom, street scene, fancy-dress party, and nursery. The museum claims to have been the first in the world devoted solely to the history of childhood. It's two blocks past the North Bridge–South Bridge junction on High Street. ⊠*42 High St., Old Town* 🕾*0131/529–4142* 🖷*0131/558–3103* ⊕*www.cac.org.uk* ⌨*Free* ☉*Mon.–Sat. 10–5, Sun. during festival 2–5.*

**㉓ Museum of Edinburgh.** A must-see if you're interested in the details of Old Town life, this former home, dating from 1570, is a fascinating museum of local history, displaying Scottish pottery and Edinburgh silver and glassware. One of the museum's most impressive documents is the National Covenant, signed by Scotland's presbyterian leadership in 1639. This "profession of faith" begins with not one, but three verses from the Bible. ⊠*142 Canongate, Old Town* 🕾*0131/529–4143* ⊕*www.cac.org.uk* ⌨*Free* ☉*Mon.–Sat. 10–5, Sun. during festival 2–5.*

**⑩ National Library of Scotland.** Founded in 1689, the library has a superb collection of books and manuscripts on the history and culture of Scotland, and also mounts regular exhibitions. Genealogists investigating family trees come here, and amateur family sleuths will find the staff helpful in their research. ⊠*George IV Bridge, Old Town* 🕾*0131/623–3700* ⊕*www.nls.uk* ⌨*Free* ☉*Mon., Tues., Thurs., and Fri. 9:30–8:30, Wed. 10–8:30, Sat. 9:30–1; exhibitions Mon.–Sat. 10–5; festival hrs weekdays 10–8, Sat. 10–5, Sun. 2–5.*

**⑭ Parliament House.** This was the seat of Scottish government until 1707, when the governments of Scotland and England were united, 104 years after the union of the two crowns. Partially hidden by the bulk of the High Kirk of St. Giles, it now houses the Supreme Law Courts of Scotland. ⊠*11 Parliament Sq., Old Town* 🕾*0131/225–2595* ⊕*www.scotcourts.gov.uk* ⌨*Free* ☉*Weekdays 10–4.*

**⑳ Scottish Storytelling Centre.** Opened in 2006, this arts center is housed in a modern building that manages to blend seamlessly with the historic structures on either side. It hosts a year-round program of storytelling, theater, and literary events. A café serves lunch and tea. ⊠*43 High St., Old Town* 🕾*0131/556–9579* ⊕*www.scottishstorytellingcentre.co.uk* ⌨*Free* ☉*Sept.–June, Mon.–Sat. 10–6; July and Aug., Mon.–Sat. 10–6, Sun. noon–6.*

**❹ Scotch Whisky Heritage Centre.** The mysterious process that turns malted barley and springwater into one of Scotland's most important exports is revealed in this museum. Although whisky-making is not in itself packed with drama, the center manages an imaginative presentation using models and tableaux viewed while riding in low-speed barrel-cars. At one point you're inside a huge vat surrounded by

> **MAPPING YOUR ROUTE**
>
> Several excellent city maps are available at bookstores. Particularly good is the *Bartholomew Edinburgh Plan,* with a scale of approximately 4 inches to 1 mi, by the long-established Edinburgh cartographic company John Bartholomew and Sons Ltd.

bubbling sounds and malty smells. The Amber Restaurant serves lunch; you can choose among 270 Scotch whiskies. ✉*354 Castlehill, Old Town* ☎*0131/220–0441* ⊕*www.whisky-heritage.co.uk* ✉*£9.25* ☻*Sept.–May, daily 9:30–6:30, last tour 5; June–Aug. daily 10–6, last tour 5:30.*

**❺ Writers' Museum.** Down a close off Lawnmarket is Lady Stair's House, built in 1622 and a good example of 17th-century urban architecture. Inside, the Writer's Museum evokes Scotland's literary past with such exhibits as the letters, possessions, and original manuscripts of Sir Walter Scott, Robert Louis Stevenson, and Robert Burns. The Stevenson collection is particularly strong. ✉*Off Lawnmarket, Old Town* ☎*0131/529–4901* ⊕*www.cac.org.uk* ✉*Free* ☻*Mon.–Sat. 10–5, last admission 4:45, Sun. during festival noon–5.*

## NEW TOWN

It was not until the Scottish Enlightenment, a civilizing time of expansion in the 1700s, that the city fathers decided to break away from the Royal Mile's rocky slope and create a new Edinburgh below the castle, a little to the north. This was to become the New Town, with elegant squares, classical facades, wide streets, and harmonious proportions. Clearly, change had to come. At the dawn of the 18th century, Edinburgh's unsanitary conditions—primarily a result of overcrowded living quarters—was becoming notorious. The well-known Scots fiddle tune "The Flooers (flowers) of Edinburgh" was only one of many ironic references to the capital's unpleasant environment, which greatly embarrassed the Scot James Boswell (1740–95), biographer and companion of the English lexicographer Dr. Samuel Johnson (1709–84). In his *Journal of a Tour of the Hebrides,* Boswell recalled that on retrieving Johnson from his grubby inn in the Canongate, "I could not prevent his being assailed by the evening effluvia of Edinburgh.... Walking the streets at night was pretty perilous and a good deal odoriferous."

To help remedy this sorry state of affairs, in 1767 James Drummond, the city's lord provost (the Scots term for mayor), urged the town council to hold a competition to design a new district for Edinburgh. The winner was an unknown young architect named James Craig (1744–95). His plan called for a grid of three main east–west streets, balanced at either end by two grand squares. These streets survive today, though some of the buildings that line them have been altered by later development. Princes Street is the southernmost, with Queen Street to the north and George Street as the axis, punctuated by St. Andrew and Charlotte squares. A look at the map will reveal a geometric symmetry unusual in Britain. Even the Princes Street Gardens are balanced by the Queen Street Gardens, to the north. Princes Street was conceived as an exclusive residential address, with an open vista facing the castle. It has since been altered by the demands of business and shopping, but the vista remains.

The New Town was expanded several times after Craig's death and now covers an area about three times larger than Craig envisioned. Indeed, some of the most elegant facades came later and can be found by strolling north of the Queen Street Gardens.

TIMING  If you want to get the most out of the National Gallery of Scotland and the Scottish National Portrait Gallery, take a whole day and allow at least an hour for each museum. The Portrait Gallery has a good restaurant, so one option is to arrive in time for lunch, then spend the afternoon there. Save time by riding the free galleries bus, which connects the National Gallery of Scotland, Scottish National Portrait Gallery, Scottish National Gallery of Modern Art, and Dean Gallery daily from 11 to 5. You can board or leave the bus at any of the galleries.

### MAIN ATTRACTIONS

OFF THE BEATEN PATH  **Britannia.** Moored on the waterfront at Leith, Edinburgh's port north of the city center, is the former Royal Yacht *Britannia,* launched in Scotland in 1953 and now retired to her home country. The Royal Apartments and the more functional engine room, bridge, galleys, and captain's cabin are all open to view. The land-based visitor center within the huge Ocean Terminal shopping mall has exhibits and photographs about the yacht's history. ⊠ *Ocean Terminal, Leith* ☎ *0131/555–5566* ⊕ *www.royalyachtbritannia.co.uk* ☎ *£9.50* ☉ *Mar.–Oct., daily 9:30–4:30; Nov.–Feb., daily 10–3:30.*

**39 ★ Georgian House.** The National Trust for Scotland has furnished this house in period style to show the elegant domestic arrangements of an affluent family of the late 18th century. The hallway was designed to accommodate sedan chairs, in which 18th-century grandees were carried through the streets. ⊠ *7 Charlotte Sq., New Town* ☎ *0131/226–3318* ⊕ *www.nts.org.uk* ☎ *£5* ☉ *Mar., daily 11–3; Apr.–June and Sept.–Oct., daily 10–5; July and Aug., daily 10–7; Nov., daily 11–3; last admission half hr before closing.*

**29** Fodor's Choice ★ **National Gallery of Scotland.** Opened to the public in 1859, the National Gallery presents a wide selection of paintings from the Renaissance to the postimpressionist period within a grand neoclassical building designed by William Playfair. Most famous are the old-master paintings bequeathed by the duke of Sutherland, including Titian's *Three Ages of Man.* All the great names are here; works by Velázquez, El Greco, Rembrandt, Goya, Poussin, Turner, Degas, Monet, and Van Gogh, among others, complement a fine collection of Scottish art, including

Sir Henry Raeburn's *Reverend Robert Walker Skating on Duddingston Loch* and other masterworks by Ramsay, Raeburn, and Wilkie. The Weston Link connects the National Gallery of Scotland to the Royal Scottish Academy and provides expanded gallery space as well as a restaurant, bar, café, information center, and shop. The free galleries bus stops here daily on the hour from 11 to 4. ✉ *The Mound, Old Town* ☎ *0131/624–6200 general inquiries, 0131/332–2266 recorded information* ⊕ *www.nationalgalleries.org* ✆ *Free* ⊘ *Fri.–Wed. 10–5, Thurs. 10–7. Print Room, weekdays 10–12:30 and 2–4:30 by appointment.*

**OFF THE BEATEN PATH**

**Royal Botanic Garden Edinburgh.** Britain's largest rhododendron and azalea gardens are part of the varied and comprehensive collection of plant and flower species in this 70-acre garden, just north of the city center. An impressive Chinese garden has the largest collection of wild-origin Chinese plants outside China. There's a cafeteria, plus a gift shop that sells plants and books. Take a taxi to the garden; or ride Bus 27 from Princes Street or Bus 23 from Hanover Street. To walk to the garden from the New Town, take Dundas Street, the continuation of Hanover Street, and turn left at the clock tower onto Inverleith Row (about 20 minutes). ✉ *Inverleith Row, Inverleith* ☎ *0131/552–7171* ⊕ *www. rbge.org.uk* ✆ *Free; greenhouses £3.50* ⊘ *Nov.–Feb., daily 10–4; Mar.–Sept., daily 10–7; Oct., daily, 10–6. Guided tours, Apr.–Sept., daily at 11 and 2.*

**㉜ Scott Monument.** What appears to be a Gothic cathedral spire chopped off and planted in the east end of the Princes Street Gardens is the nation's tribute to Sir Walter—a 200-foot-high monument looming over Princes Street. Built in 1844 in honor of Scotland's most famous author, Sir Walter Scott, the author of *Ivanhoe, Waverley,* and many other novels and poems, it's centered on a marble statue of Scott and his favorite dog, Maida. It's worth taking the time to explore the immediate area, Princes Street Gardens, one of the prettiest city parks in Britain. In the open-air theater, amid the park's trim flower beds, stately trees, and carefully tended lawns, brass bands occasionally play. Here, too, is the famous **monument to David Livingstone,** whose African meeting with H. M. Stanley is part of Scot-American history. ✉ *Princes St., New Town* ☎ *0131/529–4068* ⊕ *www.cac.org.uk* ✆ *£3* ⊘ *Apr.–Sept., Mon.–Sat. 9–6, Sun. 10–6; Oct.–Mar., Mon.–Sat. 9–3, Sun. 10–3.*

**OFF THE BEATEN PATH**

**Scottish National Gallery of Modern Art.** This handsome former school building on Belford Road, close to the New Town, displays paintings and sculpture, including works by Pablo Picasso, Georges Braque, Henri Matisse, and André Derain. The gallery also has an excellent restaurant in the basement. The free galleries bus stops here on the half hour. Across the street is the **Dean Gallery,** also part of the National Galleries of Scotland. It showcases modern art and changing exhibitions. ✉ *Belford Rd., Dean Village* ☎ *0131/556–8921* ⊕ *www.nationalgalleries.org* ✆ *Free* ⊘ *Daily 10–5; extended hrs during festival.*

**㊷ ★ Scottish National Portrait Gallery.** A magnificent red-sandstone Gothic building dating from 1889 on Queen Street houses this must-visit institution. The gallery contains a superb Thomas Gainsborough paint-

## CLOSE UP

# Leith, Edinburgh's Seaport

1

Just north of the city, Leith sits on the south shore of the Firth of Forth and was a separate town until it merged with the city in 1920. After World War II and up until the 1980s, the declining seaport had a reputation for poverty and crime. In recent years, however, it has been revitalized with the restoration of commercial buildings as well as the construction of new luxury housing, bringing a buzz of trendiness. All of the docks have been redeveloped; the Old East and West docks are now the administrative headquarters of the Scottish Executive.

In earlier times, Leith was the stage for many historic happenings. In 1560 Mary of Guise, the mother of Mary, Queen of Scots, ruled Scotland from Leith; her daughter landed in Leith the following year to embark on her infamous reign. A century later, Crom-

well led his troops to Leith to root out Scots royalists. An arch of the Leith Citadel reminds all of the Scots' victory. Leith also prides itself on being a "home of golf" because official rules to the game were devised in 1744, in what is today Links Park. The rolling green mounds here hide the former field and cannon sites of past battles.

It's worth exploring the lowest reaches of the Water of Leith (the river that flows through the town), an area where restaurants, shops, and pubs proliferate. The major attraction for visitors here is the former royal yacht *Britannia,* moored outside the huge Ocean Terminal shopping mall. Reach Leith by walking down Leith Street and Leith Walk, from the east end of Princes Street (20 to 30 minutes) or take Lothian Bus 22 (Britannia Ocean Drive, Leith).

ing and portraits by the Scottish artists Allan Ramsay (1713–84) and Sir Henry Raeburn (1756–1823), among many others. You can see portraits of classic literary figures such as Robert Burns and Sir Walter Scott, and modern portraits depict actors, sports stars, and living members of the royal family. The building's beautiful William Hole murals representing Scots from the Stone Age to the 19th century are themselves worthy of study. The free galleries bus stops here every day from 11:15 to 4:15. ⊠ *1 Queen St., New Town* ☎*0131/624–6200* ⊕*www.nationalgalleries.org* ✉*Free; charge for special exhibitions* ☉*Fri.–Wed. 10–5, Thurs. 10–7; extended hrs during festival.*

### ALSO WORTH SEEING

**36** **Calton Hill.** Robert Louis Stevenson's favorite view of his beloved city was from the top of this hill. The architectural styles represented by the extraordinary collection of monuments here include mock Gothic—the Old Observatory, for example—and neoclassical. Under the latter category falls the monument William Playfair (1789–1857) designed to honor his talented uncle, the geologist and mathematician John Playfair (1748–1819), as well as his cruciform **New Observatory.** The piece that commands the most attention, however, is the so-called **National Monument,** often referred to as "Edinburgh's [or Scotland's] Disgrace." Intended to mimic Athens's Parthenon, this monument for the dead of the Napoleonic Wars was started in 1822 to the specifications of a design by Playfair. But in 1830, only 12 columns later, money ran out, and the columned facade became a monument to high aspirations and poor fund-raising. The tallest monument on Calton Hill is the 100-foot-high **Nelson Monument,** completed in 1815 in honor of Britain's naval hero Horatio Nelson (1758–1805); you can climb its 143 steps for sweeping city views. The **Burns Monument** is the circular Corinthian temple below Regent Road. Devotees of Robert Burns may want to visit one other grave—that of Mrs. Agnes McLehose, or "Clarinda," in the Canongate Graveyard. ⊠ *Bounded by Leith St. to the west and Regent Rd. to the south, Calton* ☎ *0131/556–2716* ⊕ *www.cac.org.uk* ✉ *£3 Nelson Monument* ⊙ *Nelson Monument Apr.–Sept., Mon. 1–6, Tues.–Sat. 10–6; Oct.–Mar., Mon.–Sat. 10–3.*

**❸❽ Charlotte Square.** At the west end of George Street is the New Town's centerpiece—an 18th-century square with one of the proudest achievements of Robert Adam, Scotland's noted neoclassical architect. On the north side, Adam designed a palatial facade to unite three separate town houses of such sublime simplicity and perfect proportions that architects come from all over the world to study it. Happily, the Age of Enlightenment grace notes continue within, as the center town house is now occupied by the **Georgian House** museum, and to the west stands **West Register House.** ⊠ *West end of George St., New Town.*

**OFF THE BEATEN PATH**

**Edinburgh Zoo.** Children love to visit the some 1,000 animals that live in Edinburgh Zoo. You can even handle some of the animals from April to September. The ever-popular Penguin Parade begins at 2:15 (but since penguin participation is totally voluntary, the event is unpredictable). The zoo spreads over an 80-acre site on the slopes of Corstorphine Hill. Take buses 12, 26, or 31. ⊠ *Corstorphine Rd., next to Holiday Inn Edinburgh, Corstorphine* ✥ *3 mi west of city center* ☎ *0131/334–9171* ⊕ *www.edinburghzoo.org.uk* ✉ *£10.50* ⊙ *Apr.–Sept., daily 9–6; Oct. and Mar., daily 9–5; Nov.–Feb., daily 9–4:30.*

**❸❼ George Street.** With its upscale shops and handsome Georgian frontages, this is a more pleasant, less crowded street for wandering than Princes Street. The **statue of King George IV,** at the intersection of George and Hanover streets, recalls the visit of George IV to Scotland in 1822. He was the first British monarch to do so since King Charles II, in the 17th century. By the 19th century, enough time had passed since the Jacobite Uprising of 1745 for Scotland to be perceived at Westminster as being safe enough for a monarch to visit.

The ubiquitous Sir Walter Scott turns up farther down the street. It was at a grand dinner in the **Assembly Rooms,** between Hanover and Frederick streets, that Scott acknowledged having written the *Waverley* novels (the name of the author had hitherto been a secret, albeit a badly kept one). You can meet Scott once again, in the form of a plaque just downhill, at 39 Castle Street, his Edinburgh address before he moved to Abbotsford, in the Borders region, where he died in 1832. ⊠ *Between Charlotte and St. Andrew squares, New Town.*

**❸❸ Jenners.** Edinburgh's equivalent of London's Harrods department store, Jenners is noteworthy not only for its high-quality wares and good restaurants but also because of the building's interesting architectural detail—baroque on the outside, with a mock-Jacobean central well inside. It was one of the earliest department stores, established in 1838. The caryatids decorating the exterior were said to have been placed in honor of the store's predominantly female customers. ⊠*48 Princes St., New Town* ☎*0131/225–2442* ☽*Mon., Tues., Wed., Fri., and Sat. 9–6, Thurs. 9–8, Sun. 11–5.*

**㊶ Moray Place.** Moray Place—with its "pendants" of Ainslie Place and Randolph Crescent—was laid out in 1822 by the earl of Moray. From the start the homes were planned to be of particularly high quality, with lovely curving facades, imposing porticos, and a central secluded garden (for residents only). ⊠*Between Charlotte Sq. and Water of Leith, New Town.*

**㉘ The Mound.** This rising street originated from the need for a dry-shod crossing of the muddy quagmire left behind when Nor' Loch, the body of water below the castle, was drained (the railway now cuts through this area). The work is said to have been started by a local tailor, George Boyd, who tired of struggling through the mud en route from his New Town house to his Old Town shop. The building of a ramp was under way by 1781, and by the time of its completion, in 1830, "Geordie Boyd's mud brig [bridge]," as the street was first known, had been built up with an estimated 2 million cartloads of earth dug from the foundations of the New Town.

**㉛ Princes Street.** The south side of this well-planned street is occupied by the well-kept Princes Street Gardens, which act as a wide green moat to the castle on its rock. Unfortunately, the north side is now one long sequence of chain stores with unappealing modern fronts that can be seen in almost any large British town. ⊠*Running east–west from Waterloo Pl. to Lothian Rd., East End to West End.*

**㉞ Register House.** Scotland's first custom-built archives depository, Register House, designed by the great Robert Adam, was partly funded by the sale of estates forfeited by Jacobite landowners after their last rebellion in Britain (1745–46). Work on the Regency-style building, which marks the end of Princes Street, started in 1774. The statue in front is of the first duke of Wellington (1769–1852). It's possible to conduct genealogical research here; check online and call ahead for more information. ⊠*2 Princes St., New Town* ☎*0131/535–1314* ⊕*www.nas. gov.uk* ☜*Free* ☽*Weekdays 9–4:45.*

**NEED A BREAK?** Café Royal ( ⊠*17 W. Register St., New Town* ☎*0131/557–4792*), immediately west of Register House, serves good Scottish lagers and ales, and simple lunch items like stovies and, of course, oysters. The 18th-century building has plenty of character, with ornate tiles and stained-glass windows. Local musicians sometimes play gigs in a separate suite.

**㉚ Royal Scottish Academy.** The William Playfair–designed Academy hosts temporary art exhibitions (Monet paintings, for example), but is also worth visiting for a look at the imposing, neoclassic architecture. The underground Weston Link connects the museum to the National Gal-

## Ancestor Hunting

Are you a Cameron or a Campbell, Mackenzie or Macdonald? If so, you may be one of the more than 25 million people of Scottish descent around the world. It was the Highland clearances of the 18th and 19th century, in which tenant farmers were driven from their homes and replaced with sheep, that started the mass emigration to North America and Australia. Before or during a trip, you can do a little genealogical research or pursue your family tree more seriously.

Start at VisitScotland's Web site, www.ancestralscotland.com, for information about clans and surnames, books, and family history societies. The site steers you to key sources, such as www.scotlandspeople.gov.uk, the official government source of genealogical data; there's a charge for using that service.

You may want to do research at Edinburgh's **General Register Office for Scotland** ( ⊠ *3 W. Register St.* ☎ *0131/314–4449 for booking* ⊕ *www.gro-scotland.gov.uk*). The fee for research here, based on how long you spend there, ranges from £10 for part of a day to £17 for a full day (a week costs £65). Space is limited, and no reservations are taken for searches of less than a day; but some places are available each day on a first-come, first-served basis.

Willing to pay for help? Companies such as Scottish Ancestral Trail (www.scottish-ancestral-trail.co.uk) do the research and plan a trip around your family history. Throughout Scotland, you can check bookstores for information and visit clan museums and societies.

lery of Scotland. ⊠*The Mound, Old Town* ☎*0131/225–6671* ⊕*www.royalscottishacademy.org* ☜*Free* ☉*Fri.–Wed. 10–5, Thurs. 10–7.*

**㉟ Waterloo Place.** The fine neoclassical architecture on this street was designed as a piece by Archibald Elliot (d. 1823) in 1815. Waterloo Place extends over Regent Bridge, bounded by the 1815 **Regent Arch,** a simple, triumphal Corinthian-column war memorial at the center of Ionic screens bordering the bridge. ⊠*Eastern extension of Princes St., East End.*

**㊵ West Register House.** The former St. George's Church, in the middle of the west side of Charlotte Square, today fulfills a different role, as an extension of the original Register House on Princes Street. You may view modern records, but check online and call ahead if you wish to carry out extensive genealogical research. ⊠*17 Charlotte Sq., New Town* ☎*0131/535–1400* ⊕*www.nas.gov.uk* ☜*Free* ☉*Weekdays 9–4:30.*

# WHERE TO EAT

Edinburgh has many restaurants serving sophisticated international cuisines, but you may also notice a strong emphasis on traditional style. This tends to mean the Scottish-French style that harks back to the historical "Auld Alliance," founded in the 13th century against the English. The Scots element is the preference for fresh and local

1

foodstuffs; the French supply the sauces, often to be poured on after cooking. Restaurants tend to be small, so it's best to make reservations at the more popular ones, even on weekdays and definitely at festival time. As Edinburgh is an unusually small capital, most of the good restaurants are within walking distance of the main streets, Princes Street and the Royal Mile.

## PRICES

It's possible to eat well in Edinburgh without spending a fortune. Multicourse pretheater or prix-fixe options are common and almost always less expensive than ordering à la carte. Even at restaurants in the highest price category, you can easily spend under £30 per person. A service charge of 10% or more may be added to your bill, though this practice is not adhered to uniformly. If no charge has been added and you're satisfied with the service, a 10% tip is appropriate. People tend to eat later in Scotland than in England, around 8 PM on average, or rather they finish eating and then drink on in leisurely Scottish fashion.

| WHAT IT COSTS IN POUNDS | | | | | |
|---|---|---|---|---|---|
| | £ | ££ | £££ | ££££ | £££££ |
| AT DINNER | under £10 | £10–£14 | £15–£19 | £20–£25 | Over £25 |

Prices are per person for a main course at dinner.

## OLD TOWN

The most historic part of the city houses the grander restaurants that many people associate with this city. It is also home to some of Edinburgh's oldest pubs serving informal meals.

### FRENCH

££££ ✕**Witchery by the Castle.** The hundreds of "witches" who were executed
Fodor'sChoice on Castlehill, just yards from where you'll be seated, are the inspiration
★ for this outstanding and atmospheric restaurant. The cavernous interior, complete with flickering candlelight, is festooned with cabalistic insignia and tarot-card characters. Gilded and painted ceilings reflect the close links between France and Scotland, as does the menu, which includes roasted quail with braised endive and scallops with spiced pork belly and carrot puree. Pre- and post-theater (5:30 to 6:30 and 10:30 to 11:30) £12.50 two-course specials are an inexpensive way to sample the exceptional cuisine. (The restaurant also offers lodging in seven sumptuous suites.) ⊠*Castlehill, Royal Mile, Old Town* ☎*0131/225–5613* ▤*AE, DC, V.*

£££ ✕**Merchants.** This is a bustling, cheery cavern with bright scarlet walls, mirrors, plants, and a nonstop jazz sound track, set beneath the dramatic arch of George IV Bridge. The menu ranges from simple haggis and beef to a mille-feuille of scallops and lamb chops with raspberry-and-mint sauce. Its more ambitious dishes are reminiscent of nouvelle cuisine, but Merchants really does the basics best. Prix-fixe lunches begin at £11, dinners from £22. ⊠*17 Merchant St., Old Town* ☎*0131/225–4009* ▤*AE, DC, MC, V.*

££  ✕ **Le Sept.** This charming French bistro full of mismatched chairs and
★   Parisian art posters is an Edinburgh institution. It's friendly, lively,
unfussy, and famed for its crepes with adventurous fillings. The daily
changing menu also lists simple staples such as delicately cooked
salmon fillets and a deliciously sweet coq au vin. The wine list is similarly select, and the service is always delightful. Fixed-price lunches are
an unbeatable value, with three courses costing £10.  ⊠*5 Hunter Sq.,
Old Town* ☎*0131/225–5428* ☰*AE, DC, MC, V.*

### MEXICAN

££  ✕ **Pancho Villa.** Named after the famous revolutionary, this vibrant eatery, part of a small Scottish chain founded by Mexican-born Mayra
Nunez, focuses on large portions of flavorful, fresh food. Traditional
paintings decorate a small space that seems bigger because of the bright
blue-and-orange color scheme. To start, try an icy blended margarita
with the *costillas en naranja* (roasted ribs in a chili-and-orange sauce)
or the *ceviche* (raw fish with a citrus marinade). Main dishes include
swordfish steak with mango salsa and *enchiladas mole poblano* (torti-
llas with chicken and chocolate sauce). ⊠*240 Canongate, Old Town*
☎*0131/557–4416* ☰*MC, V.*

### SCOTTISH

££££ ✕ **The Tower.** On the rooftop of the Museum of Scotland, this restaurant
offers a feast of modern aesthetics—tweed banquettes, suede chairs,
glass walls—before you even get to the menu. It also has one of the finest vistas in the capital. The Tower has a high-powered ambience and
a sophisticated menu with an exquisite oyster and shellfish selection,
roast saddle of wild red venison, and more. The two-course pretheater (5 to 6:30) supper is an especially good value, but don't let the
lovely Edinburgh skyline distract you from making your curtain time.
⊠*Museum of Scotland, Chambers St., Old Town* ☎*0131/225–3003*
⚝*Reservations essential* ☰*AE, DC, MC, V.*

£££  ✕ **Howie's.** This chain consists of four stylish neighborhood bistros,
each with its own character. The food is Scottish contemporary—lots
of fresh local produce, fish, and game. The steaks are tender Aberdeen
beef, and the Loch Fyne herring is sweet-cured to Howie's own recipe.
⊠*10–14 Victoria St., Old Town* ☎*0131/225–1721* ⊠*29 Waterloo Pl., East End* ☎*0131/556–5766* ⊠*208 Bruntsfield Pl., South
Side* ☎*0131/221–1777* ⊠*1 Alva St., West End* ☎*0131/225–9594*
☰*AE, MC, V.*

££  ✕ **Doric Tavern.** Beyond the bar's grand entrance staircase is a languid
bistro environment enhanced by the stripped wood floor, plain wood
tables, and color scheme in subdued orange and terra-cotta. The menu
lists a selection of fresh fish, meat, and vegetarian dishes, plus a daily
special such as honey-baked salmon with oatcakes. Prix-fixe lunch and
dinner options are an excellent value. ⊠*15/16 Market St., Old Town*
☎*0131/225–1084* ⚝*Reservations essential* ☰*AE, MC, V.*

£   ✕ **Beehive Inn.** Some 400 years ago the Beehive was a coaching inn,
and outside the pub's doors once stood the gallows. Bar meals and
snacks are served throughout the day, downstairs or in the beer garden.
Upstairs, Rafters Restaurant opens at 6 for dinner; the grilled salmon

steaks are a good option. The bar can be noisy, but there's usually a quieter spot to be found. You can book literary lunch and supper packages downstairs in conjunction with the McEwan's Edinburgh Literary Pub Tour, which departs from here. ⊠ *18–20 Grassmarket, Old Town* ☎ *0131/225–7171* ⊟ *AE, MC, V.*

### THAI

££ ✕ **Thai Orchid.** The statue of a golden Buddha greets you at this stylish restaurant where each table has an orchid for its centerpiece. Rich reds and browns, a portrait of the Thai king, and the traditionally dressed staff transport you to Thailand, if only for a few hours. To start, try the *todd mun kao pode* (deep-fried corn cakes with sweet-and-sour peanut and coriander dip). Good main courses include *pla priew wan* (monkfish poached with coconut milk) or *pedt Orchid*, duck stir-fried with mango, chili, garlic, and red peppers. The sticky rice with coconut milk and mango is an unmissable dessert. ⊠ *5A Johnston Terr., Old Town* ☎ *0131/225–6633* ⊟ *MC, V.*

### VEGETARIAN

££ ✕ **David Bann.** In the heart of the Old Town, this ultrahip vegetarian and ★ vegan favorite attracts young locals with its light, airy, modern dining room and creative menu. Tap water comes with mint and strawberries; dishes are sizable and extremely colorful. The food is so flavorful that carnivores may forget they're eating vegetarian. Try the spinach and smoked cheese strudel and the malt-whisky pannacotta. ⊠ *56–58 St. Mary's St., Old Town* ☎ *0131/556–5888* ⊟ *AE, DC, MC, V.*

## NEW TOWN

The New Town, with its striking street plan, ambitious architecture, and professional crowd, has restaurants where you can get everything from a quick snack to a more formal dinner.

### CHINESE

££ ✕ **Kweilin.** This pleasant family-run restaurant serves such favorites as aromatic crispy duck, and bean curd with vegetables. The lunch menu is a pricey £15 but worth it, and the special four-course dinner menus are an even better value, starting at £23 per person. Amid the traditional Chinese decor are several large paintings depicting scenes from the Kwangsi Province, of which Kweilin is the capital. ⊠ *19–21 Dundas St., New Town* ☎ *0131/557–1875* ⊟ *AE, MC, V* ⊘ *Closed Mon. Jan.–Nov.*

### ECLECTIC

££££ ✕ **Oloroso.** In the heart of the New Town and close to the main shopping streets, this is the perfect spot for a revitalizing lunch or dinner after exploring the city. The contemporary international cooking reflects influences from Europe and Asia, service is efficient and friendly, and the bar serves some of the best cocktails in Britain. Try the roasted duck breast with braised red cabbage and apples, or the aubergine *galette* (eggplant tart) with a tomato-and-cinnamon sauce. The wine list has about 230 selections, including champagne. The dining room and roof

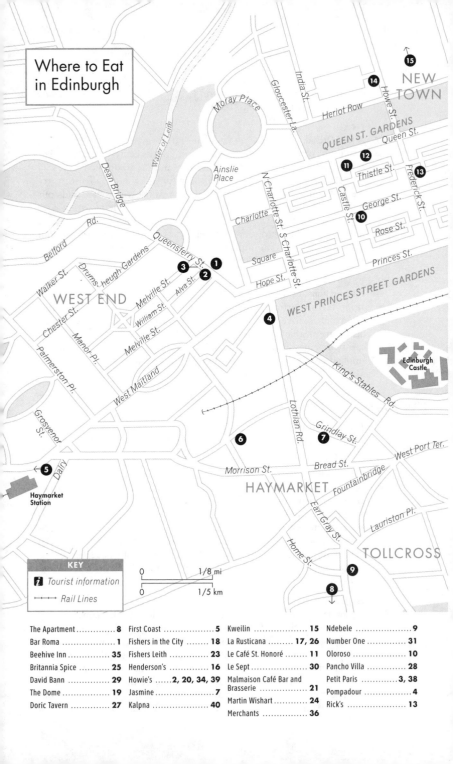

# Where to Eat
in Edinburgh

**NEW TOWN**

**WEST END**

Edinburgh Castle

Haymarket Station

**HAYMARKET**

**TOLLCROSS**

0        1/8 mi

0        1/5 km

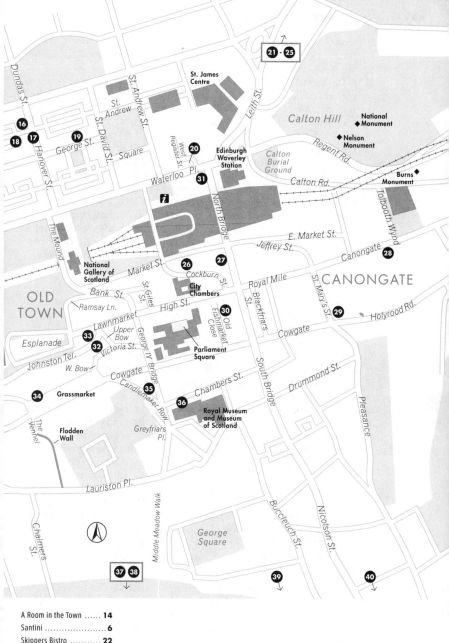

terrace have stunning views across the Firth of Forth to the hills of Fife on one side, and the castle and city rooftops on the other. ⊠ *33 Castle St., New Town* ☎ *0131/226–7614* ▤ *AE, DC, MC, V.*

£££   ✕ **The Dome.** The splendid interior of this former bank, with painted plasterwork and a central dome, provides an elegant backdrop for relaxed dining. Or you could just opt for a drink at the bar, a hot spot where sophisticates wind down after work. The toasted BLT sandwiches are almost big enough for two, but if you're ravenous the eclectic menu offers many other options: try the tortellini in a broccoli-and-blue-cheese sauce or the char-grilled chicken salad with nan bread. ⊠ *14 George St., New Town* ☎ *0131/624–8624* ▤ *AE, MC, V.*

££   ✕ **Rick's.** There's no *Casablanca* theme, and Sam doesn't play it even once, but the local office crowd makes things lively after 5 at this restaurant-bar. The minimalist design is ultrachic. An imaginative menu includes duck breast with pink peppercorn sauce, asparagus ravioli, and crispy salmon fillet with Asian fried rice. The bright lobby bar serves cocktails amid brash music and chrome-and-stone decor. ⊠ *55A Fredrick St., New Town* ☎ *0131/622–7800* ▤ *AE, MC, V.*

### FRENCH

££££   ✕ **Le Café St. Honoré.** Quintessentially Parisian in style, this restaurant reflects all that is charming about French café dining. From the moment you enter the beautifully lighted room you're transported into the decadently stylish belle epoque. A concise menu leaves more time for chat. You might start off with a warm salad of scallops, monkfish, chorizo, and pine nuts, followed by lamb confit or panfried turbot cooked with cider, green peppercorns, and prawns. ⊠ *34 N.W. Thistle Street La., New Town* ☎ *0131/226–2211* ▤ *AE, DC, MC, V.*

£££   ✕ **Pompadour.** As might be expected of a restaurant named after the
★   king's mistress, Madame de Pompadour, the dining room here is inspired by the court of Louis XV, with subtle plasterwork and rich murals. The cuisine is also classic French, with top-quality Scottish produce completing the happiest of alliances. The extensive, well-chosen wine list complements such dishes as sea bass with crispy leeks and caviar-butter sauce, whole lobster with mustard and cheese, and loin of venison with potato pancakes. This is the place to go if you want a festive night out, and it's ideal for the formal lunch that needs lightening up. ⊠ *Caledonian Hilton Hotel, Princes St., New Town* ☎ *0131/222–8777* ⌕ *Reservations essential* ▤ *AE, DC, MC, V* ☉ *Closed Sun. and Mon.*

### ITALIAN

££   ✕ **La Rusticana.** Hanover Street exists to delight lovers of Italian food; some of the best pasta and pizza restaurants compete here, but this one usually wins the day. Stronger on pasta than pizza, La Rusticana remains a good value, only marginally above average in price. Along with a sister restaurant in the Old Town, it's a fundamental part of Edinburgh's food culture, a favorite for business meetings, and a generous patron of charity events. ⊠ *90 Hanover St., New Town* ☎ *0131/225–2227* ⊠ *25 Cockburn St., Old Town* ☎ *0131/225–2832* ▤ *AE, DC, MC, V.*

### SCOTTISH

£££££  ✗ **Number One.** Within the Edwardian splendor of the Balmoral Hotel, this restaurant matches its grand surroundings with a menu that highlights the best of Scottish seafood and game. Try the roulade of organic salmon with langoustine tortellini or the hazelnut-infused pork loin with beetroot-and-chive *jus*. The wine list is extensive, the service impeccable. All in all, this is the kind of stylish yet unstuffy restaurant that is perfect for an intimate dinner. ⊠*Princes St., New Town* ☎*0131/557–2672* ⚑*Reservations essential* ▭*AE, DC, MC, V.*

£££  ✗ **A Room in the Town.** At this relaxed, friendly bistro serving Scots-French fare, there's a strong emphasis on fresh local meat, with the Scottish touch accounting for slightly sweeter-than-usual sauces. You may bring your own bottle of wine—an excellent wine shop is just a block away—to offset the somewhat high prices, although the restaurant serves wine, too, along with very nice brandy. Plain but cheerful thanks to bright colors and wooden fixtures, it's perfect for a sociable night out with friends. ⊠*18 Howe St., New Town* ☎*0131/225–8204* ⚑*Reservations essential* ▭*MC, V.*

### VEGETARIAN

£  ✗ **Henderson's.** This was Edinburgh's original vegetarian restaurant long before it was fashionable to serve healthful, meatless creations. The salad bar has more than a dozen different salads each day; a massive plateful costs less than £7. Tasty hot options include Moroccan stew with couscous and moussaka. Live mellow music plays six nights a week (seven during the festival). Around the corner on Thistle Street is the Bistro, from the same proprietors; it serves snacks, meals, and decadent desserts such as chocolate fondue. There's also an impressive organic wine list. ⊠*94 Hanover St., New Town* ☎*0131/225–2131* ▭*AE, DC, MC, V* ☾*Closed Sun. except during festival.*

## HAYMARKET

West of the Old Town and south of the West End is Haymarket, a district with its own down-to-earth character and well-worn charm. This area has many restaurants that tend to be more affordable than those in the center of town.

### CHINESE

££  ✗ **Jasmine.** Seafood is the specialty of this small, friendly Cantonese restaurant, known for rapid service that deals with the constant stream of customers, even on weekdays. The flickering candles that illuminate the interior are relaxing, although tables are quite closely spaced. Delicious dishes include mixed seafood on a bed of lettuce, and mango-flavored chicken served in the shells of two half mangos. Prix-fixe lunches, starting at £6.90 for three courses, are a good value. A take-out menu is available. ⊠*32 Grindlay St., Haymarket* ☎*0131/229–5757* ▭*AE, MC, V.*

### SCOTTISH

££   ✕ **First Coast.** This attractive, laid-back bistro, just a few minutes' walk from Haymarket Station, is a favorite with locals. Hardwood floors, stone walls, soft blue hues, and seaside paintings add to the coastal theme. Savory temptations include pumpkin stew and raisin couscous, panfried seabass with fennel, mustard, and ginger, and Aberdeen Angus sirloin steak with tomato-and-red-onion salad. The international wine list is as varied as the daily specials. ✉ *99–101 Dalry Rd., Haymarket* ☎ *0131/313–4404* ▭ *MC, V.*

## WEST END & POINTS WEST

Even after business hours, the city's commercial center is the place to find a variety of international restaurants.

### FRENCH

£££   ✕ **Petit Paris.** Don't be put off by the somewhat bland entrance of this lively 2nd-floor bistro; inside, it's cheerfully decorated with checked tablecloths, copper pots, and bunches of garlic. The staff is predominantly French, and the emphasis is on casual dining, local produce, and home cooking. The one-course lunch special plus coffee or tea for £5.90 is a real bargain. Try the traditional French black pudding and slow-baked rabbit with Dijon-mustard sauce. ✉ *17 Queensferry St., West End* ☎ *0131/226–1890* ✉ *38/40 Grassmarket, Old Town* ☎ *0131/226–2442* ▭ *MC, V.*

### ITALIAN

£££   ✕ **Bar Roma.** This is a genuine Italian experience, albeit in Scotland. The food tastes great, the place is noisy and fun, the chatty waiters are full of energy, and the hosts are always willing to squeeze you in, no matter how crowded the place may be. If you want to dine in peace and quiet, avoid early evening when the office crowd warms up for a night on the town. Specialties include ample calzone and seafood linguine. ✉ *39A Queensferry St., West End* ☎ *0131/226–2977* ▭ *AE, DC, MC, V.*

£££   ✕ **Santini.** Its dated decor and an out-of-the-way location that makes you wonder if Santini will also serve disappointing dishes. But this trattoria makes up for any shortcomings by giving you a mouthful of flavors. The Tuscan chef cooks with real passion: the tenderest steak in balsamic vinegar and the hottest, sweetest prawns with linguini are just two of the knee-tremblers on the menu. Vegetarians are catered for with classic peasant dishes, like melt-in-the-mouth *melanzane alla parmigiana* (eggplant with cheese). ✉ *8 Conference Sq., West End* ☎ *0131/221–7788* ▭ *AE, DC, MC, V.*

## SOUTH SIDE

The presence of university professors and students means eateries that are both affordable and interesting.

**1**

### AFRICAN

£ ✗**Ndebele.** This small, friendly café—named after the tribe from South Africa and Zimbabwe that has maintained the customs and language of its Zulu ancestors—is ideally placed for a snack before a trip to the nearby Cameo cinema. The tasty *boerewors* (South African sausage), smoked ostrich, and the large selection of interesting sandwiches on a choice of breads can be eaten on the spot or ordered out. Deli products, including *biltong* (strips of cured, air-dried meat), are also for sale. African art hangs on the wood-panel, geometric-pattern walls in bright shades of purple and orange. ✉*57 Home St., Tollcross* ☎*0131/221–1141* ▤*AE, MC, V.*

### ECLECTIC

££ ✗**The Apartment.** A wacky, whirlwind affair, this popular restaurant has a varied, innovative menu that materializes into huge portions. Choose from one of four menu categories: CHL (Chunky Healthy Lines), Fish Things, Other Things, and Salad. Dishes include fabulous mussels in a creamy sauce, North African spicy marinated lamb patties, *merguez* (spicy sausage) and grilled basil-wrapped goat cheese, and huge salads like *tiede* piquant (spicy olives, potatoes, roasted peppers, and chorizo, topped with a poached egg). ✉*7–13 Barclay Pl., near King's Theatre, Tollcross* ☎*0131/228–6456* ▤*MC, V.*

### INDIAN

£ ✗**Kalpna.** The unremarkable facade of this vegetarian Indian restaurant, amid an ordinary row of shops, and the low-key interior, enlivened by Indian prints and fabric pictures, belie the food—unlike anything you're likely to encounter elsewhere in the city. *Dam aloo Kashmiri* is a medium-spicy potato dish with a sauce made from honey, pistachios, and almonds. *Bangan mirch masala* is spicier, with eggplant and red chili peppers. Thaali (a variety of dishes served in bowls on a tray), a Gujarat specialty, is great value at £12.95. ✉*2–3 St. Patricks Sq., South Side* ☎*0131/667–9890* ▤*MC, V* ☺*Closed Sun. Jan.–Mar.*

FodorśChoice ★

## LEITH

Seafood lovers are drawn to the old port of Leith to sample the freshest seafood and to admire the authentic seafaring feel of the docklands.

### ASIAN

££ ✗**Britannia Spice.** A few hundred yards from the former royal yacht from which it gets its name, this restaurant is a good place to recover from the Ocean Terminal shopping experience. Britannia Spice serves dishes from India, Bangladesh, Thailand, and Nepal. Try the Thai beef or the Nepalese trout with vegetables and green chilies. The staff is friendly and attentive. ✉*150 Commercial St., Leith* ☎*0131/555–2255* ▤*AE, DC, MC, V.*

### FRENCH

£££££ ✗**Martin Wishart.** Slightly out of town but worth every penny of the taxi fare, this rising culinary star woos diners with an impeccable and varied menu of beautifully presented, French-influenced dishes. Terrine
★

of foie gras, compote of Agen prunes, and sole Murat (glazed fillet of sole with baby onions, artichoke, parsley, and lemon) with *pommes en cocotte* (potatoes cooked in a casserole) typify the cuisine. Reservations are essential on Friday and Saturday night. ⊠*54 The Shore, Leith* ☎*0131/553–3557* ⊟*AE, MC, V* ⊙*Closed Sun. and Mon. No lunch Sat.*

£££   ✕**Malmaison Café Bar and Brasserie.** Freshly made soups, crunchy salads, inventive sandwiches (try the roasted red pepper and pesto), and gooey pastries are the choices in the café at the stylish Malmaison Hotel, in Edinburgh's rejuvenated dockside area. If you fancy something more substantial (and more expensive), try the Brasserie, which serves traditional French and modern British cuisine. The "homegrown and local" menu showcases the best of Scottish produce with dishes like Buccleuch Scottish beef carpaccio. ⊠*1 Tower Pl., Leith* ☎*0131/468–5000* ⧄*Reservations essential* ⊟*AE, DC, MC, V.*

### SEAFOOD

£££   ✕**Fishers Leith.** Locals and visitors flock to this laid-back pub-cum-bistro down on the waterfront, and to its sister restaurant, **Fishers in the City,** in the New Town. The menu is the same, but Fishers Leith opened first and is still the one with the better reputation and vibe. Bar meals are served, although for more comfort and elegance sit in the cozy blue-walled dining room. Seafood is the specialty—the Loch Fyne oysters are wonderful. Watch for the daily specials: perhaps a seafood or vegetarian soup followed by North African gamba prawns as big as your hand. It's a good idea to reserve ahead for the bistro. ⊠*1 The Shore, Leith* ☎*0131/554–5666* ⊠*58 Thistle St., New Town* ☎*0131/225–5109* ⊟*AE, MC, V.*

£££   ✕**Skippers Bistro.** This superb seafood restaurant has a traditional, snug, cluttered interior with dark wood, shining brass, and lots of pictures and seafaring ephemera. For a starter, try the fragrant Cullen skink. Main dishes change daily but might include Finnan haddie, halibut, salmon, or monkfish in delicious sauces. Reservations are essential on weekends. ⊠*1A Dock Pl., Leith* ☎*0131/554–1018* ⊟*AE, MC, V.*

# WHERE TO STAY

It used to be that Scottish hotels were considered either rather better or much worse than their English counterparts; the good ones were very good, and the bad ones horrid. Today Scotland's capital has an expanding choice of delightful hotel accommodations, from elegant conversions of classic buildings to sleek modern boutique hotels. The inexpensive Scottish hotel is now at least the equal of anything that might be found in England.

Rooms are harder to find in August and September, when the Edinburgh International Festival and the Fringe Festival take place, so reserve at least three months in advance. Bed-and-breakfast accommodations may be harder to find in December, January, and February, when some proprietors close for a few weeks. Scots are trusting people—many B&B proprietors provide front-door keys and few impose curfews.

**1**

## PRICES

Weekend rates in the larger hotels are always much cheaper than mid-week rates, so if you want to stay in a plush hotel, come on the weekend. To save money and see how local residents live, stay in a B&B in one of the areas away from the city center, such as Pilrig to the north, Murrayfield to the west, or Sciennes to the south. Public buses can whisk you to the city center in 10 to 15 minutes.

| WHAT IT COSTS IN POUNDS | | | | | |
|---|---|---|---|---|---|
| | £ | ££ | £££ | ££££ | £££££ |
| FOR TWO PEOPLE | under £70 | £70–£120 | £121–£180 | £181–£250 | over £250 |

Prices are for two people in a standard double room in high season, usually including 17.5% V.A.T.

## OLD TOWN

The narrow *pends* (alleys), cobbled streets, and steep hills of the Old Town remind you that this is a city with many layers of history. Medieval to modern, these hotels all are within a stone's throw of the action.

£££££    **The Scotsman.** This magnificent turn-of-the-20th-century, gray-sand-
Fodor'sChoice    stone building, with a marble staircase and a fascinating history—it
★    was once the headquarters of the *Scotsman* newspaper—now houses a modern, luxurious hotel. Dark wood, earthy colors, tweeds, and contemporary furnishings decorate the rooms and public spaces. North Bridge, the casual-chic brasserie, serves shellfish and grill food, whereas the formal Vermilion concocts beautiful presentations of Scottish-French dishes. **Pros:** Gorgeous surroundings, personalized service. **Cons:** No air-conditioning, spa is a bit noisy. ⊠*20 N. Bridge, Old Town, EH1 1YT* ☎*0131/556–5565* ⊕*www.thescotsmanhotel.co.uk* ➫*56 rooms, 12 suites* ♿*In-room: no a/c, dial-up, Wi-Fi. In-hotel: 2 restaurants, bar, pool, gym, spa* ▤*AE, DC, MC, V* ⦿*BP.*

£££££    **The Witchery.** This lavishly theatrical lodging promises a night to remember. Each room has a theme—choices include the Library, the Armory, and to the Inner Sanctum—and is decked out with jaw-droppingly grand antiques, champagne chilling in an immense bucket, and the finest quality bedding. Dining in the dark-paneled restaurant is just as dramatic, with old-world dishes such as saddle of rabbit and roast lobster. **Pros:** A Gothic treasure, sumptuous dining. **Cons:** Can be noisy at night, ghost appearance not guaranteed. ⊠*Castlehill, Royal Mile, Old Town, EH12NF* ☎*0131/225–5613* ⊕*www.thewitchery. com* ➫*7 rooms* ♿*In-room: no a/c In-hotel: restaurant* ▤*AE, DC, MC, V* ⦿*BP.*

£££    **Knights Residence.** Ten minutes from the Grassmarket, the Knights is made up of 19 different apartments. You are greeted by a concierge who will show you to your unit, which will be pleasingly furnished and filled with the things you need for a perfect stay, including a washer-dryer and a DVD library. Breakfast can be found in the fridge. **Pros:** Comfortable apartments, secure location, kitted out to a high standard. **Cons:** Lack of staff won't suit everyone, better for stays of two or more

nights. ⊠*12 Lauriston St., Old Town, EH3 9DJ* ☎*0131/622–8120*
⊕*www.theknightresidence.co.uk* ⤢*19 apartments* &*In-room: no a/c,
Wi-Fi. In-hotel: parking (no fee)* ⧀*CP.*

£££   🖫**Radisson SAS Edinburgh.** Although it was built in the late 1980s, this
city-center hotel was designed to blend into its surroundings among the
16th-, 17th-, and 18th-century buildings on the Royal Mile. Rooms
are spacious and contemporary—practical rather than luxurious. **Pros:**
Central location, can-do staff. **Cons:** Breakfast is expensive, difficult
to reach by car. ⊠*80 High St., Royal Mile, Old Town, EH1 1TH*
☎*0131/557–9797* ⊕*www.radissonsas.com* ⤢*238 rooms, 10 suites*
&*In-room: dial-up. In-hotel: restaurant, bar, pool, gym, parking (fee)*
▤*AE, DC, MC, V* ⧀*BP.*

£££   🖫**Ten Hill Place.** This stylish hotel just around the corner from the Festival Theatre has impeccable service. The rooms are large, immaculate, and airy, filled with sleek furnishings covered in delectable colors
ranging from oatmeal to mocha. The breakfasts are satisfying, and
include plenty of top-notch coffee. **Pros:** Well kept, close to everything
but not in the midst of the broo-ha-ha. **Cons:** Rooms can be too dark,
glass doors on the bathrooms. ⊠*10 Hill Pl., Old Town, EH8 9DR*
☎*0131/662–2080* ⊕*www.tenhillplace.com* ⤢*78 rooms* &*In room:
Wi-Fi. In hotel: bar, parking (fee)* ▤*AE, MC, V* ⧀*BP.*

---

## NEW TOWN

£££££   🖫**Balmoral Hotel.** The attention to detail in the elegant rooms—colors
Fodor's Choice   were picked to echo the country's heathers and moors—and the sheer
★   élan that has re-created the Edwardian splendor of this grand, former
railroad hotel make staying at the Balmoral a special introduction to
Edinburgh. Here, below the landmark clock tower marking the east
end of Princes Street, the lively buzz makes you feel as if you're at the
center of city life. The hotel's main restaurant is the plush and stylish
Number One, serving excellent Scottish seafood and game. If you over-
indulge, recuperate at the luxurious spa. **Pros:** Big and beautiful building, top-hatted doorman, lovely touches in the rooms. **Cons:** Pool is
small, spa books up fast, the restaurants can be very busy. ⊠*1 Princes
St., New Town, EH2 2EQ* ☎*0131/556–2414* ⊕*www.thebalmoral-
hotel.com* ⤢*188 rooms, 20 suites* &*In-room: Ethernet. In-hotel: 2
restaurants, bar, pool, gym, spa, public Internet, parking (fee)* ▤*AE,
DC, MC, V* ⧀*BP*

£££££   🖫**The Glasshouse.** Glass walls extend from the 19th-century facade of
★   a former church, foreshadowing the daring interior of one of the city's
chicest boutique hotels. Rooms are decorated in a minimalist style,
with soft browns and beiges blending nicely with the wood and marble.
The bathrooms were built in Denmark and shipped as intact "pods"
that were then fitted into the rooms. A bedside control panel lets you
control the drapes, and the flat-screen TV swivels to face the bed or
the sitting area. Floor-to-ceiling windows overlook the New Town or
the rooftop garden in back. The hotel's halls and rooms serve as gallery space for 200 female nude photographs by Scottish photographers
Trevor and Faye Yerbury. **Pros:** Near all the attractions, very modern

and stylish. **Cons:** Staff can be a bit sniffy, nightclub downstairs is noisy. ⊠ *2 Greenside Pl., New Town, EH1 3AA* ☎ *0131/525–8200* ⊕ *www.theetoncollection.com* ⤵ *65 rooms, 18 suites* ⟁ *In-room: safe, dial-up. In-hotel: restaurant, room service, bar* ⊟ *AE, MC, V.*

**££££** ▦ **Caledonian Hilton Hotel.** "The Caley," a conspicuous block of red sandstone beyond the west end of West Princes Street Gardens, was built between 1898 and 1902 as the flagship hotel of the Caledonian Railway, and its imposing Victorian decor has been faithfully preserved. The public area has marbled green columns and an ornate stairwell with a burnished-metalwork balustrade. Rooms and corridors are exceptionally large and well appointed. **Pros:** Service with a smile, lots of choices at breakfast. **Cons:** Internet access is extra, rooms can be small. ⊠ *Princes St., New Town, EH1 2AB* ☎ *0131/222–8888* ⊕ *www. hilton.co.uk* ⤵ *251 rooms, 20 suites* ⟁ *In-room: dial-up, Wi-Fi. In-hotel: 3 restaurants, pool, parking (fee)* ⊟ *AE, DC, MC, V* ⧖ *BP.*

**££££** ▦ **Tigerlilly.** On hip George Street, Edinburgh's newest boutique hotel has everything a girl could imagine—bowls of fresh fruit, designer candles, hair straighteners—for a night away from home. But there's plenty for the guys, too. Everyone will enjoy the little extras, like the iPod you can borrow. The restaurant serves confidently prepared pan-Asian fare. If you fancy a postdinner snifter, the bar has a cocktail menu of biblical proportions. Don't worry if you overdo it—breakfast is served until noon. **Pros:** Chic yet not intimidating, laid-back but efficient staff. **Cons:** No views, can be noisy. ⊠ *125 George St., New Town, EH2 4JN* ☎ *0131/225–5005* ⊕ *www.tigerlilyedinburgh.co.uk* ⤵ *33 rooms* ⟁ *In-room: Wi-Fi. In-hotel: restaurant, bar* ⊟ *AE, MC, V* ⧖ *BP.*

**£££** ▦ **The Howard.** Close to Drummond Place, this hotel is in a classic
★ New Town building, elegant proportioned and superbly outfitted. Antique furniture and original art throughout make the Howard more like a swank private club. You can expect the most upscale amenities, including private butlers. Some of the best rooms overlook the garden. **Pros:** Small but grand building, staff has a great attitude. **Cons:** Some of the elegance has faded, noisy neighborhood. ⊠ *34 Great King St., New Town, EH3 6QH* ☎ *0131/557–3500* ⊕ *www. thehoward.com* ⤵ *18 rooms, 5 suites* ⟁ *In-room: no a/c, dial-up. In-hotel: restaurant, room service, laundry service, parking (no fee)* ⊟ *AE, DC, MC, V* ⧖ *BP.*

**£££** ▦ **Walton Hotel.** This B&B in a Georgian town house is a 10-minute walk from the city center. High-ceilinged, elegant rooms are furnished in an unfussy, traditional style, and there's a choice of breakfasts—traditional Scottish, Continental, or American. Four of the rooms are on the ground floor, and six are in the basement (all have windows). **Pros:** Top-class staff, bountiful breakfasts. **Cons:** Some rooms need an upgrade, some rooms are below street level. ⊠ *79 Dundas St., New Town, EH3 6SD* ☎ *0131/556–1137* ⊕ *www.waltonhotel.com* ⤵ *10 rooms* ⟁ *In-room: no a/c, dial-up, Wi-Fi. In-hotel: no elevator, parking (no fee)* ⊟ *MC, V* ⧖ *BP.*

**££** ▦ **Ardenlee Guest House.** An exquisite Victorian-tile floor is one of many original features at this gem of a guesthouse tucked away from the hustle and bustle of the city center. A cast-iron staircase leads to simple

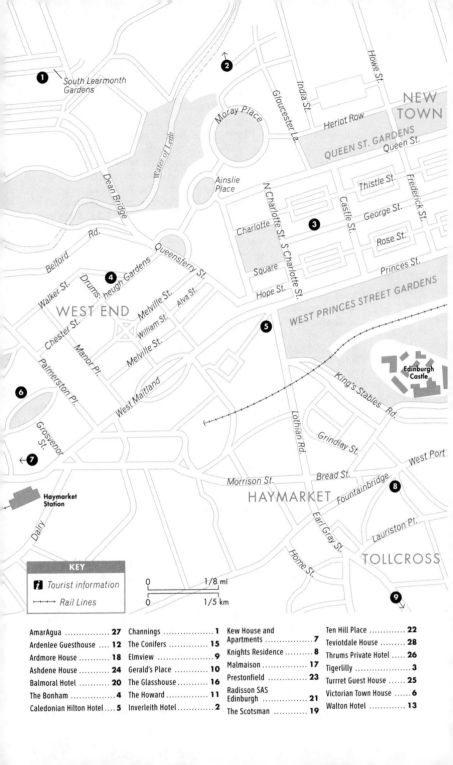

**KEY**

🛈 Tourist information

+—+—+ Rail Lines

0          1/8 mi

0          1/5 km

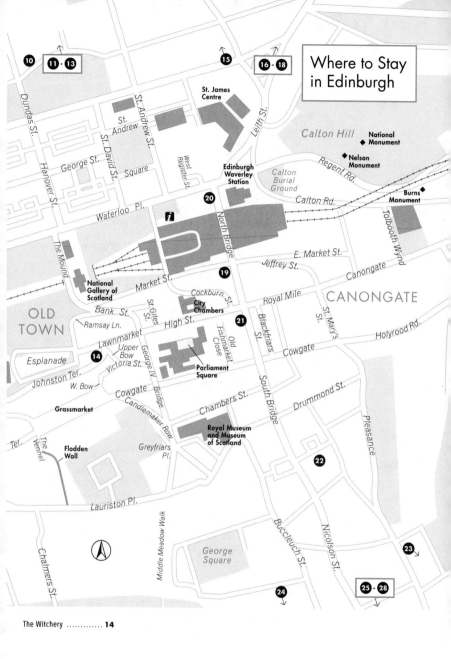

# Where to Stay in Edinburgh

**10**   **11 · 13**   **15**   **16 · 18**

St. James Centre

Calton Hill

National Monument

Nelson Monument

Dundas St.

St. Andrew St.

St. Andrew Square

George St.

St. David St.

West Register St.

Leith St.

Regent Rd.

Hanover St.

Edinburgh Waverley Station

Calton Burial Ground

Calton Rd.

Burns Monument

Waterloo Pl.

**20**

North Bridge

E. Market St.

Tolbooth Wynd

The Mound

National Gallery of Scotland

Market St.

**19**

Jeffrey St.

Canongate

CANONGATE

OLD TOWN

Bank St.

Ramsay Ln.

St. Giles St.

Cockburn St.

City Chambers

Royal Mile

High St.

**21**

Old Fishmarket Close

Blackfriars St.

St. Mary's St.

Holyrood Rd.

Esplanade

Lawnmarket

Upper Bow

George IV Bridge

Victoria St.

**14**

Parliament Square

Cowgate

South Bridge

Cowgate

Johnston Ter.

W. Bow

Candlemaker Row

Chambers St.

Drummond St.

Pleasance

Grassmarket

Greyfriars Pl.

Royal Museum and Museum of Scotland

Ter.

The Vennel

Flodden Wall

**22**

Lauriston Pl.

Chalmers St.

Middle Meadow Walk

George Square

Buccleuch St.

Nicolson St.

**23**

**24**

**25 · 28**

but spacious rooms. The owner is friendly and helpful, and has plenty of information on the sights in and around Edinburgh. **Pros:** Family-run establishment, good value for money. **Cons:** No Internet connection, uphill walk to the city center. ⊠ *9 Eyre Pl., New Town, EH3 5ES* ☎*0131/556–2838* ⊕*www.ardenlee.co.uk* ➯*9 rooms, 7 with bath* ⚿*In-room: no a/c, no phone. In-hotel: no elevator* ⊟*MC, V* ⦿*BP.*

**££** ⊞ **Gerald's Place.** Although he is not a native of the city, Gerald Della-Porta is one of those B&B owners to whom Edinburgh owes so much. Forget the cliches—you really are welcomed into his home and treated like a most welcome guest. The rooms are furnished in classic style, with huge beds, fresh flowers, and original artwork (much of it for sale). A block beyond Queen Street, this lodging has a fairly central location. Breakfast around the big table is a communal affair, and the food is healthier than at most places. **Pros:** The advice and thoughtfulness of the owner, spacious rooms. **Cons:** The stairs are difficult to manage, it's an uphill walk to the city center. ⊠ *21B Abercromby Pl.* ☎*0131/558–7017* ⊕*www.geraldsplace.com* ➯*2 rooms* ⚿*In-room: no a/c, Wi-Fi. In-hotel: no elevator* ⊟*MC, V* ⦿*BP.*

**££** ⊞ **Inverleith Hotel.** Across from the Royal Botanical Gardens, this renovated Victorian town house has cozy, well-lighted rooms with velour bedspreads, dark wooden furniture, and pale-gold curtains. In winter, when the surrounding trees loose their leaves, a couple of the south-facing rooms have views of the castle. The reception doubles as a private bar for guests and sells a fine selection of malt whiskies. Several good restaurants and cafés are nearby. **Pros:** Quiet surroundings, knowledgeable staff. **Cons:** Some of the rooms are small, narrow passageways, uphill walk to the city center. ⊠ *5 Inverleith Terr., New Town, EH3 4NS* ☎*0131/556–2745* ⊕*www.inverleithhotel.co.uk* ➯*12 rooms, 1 apartment* ⚿*In-room: no a/c. In-hotel: bar, parking (no fee), no elevator* ⊟*MC, V* ⦿*BP.*

## HAYMARKET

**£££** ⊞ **Kew House and Apartments.** With such sumptuous rooms, you might
**★** think that Kew House was a full-service hotel. Inside the elegant 1860 terraced house are unfussy rooms with nice touches like hair dryers, coffeemakers, and pants presses. Welcome luxuries include fresh flowers, decadent chocolates, and a decanter of sherry on arrival. There's also a bar for guests only. **Pros:** As clean as a whistle, thoughtful touches throughout. **Cons:** A little out of the way, longish walk to the city center. ⊠ *1 Kew Terr., Haymarket, EH12 5JE* ☎*0131/313–0700* ⊕*www.kewhouse.com* ➯*6 rooms, 2 apartments* ⚿*In-room: no a/c. In-hotel: bar, public Internet, parking (no fee)* ⊟*AE, DC, MC, V* ⦿*BP.*

**££** ⊞ **Victorian Town House.** In a leafy crescent, this house once belonged to David Alan Stevenson, cousin of Robert Louis Stevenson. The writer would doubtless be happy to lay down his head in this lovingly preserved home away from home. The bright yet calming rooms have beds that are piled with plump duvets. But those who don't sleep so easy will appreciate crystal decanter with just enough whisky to send you off. **Pros:** Serene surroundings, gracious staff. **Cons:** No parking nearby. ⊠ *14 Eglinton Terr., Haymarket, EH12 5DD* ☎*0131/337–*

1

7088 ⊕*www.thevictoriantownhouse.co.uk* ⇆*3 rooms* ⌂*In-room: no a/c. In-hotel: no elevator* ⊟*No credit cards* ⦿*BP.*

## WEST END

££££  ⚏**The Bonham.** This hotel in the elegant West End carries out a successful, sophisticated flirtation with modernity that makes it stand out from its neighbors. Bold colors and contemporary Scottish art set off its late-19th-century architecture and classic furniture. The good-size rooms are typical of an Edinburgh town house but offer peace and quiet without the noise often associated with this type of hotel. The chic, unadorned restaurant has oversize mirrors and a central catwalk of light; its focus is on beautifully presented contemporary cuisine. **Pros:** Thorough yet unobtrusive service, excellent restaurant. **Cons:** Not many common areas, can have a business-hotel feel. ⊠*35 Drumsheugh Gardens, West End, EH3 7RN* ☎*0131/226–6050* ⊕*www. thebonham.com* ⇆*48 rooms, 3 suites* ⌂*In-room: no a/c, Ethernet. In-hotel: restaurant, parking (no fee)* ⊟*AE, DC, MC, V* ⦿*BP.*

£££  ⚏**Channings.** Five Edwardian terraced town houses make up this inti-
★   mate, elegant hotel in an upscale West End neighborhood just minutes from Princes Street. Beyond the clubby, oak-paneled lobby lounge are quiet guest rooms with well-chosen antiques and marble baths. North-facing rooms have great views of Fife. Channings Restaurant offers excellent value in traditional Scottish and Continental cooking. **Pros:** Romantic surroundings, inventive color schemes. **Cons:** Not all rooms are equal, breakfasts are a bit meager. ⊠*12–16 S. Learmonth Gardens, West End, EH4 IEZ* ☎*0131/315–2226* ⊕*www.channings. co.uk* ⇆*41 rooms, 3 suites* ⌂*In-room: no a/c. In-hotel: restaurant, bar* ⊟*AE, DC, MC, V* ⦿*BP.*

## SOUTH SIDE

££££  ⚏**Prestonfield.** The cattle grazing on the hotel's 20-acre grounds let you know that you've entered a different world, even though you're five minutes by car from the Royal Mile. Inside this 1687 mansion, baroque opulence reigns in the well-restored public rooms; there are plenty of gilt treasures to relax among as you sip a whisky. Guest rooms are individually decorated, but mix antiques and the latest amenities for total indulgence. The romantic Rhubarb restaurant carries through the hedonistic note with superb Scottish fare, such as seared turbot with langoustine crushed potatoes. **Pros:** Eccentric grandeur, comfortable beds. **Cons:** Slightly haphazard service, brooding decor never looks good in the harsh light of day. ⊠*Priestfield Rd., Prestonfield, EH16 5UT* ☎*0131/225–7800* ⊕*www.prestonfield.com* ⇆*22 rooms, 2 suites* ⌂*In-room: Wi-Fi. In-hotel: restaurant, bar, parking (no fee)* ⊟*AE, MC, V* ⦿*BP.*

££  ⚏**AmarAgua.** Deep-pile carpets, floral drapes with plenty of swags, and well-designed furniture create restrained opulence in this Victorian town house, which is 10 minutes by bus from the city center. Many of the rooms look distinctly Asian, as the multilingual owners spent some time working in the Far East. Carry-out breakfasts are available for guests leaving early to catch a bus or plane. **Pros:** Quiet setting, snug rooms. **Cons:** No restaurants within walking distance, not all rooms are en suite. ⊠ *10 Kilmaurs Terr., Newington, EH16 5DR* ☎ *0131/667–6775* ⊕ *www.amaragua.co.uk* ☞ *7 rooms, 4 with bath* ⚄ *In-room: no a/c. In-hotel: no elevator, public Internet* ⊟ *MC, V* ☾ *Closed Jan. and 2 wks in Oct. and Nov.* ⫶◯⫶ *BP.*

££ ⊡ **Ashdene House.** On a quiet residential street sits this Edwardian house, one of the city's first-class B&Bs. Country-style pine furniture and vividly colored fabrics decorate the guest rooms and common areas. The owners are particularly helpful in arranging tours and evening theater entertainment, and they will recommend local restaurants. There's ample parking on the street., The city center is 10 minutes away by bus. **Pros:** Homemade breads at breakfast, spacious rooms. **Cons:** No Internet connections, not within walking distance of the center. ⊠ *23 Fountainhall Rd., The Grange, EH9 2LN* ☎ *0131/667–6026* ⊕ *www.ashdenehouse.com* ☞ *5 rooms* ⚄ *In-room: no a/c. In-hotel: no elevator, parking (no fee)* ⊟ *MC, V* ⫶◯⫶ *BP.*

££ ⊡ **Elmview.** Near Bruntsfield Links, Elmview has a verdant location that
★ completely justifies the name. Dating from the turn of the last century, the handsome stone house was designed by the celebrated architect, Sir Edwin Lutyens, as a "dignified holiday home." Guest rooms are spacious havens with furnishing that are homey but not too twee. The sociable breakfasts are great for sharing tips with your fellow travelers. They're healthy to boot, with refreshing organic and healthy alternatives. **Pros:** Next to the historic golf course, superb breakfasts, helpful owners. **Cons:** Books up in advance, doesn't cater to families with young children. ⊠ *15 Glengyle Terr., Bruntsfield, EH3 9LN* ☎ *0131/228–1973* ⊕ *www.elmview.co.uk* ☞ *4 rooms* ⚄ *In-room: no a/c, refrigerator, Wi-Fi. In-hotel: no elevator, no children under 15* ⊟ *AE, DC, MC, V* ☾ *Closed Nov.–Apr.* ⫶◯⫶ *BP.*

££ ⊡ **Teviotdale House.** The lavish interior of this 1848 town house includes canopy beds and miles of festive fabrics. You'll be greeted at the door by the Thiebauds, your friendly hosts. This warm retreat sits on a tree-lined street away from the hustle and bustle of the city. If you need an urban fix, you can head downtown via a 10-minute bus ride. The hearty egg-and-sausage breakfasts are a pleasure. **Pros:** The kind of porridge that builds a nation, owners take pride in their hospitality. **Cons:** A long walk from the city center, not all bathrooms have tubs. ⊠ *53 Grange Loan, The Grange, EH9 2ER* ☎ *0131/667–4376* ⊟ *0131/667–4763* ⊕ *www.teviotdalehouse.com* ☞ *7 rooms* ⚄ *In-room: no a/c. In-hotel: no elevator* ⊟ *AE, MC, V* ⫶◯⫶ *BP.*

££ ⊡ **Thrums Private Hotel.** Inside this detached Georgian house are small, cozy rooms decorated with antique reproductions. Breakfast is served in a large, glass-enclosed conservatory. The staff that runs the hotel is very welcoming and more than willing to advise you on what to see and do in and around Edinburgh. **Pros:** Good value, neat and tidy. **Cons:** On a busy street, some rooms need refurbishing. ⊠ *14–15 Minto St., Newington, EH9 1RQ* ☎ *0131/667–5545* ⊕ *www.thrumshotel.com*

1

🛏15 rooms 🛋In-room: no a/c. In-hotel: parking (no fee), no elevator ▤MC, V †◯⏐BP.

££ 🏠**Turret Guest House.** Modern furnishings in rooms with Victorian cornices, paneled doors, and high ceilings make this B&B, in a baronial town house, a nice combination of old-fashioned charm and contemporary comfort. Two of the rooms have four-poster beds. The inn is on a quiet residential street on the South Side, close to Commonwealth Pool and Holyrood Park. The tempting breakfast options include Scottish favorites like haggis as well as waffles, pancakes, and French toast. **Pros:** Smashing breakfasts, well-appointed rooms. **Cons:** Short beds, a bus or taxi needed to get downtown. ✉8 Kilmaurs Terr., Prestonfield, EH16 5DR ☎0131/667–6704 ⊕www. turretguesthouse.co.uk 🛏8 rooms, 5 with bath 🛋In-room: no a/c. In-hotel: no elevator, no-smoking rooms ▤MC, V †◯⏐BP.

## LEITH

£££ 🏠**Malmaison.** Once a seamen's hostel, the Malmaison now draws a more refined clientele. A dramatic black, cream, and taupe color scheme prevails in the public areas. King-size beds, CD players, and satellite TV are standard in the bedrooms, which are decorated in a bold, modern style. The French theme of the hotel, which is part of a chic British chain, is emphasized in the Café Bar and Brasserie. **Pros:** Impressive building, great location. **Cons:** The bar can be rowdy at night, service can be erratic. ✉1 Tower Pl., Leith, EH6 7DB ☎0131/468–5000 ⊕www.malmaison-edinburgh.com 🛏100 rooms, 9 suites 🛋In-room: no a/c, dial-up. In-hotel: restaurant, bar, gym, parking (no fee) ▤AE, DC, MC, V †◯⏐BP.

££ 🏠**Ardmor House.** This low-key guesthouse combines the original features of a Victorian home with stylish contemporary furnishings. Rooms are fresh and modern, with an occasional antique adding some character. The friendly owners, Robin and Colin, extend a warm welcome to all their guests. They offer a thoroughly efficient concierge service with a twist—lots of personal opinions and recommendations thrown in. Their listing of gay-friendly venues locates bars, cafés, and even saunas. **Pros:** Warm and friendly owners, decorated with great style, gay-friendly environment. **Cons:** A bit out of the way, double room on the ground floor is tiny. ✉74 Pilrig St., Leith, EH6 5AS ☎🖨0131/554–4944 ⊕www.ardmorhouse.com 🛏5 rooms 🛋In-room: no a/c. In-hotel: no elevator, public Wi-Fi ▤MC, V †◯⏐BP.

££ 🏠**The Conifers.** This trim B&B in a red-sandstone town house north of the New Town offers simple, traditionally decorated rooms. Framed prints of old Edinburgh adorn the walls. The owner, Liz Fulton, has a wealth of knowledge about what to see and do in Edinburgh. **Pros:** Nice mix of old and new, many original fittings, hearty breakfasts. **Cons:** A long walk to the city center, not all rooms have bathrooms. ✉56 Pilrig St., Leith, EH6 5AS ☎0131/554–5162 ⊕www.conifers guesthouse.com 🛏4 rooms, 3 with bath 🛋In-room: no a/c. In-hotel: no elevator ▤No credit cards †◯⏐BP.

# NIGHTLIFE & THE ARTS

## THE ARTS

Those who think Edinburgh's arts scene consists of just the elegiac wail of a bagpipe and the twang of a fiddle or two will be proved wrong by the hundreds of performing-arts options. The jewel in the crown, of course, is the famed Edinburgh International Festival, which now attracts the best in music, dance, theater, painting, and sculpture from all over the globe during three weeks from mid-August to early September. The *Scotsman* and *Herald,* Scotland's leading daily newspapers, carry listings and reviews in their arts pages every day, with special editions during the festival. Tickets are generally available from box offices in advance; in some cases they're also available from certain designated travel agents or at the door, although concerts by national orchestras often sell out long before the day of the performance. The *List* and the *Day by Day Guide,* available at the **Edinburgh and Scotland Information Centre** ( ⌂ *3 Princes St., East End* ☎ *0845/225–5121* ⊕ *www. edinburgh.org*), carry the most up-to-date details about cultural events. The *List* is also available at newsstands throughout the city.

### DANCE

The Scottish Ballet performs at the **Festival Theatre** ( ⌂ *13–29 Nicolson St., Old Town* ☎ *0131/529–6000* ⊕ *www.eft.co.uk*) when in Edinburgh. Visiting contemporary dance companies perform in the **Royal Lyceum** ( ⌂ *Grindlay St., West End* ☎ *0131/248–4848* ⊕ *www.lyceum.org.uk*).

### FESTIVALS

The **Edinburgh Festival Fringe** ( ⌂ *Edinburgh Festival Fringe Office, 180 High St., Old Town, EH1 1QS* ☎ *0131/226–0026* ⊕ *www.edfringe. com*) presents many theatrical and musical events, some by amateur groups (you have been warned), and is more of a grab bag than the official festival. Many events are free but some do require tickets; prices start at £2 and go up to £15. During festival time—roughly the same as the International Festival—it's possible to arrange your own entertainment program from morning to midnight and beyond, if you don't feel overwhelmed by the variety available.

☾ The **Edinburgh International Book Festival** ( ⌂ *Charlotte Sq. Gardens, New Town* ☎ *0131/718–5666* ⊕ *www.edbookfest.co.uk*), a two-week-long event in August, pulls together a heady mix of the biggest-selling and the most challenging authors from around the world and gets them talking about their work in a magnificent tent village. Workshops for would-be writers and children are hugely popular.

★ The **Edinburgh International Festival** ( ⌂ *The Hub, Edinburgh Festival Centre, Castlehill, Old Town* ☎ *0131/473–2009 information, 0131/473–2000 tickets* ⊕ *www.eif.co.uk*), the flagship arts event of the year, attracts performing artists of international caliber to a celebration of music, dance, drama, and artwork. Advance information, programs, tickets, and reservations are available from the Edinburgh Festival Centre, an impressive Victorian Gothic church building renamed the Hub.

CLOSE UP

1

# Festivals in Edinburgh

Walking around Edinburgh in late July, you'll likely feel the first vibrations of the earthquake that is festival time, which shakes the city throughout August and into September. You may hear reference to an "Edinburgh Festival," but this is really an umbrella term for six separate festivals all taking place around the same time. Visiting Edinburgh in August is an experience you are unlikely to forget.

**Edinburgh International Festival.** The best-known and oldest of these is the Edinburgh International Festival, founded in 1947 when Europe was recovering from World War II. In recent years the festival has drawn as many as 400,000 people to Edinburgh, with more than 100 acts by world-renowned music, opera, theater, and dance performers, filling all the major venues in the city. Tickets for the festival go on sale in April, and many sell out within the month. However, you may still be able to purchase tickets, which range from £6 to £60, during the festival.

**Edinburgh Festival Fringe.** If the Edinburgh International Festival is the parent of British festivals, then the Edinburgh Festival Fringe is its unruly child. The Festival Fringe started in 1947 at the same time as the International Festival, when eight companies that were not invited to perform in the latter decided to attend anyway. Knowing there would be an audience,

these companies found small, local theaters to host them. Since then, the Festival Fringe has grown at about the same rate as its counterpart. In 2005 there were 1,800 shows and 27,000 performances of those shows at the Fringe, making it the largest festival of its kind in the world. Its events range from the brilliant to the impossibly mundane, badly performed, and downright tacky.

While the Fringe is going on, most of the city center becomes one huge performance area, with fire eaters, sword swallowers, unicyclists, jugglers, string quartets, jazz groups, stand-up comics, and magicians all thronging into High Street and Princes Street. Every available theater and pseudo-performance space is utilized—church halls, community centers, parks, sports fields, putting greens, and nightclubs. In 1954 the Edinburgh Festival Fringe Society was formed, and it oversees everything from ticket sales to publicity.

**Festivals for all interests.** Edinburgh festival time can fill almost any artistic need. Besides the International Festival and Festival Fringe, look for the Edinburgh International Film Festival; the International Jazz & Blues Festival, the International Book Festival, and the Military Tattoo, which includes reenactments of historic events, military marching bands, Highland dancing, and more.

Tickets range from £7 to £60, depending on the event. The festival runs from mid-August through early September.

The **Edinburgh International Film Festival** ( ⌂*Edinburgh Film Festival Office, at Filmhouse, 88 Lothian Rd., West End* ☎*0131/228–4051* ⊕*www.edfilmfest.org.uk*) is yet another aspect of the busy August festival logjam in Edinburgh.

The **Edinburgh International Science Festival** (*Information:* ✉*Roxburgh's Court, off 323 High St., Edinburgh* ☎*0131/545–9830* ⊕*www.sciencefestival.co.uk Tickets:* ✉*The Hub, Castlehill, Edinburgh*), held around Easter each year, aims to make science accessible, interesting, but above all fun. Children's events turn science into entertainment and are especially popular.

★  The **Edinburgh Military Tattoo** (✉*Edinburgh Military Tattoo Office, 32 Market St., Old Town* ☎*0131/225–1188 or 08707/555–1188* ⊕*www.edintattoo.co.uk*) may not be art, but it is certainly Scottish culture. It's sometimes confused with the festival itself, partly because both events take place in August (though the Tattoo starts and finishes a week earlier). This celebration of martial music and skills with bands, gymnastics, and stunt motorcycle teams is on the castle esplanade, and the dramatic backdrop augments the spectacle. Dress warmly for late-evening performances. Even if it rains, the show most definitely goes on.

The **International Jazz Festival** (✉*29 St. Stephen St., Stockbridge* ☎*0131/225–2202* ⊕*www.edinburghjazzfestival.co.uk*), held in August, attracts international top performers and brings local enthusiasts out of their living rooms and into the pubs and clubs to listen and play.

### FILM

The **Cameo** (✉*38 Home St., Tollcross* ☎*0131/228–2800*) has one large and two small auditoriums, which are extremely comfortable, plus a bar and late-night specials. Apart from cinema chains, Edinburgh has the excellent three-screen **Filmhouse** (✉*88 Lothian Rd., West End* ☎*0131/228–2688 box office*), the best venue for modern, foreign-language, offbeat, or simply less-commercial films.

### MUSIC

The **Festival Theatre** (✉*13–29 Nicolson St., Old Town* ☎*0131/529–6000*) hosts performances by the Scottish Ballet and the Scottish Opera. The **Playhouse** (✉*Greenside Pl., East End* ☎*0870/606–3424*) leans toward popular artists and musicals. The intimate **Queen's Hall** (✉*Clerk St., Old Town* ☎*0131/668–2019*) hosts small recitals. **Usher Hall** (✉*Lothian Rd., West End* ☎*0131/228–1155*) is Edinburgh's grandest venue, and international performers and orchestras, including the Royal Scottish National Orchestra, perform here.

### THEATER

MODERN  The **Theatre Workshop** (✉*34 Hamilton Pl., Stockbridge* ☎*0131/226–5425*) hosts fringe events during the Edinburgh Festival and modern, community-based theater year-round. It's wheelchair accessible. The **Traverse Theatre** (✉*10 Cambridge St., West End* ☎*0131/228–1404*) has developed a solid reputation for new, stimulating Scottish plays, performed in a specially designed flexible space.

TRADITIONAL  Edinburgh has three main theaters. The **Festival Theatre** (✉*13–29 Nicolson St., Old Town* ☎*0131/529–6000*) presents opera and ballet but also the occasional excellent touring play. The **King's** (✉*2 Leven St., Tollcross* ☎*0131/529–6000*) has a program of contemporary and traditional dramatic works. The **Royal Lyceum** (✉ *Grindlay St., West End* ☎ *0131/248–4848*) shows traditional plays and contemporary works, often transferred from or prior to their London West End showings.

On the eastern outskirts of Edinburgh, the **Brunton Theatre** (✉ *Ladywell Way, Musselburgh* ☎ *0131/665–2240*) presents a regular program of repertory, touring, and amateur performances. The **Church Hill Theatre** (✉ *Morningside Rd., Morningside* ☎ *0131/447–7597*) hosts productions by local dramatic societies that are of a high standard. The **Playhouse** (✉ *Greenside Pl., East End* ☎ *0870/606–3424*) hosts mostly popular artists and musicals.

## NIGHTLIFE

The nightlife scene in Edinburgh is vibrant—whatever you're looking for, you'll most certainly find it here, and you won't have to go far. Expect old-style pubs as well as cutting-edge bars and clubs. Live music pours out of most watering holes on weekends, particularly folk, blues, and jazz. Well-known artists perform at some of the larger venues. *The List* magazine, available at newsstands, gives locations, dates, times, and prices. Make sure you partake in at least one ceilidh; they're fun and a good way to meet locals.

### BARS & PUBS
Edinburgh's 400-odd pubs are a study in themselves. In the eastern and northern districts of the city you can find some grim, inhospitable-looking places that proclaim that drinking is no laughing matter. But throughout Edinburgh many pubs have deliberately traded in their old spit-and-sawdust images for atmospheric revivals of the warm, oak-paneled, leather-chaired *howffs* of a more leisurely age. Most pubs and bars are open weekdays and Saturday from 11 AM to midnight, and from 12:30 to midnight on Sunday.

OLD TOWN **The Canons' Gait** (✉ *232 Canongate, Old Town* ☎ *0131/556–4481*)
★ sells Edinburgh's own special brew, Innis & Gunn, aged in American white-oak barrels. It also has live jazz and blues on Thursday and Saturday nights. **Deacon Brodie's Pub** (✉ *435 Lawnmarket, Old Town* ☎ *0131/225–6531*), named for the infamous criminal who may have inspired Robert Louis Stevenson's *Strange Case of Dr. Jekyll and Mr. Hyde,* serves traditional meals and pints.

NEW TOWN **Abbotsford** (✉ *3 Rose St., New Town* ☎ *0131/225–5276*) has lots of Victorian atmosphere, an ever-changing selection of five real ales, and bar lunches. **Café Royal Circle Bar** ( ✉ *19 W. Regent St., New Town* ☎*0131/556–1884*) has beautiful Victorian tiled murals, oysters on the half shell, and leather booths. **Cask and Barrel** ( ✉ *115 Broughton St., New Town* ☎*0131/556–3132*) is a spacious, busy pub in which to sample hand-pulled ales at the horseshoe bar, reflected in a collection of brewery mirrors. **Cumberland Bar** ( ✉ *1–3 Cumberland St., New Town* ☎*0131/558–3134*) has eight ales on tap, wood trim, typical pub mirrors, and a comfy sitting room. **80 Queen Street** ( ✉ *80 Queen St., New Town* ☎*0131/226–5097*), with dark-wood booths, is just the place for lunch with a pint of draft beer. There's a jam session on Wednesday and Saturday.

★ **Guildford Arms** ( ✉ *1 W. Register St., east end of Princes St., New Town* ☎*0131/556–4312*) is worth a visit for its interior alone: ornate plasterwork, cornices, friezes, and wood paneling form the backdrop for some excellent draft ales, including Orkney Dark Island. **Harry's Bar** ( ✉ *7B Randolph Pl., New Town* ☎*0131/539–8100*), a retro basement bar with disco music, is hugely popular with locals. **Kay's Bar** ( ✉ *39 Jamaica St., New Town* ☎*0131/225–1858*), a friendly, comfortable spot, is a good place for a bar lunch. Don't miss the selection of 50 single-malt whiskies in addition to the real ales on draft. **Milne's Bar** ( ✉ *35 Hanover St., New Town* ☎*0131/225–6738*) is known as the poets' pub because of its popularity with the Edinburgh literati. Pies and baked potatoes go well with seven real ales and varying guest beers (beers not of the house brewery). Victorian advertisements and photos of old Edinburgh give the place an old-time feel.

**Standing Order** ( ✉ *62–66 George St., New Town* ☎*0131/225–4460*), in a former banking hall with a magnificent painted-plasterwork ceiling, is one of the popular and expanding J.D. Wetherspoon chain of pubs, priding itself on friendly, music-free watering holes with cheap beer—you can even lounge on leather sofas. Children are welcome. **Tiles** ( ✉ *1 St. Andrew Sq., New Town* ☎*0131/558–1507*), in a converted bank, gets its name from the wealth of tiles covering the walls, which are topped by elaborate plasterwork. The large selection of real ales complements a choice of bar meals or a table d'hôte menu specializing in fresh Scottish poultry, game, and fish. **Tonic** ( ✉ *34A Castle St., New Town* ☎*0131/225–6431*), is a stylish basement bar with bouncy stools and comfy sofas, pale wood, and chrome—and more than 200 cocktails from which to choose.

SOUTH SIDE **Cloisters** ( ✉ *26 Brougham St., Tollcross* ☎*0131/221–9997*) prides itself on the absence of music, gaming machines, and any other modern pub gimmicks; it specializes instead in real ales, malt whiskies, and good food, all at reasonable prices. **Leslie's Bar** ( ✉ *45 Ratcliffe Terr., South Side* ☎*0131/667–7205*) is an unspoiled Victorian bar near the hotels and guesthouses of Newington, with a good range of traditional Scottish ales and whiskies. **Southsider** ( ✉ *3–7 W. Richmond St., South Side* ☎*0131/667–2003*), near the antiques and junk shops of Causewayside, is popular with locals and students.

LEITH  The **Cameo Bar** (⌗*23 Commercial St., Leith* ☎*0131/554–9999*), is a bright and airy haven for the young and hip. **Malt and Hops** (⌗*45 The Shore, Leith* ☎*0131/555–0083*), more than 260 years old, has its own cask ales and ghost, and overlooks the waterfront. **Waterline** (⌗*58 The Shore, Leith* ☎*0131/554–2425*) has leather sofas to recline on, nautical charts pasted to the ceiling, and a great pub quiz every Thursday night.

## CEILIDHS & SCOTTISH EVENINGS

For those who feel a trip to Scotland is not complete without hearing the "Braes of Yarrow" or "Auld Robin Gray," several hotels present traditional Scottish-music evenings in the summer season. Head for the **Edinburgh Thistle Hotel** (⌗*107 Leith St., New Town* ☎*0131/556–0111*) to see *Jamie's Scottish Evening,* an extravaganza of Scottish song, tartan, plaid, and bagpipes that takes place nightly. The cost is £59.50, including a three-course dinner.

## COMEDY CLUBS

The Edinburgh Fringe Festival has become one of the world's most famous events for comedy. But throughout the year you can laugh until your sides split at the **Stand** (⌗*5 York Pl., East End* ☎*0131/558–7272*), which hosts names, up-and-coming acts and, of course, central to any comedy performance, the audience.

## FOLK CLUBS

You can usually find folk musicians performing in pubs throughout Edinburgh, although there's been a decline in the live-music scene because of dwindling profits and the predominance of popular theme bars.

The friendly "folk at the Oak" make the **Royal Oak** (⌗*1 Infantry St., Old Town* ☎*0131/557–2976*) so special. This cozy bar has live blues and folk most nights. **Whistle Binkies Pub** (⌗*South Bridge, Old Town* ☎*0131/557–5114*), a friendly basement bar with great rock and folk music every night of the week, is the place for a bit of *wellie* (volume, energy).

## GAY & LESBIAN CLUBS

There's a burgeoning gay and lesbian scene in Edinburgh, and the city has many predominantly gay clubs, bars, and cafés. However, don't expect the scene to be as extrovert or open as it is in London, New York, or even Glasgow. The *List* has a section that focuses on the gay and lesbian venues.

**Blue Moon Café** (⌗*36 Broughton St., New Town* ☎*0131/557–0911*), Edinburgh's longest running gay café, is still the best. **CC Blooms** (⌗*23–24 Greenside Pl., East End* ☎*0131/556–9331*), modern, colorful, and open nightly, plays a mix of musical styles. Once a month there's an ice-breaker evening for those new to the gay scene. The **Honeycomb** (⌗*Niddry St., off High St., Old Town* ☎*0131/556–2442*), a hot spot with a live DJ, gets a mixed gay and straight crowd; it's open Friday through Sunday. **The Regent** (⌗*2 Montrose Terr., Abbeyhill* ☎*0131/661–8198*) has a friendly vibe and a good selection of ales.

### NIGHTCLUBS

For the young and footloose, many Edinburgh dance clubs offer reduced admission and/or less expensive drinks for early revelers. Consult the *List* for special events.

The well-liked **Club Massa** ( ⊠ *36–39 Market St., Old Town* ☎ *0131/226–4224*) has theme nights covering the full spectrum of musical sounds; it's open Wednesday through Sunday. The **Opal Lounge** ( ⊠ *51A George St., New Town* ☎ *0131/226–2275*), a casual but stylish nightspot, evolves by a subtle change of mood and lighting from a restaurant to a club for drinks and dancing to soul or funk. **Po Na Na Souk Bar** ( ⊠ *43B Frederick St., New Town* ☎ *0131/226–2224*) has a cool but cozy atmosphere, and a distinctly North African atmosphere, with its secluded booths and Bedouin furnishings. The music is a mix of funk, hip hop, R&B, house, and disco. **Venue** ( ⊠ *15–21 Calton Rd., Old Town* ☎ *0131/557–3073*) blares all forms of live and DJ–ed music.

# SPORTS & THE OUTDOORS

### BICYCLING

Edinburgh is not the friendliest city for bikes; there's a lot of traffic, even on weekends. The tourist information center can point you toward some quieter routes just beyond the city center. Rentals cost £70 per week for a 21-speed or mountain bike. Daily rates (24 hours) are about £16, with half days costing £12. **Bike Trax** ( ⊠ *11–13 Lochrin Pl., Tollcross* ☎ *0131/228–6333*) has a variety of rental bikes. **Pedal Culture** ( ☎ *0796/644–7206*) leads guided bicycle tours of the city. A three-hour tour runs twice a day and costs £15, which includes bike hire, a helmet, and waterproof gear.

For longer rides, consider the **Bike Station** ( ⊠ *250 Causewayside, Newington* ☎ *0131/ 668–1996*), which will sell you a reconditioned bike for around £45 that you can sell back when you're finished.

### GOLF

For the courses listed below, *SSS* indicates the "standard scratch score," the score a scratch golfer could achieve in ideal conditions. VisitScotland provides a free leaflet on golf in Scotland, available from the **Edinburgh and Scotland Information Centre** ( ⊠ *3 Princes St., East End* ☎ *0131/473–3800* ⊕ *www.edinburgh.org*), or check online at golf.visitscotland.com. *See Chapter 11 for an overview of the best golf near the capital.*

**Braids.** This 18-hole course was founded in 1897 and laid out over several small hills 3 mi south of Edinburgh. The 9-hole course opened in 2003. ⊠ *Braids Hill Rd., Braidburn* ☎ *0131/447–6666* ⚑ *Course 1: 18 holes, 5,865 yds, SSS 67. Course 2: 9 holes.*

**Bruntsfield Links.** Several tournaments are held each year at this championship course, opened in 1898 a couple miles northwest of the city. ⊠ *32 Barnton Ave., Davidson's Mains* ☎ *0131/336–4050* 🖶 *0131/336–5538* ⚑ *18 holes, 6,407 yds, SSS 71.*

**Duddingston.** You can find this public parkland course, founded in 1895, 2 mi east of the city. ⊠*Duddingston Rd. W, Duddingston* ☎*0131/661–7688* ⚐*18 holes, 6,420 yds, SSS 72.*

**Liberton.** This public parkland course was built in 1920, 4 mi south of the city. ⊠*Kingston Grange, 297 Gilmerton Rd., Liberton* ☎*0131/664–3009* 🖶*0131/666–0853* ⚐*18 holes, 5,412 yds, SSS 69.*

**Lothianburn.** You can see good views of the Midlothian countryside from this hillside course, founded in 1893, 6 mi south of the city. ⊠*Biggar Rd., Fairmilehead* ☎*0131/445–5067* ⚐*18 holes, 5,662 yds, SSS 68.*

**Portobello.** Short and sweet, Portobello has welcomed amateur golfers since 1826. ⊠*Stanley St., Portobello* ⊹*2 mi east of city* ☎*0131/669–4361* ⚐*9 holes, 2,449 yds, SSS 32.*

### RUGBY

At **Murrayfield Stadium** ( ⊠*Roseburn Terr., Murrayfield* ☎*0131/346–5000*), home of the Scottish Rugby Union, Scotland's international rugby matches are played in early spring and fall. During that time of year, crowds of good-humored rugby fans from all over the world add greatly to the sense of excitement in the streets of Edinburgh.

### SOCCER

Like Glasgow, Edinburgh is soccer-mad, and there's an intense rivalry between the city's two professional teams. Remember, the game is called football in Britain. The **Heart of Midlothian Football Club ("Hearts")** ( ☎*0131/200–7200*) plays in maroon and white and is based at Tynecastle. The green-bedecked **Hibernian ("Hibs") Club** ( ☎*0131/661–2159*) plays its home matches at Easter Road.

# SHOPPING

Despite its renown as a shopping street, **Princes Street** in the New Town may disappoint some visitors with its dull, anonymous modern architecture, average chain stores, and fast-food outlets. One block north of Princes Street, **Rose Street** has many smaller specialty shops; part of the street is a pedestrian zone, so it's a pleasant place to browse. The shops on **George Street** tend to be fairly upscale. London names, such as Laura Ashley and Penhaligons, are prominent, though some of the older independent stores continue to do good business.

The streets crossing George Street—Hanover, Frederick, and Castle—are also worth exploring. **Dundas Street,** the northern extension of Hanover Street, beyond Queen Street Gardens, has several antiques shops. **Thistle Street,** originally George Street's "back lane," or service area, has several boutiques and more antiques shops. As may be expected, many shops along the **Royal Mile** sell what may be politely or euphemistically described as tourist-ware—whiskies, tartans, and tweeds. Careful exploration, however, will reveal some worthwhile establishments. Shops here also cater to highly specialized interests and hobbies.

Close to the castle end of the Royal Mile, just off George IV Bridge, is **Victoria Street,** with specialty shops grouped in a small area. Follow the tiny West Bow to **Grassmarket** for more specialty stores. North of Princes Street, on the way to the Royal Botanic Garden Edinburgh, is **Stockbridge,** an oddball shopping area of some charm, particularly on St. Stephen Street. To get here, walk north down Frederick Street and Howe Street, away from Princes Street, then turn left onto North West Circus Place. **Stafford and William streets** form a small, upscale shopping area in a Georgian setting. Walk to the west end of Princes Street and then along its continuation, Shandwick Place, then turn right onto Stafford Street. William Street crosses Stafford halfway down.

## ARCADES & SHOPPING CENTERS

Like most large towns, Edinburgh has succumbed to the fashion for under-one-roof shopping. **Cameron Toll** (⌧*Bottom of Dalkeith Rd., Mayfield*), in the city's South Side, caters to local residents, with food stores and High Street brand names. If you don't want to be distracted by wonderful views between shops—or if it's raining—try the upscale **Princes Mall** (⌧*East end of Princes St., East End*), with a fast-food area, designer-label boutiques, and shops that sell Scottish woolens and tweeds, whisky, and confections. The **Ocean Terminal** (⌧*Ocean Dr., Leith*) houses a large collection of shops as well as bars and eateries. Here you can also visit the former royal yacht *Britannia*. The **St. James Centre** (⌧*Princes St., East End*) has Dorothy Perkins, HMV, and numerous other chain stores. **South Gyle** (⌧*Off A720, near airport, Gyle*) is like a typical U.S.–style shopping mall. Here you can find the usual High Street brand names, including a huge Marks & Spencer.

## DEPARTMENT STORES

In contrast to other major cities, Edinburgh has few true department stores. If you plan on a morning or a whole day of wandering from department to department, trying on beautiful clothes, buying crystal or china, or stocking up on Scottish food specialties, with a break for lunch at an in-store restaurant, Jenners is your best bet.

★ **Aitken and Niven** (⌧*6 Selcon Rd., Morningside* ☎*0131/477–3922*) is an Edinburgh institution: a small department store where the well-heeled come to buy upscale clothing, shoes, and accessories. **Harvey Nichols** (⌧*30–34 St. Andrew Sq., New Town* ☎*0131/524–8388*) is the local outpost of the high-style British chain. **Jenners** (⌧*48 Princes St., New Town* ☎*0131/225–2442*) specializes in traditional china and glassware, as well as Scottish clothing (upscale tweeds and tartans). Its justly famous food hall sells shortbreads and Dundee cakes (a light fruit cake with a distinctive pattern of split almonds arranged in circles on the top), honeys, and marmalades, as well as high-quality groceries. **John Lewis** (⌧*69 St. James Centre, East End* ☎*0131/556–9121*), part of a U.K.–wide chain, specializes in furniture and household goods but also stocks designer clothes. **Marks & Spencer** (⌧*54 and 91 Princes St., New Town* ☎*0131/225–2301*) sells well-priced, stylish everyday clothes and accessories. You can also buy food items and household goods here.

## SPECIALTY SHOPS

### ANTIQUES

Antiques dealers tend to cluster together, so it may be easiest to concentrate on one area—St. Stephen Street, Bruntsfield Place, Causewayside, or Dundas Street, for example—if you're short on time.

**Courtyard Antiques** ( ⊠*108A Causewayside, Sciennes* ☎*0131/662–9008*) stocks a mixture of high-quality antiques, toys, and militaria.

### BOOKS, PAPER, MAPS & GAMES

As a university city and cultural center, Edinburgh is endowed with excellent bookstores.

Near the Grassmarket, **Armchair Books** ( ⊠*72–74 W. Port, Old Town* ☎*0131/229–5927*) is a chaotic secondhand bookshop heaving with tomes from your youth. **Beyond Words** ( ⊠*42–44 Cockburn St., Old Town* ☎*0131/226–6636*) has an awe-inspiring selection of photography books. **Carson Clark Gallery** ( ⊠*181–183 Canongate, Old Town* ☎*0131/556–4710*) specializes in antique maps, sea charts, and prints.

### CLOTHING BOUTIQUES

Edinburgh is home to several top-quality designers—although, it must be said, probably not as many as are found in Glasgow, Scotland's fashion center—some of whom make a point of using Scottish materials in their creations.

**Bill Baber** ( ⊠*66 Grassmarket, Old Town* ☎*0131/225–3249*) is one of the most imaginative of the many Scottish knitwear designers, and a long way from the conservative pastel woolies sold at some of the large mill shops. The **Extra Inch** ( ⊠*12 William St., West End* ☎*0131/226–3303*) stocks a full selection of clothes in European sizes 16 (U.S. size 14) and up.

**Herman Brown's** ( ⊠*151 W. Port, West End* ☎*0131/228–2589*) is a secondhand clothing store where cashmere twin sets and classic luxe labels are sought and found. If you don't make it up to the main shop in Skye, **Ragamuffin** ( ⊠*278 Canongate, Old Town* ☎*0131/557-6007*) sells the funkiest and brightest knits produced in Scotland.

### JEWELRY

**Clarksons** ( ⊠*87 W. Bow, Old Town* ☎*0131/225–8141*), a family firm, handcrafts a unique collection of jewelry, including Celtic styles. The jewelry here is made with silver, gold, platinum, and precious gems, with a particular emphasis on diamonds. **Hamilton and Inches** ( ⊠*87 George St., New Town* ☎*0131/225–4898*), established in 1866, is a silver- and goldsmith worth visiting not only for its modern and antique gift possibilities, but also for its late-Georgian interior, designed by David Bryce in 1834—all columns and elaborate plasterwork. **Joseph Bonnar** ( ⊠*72 Thistle St., New Town* ☎*0131/226–2811*), tucked behind George Street, has Scotland's largest collection of antique jewelry, including 19th-century agate jewels.

### LINENS, TEXTILES & HOME FURNISHINGS

**And So To Bed** ( ⊠ *30 Dundas St., New Town* ☎ *0131/652–3700*) has a wonderful selection of embroidered and embellished bed linens, cushion covers, and the like. **In House** ( ⊠ *28 Howe St., New Town* ☎ *0131/225–2888*) sells designer furnishings and collectibles at the forefront of modern design for the home. **Studio One** ( ⊠ *10–16 Stafford St., New Town* ☎ *0131/226–5812*) has a well-established and comprehensive inventory of gift articles.

### OUTDOOR SPORTS GEAR

**Tiso** ( ⊠ *123–125 Rose St., New Town* ☎ *0131/225–9486* ⊠ *41 Commercial St., Leith* ☎ *0131/554–0804*) stocks outdoor clothing, boots, and jackets ideal for hiking or camping in the Highlands or the islands.

### SCOTTISH SPECIALTIES

If you want to identify a particular tartan, several shops on Princes Street will be pleased to assist. The **Clan Tartan Centre** ( ⊠ *70–74 Bangor Rd., Leith* ☎ *0131/553–5516*) has a database containing details of all known tartans, plus information on clan histories. At the **Edinburgh Old Town Weaving Company** ( ⊠ *555 Castlehill, Old Town* ☎ *0131/226–1555*), you can watch and even talk to the cloth and tapestry weavers as they work, then buy the products. The company can also provide information on clan histories, and, if your name is a relatively common English or Scottish one, tell you which tartan you're entitled to wear. **Geoffrey (Tailor) Highland Crafts** ( ⊠ *57–59 High St., Old Town* ☎ *0131/557–0256*) can clothe you in full Highland dress, with kilts made in its own workshops. The affiliated **21st Century Kilts** crafts contemporary kilts in leather, denim, and even camouflage.

# SIDE TRIPS FROM EDINBURGH

If you stand on an Edinburgh eminence—the castle ramparts, Arthur's Seat, Corstorphine Hill—you can plan a few Lothian excursions without even the aid of a map. The Lothians is the collective name given to the swath of countryside south of the Firth of Forth and surrounding Edinburgh. Many courtly and aristocratic families lived here, and the region still has the castles and mansions to prove it. The rich arrived and with them came deer parks, gardens in the French style, and Lothian's fame as a seed plot for Lowland gentility. Although the region has always provided rich pickings for historians, it also used to offer even richer pickings for coal miners—for a century after the start of the industrial revolution, gentle streams in fairy glens (so the old writings describe them) steamed and stank with pollution. Although some black spots still remain, most of the rural countryside is once again a fitting setting for excursions. When the coal miners left, admirals came here to retire, and today the area happily holds many delights.

The 70-mi round-trip exploration of the historic houses and castles of West Lothian and the Forth Valley, and territory north of the River Forth, can be accomplished in a full day with select stops, or you can just pick one or two. Stretching east to the sea and south to the Lowlands from Edinburgh, Midlothian and East Lothian are no more than one hour from Edinburgh. The inland river valleys, hills, and castles of Midlothian and East Lothian's delightful waterfronts, dunes, and golf links offer a taste of Scotland close to the capital.

| WHAT IT COSTS IN POUNDS | | | | | |
|---|---|---|---|---|---|
| | £ | ££ | £££ | ££££ | £££££ |
| RESTAURANTS | under £10 | £11–£14 | £15–£19 | £20–£25 | over £25 |
| HOTELS | under £70 | £70–£120 | £121–£160 | £161–£220 | over £220 |

Restaurant prices are for a main course at dinner. Hotel prices are for two people in a standard double room in high season, generally including 17.5% V.A.T. These are different from the Edinburgh city prices.

## WEST LOTHIAN & THE FORTH VALLEY

West Lothian comprises a good bit of Scotland's central belt. The River Forth snakes across a widening floodplain on its descent from the Highlands, and by the time it reaches the western extremities of Edinburgh, it has already passed below the mighty Forth bridges and become a broad estuary. Castles and stately homes sprout thickly on both sides of the Forth.

### CRAMOND
*4 mi west of Edinburgh.*

At this compact coastal settlement, you can watch summer sunsets upriver of where the Almond joins the Firth of Forth. The river's banks, once the site of mills and industrial works, now have pleasant, leafy walks.

#### WHERE TO EAT

££  ✕ **Cramond Inn.** After a bracing walk along the seaside promenade, stop by this dark, 17th-century village inn—once the haunt of Robert Louis Stevenson—for a pint at the bar or a selection from the small but varied pub menu. Among the options are grilled halibut and new potatoes, sole and salmon rolls, chicken with mango chutney and rice, and steak. ⊠ *Cramond Glebe Rd.* ☎ *0131/336–2035* ▤ *MC, V.*

#### DALMENY HOUSE
*6 mi west of Edinburgh.*

The first of the stately houses clustered on the western edge of Edinburgh, Dalmeny House is the home of the earl and countess of Rosebery. This 1815 Tudor Gothic mansion displays among its sumptuous contents the best of the family's famous collection of 18th-century French furniture. Highlights include the library, the Napoléon Room, the Vincennes and Sevres porcelain collections, and the drawing room, with its tapestries and intricately wrought French furniture. ⊠ *B924, by South Queensferry* ☎ *0131/331–1888* ⊕ *www.dalmeny.co.uk* ☞ *£5* ♥ *July and Aug., Sun.–Tues. 2–5:30; last admission at 4:30.*

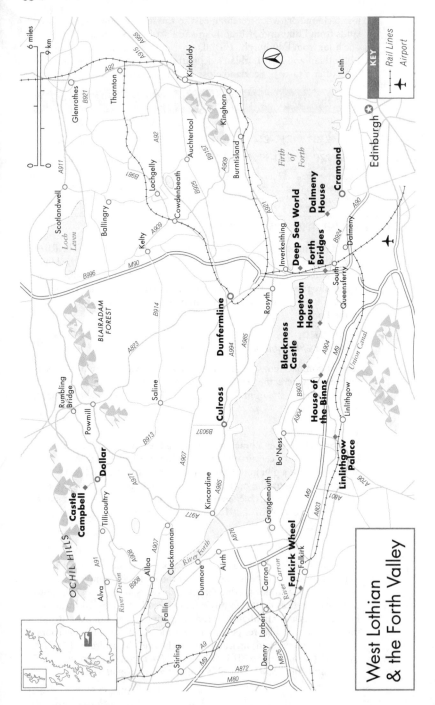

KEY
— Rail Lines
✈ Airport

West Lothian
& the Forth Valley

**1**

### SOUTH QUEENSFERRY
*7 mi west of Edinburgh.*

★ This pleasant little waterside community, a former ferry port, is completely dominated by the **Forth Bridges,** dramatic structures of contrasting architecture that span the Firth of Forth at this historic crossing point. The **Forth Rail Bridge** was opened in 1890 and at the time hailed as the eighth wonder of the world, at 2,765 yards long—except on a hot summer's day when it expands by about another yard. Its neighbor is the 1,993-yard-long **Forth Road Bridge,** in operation since 1964.

### WHERE TO EAT

££ ✕**The Hawes Inn.** In his novel *Kidnapped,* Robert Louis Stevenson describes a room at this inn as "a small room, with a bed in it, and heated like an oven by a great fire of coal." The dramatic setting and history alone are well worth the trip to the inn, which is 10 mi from the city center of Edinburgh and 1 mi from Dalmeny Railway station. It sits right under the girders of the Forth Rail Bridge. The open fireplaces at this 1638 pub create a sense of comfort and coziness. You can find traditional pub fare here, such as steak pie and fish-and-chips. ✉*7 Newhalls Rd.* ☎*0131/331–1990* ▭*AE, MC, V.*

### HOPETOUN HOUSE
★ *10 mi west of Edinburgh.*

The palatial premises of Hopetoun House, probably Scotland's grandest courtly seat and home of the marquesses of Linlithgow, are considered to be among the Adam family's finest designs. The enormous house was started in 1699 to the original plans of Sir William Bruce (1630–1710), then enlarged between 1721 and 1754 by William Adam (1689–1748) and his sons Robert and John. There's a notable painting collection, and the house has decorative work of the highest order, plus all the trappings to keep you entertained: a nature trail, a restaurant in the former stables, and a museum. Much of the wealth that created this sumptuous building came from the family's mining interests in the surrounding regions. ✉*Off A904, 6 mi west of South Queensferry* ☎*0131/331–2451* ⊕*www.hopetounhouse.com* ✉*£8* ☼*Apr.–Sept., daily 10–5:30, last admission at 4; Oct., daily 11–4, last admission at 3:30.*

### HOUSE OF THE BINNS
*12 mi west of Edinburgh.*

The 17th-century general "Bloody Tam" Dalyell (circa 1599–1685) transformed a fortified stronghold into a gracious mansion, the House of the Binns (the name derives from *bynn,* the old Scottish word for hill). The present exterior dates from around 1810 and shows a remodeling into a kind of mock fort with crenellated battlements and turrets. Inside, magnificent plaster ceilings are done in the Elizabethan style. The house is cared for by the National Trust for Scotland. ✉*Off A904, 4 mi east of Linlithgow* ☎*01506/834255* ⊕*www.nts.org.uk* ✉*£8* ☼*House June–Sept., Sat.–Wed. 2–5. Park Apr.–Oct., daily 10–7; Nov.–Mar., daily 10–4.*

### BLACKNESS CASTLE
*12 mi west of Edinburgh.*

The castle of Blackness stands like a grounded ship on the very edge of the Forth. A curious 15th-century structure, it has had a varied career as a strategic fortress, state prison, powder magazine, and youth hostel. The countryside is gently green and cultivated, and open views extend across the blue Forth to the distant ramparts of the Ochil Hills. The castle is run by Historic Scotland, a government organization that looks after many historic properties in Scotland. ⊠*B903, 4 mi northeast of Linlithgow* ☎*01506/834807* ⊕*www.historic-scotland.gov.uk* ⊠*£4* ⊘*Apr.–Sept., daily 9:30–5:30; Oct.–Mar., Sat.–Wed. 9:30–4:30.*

### LINLITHGOW PALACE
*12 mi west of Edinburgh.*

On the edge of Linlithgow Loch stands the splendid ruin of Linlithgow Palace, the birthplace of Mary, Queen of Scots in 1542. Burned, perhaps accidentally, by Hanoverian troops during the last Jacobite rebellion in 1746, this impressive shell stands on a site of great antiquity, though nothing for certain survived an earlier fire in 1424. The palace gatehouse was built in the early 16th century, and the central courtyard's elaborate fountain dates from around 1535. The halls and great rooms are cold, echoing stone husks now in Historic Scotland's care. ⊠*A706, south shore of Linlithgow Loch* ☎*01506/842896* ⊕*www. historic-scotland.gov.uk* ⊠*£5* ⊘*Apr.–Sept., daily 9:30–5:30; Oct.– Mar., daily 9:30–4:30.*

### FALKIRK WHEEL
★ *25 mi west of Edinburgh.*

In 2002, British Waterways opened the only rotating boatlift in the world, linking two major waterways, the Forth and Clyde Canal and the Union Canal, between Edinburgh and Glasgow. Considered an engineering marvel, the wheel transports eight or more boats at a time overland from one canal to the other in about 45 minutes. The boats float into a cradlelike compartment full of water; as the wheel turns, they're transported up or down to meet the destination canal. You can board tour boats at Falkirk to ride the Wheel, or you can take a multiday barge cruise between Edinburgh and Glasgow; book in advance. At Falkirk, allow 30 minutes before your scheduled departure time to pick up your tickets and choose your boat. ⊠*Lime Rd., Tamfourhill* ☎*01324/619888, 08700/500208 reservations* ⊕*www. thefalkirkwheel.co.uk* ⊠*Boat trips £8; visitor center free* ⊘*Boat trips, Apr.–Oct., daily 9:30–5; Nov.–Mar., daily 10–3. Visitor center, Apr.–Oct., daily 9–5; Nov.–Mar., daily 10–5.*

### OCHIL HILLS
*24 mi northwest of Edinburgh.*

The scarp face of the Ochil Hills looms unmistakably. It's an old fault line that yields up hard volcanic rocks and contrasts with the quantities of softer coal immediately around the River Forth. The steep Ochils provided grazing land and water power for Scotland's second-largest textile area. Some mills still survive in the so-called Hillfoots towns, on the scarp edge east of Stirling. The **Mill Trail Visitor Centre** ( ✉ W. *Stirling St., Alva* ☎ 01259/769696), has information about the area's mill shops.

Behind the town of Alva (on A91) sits **Alva Glen** ( ⊕ *www.alvaglen.org. uk*), a park near the converted Strude Mill, at the top and eastern end of the little town.

East of Alva Glen is the **Ochil Hills Woodland Park** ( ⊕ *www.clacksweb. org.uk*), which provides access to Silver Glen.

The **Mill Glen,** behind Tillicoultry (pronounced tilly-*coot*-ree), with its giant quarry, fine waterfalls, and interesting plants, is a good hiking option for energetic explorers.

## DOLLAR
*30 mi northwest of Edinburgh.*

This *douce* (Scots for well-mannered or gentle) and tidy town below the Ochil Hills lies at the mouth of Dollar Glen.

With green woods below, bracken hills above, and a view that on a clear day stretches right across the Forth Valley to the tip of Tinto Hill near Lanark, **Castle Campbell** is certainly the most atmospheric fortress within easy reach of Edinburgh. Formerly known as Castle Gloom, Castle Campbell stands out among Scottish castles for the sheer drama of its setting. The sturdy square of the tower house survives from the 15th century, when the site was fortified by the first earl of Argyll (died 1493). Other buildings and enclosures were subsequently added, but the sheer lack of space on this rocky eminence ensured that there would never be any drastic changes. John Knox, the fiery religious reformer, once preached here. In 1654 the castle was captured by Oliver Cromwell and garrisoned with English troops. It's now cared for by Historic Scotland. To get here, follow a road off the A91 that angles sharply up the east side of the wooded defile. ✉ *Off A91, Dollar Glen* ✛ *1 mi north of Dollar* ☎ 01259/742408 ⊕ *www.historic-scotland.gov.uk* ⛛ *£4.50* ☉ *Apr.–Sept., daily 9:30–5:30; Oct.–Mar., daily 9:30–4:30.*

## CULROSS
★ *17 mi northwest of Edinburgh.*

With its Mercat Cross, cobbled streets, tolbooth, and narrow wynds (alleys), Culross, on the muddy shores of the Forth, is now a living museum of a 17th-century town and one of the most remarkable little towns in Scotland. It once had a thriving industry and export trade in coal and salt (the coal was used in the salt-panning process). It also had, curiously, a trade monopoly in the manufacture of baking *girdles* (griddles). As local coal became exhausted, the impetus of the industrial revolution passed Culross by, and other parts of the Forth Valley prospered. Culross became a backwater town, and the merchants' houses of the 17th and 18th centuries were never replaced by Victorian developments or modern architecture. In the 1930s the then-new and also very poor National Trust for Scotland started to buy up the decaying properties. With the help of other agencies, these buildings were conserved and brought to life. Today ordinary citizens live in many of the National Trust properties. A few—the Palace, Study, and Town House—are open to the public. ⊠ *Off A985, 8 mi south of Dollar* ☎ *01383/880359* ⊕ *www.nts.org.uk* ☜ *Palace, Study, and Town House £8* ⊘ *Palace, Study, and Town House June–Aug., daily 10–6; Apr. and May, Thurs.–Mon. noon–5; Sept.–late Oct., Thurs.–Mon. noon–4; last admission 1 hr before closing.*

## DUNFERMLINE
*16 mi northwest of Edinburgh.*

Dunfermline was once the world center for the production of damask linen, but the town is better known today as the birthplace of millionaire industrialist and philanthropist Andrew Carnegie (1835–1919). Undoubtedly Dunfermline's most famous son, Carnegie endowed the town with a park, library, health and fitness center, and, naturally, a Carnegie Hall, still the focus of culture and entertainment.

The 18th-century weaver's cottage where Carnegie was born in 1835 is now the **Andrew Carnegie Birthplace Museum.** Don't be misled by the cottage's simple exterior. Inside it opens into a larger hall, where documents, photographs, and artifacts relate Carnegie's fascinating life story. You can learn such obscure details as the claim that Carnegie was one of only three men in the United States then able to translate Morse code by ear as it came down the wire. ⊠ *Moodie St.* ☎ *01383/724302* ⊕ *www.carnegiebirthplace.com* ☜ *Free* ⊘ *Apr.–Oct., Mon.–Sat. 11–5, Sun. 2–5.*

The **Pittencrieff House Museum** tells the story of the town's damask linen industry. ⊠ *Pittencrieff Park* ☎ *01383/313838 or 01383/722935* ⊕ *www.scottishmuseums.org.uk* ☜ *Free* ⊘ *Apr.–Sept., daily 11–5; Oct.–Mar., daily 11–4.*

The **Dunfermline Abbey and Palace** complex was founded in the 11th century by Queen Margaret, the English wife of the Scots king Malcolm III. Some Norman work can be seen in the present church, where Robert the Bruce (1274–1329) lies buried. The palace grew from the abbey guesthouse and was the birthplace of Charles I (1600–49). Dunfermline was the seat of the royal court of Scotland until the end of the 11th century, and its central role in Scottish affairs is explored by means of display panels dotted around the drafty but hallowed buildings. ⊠ *Monastery St.* ☎ *01383/739026* ⊕ *www.historic-scotland.gov.uk* ☜ *£3.50* ⊘ *Apr.–Sept., daily 9:30–5:30; Oct.–Mar., Mon.–Wed. and Sat. 9:30–4, Thurs. 9:30–noon and Sun. 2–4:30; last admission half hr before closing.*

## DEEP SEA WORLD
*9 mi northwest of Edinburgh.*

The former ferry port in North Queensferry dropped almost into oblivion after the Forth Road Bridge opened, but was dragged abruptly back into the limelight by the hugely popular Deep Sea World. This sophisticated aquarium—for want of a better word—on the Firth of

Forth offers a fascinating view of underwater life. Go down a clear acrylic tunnel for a diver's-eye look at more than 5,000 fish, including 250 sharks (some over 9 feet long); and visit the exhibition hall, which has an Amazon-jungle display and an audiovisual presentation on local marine life. Ichthyophobes will feel more at ease in the adjacent café and gift shop. ✉*North Queensferry* ☎*01383/411880* ⊕*www.deep-seaworld.com* ⊒*£10* ⊙ *Weekdays 10–5; weekends 10–6; last admission 1 hr before closing.*

## WEST LOTHIAN & THE FORTH VALLEY ESSENTIALS

### TRANSPORTATION

BY BUS First bus services link most of this area, but working out a detailed itinerary by bus is tricky and may be best left to your travel agent or guide.

Information **First** (☎*0870/872-7271* ⊕*www.firstgroup.com*).

BY CAR What follows is a route for the main sights in this section. Leave Edinburgh by Queensferry Road—the A90—and follow signs for the Forth Bridge. At Cramond take the slip road, B924, for South Queensferry, watching for signs to Dalmeny House. After turning right onto A904, follow signs for Hopetoun House, House of the Binns, and Blackness Castle. Join the M9, which will speed you west, and look for signs leading to the Falkirk Wheel, southwest of the motorway. Then return to the M9 and cross the Forth.

At this point you'll leave the industrial northern shore of the Forth and enter the Ochil Hills, which you can explore by following the A91 east at Alva; the road continues to Dollar, where you should follow signs to Castle Campbell. From the castle, retrace your route to A91 and turn left. A few minutes outside Dollar, follow A823 through Powmill (follow the signs for Dunfermline); turn right off A823, following the signs for Saline, and then join the A907. Take the B9037 to Culcross and east to join the A994, which leads to Dunfermline. From here follow the Edinburgh signs to the A823 and return via North Queensferry and the Forth Road Bridge (toll £1 traveling north into Fife only).

BY TRAIN Dalmeny, Linlithgow, and Dunfermline all have rail stations and can be reached from Edinburgh Waverley station.

Information **National Rail Enquiries** (☎*08457/484950* ⊕*www.nationalrail. co.uk*).

### CONTACTS & RESOURCES

VISITOR The Mill Trail Visitor Centre, at Alva, can provide information on the
INFORMATION region's textile establishments as well as a *Mill Trail* brochure, which directs you to mill shops selling bargain woolen and tweed goods.

Information **Mill Trail Visitor Centre** (✉ *W. Stirling St., Alva* ☎*01259/769696*).

## MIDLOTHIAN & EAST LOTHIAN

In spite of the finest stone carving in Scotland at Rosslyn Chapel, associations with Sir Walter Scott, outstanding castles, and miles of rolling countryside, Midlothian, the area immediately south of Edinburgh, for years remained off the beaten path. Perhaps a little in awe of sophisticated Edinburgh to the north and the well-manicured charm of the stockbroker belt of nearby upmarket East Lothian, Midlothian was quietly preoccupied with its own workaday little towns and dormitory suburbs.

As for East Lothian, it started with the advantage of golf courses of world rank, most notably Muirfield, plus a scattering of stately homes and interesting hotels. It's an area of glowing grain fields in summer and quite a few discreetly polite STRICTLY PRIVATE signs at the end of driveways. Still, it has plenty of interest, including photogenic villages, active fishing harbors, and vistas of pastoral Lowland Scotland, seemingly a world away (but much less than an hour by car) from bustling Edinburgh.

### NEWHAILES
*5 mi east of Edinburgh.*

This fine late-17th-century house (with 18th-century additions), owned and run by the National Trust for Scotland, was designed by Scottish architect James Smith (circa 1645–1731) in 1686 as his own home. He later sold it to Lord Bellendon, and in 1707 it was bought by Sir David Dalrymple (c. 1665–1721), first baronet of Hailes, who improved and extended the house, adding one of the finest rococo interiors in Scotland. The library played host to many famous figures from the Scottish Enlightenment, including inveterate Scot-basher Dr. Samuel Johnson, who dubbed the library "the most learned room in Europe." Most of the original interiors and furnishings remain intact, creating great authenticity. ⊠ *Newhailes Rd., Musselburgh, EH21 6RY* ☎ *0131/665–1546* ⊕ *www.nts.org.uk* ⊠ *House £10, grounds free* ⊙ *House May–Oct., Thurs.–Mon. noon–5; grounds daily year-round.*

### ROSLIN
*7 mi south of Edinburgh.*

Fodor'sChoice
★    **Rosslyn Chapel** has always beckoned curious visitors intrigued by the various legends surrounding its magnificent carvings, but today it pulses with tourists as never before. Dan Brown's bestselling novel *The Da Vinci Code* has made visiting this Episcopal chapel (services continue to be held here) an imperative stop for many of its enthusiasts. Whether you're a fan of the book or not—and of the book's theory that

the chapel has a secret sign that can lead you to the Holy Grail—this is a site of immense interest. Originally conceived by Sir William Sinclair (circa 1404–80) and dedicated to St. Matthew in 1446, the chapel is outstanding for the quality and variety of the carving inside. Covering almost every square inch of stonework are human figures, animals, and plants. The meaning of these remains subject to many theories; some depict symbols from the medieval order of the Knights Templar and from Freemasonry. The chapel's design called for a cruciform structure, but only the choir and parts of the east transept walls were completed. ✉Roslin ✛Off A703 ☎0131/440–2159 ⊕www.rosslyn-chapel.com ▣£7 ⊙Mon.–Sat. 9:30–5, Sun. noon–4:45.

## SCOTTISH MINING MUSEUM
*9 mi southeast of Edinburgh.*

The Scottish Mining Museum, in the former mining community of Newtongrange, provides a good introduction to the history of Scotland's mining industry. With the help of videos you can go on shift as a coal miner and experience life deep below the ground. There are also interactive displays and "magic helmets" that bring the tour to life and relate the power that the mining company had over the lives of the individual workers here, in Scotland's largest planned-mining village. This frighteningly autocratic system survived well into the 1930s—the company owned the houses, shops, and even the pub. The scenery is no more attractive than you would expect, though the green Pentland Hills hover in the distance. ✉A7, Newtongrange ☎0131/663–7519 ⊕www.scottishminingmuseum.com ▣£5.95 ⊙Daily 10–5; last admission 1½ hrs before closing.

## BORTHWICK CASTLE
*12 mi southeast of Edinburgh.*

Set in green countryside with scattered woods and lush hedgerows, the village of Borthwick is dominated by Borthwick Castle, which dates from the 15th century and is still occupied. Mary, Queen of Scots, came to this stark, tall, twin-towered fortress on a kind of honeymoon with her ill-starred third husband, the earl of Bothwell. Their already-dubious bliss was interrupted by Mary's political opponents, often referred to as the Lords of the Congregation, a confederacy of powerful nobles who favored the crowning of her young son, James. Rather insensitively, they laid siege to the castle while the newlyweds were there. Mary subsequently escaped disguised as a man. She was not free for long, however. It was only a short time before she was defeated in battle and imprisoned. She languished in prison for 21 years before Queen Elizabeth I of England (1558–1603) signed her death warrant in 1587. Bothwell's fate was equally gloomy: he died insane in a Danish prison. The castle now functions as a hotel, but it's well worth a look around. ✉Borthwick ✛1 mi south of Gorebridge ☎01875/820514 ⊕www.borthwickcastlehotel.com ▣Free ⊙Tour hrs vary.

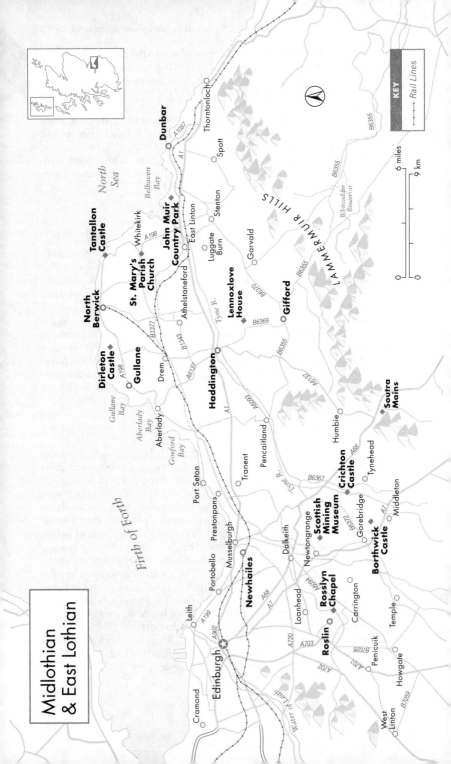

# Midlothian & East Lothian

**KEY**

Rail Lines

North Sea

*Belhaven Bay*

*North Sea*

Dunbar

Thorntonloch

Spott

A1087

A1

Whitekirk

John Muir Country Park

Tantallon Castle

St. Mary's Parish Church

A198

East Linton

Stenton

Luggate Burn

Garvald

LAMMERMUIR HILLS

*Whiteadder Reservoir*

B6355

B6355

North Berwick

Dirleton Castle

Gullane

Athelstaneford

*Tyne R.*

Lennoxlove House

B6369

Gifford

B6370

B6355

A198

Drem

B1377

B1343

A6137

Haddington

A1

A6093

A6137

*Gullane Bay*

*Aberlady Bay*

Aberlady

*Gosford Bay*

Pencaitland

Humbie

Soutra Mains

A68

Tynehead

Middleton

A7

*Firth of Forth*

Port Seton

Prestonpans

Tranent

*Tyne R.*

B6367

Crichton Castle

Gorebridge

Portobello

Musselburgh

Dalkeith

Newtongrange

Scottish Mining Museum

B6372

Borthwick Castle

Leith

A199

Newhailes

A68

A7

Loanhead

A6094

Rosslyn Chapel

Carrington

Temple

Cramond

A902

Edinburgh

A720

A703

Roslin

A702

B7026

Penicuik

A701

Howgate

B7059

West Linton

*Water of Leith*

6 miles
9 km

## CRICHTON CASTLE
*11 mi southeast of Edinburgh.*

Crichton Castle stands amid rolling hills that are interrupted here and there by patches of woodland. Crichton was a Bothwell family castle; Mary, Queen of Scots, attended the wedding here of Bothwell's sister, Lady Janet Hepburn, to Mary's brother, Lord John Stewart. The curious arcaded range reveals diamond-faceted stonework; this particular geometric pattern is unique in Scotland and is thought to have been inspired by Renaissance styles on the Continent, particularly Italy. The oldest part of the work is the 14th-century keep (square tower). You can reach this castle from Borthwick Castle by taking a peaceful walk through the woods (there are signposts along the way). ⊠ *B6367, near Pathhead, 7 mi southeast of Dalkeith* ☎ *01875/320017* ⊕ *www.historic-scotland.gov.uk* ⊠ *£3.50* ⊙ *Apr.–Sept., daily 9:30–5:30.*

**EN ROUTE** If you follow the A68 5 mi south from Pathhead, you reach the very edge of the Lammermuir Hills. Just beyond the junction with the A6368 is a spot called **Soutra Mains** ( ⊠ *16 mi southeast of center of Edinburgh*). From the small parking lot here, you can enjoy glorious unobstructed views extending northward over the whole of the Lothian plain.

## GIFFORD
*25 mi southeast of Edinburgh.*

With its 18th-century kirk and Mercat Cross, Gifford is a good example of a tweedily respectable East Lothian village. John Witherspoon (1723–94), a signatory of the U.S. Declaration of Independence, was born here. A narrow road from Gifford leads up into the Lammermuir Hills and down into Berwickshire, passing the Whiteadder Reservoir.

## DUNBAR
*25 mi east of Edinburgh.*

In the days before tour companies started offering package deals to the Mediterranean, Dunbar was a popular holiday beach resort. Now a bit faded, the town is still lovely for its spacious Georgian-style properties, characterized by the astragals, or fan-shape windows, above the doors; the symmetry of the house fronts; and the parapeted roof lines. Though not the popular seaside playground it once was, Dunbar has an attractive beach and a picturesque harbor.

Taking in the estuary of the River Tyne winding down from the Moorfoot Hills, the **John Muir Country Park** encompasses varied coastal scenery: rocky shoreline, golden sands, and the mixed woodlands of Tyninghame, teeming with wildlife. Dunbar-born conservationist John Muir (1838–1914), whose family moved to the United States when he was a child, helped found Yosemite and Sequoia national parks in California. ⊠ *Off A1087, 2 mi west of Dunbar.*

## NORTH BERWICK
*20 mi northeast of Edinburgh.*

The pleasant little seaside resort of North Berwick manages to retain a small-town personality even when it's thronged with city visitors on warm summer Sunday afternoons. Eating ice cream, the city folk stroll on the beach and in the narrow streets or gaze at the sailing craft in the small harbor. The town is near a number of castles and other sights.

An observation deck, exhibits, and films at the **Scottish Seabird Centre** provide a good introduction to the world of the gannets and puffins that nest on nearby Bass Rock. Live interactive cameras let you take an even closer look at the bird. ⊠ *The Harbour* ☎ *01620/890202* ⊕ *www. seabird.org* 🎫 *£6.95* ⊘ *Apr.–Sept., daily 10–6; Feb., Mar., and Oct., weekdays 10–5, weekends 10–5:30; Nov.–Jan., weekdays 10–4, weekends 10–5:30; last admission 45 min before closing.*

In the center of tiny Dirleton sits the 12th-century **Dirleton Castle,** surrounded by a high outer wall. Within the wall you can find a 17th-century bowling green, set in the shade of yew trees and surrounded by a herbaceous flower border that blazes with color in high summer. Dirleton Castle, now in Historic Scotland's care, was occupied in 1298 by King Edward I of England as part of his campaign for the continued subjugation of the unruly Scots. ⊠ *On A198, 2 mi west of North Berwick* ☎ *01620/850330* ⊕ *www.historic-scotland.gov.uk* 🎫 *£4.50* ⊘ *Apr.–Sept., daily 9:30—5:30; Oct.–Mar., daily 9:30—4:30.*

Rising on a cliff beyond the flat fields east of North Berwick, **Tantallon Castle** is a substantial ruin defending a headland with the sea on three sides. The red sandstone is pitted and eaten by time and sea spray, with the earliest surviving stonework dating from the late 14th century. The fortress was besieged in 1529 by the cannons of King James V (1512–42). Rather inconveniently, the besieging forces ran out of gunpowder. Cannons were used again, to deadlier effect, in a later siege during the Civil War in 1651. Twelve days of battering with the heavy guns of Cromwell's General Monk greatly damaged the flanking towers. Fortunately much of the curtain wall of this former Douglas stronghold, now cared for by Historic Scotland, survives. ⊠ *A198, 3 mi east of North Berwick* ☎ *01620/892727* ⊕ *www.historic-scotland. gov.uk* 🎫 *£4.50* ⊘ *Apr.–Sept., daily 9:30–5:30; Oct.–Mar., Sat.–Wed. 9:30–4:30; last admission half hr before closing.*

The unmistakable red-sandstone **St. Mary's Parish Church,** with its Norman tower, stands in the village of Whitekirk, 6 mi south of North Berwick, on a site occupied since the 6th century. It was a place of pilgrimage in medieval times because of its healing well. Behind the kirk, in a field, stands a tithe barn. Tithe barns originated with the practice of giving to the church a portion of local produce, which then required storage space. In the 15th century, the church was visited by a young Italian nobleman, Aeneas Sylvius Piccolomini, after he was shipwrecked off the East Lothian coast. Two decades later, Piccolomini became Pope Pius II. At one end of the barn stands a 16th-century tower house, which at one point in its history accommodated visiting pilgrims. The large three-story barn was added to the tower house in the 17th century. ⊠ *A198, Whitekirk* 🎫 *Free* ⊘ *Daily 9 AM–sunset.*

**WHERE TO STAY**

££ 　Glebe House. This dignified 18th-century manse sits amid its own secluded grounds, yet it's in the heart of town, a 10-minute walk east of the station. It's also close to the beach and 18 golf courses, including nearby Muirfield. The elegant bedrooms, one of which has a four-poster bed, are in keeping with the Georgian style of the house. Grand period furniture, paintings, and ornaments fill the sitting and dining rooms. **Pros:** Peaceful atmosphere, interesting antiques, sociable breakfast around a mahogany table. **Cons:** Books up well in advance, too twee for some. ⊠*Law Rd., EH39 4PL* ☎*01620/892608* ⊕*www.glebehouse-nb.co.uk* ➔*4 rooms* ⌂*In-room: no a/c, no TV In-hotel: no elevator* ⊟*No credit cards* ¶◎*BP.*

## GULLANE
*15 mi northeast of Edinburgh.*

Very noticeable along this coastline are the golf courses of East Lothian, laid out wherever there is available links space. Ultrarespectable Gullane is surrounded by them, and its inhabitants are typically clad in expensive golfing sweaters. **Muirfield** *(⇨ Chapter 11)*, a course that hosts the British Open championship, is to the north of the village. Greywalls, now a hotel, was originally a private house, designed by Sir Edwin Lutyens (1869–1944). Apart from golf, you can enjoy restful summer evening strolls at Gullane's beach, well within driving distance of the village.

**WHERE TO STAY**

££££–£££££ 　Greywalls. This is the ideal hotel for a golfing vacation: comfortable, ★ with attentive service and fine modern British cuisine that makes the most of local produce. The turn-of-the-20th-century house, designed by Sir Edwin Lutyens in the shape of a crescent and with a walled garden, is an architectural treasure. Edward VII stayed here, as did Jack Nicklaus, Lee Trevino, Arnold Palmer, and a host of other golfing greats. Shades of restful green predominate in the stylish fabrics from the likes of Nina Campbell, Colefax and Fowler, and Osborne and Little. A separate lodge house can accommodate up to eight people. **Pros:** Golfing stories abound, restful ambience, secluded gardens. **Cons:** Not ideal if you dislike golf, expensive rates. ⊠*Muirfield, Gullane, EH31 2EG* ☎*01620/842144* ⊕*www.greywalls.co.uk* ➔*23 rooms, 1 lodge* ⌂*In-room: no a/c. In-hotel: restaurant, tennis courts, no elevator* ⊟*AE, DC, MC, V* ⊗*Closed mid-Oct.–late Mar.* ¶◎*BP* .

## HADDINGTON
*15 mi east of Edinburgh.*

One of the best-preserved medieval street plans in the country can be explored in Haddington. Among the many buildings of architectural or historical interest is the Town House, designed by William Adam in 1748 and enlarged in 1830. A wall plaque at the Sidegate recalls the great heights of floods from the River Tyne. Beyond is the medieval Nungate footbridge, with the Church of St. Mary a little way upstream.

Just to the south of Haddington stands **Lennoxlove House,** the grand ancestral home of the very grand dukes of Hamilton since 1947 and the Baird family before them. A turreted country house, part of it dating from the 15th century, Lennoxlove is a cheerful mix of family life and Scottish history. The beautifully decorated rooms house portraits, furniture, porcelain, and items associated with Mary, Queen of Scots, including her supposed death mask. Sporting activities from falconry to fishing take place on the stunning grounds. ⊠ *B6369, 1 mi south of Haddington* ☎ *01620/823720* ⊕ *www.lennoxlove.com* 🖾 *£4.50* ⊙ *Tours Apr.–Oct., Wed., Thurs, and Sun. 1:30–4.*

## MIDLOTHIAN & EAST LOTHIAN ESSENTIALS

### TRANSPORTATION

BY BUS  City buses travel as far as Swanston and the Pentland Hills. First buses run to towns and villages throughout Midlothian and East Lothian. For details of all services, inquire at the St. Andrew Square bus station in Edinburgh.

**Information First** ( ☎ *0870/872-7271* ⊕ *www.firstgroup.com*).

BY CAR  If traveling by car, here are the roads you'll need to know for visiting the region's main attractions. For Rosslyn Chapel, leave Edinburgh via the A701 (Liberton Road), then turn left to Roslin on the B7006. For a scenic route beneath the Pentland Hills, take the A766 and A702, which runs from Penicuik to West Linton. At the junction of B6372 with A7, just before Gorebridge, you can head to either the Scottish Mining Museum or Borthwick Castle.

West of Dunbar, on the way back to Edinburgh, the A1087 leads to the sandy reaches of Belhaven Bay, signposted from the main road, and to the John Muir Country Park. Beyond the park turn right onto the A1, then turn right onto the A198 to reach St. Mary's Parish Church at Whitekirk, Tantallon Castle, North Berwick, Dirleton, and Gullane. A198 eventually leads to Aberlady, from which you can take the A6137 south to the former county town of Haddington and, by way of B6369, to Lennoxlove House.

BY TRAIN  There is no train service in Midlothian. In East Lothian, the towns of North Berwick, Drem, and Dunbar have train stations with regular service from Edinburgh.

# EDINBURGH & THE LOTHIANS ESSENTIALS

### AIR TRAVEL

Airlines serving Edinburgh include Aer Arann, Aer Lingus, British Airways, British Midland, easyJet, flybe, Flyglobespan, KLM, Lufthansa, Ryanair, Scandinavian Airlines, and ScotAirways. A few transatlantic flights come through Edinburgh (Continental has service from Newark Liberty, near New York City; Delta flies from Atlanta and Flyglobespan travels from Toronto). Except for these fights, you'll probably have to fly into Glasgow, 50 mi away. Ryanair and easyJet have sparked a major price war on the Anglo-Scottish routes. They offer unbeatable, no-frills airfares on routes connecting Edinburgh Airport, Glasgow International, Prestwick Airport (30 mi south of Glasgow), and London's major airports.

**Contacts** **Aer Arann** ( ☎ *0800/587–2324* ⊕ *www.aerarann.com*). **Aer Lingus** ( ☎ *0845/084–4444* ⊕ *www.aerlingus.com*). **British Airways** ( ☎ *0870/850–9850* ⊕ *www.britishairways.com*). **British Midland** ( ☎ *0870/607–0555* ⊕ *www.flybmi.com*). **easyJet** ( ☎ *0871/244–2366* ⊕ *www.easyjet.com*). **flybe** ( ☎ *0870/567–6676* ⊕ *www.flybe.com*). **Flyglobespan** ( ☎ *0131/466–7612* ⊕ *www.flyglobespan.com*). **KLM** ( ☎ *0870/507–4074* ⊕ *www.klm.com*). **Lufthansa** ( ☎ *0845/773–7747* ⊕ *www.lufthansa.com*). **Ryanair** ( ☎ *0906/270–5656* ⊕ *www.ryanair.com*). **Scandinavian Airlines** ( ☎ *201/896–3735* ⊕ *www.flysas.com*). **ScotAirways** ( ☎ *0870/606–0707* ⊕ *www.scotairways.co.uk*).

AIRPORTS Edinburgh Airport, 7 mi west of the city center, offers only a few transatlantic flights. It does, however, have air connections throughout the United Kingdom—London (Heathrow, Gatwick, Stansted, Luton, and City), Birmingham, Bristol, East Midlands, Humberside, Jersey, Kirkwall (Orkney), Inverness, Leeds–Bradford, Manchester, Norwich, Sumburgh (Shetlands), Southampton, Wick, and Belfast (in Northern Ireland)—as well as with a number of European cities, including Amsterdam, Brussels, Copenhagen, Cork, Dublin, Frankfurt, Paris, Rome, Stockholm, and Zurich. Flights take off for Edinburgh Airport virtually every hour from London's Gatwick and Heathrow airports; it's usually faster and less complicated to fly through Gatwick, which has excellent rail service from London's Victoria Station.

Glasgow Airport, 50 mi west of Edinburgh, serves as the major point of entry into Scotland for transatlantic flights. Prestwick Airport, 30 mi southwest of Glasgow, after some years of eclipse by Glasgow Airport, has grown in importance, not least because of the activities of Ryanair.

**Information** **Edinburgh Airport** ( ☎ *0870/040–0007* ⊕ *www.baa.com*). **Glasgow Airport** ( ☎ *0870/040–0008* ⊕ *www.baa.com*). **Prestwick Airport** ( ☎ *0871/223–0700* ⊕ *www.gpia.co.uk*).

TRANSFERS FROM EDINBURGH AIRPORT There are no rail links to the city center, even though the airport sits between two main lines. By bus or car you can usually make it to Edinburgh in a half hour, unless you hit the morning (7:30 to 9) or evening (4 to 6) rush hours. Lothian Buses run between Edinburgh Airport and the city center every 15 minutes daily from 9 to 5 and less frequently (roughly every hour) during off-peak hours. The trip takes about 30 minutes, or about 45 minutes during rush hour. A single-fare ticket costs £1. Airport 100 runs an express service to Waverley Station via Haymarket that takes 25 minutes. Buses run every 10 minutes and single-fare tickets cost £3.

You can arrange for a chauffeur-driven limousine to meet your flight at Edinburgh Airport through David Grieve Chauffeur Drive, Little's Chauffeur Drive, or WL Sleigh Ltd., for about £50.

Taxis are readily available outside the terminal. The trip takes 20 to 30 minutes to the city center, 15 minutes longer during rush hour. The fare is roughly £20. Note that airport taxis picking up fares from the terminal are any color, not the typical black cabs.

Contact **David Grieve Chauffeur Drive** (✉ *5B Polworth Gardens, Tollcross* ☎ *0131/229-8666*). **Little's Chauffeur Drive** (✉ *1282 Paisley Rd. W, Paisley* ☎ *0141/883-2111* ⊕ *www.littles.co.uk*). **W L Sleigh Ltd.** (✉ *6 Devon Pl., West End* ☎ *0131/337-3171* ⊕ *www.sleigh.co.uk*).

TRANSFERS FROM GLASGOW AIRPORT
Scottish Citylink buses leave Glasgow Airport every 15 minutes to travel to Glasgow's Buchanan Street (journey time is 25 minutes), where you can transfer to an Edinburgh bus (leaving every 20 minutes). The trip to Edinburgh takes 70 minutes and costs £8.50 one-way. ■TIP→ **A far more pleasant option is to take a cab from Glasgow Airport to Glasgow's Queen Street train station (20 minutes and costs about £18) and then take the train to Waverley Station in Edinburgh.** Trains depart about every 30 minutes; the trip takes 50 minutes and costs about £9. Another, less-expensive alternative—best for those with little luggage—is to take the bus from Glasgow Airport to Glasgow's Buchanan bus station, walk five minutes to the Queen Street train station, and catch the train to Edinburgh. Taxis from Glasgow Airport to downtown Edinburgh take about 70 minutes and cost around £100.

Contact **Scottish Citylink** (☎ *08705/505050* ⊕ *www.citylink.co.uk*).

## BY BUS

National Express provides bus service to and from London and other major towns and cities. The main terminal, St. Andrew Square bus station, is a couple of minutes (on foot) north of Waverley station, immediately east of St. Andrew Square. Long-distance coaches must be booked in advance from the booking office in the terminal. Edinburgh is approximately eight hours by bus from London.

Lothian Buses provides much of the service between Edinburgh and the Lothians and conducts day tours around and beyond the city. First Ltd. runs buses out of Edinburgh into the surrounding area. Megabus offers dirt-cheap fares if you book in advance. However, the buses can be grubby inside.

Information **First** (☎ *0870/872-7271* ⊕ *www.firstgroup.com*). **Lothian Buses** (☎ *0131/555-6363* ⊕ *www.lothianbuses.co.uk*). **Megabus** (☎ *0900/160-0900* ⊕ *www.megabus.com*). **National Express** (☎ *08705/808080* ⊕ *www.national express.co.uk*).

TRAVEL WITHIN EDINBURGH
Lothian Buses is the main operator within Edinburgh. You can buy tickets on the bus. The Day Ticket (£2.50), allowing unlimited one-day travel on the city's buses, can be purchased in advance or from the driver on any Lothian bus (exact fare is required when purchasing on a bus). The Ridacard (for which you'll need a photo) is valid on all buses for seven days (Sunday through Saturday night) and costs £13; the four-week Rider costs £37. ■TIP→ **Buses are great for cheap daytime travel, but in the evening you'll probably want to take a taxi.**

Information **Lothian Buses** (✉ *Waverley Bridge, Old Town* ☎ *0131/555-6363* ⊕ *www.lothianbuses.co.uk*).

### BY CAR

Driving in Edinburgh has its quirks and pitfalls, but competent drivers should not be intimidated. Metered parking in the city center is scarce and expensive, and the local traffic wardens are a feisty, alert bunch. Note that illegally parked cars are routinely towed away, and getting your car back will be expensive. After 6 PM the parking situation improves considerably, and you may manage to find a space quite near your hotel, even downtown. If you park on a yellow line or in a resident's parking bay, be prepared to move your car by 8 the following morning, when the rush hour gets under way. Parking lots are clearly signposted; overnight parking is expensive and not permitted in all lots.

### BY TAXI

Taxi stands can be found throughout the downtown area. The following are the most convenient: the west end of Princes Street; South St. David Street, and North St. Andrew Street (both just off St. Andrew Square); Princes Mall; Waterloo Place; and Lauriston Place. Alternatively, hail any taxi displaying an illuminated FOR HIRE sign.

### BY TRAIN

Edinburgh's main train hub, Waverley Station, is downtown, below Waverley Bridge and around the corner from the unmistakable spire of the Scott Monument. Travel time from Edinburgh to London by train is as little as 4½ hours for the fastest service.

Edinburgh's other main station is Haymarket, about four minutes (by rail) west of Waverley. Most Glasgow and other western and northern services stop here. Haymarket can be more convenient if you're staying in hotels beyond the west end of Princes Street.

Information **First ScotRail** (☎ 0845/601–5929 ⊕ www.firstgroup.com/scotrail). **National Rail Enquiries** (☎ 08457/495051 ⊕ www.nationalrail.co.uk).

## CONTACTS & RESOURCES

### CONSULATES

The London office of the Canadian High Commission can provide local information for visitors.

Information **Canadian High Commission** (✉ 50 Lothian Rd., Festival Sq., West End ☎ 0131/473–6320 ⊕ www.dfait-maeci.gc.ca/canadaeuropa/united_kingdom). **United States Consulate General** (✉ 3 Regent Terr., Calton ☎ 0131/556–8315 ⊕ www.usembassy.org.uk/scotland).

### EMERGENCIES

In an emergency dial **999** for an ambulance or for the police or fire departments (no coins are needed for emergency calls made from pay phones). The accident and emergency department of Edinburgh Royal Infirmary is at Lauriston Place in the city center, though the main buildings are 6 mi to the southeast in an area known as Little France.

You can find out which pharmacy is open late on a given night by looking at the notice posted on every pharmacy door. A pharmacy—or dispensing chemist, as it's called here—is easily identified by its sign, showing a green cross on a white background. Boots, a large British chain, is open weekdays from 8 AM to 9 PM, Saturday from 8 to 6, and Sunday from 10:30 to 4:30.

To retrieve lost property, try the Lothian and Borders police headquarters, open weekdays from 9 to 5. If you lose something on a public bus, contact Lothian Buses, open weekdays from 10 to 1:30.

**Hospital Edinburgh Royal Infirmary** ( ⊠ *Dalkeith Rd., Little France* ⊠ *Accident and Emergency, Lauriston Pl., Old Town* ☎ *0131/536-1000*).

**Late-Night Pharmacy Boots** ( ⊠ *48 Shandwick Pl., west end of Princes St., West End* ☎ *0131/225-6757*).

**Lost & Found Lothian and Borders police headquarters** ( ⊠ *Fettes Ave., Inverleith* ☎ *0131/311-3131*). **Lothian Buses** ( ⊠ *55 Annandale St., New Town* ☎ *0131/558-8858*).

## MAIL & SHIPPING
The post office in St. James Centre is the most central and is open Monday from 9 to 5:30, Tuesday through Friday from 8:30 to 5:30, and Saturday from 8:30 to 6. There are two other main post offices in the city center. Many newsstands also sell stamps.

**Post Offices City Center** ( ⊠ *40 Frederick St., New Town* ☎ *0845/722-3344* ⊠ *7 Hope St., West End* ☎ *0131/226-6823*). **St. James Centre** ( ⊠ *St. Andrew Sq., East End* ☎ *0845/722-3344*).

## SIGHTSEEING TOURS
ORIENTATION TOURS  The best way to get oriented in Edinburgh is to take a bus tour, most of which are operated by Lothian Buses. City Sightseeing open-top bus tours (£9) include multilingual commentary; MacTours (£9) are conducted in vintage open-top buses. All tours take you to the main attractions, including Edinburgh Castle, the Royal Mile, Palace of Holyroodhouse, city museums and galleries, and the Old and New towns. They depart from Waverley Bridge, and are hop on/hop off services, with tickets lasting 24 hours. The 60-minute Majestic Tour (£12) operates with a professional guide, and takes you from Waverly Bridge to the New Town, past Charlotte Square, art galleries, the Royal Botanic Garden Edinburgh, and Newhaven Heritage Museum, until it reaches the royal yacht *Britannia* moored at Leith. Tickets for all tours are available from ticket sellers on Waverley Bridge or on the buses themselves.

**Information Lothian Buses** ( ☎ *0131/555-6363* ⊕ *www.edinburghtour.com*).

PERSONAL GUIDES  Scottish Tourist Guides can supply guides (in 19 languages) who are fully qualified and will meet clients at any point of entry into the United Kingdom or Scotland. They can also tailor tours to your interests.

**Contact Scottish Tourist Guides** (*Contact Doreen Boyle* ⊠ *Old Town Jail, St. John St., Stirling FK8 1EA* ☎ *01786/451953* ⊕ *www.stga.co.uk*).

WALKING
TOURS
Cadies and Witchery Tours, a fully qualified member of the Scottish Tourist Guides Association, has built a reputation for combining entertainment and historical accuracy in its lively and enthusiastic Ghosts & Gore Tour and Murder & Mystery Tour (£7.50 each), which take you through the narrow Old Town alleyways and closes, with costumed guides and other theatrical characters showing up en route. The Scottish Literary Tour Company takes you around Edinburgh's Old and New Town, with guides invoking Scottish literary characters; it also has regional tours around Scotland.

**Contact Cadies and Witchery Tours** ( ✉84 W. Bow, Edinburgh ☎0131/225–6745 ⊕ www.witcherytours.com). **Scottish Literary Tour Company** ( ✉97B W. Bow, Suite 2, Edinburgh ☎0131/226–6665 ⊕ www.edinburghliterarypubtour.co.uk).

### VISITOR INFORMATION

The Edinburgh and Scotland Information Centre, next to Waverley Station (follow the TIC signs in the station and throughout the city), offers an accommodations service (Book-A-Bed-Ahead) in addition to the more typical services. It's open May through June and September, from Monday to Saturday 9 to 7, Sunday 10 to 5; July and August, from Monday to Saturday 9 to 8, Sunday 10 to 8; October and April, from Monday to Saturday 9 to 6, Sunday 10 to 5; November through March, from Monday to Wednesday 9 to 5, Thursday to Saturday 9 to 6, and Sunday 10 to 5.

Complete information is also available at the information desk at the Edinburgh Airport.

**Information Edinburgh and Scotland Information Centre** ( ✉3 Princes St., East End ☎0845/225–511 ⊕ www.edinburgh.org).

# Glasgow

Updated by
Fiona G.
Parrott

**IN THE DAYS WHEN BRITAIN** still ruled over an empire, Glasgow pronounced itself the Second City of the Empire. Its people were justifiably proud of Glasgow, as it was here that Britain's great steamships, including the 80,000-ton *Queen Elizabeth*, were built. The term "Clyde-built" (from Glasgow's River Clyde) became synonymous with good workmanship and lasting quality. Scots engineers were to be found wherever there were engines—Glaswegians built the railway locomotives that opened up the Canadian prairies, the South African veldt, the Australian plains, and the Indian subcontinent. Some of the world's greatest industrial and scientific thinkers, such as Lord Kelvin and James Watt, tested their groundbreaking theories and discoveries as young men in Glasgow.

A 16th-century traveler described Glasgow as "a flourishing cathedral city reminiscent of the beautiful fabrics and florid fields of England." Daniel Defoe in 1727 described it as "one of the cleanliest and most beautiful and best-built of cities." Massive industrialization in the 19th century, however, was soon to create a Glasgow less clean and less beautiful.

Stretching along the heavily industrialized banks of the River Clyde, Glasgow had fallen into a severely depressed state by the early 20th century. By the middle of the century its dockland slums were notorious seedbeds of inner-city decay. "All Glasgow needs," said an architecture pundit then, "is a bath and a little loving care." During the last two decades of the 20th century, happily, the city received both. Modern Glasgow has undergone an urban renaissance: trendy downtown stores, a booming and diverse cultural life, stylish restaurants, and an air of confidence make it Scotland's most exciting city.

The city's development has been unashamedly commercial, tied up with the wealth of its manufacturers and merchants, who constructed a vast number of civic buildings throughout the 19th century. Among those who helped shape Glasgow's unique Victorian cityscape during that great period of civic expansion was the local-born architect Alexander "Greek" Thomson (1817–75). Side by side with the overly Victorian, Glasgow had an architectural vision of the future in the work of Charles Rennie Mackintosh (1868–1928). The Glasgow School of Art, the Willow Tearoom, the *Glasgow Herald* building (now home to the Lighthouse architecture and design center), and the churches and schools he designed point clearly to the clarity and simplicity of the best of 20th-century design.

## A BRIEF HISTORY

Glasgow first came into prominence in Scottish history somewhere around 1,400 years ago, and typically for this rambunctious city it all had to do with an argument between a husband and wife. When the king of Strathclyde gave his wife a ring, she was rash enough to present it to an admirer. The king, having surreptitiously repossessed it, threw it into the Clyde before quizzing his wife about its disappearance. In her distress, the queen turned to her confessor, St. Mungo, for advice. He instructed her to fish in the river and—surprise—the first salmon she landed had the ring in its jaws. Glasgow's coat of arms is dominated by three salmon, one with a ring in its mouth. Not surprisingly, Mungo became the city's patron saint. His tomb lies in the mighty medieval cathedral that bears his name.

Glasgow flourished quietly during the Middle Ages. Its cathedral was the center of religious life, its university a center of serious academia. Although the city was made a burgh (i.e., granted trading rights) in 1175 by King William the Lion, its population never numbered more than a few thousand people. What changed Glasgow irrevocably was the Treaty of Union between Scotland and England, in 1707, which allowed Scotland to trade with the essentially English colonies in America. Glasgow, with its advantageous position on Scotland's west coast, prospered. In came cotton, tobacco, and rum; out went various Scottish manufactured goods and clothing. The key to it all was tobacco. The prosperous merchants known as tobacco lords ran the city, and their wealth laid the foundation for the manufacturing industries of the 19th century.

As Glasgow prospered, its population grew. The "dear green place" (the literal meaning of the Gaelic *Glas Cu,* from which the name "Glasgow" purportedly derives) expanded beyond recognition, extending westward and to the south of the original medieval city, which centered around the cathedral and High Street. The 18th-century Merchant City, now largely rejuvenated, lies just to the south and east of George Square, where all but a few of the original merchants' houses remain in their original condition. As the merchants moved to quieter areas in the west of the city, the Beaux-Arts elegance of their mansions and quiet streets gave way to larger municipal buildings and commercial warehouses. During the 19th century the population grew from 80,000 to more than 1 million, and along with this enormous growth there developed a sense of exuberance and confidence that's still reflected in the city's public buildings. The City Chambers, built in 1888, are a proud statement in marble and gold sandstone, a clear symbol of the wealthy and powerful Victorian industrialists' hopes for the future.

**PRESENT & FUTURE**

Today, as always, Glasgow's eye is trained on the future. The city is Scotland's major business destination, with the Scottish Exhibition and Conference Centre serving as the hub of activity. It's also a nexus of rail routes and motorways that can deliver you in less than an hour to Edinburgh, Stirling, Loch Lomond, the Burns Country, and the Clyde coast golfing resorts. Still, Glasgow has learned to take the best of its past and adapt it for the needs of the present day. The dear green places still remain in the city-center parks; the medieval cathedral stands proud, as it has done for 800 years; the Merchant City is revived and thriving; the Victorian splendor has been cleansed of its grime; and the cultural legacy of museums and performing arts is stronger than ever.

## TOP REASONS TO GO

**Inspiring architecture:** The ambitious Victorians left a legacy of striking architecture, and Glasgow's buildings manifest the city's enduring love of grand artistic statements—just remember to look up. The Arts and Crafts buildings and interiors by Charles Rennie Mackintosh are reason alone to visit the city.

**Artistic treasures:** Some of Britain's best museums and art galleries are in Glasgow. The Burrell Collection and the stunningly renovated Kelvingrove Art Gallery are definitely worth a visit even on a sunny day.

**Gorgeous gardens:** From the Kelvingrove to the Botanic Garden, Glasgow has more parks per square mile than any other in Europe. Stop by during one of the music festivals or outdoor theatrical productions in summer.

**Wetting your whistle:** Whether you fancy a cold pint of Guinness in a traditional old-man's pub like the Scotia or an icy gin and tonic at one of Glasgow's many churches turned trendy watering holes like Òran Mór, there's a pub in Glasgow to fit every kind of thirst.

**Retail therapy:** The city has become known for cutting-edge design. Look for everything from Scottish specialties to stylish fashions on the city center's hottest shopping streets, Buchanan and Sauchiehall, as well as in Princes Square.

**Great grub:** Serving local food and international favorites, Glasgow has restaurants to satisfy every palate and occasion. Locals love their cafés and tearooms; check out the scene at the Willow Tearoom as a break from sightseeing.

**Explore Burns Country:** Outside the city are scenic landscapes from coastlines to cottages to castles. Here you can learn about the life and legacy of Robert Burns, Scotland's most renowned poet. Alloway and Ayr are the places to start.

# EXPLORING GLASGOW

Glasgow's layout is hard to read in a single glance. The city center is roughly defined by the M8 motorway to the north and west, the River Clyde to the south, and Glasgow Cathedral and High Street to the east. Glaswegians tend to walk a good deal, and the relatively flat and compact city center, most of which follows a grid plan, is designed for pedestrians. Good street maps are available from bookstores and the helpful Greater Glasgow and Clyde Valley Tourist Board. If you do get lost, though, just ask a local for help. Most people will be more than happy to help you find your way. The streets are also relatively safe, even at night.

The River Clyde, on which Glasgow's trade across the Atlantic developed, runs through the center of the city—literally cutting it in two and offering intriguing views of South Side buildings. In Glasgow always look up: your reward is much ornate detailing above eye level. Remember to bring plenty of insect repellent as the midges (Scotland's own version of the mosquito) are found not only in the country but the city as well. Their favorite season is summer and they tend to travel in swarms.

In the quieter, slightly hillier western part of the city is Glasgow University and the often forgotten bohemian side of Glasgow. Some form of transportation is required to go to either the West End or the South Side, and you should have no qualms in using Glasgow's integrated transport network of buses, subways, and trains. Information is available from Strathclyde Passenger Transport (SPT) Travel Centre. ■TIP→ **The Discovery Ticket one-day pass for the subway (£1.90, after 9:30) is a good deal if you're traveling around. Glasgow's buses have a similar deal (£2.45, after 9:30).**

## MEDIEVAL GLASGOW & THE MERCHANT CITY

In this central part of the city, alongside the relatively few surviving medieval buildings, are some of the best examples of the architectural confidence and exuberance that so characterized the burgeoning Glasgow of the turn of the 20th century. A lot of the city's most important historical buildings are found here, as well as plenty of trendy eateries and pubs. Every form of public transportation can bring you here, from bus to train to subway. Get off at the stop or station closest to George Square and then walk from there.

### MAIN ATTRACTIONS

**8** **Barras.** Scotland's largest indoor market—named for the barrows, or pushcarts, formerly used by the stall holders—is a must-see for anyone addicted to searching through piles of junk for bargains. The century-old institution, open weekends, consists of nine markets. The atmosphere is always good-humored, and you can find just about anything here, in any condition, from dusty model railroads to antique jewelry. Haggling is compulsory! You can reach the Barras by walking from the Argyle Street train station, or take any of the various buses to Glasgow Cross at the foot of the Gallowgate. ⊠¼ *mi east of Glasgow Cross on London Rd., Glasgow Cross* ☎*0141/552–4601* ⊕*www.glasgowbarras.com* ⊠*Free* ⊙*Weekends 10–5.*

**2** **City Chambers.** Dominating the east side of George Square, this exuberant expression of Victorian confidence, built by William Young in Italian Renaissance style, was opened by Queen Victoria (1819–1901) in 1888. Among the interior's outstanding features are the entrance hall's vaulted ceiling, the marble-and-alabaster staircases, the banqueting hall, and Venetian mosaics. The debating chamber has gleaming oak panels and fixtures. Free guided tours lasting about 45 minutes depart weekdays at 10:30 and 2:30. ■TIP→ **Note that the building is closed to all visitors during occasional civic functions.** ⊠*George Sq., City Center* ☎*0141/287–4020* ⊕*www.glasgow.gov.uk* ⊠*Free* ⊙*Weekdays 9–5.*

Fodor'sChoice
★

**1** **George Square.** The focal point of Glasgow's business district is lined with an impressive collection of statues of worthies: Queen Victoria; Scotland's national poet, Robert Burns (1759–96); the inventor and developer of the steam engine, James Watt (1736–1819); Prime Minister

## GREAT ITINERARIES

To take advantage of Glasgow's wealth of cultural sites and shopping, you could easily spend four or five days here, but it's possible to see the city's greatest hits in only two days.

### IF YOU HAVE 2 DAYS

On the first day explore the core of historic Glasgow—the medieval area, dominated by Glasgow's cathedral, and Merchant City. Shoppers should head for Buchanan Street, including the Princes Square development and the Buchanan Galleries. Art lovers should make a bee-line to the Burrell Collection in Pollock Country Park on the South Side. On the second day, see the West End, including the artwork and Charles Rennie Mackintosh furniture at the Hunterian Art Gallery. If you haven't yet seen the city-center parks, venture to Glasgow Green, the art collections at Pollok Country Park, or the House for an Art Lover, at Bellahouston

Park. Remember that Glasgow's pubs and clubs serve up entertainment until late in the evening.

### IF YOU HAVE 5 DAYS

Five days will allow enough time to enjoy more of Glasgow's key museums and cultural attractions: the Glasgow Gallery of Modern Art, the Centre for Contemporary Arts, and the McLellan Galleries, in the city center; or the St. Mungo Museum of Religious Life and Art, to the east. You could easily take a full day to see the cluster of West End museums by Kelvingrove Park (the Kelvingrove Art Gallery and Museum, Hunterian Art Gallery and Hunterian Museum, and the Museum of Transport). For a good day trip take the hour-long train ride to Wemyss Bay, and from there take the ferry to the Isle of Bute, where you can visit Mount Stuart, a spectacular, stately Victorian home.

William Gladstone (1809–98); and towering above them all, Scotland's great historical novelist, Sir Walter Scott (1771–1832). The column was intended for George III (1738–1820), after whom the square is named, but when he was found to be insane toward the end of his reign, his statue was never erected. On the square's east side stands the magnificent Italian Renaissance–style **City Chambers**; the handsome **Merchants' House** fills the corner of West George Street.

Off and around George Square, several streets—Virginia Street, Miller Street, Glassford Street—recall the yesterdays of mercantile wealth. The French-style palaces, with their steep mansard roofs and cupolas, were once tobacco warehouses. Inside are shops and offices; here and there you may trace the elaborately carved mahogany galleries where auctions once took place. ⊠*Between St. Vincent and Argyle Sts., City Center.*

**❸** **Glasgow Cathedral.** The most complete of Scotland's cathedrals (it would
★ have been more complete had 19th-century vandals not pulled down its two rugged towers), this is an unusual double church, one above the other, dedicated to Glasgow's patron saint, St. Mungo. Consecrated in 1136 and completed about 300 years later, it was spared the ravages of the Reformation—which destroyed so many of Scotland's medieval churches—mainly because Glasgow's trade guilds defended it. In the

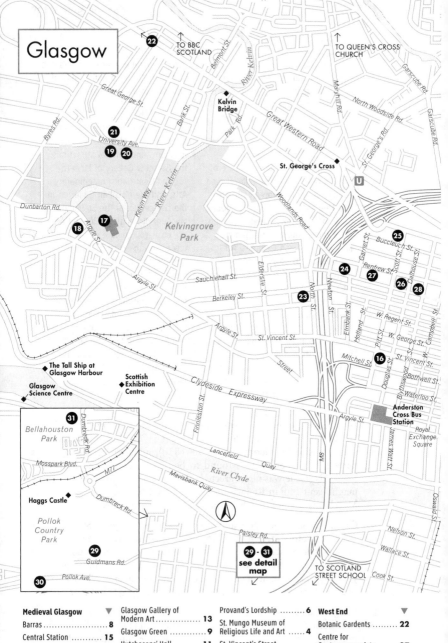

# Glasgow

TO BBC
SCOTLAND

TO QUEEN'S CROSS
CHURCH

Kelvin
Bridge

Belmont St.

River Kelvin

Great Western Road

St. George's Cross

Great George St.

Byres Rd.

University Ave.

Bank St.

Park Rd.

Maryhill Rd.

North Woodside Rd.

Garscube Rd.

Garscube Rd.

St. George's Rd.

U

Dunbarton Rd.

Kelvin Way

River Kelvin

Kelvingrove
Park

Woodlands Road

Buccleuch St.

Scott St.

Dalhousie St.

Garnet St.

Renfrew St.

Argyle St.

Sauchiehall St.

Berkeley St.

Elderslie St.

North St.

Newton St.

Embank St.

Holland St.

W. Regent St.

W. George St.

Hill St.

Argyle St.

St. Vincent St.

Street

Pitt St.

Mitchell St.

St. Vincent St.

Bothwell St.

Douglas St.

Blythswood

Wood St.

Waterloo St.

The Tall Ship at
Glasgow Harbour

Scottish
Exhibition
Centre

Clydeside    Expressway

Anderston
Cross Bus
Station

Glasgow
Science Centre

Argyle St.

James Watt St.

Royal
Exchange
Square

Finnieston St.

Lancefield    Quay

M8

Bellahouston
Park

Dumbreck Rd.

Mosspark Blvd.

M77

River Clyde

Mavisbank Quay

Haggs Castle

Dumbreck Rd.

Pollok
Country
Park

Guldmans Rd.

Pollok Ave.

Paisley Rd.

TO SCOTLAND
STREET SCHOOL

Nelson St.

Wallace St.

Oswald St.

Cook St.

29 - 31
see detail
map

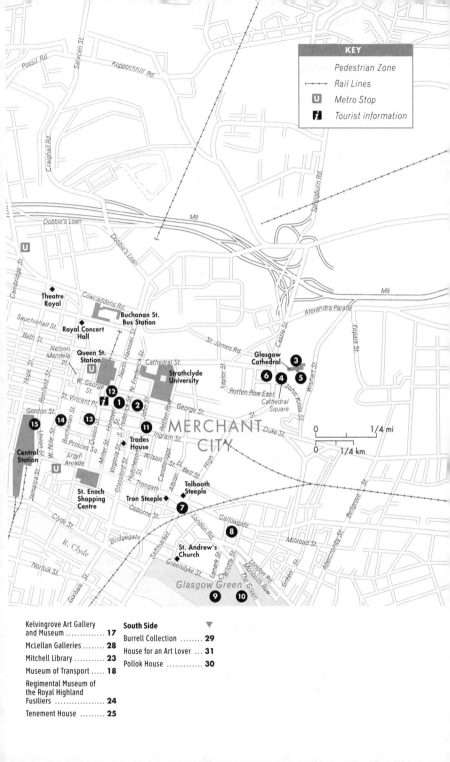

KEY

Pedestrian Zone
Rail Lines
Ⓤ Metro Stop
ℹ Tourist information

Possil Rd.
Saracen St.
Keppochhill Rd.
Craighall Rd.
Dobbie's Loan
M8
Spreyburn Rd.
Cambridge St.
Ⓤ
Dobbie's Loan
M8
Cowcaddens Rd.
Alexandra Parade
Theatre Royal
Sauchiehall St.
Royal Concert Hall
Bath St.
Buchanan St. Bus Station
St. James Rd.
Castle St.
Filpark St.
Nelson Mandela Pl.
Queen St. Station
Ⓤ
St. James Rd.
Glasgow Cathedral ③
Hope St.
Renfield St.
W. George St.
Cathedral St.
Taylor St.
⑥ ④ ⑤
Strathclyde University
Rotten Row East
John Knox St.
Wishart St.
St. Vincent Pl.
⑫
N. Frederick St.
Cathedral Square
Gordon St.
⑦ ① ②
Hanover St.
North Hanover St.
Rotten Row
George St.
Duke St.
0        1/4 mi
⑭  ⑬
Buchanan St.
John St.
⑪
MERCHANT CITY
0     1/4 km
⑮
Princes St.
W. Nile St.
Queen St.
Miller St.
Hutcheson St.
Ingram St.
High St.
Central Station
Union St.
Argyll Arcade
Glassford St.
Trades House
Wilson St.
Candleriggs
Albion St.
Bell St.
Jamaica St.
Trongate
Tolbooth Steeple
Bridgegate
St. Enoch Shopping Centre
Osborne St.
Tron Steeple ◆
⑦
Bellgrove St.
Clyde St.
Saltmarket
London Rd.
Gallowgate
⑧
Norfolk St.
R. Clyde
Greendyke St.
St. Andrew's Church
Lanark St.
Charlotte St.
Monteith Row
The Green
Millroad St.
Green
Abercromby St.
Corbals St.
Glasgow Green
⑨    ⑩

lower church is the splendid crypt of St. Mungo, who was originally known as St. Kentigern (*kentigern* means "chief word,") but who was nicknamed St. Mungo (meaning "dear one") by his early followers in Glasgow. The site of the tomb has been revered since the 6th century, when St. Mungo founded a church here. Mungo features prominently in local legends; one such legend is about a pet bird that he nursed back to life, and another tells of a bush or tree, the branches of which he used to miraculously relight a fire. Bird, tree, and the salmon with a ring in its mouth (from the famous tale related in the introduction to this chapter) are all to be found on the city of Glasgow's coat of arms, together with a bell that Mungo brought from Rome. ⊠ *Cathedral St., City Center* ☎ *0141/552–6891* ⊕ *www.glasgow-cathedral.com* ☜ *Free* ⊙ *Apr.–Sept., Mon.–Sat. 9:30–5:30, Sun. 1–5; Oct.–Mar., Mon.–Sat. 9:30–4:30, Sun. 1–4:30.*

**NEED A BREAK?** Café Cossachok (⊠ *38 Albion St., Glasgow Cross* ☎ *0141/553–0733*) is a colorful café serving excellent borscht, a selection of refreshing European beers, and about 25 kinds of heartwarming Russian vodka. The deep-red walls are peppered with artwork and the low buzz of conversation keeps the place lively.

🔞 **Glasgow Gallery of Modern Art.** One of Glasgow's boldest galleries occupies the former Royal Exchange building. The Exchange, designed by David Hamilton (1768–1843) and finished in 1829, was a meeting place for merchants and traders; later it became Stirling's Library. It incorporates the mansion built in 1780 by William Cunninghame, one of the wealthiest tobacco lords. The modern art, craft, and design collections contained within this handsome building include works by Scottish conceptual artists such as David Mach, and also paintings and sculptures from around the world, including Papua New Guinea, Ethiopia, and Mexico. The display scheme is designed for each floor to reflect the elements—air, fire, and water—which creates some unexpected juxtapositions and also allows for various interactive exhibits. ⊠ *Queen St., City Center* ☎ *0141/229–1996* ⊕ *www.glasgowmuseums.com* ☜ *Free* ⊙ *Mon.–Wed. and Sat. 10–5, Thurs. 10–8, Fri. and Sun. 11–5.*

❾ **Glasgow Green.** Glasgow's oldest park, on the northeast side of the River Clyde, has a long history as a favorite spot for public recreation and political demonstrations. Note the Nelson Column, erected long before London's; the McLennan Arch, originally part of the facade of the old Assembly Halls in Ingram Street; and the Templeton Business Centre, a former carpet factory built in the late 19th century in the style of the Doge's Palace in Venice. The most significant building in the park is the **People's Palace.** ⊠ *Between Greendyke St. to north and River Clyde to south, and between Green to east and Saltmarket to west, Glasgow Cross.*

🔞 **The Lighthouse.** Charles Rennie Mackintosh designed these former offices of the *Glasgow Herald* newspaper in 1893. Mackintosh's building now serves as a fitting setting for Scotland's **Centre for Architecture, Design** and the City, which celebrates all facets of the architectural profession. The **Mackintosh Interpretation Centre** is a great starting point for discovering more about his other buildings in the city. As you ascend the helical staircase you can take a look at Mackintosh's original designs for the building. ⊠*11 Mitchell La., City Center* ☎*0141/225–8414* ⊕*www.the lighthouse.co.uk* ✉*£3 for Mackintosh Interpretation Centre* ⊙*Mon. and Wed.–Sat. 10:30–5, Tues. 11–5, Sun. noon–5.*

---

**MACKINTOSH TRAIL**

If you're interested in the work of architect Charles Rennie Mackintosh, you might purchase a £12 **Mackintosh Trail Ticket** at major sites, visitor centers, or online from the Mackintosh Society. It includes transportation and one-day admission to many sites. Strathclyde Passenger Transport ( ⊕*www.spt.co.uk*) has more information.

---

**Merchant City.** Among the preserved Georgian and Victorian buildings of this city-center neighborhood are many elegant designer boutiques. The **City and County buildings,** on Ingram Street, were built in 1842 to house civil servants; note the impressive arrangement of bays and Corinthian columns. To see more interesting architecture, explore the roads off Ingram Street—including Candleriggs, Wilson, and Glassford. ⊠*Between George, Argyle, Buchanan, and High Sts., City Center.*

**❺ Necropolis.** A burial ground since the beginning of recorded history, the Necropolis, modeled on the famous Père-Lachaise Cemetery in Paris, contains some extraordinarily elaborate Victorian tombs. A statue of John Knox (circa 1514–72), leader of the Scottish Reformation, watches over the cemetery, which includes the tomb of 19th-century Glasgow merchant William Miller (1810–72), author of the "Wee Willie Winkie" nursery rhyme. ⊠*Behind Glasgow Cathedral, City Center.*

**❿ People's Palace.** An impressive Victorian red-sandstone building dating from 1894 houses an intriguing museum dedicated to the city's social history. Included among the exhibits is one devoted to the ordinary folk of Glasgow, called the *People's Story.* Also on display are the writing desk of John McLean (1879–1923), the "Red Clydeside" political activist who came to Lenin's notice, and the famous banana boots worn on stage by Glasgow-born comedian Billy Connolly. Behind the museum are the well-restored Winter Gardens, a relatively sheltered spot where you can escape the often chilly winds whistling across the green. ⊠*Glasgow Green, Glasgow Cross* ☎*0141/271–2951* ⊕*www. glasgowmuseums.com* ✉*Free* ⊙*Mon.–Thurs. and Sat. 10–5, Fri. and Sun. 11–5.*

**❻ Provand's Lordship.** Glasgow's oldest house was built in 1471 by Bishop Andrew Muirhead as a residence for churchmen. Mary, Queen of Scots (1542–87) is said to have stayed here. After her day, however, the house fell into decline and was used as a sweets shop, a soft-drink factory, the home of the city hangman, and a junk shop. The city finally rescued it and turned it into a museum. Exhibits show the house as it might have looked in its heyday, with period rooms and a spooky re-creation of the old hangman's room. ✉ *3 Castle St., City Center* ☎ *0141/552–8819* ⊕ *www.glasgowmuseums.com* 🖾 *Free* ☾ *Mon.–Thurs. and Sat. 10–5, Fri. and Sun. 11–5.*

❹ **St. Mungo Museum of Religious Life and Art.** An outstanding collection of
★ artifacts, including Celtic crosses and statuettes of Hindu gods, reflects the many religious groups that have settled throughout the centuries in Glasgow and the west of Scotland. This rich history is depicted in the stunning Sharing of Faiths Banner, which celebrates the city's many different faiths. A Zen Garden creates a peaceful setting for rest and contemplation, and elsewhere stained-glass windows include a depiction of St. Mungo himself. ✉ *2 Castle St., City Center* ☎ *0141/553–2557* ⊕ *www.glasgowmuseums.com* 🖾 *Free* ☾ *Mon.–Thurs. and Sat. 10–5, Fri. and Sun. 11–5.*

## ALSO WORTH SEEING

⓯ **Central Station.** The railway bridge supporting the tracks going into the station is known as the Highlandman's Umbrella because it was the traditional gathering place for immigrant Highlanders looking for work in Glasgow in the early 20th century. There are several interesting shops in the depot, which serves as the departure point for trains to England and the Ayrshire coast. ✉ *Bounded by Gordon, Union, Argyle, Jamaica, Clyde, Oswald, and Hope Sts., City Center.*

❼ **Glasgow Cross.** This crossroads was the center of the medieval city. The Mercat Cross (*mercat* means "market"), topped by a unicorn, marks the spot where merchants met, where the market was held, and where criminals were executed. Here, too, was the *tron,* or weigh beam, installed in 1491 and used by merchants to check weights. The Tolbooth Steeple dates from 1626 and served as the civic center and the place where travelers paid tolls. ✉ *Intersection of Saltmarket, Trongate, Gallowgate, and London Rds., Glasgow Cross.*

⓫ **Hutchesons' Hall.** Now a visitor center and shop for the National Trust for Scotland, this elegant neoclassical building was designed by David Hamilton in 1802. The hall was originally a hospice founded by two brothers, George and Thomas Hutcheson; you can see their statues in niches in the facade. ✉ *158 Ingram St., Merchant City* ☎ *0141/552–8391* ⊕ *www.nts.org.uk* 🖾 *Free* ☾ *Mon., Tues., Thurs., and Fri. 10–5.*

⓬ **Merchants' House.** A golden sailing ship, a reminder of the importance of sea trade to Glasgow's prosperity, tops this handsome 1874 Victorian building, home to Glasgow's chamber of commerce. The interior isn't open, but the exterior is impressive. ✉ *West side of George Sq., Merchant City.*

⓰ **St. Vincent's Street Church.** Dating from 1859, this church, the work of Alexander Thomson, exemplifies his Greek-revival style, replete with Ionic temple, sphinx-esque heads, Greek ornamentation, and rich interior color. ✉ *Pitt and St. Vincent Sts., City Center.*

# THE WEST END

Glasgow's West End has a stellar mix of education, culture, art, and parkland. The neighborhood is dominated by Glasgow University, founded in 1451, making it the third-oldest in Scotland, after St. Andrews and Aberdeen, and at least 130 years ahead of the University of Edinburgh. It has thrived as a center of educational excellence, particularly in the sciences. The university buildings sit amid parkland, reminding you that Glasgow is a city with more green space per citizen than any other in Europe. ■TIP➜ **A good way to save money is to take a picnic lunch to the park (weather permitting, of course). You can buy sandwiches, salads, and other portable items at several shops on Byres Road.**

> **GETTING AROUND**
>
> The many bus companies cooperate with the Underground and ScotRail to produce the **Family Day Tripper Ticket** (£15 for two adults), which gets you around the whole area, from Loch Lomond to Ayrshire. The tickets are a good value and are available from rail and bus stations and at Strathclyde Passenger Transport Travel Centre (⊠ *St. Enoch Sq., City Center* ☎ *0141/333-3708* ⊕ *www. spt.co.uk*).

The West End is a neighborhood of museums and art galleries, having benefited from the generosity of industrial and commercial philanthropists and from the deep-seated desire of the city founders to place Glasgow at the forefront of British cities. The best way to get to the West End is by subway. Get off at the Hillhead station.

## MAIN ATTRACTIONS

**㉒** **Botanic Gardens.** The Royal Botanical Institute of Glasgow began to display plants here in 1842, and today the gardens include herbs, tropical plants, and a world-famous collection of orchids. The most spectacular building in the complex is the **Kibble Palace,** which reopened in 2007 after extensive renovation. Originally built in 1873, it was the conservatory of a Victorian eccentric named John Kibble. Its domed, interlinked greenhouses contain tree ferns, palm trees, temperate plants, and the Tropicarium, where you can experience the lushness of a rain forest. Elsewhere around the grounds are more conventional greenhouses, as well as immaculate lawns and colorful flower beds. ⊠ *Great Western Rd., West End* ☎ *0141/334–2422* ⊕ *www.glasgow.gov.uk* 🗺 *Free* ⊗ *Gardens Mar.–mid-Oct., daily 7–dusk; mid-Oct.–Feb., daily 7–4:15. Kibble Palace and other greenhouses Mar.–mid-Oct., daily 10–6; mid-Oct.–Feb., daily 10–4:15.*

**NEED A BREAK?**

The Willow Tearoom (⊠ *217 Sauchiehall St., City Center* ☎ *0141/332– 0521*) has been restored to its original Charles Rennie Mackintosh art-nouveau design, right down to the decorated tables and chairs. The building was designed by Mackintosh in 1903 for Kate Cranston, who ran a chain of tearooms. The tree motifs reflect the street address—*sauchie* is an old Scots word for willow.

## A GOOD WALK

This tranquil stroll, taking about an hour if you don't poke into the museums, showcases all of the beauty the West End has to offer. Start in Kelvingrove Park, at the junction of Sauchiehall (pronounced *socky*-hall) and Argyle streets, where the city's main art museum, Kelvingrove Art Gallery and Museum stands. The impressive red-sandstone building and its leafy surroundings are well worth a visit as is the Museum of Transport, on the opposite side of the street. From here stroll up tree-lined Kelvin Way; the skyline to your left is dominated dramatically by Glasgow University.

Turn left onto University Avenue and walk past the Memorial Gates. On the south side of University Avenue, is the Hunterian Museum. Across University Avenue, is the even more interesting Hunterian Art Gallery. From here make your way up to the Botanic Gardens, where 12 Victorian conservatories and their fragrant collections await you. To get there continue west along University Avenue, turn right at Byres Road, and walk as far as Great Western Road. The 40 acres of gardens are across the busy intersection. Its peaceful garden makes you feel a million miles away from the city center.

**26 ★ Glasgow School of Art.** The exterior and interior, structure, furnishings, and decoration of this art-nouveau building, built between 1897 and 1909, form a unified whole, reflecting the inventive genius of Charles Rennie Mackintosh, who was only 28 years old when he won the competition for its design. Architects and designers from all over the world come to admire it, but because it's a working school of art, general access is sometimes limited. Guided tours beginning at the top of the hour are available; it's best to make reservations. You can always visit the four on-site galleries that host frequently changing exhibitions. The shop sells a good selection of Mackintosh prints, postcards, and books, plus a selection of contemporary art by the school's students and graduates. A block away is Mackintosh's Willow Tearoom. ⊠ *167 Renfrew St., City Center* ☎ *0141/353–4526* ⊕ *www.gsa.ac.uk* ☎ *£6.50* ⊙ *Tours Oct.–Apr., Mon.–Sat. 11 and 2; Apr.–Sept., daily 10–4.*

**OFF THE BEATEN PATH**

**Glasgow Science Centre.** Families with children love this center, which has a fun-packed Science Mall, an IMAX theater, and the futuristic Glasgow Tower. The 417-foot spire—with an aerodynamic profile that twists 360 degrees—is a marvel. In the three-level Science Mall, state-of-the-art displays educate kids and adults about exploration, discovery, and the environment. The ScottishPower Planetarium has a fantastic Zeiss Starmaster projector, which allows visitors to gaze at the glittering stars. Set aside half a day to see everything. ⊠ *50 Pacific Quay, South Side* ☎ *0141/420–5000* ⊕ *www.gsc.org.uk* ☎ *IMAX film, Science Mall, or Glasgow Tower £7; any 2 attractions £10* ⊙ *Daily 10–6.*

**19 Glasgow University.** The architecture, grounds, and great views of Glasgow all warrant a visit to the university. The Gilbert Scott Building, the university's main edifice, was built more than a century ago and is a good example of the Gothic-revival style. **Glasgow University Visitor Centre** has exhibits on the university, a coffee bar, and a gift shop and is the starting point for one-hour guided walking tours of the campus. A self-guided tour starts at the visitor center and takes in the east and west quadrangles, the cloisters, Professor's Square, Pearce Lodge, and the not-to-be-missed University Chapel. ⊠ *University Ave., West End* ☎ *0141/330–5511* ⊕ *www.glasgow.ac.uk* ⊠ *tour £3.50* ⊗ *May–Sept., Mon.–Sat. 9:30–5.*

**㉑ Hunterian Art Gallery.** This Glasgow University gallery houses William
★ Hunter's (1718–83) collection of paintings (his antiquarian collection is housed in the nearby Hunterian Museum), together with prints and drawings by Tintoretto, Rembrandt, Sir Joshua Reynolds, and Auguste Rodin, as well as a major collection of paintings by James McNeill Whistler, who had a great affection for the city that bought one of his earliest paintings. Also in the gallery is a replica of **Charles Rennie Mackintosh's town house,** which once stood nearby. The rooms contain Mackintosh's distinctive art-nouveau chairs, tables, beds, and cupboards, and the walls are decorated in the equally distinctive style devised by him and his artist wife, Margaret. ⊠ *Hillhead St., West End* ☎ *0141/330–5431* ⊕ *www. hunterian.gla.ac.uk* ⊠ *Free* ⊗ *Mon.–Sat. 9:30–5.*

**㉒ Hunterian Museum.** The city's oldest museum reopened in 2007, just in time for its bicentenary. Part of Glasgow University, the museum showcases part of the collections of William Hunter, an 18th-century Glasgow doctor who assembled a staggering quantity of valuable material. (The doctor's art treasures are housed in the nearby Hunterian Art Gallery.) The museum displays Hunter's hoards of coins, manuscripts, scientific instruments, and archaeological artifacts in a striking Gothic building. ⊠ *University Ave., West End* ☎ *0141/330–4221* ⊕ *www. hunterian.gla.ac.uk* ⊠ *Free* ⊗ *Mon.–Sat. 9:30–5.*

**㉑ Kelvingrove Art Gallery and Museum.** Following Glasgow's successful
⟳ 1888 International Exhibition of Science, Art, and Industry, city offi-
Fodor'sChoice cials resolved to build a museum and gallery worthy of a world-class
★ art collection and future international exhibitions. This magnificent combination of cathedral and castle was designed in the Renaissance style and built between 1891 and 1901. J. W. Simpson and E. J. Milner Allen were the main architects; Sir George Frampton designed the central porch; and James Harrison Mackinnon designed the decorative carving on the exterior. The stunning red-sandstone edifice is an appropriate home for an art collection—including works by Botticelli, Rembrandt, and Monet—hailed as "one of the greatest civic collections in Europe." The Glasgow Room houses extraordinary works by local artists. The entire museum reopened in 2006 after a complete renovation that added gallery space, a theater, a visitor center, a café, and a restaurant. ⊠ *Argyle St., Kelvingrove Park, West End* ☎ *0141/276–9599* ⊕ *www.glasgowmuseums.com* ⊠ *Free* ⊗ *Mon.–Thurs., and Sat. 10–5, Fri. and Sun. 11–5.*

⟳ **Kelvingrove Park.** A peaceful retreat, the park was purchased by the city in 1852 and takes its name from the River Kelvin, which flows through it. Among the numerous statues of prominent Glaswegians is one of Lord Kelvin (1824–1907), the Scottish mathematician and physicist who pioneered a great deal of work in electricity. The park also has a massive fountain commemorating a lord provost of Glasgow from the 1850s, a duck pond, a play area, a small open-air theater, and lots of exotic trees. ⊠*Bounded roughly by Sauchiehall St., Woodlands Rd., and Kelvin Way, West End.*

🞷 **McLellan Galleries.** In an understated Victorian building designed by
★ James Smith (1808–63), the McLellan hosts temporary exhibitions. (It's not always open, so call ahead.) Past shows have showcased 16th- and 17th-century paintings by Dutch and Italian masters, as well as contemporary work by both Scottish and international artists, such as David Hockney and David Mach. ⊠*270 Sauchiehall St., City Center* 🕾*0141/565–4137* ⊕*www.glasgowmuseums.com* ⊠*Free* ☾*Mon.– Thurs. and Sat. 10–5, Fri. and Sun. 11–5.*

🞷 **Mitchell Library.** The largest public reference library in Europe houses more than a million volumes, including what's claimed to be the world's largest collection about Robert Burns. A bust in the entrance hall commemorates the library's founder, Stephen Mitchell, who died in 1874. Minerva, goddess of wisdom, looks down from the library's dome, encouraging the library's users and frowning at the drivers thundering along the motorway just in front of her. The western facade (at the back), with its sculpted figures of Mozart, Beethoven, Michelangelo, and other artistic figures, is particularly beautiful. ⊠*North St., City Center* 🕾*0141/287-2999* ⊕*www.mitchelllibrary.org* ⊠*Free* ☾*Mon.–Thurs. 9–8, Fri. and Sat. 9–5.*

🞷 **Museum of Transport.** Here Glasgow's history of locomotive building is
Ⓒ dramatically displayed with impressive full-size exhibits. The collection of Clyde-built ship models is world famous. Anyone who knows what Britain was like in the 1930s will wax nostalgic at the re-created street scene from that era. ⊠*Kelvin Hall, 1 Bunhouse Rd., West End* 🕾*0141/287-2720* ⊕*www.glasgowmuseums.com* ⊠*Free* ☾*Mon.– Thurs. and Sat. 10–5, Fri. and Sun. 11–5.*

**ALSO WORTH SEEING**

🞷 **Centre for Contemporary Arts.** This arts, cinema, and performance venue is in a post-industrial-revolution Alexander Thomson building. It has a reputation for unusual visual-arts exhibitions, from paintings and sculpture to new media, and has championed a number of emerging talents, including Toby Paterson, one of Scotland's most successful contemporary artists. Simon Starling, the Scottish representative at the Venice Biennale in 2003, has also exhibited work here. The vibrant Tempus Bar Café is designed by Los Angeles–based artist, Jorge Pardo. ⊠*350 Sauchiehall St., City Center* 🕾*0141/352-4900* ⊕*www. cca-glasgow.com* ⊠*Free* ☾*Tues.–Fri. 11–6, Sat. 10–6.*

**OFF THE
BEATEN
PATH**

**Queen's Cross Church.** Head for the Charles Rennie Mackintosh Society Headquarters, in the only church Mackintosh designed, to learn more about the famous Glasgow-born architect and designer. Although one of the leading lights in the turn-of-the-20th-century art-nouveau movement, Mackintosh died in relative obscurity in 1928. Today he's widely accepted as a brilliant innovator. The church has beautiful stained-glass windows and a light-enhancing, carved-wood interior. The center's library and shop provide further insight into Glasgow's other Mackintosh-designed buildings, which include Scotland Street School, the Martyrs Public School, and the Glasgow School of Art. The church sits on the corner of Springbank Street at the junction of Garscube Road with Maryhill Road; a cab ride can get you here, or take a bus toward Queen's Cross from stops along Hope Street. ⊠*870 Garscube Rd., West End* ☎*0141/946–6600* ⊕*www.crm-society.com* ⊠*£2* ⊗*Mar.–Oct., weekdays 10–5, Sun. 2–5; Nov.–Feb., weekdays 10–5.*

**24 Regimental Museum of the Royal Highland Fusiliers.** Exhibits of medals, badges, and uniforms relate the history of a famous, much-honored regiment and the men who served in it. ⊠*518 Sauchiehall St., City Center* ☎*0141/332–0961* ⊕*www.army.mod.uk/rhf/* ⊠*Free* ⊗*Mon.–Thurs. 9–4:30, Fri. 9–4, weekends by appointment only.*

> ### GLASGOW'S UNDERGROUND
>
> Glasgow is the only city in Scotland with a subway (or underground, as it's called here). The system was built at the end of the 19th century and takes the simple form of two circular routes, one going clockwise and the other counterclockwise. All trains eventually bring you back to where you started, and the complete circle takes 24 minutes. The tunnels are small, and so are the trains. This, together with the affection in which the system is held and the bright orange paints of the trains, gave the system the nickname the "Clockwork Orange."

**OFF THE BEATEN PATH**

**The Tall Ship at Glasgow Harbor.** This maritime attraction centers around the restored tall ship the *Glenlee*, a former cargo ship originally built in Glasgow in 1896, purchased by the Spanish navy, and bought back by the Clyde Maritime Trust in 1993. The ship itself is fascinating, but take time to explore the Pumphouse Exhibition and Gallery, which screens films of the restoration process and hosts interactive exhibits. A bus (No. 100) runs every half hour from the Buchanan Street bus station. ⊠*100 Stobcross Rd., West End* ☎*0141/222–2513* ⊕*www.thetallship.com* ⊠*£5* ⊗*Mar.–Oct., daily 10–5; Nov.–Feb., daily 11–4.*

**25 Tenement House.** This ordinary apartment building is anything but ordinary inside: it was occupied from 1911 to 1965 by Agnes Toward, who seems never to have thrown anything away. Her legacy is a fascinating time capsule, painstakingly preserved with her everyday furniture and belongings. The red-sandstone building dates from 1892 and can be found in the Garnethill area north of Charing Cross station. ⊠*145 Buccleuch St., City Center* ☎*0141/333–0183* ⊕*www.nts.org.uk* ⊠*£5* ⊗*Mar.–Oct., daily 1–5; last admission at 4:30.*

## THE SOUTH SIDE: ART-FILLED PARKS WEST

Just southwest of the city center in the South Side are two of Glasgow's dear green places—Bellahouston Park and Pollok Country Park—which have important art collections: Charles Rennie Mackintosh's House for an Art Lover, the Burrell Collection, and Pollok House. A respite from the buzz of the city can also be found in the parks, where you can have a picnic or ramble through greenery and gardens. Both parks are off Paisley Road, about 3 mi southwest of the city center. You can take a taxi or car, city bus, or a train from Glasgow Central Station to Pollokshaws West Station or Dumbreck.

### MAIN ATTRACTIONS

**㉙ Burrell Collection.** An elegant, ultramodern building of pink-sandstone and stainless steel houses thousands of items of all descriptions, from ancient Egyptian, Greek, and Roman artifacts to Chinese ceramics, bronzes, and jade. You can also find medieval tapestries, stained-glass windows, Rodin sculptures, and exquisite French-impressionist paintings—Degas's *The Rehearsal* and Sir Henry Raeburn's *Miss Macartney*, to name a few. Eccentric millionaire Sir William Burrell (1861–1958) donated the magpie collection to the city in 1944. The 1983 building's exterior and interior were designed with large glass walls so that the items on display could relate to their surroundings in Pollok Country Park: art and nature, supposedly in perfect harmony. You can get there via buses 45, 48, and 57 from Union Street. ✉*2060 Pollokshaws Rd., South Side* ☎*0141/287–2550* ⊕*www.glasgowmuseums.com* ✉*Free* ⊙*Mon.–Thurs. and Sat. 10–5, Fri. and Sun. 11–5.*

Fodor'sChoice
★

**㉛ House for an Art Lover.** Within Bellahouston Park is a "new" Mackintosh house: based on a competition entry Charles Rennie Mackintosh submitted to a German magazine in 1901, but which was never built in his lifetime. The building houses Glasgow School of Art's postgraduate study center and exhibits of designs for the various rooms and decorative pieces Mackintosh and his wife, Margaret, created. There's also a café and shop filled with artworks. Buses 9, 53, and 54 from Union Street will get you here. Call ahead, as the building is often closed for official functions. ✉*Bellahouston Park, 10 Dumbreck Rd., South Side* ☎*0141/353–4770* ⊕*www.houseforanartlover.co.uk* ✉*£3.50* ⊙*Apr.–Sept., Mon.–Wed. 10–4, Thurs.–Sun. 10–1; Oct.–Mar., weekends 10–1.*

### ALSO WORTH SEEING

OFF THE
BEATEN
PATH

**Holmwood House.** The National Trust for Scotland has undertaken the restoration of this large mansion house, designed by Alexander "Greek" Thomson for the wealthy owner of a paper mill. Its classical Greek architecture and stunningly ornamented wood and marble features are among his finest. You can witness the ongoing restoration process one or two days a week; call to check the dates. ✉*61–63 Netherlee Rd., South Side* ☎*0141/637–2129* ⊕*www.nts.org.uk* ✉*£5* ⊙*Apr.–Oct., Thurs.–Mon. noon–5:30; last admission at 5.*

**㉚ Pollok House.** The classic Georgian Pollok House, dating from the mid-1700s, contains the Stirling Maxwell Collection of paintings, including works by El Greco, Murillo, Goya, Signorelli, and William Blake. Fine 18th- and early-19th-century furniture, silver, glass, and porcelain are also on display. The house has lovely gardens and looks over the White Cart River and Pollok Country Park, where, amid mature trees and

# Charles Rennie Mackintosh

Not so long ago, the furniture of innovative Glasgow-born architect Charles Rennie Mackintosh (1868–1928) was broken up for firewood. Today his major bookcases and chairs go for hundreds of thousands of pounds at auction, art books are devoted to his astonishingly elegant Arts and Crafts interiors, and artisans around the world look to his theory that "decoration should not be constructed, rather construction should be decorated" as holy law. Mackintosh's stripped-down designs slammed the door on Victorian antimacassars and floral chintz, ushering in the modern age with their deceptively stark style.

Mackintosh trained in architecture at the Glasgow School of Art and was apprenticed to the Glasgow firm of John Hutchison at the age of 16. Early influences on his work included the Pre-Raphaelites, James McNeill Whistler (1834–1903), Aubrey Beardsley (1872–98), and Japanese art, but by the 1890s a distinct Glasgow style had been developed by Mackintosh and others.

The building for the *Glasgow Herald* newspaper, which he designed in 1893 and which is now the Lighthouse Centre for Architecture, Design and the City, was soon followed by other major Glasgow buildings: Queen Margaret's Medical College; the Martyrs Public School; tearooms for Catherine Cranston, including the famous Willow Tearoom; the Hill House, Helensburgh, now owned by the National Trust for Scotland; and Queen's Cross Church, completed in 1899 and now the headquarters of the Charles Rennie Mackintosh Society. In 1897 Mackintosh began work on a new home for the Glasgow School of Art, recognized as one of his major achievements.

Mackintosh married Margaret Macdonald in 1900, and in later years her decorative work enhanced the interiors of his buildings. In 1904 he became a partner in Honeyman and Keppie and designed Scotland Street School, now the Museum of Education, in the same year. Until 1913, when he left Honeyman and Keppie and moved to England, Mackintosh's projects included buildings and/or interiors over much of Scotland, but especially in the Central Belt: Comrie, Bridge of Allan, Kilmacolm, and many other places. He preferred wherever possible to include interiors—furniture and fittings—as part of his overall design.

Commissions in England after 1913 included a variety of design challenges not confined to buildings, including fabrics, furniture, and even bookbindings. In 1923 Mackintosh settled in France, but he returned to London in 1927 and died there in 1928.

Glasgow is the best place in the world to admire Mackintosh's work: in addition to the buildings mentioned above, most of which can be visited, the Hunterian Art Gallery contains magnificent reconstructions of the principal rooms at 78 Southpark Avenue, Mackintosh's Glasgow home, and original drawings, documents, and records, plus the re-creation of a room at 78 Derngate, Northampton. To take it all in, purchase a £12 **Mackintosh Trail Ticket** at major sites, visitor centers, or online from the Mackintosh Society (www.crmsociety.com). It includes transportation and one-day admission to many sites.

abundant wildlife, the city of Glasgow's own cattle peacefully graze. Take buses 45, 47, or 57 to the Gate of Pollok County Park. ✉*2060 Pollokshaws Rd., South Side* ☎*0141/616–6410* ⊕*www.nts.org.uk* 📷*Apr.–Oct., £8; Nov.–Mar., free* ⊗*Daily 10–5.*

OFF THE BEATEN PATH **Scotland Street School.** A former school designed by Charles Rennie Mackintosh, this building houses a fascinating museum of education. Classrooms re-create school life in Scotland during Victorian times and World War II, and a cookery room recounts a time when education for Scottish girls consisted of little more than learning how to become a housewife. An exhibition space and café are also here. The building sits opposite Shields Road underground station. ✉*225 Scotland St., South Side* ☎*0141/287–0500* ⊕*www.glasgowmuseums.com* 📷*Free* ⊗*Apr.–Sept., Mon.–Thurs. and Sat. 10–5, Fri. and Sun. 11–5.*

# WHERE TO EAT

The key to Glaswegian cuisine is not Glasgow, but the world beyond. A flurry of foreign restaurants line the streets—from late-night crepe stalls and *pakora* (Indian fried-chickpea cakes) bars to elegant restaurants with worldly menus. And because of the new smoking ban that doesn't allow smoking in any enclosed space, many restaurants have decided to place tables outside under awnings during the warm(ish) summer months. With this type of outdoor dining come fresher, more Mediterranean-style meals.

Dining in Glasgow is now an all-evening affair. Although some celebrity chefs and chain restaurants have left their mark, it's the small, independent eateries like An Lochan and City Merchant that are making all the waves. They focus on what's seasonal and, in many cases, organic. Glasgow's food scene is a far cry from the black puddings of its past. Today's Glasgow is a city with an appetite, so wherever you go be sure to make a reservation.

## PRICES
Eating in Glasgow can be casual or lavish, with much the same prices and variety as you'll find in Edinburgh. For inexpensive dining, consider the benefit of pretheater menus. Beer and spirits cost much the same as they would in a bar, but wine is relatively expensive in restaurants. ■TIP➔ **Many restaurants allow you to bring your own bottle of wine, charging just a small corkage fee. It's worth the effort, as it can save you quite a bit of money.**

| WHAT IT COSTS IN POUNDS | | | | | |
|---|---|---|---|---|---|
| | £ | ££ | £££ | ££££ | £££££ |
| AT DINNER | under £10 | £10–£14 | £15–£19 | £20–£25 | over £25 |

Prices are per person for a main course at dinner.

## MEDIEVAL GLASGOW & MERCHANT CITY

This part of the city has restaurants catering to the 9-to-5 crowd, meaning there are a lot of fine dining establishments catching people as they leave work. You can however, always find a fish-and-chips shop on any busy street corner.

### ASIAN

££££ ✕**Khublai Khan Barbecue.** Wild boar, ostrich, shark, and other exotic flavors feature prominently at this eclectic eatery. Odds are you'll devour the legendary Mongolian Feast, which includes an unlimited supply of barbecued meats cooked on a giant hotplate. The massive space is festooned with handwoven rugs and a huge mural of Mongolian warriors advancing threateningly. Don't worry: the service is friendly. This place is popular with groups, so it can get noisy. ⊠26 *Candleriggs St., Merchant City* ☎*0141/552–5646* ⊟*AE, DC, MC, V* ⊘*No lunch weekdays.*

### CHINESE

££ ✕**Amber Regent.** This may not be the cheapest Chinese restaurant in town, but it's certainly one of the finest and most formal. For a start, the meticulously sculpted vegetables that accompany the hors d'oeuvres seem almost too artful to eat. Succulent king prawns or duck with mashed prawns in an oyster sauce readily attest to the kitchen's skill in preparing excellent Cantonese and Szechuan cuisine. Its reputation means that the restaurant can get very busy, however. For the best value, try the two- and three-course menus served between noon and 2:15. ⊠*50 W. Regent St., City Center* ☎*0141/331–1655* ⊟*AE, MC, V* ⊘*Closed Sun.*

££ ✕**Loon Fung.** The pleasant, enthusiastic staff at this popular Cantonese eatery guides you through the house specials, including the famed dim sum. If you like seafood, try the deep-fried wonton with prawns, crispy stuffed crab claws, or lobster in garlic-and-cheese sauce. The first-rate three-course business lunch, available until 6:30 PM, is a bargain at £9. ⊠*417 Sauchiehall St., City Center* ☎*0141/332–1240* ⊟*AE, MC, V.*

### CONTINENTAL

££ ✕**Brasserie.** A hotel basement fitted with wooden booths makes for a quiet, relaxed environment in which to appreciate a varied modern European menu. The fish cakes are the traditional favorite here, but also good are the spaghetti with mussels and clams, and the grilled rib-eye steak. Be sure to leave room for desserts such as the pineapple mille-feuille and homemade coconut sorbet. The two-course lunch is an excellent deal at £13.50. ⊠*Malmaison Hotel, 278 W. George St., City Center* ☎*0141/572–1001* ⚲*Reservations essential* ⊟*AE, DC, MC, V.*

££ ✕**Drum and Monkey.** A glorious former bank building dating from the Victorian era houses this busy and friendly bar-restaurant. The food ranges from pub fodder to some Scottish-French delights. Try the excellent fish cakes, the smoked salmon with spinach and lemon-butter sauce, or the chicken stuffed with smoked cheese and rosemary. ⊠*93–95 St. Vincent St., City Center* ☎*0141/221–6636* ⊟*AE, DC, MC, V.*

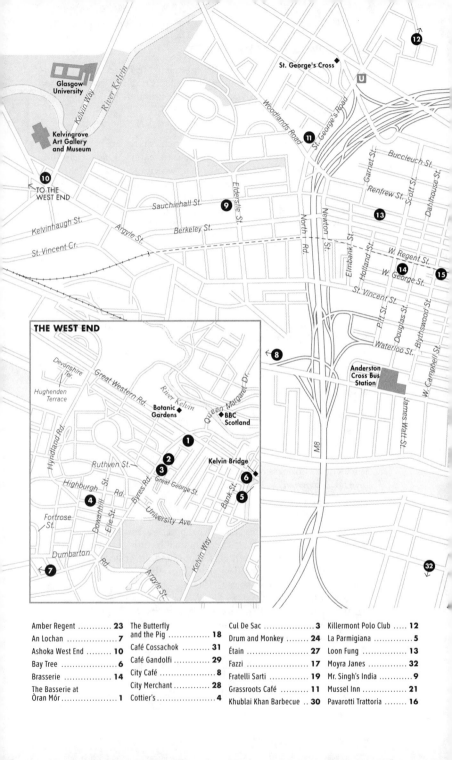

Glasgow University

Kelvingrove Art Gallery and Museum

St. George's Cross

Kelvin Way

River Kelvin

Woodlands Rd.

St. George's Road

Garnet St.

Buccleuch St.

Scott St.

Dalhousie St.

Renfrew St.

Sauchiehall St.

Elderslie St.

North Rd.

Newton St.

W. Regent St.

Kelvinhaugh St.

Argyle St.

Berkeley St.

St. Vincent Cr.

Elmbank St.

Holland St.

Pitt St.

Douglas St.

Blythswood St.

W. George St.

St. Vincent St.

Waterloo St.

Anderston Cross Bus Station

James Watt St.

W. Campbell St.

M8

TO THE WEST END

**THE WEST END**

Devonshire Ter.

Hughenden Terrace

Great Western Rd.

River Kelvin

Botanic Gardens

Queen Margaret Dr.

BBC Scotland

Hyndland Rd.

Ruthven St.

Byres Rd.

Great George St.

Kelvin Bridge

Highburgh Rd.

Dowanhill St.

Elie St.

University Ave.

Bank St.

Fortrose St.

Kelvin Way

Dumbarton Rd.

Argyle St.

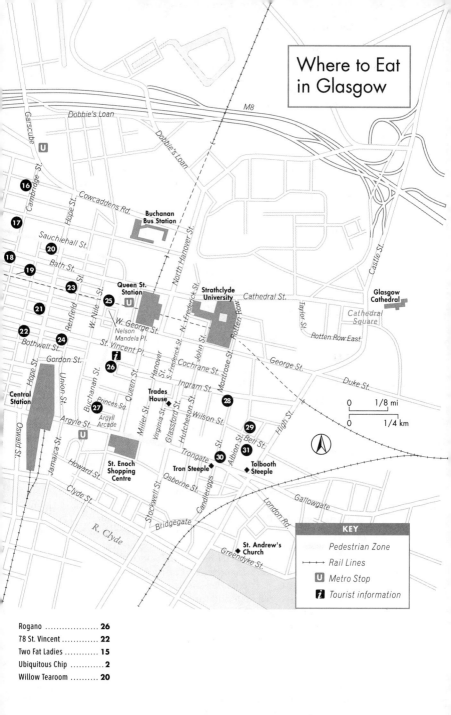

# Where to Eat in Glasgow

**KEY**

*Pedestrian Zone*

+—+—+ *Rail Lines*

**U** *Metro Stop*

**𝑖** *Tourist information*

### FRENCH

£££  ✕**Étain.** Sir Terence Conran's glamorous establishment is still the talk of the town. A futuristic steel-and-glass elevator whisks you up to an elegant and serene dining room with tables set amid sexy metal pillars. The sophistication is reflected in Chef Geoffrey Smeddle's contemporary take on French cusine, always using the freshest of local produce. Expect revelatory tastes in creations such as venison with a pomegranate-and-chocolate sauce or fillet of sea bream with broad-bean risotto and red-pepper oil. Set aside three hours for a truly epicurean experience. A two-course set meal costs £26, and a three-course meal costs £32. ⊠*Princes Sq., Buchanan St., City Center* ☎*0141/225–5630* ☐*AE, DC, MC, V* ☽*No dinner Sun.*

### INDIAN

££  ✕**Mr. Singh's India.** Three generations of an Indian family have transformed this into one of Glasgow's most popular eateries. It's a restful haven in creams and blues and plenty of beech wood, rather quirkily combined with waiters in kilts and a menu including haggis *pakora* (deep-fried haggis parcels). Meats and vegetables can be cooked in a number of different delicious sauces; try the lamb *mazadar* (hot and spicy, with Rémy Martin) or the pistachio *korma* (curried meat with onions and vegetables). ⊠*149 Elderslie St., City Center* ☎*0141/204–0186 or 0141/221–1452* ☐*AE, DC, MC, V.*

### ITALIAN

££  ✕**Fratelli Sarti.** Glasgow's large Italian immigrant population is never
**Fodor'sChoice** more visible—or audible—than here. The cavernous surroundings are
★ cluttered and the tables are pressed close together, so this is not really the place for an intimate dinner, but the food is authentic, with all of the classic dishes on an extensive menu. If you like seafood, try the wonderfully fresh and piquant pasta *vongole* (with small clams). Finish off with the light, creamy tiramisu. Note that the service can be a bit leisurely. ⊠*121 Bath St., City Center* ☎*0141/204–0440* ☐*AE, DC, MC, V* ☽*No lunch Sun.*

££  ✕**Pavarotti Trattoria.** Despite the somewhat silly name, no doubt arising from the restaurant's proximity to Scottish Opera's Theatre Royal, this is not a kitschy affair, but a very good Italian restaurant. The menu changes regularly because the kitchen uses only the freshest ingredients. Consequently, the standard meat and fish dishes are unusually succulent. The lunch and pretheater set menus—£7 and £10—are an exceptionally good value. ⊠*91 Cambridge St., City Center* ☎*0141/332–9713* ☐*AE, DC, MC, V* ☽*No lunch Sun.*

£  ✕**Fazzi.** With its red tablecloths, tile floors, and bentwood chairs, this inexpensive Italian café-bar is a cheerful place for a plateful of gnocchi *alla Emiliana* (with tomato, basil, and cheese sauce) or spinach-and-ricotta ravioli. The delicatessen here sells takeout. ⊠*65–67 Cambridge St., City Center* ☎*0141/332–0941* ☐*AE, DC, MC, V.*

### RUSSIAN

££  ✕**Café Cossachok.** Near the Tron Theatre, this is a willfully arty place:
★ the tables are hand-carved, the lighting is courtesy of candles, and the decor is a sea of shawls. The Russian owner pays homage to his home-

land with a menu that includes delicious blintzes and trout à la Pushkin (in a thirst-rousing salty sauce). Another welcome touch is the nicely chilled selection of vodkas. This fun venue is fashionable among the fashionable, so it's best to book ahead. ⊠ *38 Albion St., Merchant City* ☎ *0141/553–0733* ⊟ *AE, MC, V* ⊙ *Closed Mon. No lunch Sun.*

2

### SCOTTISH

£££ ✕ **City Café.** This bright, contemporary Scottish restaurant, boasts crisp white table cloths, lots of light, and one of the best riverside locations in Glasgow. Its location is ideal as it's adjacent to the Scottish Exhibition and Conference Centre and the Glasgow Science Centre. In good weather you can dine outside by the banks of the Clyde, and in the shadow of the mighty Finnieston Crane, the 195-foot-high hammerhead crane formerly used to load heavy cargo onto freighters. The menu dresses up traditional dishes with modern touches: roast salmon wrapped in prosciutto and served with a fennel compote, for example, or fillet of lamb with caramelized onions, broad beans, and a morel sauce. ⊠ *Finnieston Quay, City Center* ☎ *0141/227–1010* ⊟ *AE, DC, MC, V.*

£££ ✕ **City Merchant.** If you have a penchant for fresh and flavorful cuisine, this place is a joy. The secret is the kitchen's use of only local ingredients. You can sample the tasty cuts of venison and beef, but seafood remains the star attraction. The mussels and oysters from Loch Etive are wondrous, as is the sea bass. There's a relatively inexpensive selection of wines and a wonderful cheeseboard served, as the locals like it, with oatcakes, celery, and quince. ⊠ *97–99 Candleriggs St., Merchant City* ☎ *0141/553–1577* ⊟ *AE, DC, MC, V* ⊙ *No lunch Sun.*

£££ ✕ **78 St. Vincent.** This former bank building with strikingly carved griffins on the facade is now a stylish restaurant where you can enjoy contemporary French-influenced Scottish cuisine. As your eyes feast on the slender Doric columns or the wall-length modern mural by Glasgow artist Donald McLean, your palate can relish the Highland venison with gin-scented *jus*, or smoked duck salad with egg, scallops, prawns, and soy-sauce dressing. The pretheater menu, served from 4 to 7, is well worth considering. ⊠ *78 St. Vincent St., City Center* ☎ *0141/248–7878* ⊟ *AE, DC, MC, V.*

£££ ✕ **Two Fat Ladies.** A Glasgow institution, this spot has the same name as the owner's other restaurant at 88 Dumbarton Road, but this branch on Blythswood Street deserves a visit because it has more space, more light, and a better location than its older sister. The menu is predominantly fish, from the delicate smoked salmon, crab and asparagus salad to the fresh whole sea bream stuffed with red pepper, oregano, and garlic salsa. But if fish doesn't rock your boat, then fillets of Angus beef with wild mushrooms and spinach jus or a roast breast of chicken with a chorizo and basil stew are also good choices. The Two Fats trio of berry crème brûlées is the perfect dessert. Reservations are a good idea. ⊠ *118A Blythswood St., City Center* ☎ *0141/847–0088* ⊟ *AE, DC, MC, V.*

££ ✕ **Café Gandolfi.** Once the offices of a cheese market, this trendy café ★ is now popular with the style-conscious crowd. Wooden tables and chairs crafted by Scottish artist Tim Stead are so fluidly shaped it's hard to believe they're inanimate. The café opens early for breakfast, serving croissants, eggs *en cocotte* (casserole style), and cups of strong espresso. Don't miss the smoked venison or the finnan haddie (smoked haddock). In 2007 the owners opened up a new establishment next door, called Gandolfi Fish. Although the menu is more expensive, it's definitely worth a visit if you enjoy seafood. The scallops with parsley and tomato risotto literally melt in your mouth, and the whole baked mackerel with lime, chili, and coriander has a perfectly balanced kick. This is a very popular eatery, so it's a good idea to make reservation. ⊠ *64 Albion St., Merchant City* ☎ *0141/552–6813* ▭ *MC, V.*

> ### TAKE TIME FOR TEA
>
> In the Victorian tradition, while men went to pubs, Glasgow women's social interaction would take place in the city's many tearooms and cafés. Today *everyone* goes to the café. Glaswegians have succumbed to the worldwide love for Italian-style, espresso-based coffees, but they'll never give up the comfort of a nice cup of tea, so you'll find both at most tearooms, along with scones, Scottish pancakes, other pastries, and light lunch fare like sandwiches and soup.

£ ✕ **The Butterfly and the Pig.** You can find this intimate restaurant down an innocuous-looking flight of stairs in the city center. It's the type of place the locals love: warm colors, flickering candles, mix-and-match crockery, and a selection of dishes that are inventive, inexpensive, and original. The menu reads like a comedic narrative, with descriptions like "traditional fish and chips, battered to death place or soul with mushy peas, kitchen-made tartar sauce and a slice of lemon, beans today as the peas don't want to cook." You can also find dishes such as hearty Portobello-mushroom burgers with extra-thick potato chips or black pudding with bacon, Parmesan cheese, and apples. The chef uses only local ingredients, so the menu changes daily. ⊠ *153 Bath St., City Center* ☎ *0141/221–7711* ▭ *AE, DC, MC, V.*

£ ✕ **Willow Tearoom.** There are two branches of this restaurant, but the Sauchiehall Street location is the real deal. Conceived by the great Charles Rennie Mackintosh, the Room De Luxe (the original tearoom) is kitted out with his trademark furnishings, including highback chairs with elegant lines and subtle curves. The St. Andrew's Platter is an exquisite selection of trout, salmon, and prawns. Scottish and continental breakfasts are available throughout the day, and the scrambled eggs with salmon is traditional Scots food at its finest. The in-house baker guarantees fresh scones, cakes, and pastries. ⊠ *217 Sauchiehall St., City Center* ☎ *0141/332–0521* ▭ *MC, V* ⊗ *No dinner.*

#### SEAFOOD

££££   ✕ **Rogano.** The spacious art-deco interior, modeled after the style of the
Fodor'sChoice   *Queen Mary* ocean liner—maple paneling, chrome trim, and dramatic
★   ocean murals—is enough to recommend this restaurant. Portions are generous in the main dining area, where impeccably prepared favorites include roast rack of lamb and classic seafood dishes like seared scallops. Downstairs in the Café Rogano (£–££), the brasserie-style food is more modern and imaginative. The theater menu provides early eve-

ning and late-night bargains, and the fixed-price lunch menu is popular with locals. You can also order one of the fabulous cocktails and prop up the swank oyster bar. ⊠ *11 Exchange Pl., City Center* ☎*0141/248– 4055* ▭*AE, DC, MC, V.*

£££ ╳ **Mussel Inn.** West coast shellfish farmers own this restaurant and feed
Fodor'sChoice their customers incredibly succulent oysters, scallops, and mussels. The
★ kilo pots of mussels, beautifully steamed to order and served with any of a number of sauces, are revelatory. The surroundings are stylish, with cool ceramic tiles and plenty of sleek wooden furniture. The staff is helpful yet unpretentious. This is the type of place locals take their friends, family, and favorite out-of-towners. ⊠ *157 Hope St., City Center* ☎*0141/572–1405* ▭*AE, MC, V* ⊗ *No lunch Sun.*

## WEST END & ENVIRONS

Because of the university, the food in this area was once just for students. That has changed in recent years. You can still find fast food at any hour of the day, but you'll discover some of the best Scottish food served at some of the city's most respected restaurants.

### INDIAN

££ ╳ **Ashoka West End.** This Punjabi restaurant outperforms its many competitors in quality, range, and taste. All portions are large enough to please the ravenous, but there's nothing heavy-handed about the cooking here: vegetable *samosas* (stuffed savory deep-fried pastries) are crisp and light, the selection of breads is superb, and the spicing for the lamb, chicken, and prawn dishes is fragrant. The eclectic decor—involving a bizarre mixture of plants, murals, rugs, and brass lamps—and inappropriate Western music simply emphasize Ashoka's idiosyncrasy. Reservations are a good idea on weekends. ⊠ *1284 Argyle St., West End* ☎*0141/339–3371* ▭*AE, MC, V* ⊗ *No lunch Sat.–Tues.*

££ ╳ **Killermont Polo Club.** Though not the most likely setting for an Indian restaurant, this Victorian manse on the outskirts of Glasgow's West End has the restful and romanticized atmosphere of colonial India. It specializes in the rather unique *dum pukht* cooking tradition, which for a time was held secret by the Mughal royal family. The appetizer *shammi kebab badami* consists of firm patties of minced lamb shot through with cinnamon, coriander, and almonds. The gently prepared *chandi kaliyan* main course mixes lamb with a gravy of poppy seeds, cashews, and saffron. Finish off with the gorgeous, spongy dessert, *gulab jamin* (fried milk balls in a sweet syrup). ⊠ *2022 Maryhill Rd., West End* ☎*0141/946–5412* ▭*AE, DC, MC, V.*

### ITALIAN

£££ ╳ **La Parmigiana.** The refreshing elegance of the surroundings is mir-
★ rored by the consistently exquisite fare at this longtime favorite. The Giovanazzis pride themselves on using the freshest of ingredients—this means you may be able to enjoy simply prepared sea bass or veal one day, guinea fowl or scallops the next. This expertise in the kitchen is reflected in the well-balanced wine list and the impeccable attentive-

ness of the black-jacketed waiters. ✉ *447 Great Western Rd., West End* ☎ *0141/334–0686* 🍴*AE, DC, MC, V* ☺*Closed Sun.*

## LATIN-AMERICAN

££  ✕**Cottier's.** A converted Victorian church decorated by Glasgow artist Daniel Cottier is the unusual setting for this theater-bar-restaurant (the Arts Theatre is attached). Red walls and beamed ceilings warm the downstairs bar, where the pub grub has Tex-Mex flavors. In the restaurant try the spicy lamb cooked with coconut, lime, and cilantro, or the tuna and snapper fillets with anchovies, chili peppers, and citrus butter—two excellent choices from the South American dishes on the menu. Reservations are advised on weekends. ✉ *93 Hyndland St., West End* ☎ *0141/357–5825* 🍴*AE, MC, V.*

## MIDDLE EASTERN

£  ✕**Bay Tree.** This small café in the university area serves wonderful Middle Eastern food—mostly vegetarian dishes, but there are a few lamb and chicken creations as well. Egyptian *phool* (broad beans dressed with spices and herbs), Turkish *mulukia* (fried eggplant with a tomato-and-herb sauce), and *kurma* (stew with spinach, herbs, and beans) are among its delights. ✉ *403 Great Western Rd., West End* ☎ *0141/334–5898* 🍴*AE, MC, V.*

## SCOTTISH

£££££  ✕**Ubiquitous Chip.** Occupying a converted mews stable behind the
★  Hillhead underground station, this restaurant is an institution among members of Glasgow's media and thespian communities. The service is friendly, and the interior very outdoorsy, with a glass roof, much greenery, and a fishpond. The menu specializes in game but has something for everyone (even vegetarian haggis); smoked salmon in Darjeeling tea is typical of the chef's clever blending of authentic Scots fare with unusual elements. For a more casual and inexpensive experience, try the brasserie and pub area upstairs (££). ✉ *12 Ashton La., West End* ☎ *0141/334–5007* 🍴*AE, DC, MC, V.*

£££  ✕**An Lochan.** Friendly and stylish, this West End eatery is a favorite among in-the-know locals. The chef uses fresh seafood and game shipped in daily from the Kyles of Bute. She also uses seasonal ingredients to create an ever-changing list of dishes. The tasting menu at £30 is a real treat, and you'll feel as if you're actually tasting Scotland. From the balsamic vinegar and orange-marinated-duck breast to the trout fillet with horseradish dressing to the rhubarb and apple crumble with vanilla-bean ice cream, this is a restaurant that satisfies all the senses. ✉ *340 Crow Rd., West End* ☎ *0141/384–6606* 🍴*AE, DC, MC, V.*

£££  ✕**The Brasserie at Òran Mór.** This is the more formal eatery (the other
★  being the bistro-style Conservatory) within this handsome church-turned-cultural-center. There's lots of elegantly curved dark wood and high-backed bench seating, as well as some Alasdair Gray murals to savor. The food is equally well crafted. Expect contemporary treats using Angus beef, Gressingham duck, and sea bass. ✉ *731–735 Great Western Rd., West End* ☎ *0141/357–6226* ⚍*Reservations essential* 🍴*AE, MC, V.*

££ ✕ **Cul De Sac.** At the end of a quiet cobbled lane, this is one of the most relaxing of Glasgow's trendy West End eateries. Right on the edge of the Glasgow University campus, it's a nice alternative to the more formal restaurants in the area. Large French windows add to the friendly street-café atmosphere. The menu of updated Scottish and European fare includes everything from affordable pasta dishes to red snapper to seared medallion of pork. ✉ *44–46 Ashton La., West End* ☎ *0141/334–6688* ▭ *AE, DC, MC, V.*



### VEGETARIAN

£ ✕ **Grassroots Café.** One of Glasgow's most relaxing eateries serves vegetarian fare that is wholesome, fresh, and above all, interesting. Unlike the food, which includes specialties like Thai-style potatoes and vegetarian chili, the interior is simple and rather plain. The list of fruit juices is extensive, and ingredients are all organic. Set aside plenty of time, as nothing is hurried, especially for the popular weekend breakfasts. ✉ *97 St. George's Rd., West End* ☎ *0141/333–0534* ▭ *AE, MC, V.*

## SOUTH SIDE

### SCOTTISH

££ ✕ **Moyra Janes.** Pull up a chair to one of the marble-topped tables in this former bank building and soak up the genteel Scots charm. This South Side favorite serves a splendid tea with mouthwatering cakes. There's a healthy dash of cosmopolitan flair to boot: alongside the all-day breakfast menu are Thai fish cakes and Italian pasta creations. ✉ *20 Kildrostan St., South Side* ☎ *0141/423–5628* ▭ *MC, V* ⏲ *No dinner Sun. and Mon.*

# WHERE TO STAY

You won't have trouble finding a place to stay in Glasgow. Over the next few years, tourism officials say, the city will add about 2,400 rooms. New on the horizon are a boutique hotel called Blythswood Square (set to open in 2008) and a pair of business hotels in the Bothwell Plaza complex (slated for 2009). Most of these projects are in the City Center.

Central Glasgow never sleeps, so downtown hotels will be noisier than those in the leafy and genteel West End. Downtown hotels are within walking distance of all the main sights; the West End is convenient for museums and art galleries. Although big hotels are spread out all around the city, B&Bs are definitely a more popular, personal, and cheaper option. For country-house luxury you should look beyond the city—try Mar Hall, near Paisley.

### PRICES

Most smaller hotels and all guesthouses include breakfast in the room rate. Larger hotels usually charge extra for breakfast.

| WHAT IT COSTS IN POUNDS | | | | |
| --- | --- | --- | --- | --- |
| £ | ££ | £££ | ££££ | £££££ |
| FOR TWO PEOPLE | under £70 | £70–£120 | £121–£179 | £181–£250 | over £250 |

Hotel prices are for two people in a standard double room in high season, generally including the 17.5% V.A.T.

## MEDIEVAL GLASGOW & MERCHANT CITY

££££ **Radisson SAS.** You can't miss this eye-catching edifice behind Central Station in the city's up-and-coming financial quarter. Its glass front makes the interior, particularly the lounge, seem as though it were part of the street. Rooms are decorated in several styles—the Nordic rooms, for example, are done up in an icy shade of blue. Both restaurants—the pop-art-inspired Collage, serving Continental cuisine, and Tapaell'Ya, the tapas bar—are popular with business and artist types, as is the sleek street-level bar. **Pros:** Two minutes from everything, imaginative decor, good dining options. **Cons:** Neighborhood can be noisy, traffic on the weekends can be overwhelming. ⊠ *301 Argyle St., City Center, G2 8DL* ☎*0141/204–3333* ⊕*www.radissonsas.com* ⊋*247 rooms, 3 suites* ⊘*In-room: safe, refrigerator, Ethernet. In-hotel: 2 restaurants, room service, bar, pool, gym, public Wi-Fi, parking (fee)* ⊟*AE, DC, V* ⦿*CP.*

£££ **Hilton Glasgow.** On first impression this is a typical international hotel, but Glasgow friendliness permeates its professional facade. The rooms are spacious, but lack individuality, although the fittings and furniture are high quality. There are two restaurants: Cameron's is designed to resemble a Highland shooting lodge, and Minsky's is a New York–style deli. Raffles bar, with its colonial Singapore theme, is a popular hangout for local and visiting celebrities. **Pros:** Fabulous service, great pool, interesting bar. **Cons:** Uninspiring room decor, mediocre location beside motorway. ⊠ *1 William St., City Center, G3 8HT* ☎*0141/204–5555* ⊕*www.hilton.com* ⊋*319 rooms* ⊘*In-room: safe, refrigerator, Ethernet. In-hotel: 2 restaurants, bar, pool, gym, laundry service, public Wi-Fi, parking (no fee)* ⊟*AE, DC, MC, V* ⦿*BP.*

£££ **Langs.** The minimalist look here extends from the sleek wood reception desk to the sophisticated platform beds in the bright bedrooms. The suites on the top floor come in three flavors, ranging from monochrome to pop art. Contemporary Scottish cooking is the forte of the Aurora restaurant, whereas the Oshi restaurant serves excellent Japanese food, including three-course pre- and posttheater meals. Japanese body treatments are available in the Oshi Spa. The downtown location puts you close to Glasgow Royal Concert Hall and the Buchanan Galleries shopping mall. **Pros:** Perfectly situated for downtown outings, modern rooms, excellent spa. **Cons:** Next door to bus station, neighborhood can get noisy, some rooms have disappointing views. ⊠ *2 Port Dundas St., City Center, G2 3LD* ☎*0141/333–1500* ⊕*www.parkinn. co.uk* ⊋*70 rooms, 30 suites* ⊘*In-room: no a/c, dial-up. In-hotel: restaurant, room service, bar, gym, spa, public Wi-Fi, no-smoking rooms* ⊟*AE, DC, MC, V* ⦿*CP.*

**2**

£££ ⊞**Malmaison.** Housed in a converted church, this modern boutique hotel prides itself on personal service and outstanding amenities: each room has nice touches like plasma televisions and music systems. The art-deco interior employs bold colors in playful prints and geometric shapes all balanced out by traditional fabrics and furnishings. The lobby's splendid staircase has a wrought-iron balustrade illustrating Napoléon's exploits (the hotel takes its name from his home). The warm Brasserie offers British-French cooking. Café Mal serves savory pasta dishes in an airy terra-cotta-hue room with iron fixtures and a spiral staircase. **Pros:** Modern rooms, close to the city center, quiet location. **Cons:** Suites are overpriced, no on-site parking, some rooms suffer from traffic noise. ⊠*278 W. George St., City Center, G2 4LL* ☎*0141/572–1000* ⊕*www.malmaison.com* ⇆*72 rooms, 8 suites* ⌂*In-room: refrigerator. In-hotel: restaurant, bar, gym* ⊟*AE, DC, MC, V* ¶◎¶*CP.*

££ ⊞**ABode Glasgow.** Part of the stylish ABode minichain, this 1911 build- ★ ing near the boutiques of Buchanan Street has retained and embellished its best features, like the wrought-iron elevator and gold-leaf lions, while modernizing the rooms to meet today's sense of luxury. Rooms have dramatic yet tasteful decor highlighted by leaded-glass windows and contemporary artwork. Noted chef Michael Caines supervises the chain's restaurants: the Café Bar has a modish, international menu, and the Bar MC downstairs is one of Glasgow's hot spots. **Pros:** Stylish rooms, great location, beautiful stained-glass windows. **Cons:** Food is overpriced, parking is a pricey £10 a day. ⊠*129 Bath St., City Center, G2 2SY* ☎*0141/221–6789* ⊕*www.abodehotels.co.uk* ⇆*60 rooms, 1 suite* ⌂*In-room: DVD, Ethernet. In-hotel: restaurant, room service, bars, parking (fee)* ⊟*AE, DC, MC, V* ¶◎¶*CP.*

££ ⊞**Marks Hotel.** This elegant hotel has a lot to recommend it, not the ★ least of which is its location, just a stone's throw away from Sauchiehall Street. The rooms are spacious and have nice touches such as plasma televisions and fresh cut flowers. The One Ten Bar and Grill serves breakfast, lunch, and dinner, including specialties such as mushroom bruschetta and grilled rib-eye steak. **Pros:** Good location, spacious rooms. **Cons:** Limited room service, busy wallpaper in rooms. ⊠*110 Bath St., City Center, G2 2EN* ☎*0141/353–0800* ⊕*www.marks hotels.com* ⇆*103 rooms* ⌂*In-room: no a/c, Wi-Fi. In-hotel: restaurant, bar* ⊟*AE, MC, V* ¶◎¶*CP.*

£ ⊞**Babbity Bowster's.** The popular on-site restaurant and bar make this restored 18th-century Robert Adam town house a lively place to stay. The rooms have modern furniture and beds with starched, white linens. A 1st-floor gallery displays many works by Glaswegian artists. **Pros:** Centrally located, quiet street, great downstairs bar and restaurant. **Cons:** Can get noisy on weekends, no elevator, no computer hook-ups. ⊠*16–18 Blackfriars St., Merchant City, G1 1PE* ☎*0141/552–5055* ⇆*6 rooms* ⌂*In-room: no a/c. In-hotel: restaurant, bar, no elevator* ⊟*AE, MC, V* ¶◎¶*BP.*

£ ⊞**Brunswick.** In a contemporary town house, this six-story hotel show-cases quintessential Glasgow style and ambition. The rooms are done in a mostly minimalist style, but squared-off wall fixtures and occa-

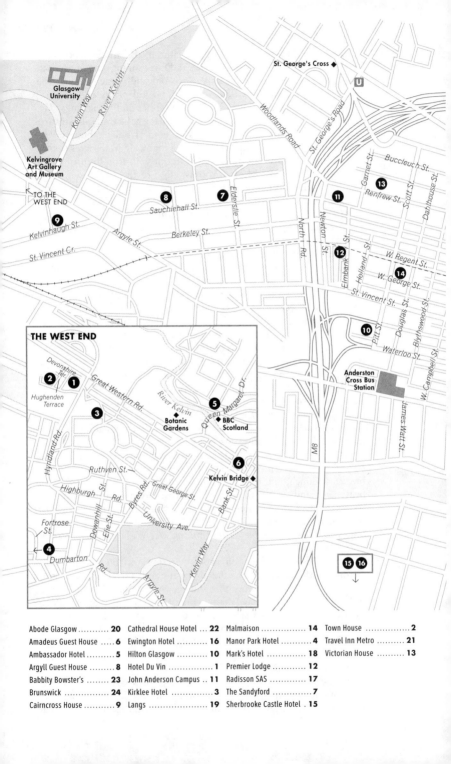

THE WEST END

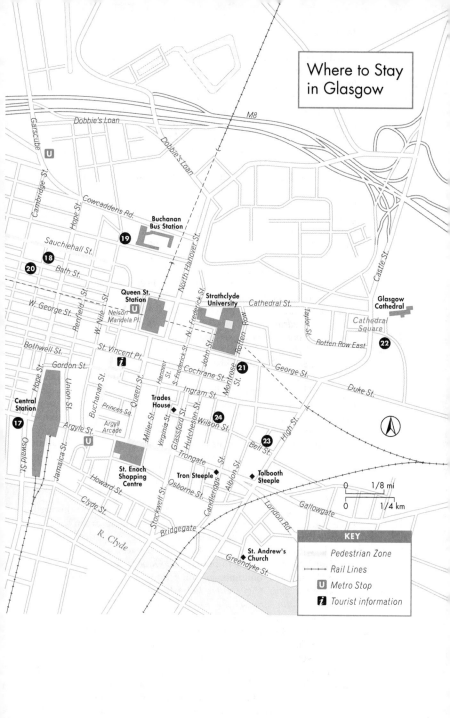

Where to Stay
in Glasgow

Dobbie's Loan

M8

Garscube

Dobbie's Loan

Cowcaddens Rd.

Cambridge St.

Hope St.

Buchanan
Bus Station

Sauchiehall St.

Bath St.

Strathclyde
University

Cathedral St.

Castle St.

Glasgow
Cathedral

W. George St.

Queen St.
Station

Nelson
Mandela Pl.

Cathedral
Square

Renfield St.

W. Nile St.

North Hanover St.

N. Frederick St.

Rotten Row

Taylor St.

Rotten Row East

Bothwell St.

Gordon St.

St. Vincent Pl.

Cochrane St.

George St.

Duke St.

Hope St.

Union St.

Buchanan St.

Queen St.

Hanover St.

S. Frederick St.

John St.

Montrose St.

Ingram St.

Central
Station

Princes Sq.

Argyll
Arcade

Trades
House

Virginia St.

Glassford St.

Hutcheson St.

Wilson St.

High St.

Argyle St.

Miller St.

Bell St.

Jamaica St.

Oswald St.

Trongate

St. Enoch
Shopping
Centre

Howard St.

Stockwell St.

Tron Steeple

Osborne St.

Candleriggs

Albion St.

Tolbooth
Steeple

London Rd.

Gallowgate

Clyde St.

Bridgegate

R. Clyde

0     1/8 mi

0     1/4 km

St. Andrew's
Church

Greendyke St.

KEY

Pedestrian Zone

Rail Lines

U Metro Stop

i Tourist information

sional splashes of color make bold statements. The three-bedroom penthouse suite has a separate kitchen and a sauna. The downstairs Brutti ma Buoni (meaning "ugly but good" in Italian), has an eclectic menu, a compact but complete wine list, and a selection of draught lagers. **Pros:** Excellent location; attentive staff. **Cons:** Neighborhood is loud on weekends, some rooms need to be freshened up. ⊠*106–108 Brunswick St., Merchant City, G1 1TF* ☎*0141/552–0001* ⊕*www. brunswickhotel.co.uk* ⇙*18 rooms, 1 suite* ♿*In-room: no a/c. In-hotel: café, bar* ▤*AE, MC, V* ⭘*CP.*

£ ⛨ **Cathedral House Hotel.** Adjacent to Glasgow Cathedral, this Scot-
★ tish Baronial–style building once served as the church's ecclesiastical headquarters—hence the name. It's suitably grand, with crow-stepped gables and towering turrets. The rooms, accessed by a spiraling stone staircase, are of varying size, but all are smartly decorated with dark-wood furnishings. The splendid restaurant and bar downstairs are very popular, but they are far enough from the rooms that the noise won't keep you up at night. A full Scottish breakfast—or a vegetarian option, if you prefer—is served in the café. **Pros:** Splendid atmosphere, quiet location, good value. **Cons:** No elevator, no Internet connections. ⊠*28–32 Cathedral Sq., Merchant City, G4 0XA* ☎*0141/552–3519* ⊕*www.cathedralhouse.com* ⇙*8 rooms* ♿*In-hotel: restaurant, bar, no elevator, laundry service, parking (no fee), no-smoking rooms* ▤*AE, MC, V* ⭘*BP.*

£ ⛨ **John Anderson Campus.** This University of Strathclyde's Campus Vil-
lage residence has more than 500 rooms available during the summer months. These modern buildings are set within landscaped gardens near Queen Street railway station and George Square. There are rooms with one, two, or three single beds, and basic, respectable furnishings. Five singles are available for guests with mobility problems. The recep-tion area is open 24 hours. **Pros:** Bargain price, convenient location. **Cons:** Dorm-style accommodations, bland decor. ⊠*Sauchiehall St., City Center, G1 1XQ* ☎*0141/553–4148* ⊕*www.rescat.strath.ac.uk* ⇙*500 rooms* ♿*In-room: no a/c, no phone, no TV. In-hotel: bar, laun-dry facilities* ▤*AE, MC, V.*

£ ⛨ **Premier Lodge.** Excellent views over the city are a plus at this well-
priced hotel in a converted office building. The rooms are in standard chain-hotel style, but you can be assured that they're spotless and com-fortable, with modern facilities. The hotel is between the city center and the West End, convenient to both. **Pros:** Good value, fantastic views. **Cons:** Unattractive building, so-so location near a gas station. ⊠*10 Elmbank Gardens, City Center, G2 4PP* ☎*0870/990–6312* ⊕*www. premiertravelinn.com* ⇙*278 rooms* ♿*In-room: no a/c, Wi-Fi. In-hotel: restaurant, bar, no-smoking rooms* ▤*AE, MC, V.*

£ ⛨ **Travel Inn Metro.** It may be a chain hotel, but the bright rooms and
low prices appeal to savvy travelers. The rooms are larger than most in this 1,400-year-old city, and have nice touches like coffeemakers. Rooms facing the street can be noisy at night, so ask for one that looks out onto the graveyard, where rabblerousers are highly unlikely. **Pros:** Great location, bargain price, bright reception area. **Cons:** Some front rooms are noisy, you pay extra for parking. ⊠*187 George St., Mer-*

2

*chant City, G1 1YU* ☎0870/238–3320 ⊕*www.premiertravelinn.com* ⤴239 rooms ♿*In-room: no a/c. In-hotel: restaurant, bar, public Wi-Fi, parking (fee), no-smoking rooms* ⊟*AE, MC, V.*

£ 🏨**Victorian House.** Compared with the bright-yellow entrance hall, the rooms in this hotel are rather plain. But its location—on a quiet residential street only a block from the Charles Rennie Mackintosh–designed Glasgow School of Art—is prime. There are plenty of restaurants and bars on nearby Sauchiehall Street, and the friendly staff is more than happy to help you choose one. **Pros:** Next to the Glasgow School of Art, tasty breakfast, basement rooms very spacious. **Con:** Some rooms need to be freshened up. ✉*212 Renfrew St., City Center, G3 6TX* ☎*0141/332–0129* ⊕*www.thevictorian.co.uk* ⤴*58 rooms* ♿*In-room: no a/c. In-hotel: no elevator* ⊟*MC, V* ⦿|*BP.*

## WEST END & ENVIRONS

£££ 🏨**Hotel Du Vin.** Once the legendary One Devonshire Gardens, frequented by such celebrities as Luciano Pavarotti and Elizabeth Taylor, the Hotel Du Vin is still a destination for those in search of luxury. Made up of a group of Victorian houses on a tree-lined street, the hotel is all about elegance, from the sophisticated drawing room to the individually decorated guest rooms with flowing draperies, Egyptian linens, and mahogany furnishings like four-poster beds. The Bistro restaurant is equally stylish; expect such delights as poached lobster and air-dried duck followed by a warm chocolate tart with pear sorbet. The beverage menu is also impressive: there are more than 600 wines and 300 whiskies. **Pros:** Stunning rooms, doting service, excellent restaurant. **Cons:** Near a busy street, no elevator. ✉*1 Devonshire Gardens, West End, G12 0UX* ☎*0141/339–2001* ⊕*www.onedevonshiregardens. com* ⤴*49 rooms* ♿*In-room: refrigerator, no a/c. In-hotel: restaurant, room service, bar, parking (no fee), spa, gym, no elevator, public Wi-Fi* ⊟*AE, DC, MC, V* ⦿|*BP.*

££ 🏨**Ambassador Hotel.** Opposite the West End's peaceful Botanic Gardens, the Ambassador is part of a string of elegant town houses on the banks of the River Kelvin. The interior echoes the peacefulness of the location and the traditional Victorian ethos of the spacious former family home. Though largely traditional, the rooms have a contemporary edge, with rich red-and-gold fabrics and beech furniture. **Pros:** Lovely views, great for kids, near public transportation. **Con:** Some of the decor is dated. ✉*7 Kelvin Dr., West End, G20 8QG* ☎*0141/946–1018* ⊕*www.glasgowhotelsandapartments.co.uk* ⤴*17 rooms* ♿*In-room: no a/c, safe, refrigerator, Wi-Fi. In-hotel: bar, laundry facilities, no elevator, parking (no fee), no-smoking rooms* ⊟*MC, V* ⦿|*BP.*

££ 🏨**Kirklee Hotel.** This West End B&B occupies a small and cozy Edwardian town house filled with home-away-from-home comforts. A bay window in the lounge overlooks a garden, and the old-fashioned morning room is adorned with embroidered settees and silk-wash wallpapers. Engravings on the walls and shelves of books in the library offer touches that any university don would appreciate. The owners are friendly and helpful. A neighboring gym charges guests £7.50 per session. **Pros:** Friendly service, quiet street, close to West End attractions. **Con:** Some rooms are a bit shabby. ⊠ *11 Kensington Gate, West End, G12 9LG* ☎*0141/334–5555* ⊕*www.kirkleehotel.co.uk* ➟*9 rooms* ♿*In-room: no a/c. In-hotel: no elevator, public Wi-Fi, no-smoking rooms* ☰*AE, DC, MC, V* �‖*BP.*

££    🏠**Town House.** This B&B is in a handsome terraced house on a quiet cul-de-sac. The owners are welcoming, which explains why this place thrives on repeat business. Restrained cream-and-pastel-stripe decor, stripped pine doors, and neutral fabrics complement the high ceilings, ornate plasterwork, and other original architectural features of the house. There's a comfortable sitting room with books, a coal-burning fireplace, and informative leaflets. **Pros:** Nice neighborhood, spacious rooms, close to park. **Con:** On a noisy street. ⊠ *4 Hughenden Terr., West End, G12 9XR* ☎*0141/357–0862* ⊕*www.thetown houseglasgow.com* ➟*10 rooms* ♿*In-room: no a/c. In-hotel: bar, no elevator, public Internet, parking (no fee)* ☰*AE, DC, MC, V* �‖*BP.*

£–££    🏠**Manor Park Hotel.** On a quiet street close to Victoria Park, one of
★    Glasgow's most idyllic public spaces, this stately terraced town house combines urban spaciousness with proximity to city action. Each of the neat and airy bedrooms, even the bright attic ones, bears the name in Gaelic of a Scottish island. The friendly owners themselves are Gaelic speakers, and tartan plays its part subtly in the homey interior. **Pros:** Quiet residential area, helpful staff, delicious breakfast. **Cons:** Far from city center, close to motorway. ⊠ *28 Balshagray Dr., West End, G11 7DD* ☎*0141/339–2143* ⊕*www.manorparkhotel.com* ➟*10 rooms* ♿*In-room: no a/c. In-hotel: bar, no elevator, parking (no fee)* ☰*AE, MC, V* �‖*BP.*

£    🏠**Amadeus Guest House.** This adorable Victorian town house is on a leafy residential street overlooking the River Kelvin. Rooms are comfortable and have plenty of natural light. Flickering candles and Mozart playing in the background add a nice touch to the breakfast buffet. **Pros:** Near West End attractions, two-minute walk from subway. **Cons:** Some rooms are small, finding parking can be difficult. ⊠*441 N. Woodside Rd., West End, G20 6NN* ☎*0141/339–8257* ⊕*www. amadeusguesthouse.co.uk* ➟*9 rooms* ♿*In-room: no a/c. In-hotel: no elevator* ☰*AE, MC, V* �‖*CP.*

£    🏠**Argyll Guest House.** At this small but cozy hotel, all the rooms are spacious and filled with Victorian-inspired furnishings. The breakfast room overlooks Kelvingrove Park, and you're welcome to have dinner at the restaurant in the Argyll Guest House's sister hotel, the Argyll Hotel, across the street. The best attraction, however, is the caring staff. **Pros:** Close to Kelvingrove Park, near public transportation. **Cons:** Front rooms noisy on weekends, longish walk to the attractions. ⊠*966–970 Sauchiehall St., West End, G3 7TH* ☎*0141/357–5155* ⊕*www.argyllguesthouseglasgow.co.uk* ➟*19 rooms* ♿*In-room: no a/c. In-hotel: bar, laundry service, no elevator* ☰*AE, MC, V* �‖*BP.*

£    🏠**Cairncross House.** On Glasgow University's West End campus, this modern dormitory provides affordable accommodation for visitors from July through mid-September. Small rooms have one or two single beds and inexpensive modern furniture. The dorm is a few minutes' walk from the Botanic Gardens and Kelvingrove Park. **Pros:** Ideal location, bargain price. **Cons:** Dorm-style rooms, cheap furnishings. ✉ *20 Kelvinhaugh Pl., West End, G3 8NH* ☎ *0141/330–3123* ⊕ *www.cvso. co.uk* ⟿ *155 rooms with shared bath* ⟁ *In-room: no a/c, no phone, kitchen, no TV, dial-up. In-hotel: laundry facilities, parking (no fee)* ⊙ *Closed Oct.–June* ▤ *AE, MC, V* ⏋⃝*CP.*

£   ⛫**The Sandyford.** The red-trimmed Victorian exterior of this simple B&B foretells the colorful interior. Each room is decorated with basic pine furnishings. On the western end of famous Sauchiehall Street, the hotel is convenient to all city-center sights, including the Scottish Exhibition Centre and many art galleries. **Pros:** Close to Kelvingrove Park, near public transportation. **Cons:** Some rooms are dingy, front rooms let in street noise, no elevator. ✉ *904 Sauchiehall St., West End, G3 7TF* ☎ *0141/334–0000* ⊕ *www.sandyfordhotelglasgow.com* ⟿ *55 rooms* ⟁ *In-room: no a/c. In-hotel: bar, no elevator* ▤ *MC, V* ⏋⃝*BP.*

## SOUTH SIDE

£££   ⛫**Sherbrooke Castle Hotel.** At this architectural flight of fantasy, the
★   cavernous rooms hark back to grander times when the South Side of Glasgow was home to the immensely wealthy tobacco barons whose homes boasted turrets and towers. The spacious grounds are far from the noise and bustle of downtown yet only a 10-minute drive from the city center. The hotel's proprietor insists on tasteful interior styling and good traditional cooking. The restaurant serves fine food, made with fresh ingredients. Everything is prepared right on the premises, including the breads. Locals flock to the busy bar. **Pros:** Great atmosphere, top-notch service, exceptional food. **Cons:** Some rooms are small, 10-minute drive from center of town, weekends functions can get very loud. ✉ *11 Sherbrooke Ave., Pollokshields, South Side, G41 4PG* ☎ *0141/427–4227* ⊕ *www.sherbrooke.co.uk* ⟿ *25 rooms* ⟁ *In-room: no a/c. In-hotel: restaurant, bar, no elevator, public Wi-Fi* ▤ *AE, DC, MC, V* ⏋⃝*BP.*

££   ⛫**Ewington Hotel.** This quiet row of town houses opposite Queen's Park is known for its traditional demeanor. Victorian-style furniture, ornately decorated bedrooms with heavy and elaborate pink-and-green floral fabrics, and an open fire in the spacious lobby all add to the relaxed, elegant character. Downtown Glasgow is only a short bus or train ride away. **Pros:** Lovely reception area, nice views of Queens's Park, most rooms are spacious and stylish. **Cons:** Need to drive to city center, slow service, rear facing rooms get noisy. ✉ *132 Queen's Dr., South Side, G42 8QW* ☎ *0141/423–1152* ⊕ *www.mckeverhotels. co.uk* ⟿ *43 rooms* ⟁ *In-room: no a/c. In-hotel: restaurant, bar, public Wi-Fi, parking (no fee)* ▤ *AE, DC, MC, V* ⏋⃝*BP.*

# NIGHTLIFE & THE ARTS

Home to Scotland's national orchestra, and opera and dance companies, Glasgow is truly the artistic hub of the country. The city's mix of university students, artists, and professionals has created a spirited pub-and-club scene at night.

## THE ARTS

Because Glasgow is home to the Royal Scottish Academy of Music and Drama, there is always a pool of impressive young talent that's pressing the city's artistic boundaries in theater, music, and film. Glasgow is known for having vibrant theater, with everything from cutting-edge one-act plays to over-the-top pantomines. And the arts don't end with theater, as Glasgow's music scene is eclectic and constantly growing. Most bars host live bands whose music ranges from traditional Scottish to the blues to rock and roll. There are, of course, plenty of places to enjoy classical music.

### CONCERTS

Glasgow's **Royal Concert Hall** ( ⊠*2 Sauchiehall St., City Center* ☎*0141/353–8000*) has 2,500 seats and is the main venue of the Royal Scottish National Orchestra, which performs winter and spring. The **Royal Scottish Academy of Music and Drama** ( ⊠*100 Renfrew St., City Center* ☎*0141/332–4101*) is one of the most important small venues for concerts, recitals, and theater productions. The **Scottish Exhibition and Conference Centre** ( ⊠*Finnieston, West End* ☎*0141/248–3000*) regularly hosts large-scale pop concerts.

### DANCE & OPERA

Glasgow is home to the Scottish Opera and Scottish Ballet, both of which perform at the **Theatre Royal** ( ⊠*282 Hope St., City Center* ☎*0141/332–9000*). Visiting dance companies from many countries appear here as well.

### FESTIVALS

**Celtic Connections** ( ⊠*Glasgow Royal Concert Hall, 2 Sauchiehall St., City Center, G2 3NY* ☎*0141/353–8000* ⊕*www.celticconnections. com*) is an ever-expanding Celtic music festival held in the second half of January. Musicians from Africa, France, Canada, Ireland, and Scotland perform and conduct hands-on workshops on topics such as how to make a harp. **Glasgay** ( ☎*0141/552–7575* ⊕*www.glasgay.co.uk*), held between late-October and mid-November, is the United Kingdom's largest multi-arts festival focusing on gay and lesbian issues. The international and Scottish line-up is always impressive and draws a huge audience.

### FILM

The **Center for Contemporary Arts** ( ⊠*350 Sauchiehall St., City Center* ☎*0141/352–4900*) screens classic, independent, and children's films. The **Glasgow Film Theatre** ( ⊠*12 Rose St., City Center* ☎*0141/332–8128*), an independent public cinema, screens the best new-release films from all over the world. The **Grosvenor** ( ⊠*Ashton La., West End*

☎*0141/339–8444*) is a popular, compact cinema in Glasgow's West End. **UGC** ( ✉*145–159 W. Nile St., City Center* ☎*0870/907–0789*), an 18-screen multilevel facility, is Glasgow's busiest movie complex. At 170 feet tall, it's also the world's tallest cinema building.

**THEATER**

Tickets for theatrical performances can be purchased at theater box offices or by telephone through the booking line: **Ticket Center** (☎*0141/287–5511*).

★ The **Arches** ( ✉*253 Argyle St., City Center* ☎*0870/240–7528*) stages challenging yet accessible drama from around the world. Some of the most exciting theatrical performances take place at the internationally renowned **Citizens' Theatre** ( ✉*119 Gorbals St., South Side* ☎*0141/429–0022*), where productions, and their sets, are often of hair-raising originality. Behind the theater's striking contemporary glass facade is a glorious Victorian red-and-gilded auditorium. Contemporary works are staged at **Cottier's Arts Theatre** ( ✉*93 Hyndland St., West End* ☎*0141/357–5825*), in a converted church.

The **King's Theatre** ( ✉*297 Bath St., City Center* ☎*0141/240–1111*) puts on dramas, variety shows, and musicals. **Òran Mór** ( ✉*At top of Byres Rd., West End* ☎*0141/357–6200*) puts on a variety of plays during lunch and dinnertime. The "Play, Pie and Pint" and "Dinner, Drama and Dram" run in 10-week blocks. Both sell out quickly, so book in advance. The **Pavilion** ( ✉*121 Renfield St., City Center* ☎*0141/332–1846*) hosts family variety entertainment along with rock and pop concerts.

The **Royal Scottish Academy of Music and Drama** ( ✉*100 Renfrew St., City Center* ☎*0141/332–4101*) stages international and student performances. The **Theatre Royal** ( ✉*282 Hope St., City Center* ☎*0141/332–1133*) hosts performances of major dramas, as well as opera and ballet. The **Tron Theatre** ( ✉*63 Trongate, Merchant City* ☎*0141/552–4267*) puts on contemporary theater from Scotland and around the world.

## NIGHTLIFE

Glasgow's nightlife scene is impressive and there's something here for everyone. Bars and pubs often close at midnight on the weekends, but nightclubs often stay open until 3 or 4 AM. Traditional *ceilidh* (a mix of country dancing, music, and song; pronounced *kay*-lee) is not as popular as it used to be (unless you're at a wedding), but you can still find it at many establishments. Consult the biweekly magazine the *List,* available at newsstands and bookstores, and the *Scotsman, Herald,* and *Evening Times* newspapers for up-to-date performance and event listings.

**BARS & PUBS**

Glasgow's pubs were once hangouts for serious drinkers who demanded few comforts. Times have changed, and many of these gritty establishments have been transformed into trendy cocktail bars. Bars and pubs vary according to location: those in the city center tend to cater to business types, although some still cater to a more traditional clientele. The bars and pubs in the West End were once favored by students; however, that is slowly changing as thirty-, forty-, and even fifty-something crowds have moved in.

First-timers to Glasgow's pub scene should order a pint, meaning a pint of lager. Bottled beers are available, but draft beer is the most popular beverage for men; women tend to drink wine or cocktails (yes, this gender difference is extremely obvious). Most bars and pubs are open daily from 11 AM to 11 PM and also serve food. Keep in mind opening hours are often extended by an hour on weekends.

CITY CENTER  Many of the most popular bars are in the center of the city. **Babbity Bowster's** ( ⊠ *16–18 Blackfriars St., Merchant City* ☎ *0141/552–5055*), a busy, friendly spot, serves interesting beers and good food. At **Bloc** ( ⊠ *117 Bath St., City Center* ☎ *0141/574–6066*), you can step behind a curious version of the Iron Curtain where Tex-Mex diner food mixes with an eclectic musical mash of DJs and live rock and folk bands. The classic **Drum and Monkey** ( ⊠ *93 St. Vincent St., City Center* ☎ *0141/221–6636*) attracts an after-work crowd of young professionals. **King Tut's Wah Wah Hut** ( ⊠ *227a St. Vincent St., City Center* ☎ *0141/221–5279*), which hosts live music most nights, claims to have been the venue that discovered the U.K. pop band Oasis. It's a favorite with students, but the cozy and traditional pub setting draws people of all ages.

**Lab** ( ⊠ *26 Springfield Ct., City Center* ☎ *0141/222–2116*) is an intimate drinking den with a vaguely scientific theme and a beguiling courtyard. For a splash of Mediterranean style, head to **Moskito** ( ⊠ *200 Bath St., City Center* ☎ *0141/331–1777*). Amid the cool, aquatic hues you can see people dancing to laid-back tunes Thursday to Sunday nights. **Nico's** ( ⊠ *375 Sauchiehall St., City Center* ☎ *0141/332–5736*), designed to resemble a Parisian café, is a favorite with art students and young Glaswegian professionals.

★  The **Riverside Club** ( ⊠ *33 Fox St., off Clyde St., City Center* ☎ *0141/248–3144*) hosts traditional bands on Friday and Saturday evenings; get there early, as it's very popular. **Rogano** ( ⊠ *11 Exchange Pl., City Center* ☎ *0141/248–4055*) is famous for its champagne cocktails and general air of 1920s decadence. The **Scotia Bar** ( ⊠ *112 Stockwell St., Merchant City* ☎ *0141/552–8681*) serves up a taste of an authentic Glasgow pub, with some traditional folk music occasionally thrown in.

WEST END  There's also a thriving scene in the West End. Despite its former austere existence as a church, the always-busy **Cottiers** ( ⊠ *Hyndland St., West End* ☎ *0141/357–5825*) is a famous haunt of the young. The best seat is outside in the popular beer garden. There's often a good lineup of established and up-and-coming rock groups at the **Halt** ( ⊠ *160 Woodlands Rd., West End* ☎ *0141/564–1527*), which attracts an older clientele. **Òran Mór** ( ⊠ *At top of Byres Rd., West End* ☎ *0141/357–6200*) is popular with all ages. Situated in a massive church, the bar has beautiful stained-glass windows. The beer garden fills up quickly in good weather.

★ **Tennents** ( ⊠*191 Byres Rd., West End* ☏*0141/341–1021*), a spacious street-corner bar, prides itself on a comprehensive selection of beers, lively conversation, and a refreshing lack of loud music. The best Gaelic pub is **Uisge Beatha** ( ⊠*232–246 Woodlands Rd., West End* ☏*0141/564–1596*). The name, pronounced *oos*-ki *bee*-ha, means "water of life" and is said to be the origin of the word "whisky." The bar serves *fraoch* (heather beer) in season and has live music on Wednesday and Sunday.

### NIGHTCLUBS

★ As elsewhere in Britain, electronic music—from house to techno to drum and bass—is par for the course in Glasgow's dance clubs. Much of the scene revolves around Center City. **Archaos** ( ⊠*25 Queen St., City Center* ☏*0141/204–3189*), the city's most cavernous club, has three dance floors blasting house, garage, indie, R&B, soul, and hip-hop music. It's open Wednesday through Sunday from 11 PM to 4 AM. The **Arches** ( ⊠*253 Argyle St., City Center* ☏*0901/022–0300*) is one of the city's largest arts venues, but on Friday (from 11 PM to 3 AM) and Saturday (from 10:30 PM to 4 AM) it thumps with house and techno. The club welcomes big music names like Colours and Inside Out at legendary parties. A few times a month it holds dressed-up gay nights.

Oozing with Edwardian style, the **Polo Lounge** ( ⊠*84 Wilson St., Merchant City* ☏*0141/553–1221*) is Glasgow's largest gay club. Upstairs is a bar that resembles an old-fashioned gentlemen's club and downstairs two dance floors that play something for everyone. The festivities run Monday through Thursday from 5 PM to 1 AM, Friday from 5 PM to 3 AM, and weekends from noon to 3 AM.

The **Sub Club** ( ⊠*22 Jamaica St., City Center* ☏*0141/248–4600*) is an atmospheric underground venue that has staged cutting-edge music events since its jazz club days in the '50s. Legendary favorites like Saturday's SubCulture (House) and Sunday's Optimo (a truly eclectic mix for musical hedonists) pack in friendly and sweaty crowds.

# SPORTS & THE OUTDOORS

Until recently, Glasgow wasn't a city known for its exercise enthusiasts. Times have most definitely changed, as you can't go far these days without seeing a runner or cyclist. Because of the city's numerous parks, there is plenty of space. Rarely is the weather conducive for outdoor exercise; it rains a lot in Glasgow, but don't let that deter you. It doesn't deter the locals who play soccer, tennis, hike, bike, run, swim and walk in the rain. Alternatively, there are plenty of indoor gyms for those who prefer to stay dry. The **Greater Glasgow and Clyde Valley Tourist Board** ( ⊠*11 George Sq., near Queen Street station, City Center* ☏*0141/204–4400*) provides information on outdoor activities.

### GOLF

Several municipal courses are operated within Glasgow proper by the local authorities. Bookings are relatively inexpensive and should be made directly to the course 24 hours in advance to ensure prime tee times (courses open at 7 AM). A comprehensive list of contacts, facilities, and greens fees of the 30 or so other courses near the city is available from the tourist board. The abbreviation SSS used below means standard scratch score, which is often used here instead of par.

**Douglas Park.** North of the city near Milngavie, Douglas Park is a long, attractive course set among birch and pine trees with masses of rhododendrons blooming in early summer. ⊠*Hillfoot, Bearsden* ☏*0141/942–0985* ⊕*www.douglasparkgolfclub.co.uk* ⚑*18 holes, 5,962 yds, par 69.*

**Lethamhill.** The fairways of this city-owned parkland course overlook Hogganfield Loch. To get there, take the M8 north to Junction 12, and drive up the A80 about a quarter mile. ⊠*1240 Cumbernauld Rd., North City* ☏*0141/770–6220* ⊕*www.scottishgolfcourses.com* ⚑*18 holes, 5,836 yds, SSS 68.*

**Littlehill.** Level fairways and greens make this municipal course not too difficult to play. It's on the A803 about 4 mi north of the city center. ⊠*Auchinairn Rd., North City* ☏*0141/772–1916* ⊕*www.scottishgolfcourses.com* ⚑*18 holes, 6,240 yds, SSS 70.*

### SOCCER

The city has been sports mad, especially for soccer, for more than 100 years. The rivalry between its two main football clubs, the Rangers and the Celtic, is legendary. Matches are held usually on Saturday in winter. Admission prices start at about £20. Don't go looking for the family-day-out atmosphere of many American football games; soccer remains a fiercely contested game attended mainly by males, though the stadiums at Ibrox and Celtic Park are fast becoming family-friendly. Rangers wear blue and play at **Ibrox** ( ⊠*Edmiston Dr., South Side* ☏*08706/001993*), pronounced *eye*-brox, to the west of the city. The Celtic wear white and green stripes and play in the east at **Celtic Park** ( ⊠*95 Kerrydale St., East End* ☏*0141/551–8653*). But the glorious game in Glasgow isn't just blue or green, nor is it dominated by international players and big money. Partick Thistle (the Jags) wear red and yellow and their ground is **Firhill Park** ( ⊠*80 Firhill, West End* ☏*0141/579–1971*).

# SHOPPING

Glaswegians love to dress up, and you'll find the mark of the fashion industry on the city center's hottest shopping streets, Buchanan and Sauchiehall, as well as in Princes Square. Glasgow is the biggest and most popular U.K. retail center outside London. Besides straight-off-the-runway couture, Glasgow has an impressive number of antiques stores, and Scottish specialty shops selling woolen, cashmere, and tartan dress.

Should the weather turn *dreich* (dismal) you can avoid getting *drookit* (wet) by sheltering in one of the many covered arcades in the city center. For more unusual items, head to the West End's Byres Road and Great

Western Road. ■TIP➜If you're here in late June and early July, there are always big sales. You can pick up some fantastic bargins.

## ARCADES & SHOPPING CENTERS

The **Buchanan Galleries** ( ✉*220 Buchanan St., City Center* ☎*0141/333–9898*), at the top end of Buchanan Street next to the Royal Concert Hall, is packed with high-quality shops; its magnet attraction is the John Lewis department store. By far the best complex is the art nouveau **Princes Square** ( ✉*48 Buchanan St., City Center* ☎*0141/204–1685*), with high-quality shops alongside pleasant cafés and a tony restaurant or two. Look for the Scottish Craft Centre, which carries an outstanding collection of work created by some of the nation's best craftspeople. **St. Enoch's Shopping Centre** ( ✉*55 St. Enoch Sq., City Center* ☎*0141/204–3900*) is eye-catching if not especially pleasing—it's a modern glass building that resembles an overgrown greenhouse. It houses various stores, but most are also found elsewhere.

## SHOPPING DISTRICTS

On the main, often-crowded pedestrian area of **Argyle Street,** you'll find chain stores such as Debenham's. An interesting diversion off Argyle Street is the covered **Argyll Arcade,** which has the largest collection of jewelers under one roof in Scotland. The L-shape arcade, built in 1904, houses several locally based jewelers and a few shops specializing in antique jewelry. **Buchanan Street,** off the Argyll Arcade, is Glasgow's premier shopping street and almost totally a pedestrian area. The usual suspects are here: Monsoon, Topshop, Burberry's, Jaeger, and other household names, some with premises in Buchanan Galleries, at the top end of the street. **St. Enoch Square,** which is also the main underground station, houses the St. Enoch Shopping Centre.

The huge **Barras** indoor market, on London Road in the Glasgow Cross neighborhood, prides itself on selling everything "from a needle to an anchor." Stalls hawk antique (and not-so-antique) furniture, bric-a-brac, good and not-so-good jewelry, and textiles—you name it, it's here. Many of Glasgow's young and upwardly mobile make their home in **Merchant City,** on the edge of the city center. Shopping here is expensive, but the area is worth visiting if you're seeking the youthful Glasgow style. The university dominates the area around **West End,** and the shops cater to local and student needs. The easiest way to get here is by the underground system to Hillhead. If you're an antiques connoisseur and art lover, a walk along **West Regent Street,** particularly its **Victorian Village,** is highly recommended, as there are various galleries and shops, some specializing in Scottish antiques and paintings.

## DEPARTMENT STORES

★ **British Home Stores** ( ✉*67–81 Sauchiehall St., City Center* ☎*0141/332–0401*) carries typical department-store goods: clothes, household gadgets, linens, and foodstuffs. **Debenham's** ( ✉*97 Argyle St., City Center*

☎*0844/561–6161*) is one of Glasgow's principal department stores, with fine china and crystal as well as women's and men's clothing. You can get here from St. Enoch Centre. **Frasers** (✉*21–45 Buchanan St., City Center* ☎*0141/221–3880*), a Glasgow institution, stocks wares that reflect the city's material aspirations—leading European designer clothes and fabrics combined with home-produced articles, such as tweeds, tartans, glass, and ceramics. The magnificent interior, set off by the grand staircase rising to various floors and balconies, is itself worth a visit.

★ **John Lewis** (✉*Buchanan Galleries, 220 Buchanan St., City Center* ☎*0141/353–6677*) is a favorite for its stylish mix of clothing and household items. **Marks & Spencer** (✉*2–12 Argyle St., City Center* ☎*0141/552–4546* ✉*172 Sauchiehall St., City Center* ☎*0141/332–6097*) sells sturdy, practical clothes and accessories at moderate prices; you can also buy food items and household goods here.

## SPECIALTY SHOPS

Scotland has fantastic specialty shops, and Glasgow is home to many of them. Antiques shops are a big draw, as are bookstores and gourmet food emporiums. And don't forget kilts! Glasgow has plenty of kilt shops, especially in the city center.

### ANTIQUES & FINE ART

★ The **Compass Gallery** (✉*178 W. Regent St., City Center* ☎*0141/221–6370*) hosts exhibitions focusing on abstract and expressionist art. **Cyril Gerber Fine Art** (✉*148 W. Regent St., City Center* ☎*0141/221–3095 or 0141/204–0276*) specializes in British paintings from 1880 to the present; they will ship your purchase for you, as will most galleries. **De Courcys** (✉*5–21 Cresswell La., West End*), an antiques and crafts arcade, has quite a few shops to visit, and lots of goods, including paintings and jewelry, are regularly auctioned. It's on one of the cobblestone lanes to the rear of Byres Road.

### BOOKS & PAPER

**Borders** (✉*98 Buchanan St., City Center* ☎*0141/222–7700*), set in a former bank building, has a particularly friendly atmosphere and carries a wide selection of Scottish books. The **Glasgow School of Art** (✉*167 Renfrew St., City Center* ☎*0141/353–4526*) sells books, cards, jewelry, and ceramics. Students often display their work during the degree shows in June. For the latest literature on the city's ever-thriving music scene, try **Monorail Music** (✉*12 Kings Ct., King St., City Center* ☎*0141/552–9458*). You can also find rare soundtracks and eclectic grooves, listen to occasional live music, or grab a microbrew beer and veggie burger at the city's only vegan restaurant. Both branches of **Papyrus** (✉*374 Byres Rd., West End* ☎*0141/334–6514* ✉*10 Sauchiehall St., City Center* ☎*0141/332–6788*) carry designer cards, as well as a good selection of books.

## CLOTHING BOUTIQUES

Male and female fashionista must not miss **Cruise** ( ⊠*180 Ingram St., City Center* ☎*0141/572–3280*), which stocks hot labels at cool prices. An eclectic array of designer clothing and accessories for women fills **Moon** ( ⊠*10 Ruthven La., off Byers Rd., West End* ☎*0141/339–2315*). **Mr. Benn** ( ⊠*6 King's Ct., King St., City Center* ☎*0141/553–1936*) has a funky selection of vintage clothing. **Strawberry Fields** ( ⊠*517 Great Western Rd., West End* ☎*0141/339–1121*) sells colorful children's wear.

## FOOD

**Iain Mellis Cheesemonger** ( ⊠*492 Great Western Rd., West End* ☎*0141/339–8998*) has a seemingly endless selection of fine Scottish cheeses. **Peckham's Delicatessen** ( ⊠*100 Byres Rd., West End* ☎*0141/357–1454* ⊠*43 Clarence Dr., West End* ☎*0141/357–2909* ⊠*Central Station, City Center* ☎*0141/248–4012* ⊠*Glassford St., Merchant City* ☎*0141/553–0666*) is *the* place for Continental sausages, cheeses, and anything else you'd need for a delicious picnic.

## HOME FURNISHINGS & TEXTILES

**Fancy Dans** ( ⊠*362 Great Western Rd., West End* ☎*0141/339–0660*) is crammed with stylish jewelry, stationery, and skin-care products. **Linens Fine** ( ⊠*The Courtyard, Princes Sq., City Center* ☎*0141/248–7082*) carries wonderful embroidered and embellished bed linens and other textiles. At the shop for the **National Trust for Scotland** ( ⊠*Hutchesons' Hall, 158 Ingram St., Merchant City* ☎*0141/552–8391*) many of the items for sale, such as china, giftware, textiles, toiletries, and housewares, are designed exclusively for trust properties and are often handmade.

## SCOTTISH SPECIALTIES

For high-quality gifts in Charles Rennie Mackintosh style, head to **Catherine Shaw** ( ⊠*24 Gordon St., City Center* ☎*0141/204–4762* ⊠*32 Argyll Arcade, City Center* ☎*0141/221–9038*). **Hector Russell Kiltmakers** ( ⊠*110 Buchanan St., City Center* ☎*0141/221–0217*) specializes in Highland outfits, wool and cashmere clothing, and women's fashions. **MacDonald MacKay Ltd.** ( ⊠*161 Hope St., City Center* ☎*0141/204–3930*) makes, sells, and exports Highland dress and accessories.

## SPORTS GEAR

You'll find good-quality outerwear at **Tiso Sports** ( ⊠*129 Buchanan St., City Center* ⊕*www.tiso.com* ☎*0141/248–4877*), handy if you're planning some Highland walks.

## TOBACCO

Much of Glasgow's wealth was generated by the tobacco lords during the 17th and 18th centuries. At **Robert Graham** ( ⊠*71 St. Vincent St., City Center* ☎*0141/221–6588*) you'll experience a little of that colorful history. The shop carries a tremendous variety of tobaccos and pipes.

# SIDE TRIPS: AYRSHIRE, CLYDE COAST & ROBERT BURNS COUNTRY

The jigsaw puzzle of firths and straits and interlocking islands that you see as you fly into Glasgow Airport harbors numerous tempting one-day excursion destinations. You can travel south to visit the fertile farmlands of Ayrshire—Robert Burns country—or west to the Firth of Clyde, or southeast to the Clyde Valley, all by car or by public transportation. You may want to begin with the town of Paisley. Once a distinct burgh but now part of the Glasgow suburbs, it has plenty of gritty character, largely from vestiges of its industrial heritage. It was once famous for its paisley shawl manufacturing; its museum displays a fine collection of these garments. Besides the Burns sites, key treasures in this area include the Marquess of Bute's Mount Stuart House on the Isle of Bute, and Culzean Castle, a favored retreat for Eisenhower and Churchill that is as famous for its Robert Adam (1728–92) design as it is for its spectacular seaside setting.

The highlight of this region is Robert Burns country, a 40-minute drive from the Glasgow. The poet was born in Alloway, beside Ayr, and the towns and villages where he lived and loved make for an interesting day out. English children learn that Burns (1759–96) is a good minor poet. But Scottish children know that he's Shakespeare, Dante, Rabelais, Mozart, and Karl Marx rolled into one. As time goes by, it seems that the Scots have it more nearly right. As poet and humanist, Burns increases in stature. When you plunge into Burns country, don't forget that he's held in extreme reverence by Scots of all backgrounds. They may argue about Sir Walter Scott and Bonnie Prince Charlie, but there's no disputing the merits of the poet of "Bonnie Doon."

On your way here you travel beside the estuary and firth of the great River Clyde and will be able to look across to Dumbarton and its Rock, a nostalgic farewell point for emigrants leaving Glasgow. The river is surprisingly narrow here, considering that the *Queen Elizabeth II* and the other great ocean liners sailed these waters from the place of their birth. Farther along the coast, the views north and west to Loch Long, Holy Loch, and the Argyll Forest Park are outstanding on a clear day.

## PAISLEY

*7 mi south of Glasgow.*

The industrial prosperity of Paisley came from textiles and, in particular, from the woolen paisley shawl. The internationally recognized paisley pattern is based on the shape of a palm shoot, an ancient Babylonian fertility symbol brought from Kashmir.

★ The full story of the pattern and of the innovative weaving techniques introduced in Paisley is told in the **Paisley Museum & Art Gallery,** which has a world-famous shawl collection. ⊠ *High St.* ☎ *0141/889–3151* ⊕ *www.paisley.org.uk* ⊠ *Free* ☯ *Tues.–Sat. 10–5, Sun. 2–5.*

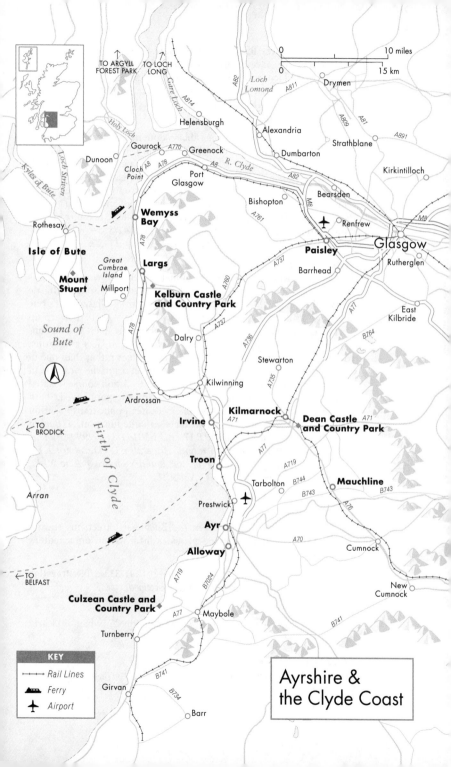

Ayrshire &
the Clyde Coast

To get an idea of the life led by textile industry workers, visit the **Sma' Shot Cottages.** These re-creations of mill workers' houses contain displays of linen, lace, and paisley shawls. An 18th-century weaver's cottage is also open to visitors. ⊠ *11–17 George Pl.* ☎ *0141/889–1708* ⊕ *www.paisley.org.uk* ⊒ *Free* ☯ *Apr.–Sept., Wed. and Sat. noon–4; Oct.–Mar. by appointment.*

Paisley's 12th-century Cluniac **Abbey** dominates the town center. Almost completely destroyed by the English in 1307, the abbey was not totally restored until the early 20th century. It's associated with Walter Fitzallan, the high steward of Scotland, who gave his name to the Stewart monarchs of Scotland (Stewart is a corruption of "steward"). Outstanding features include the vaulted stone roof and stained glass of the choir. Paisley Abbey is today a busy parish church; if you're visiting with a large group you should call ahead. ☎ *0141/889–7654* ⊒ *Free* ☯ *Mon.–Sat. 10–3:30, Sun. services 11, 12:15, and 6:30.*

## WHERE TO STAY & EAT

££££ ✕◻ **Mar Hall.** Set amid 240 acres of formal gardens and woodlands, this neo-Gothic manor on the River Clyde seems isolated from the bustle of daily life, even though it's only 20 minutes from Glasgow. It's one of Scotland's most dramatic lodgings, with stone steps that sweep up to the massive, mid-19th-century stone house. The guest rooms continue the romance, with four-poster beds draped in silks and satins; you may prefer a room that overlooks the gardens rather than one in the spa annex. Dining choices include afternoon tea in the Grand Hall and sophisticated Scottish fare at Cristal (££££). A golf course is slated to open in 2009. **Pros:** Spacious rooms, fantastic pool, Aveda bath products. **Cons:** You need to drive to city center, public transportation is difficult, service can be patchy if there's a large function. ⊠ *Earl of Mar Estate, Bishopton, Renfrew PA7 5PU* ☎ *0141/812–9999* ⊕ *www.marhall.com* ⊠ *53 rooms* ⚬ *In-room: refrigerator, DVD, Ethernet. In-hotel: 2 restaurants, bar, pool, gym, spa, laundry service, public Wi-Fi, parking (no fee)* ▭ *AE, DC, MC, V* ◉ *BP.*

## PAISLEY ESSENTIALS

### BY BUS

Paisley-bound buses depart from the Buchanan Street bus station in Glasgow. Traveline Scotland provides information on schedules and fares.

**Information** **Buchanan Street bus station** (☎ *0141/333–3708*). **Traveline Scotland** (☎ *0870/608–2608* ⊕ *www.travelinescotland.com*).

### BY CAR

Take the M8 westbound and turn off at Junction 27, which is clearly signposted to Paisley.

### BY TRAIN

Trains to Paisley depart daily every 5 to 10 minutes from Glasgow Central Station.

**Information Glasgow Central Station** (☎ 0845/748–4950). **National Rail** (☎ 0845/748–4950 ⊕ www.nationalrail.co.uk).

## VISITOR INFORMATION

The tourist information center, which is open daily from 10 to 5, except on Sunday from October through March, is near Paisley Gilmour Street railway station.

**Information Paisley Tourist Information Center** (⊠ 9A Gilmour St. ☎ 0141/889–0711 ⊕ www.seeglasgow.com).

# WEMYSS BAY

*15 mi west of Paisley, 31 mi west of Glasgow.*

From the old Victorian village of Wemyss Bay there's ferry service to the Isle of Bute, a favorite holiday spot for Glaswegians before air travel made it easier to go abroad. The many handsome buildings, especially the station and its covered walkway between the train platform and steamer pier, are a reminder of the Victorian era's grandeur and style and of the generations of visitors who used trains and ferries for their summer holidays. South of Wemyss Bay, you can look across to the Isle of Arran, another Victorian holiday favorite, and then to the island of Great Cumbrae, a weighty name for a tiny island.

# ISLE OF BUTE

*75 mi west of Glasgow.*

The Isle of Bute affords a host of relaxing walks and scenic vistas. **Rothesay,** a faded but appealing resort, is the main town.

Bute's biggest draw is spectacular **Mount Stuart,** ancestral home of the marquesses of Bute, about 5 mi south of Rothesay. The massive Victorian Gothic palace, built in red sandstone, has ornate interiors, including the Marble Hall, with a star-studded vault, stained glass, arcaded galleries, and magnificent tapestries woven in Edinburgh in the early 20th century. The paintings and furniture throughout the house are equally outstanding. ⊠ *Isle of Bute* ☎ *01700/503877* ⊕ *www.mountstuart.com* 🎫 *Gardens £3.50; house and gardens £7.50* ⊙ *Gardens May–Sept., daily 10–6; house May–Sept., Sun.–Fri. 11–5, Sat. 10–2:30.*

### WHERE TO STAY

££ 🏠 **Munro's Bed and Breakfast.** Surrounded by colorful gardens, this small B&B in a peaceful residential area has a home-away-from-home feel. The newly refurbished rooms are stylish with all the modern touches like flat-screen TVs and under floor heating in the bathrooms. Muted dark purples and browns give the spacious rooms an elegant, warm feel. Room number 2 is the best as it has a small lounge area attached. Downstairs, a cozy bar with an open fire welcomes guests. Dinner is on a request-only basis and includes organic and local produce when available; locally grown beef and langoustines are a few of the specialties. **Pros:** Beautiful location, newly remodeled, environmentally aware. **Cons:** Far out of town, hilltop location a problems for those with trouble walking. ✉ *Ardmory Rd., Ardbeg, Isle of Bute PA20 0PG* ☎ *01700/502346* ⊕ *www.visitmunros.co.uk* ⇨ *6 rooms* ⚬ *In-room: no a/c, Wi-Fi. In-hotel: restaurant, bar, no elevator* ⊟ *MC, V* ⦿ *BP.*

## LARGS

*42 mi southwest of Glasgow.*

At the coastal resort of Largs, the community makes the most of the town's Viking history. This was the site in 1263 of a major battle that finally broke the power of the Vikings in Scotland, and every September a commemorative Viking Festival is held.

⟳ **Vikingar!** tells the story of the Viking influence in Scotland by way of film, tableaux, and displays. ✉ *Barrfields, Greenock Rd.* ☎ *01475/689777* ⊕ *www.vikingar.co.uk* ⛭ *£4.20* ⊗ *Apr.–Sept., daily 10:30–5:30, Sat. 12:30–3:30; Oct. and Mar., daily 10:30–3:30; Nov.–Feb., weekends 10:30–3:30.*

If you're in Largs on the seafront on a summer's afternoon, take time to visit the **Clark Memorial Church** ( ✉ *Bath St.* ☎ *01475/675186*), which has a particularly splendid array of Glaswegian Arts and Crafts stained glass of the 1890s in its windows. Among the studios involved in their design were those of Stephen Adam (1848–1910) and his contemporary Christopher Wall.

⟳ Just south of Largs is **Kelburn Castle and Country Park,** the historic estate of the earl of Glasgow. There are walks and trails through the mature woodlands, including the mazelike Secret Forest, which leads deep into the thickets. There are many surprises along the way for kids, including the Crocodile Swamp, the Gingerbread House, and mysterious Castle with No Entrance. The adventure center and commando-assault course wear out even the most overexcited of children. The excellent riding school provides year-round activities including paddock rides, hacks around the grounds, jumps in the arena, and lessons for all ages and abilities. ✉ *Fairlie, Ayrshire* ☎ *01475/568685* ⊕ *www.kelburncountrycentre.com* ⛭ *Grounds and castle £7* ⊗ *Grounds Easter–Oct., daily 10–6; Nov.–Easter, daily 11–5. Castle July and Aug., daily tours at 1:30, 2:45, and 4.*

## IRVINE

*24 mi south of Glasgow.*

Beyond Irvine's cobbled streets and grand Victorians, look for a peaceful crescent-shape harbor and fishermen's cottages huddled in solidarity against the Atlantic winds.

Founded in 1826, the **Irvine Burns Club** is one of the oldest Burns clubs in the world. Today its gallery displays a collection of original manuscripts, plus murals and stained-glass windows that narrate Burns's life and work. The author lived in Irvine when he was 22. ⊠*28 Eglinton St.* ☎*01294/274511* ⊕*www.irvineayrshire.org* ⬚*Free* ☽*Apr.–Sept., Mon., Wed., Fri., and Sat. 2:30–4:30; Oct.–Mar., Sat. 2:30–4:30.*

The **Vennel Art Gallery** is in the house where Burns came to live and the shed where he learned to heckle—or dress—flax (the raw material for linen). Both buildings have on display paintings, photographs, and sculpture by mainly Scottish artists. ⊠*10 Glasgow Vennel* ☎*01294/275059* ⬚*Free* ☽*Thurs.–Sat. 10–1 and 2–5.*

## TROON

*4 mi south of Irvine, 28 mi south of Glasgow.*

The small coastal town of Troon is famous for its international golf course, Royal Troon. You can easily see that golf is popular here: at times, the whole 60-mi-long Ayrshire coast seems one endless course.

### WHERE TO STAY & EAT

£££ ✕**MacCallums Oyster Bar.** The main ingredients at MacCallums come
★  straight from the sea, and the menu varies depending on the day's catch. You can usually count on lobster in garlic butter; seared scallops; or grilled langoustines. Excellent light white wines match the freshness of the food. Solid wooden tables and other simple furniture add a rustic touch to the dining room. Hidden among the boatyards and customs buildings of Troon Harbour, this top-class restaurant is easy to miss, but you can find it next to the Seacat Ferry Terminal. ⊠*The Harbour* ☎*01292/319339* ▭*DC, MC, V* ☽*Closed Sun. evening and Mon.*

£££ ✕▣**Piersland House Hotel.** A late-Victorian mansion, formerly the home of a whisky magnate, is now a country-house hotel. All the bedrooms in the half-timbered main house are furnished in traditional style, and many have romantic four-poster or canopy beds. Oak paneling and log fires in the restaurant provide a warm backdrop for Scottish cuisine (£££), including specialties such as beef medallions in pickled walnut sauce. **Pros:** Gorgeous grounds, close to golf courses, near Prestwick Airport. **Cons:** Helps to have a car to get around, some of the decor is dated, gets very crowded with private functions. ⊠*15 Craigend Rd., just north of Ayr, KA10 6HD* ☎*01292/314747* ⊕*www.piersland. co.uk* ⤶*30 rooms* ⬚*In-room: no a/c, refrigerator. In-hotel: restaurant, no elevator* ▭*AE, DC, MC, V* ⭐*BP.*

### GOLF

Founded in 1878, **Royal Troon** has two 18-hole courses: the Old, or Championship, Course and the Portland Course. The views are magnificent, but the courses can get windy. Access for nonmembers is limited between May and mid-October to Monday, Tuesday, and Thursday only; day tickets cost £200 and include two rounds, morning coffee, and a buffet lunch. ⊠*Craigend Rd.* ☎*01292/311555* ⊕*www.royal troon.co.uk* ⛳*Old Course: 18 holes, 7,150 yds, SSS 74. Portland Course: 18 holes, 6,289 yds, SSS 70.*

## SHOPPING

Many Glaswegians frequent **Regalia Fashion Salon** ( ⊠ *44 Church St.* ☎ *01292/312162*) for its unusual collection of designer clothing for women. For a fascinating look at local antiquities, visit **Tantalus Antiques** ( ⊠ *79 Templehill* ☎ *01292/315999*).

# AYR

*6 mi south of Troon, 34 mi south of Glasgow.*

The commercial port of Ayr is Ayrshire's chief town, a peaceful and elegant place with an air of prosperity. Robert Burns was baptized in the Auld Kirk (Old Church) here and wrote a humorous poem about the Twa Brigs (Two Bridges) that cross the river nearby. He described Ayr as a town unsurpassed "for honest men and bonny lasses." If he were to visit today, he might also mention the good shopping.

If you're on the Robert Burns trail, head for **Alloway,** on B7024 in Ayr's southern suburbs. A number of sights here are part of the **Burns National Heritage Park** (www.burnsheritagepark.com).

In Alloway, among the middle-class residences, you'll find the one-room thatched **Burns Cottage,** where Scotland's national poet was born in 1759 and which his father built. Not many outside Scotland appreciate the depth of affection Scotland has for Burns. To his fellow Scots he's more than a great lyric bard; he's the champion of the underdog, the lover of noble causes, the hater of pomposity and cant, the prophet of social justice. "A man's a man for a' that"—such phrases have exalted the Scottish character, while his love songs warm the coldest hearts. January 25, Burns Night, is an anniversary of importance in Scotland. A **museum** next to the cottage contains an original manuscript of "Auld Lang Syne" and other important Burns manuscripts and artifacts. ⊠ *Murdoch's Lone, Alloway* ☎ *01292/441215* ⊕ *www. robertburns.org* 🎟 *£5 ticket includes admission to Tam o' Shanter Experience and Burns Monument* ☉ *Apr.–Sept., daily 9:30–5:30; Oct.–Mar., daily 10–5.*

Find out all about Burns at the **Tam o' Shanter Experience.** Here you can enjoy a 10-minute audiovisual journey through his life and times, then watch as one of Burns's most famous poems, "Tam o' Shanter," is brought to life on a three-screen theatrical set. It's down the road from Burns Cottage and around the corner from Alloway's ruined church. ⊠ *Murdoch's Lone, Alloway* ☎ *01292/443700* ⊕ *www.robertburns. org* 🎟 *£5 ticket includes Burns Cottage and Burns Monument* ☉ *Apr.– Sept., daily 10–5:30; Oct.–Mar., daily 10–5.*

**Auld Kirk Alloway** is where Tam o' Shanter, in Burns's eponymous poem, unluckily passed a witches' revel—with Old Nick himself playing the bagpipes—on his way home from a night of drinking. Tam, in flight from the witches, managed to cross the **Brig o' Doon** (*brig* is Scots for *bridge*) just in time. His gray mare, Meg, lost her tail to the closest witch. (Any resident of Ayr will tell you that witches cannot cross running water.)

**2**

The **Burns Monument** overlooks the Brig o' Doon in Alloway. ☏ *No phone* ⊕*www.robertburns.org* 🎟️*£1; £5 ticket includes Burns Cottage and Tam o' Shanter Experience* ⊙*Apr.–Sept., daily 9:30–5; Nov.–Mar., daily 10–4.*

At Tarbolton, 8 mi northeast of Ayr and 28 mi southwest of Glasgow, is the **Bachelors' Club**, the 17th-century house where Robert Burns learned to dance, founded a debating and literary society, and became a Freemason. ✉*Sandgate St., Tarbolton* ☏*01292/541940* ⊕*www.nts.org.uk* 🎟️*£5* ⊙*Apr.–late Sept., Fri.–Tues. 1–5.*

### WHERE TO EAT

£££ ✕**Fouter's Bistro.** Fouter's is in a long
★ and narrow cellar, yet its white walls and decorative stenciling create a sense of airiness. The cuisine is also light and skillful—no heavy sauces here. Try the roast Ayrshire lamb with pan juices, red wine, and mint, or sample the "Taste of Scotland" appetizer—smoked salmon, trout, and other goodies. This is modern Scottish and French cooking at its best. ✉*2A Academy St.* ☏*01292/261391* 🍴*DC, MC, V* ⊙*Closed Sun. and Mon.*

### SHOPPING

Ayr has a good range of shops. The **Begg & Co.** (✉*Viewfield Rd.* ☏*01292/267615*) sells a good selection of scarves, stoles, plaids, and travel rugs handmade on the premises. You can watch craftspeople at work at the jewelry workshop **Diamond Factory** (✉*26 Queen's Ct.* ☏*01292/280476*). Particularly coveted are the handmade Celtic wedding bands. The store will export your purchases if you don't have time to wait for the work to be completed.

> ## REMEMBERING MR. BURNS
>
> Born in Ayrshire, Robert Burns (1759–96) is one of Scotland's treasures. The poet and balladeer had a style that was his and his alone. His most famous song, "Auld Lang Syne," is heard everywhere on New Year's Day. Burns's talent, charisma, and good looks made him an icon to both the upper and lower classes (and made him quite popular with the ladies). Today his birthday (January 25) is considered a national holiday; on "Burns Night" young and old alike get together for Burns Suppers and recite his work over neeps, tatties, and drams of the country's finest whisky.

## CULZEAN CASTLE & COUNTRY PARK

★ 16 mi south of Alloway, 50 mi south of Glasgow.

The dramatic cliff-top Culzean (pronounced ku-*lain*) Castle and Country Park is the National Trust for Scotland's most popular property, yet it remains unspoiled. Robert Adam designed the neoclassical mansion, complete with a walled garden, in 1777. In addition to its marvelous interiors, it contains the National Guest Flat, donated by the people of Scotland in appreciation of General Eisenhower's (1890–1969) services during World War II. As president he stayed here once or twice, and his relatives still do so occasionally. Between visits it's used by the National

Trust for official entertaining. The rooms on the approach to this apartment evoke the atmosphere of World War II: mementos of Glenn Miller (1904–44), Winston Churchill (1874–1965), and other personalities of the era all help create a suitably 1940s mood. On the estate grounds, shrubberies reflect the essential mildness of this coast, though some visitors, meeting the

full force of a westerly gale, might think otherwise. Culzean's perpendicular sea cliff affords views across the Firth of Clyde to Arran and the Irish coast. Not a stone's throw away, it seems, the pinnacle of Ailsa Craig rears from midchannel. There are guided tours of the castle from July to September at 11 and 3 and from October to June at 3. ☎01655/884400 ⊕*www.nts.org.uk* ✉*Park £8; park and castle £12* ☉*Park, daily 9:30–sunset; castle, Mar.–Oct., daily 10:30–5, last admission at 4.*

## MAUCHLINE

*26 mi south of Glasgow.*

Mauchline has strong connections with Robert Burns. There's a **Burns House** here and four of his daughters are buried in the churchyard. **Poosie Nansie's Pub,** where Burns used to drink, is still serving pints today. The village is also famous for making curling stones.

## KILMARNOCK

*20 mi south of Glasgow.*

This industrial town, home of Johnny Walker whisky, has more enjoyment for Burns enthusiasts: the Dick Institute, which houses the Burns Museum and the Burns Federation.

**Dean Castle and Country Park** is a 14th-century castle with a wonderful collection of medieval arms and armor and an attractive visitor center. Burns also inevitably gets a mention. ✉*Off Glasgow Rd.* ☎01563/522702 ⊕*www.deancastle.com* ✉*Free* ☉*Apr.–Oct., daily 11–5; Nov.–Mar., weekends noon–4.*

## AYRSHIRE & THE CLYDE COAST ESSENTIALS

### TRANSPORTATION

#### BY BUS

From Glasgow, take the bus to Largs for Cumbrae; Ardrossan for Arran; Ayr and Kilmarnock for the Burns Heritage Trail; and Troon, Prestwick, and Ayr to play golf. Bus companies also operate one-day guided excursions; for details contact the tourist information center

**2**

in Glasgow, Strathclyde Passenger Transport Travel Centre. Traveline Scotland has a very helpful Web site.

**Information** **Traveline Scotland** ( ☎ *0870/608–2608* ⊕ *www.travelinescotland. com*). **SPT Travel Centre** ( ⊠ *Buchanan Bus Station, Killermont St.* ☎ *0141/333– 3708* ⊕ *www.spt.co.uk*).

### BY CAR

Begin your trip from Glasgow westbound on the M8, signposted for Glasgow Airport and Greenock. Join the A8 and follow it from Greenock to Gourock and around the coast past the Cloch Lighthouse. Head south on the A78 to the old Victorian village of Wemyss Bay and take the ferry over to Bute to see Mount Stuart (leave your car behind: a bus service takes you there from the ferry). Then continue down the A78 through Largs, Irvine, Troon, and on to Ayr and Alloway. Head to Culzean Castle, then return to Ayr and turn eastward on the B743, the Mauchline Road; but before you get here, turn left on a little road to Tarbolton and the Bachelors' Club. Return to the B743, visit Mauchline, and then head north on A76 to Kilmarnock. Glasgow is only a half hour away on the fast A77.

### BY TRAIN

You can travel via train to Largs for Cumbrae; Ardrossan for Aryan; Ayr and Kilmarnock for the Burns Heritage Trail; and Troon, Prestwick, and Ayr to play golf.

**Information** **National Rail** ( ☎ *0845/748–4950* ⊕ *www.nationalrail.co.uk*).

## CONTACTS & RESOURCES

### VISITOR INFORMATION

All of the visitor centers in the area can provide you with brochures on the Burns Heritage Trail.

**Information** **Ayr** ( ⊠ *22 The Sandgate* ☎ *08452/255121* ⊕ *www.ayrshire-arran. com*). **Irvine** ( ⊠ *New St.* ☎ *08452/255121* ⊕ *www.aboutbritain.com*). **Kilmarnock** ( ⊠ *62 Bank St.* ☎ *08452/255121* ⊕ *www.aboutbritain.com*). **Largs** ( ⊠ *Promenade* ☎ *08452/255121* ⊕ *www.largsonline.co.uk*). **Rothesay** ( ⊠ *The Winter Gardens, Rothesay, Isle of Bute* ☎ *08452/255121* ⊕ *www.isle-of-bute.com*).

# SIDE TRIPS: THE CLYDE VALLEY

The River Clyde is (or certainly was) famous for its shipbuilding and heavy industries, yet its upper reaches flow through some of Scotland's most fertile farmlands, rich with tomato crops. It's an interesting area, with ancient castles as well as museums that tell the story of manufacturing and mining prosperity.

## BLANTYRE

*8 mi southeast of Glasgow.*

In the not-very-pretty town of Blantyre, look for signs to the **David Livingstone Centre,** a park area around the tiny tenement apartment where

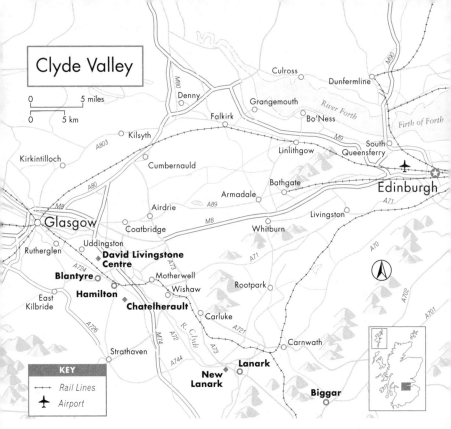

the great explorer of Africa (1813–73) was born. Displays tell of his journeys, of his meeting with Stanley ("Dr. Livingstone, I presume"), of Africa, and of the area's industrial heritage. In winter it's a good idea to call ahead. ⊠ *165 Station Rd.* ☎ *01698/823140* ⊕ *www.nts.org.uk* 🎫 *£5* ⏲ *Apr.–late Dec., Mon.–Sat. 10–5, Sun. 12:30–5.*

**Bothwell Castle,** with its well-preserved walls, dates to the 13th century and stands above the River Clyde. It's close to the David Livingstone Centre. ⊠ *Uddingston* ☎ *01698/816894* ⊕ *www.historic-scotland.gov. uk* 🎫 *£3.50* ⏲ *Apr.–Sept., daily 9:30–6.30; Oct.–Mar., Mon.–Wed. and Sat. 9:30–4.30, Sun. 2–4.30, Thurs. 9:30–noon.*

## HAMILTON

*9 mi southeast of Glasgow.*

The **Hamilton Mausoleum,** in Strathclyde Country Park near the industrial town of Hamilton, was built in the 1840s as an extraordinary monument to the lavish eccentricities of the dukes of Hamilton, who had more money than sense.

Near Hamilton is **Chatelherault** (pronounced *shat*-lerro), a unique one-room-deep facade—part shooting lodge, part glorified dog kennel—

designed in elegant Georgian style by William Adam (1689–1748) for the dukes of Hamilton. Within Chatelherault is an exhibition describing the glories of estate life. ✉*Carlisle Rd., Ferniegar* ☎*01698/426213* ☞*Free* ⊙*Mon.–Sat. 10–5, Sun. noon–5.*

## LANARK

*19 mi east of Glasgow.*

★ Set in pleasing, rolling countryside, Lanark is a typical old Scottish town. It's now most often associated with its unique neighbor **New Lanark,** a World Heritage Site that was home to a social experiment—a model community with well-designed workers' homes, a school, and public buildings. The River Clyde powers its way through a beautiful wooded gorge, and its waters were harnessed to drive textile-mill machinery before the end of the 18th century. The owner, David Dale (1739–1806), was noted for his caring attitude toward the workers, unusual for that era. Later, his son-in-law, Robert Owen (1771–1858), took this attitude even further, founding a benevolent doctrine known as Owenism and eventually crossing the Atlantic to become involved in a similar planned-community project in Indiana, called New Harmony, which, unlike New Lanark, failed. Robert Owen's son Robert Dale Owen (1801–77) helped found the Smithsonian Institution.

After many changes of fortune the mills eventually closed and were converted into a hotel and private residential properties. As a result, residents have moved in and New Lanark has maintained its unique environment, where those leading normal everyday lives mix easily with the tourists.

One of the mills has been converted into an **interpretive center,** which tells the story of this brave social experiment. Upstream, the Clyde flows through some of the finest river scenery anywhere in Lowland Scotland, with woods and spectacular waterfalls. ☎*01555/665876* ⊕*www.newlanark.org* ☞*£5.95* ⊙*Daily 11–5.*

### WHERE TO STAY

££ 🏨**New Lanark Mill Hotel.** Housed in a converted cotton mill at the 18th-century model village of New Lanark, this hotel is decorated in a spare, understated style that allows the impressive architecture of barrel-vaulted ceilings and elegant Georgian windows to speak for itself. Right next to the river in the heart of the village, the hotel has all the attractions—visitor center, shops, Falls of Clyde Wildlife Reserve—at its doorstep. **Pros:** Beautiful views of the river, large rooms, impressive spa. **Cons:** Bland bar, some rooms get cold. ✉*New Lanark, ML11 9DB* ☎*01555/667200* ⊕*www.newlanark.org* ⇋*38 rooms, 8 cottages* ⌂*In-room: no a/c. In-hotel: restaurant, pool, gym, public Wi-Fi* ▤*AE, DC, MC, V* ⊙*BP.*

### SHOPPING

Lanark has an interesting selection of shops within walking distance of each other. **McKellar's** ( ✉*41 High St.* ☎*01555/661312*) sells Charles Rennie Mackintosh–inspired designs in gold and silver. **Strands** ( ✉*8*

*Bloomgate*  ☎*01555/665757)* carries yarns and knitwear, including Arran designs and one-of-a-kind creations by Scottish designers.

## BIGGAR

*34 mi southeast of Glasgow.*

A pleasant town built of stone, Biggar is a rewarding place to spend an hour or two, out of all proportion to its size. At Biggar you are near the headwaters of the Clyde, on the moors in the center of southern Scotland. The Clyde flows west toward Glasgow and the Atlantic Ocean, and the Tweed, only a few miles away, flows east toward the North Sea. There are fine views around Biggar: to Culter Fell and to the Border Hills in the south.

**Gladstone Court Museum** paints a fascinating picture of life in the town in years past, with reconstructed Victorian-era shops, a bank, a phone exchange, and a school. ⊠*Gladstone Ct.*  ☎*01899/221050* 🖃*£2* ☉*Easter weekend, May.–Sept., Mon.–Sat. 11–4:30, Sun. 2–4:30.*

For Biggar's geology and prehistory, plus an interesting embroidery collection (including samplers and fine patchwork coverlets), visit the **Moat Park Heritage Centre,** also in the town center, in a former church. ⊠*Moat Park Church, Moat Park*  ☎*01899/221050* 🖃*£2* ☉*May–Sept., Mon.–Sat. 11–4:30, Sun. 2–5.*

The **Gasworks,** built in 1839, is a fascinating reminder of the efforts once needed to produce gas for light and heat. ⊠*Moat Park*  ☎*01899/221050* 🖃*£1.50* ☉*June–Sept., daily 2–5.*

The **Greenhill Covenanters' House** is a farmhouse filled with 17th-century furnishings, costume dolls, and rare farm breeds. The Covenanters were breakaway supporters of Presbyterianism in the 17th century. ⊠*Moat Park*  ☎*01899/221050* 🖃*£1* ☉*May–Sept., weekends 2–4:30.*

☽ **Biggar Puppet Theatre** regularly presents performances by Purves Puppets. Before and after performances, two half-hour hands-on tours led by the puppeteers are available. One tour goes backstage with the puppets being demonstrated on stage; the other tours the puppet museum. The theater also has games and a picnic area. ⊠*B7016, east of Biggar* ☎*01899/220631* ⊕*www.purvespuppets.com* 🖃*Tours £2.50; performances £6.50* ☉*Call ahead for tours.*

### WHERE TO STAY

££  🏠 **Shieldhill Castle.** This Norman manor has stood on this spot since 1199, though it was greatly enlarged in 1560. It's in an ideal location for touring the Borders—27 mi from Edinburgh and 31 mi from Glasgow. The rooms are named after great Scottish battles—Culloden, Glencoe, Bannockburn—and are furnished very comfortably, with miles of Laura Ashley–style fabrics and wallpaper. **Pros:** Charming Scottish theme, plenty of character, beautiful gardens. **Cons:** Shabby lobby, too much wallpaper, some rooms need a makeover. ⊠*Quothquan ML12 6NA* ✚*Near Biggar* ☎*01899/220035* ⊕*www.shieldhill.co.uk* ⇙*26* *rooms* &*In-room: no a/c, Wi-Fi. In-hotel: 2 restaurants, no elevator* ═MC, V ¶◎⎪BP.

## CLYDE VALLEY ESSENTIALS

### TRANSPORTATION

#### BY BUS

Buses run between Glasgow and Hamilton. Inquire at the Buchanan Street bus station for details. Traveline Scotland can provide information on schedules and fares.

Information **Buchanan Street bus station** (☎ *0141/333–3708*). **Traveline Scotland** (☎ *0870/608–2608* ⊕ *www.travelinescotland.com*).

#### BY CAR

Take the A724 east out of Glasgow, south of the river through Rutherglen toward Hamilton; it's not a very pretty route. In Blantyre look for signs to the David Livingstone Centre. From Blantyre take the main road to Hamilton. Then travel on the A72 past Chatelherault toward Lanark. You pass the ruins of medieval Craignethan Castle, lots of greenhouses, nurseries, and gnarled old orchards running down to the Clyde. Before reaching Lanark, follow the signs down a long winding hill, to New Lanark. The A72 continues south of Lanark to join the A702 near Biggar. At the end of a full day of touring you can return to Glasgow the quick way by joining the M74 from the A744 west of Lanark (the Strathaven road). Or take a more scenic route through Strathaven (pronounced *stra*-ven) itself, A726 to East Kilbride, and enter Glasgow from south of the river.

#### BY TRAIN

Service runs from Glasgow Central Station to Hamilton and Lanark; for details call National Rail, or check out the timetable online. There are no trains to Biggar, but there's a connecting bus from Hamilton to Biggar.

Information **National Rail** (☎ *0845/748–4950* ⊕ *www.nationalrail.co.uk*).

### CONTACTS & RESOURCES

#### VISITOR INFORMATION

Information **Abington** (✉ *Welcome Break Services, M74 Junction 13* ☎ *01864/502436* ⊕ *guide.visitscotland.com*). **Biggar** (✉ *155 High St.* ☎ *01899/221066* ⊕ *guide.visitscotland.com*). **Lanark** (✉ *Horsemarket, Ladyacre Rd.* ☎ *01555/661661* ⊕ *guide.visitscotland.com*).

# GLASGOW ESSENTIALS

## TRANSPORTATION

#### BY AIR

Airlines flying from Glasgow Airport to the rest of the United Kingdom and to Europe include Aer Lingus, Air Malta, British Airways, bmi/

British Midland, easyJet, Icelandair, KLM, and Zoom. Several carriers fly from North America, including Air Canada, American Airlines, Continental, and Icelandair (service via Reykjavík).

Ryanair and easyJet have sparked a major price war on the Anglo-Scottish routes (e.g., between London and Glasgow). Ryanair offers rock-bottom airfares between Prestwick and London's Stansted Airport. Budget-minded easyJet has similar services from Glasgow to Stansted and Luton, respectively.

**Information Aer Lingus** (☎ 0845/084–4444 ⊕ www.aerlingus.com). **Air Canada** (☎ 800/8712–7786 ⊕ www.aircanada.com). **Air Malta** (☎ 0845/607–3710 ⊕ www.airmalta.com). **American Airlines** (☎ 0845/778–9789 ⊕ www.aa.com). **bmi/British Midland** (☎ 0870/607–0555 ⊕ www.flybmi.com). **British Airways** (☎ 0870/850–9850 ⊕ www.ba.com). **Continental** (☎ 0845/607–6760 ⊕ www.continental.com). **easyJet** (☎ 0870/600–0000 ⊕ www.easyjet.com). **Icelandair** (☎ 0845/758–1111 ⊕ www.icelandair.com). **KLM** (☎ 0870/507–4074 ⊕ www.klm.com). **Ryanair** (☎ 0871/246–0000 ⊕ www.ryanair.com). **Zoom** (☎ 0870/240–0055 ⊕ www.flyzoom.com).

## AIRPORTS

Glasgow Airport is about 7 mi west of the city center on the M8 to Greenock. The airport serves international and domestic flights, and most major European carriers have frequent and convenient connections (some via airports in England) to many cities on the Continent. There's frequent shuttle service from London, as well as regular flights from Birmingham, Bristol, East Midlands, Leeds/Bradford, Manchester, Southampton, Isle of Man, and Jersey. There are also flights from Wales (Cardiff) and Ireland (Belfast, Dublin, and Londonderry). Local Scottish connections can be made to Aberdeen, Barra, Benbecula, Campbeltown, Inverness, Islay, Kirkwall, Shetland (Sumburgh), Stornoway, and Tiree.

Prestwick Airport, on the Ayrshire coast about 30 mi southwest of Glasgow and for some years eclipsed by Glasgow Airport, has grown in importance, not least because of lower airfares from Ryanair.

**Information Glasgow Airport** (☎ 0870/040–0008 ⊕ www.baa.co.uk). **Prestwick Airport** (☎ 01292/511006 ⊕ www.gpia.co.uk).

TRANSFERS **From Glasgow Airport:** Although there's a railway station about 2 mi from Glasgow Airport (Paisley Gilmour Street), most people travel to the city center by bus or taxi. It takes about 20 minutes, slightly longer at rush hour. Metered taxis are available outside domestic arrivals. The fare should be £15 to £18.

Express buses run from Glasgow Airport (outside departures lobby) to near the Central railway station, to Queen Street railway station, and to the Buchanan Street bus station. There's service every 15 minutes throughout the day. The fare is £3.30 on both Scottish Citylink and Fairline buses.

The drive from Glasgow Airport into the city center is normally quite easy, even if you're used to driving on the right. The M8 motorway runs beside the airport (Junction 29) and takes you straight into the Glasgow city center. Thereafter Glasgow's streets follow a grid pattern, at least in the city center. A map is useful—get one from the car-rental company.

Most companies that provide chauffeur-driven cars and tours will also do limousine airport transfers. Companies that are currently members of the Greater Glasgow and Clyde Valley Tourist Board are Charlton, Little's, and Peter Holmes.

**From Prestwick Airport:** An hourly coach service makes trips to Glasgow but takes much longer than the train. There's a rapid half-hourly train service (hourly on Sunday) direct from the terminal building to Glasgow Central. Strathclyde Passenger Transport and ScotRail offer an AirTrain discount ticket that allows you to travel for 50% off the standard rail fare. Just show a valid airline ticket (boarding cards are not accepted), for a flight to or from Prestwick Airport when you purchase your rail ticket from a booking office or conductor.

By car the city center is reached via the fast A77 in about 40 minutes (longer in rush hour). Metered taxi cabs are available at the airport. The fare to Glasgow is about £40.

Contact **Charlton** (☎ 0141/570–2000 ⊕ www.charltonlimo.com). **Little's** ( ☎ 0141/883–2111 ⊕ www.littles.co.uk). **Peter Holmes** ( ☎ 01389/830688).

## BY BUS
Glasgow's bus station is on Buchanan Street at Argyle Street, not far from Central Station. The main intercity operators are National Express and Scottish Citylink, which serve numerous towns and cities in Scotland, Wales, and England, including London; there's also service to Edinburgh. Buchanan Street is close to the underground station of the same name and to the Queen Street station. Traveline Scotland can provide information on schedules and fares.

Bus service is reliable within Glasgow, and connections are convenient from buses to trains and the underground. Note that buses require exact fare, which varies by the destination, though it's usually around £1.50

Information **Buchanan Street bus station** ( ☎ 0141/333–3708). **National Express** ( ☎ 0870/580–8080 ⊕ www.nationalexpress.co.uk). **Scottish Citylink** ( ☎ 0870/550–5050 ⊕ www.citylink.co.uk). **Traveline Scotland** ( ☎ 0870/608–2608 ⊕ www.travelinescotland.com).

## BY CAR
If you come to Glasgow from England and the south of Scotland, you'll probably approach the city from the M6, M74, and A74. The city center is clearly marked from these roads. From Edinburgh the M8 leads to the city center and is the route that cuts straight across the city center and into which all other roads feed. From the north either the A82 from Fort William or the A/M80 from Stirling also feed into the M8 in the Glasgow city center. From then on you only have to know your exit: Exit 16 serves the northern part of the city center, Exit 17/18 leads to the northwest and Great Western Road, and Exit 18/19 takes

you to the hotels of Sauchiehall Street, and the Scottish Exhibition and Conference Centre.

You don't need a car in the city center, and you're probably better off without one; though most modern hotels have their own lots, parking here can be trying. More convenient are the park-and-ride operations at underground stations (Kelvinbridge, Bridge Street, and Shields Road), which will bring you into the city center in a few minutes. The West End museums and galleries have their own lots, as does the Burrell. Parking wardens are constantly on patrol, and fines cost upward of £26 for parking illegally. Multistory garages are open 24 hours a day at the following locations: Anderston Centre, George Street, Waterloo Place, Mitchell Street, Cambridge Street, and Concert Square. Rates run between £1 and £2 per hour.

### BY SUBWAY

On Glasgow's subway lines, you can choose between flat fares (£1) and the Discovery Ticket one-day pass (£1.90, after 9:30 AM). Trains run regularly from Monday through Saturday from early morning to late evening, with a limited Sunday service, and connect the city center with the West End (for the university) and the city south of the River Clyde. Look for the orange U signs marking the 15 stations. Further information is available from Strathclyde Passenger Transport Travel Centre.

Information **Strathclyde Passenger Transport Travel Centre** ( ⊠ *St. Enoch Sq., City Center* ☎ *0870/608–2608* ⊕ *www.spt.co.uk*).

### BY TAXI

You'll find metered taxis (usually black and of the London sedan type) at stands all over the city center. Most have radio dispatch. Some have also been adapted to take wheelchairs. You can hail a cab on the street if its FOR HIRE sign is illuminated. A typical ride from the city center to the West End or the South Side costs around £6.

Contact **Glasgow Taxis** ( ☎ *0141/429–7070* ⊕ *www.glasgowtaxisltd.co.uk*).

### BY TRAIN

Glasgow has two main rail stations: Central and Queen Street. Central is the arrival and departure point for trains from London's Euston station (five hours), which come via Crewe and Carlisle in England, as well as via Edinburgh from King's Cross. It also serves other cities in the northwest of England and towns and ports in the southwest of Scotland: Kilmarnock, Dumfries, Ardrossan (for the island of Arran), Gourock (for Dunoon), Wemyss Bay (for the Isle of Bute), and Stranraer (for Ireland). The Queen Street station has frequent connections to Edinburgh (50 minutes) and onward by the east-coast route to Aberdeen or south via Edinburgh to Newcastle, York, and London's King's Cross. Other services from Queen Street go to Stirling, Perth, and Dundee; northward to Inverness, Kyle of Lochalsh, Wick, and Thurso; along the Clyde to Dumbarton and Balloch (for Loch Lomond); and on the scenic West Highland line to Oban, Fort William, and Mallaig. Oban and Mallaig have island ferry connections. For details contact National Rail.

A regular bus service links the Queen Street and Central stations. Both are close to stations on the Glasgow underground. At Queen Street go to Buchanan Street, and at Central go to St. Enoch. City taxis are available at both stations.

The Glasgow area has an extensive network of suburban railway services. Locals still call them the Blue Trains, even though most are now painted maroon and cream. Look for signs to LOW LEVEL TRAINS at the Queen Street and Central stations. For more information and a free map, call Strathclyde Passenger Transport Travel Centre or the National Rail Enquiry Line. Details are also available from the Greater Glasgow and Clyde Valley Tourist Board.

Information **Greater Glasgow and Clyde Valley Tourist Board** (⊠ *11 George Sq., near Queen Street station, City Center* ☎ *0141/204–4400* ⊕ *www.seeglasgow. com*). **National Rail** (☎ *0870/748–4950* ⊕ *www.nationalrail.co.uk*). **Strathclyde Passenger Transport Travel Centre** (⊠ *St. Enoch Sq., City Center* ☎ *0870/608– 2608* ⊕ *www.spt.co.uk*).

## CONTACTS & RESOURCES

### EMERGENCIES
In case of any emergency, dial **999** to reach an ambulance or the police or fire departments (no coins are needed for emergency calls from public phones). Note that pharmacies generally operate on a rotating basis for late-night opening; hours are posted in storefront windows. Alliance Pharmacy is open daily 9 to 9.

Dentists **Glasgow Dental Hospital** (⊠ *378 Sauchiehall St., City Center* ☎ *0141/211–9600*).

Hospitals **Glasgow Royal Infirmary** (⊠ *Castle St., near cathedral, City Center* ☎ *0141/211–4000*). **Glasgow Western Infirmary** (⊠ *Dumbarton Rd., near university, West End* ☎ *0141/211–2000*). **Southern General Hospital** (⊠ *1345 Govan Rd., south side of Clyde Tunnel, South Side* ☎ *0141/201–1100*). **Stobhill Hospital** (⊠ *133 Balornock Rd., near Royal Infirmary and Bishopriggs, North City* ☎ *0141/201–3000*).

Pharmacy **Alliance Pharmacy** (⊠ *693 Great Western Rd., West End* ☎ *0141/339– 0012*).

### INTERNET, MAIL & SHIPPING
The main post office is at St. Vincent Street, and there are many smaller post offices around the city. Internet cafés are scattered throughout the city.

Post Office **Main post office** (⊠ *St. Vincent St., City Center* ☎ *0845/722-3344*).

Internet Cafés **Easyinternetcafe** (⊠ *56–72 St. Vincent St., City Center* ☎ *0141/222-2365* ⊕ *www.glasgowontheweb.com*). **Sip n Surf** (⊠ *521 Great Western Rd., West End* ☎ *0141/339-4449* ⊕ *www.glasgowontheweb.com*). **Yehaa Internet** (⊠ *48 W. George St., City Center* ☎ *0141/332-6543* ⊕ *www. glasgowontheweb.com*).

### SIGHTSEEING TOURS

BOAT TOURS   Cruises are available on Loch Lomond and to the islands in the Firth of Clyde; contact the Greater Glasgow and Clyde Valley Tourist Board for details. Contact the *Waverley* paddle steamer from June through August, and Clyde Marine Cruises from May through September.

Contact **Clyde Marine Cruises** (⌧ *Victoria Harbour, Greenock* ☎ *01475/721281* ⊕ *www.clyde-marine.co.uk*). **Greater Glasgow and Clyde Valley Tourist Board** (⌧ *11 George Sq., near Queen Street station, City Center* ☎ *0141/204–4400* ⊕ *www.seeglasgow.com*). Waverley (⌧ *36 Anderston Quay* ☎ *0845/130–4647* ⊕ *www.waverleyexcursions.co.uk*).

BUS TOURS   City Sightseeing bus tours leave daily from the west side of George Square. The Greater Glasgow and Clyde Valley Tourist Board can give further information and arrange reservations. Details of longer tours northward to the Highlands and islands can be obtained from the tourist board or Strathclyde Passenger Transport Travel Centre.

Classic Coaches operates restored coaches from the 1950s, '60s, and '70s on tours to the north and west and to the islands. The following Glasgow companies run regular bus tours around the region: Greater Glasgow and Clyde Valley Tourist Board, Southern Coaches, and Strathclyde Passenger Transport Travel Centre.

Contact **Greater Glasgow and Clyde Valley Tourist Board** (⌧ *11 George Sq., near Queen Street station, City Center* ☎ *0141/204–4400* ⊕ *www.seeglasgow. com*). **Southern Coaches** (⌧ *Barshagra Garage, Lochlibo Rd.* ☎ *0800/298–1655* ⊕ *www.southerncoaches.co.uk*). **Strathclyde Passenger Transport Travel Centre** (⌧ *St. Enoch Sq., City Center* ☎ *0870/608–2608* ⊕ *www.spt.co.uk*).

PRIVATE GUIDES   Little's Chauffeur Drive arranges personally tailored car-and-driver tours, both locally and throughout Scotland. The Scottish Tourist Guides Association also provides a private-guide service. Taxi firms offer city tours. If you allow the driver to follow a set route, the cost is £16 per hour for up to five people. If you wish the driver to follow your own route, the charge will be £16 an hour or the reading on the meter, whichever is greater. You can book tours in advance and be picked up and dropped off wherever you like. Contact Glasgow Taxis.

Contact **Glasgow Taxis** (☎ *0141/429–7070* ⊕ *www.glasgowtaxisltd.co.uk*). **Little's Chauffeur Drive** (⌧ *1282 Paisley Rd. W, South Side* ☎ *0141/883–2111* ⊕ *www.littles.co.uk*). **Scottish Tourist Guides Association** (☎ *01786/451953* ⊕ *www.stga.co.uk*).

WALKING TOURS   The Greater Glasgow and Clyde Valley Tourist Board can provide information on special walks on a given day. Glasgow Walking organizes specialized tours of the city's architectural treasures. For spine-chilling tales about the city accompanied by costumed characters like Mary, Queen of Scots, contact Mercat Glasgow.

Contact **Glasgow Walking Tour** ( ☎ *01620/825722* ⊕ *www.glasgowarchitecture. co.uk/glasgow_walking_tours.htm*). **Greater Glasgow and Clyde Valley Tourist Board** ( ✉ *11 George Sq., near Queen Street station, City Center* ☎ *0141/204–4400* ⊕ *www.seeglasgow.com*). **Mercat Glasgow** ( ☎ *0141/586–5378* ⊕ *www.mercat-glasgow.co.uk*).

## VISITOR INFORMATION

The Greater Glasgow and Clyde Valley Tourist Board provides information and has an accommodations-booking service, a currency-exchange office, a Western Union money-transfer service, city bus tours, guided walks, boat trips, and coach tours around Scotland. Books, maps, and souvenirs are also available. The office is open October through May, Monday to Saturday 9 to 6; June and September, Monday to Saturday 9 to 7, Sunday 10 to 6; and July and August, Monday to Saturday 9 to 8, Sunday 10 to 6. The tourist board's branch office at the airport is open from Monday to Saturday 7:30 to 5, Sunday 8 to 3:30 (Sunday 7:30 to 5, April through September).

Information **Greater Glasgow and Clyde Valley Tourist Board** ( ✉ *11 George Sq., near Queen St. station, City Center* ☎ *0141/204–4400* ⊕ *www.seeglasgow.com*).

# The Borders & the Southwest

Updated by
Fiona G.
Parrott

**IF YOU'RE COMING TO SCOTLAND** by road or rail from England, you'll first encounter either the Borders area or the Southwest, also known as Dumfries and Galloway, depending on the route you take. Although you'll find no checkpoints or customs posts, the Scottish tourist authorities firmly promulgate the message that this land is indeed Scottish. And you begin to notice all the idiosyncracies that distinguish Scotland—like its myriad names for things—just as soon as you pass the first Scottish signs by the main roads heading north.

Many people rush through this area, stop in Edinburgh or Glasgow, and then plunge northward to the Highlands, thus missing portions of Scotland that are as beautiful and historically important as elsewhere. After all, the Borders and the Southwest have more stately homes, fortified castles, and medieval monastic houses than anywhere else in Scotland. If you take the time to explore, you'll see that there's more to Scotland than brooding lochs and glens.

The Borders region embraces the whole 90-mi course of one of Scotland's greatest rivers, the Tweed, and its tributaries. Passing mill chimneys, peel towers (small fortified towers), ruined abbeys, stately homes, and woodlands luxuriant with game birds, the rivers flow in a series of fast-rushing torrents and dark serpentine pools through the history of two nations. For at different times, parts of the region have been in English hands, just as slices of northern England (Berwick-upon-Tweed, for example) have been in Scottish hands.

All the main routes from London to Edinburgh traverse the Borders region, whose hinterland of undulating pastures, woods, and valleys is enclosed within three lonely groups of hills: the Cheviots, the Moorfoots, and the Lammermuirs. Innumerable hamlets and towns dot the land, giving valley slopes a lived-in look, yet the total population is still relatively sparse. Sheep outnumber human beings by 14 to 1—which is just as Sir Walter Scott, the region's most famous resident, would have wanted it. His pseudo-baronial home at Abbotsford is the most visited of Scottish literary landmarks.

To the west is the region of Dumfries and Galloway, on the shores of the Solway Firth. It might appear to be an extension of the Borders, but the Southwest has a history all its own. Inland, the earth rises toward high hills, forest, and bleak but captivating moorland, whereas nearer the coast you can find pretty farmlands, small villages, and unassuming towns. The shoreline is washed by the North Atlantic Drift (Scotland's answer to the Gulf Stream), and first-time visitors are always surprised to see palm trees and exotic plants thriving in gardens and parks along the coast.

## EXPLORING THE BORDERS & THE SOUTHWEST

The Borders region is characterized by upland moors and hills, with fertile, farmed, and forested river valleys. Borders towns cluster around and between two great rivers—the Tweed and its tributary, the Teviot. These are mostly textile towns with plenty of personality—Borders folk

## TOP REASONS TO GO

**Ancient abbeys:** The region's four ruined abbeys—Melrose, Dryburgh, Jedburgh, and Kelso—tell of a long history of struggle. Vestiges of intricately carved capitals, decorative gargoyles, and painstakingly exquisite tracery reveal a flicker of the abbeys' former brilliance.

**Country biking:** Away from busy roads, the Borders area is ideal for bicycling. In the Southwest, once you're off the beaten track, you'll discover quiet roads and country lanes that beg to be explored. There are bike-rental shops in many towns, including Pebbles, Dumfries, and Castle Douglas.

**Stately homes and castles:** Transport yourself back to a more gracious time. Paxton and Manderston Houses hold well-preserved

treasures from a bygone era, and you can sip ale on the grounds of the 12th-century Traquair House. Splendid Floors Castle is the largest inhabited castle in Scotland.

**Scott's Scotland:** This part of the country has enough monuments and sites dedicated to Sir Walter Scott to make his life and works a theme of your visit. Don't miss the epic Abbotsford House, Smailholm Tower, Dryburgh Abbey, and Scott's View.

**Sweaters and sweets:** The Borders is well known for its knitwear industry, and mill shops are abundant. Throughout the region also look for specialty peppermint or fruit-flavor boiled sweets (hard candies), tablet (a sugary caramel-like candy), and fudges. Don't worry; you won't go home empty-handed.

are sure of their own identity and are fiercely partisan toward their own native towns.

Dumfries and Galloway, especially inland, shares the upland characteristics and, if anything, has a slightly wilder air—the highest hill in Dumfries and Galloway is the Merrick, at 2,765 feet. Easygoing and peaceful, towns in this region are usually very attractive, with wide streets and colorful frontages.

The best way to explore the region is to get off the main, and often crowded, arterial roads—the A1, A697, A68, A76, A7, M74/A74, and A75—and onto the little back roads. You may occasionally be delayed by a herd of cows on their way to the milking parlor, but this is often far more pleasant than, for example, tussling on the A75 with heavy-goods vehicles rushing to make the Irish ferries.

### ABOUT THE RESTAURANTS & HOTELS

From top-quality, full-service hotels to quaint 18th-century drovers' inns to cozy bed-and-breakfasts, the Borders has all manner of lodging options. Most good restaurants in the region tend to be within hotels rather than independent establishments. Lodging in Dumfries and Galloway may be a little less expensive than in the Borders. There are farmhouse B&Bs, where mornings start with hearty, extra-fresh breakfasts. Keep in mind, though, that many of these B&Bs are *working* farms, where early-morning activity and the presence of animals are an inescapable part of the scene.

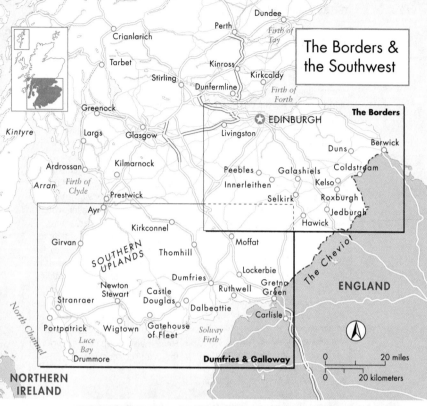

| WHAT IT COSTS IN POUNDS | | | | | |
|---|---|---|---|---|---|
| | £ | ££ | £££ | ££££ | £££££ |
| RESTAURANTS | under £10 | £10–£14 | £15–£19 | £20–£25 | over £25 |
| HOTELS | under £70 | £70–£120 | £121–£160 | £161–£220 | over £220 |

Restaurant prices are for a main course at dinner. Hotel prices are for two people in a standard double room in high season, generally including the 17.5% V.A.T.

### TIMING

Because many properties are privately owned and shut down from early autumn until early April, the area is less well suited to off-season touring than some other parts of Scotland. The region does look magnificent in autumn, however, especially along the wooded river valleys of the Borders. Late spring is the time to see the rhododendrons in the gardens of Dumfries and Galloway.

# THE BORDERS

Although the Borders has many attractions, it's most famous for being the home base for Sir Walter Scott (1771–1832), the early-19th-century poet, novelist, and creator of *Ivanhoe,* who single-handedly

# GREAT ITINERARIES

The driving distances between towns in the Borders and the Southwest are not lengthy, but traveling on narrow country roads can take a little longer than you might expect. Five days should be enough to see the most important sights of both regions. If you particularly enjoy sketching or taking photographs, this is not an area to be rushed; three days is the minimum time needed to sample an abbey or two and see the settings of Dumfries and Galloway towns.

## IF YOU HAVE 2 DAYS

If you have only two days, then you'll have to concentrate on either the Borders or Dumfries and Galloway. ⬛ **Jedburgh** is the best place to get an idea of how important the Borders abbeys were. If you cross the border to the west, head for **Kirkcudbright**, near the ⬛ Gatehouse of Fleet, for a flavor of Dumfries and Galloway.

## IF YOU HAVE 5 DAYS

Plan to divide your time between the Borders and Dumfries and Galloway; you'll have to be selective about which abbeys and stately homes you can fully explore. Jedburgh Abbey, in **Jedburgh**, is a must-see, as is the abbey at ⬛ **Melrose**. Melrose also has gardens to enjoy, several museums, and famous homes nearby, including **Abbotsford House**, home of Sir Walter Scott. Finish up at ⬛ **Peebles**, where you should allow plenty of time to shop. In Dumfries and Galloway, two full days will give you time to visit **Sweetheart Abbey**, in New Abbey, and **Caerlaverock Castle**, near Ruthwell. Try to fit in Castle Douglas and **Threave Gardens**. **Kirkcudbright**, near the ⬛ Gatehouse of Fleet, is also worth even a quick visit for its artistic connections.

transformed Scotland's image from that of a land of brutal savages to one of romantic and stirring deeds and magnificent landscapes. One of the best ways to approach this district is to make the theme of your tour the life and works of Scott. The novels of Scott are not read much nowadays—frankly, some of them are difficult to wade through—but the mystique that he created, the aura of historical romance, has outlasted his books and is much in evidence in the ruined abbeys, historical houses, and grand vistas of the Borders.

A visit to at least one of the region's four great ruined abbeys makes the quintessential Borders experience. The monks in these striking, long-abandoned religious orders were the first to work the fleeces of their sheep flocks, thus laying the groundwork for what is still the area's main manufacturing industry.

Borders folk take great pride in the region's fame as Scotland's main woolen-goods manufacturing area. To this day the residents possess a marked determination to defend their towns and communities. Changing times have allowed them to reposition their priorities: instead of guarding against southern raiders, they now concentrate on maintaining a competitive rugby team for the popular intertown rugby matches.

# The Borders

*North Sea*

ENGLAND

CHEVIOT HILLS

PENTLAND HILLS

Cockburnspath
Haddington
Fala
Dalkeith
Edinburgh
Kirkliston
Livingston
Penicuik
Heriot
Lauder
Innerleithen
Peebles
Galashiels
Abbotsford House
Melrose
Selkirk
Scott's View
Dryburgh Abbey
Bowhill
Ashkirk
Roberton
Hawick
Jedburgh
Lanton
Ancrum
Harestanes Countryside Visitor Center
Waterloo Monument
Roxburgh
Morebattle
Kelso
Roxburghe Castle
Floors Castle
Smailholm Tower
Mellerstain House
Eccles
Duns
Swinton
Coldstream
Manderston House
Paxton House

Roslin
Dundee
TO HERMITAGE CASTLE
TO CRAIK FOREST

R. Tweed
Black adder
Kale Wt.
Teviot
R. Tweed
S. Esk
N. Esk

A1
A11
M9
M8
A6093
A68
A7
A72
A703
A708
A707
A699
A698
A68
A7
A6088
B709
B6400
B6404
B6356
B6360
B6397
B6352
A698
A699
A697
A6089
A697
A6112
A6105
B6461
B6437

KEY
✈ Airport

0    10 miles
0    10 kilometers

## JEDBURGH

*50 mi south of Edinburgh, 95 mi southeast of Glasgow.*

The town of Jedburgh (*-burgh* is always pronounced *burra* in Scots) was for centuries the first major Scottish target of invading English armies. In more peaceful times it developed textile mills, most of which have since languished. The large landscaped area around the town's tourist information center was once a mill but now provides an encampment for the armies of modern tourists. The past still clings to this little town, however. The ruined abbey dominates the skyline and remains a reminder of the formerly strong, governing role of the Borders abbeys.

★ **Jedburgh Abbey,** the most impressive of the Borders abbeys, was nearly destroyed by the English earl of Hertford's forces in 1544–45, during the destructive time known as the Rough Wooing. This was English king Henry VIII's (1491–1547) armed attempt to persuade the Scots that it was a good idea to unite the kingdoms by the marriage of his young son to the infant Mary, Queen of Scots (1542–87); the Scots disagreed and sent Mary to France instead. The full story is explained in vivid detail at the **Jedburgh Abbey Visitor Centre,** which also provides information on interpreting the ruins. Ground patterns and foundations are all that remain of the once-powerful religious complex. ⊠*High St.* ☏*01835/863925* ⊕*www.historic-scotland.gov.uk* ▨*£5* ⊙*Apr.–Sept., daily 9:30–5; Oct.–Mar., daily 9:30–4.*

The **Mary, Queen of Scots House,** a *bastel* (from the French *bastille*), was the fortified town house in which, as the story goes, Mary stayed before embarking on her famous 20-mi ride to Hermitage Castle to visit her wounded lover, the earl of Bothwell (circa 1535–78). Interpretive displays relate the tale and illustrate other episodes in her life. Some of her possessions are also on display, as well as tapestries and furniture of the period. ⊠*Queen St.* ☏*01835/863331* ▨*£3* ⊙*Mar.–Nov., Mon.–Sat. 10–4:30, Sun. 11–4:30.*

**Jedburgh Castle Jail** was the site of the Howard Reform Prison established in 1820. Today you can inspect prison cells, rooms arranged with period furnishings, and costumed figures. Audiovisual displays recount the history of the Royal Burgh of Jedburgh. ⊠*Castlegate* ☏*01835/864750* ▨*£2* ⊙*Mar.–Oct., Mon.–Sat. 10–4:30, Sun. 1–4; last admission half hr before closing.*

⟳ The **Harestanes Countryside Visitor Centre,** in a former farmhouse 3 mi north of Jedburgh, conveys life in the Scottish Borders with changing art exhibitions and interpretive displays on the natural history of the region. Crafts such as woodworking and tile-making are taught at the center, and finished projects are often on display. There's a gift shop and tearoom, and outside are paths for countryside walks, plus the biggest children's play area in the Borders. The quiet roads are suitable for bicycle excursions. ⊠*Near junction of A68 and B6400* ☏*01835/830306* ▨*Free* ⊙*Apr.–Oct., daily 10–5.*

From Harestanes Countryside Visitor Centre you can see the **Waterloo Monument** on the horizon about 3 mi to the northeast. The imposing tower is an enduring reminder of the power of the landowning gentry: a marquis of Lothian built the monument in 1815, with the help of his tenants, in celebration of the victory of Wellington at Waterloo. If you have time, you can walk to the tower from the visitor center in about an hour. ⊠ *Off B6400, 5 mi north of Jedburgh.*

> **RIDING THE MARCHES**
>
> Borders communities have reestablished their identities through the gatherings known as the Common Ridings. Long ago it was essential that each town be able to defend its area, and this need became formalized in mounted gatherings to "ride the marches," or patrol the boundaries. The Common Ridings possess much more authenticity than the concocted Highland Games, so often taken to be the essence of Scotland. You can watch the excitement of clattering hooves and banners proudly displayed, but this is essentially a time for native Borderers.

**OFF THE BEATEN PATH**

**Hermitage Castle.** To appreciate the famous 20-mi ride of Mary, Queen of Scots, to visit her wounded lover, the earl of Bothwell, travel southwest from Jedburgh to this, the most complete remaining example of the bare and grim medieval border castles, full of gloom and foreboding. Restored in the early 19th century, it was built in the 14th century to guard what was at the time one of the important routes from England into Scotland. The original owner, Lord Soulis, notorious for diabolical excess, was captured by the local populace, which wrapped him in lead and boiled him in a cauldron—or so the tale goes. ⊠ *On an unnamed road 2 mi west of B6399, about 15 mi south of Hawick near Liddesdale* ☎ *01387/376222* ⊕ *www.historic-scotland.gov.uk* ⊿ *£3.50* ⊙ *Apr.–Sept., daily 9:30–5:30; last admission half hr before closing.*

**WHERE TO STAY & EAT**

££ ✕ **Cross Keys.** This traditional pub, a national treasure, specializes ★ in local ingredients, from fish to game. A splendid array of Scottish beers—real ale, as it's known here—is served. This is the quintessential village inn, right down to the green outside the front door. ⊠ *The Green, Ancrum* ☎ *01835/830344* ⊕ *www.ancrumcrosskeys.co.uk* 🞀 *DC, MC, V.*

£ ⬚ **Hundalee House.** This B&B in an 18th-century manor has richly decorated Victorian-style rooms with nice touches like four-poster beds and cozy fireplaces. Fifteen acres of gardens and woods surround the house, and there are splendid views across to the English border at Carter Bar and to the Cheviot hills in the southeast. **Pros:** Fantastic views of apple orchards, hearty breakfasts with homemade jams and honey, good children's facilities. **Cons:** Farm aromas, far from shops and restaurants. ⊠ *Off A68, 1 mi south of Jedburgh, TD8 6PA* ☎ *01835/863011* ⊕ *www.accommodation-scotland.org* 🛏 *4 rooms* ⬚ *In-room: no a/c, no phone. In-hotel: bar, no elevator* 🞀 *No credit cards* ⊙ *Closed Nov.– Mar.* ⎓ *BP.*

£ Spinney Guest House. A converted farm cottage, this B&B offers simple but carefully decorated rooms. Additionally, there are two one-bedroom wood cabins that are perfect for couples who like privacy, and a two-bedroom cabin where three people can sleep comfortably. Each cabin has a kitchenette and a small patio. The common room in the main house has several welcoming armchairs. **Pros:** Close to Jedburgh, plenty of peace and quiet, pristine cabins. **Cons:** Miles from nearest restaurant, dated decor. ⊠*The Spinney, Langlee, TD8 6PB* ☎*01835/863525* ⊕*www.thespinney-jedburgh.co.uk* ↩*3 rooms, 3 cabins* ⚒*In-room: no a/c, no phone, kitchen (some), refrigerator (some). In-hotel: no elevator* ⊟*MC, V* ⦿*BP.*

### BICYCLING

**Christopher Rainbow Tandem & Bike Hire** (⊠*8 Timpendean Cottages* ☎*01835/830326 or 07799/525123*) rents tandem bikes, mountain bikes, and touring bikes. It's on the A698 between Jedburgh and Ancrum, making it ideal for exploring the four abbeys as well as the Tweed Cycleway and Borderloop Cycleway. The company provides tour itineraries, as well as extra services such as luggage forwarding.

■TIP➡Remember that cars drive on the left side of the road; this rule applies to cyclists as well.

## KELSO

*12 mi northeast of Jedburgh.*

One of the most charming Borders burghs, Kelso is often described as having a Continental flavor—some people think its broad, paved square makes it resemble a Belgian-market town. The community has some fine examples of Georgian and Victorian Scots town architecture.

**Kelso Abbey** is the least intact ruin of the four great abbeys—just a bleak fragment of what was once the largest of the group. It was here in 1460 that the nine-year-old James III was crowned king of Scotland. On a main invasion route, the abbey was burned three times in the 1540s alone, on the last occasion by the English earl of Hertford's forces in 1545, when the 100 men and 12 monks of the garrison were butchered and the structure all but destroyed. ⊠*Bridge St.* ☎*0131/668–8800* ⊕*www.kelso.bordernet.co.uk* ⊠*Free* ⊙*Apr.–Dec., daily 24 hrs.*

Fodor'sChoice On the outskirts of Kelso stands the palatial **Floors Castle,** the largest
★ inhabited castle in Scotland. The ancestral home of the dukes of Roxburghe, Floors is an architectural extravagance bristling with pepper-mill turrets and towers. It stands on the "floors," or flat terrain, on the banks of the River Tweed opposite the barely visible ruins of Roxburghe Castle. The enormous home was built in 1721 by William Adam (1689–1748) and modified by William Playfair (1789–1857), who added the turrets and towers in the 1840s. A holly tree in the deer park marks the place where King James II of Scotland (1430–60) was killed by a cannon that "brak in the shooting." ⊠*A6089* ☎*01573/223333* ⊕*www.floorscastle.com* ⊠*Grounds £3; castle and grounds £6.50* ⊙*May–Oct., daily 11–5; last admission half hr before closing.*

Don't confuse 12th-century **Roxburghe Castle** with the comparatively youthful Floors Castle. Only traces of rubble and earthworks remain of this ancient structure. Although the modern-day village of **Roxburgh** is young, the original Roxburgh, one of the oldest burghs in Scotland, has virtually disappeared. Its name lives on in the duke's title and in the name of the old county of Roxburghshire. ✉ *Off A699, 4 mi southwest of Kelso* ☎ *No phone* ⊕ *www.discovertheborders.co.uk* ✆ *Free* ☉ *Daily sunrise–sunset.*

**3**

### WHERE TO STAY & EAT

££ ✕▦ **Edenwater House.** This handsome stone house overlooks Edenwa-
★ ter, a trout stream that runs into the River Tweed. Four well-appointed guest rooms afford superb views of the river and two of the Cheviot hills. The inn's restaurant (£££££) is filled with antiques and serves what some connoisseurs regard as the best food in the Borders. Roast saddle of hare with foie gras and fillet of monkfish crusted with basil and coriander in beurre blanc are two of the dishes you might find on the menu. The restaurant, open to nonguests on weekends, offers a £35 three-course dinner. Children under 10 are not admitted to the restaurant. **Pros:** Excellent food, romantic atmosphere, peaceful surroundings. **Cons:** Not good for families with small children, far from urban amenities. ✉ *Off B6461, Ednam, TD5 7QL* ☎ *01573/224070* ⊕ *www.edenwaterhouse.co.uk* ⬎ *4 rooms* ☖ *In-room: no a/c, no phone. In-hotel: restaurant, bar, no elevator* ▤ *MC, V* ☉ *Closed Sun.– Tues. and Jan. 1–14* ¶◯¶ *BP.*

££ ✕▦ **Ednam House Hotel.** People return again and again to this large,
★ stately hotel on the banks of the River Tweed, close to Kelso's grand abbey and sprawling Market Square. The main hall, part of the original 1761 home, welcomes you with deep-seated armchairs, lovely paintings, and an open fire. The restaurant's three windowed walls overlook the garden and river, and its Scottish fare (£££££) includes Borders beef, Highland venison, smoked wild salmon, and homemade traditional puddings. **Pros:** Great outdoor activities, atmospheric lobby, impressive restaurant. **Cons:** Hunting is popular, so dead pheasants are a common sight; some rooms need a makeover. ✉ *Bridge St., TD5 7HT* ☎ *01573/224168* ⊕ *www.ednamhouse.com* ⬎ *32 rooms* ☖ *In-room: no a/c. In-hotel: restaurant, bars, no elevator* ▤ *MC, V* ☉ *Closed late Dec. and early Jan.* ¶◯¶ *BP.*

## MELLERSTAIN HOUSE

*7 mi northwest of Kelso.*

One fine example of the Borders area's ornate country homes is Mellerstain House. Begun in the 1720s, it was finished in the 1770s by Robert Adam (1728–92) and is considered one of his finest creations. Sumptuous plasterwork covers almost all interior surfaces, and there are outstanding examples of 18th-century furnishings. The beautiful terraced gardens, open an hour before the house itself, are as renowned as the house. ✉ *Off A6089* ☎ *01573/410225* ⊕ *www.mellerstain.com* ✆ *Gardens £3.50; house and gardens £6* ☉ *May, June, and Sept., Sun.*

*and Wed. 12:30–5; July and Aug., Sun., Mon., Wed., and Thur. 12:30–5; Oct., Sun. 12:30–5; last admission half hr before closing.*

## SMAILHOLM TOWER

*6 mi south of Mellerstain House, 8 mi northwest of Kelso.*

This characteristic Borders structure stands uncompromisingly on top of a barren, rocky ridge in the hills south of Mellerstain. The 16th-century peel was built solely for defense, and its unadorned stones contrast with the luxury of Mellerstain House. If you let your imagination wander in this windy spot, you can almost see the flapping pennants and rising dust of an advancing raiding party and hear the anxious securing of doors and bolts. Sir Walter Scott found this spot inspiring. His grandfather lived nearby, and the young Scott visited the tower often during his childhood. A museum here displays costumed figures and tapestries relating to Scott's Borders folk ballads. ⊠ *Off B6404* ☎ *01573/460365* ⊕ *www.historic-scotland.gov.uk* ✆ *£3.50* ☉ *Apr.–Sept., daily 9:30–5:30; Oct., Sat.–Wed. 9:30–4:30; Nov.–Mar., weekends 9:30–4:30; last admission half hr before closing.*

## COLDSTREAM

*9 mi east of Kelso.*

Three miles west of Coldstream, the England–Scotland border comes down from the hills and runs beside the Tweed for the rest of its journey to the sea. Coldstream itself, like Gretna Green, was once a Las Vegas of sorts, where runaway couples from the south could come to get married in a time when the marriage laws of Scotland were more lenient than those of England. A plaque on the former bridge tollhouse recalls this fact. The town is also celebrated in military history: in 1659 General Monck raised a regiment of foot guards here on behalf of his exiled monarch, Charles II of England (1630–85). Known as the Coldstream Guards, the successors to this regiment have become an elite corps in the British army. Today Coldstream is still a small town, with a mix of attractive 18th- and 19th-century buildings.

The **Coldstream Museum,** in the Coldstream Guards' former headquarters, examines the history of the community. You can see 18th-century marriage contracts, pieces of masonry from the village's lost medieval convent, weapons, uniforms, and photographs. A children's play area has toys and costumes, including a child-size Coldstream Guard uniform and bearskin hat made by the Guards' regimental tailor. ⊠ *12 Market Sq.* ☎ *01890/882630* ⊕ *www.scotborders.gov.uk* ✆ *Free* ☉ *Apr.–Sept., Mon.–Sat. 10–4, Sun. 2–4; Oct., Mon.–Sat. 1–4.*

Dignified houses and gardens line the stretch of the Tweed near Coldstream. The best-known house is the **Hirsel,** where a complex of farmyard buildings now serves as a crafts center and museum, with interesting walks on the extensive grounds. It's a favorite spot for bird-watchers, and superb rhododendrons bloom here in late spring.

The house itself is not open to the public. ⊠ *A697, immediately west of Coldstream* ☎ *01890/882834* ⊕ *www.hirselcountrypark.co.uk* ⌑ *Free; parking £2.50* ⊙ *Grounds daily sunrise–sunset; museum and crafts center weekdays 10–5, weekends noon–5.*

### WHERE TO STAY & EAT

££ ✕⊡ **Wheatsheaf Hotel and Restaurant.** The Wheatsheaf is a dining estab-
★ lishment that also provides accommodation—an important distinction, according to the owner. You can have an outstanding casual meal in the black-beamed bar, but the real treat is the formal restaurant. Here, the sheer excellence of the Scottish cuisine, whether you order beef, salmon, or venison, has won widespread praise yet neither the food nor the small but carefully chosen wine list is overpriced. If you don't want to leave after your meal, stay in one of the seven country-style bedrooms. The inn is on the main street of Swinton, 6 mi north of Coldstream. **Pros:** Every detail is seen to with an attentive eye, cozy rooms, wonderful restaurant. **Cons:** Some rooms need new carpeting; on a busy road. ⊠ *Main St., Swinton TD11 3JJ* ☎ *01890/860257* ⊕ *www. wheatsheaf-swinton.co.uk* ⌑ *10 rooms* ⊘ *In-room: no a/c, DVD. In-hotel: 2 restaurants, bar, no elevator* ⊟ *MC, V* ⊙ *Restaurant closed to nonguests on Sun. in Dec. and Jan.* ⦾ *BP.*

## PAXTON HOUSE

*15 mi northeast of Coldstream.*

Stately Paxton House is a comely Palladian mansion designed in 1758 by James and John Adam, with interiors designed by their brother Robert. There's Chippendale and Trotter furniture, and the splendid Regency picture gallery, an outstation of the National Galleries of Scotland, has a magnificent collection of paintings. The garden is delightful, with a squirrel hide and a restored boathouse containing a museum of salmon fishing. The adjacent crafts shop and tearoom are open daily 9 to 5. ⊠ *Paxton* ⊹ *15 mi northeast of Coldstream, take A6112 and B6461* ☎ *01289/386291* ⊕ *www.paxtonhouse.com* ⌑ *Grounds £3; house and grounds £6* ⊙ *Apr.–Oct., daily 11–5; last tour at 4.*

## MANDERSTON HOUSE

*15 mi north of Coldstream.*

Manderston House is a good example of the grand, no-expense-spared Edwardian country house. The family that built it made its fortune selling herring to Russia. A Georgian house from the 1790s was completely rebuilt from 1903 to 1905 to the specifications of John Kinross. The silver-plated staircase was modeled after the one in the Petit Trianon, at Versailles. Look for the collection of late-19th- and early-20th-century cookie tins. There's much to see downstairs in the kitchens, and outside, among a cluster of other buildings, is the octagonal, one-of-a-kind marble dairy where lunch, dinner, or afternoon tea can be arranged for groups. You can reach the house by traveling northeast from Coldstream along the A6112 to Duns, then taking the A6105 east. ⊠ *Off A6105* ☎ *01361/882636* ⊕ *www.manderston. co.uk* ✉ *Grounds £4.50; house and grounds £8* ⊙ *Mid-May–Sept., Thurs. and Sun. 1:30–5; last entry 4:15.*

## DRYBURGH ABBEY

★  8 mi southeast of Melrose.

The final resting place of Sir Walter Scott and his wife, and the most peaceful and secluded of the Borders abbeys, Dryburgh Abbey sits on gentle parkland in a loop of the Tweed. The abbey suffered from English raids until, like Melrose, it was abandoned in 1544. The style is transitional, a mingling of rounded Romanesque and pointed early English. The north transept, where the Haig and Scott families lie buried, is lofty and pillared, and once formed part of the abbey church. ⊠ *On B6404, off A68* ☎ *01835/822381* ⊕ *www.historic-scotland.gov.uk* ✉ *£4.50* ⊙ *Apr.–Sept., daily 9:30–5:30; Oct.–Mar., daily 9:30–4:30; last entry half hr before closing.*

**OFF THE BEATEN PATH**

**Scott's View.** There's no escaping Sir Walter in this part of the country: 3 mi north of Dryburgh on the B6356 is possibly the most photographed rural view in the south of Scotland. (Perhaps the only view used more often to summon a particular interpretation of Scotland is that of Eilean Donan Castle, far to the north.) The sinuous curve of the River Tweed and the gentle landscape unfolding to the triple peaks of the Eildons and then rolling out into shadows beyond are certainly worth seeking. You arrive at this peerless vista, where Scott often came to meditate, by taking the B6356 north from Dryburgh. A poignant tale is told about the horses of Scott's funeral cortege: on their way to Dryburgh Abbey they stopped here out of habit as they had so often in the past.

### WHERE TO STAY & EAT

££££  ✕ Dryburgh Abbey Hotel. Mature woodlands and verdant lawns surround this imposing, 19th-century mansion, which is adjacent to the abbey ruins on a sweeping bend of the River Tweed. Throughout the hotel you'll feel a sense of peace and quiet in keeping with the location. The rooms are large and sumptuous, with canopy beds and lace-trimmed curtains. The restaurant (££££) specializes in Scottish fare such as roasted lamb or belly of pork. A four-course meal is a bargain at £32.50. **Pros:** Beautiful grounds, romantic setting. **Cons:** A bit isolated, not much nightlife. ⊠ *Off B6404, St. Boswells TD6 0RQ* ☎ *01835/822261* ⊕ *www. dryburgh.co.uk* ✒ *36 rooms, 2 suites* ⌂ *In-room: no a/c. In-hotel: restaurant, pool, public Wi-Fi* ⊟ *AE, MC, V* ⊠ *BP.*

## MELROSE

*15 mi west of Coldstream, 5 mi southeast of Galashiels.*

Though it's small, there is nevertheless a bustle about Melrose, the perfect example of a prosperous Scottish-market town and one of the loveliest in the Borders. It's set round a square lined with 18th- and 19th-century buildings housing myriad small shops and cafés. Despite its proximity to the much larger Galashiels, Melrose has rejected industrialization. You'll likely hear local residents greet each other by first name in the square.

★ Just off the square, down Abbey Street, sit the ruins of **Melrose Abbey,** one of the four Borders abbeys. "If thou would'st view fair Melrose aright, go visit it in the pale moonlight," wrote Scott in *The Lay of the Last Minstrel,* and so many of his fans took the advice literally that a sleepless custodian begged him to rewrite the lines. Today the abbey is still impressive: a red-sandstone shell with slender windows, delicate tracery, and carved capitals, all carefully maintained. Among the carvings high on the roof is one of a bagpipe-playing pig. An audio tour is included in the admission price. ✉ *Abbey St.* ☏ *01896/822562* ⊕ *www.historic-scotland.gov.uk* 🎫 *£5* ⊙ *Apr.–Sept., daily 9:30–5:30; Oct.–Mar., daily 9:30–4:30; last entry half hr before closing.*

The National Trust for Scotland's **Priorwood Gardens,** next to Melrose Abbey, specializes in flowers for drying. Dried flowers are on sale in the shop. Next to the gardens is an orchard with some old apple varieties. ✉ *Abbey St.* ☏ *01896/822493* ⊕ *www.nts.org.uk* 🎫 *£3* ⊙ *Jan.–Mar., Mon.–Sat. noon–4; Apr.–Dec., Mon.–Sat. 10–5, Sun. 1–5.*

☾ **Thirlestane Castle** is a large, turreted, and castellated house, part of which was built in the 13th century and part in the 16th century. It looks for all the world like a French château, and it brims with history. The former home of the Duke of Lauderdale (1616–82), one of Charles II's advisors, Thirlestane is said to be haunted by the duke's ghost. Exquisite 17th-century plaster ceilings and rich collections of paintings, porcelain, and furniture fill the rooms. In the nursery, children are invited to play with Victorian-style toys and to dress up in masks and costumes. Guided tours are available 11 to 2. ✉ *Off A68, Lauder* ✛ *9 mi north of Melrose* ☏ *01578/722430* ⊕ *www.thirlestanecastle.co.uk* 🎫 *Grounds £3; castle and grounds £7* ⊙ *May, June, and early Sept., Wed., Thurs., and Sun. 10–3; July and Aug., Sun.–Thurs., daily 10–3.*

The **Three Hills Roman Heritage Centre** exhibits such artifacts as tools, weapons, and armor, retrieved from the largest Roman settlement in Scotland, which was at nearby Newstead. A blacksmith's shop, several examples of pottery, and scale models of the fort are also on display. A guided four-hour walk along the 5-mi trail to the site departs at 1:30 on Thursday (also on Tuesday in July and August). The cost is £3. ✉ *The Ormiston, Melrose Sq.* ☏ *01896/822463* ⊕ *www.trimontium. freeserve.co.uk* 🎫 *£1.50* ⊙ *Apr.–Oct., daily 10:30–4:30.*

## WHERE TO STAY & EAT

£££ ✕ **Hoebridge Inn.** Whitewashed walls, oak-beamed ceilings, and an open
**Fodor's Choice** fire welcome you into this converted 19th-century bobbin mill. The
★ cuisine is a blend of British and Mediterranean styles with occasional Asian influences. You might have lamb served with rosemary mashed potatoes and red-currant sauce or pan-fried tiger prawns with chili and lime syrup, accompanied by a salad of bean sprouts and *mangetout* (peas in their edible pods). The inn lies in Gattonside, next to Melrose but a 2-mi drive along the B6360, thanks to the intervention of

the Tweed; you can also reach the inn by a footbridge from the town. ⊠*B360, Gattonside* ☎*01896/823082* ⊕*www.thehoebridgeinn.com* ☰*MC, V* ☽*Closed Mon. No dinner Sun.*

££   ✕⌐⌐ **Burts Hotel.** This charming whitewashed building dating from the 18th century sits in the center of Melrose. Floral pastels fill the rooms and public areas. The bar is welcoming, with a cheerful open fire and a wide selection of fine malt whiskies; it's ideal for a quiet dram before or after a meal. The vast restaurant (££££) has high-back upholstered chairs and white-linen tablecloths. Lamb with apple sauce and lentils or chicken breast with truffle foam are typical entrées on the prix-fixe menu costing £33. Fishing can be arranged. **Pros:** Walking distance to restaurants and pubs, good menu in restaurant. **Cons:** Some rooms are tiny, bland room decor. ⊠*Market Sq., TD6 9PL* ☎*01896/822285* ⊕*www.burtshotel.co.uk* ⇗*20 rooms* ♿*In-room: no a/c. In-hotel: restaurant, bar, no elevator, public Wi-Fi* ☰*AE, MC, V* ⦿*BP.*

**THE ARTS**

**The Wynd Theatre** ( ⊠*3 Buccleuch St.* ☎*01896/823854*) has a monthly program of four nights of drama from national touring companies, two concerts of folk, blues, jazz, or classical from touring national and international companies, plus screenings of classic films on two Fridays. There's an art gallery highlighting top contemporary Scottish artists. Tickets cost £10 to £12 for performances or £6 for films.

## ABBOTSFORD HOUSE

Fodor'sChoice   *2 mi west of Melrose.*
★

In 1811 Sir Walter Scott, already an established writer, bought a farm on this site named Cartleyhole, which was a euphemism for the real name, Clartyhole (*clarty* is Scots for "muddy" or "dirty"). The name was surely not romantic enough for Scott, who renamed the property Abbotsford House after a ford in the nearby Tweed used by the abbot of Melrose. Scott eventually had the house entirely rebuilt in the Scots baronial style. The result was called "the most incongruous pile that gentlemanly modernism ever devised" by art critic John Ruskin. That was Mr. Ruskin's idiosyncratic take; most people have found this to be one of the most fetching of all Scottish abodes. A gently seedy mansion chock-full of Scottish curios, paintings, and mounted deer heads, it seems an appropriate domicile for a man of such an extraordinarily romantic imagination. It's worth visiting just to feel the atmosphere that the most successful writer of his day created and to see the condition in which he wrote, driving himself to pay off his endless debts. To Abbotsford came most of the famous poets and thinkers of Scott's day, including Wordsworth and Washington Irving. With some 9,000 volumes in the library, Abbotsford is the repository for the writer's collection of Scottish memorabilia and historic artifacts. Scott died here in 1832, and the house is today owned by his descendants. ⊠*B6360, Galashiels* ☎*01896/752043* ⊕*www.scottsabbotsford.co.uk* ⊠*Grounds £2; house and grounds £6* ☽*Late Mar.–Oct., Mon.–Sat. 9:30–5, Sun., 2–5; Nov.–early Mar., weekdays by appointment only.*

## The World of Sir Walter Scott

Sir Walter Scott (1771–1832) was probably Scottish tourism's best propagandist. Thanks to his fervid "Romantik" imagination, his long narrative poems—such as *The Lady of the Lake*—and a long string of historical novels, including *Ivanhoe, Waverley, Rob Roy, Redgauntlet*, and *The Heart of Midlothian*, the world fell in love with the image of heroic Scotland. Scott wrote of Scotland as a place of Highland wilderness and clan romance, shaping outsiders' perceptions of Scotland in a way that to an extent survives even today.

Scott was born in College Wynd, Edinburgh. A lawyer by training, he was an assiduous collector of old ballads and tales. *The Lay of the Last Minstrel*, a romantic poem published in 1805, brought him fame. In 1811 Scott bought the house that was to become Abbotsford, his Borders mansion near Melrose.

Scott started on his series of Waverley novels in 1814, at first anonymously, and by 1820 had produced *Waverley, Guy Mannering, The Antiquary, Tales of My Landlord* (three series), and *Rob Roy*. Between 1820 and 1825

there followed an additional 11 titles, including *Ivanhoe* and *The Pirate*. Many of his verse narratives and novels focused on real-life settings, in particular the Trossachs, northwest of Stirling, an area that rapidly became, and still remains, popular with visitors.

Apart from his writing, Scott is also remembered for rediscovering the Honours of Scotland—the crown, scepter, and sword of state of the Scottish monarchs—in 1819. These symbols had languished at the bottom of a chest in Edinburgh Castle since 1707, when Scotland lost its independence. Today they're on display in the castle.

Abbotsford can be visited in spring and summer, and other houses associated with Scott can be seen in Edinburgh: 25 George Square, which was his father's house, and 39 Castle Street. The site of his birthplace, in College Wynd, is marked with a plaque. The most obvious structure associated with Scott is the Scott Monument on Princes Street, which looks like a Gothic rocket ship with a statue of Scott and his pet dog as passengers.

## GALASHIELS

*5 mi northwest of Melrose.*

A busy gray-stone Borders town, Galashiels is still active with textile mills and knitwear shops.

Dating from 1583, **Old Gala House** is the former home of the lairds (landed proprietors) of Galashiels. It now serves as a museum with displays on the building's history and the town of Galashiels, as well as a contemporary art gallery. You can trace your family history at a comprehensive genealogy facility. The house is a short walk from the town center. ⊠*Scott Crescent* ☎*01750/20096* ⊕*www.galashiels.bordernet. co.uk* ⊠*Free* ⊗*Apr., May, and Sept., Tues.–Sat. 10–4; June–Aug., Mon.–Sat. 10–4, Sun. 1–4; Oct., Tues.–Fri. 1–4, Sat. 10–4.*

# SELKIRK

*7 mi south of Galashiels.*

Selkirk is a hilly outpost with a smattering of antiques shops and an assortment of bakers selling the Selkirk Bannock (fruited sweet bread-cake) and other cakes. Sir Walter Scott was sheriff (judge) of Selkirkshire from 1800 until his death in 1832, and his statue stands in Market Place. The town is also near Bowhill, a stately home.

**Sir Walter Scott's Courtroom,** where he presided, contains a display examining Scott's life, his writings, and his time on the bench, and it includes an audiovisual presentation. ⊠*Market Pl.* ☎*01750/20096* ⊕*www.scottishmuseums.org.uk* ⊠*Free* ☉*Apr. and Sept., weekdays 10–4, Sat. 10–2; May–Aug., weekdays 10–4, weekends 10–2; Oct., Mon.–Sat. 1–4.*

**Halliwell's House Museum,** tucked off the main square, was once an ironmonger's shop, which is now re-created downstairs. Upstairs, an exhibit tells the town's tale, with useful background information on the Common Ridings. ⊠*Market Pl.* ☎*01750/20096* ⊕*www.scotborders.gov.uk* ⊠*Free* ☉*Apr.–June and Sept., Mon.–Sat. 10–5, Sun. 10–noon; July and Aug., Mon.–Sat. 10–5:30, Sun. 10–noon; Oct., Mon.–Sat. 10–4.*

The **Lochcarron of Scotland Cashmere and Wool Centre** houses a museum where you can tour a mill and learn about the manufacture of tartans and tweeds. ⊠*Waverley Mill, Rodgers Rd.* ☎*01750/726000* ⊕*www.lochcarron.com* ⊠*Free; tour £2.50* ☉*June–Sept., Mon.–Sat. 9–5, Sun. 11–4; Oct.–May, Mon.–Sat. 9–5. Guided tours Mon.–Thurs. at 10:30, 11:30, 1:30, and 2:30; Fri. at 10:30 and 11:30.*

**Bowhill,** one of the stately homes in the Borders, and home of the duke of Buccleuch, dates from the 19th century and houses an outstanding collection of works by Gainsborough, Van Dyck, Canaletto, Reynolds, and Raeburn, as well as porcelain and period furniture. The house itself is only open in July; the grounds have more friendly hours. It's 3 mi west of Selkirk. ⊠*Off A708* ☎*01750/22204* ⊕*www.discovertheborders.co.uk* ⊠*Grounds £3; house and grounds £7* ☉*House: July, daily 1–5; Aug., daily 10–5. Grounds: Easter holidays, weekends, and bank holidays, May and June daily 10–5; July and Aug., daily 10–5.*

# INNERLEITHEN

*15 mi northwest of Selkirk.*

☼ The main reason to come to Innerleithen is to see **Robert Smail's Printing Works.** The fully operational, restored print shop with a reconstructed waterwheel fascinates adults and older children, who can try their hand at old-fashioned typesetting. ⊠*7–9 High St.* ☎*01896/830206*

⊕*www.nts.org.uk* ☒*£5* ☉*Apr.–Oct., Thurs.–Sat. and Mon.. noon–5, Sun. 1–5; last admission at 4:15.*

Fodor'sChoice ★ Near the town of Innerleithen stands **Traquair House,** said to be the oldest continually occupied home in Scotland. Inside you're free to discover secret stairways, a maze, more than 3,000 books, and a bed used by Mary, Queen of Scots, in 1566. The 18th-century brew house still makes highly recommended ale. You may even spend the night, if you wish. ☒*B709, Traquair* ✚*1 mi from Innerleithen* ☏*01896/830323* ⊕*www.traquair.co.uk* ☒*Grounds £3.50; house and grounds £6.30* ☉*Apr. and May, daily noon–5; June–Aug., daily 10:30–5; Sept., daily noon–5; Oct., daily 11–4; Nov., weekends 11–3; last admission half hr before closing.*

#### WHERE TO STAY

££££ ▦ **Traquair House.** To stay in one of the guest rooms in the 12th-century part of Traquair House is to experience a slice of Scottish history. Each spacious room is individually decorated with antiques and canopied beds. During your stay you may explore those parts of the house that are open to the public, or walk in the parkland and gardens. In the 18th-century lower drawing room you can savor a glass of the house ale before an open fire. Dinner can be arranged. **Pros:** Stunning grounds, spacious rooms, great breakfast. **Cons:** Far from restaurants and shops, rooms fill up quickly in summer. ☒*B709, Traquair EH44 6PW* ☏*01896/830323* ⊕*www.traquair.co.uk* ⇦*3 rooms* ⌂*In-room: no a/c. In-hotel: no elevator* ▭*MC, V* ⅋*BP.*

## PEEBLES

*6 mi west of Innerleithen.*

Thanks to its excellent though pricey shopping, Peebles gives the impression of catering primarily to leisured country gentlefolk. Architecturally the town is nothing out of the ordinary, just a very pleasant burgh. Don't miss the splendid dolphins ornamenting the bridge crossing the River Tweed.

**Neidpath Castle,** a 15-minute walk upstream along the banks of the Tweed, perches artistically above a bend in the river. It comes into view as you approach through the tall trees. The castle is a medieval structure remodeled in the 17th century, with dungeons hewn from solid rock. You can return on the opposite riverbank after crossing an old, finely skewed railroad viaduct. ☒*Off A72* ☏*01721/720333* ⊕*www. discovertheborders.co.uk* ☒*£3* ☉*May–Sept., Mon.–Sat. 10:30–5, Sun. 12:30–5; last admission half hr before closing.*

The exotic, almost Moorish mosaics of the **Peebles War Memorial** ( ☒*Chambers Quadrangle, High St.*) are unique in Scotland, although most towns have a memorial to honor those killed in service. It's a remarkable tribute to the 225 Peebleans killed in World War II.

## WHERE TO STAY & EAT

**£££££** ✕⌂ **Cringletie House.** With medieval-style turrets and crow-step gables,
★ this small-scale, peaceful retreat manages to be fancy *and* homey, Victorian (it was built in the 1860s) and modern (flat-screen TVs). A British-country-house style predominates. Some of the individually decorated bedrooms have fireplaces and four-posters, and all overlook the 28-acre grounds. From the drawing room there are views over the valley. A walled garden grows produce used in the excellent restaurant (£££££), which draws locals for Scottish fare such as boned quail stuffed with trompette mushrooms, and loin of deer from the neighboring estate. The afternoon tea, served in the conservatory, is especially recommended. **Pros:** Elegant bedrooms, cozy fireplaces, decadent dining. **Cons:** Some bedrooms have low ceilings; atmosphere can be almost too quiet. ✉*Edinburgh Rd., off A703, EH45 8PL* ☎*01721/725750* ⏚*www.cringletie.com* ⤶*13 rooms* ⌂*In-room: no a/c. In-hotel: restaurant, bar, public Wi-Fi, some pets allowed* ⊟*AE, MC, V* ⦾*BP.*

**££££** ✕⌂ **Peebles Hydro.** Not only does the Hydro have something for everyFodor'sChoice one, but it has it in abundance: pony rides, a putting green, and a
★ giant chess and checkers game are just a few of the diversions. The elegant Edwardian building stands on 30 acres of land, and you're welcome to explore every inch. The public areas and most rooms have lofty ceilings and elegant, antique-reproduction furnishings. The restaurant (£££££) has a Scottish menu that includes local salmon, lamb, and beef. **Pros:** Plenty of activities, good children's programs, delicious breakfast. **Cons:** Can feel impersonal, some rooms have bland decor, reception area in need of a makeover. ✉*Innerleithen Rd., EH45 8LX* ☎*01721/720602* ⏚*www.peebleshotelhydro.com* ⤶*132 rooms* ⌂*Inroom: no a/c. In-hotel: restaurant, bar, tennis court, pool, gym, bicycles, children's programs (ages infant–16), laundry service, public Wi-Fi* ⊟*AE, DC, MC, V* ⦾*BP.*

**£££** ✕⌂ **Park Hotel.** An intimate retreat on the banks of the River Tweed at the northern tip of the Ettrick Forest, the Park Hotel offers tranquil, green surroundings and airy, modern rooms. The restaurant (£££££) serves superior Scottish cuisine; many of the dishes use locally caught salmon and trout. You are welcome to use the facilities at the Peebles Hydro Hotel, ½ mi away. **Pros:** Homey feel, great views of golf course, complimentary sherry upon arrival. **Cons:** Needs to be redecorated, some rooms have a slight doggy smell. ✉*Innerleithen Rd., EH45 8BA* ☎*01721/720451* ⏚*www.parkpeebles.co.uk* ⤶*24 rooms* ⌂*In-room: no a/c. In-hotel: restaurant, bar, some pets allowed* ⊟*AE, DC, MC, V* ⦾*BP.*

## SHOPPING

Be prepared for temptations at every turn as you browse the shops on High Street and in the courts and side streets leading off it.

If you need a rest after a heavy day of shopping, repair to the **Country Shop** ( ✉*56 High St.* ☎*01721/720630*), a gift store with a coffee shop upstairs overlooking bustling High Street. There are also cooking and garden departments. **Head to Toe** ( ✉*43 High St.* ☎*01721/722752*) stocks natural beauty products, handmade pine furniture, and handsome linens—from patchwork quilts to silk flowers. Among the many jewelers on High Street is **Keith Walter** (⊠*28 High St.* ☎*01721/720650*), a gold- and silversmith who makes items on the premises. He also stocks jewelry made by other local designers.

# DUMFRIES & GALLOWAY

Galloway covers the southwestern portion of Scotland, west of the main town of Dumfries. Here a gentle coastline gives way to farmland and then breezy uplands that gradually merge with coniferous forests. Use caution when negotiating the A75—you're liable to find aggressive trucks bearing down on you as these commercial vehicles race for the ferries at Stranraer and Cairnryan. Trucks notwithstanding, once you're off the main roads, Dumfries and Galloway offer some of the most pleasant drives in Scotland—though the occasional herd of cows on the way to be milked is a potential hazard.

## GRETNA GREEN

*10 mi north of Carlisle, 87 mi south of Glasgow, 92 mi southwest of Edinburgh.*

Gretna Green is, quite simply, an embarrassment to native Scots. What else can you say about a place that advertises "amusing joke weddings," as does one of the visitor centers here? These strange goings-on are tied to the reputation this community developed as a refuge for runaway couples from England, who once came north to take advantage of Scotland's more lenient marriage laws. This was the first place they reached on crossing the border. At one time anyone could perform a legal marriage in Scotland, and the village blacksmith (known as the "anvil priest") did the honors in Gretna Green. The blacksmith's shop is still standing, and today it contains a collection of blacksmithing tools, including the anvil over which many weddings were conducted.

## RUTHWELL

*21 mi west of Gretna, 83 mi south of Glasgow, 88 mi southwest of Edinburgh.*

North of the upper Solway Firth the countryside is flat, fertile farmland. Progressing west, however, a pleasant landscape of low, round hills begins to take over. But there are two historical features among the flatlands that should not be ignored.

Inside **Ruthwell Parish Church** is the 8th-century Ruthwell Cross, a Christian sculpture admired for the detailed biblical scenes carved onto its north and south faces. The east and west faces have carvings of vines, birds, and animals, plus verses from an Anglo-Saxon poem called *The Dream of the Rood.* Considered an idolatrous monument, it was

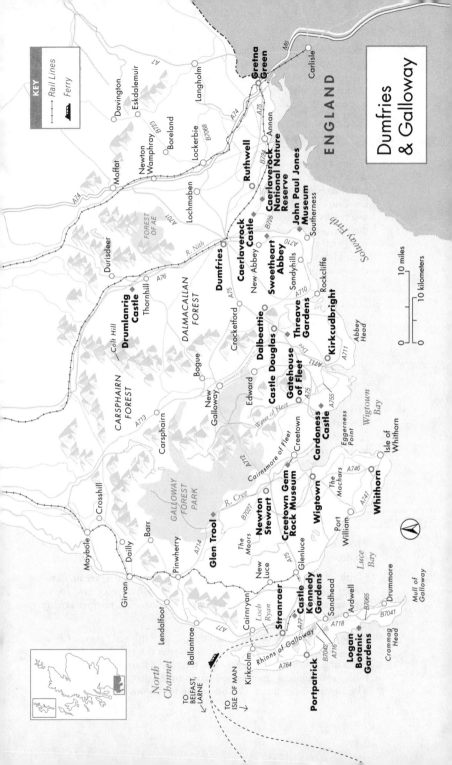

# Dumfries & Galloway

ENGLAND

## KEY

+ Rail Lines
⚓ Ferry

Carlisle

Gretna Green

Langholm

Davington

Eskdalemuir

Boreland

Lockerbie

Moffat

Newton Wamphray

Durisdeer

Thornhill

Drumlanrig Castle

Colt Hill

DALMACALLAN FOREST

FOREST OF AE

Lochmaben

Ruthwell

Annan

Caerlaverock National Nature Reserve

John Paul Jones Museum

Southerness

Solway Firth

Caerlaverock Castle

New Abbey

Sweetheart Abbey

Sandyhills

Rockcliffe

Abbey Head

Dumfries

R. Nith

Crocketford

Bogue

CARSPHAIRN FOREST

Carsphairn

Crosshill

Barr

Dailly

Maybole

Girvan

Lendalfoot

Ballantrae

North Channel

Pinwherry

Dalbeattie

Castle Douglas

Threave Gardens

Kirkcudbright

Edward

Dee

New Galloway

Water of Fleet

Gatehouse of Fleet

Cardoness Castle

Creetown

Cairnsmore of Fleet

GALLOWAY FOREST PARK

R. Cree

The Moors

Newton Stewart

Creetown Gem Rock Museum

Wigtown

Port William

The Machars

Isle of Whithorn

Eggerness Point

Wigtown Bay

Whithorn

Glen Trool

New Luce

Glenluce

Stranraer

Cairnryan

Loch Ryan

Rhinns of Galloway

Portpatrick

Kirkcolm

Castle Kennedy Gardens

Sandhead

Ardwell

Luce Bay

Drummore

Logan Botanic Gardens

Mull of Galloway

Crammag Head

TO BELFAST, LARNE

TO ISLE OF MAN

10 miles

10 kilometers

removed and demolished by Church of Scotland zealots in 1642 but was later reassembled. ⊠*6½ mi west of Annan* ☎*No phone.*

The **Savings Banks Museum,** near the church in Ruthwell, tells the story of the savings-bank movement, founded by the Reverend Dr. Henry Duncan in 1810. It's said that Duncan's bank was the first in Western history to encourage ordinary people to invest their money in savings accounts in return for interest. ⊠*6½ mi west of Annan* ☎*01387/870640* ⊕*www.savingsbanksmuseum.co.uk* ☞*Free* ♥*Apr.–Sept., Tues.–Sat. 10–4; Oct–Mar., Thurs.–Sat. 10–4.*

## CAERLAVEROCK CASTLE

Fodor'sChoice *5 mi (8 km) west of Ruthwell.*
★

The moated Caerlaverock Castle overlooks a nature reserve on a coastal loop of the B725. Built in a triangular design unique to Britain, this 13th-century fortress has solid-sandstone masonry and an imposing double-tower gatehouse. King Edward I of England (1239–1307) besieged the castle in 1300, when his forces occupied much of Scotland at the start of the Wars of Independence. The castle suffered many times in Anglo-Scottish skirmishes, as the video presentation attests. ⊠*Off B725, 5 mi west of Ruthwell* ☎*01387/770244* ⊕*www. historic-scotland.gov.uk* ☞*£5* ♥*Apr.–Sept., daily 9:30–5:30; Oct.–Mar., daily 9:30–4:30.*

The **Caerlaverock National Nature Reserve** lets you observe wintering wildfowl, including various species of geese, ducks, swans, and raptors. There are free guided walks throughout the year. ⊠*Off B725, east of Caerlaverock Castle* ☎*01387/770275* ☞*Free* ♥*Daily 24 hrs.*

## DUMFRIES

*15 mi northwest of Ruthwell, 76 mi south of Glasgow, 81 mi southwest of Edinburgh.*

Author J. M. Barrie (1860–1937) spent his childhood in Dumfries, and the garden of Moat Brae House is said to have inspired his boyish dreams in *Peter Pan*. The River Nith meanders through Dumfries, and the pedestrians-only town center makes wandering and shopping a pleasure. The town also contains the Globe Inn, a favorite *howff* (pub) of Scotland's national poet Robert Burns (1759–96), as well as one of the houses he lived in and his mausoleum.

Not surprisingly, in view of its close association to the poet, Dumfries has a **Robert Burns Centre,** housed in a sturdy former mill overlooking the river. The center has an audiovisual program and an extensive exhibit on the life of the poet. During the Dumfries Festival, held late May to early June, films are screened in the theater. ⊠*Mill Rd.* ☎*01387/264808* ⊕*www.dumfriesmuseum.demon.co.uk* ☞*Free; £1.60 for audiovisual show* ♥*Apr.–Sept., Mon.–Sat. 10–8, Sun. 2–5; Oct.–Mar., Tues.–Sat. 10–1 and 2–5.*

At the center of the village of New Abbey, 7 mi south of Dumfries, is the red-tinted and roofless **Sweetheart Abbey.** The odd name is a translation of the abbey's previous name, St. Mary of the Dolce Coeur. The abbey was founded in 1273 by the Lady of Galloway, Devorgilla (1210–90), in memory of her husband, John Balliol (?–1269), who was buried in Bardard Castle in England. It's said Devorgilla had her husband's heart embalmed and placed in a tiny casket that she carried everywhere. After she died, Devorgilla was laid to rest before the High Altar of Sweetheart Abbey with the casket resting on her breast. The couple's son, also named John (1249–1315), was the puppet king installed in Scotland by Edward of England when the latter claimed sovereignty over Scotland. After John's appointment the Scots gave him a scathing nickname that would stay with him for the rest of his life: Toom Tabard (Empty Shirt). ⊠ *A710 at New Abbey* ☎ *01387/850397* ⊕ *www.dumfriesmuseum.demon.co.uk* ⊠ *£3* ⊙ *Apr.–Sept., daily 9:30–5:30; Oct.–Mar., Sat.–Wed. 9:30–4:30.*

The little community of Kirkbean (blink and you'll miss it), 12 mi south of Dumfries, is the backdrop for Arbigland estate. It was in a cottage, now the **John Paul Jones Museum,** in this bright green landscape that John Paul (1747–92), the son of an estate gardener, was born. He eventually left Scotland, added "Jones" to his name, and became the founder of the U.S. Navy. The cottage where he was born is furnished as it would have been when John was a boy. An audio tour describes what life was like in the mid-18th century. John Paul Jones returned to raid the coastline of his native country in 1778. This exploit is described in an adjoining visitor center, where there's a replica of Jones's ship cabin. ⊠ *Off A710 near Kirkbean* ☎ *01387/880613* ⊕ *www.dumfries museum.demon.co.uk* ⊠ *£2.50* ⊙ *Apr.–June and Sept., Tues.–Sun. 10–5; July and Aug., daily 10–5.*

**OFF THE BEATEN PATH**

**Drumlanrig Castle.** This spectacular estate is as close as Scotland gets to the treasure houses of England—which is not surprising, since it's owned by the dukes of Buccleuch, one of the wealthiest British peerages. Resplendent with romantic turrets, this pink-sandstone palace was constructed between 1679 and 1691 by the first duke of Queensbury, who, after nearly bankrupting himself building the place, found it disappointing on his first overnight stay and never returned. The Buccleuchs inherited the palace and soon filled the richly decorated rooms with French furniture from the period of Louis XIV, family portraits, and a valuable collection of paintings by Holbein, Rembrandt, and Murillo. Because of the theft of a da Vinci painting in 2003, all visits are conducted by guided tour. There's also a playground, a gift shop, and a tearoom. ⊠ *Off A76 near Thornhill, about 18 mi northwest of Dumfries* ☎ *01848/600283* ⊕ *www.drumlanrig.co.uk* ⊠ *Park £4; castle and park £7* ⊙ *Grounds Apr.–Sept., daily 11–5. Castle May and June, daily noon–4; July and Aug., daily 11–4.*

## THE ARTS

**Gracefield Arts Centre** ( ⊠*28 Edinburgh Rd.* ☎*01387/262084*) has galleries with constantly changing exhibits. The **Dumfries and Galloway Arts Festival** ( ☎*01387/260447* ⊕*www.dgartsfestival.org.uk*) is usually held at the end of May at several venues throughout the region.

## BICYCLING

Cycles can be rented from **G&G Cycle Centre** ( ⊠*10–12 Academy St.* ☎*01387/259483*). The staff gives good advice on where to ride.

## SHOPPING

Dumfries is the main shopping center for the region, with all the big-name chain stores as well as specialty shops. For a souvenir that's easy to pack, try **David Hastings** ( ⊠*Maryng, Shieldhill, near Amisfield* ☎*01387/710451*), with more than 100,000 old postcards and postal history items. The store is open weekdays 10 to 3 or by appointment. The shop is in a house called Maryng in a group of houses called Shieldhill. **Greyfriars Crafts** ( ⊠*56 Buccleuch St.* ☎*01387/264050*) sells mainly Scottish goods, including glass, ceramics, and jewelry.

# DALBEATTIE

*12 mi northwest of Southerness, 89 mi south of Glasgow, 95 mi southwest of Edinburgh.*

Like the much larger Aberdeen, far to the northeast, Dalbeattie contains buildings constructed with local gray granite from the town's quarry. The well-scrubbed gray glitter makes Dalbeattie atypical of Galloway towns, where housefronts are usually painted in pastels.

## WHERE TO STAY

££ **Auchenskeoch Lodge.** This quaint and informal Victorian country
★ house, a former hunting lodge, has four cozy bedrooms. The antique furnishings have a faded elegance that will make you feel at home. You'll find full bookshelves in the sitting room, a billiards table in the game room, and a private loch and croquet lawn outdoors. The dining room serves delicious breakfasts and dinners for its guests. Many of the vegetables and herbs used in the kitchen are grown in the hotel's own gardens. **Pros:** Spacious rooms, peaceful surroundings, lovely scenery. **Cons:** Guests dine at one long table, several miles from urban amenities. ⊠*B793, 5 mi southeast of Dalbeattie, DG5 4PG* ☎*01387/780277* ⊕*www.auchenskeoch.co.uk* ⇆*4 rooms* ⌂*In-room: no a/c. In-hotel: no elevator* ⊟*No credit cards* ☉*Closed Nov.–Easter* ⏺*MAP.*

## SPORTS & THE OUTDOORS

**Barend Riding School and Trekking Centre** ( ⊠*Sandyhills* ☎*01387/780632*) helps you to a "horse-high" view of the beautiful coast and countryside. The school is 6 mi southeast of Dalbeattie on A710.

## CASTLE DOUGLAS

*6 mi west of Dalbeattie, 94 mi south of Glasgow, 99 mi southwest of Edinburgh.*

★ The main reason to come to this pleasant town is to visit **Threave Gardens.** The National Trust for Scotland cares for several garden properties, including the sloping parkland around the 1867 mansion built by William Gordon, a Liverpool businessman. Today a large section of the house has been converted into accommodations for students studying under the NTS's practical gardening program. The garden's horticultural undertaking demands the employment of many gardeners—and it's here that the gardeners train, thus ensuring there's always some fresh development or experimental planting here. You can stop by the restaurant and visitor center as well. ⊠*South of A75, 1 mi west of Castle Douglas* ☎*01556/502575* ⊕*www.nts.org.uk* ⊠*Gardens £6; house and gardens £10* ⊙*House Apr.–Oct., Wed., Thurs., Fri., and Sun. 11–3:30. Visitor center Feb., Mar., Nov., and Dec., daily 10–4; Apr.–Oct. daily 9:30–5:30.*

**Threave Castle,** not to be confused with the mansion in Threave Gardens, was an early home of the Black Douglases, who were the earls of Nithsdale and lords of Galloway. The castle was dismantled in the religious wars of the mid-17th century, though enough of it remains to have housed prisoners from the Napoleonic Wars of the 19th century. It's a few minutes from Castle Douglas by car and is signposted from the main road. To get there, you must leave your car in a farmyard and walk the rest of the way. Make your way down to the reeds by the river on an occasionally muddy path. At the edge of the river you can then ring a bell, and, rather romantically, a boatman will come to ferry you across to the great stone tower looming from a marshy island in the river. ⊠*North of A75, 3 mi west of Castle Douglas* ☎*07711/223101* ⊠*£4, includes ferry* ⊙*Castle Apr.–Sept., daily 9:30–5:30.*

### SPORTS & THE OUTDOORS

BICYCLING  You can rent bicycles from **Castle Douglas Cycle Centre** ( ⊠*Church St.* ☎*01556/504542* ⊕*www.cdbikes.co.uk*).

BOATING  The **Galloway Sailing Centre** ( ⊠*Loch Ken* ☎*01644/420626* ⊕*www. lochken.co.uk*) rents dinghies, kayaks, and canoes. It also offers sailing, windsurfing, canoeing, mountain biking, archery, and rock-climbing courses.

### SHOPPING

It's well worth the short drive north from Castle Douglas (A75 then B794) to visit **Benny Gillies Books, Maps, and Prints** ( ⊠*31–33 Victoria St., Kirkpatrick Durham* ☎*01556/650412*). The shop has an outstanding selection of secondhand and antiquarian Scottish books, hand-colored antique maps, and prints depicting areas throughout Scotland.

**Galloway Gems** ( ⊠*130–132 King St.* ☎*01556/503254*) sells mineral specimens, polished stone slices, and a range of Celtic- and Nordic-inspired jewelry. The **Posthorn** ( ⊠*26–30 St. Andrew St.* ☎*01556/502531*) is renowned for its display of figurines by Border

Fine Art as well as Scotland's biggest display of Moorcroft glazed and enamel pottery.

## KIRKCUDBRIGHT

*11 mi southwest of Castle Douglas, 103 mi south of Glasgow, 109 mi southwest of Edinburgh.*

Kirkcudbright (pronounced "Kirk-*coo*-bray") is an 18th-century town of Georgian and Victorian houses, some of them washed in pastel shades and roofed with the blue slates of the district. Since the early 20th century it has been known as a haven for artistic types, and its L-shape main street is full of crafts and antiques shops.

The **Tolbooth Arts Centre,** in the old tolbooth, gives a history of the town's artists' colony and its leaders, E. A. Hornel, Jessie King, and Charles Oppenheimer. Some of their paintings are on display, as are works by modern artists and craftspeople. ⊠*High St.* ☎*01557/331556* ⊕*www. kirkcudbright.co.uk* ☜*Free* ☉ *Oct.–May, Mon.–Sat. 11–4; June–Sept., Mon.–Sat. 11–4, Sun. 2–5.*

The 18th-century **Broughton House** was once the home of the artist E. A. Hornel, one of the "Glasgow Boys" of the late 19th century. Many of his paintings hang in the house, which is furnished in period style and contains an extensive library specializing in local history. There's also a Japanese garden. ⊠*12 High St.* ☎*01557/330437* ⊕*www.nts.org.uk* ☜*£8* ☉ *Garden: Feb. and Mar., weekdays 11–4; Apr.–June, Sept., and Oct., Thurs.–Mon. noon–5; July and Aug., daily noon–5. House: Apr.–June, Sept., and Oct., Thurs.–Mon. noon–5; July and Aug., daily noon–5.*

Conspicuous in the town center are the stone walls of **MacLellan's Castle,** a once-elaborate castellated mansion dating from the 16th century. You can walk around the interior, though the rooms are bare. There are lovely views over the town from the windows. ⊠*Off High St.* ☎*01557/331856* ⊕*www.historic-scotland.gov.uk* ☜*£3.50* ☉ *Apr.– Sept., daily 9:30–5:30.*

Stuffed with all manner of local paraphernalia, the delightfully old-fashioned **Stewartry Museum** allows you to putter and absorb as much or as little as takes your interest in the display cases. ⊠*St. Mary St.* ☎*01557/331643* ⊕*www.dum-friesmuseum.demon.co.uk* ☜*Free* ☉ *May, June, and Sept., Mon.–Sat. 11–5, Sun. 2–5; July and Aug., Mon.–Sat. 10–5, Sun. 2–5; Oct., Mon.–Sat. 11–4, Sun. 2–5; Nov.– Apr., Mon.–Sat. 11–4.*

> ### WORD OF MOUTH
>
> "So how pleasant a town to fall in. [Kirkcudbright has] nice wee shops, a good bookstore, lovely view of the river, multicolored 200-year-old houses, and dozens of little galleries." –sheila

## GATEHOUSE OF FLEET

*9 mi west of Kirkcudbright, 108 mi southwest of Glasgow, 114 mi southwest of Edinburgh.*

A peaceful, pleasant backwoods sort of place, Gatehouse of Fleet has a castle guarding its southern approach.

**Cardoness Castle** is a typical Scottish tower house, severe and uncompromising. The 15th-century structure once was the home of the McCullochs of Galloway, then the Gordons—two of the area's important and occasionally infamous families. ⊠*A75, 1 mi southwest of Gatehouse of Fleet* ☎*01557/814427* ⊕*www.historic-scotland.gov.uk* ⊠*£3.50* ⊙*Apr.–Sept., daily 9:30–5:30; Oct., Sat.–Wed. 9:30–4:30; Nov.–Mar., weekends 9:30–4:30.*

The **Mill on the Fleet** is a converted mill in which you can learn the history behind this small town's involvement in the cotton industry. Arts and crafts are on display, and the tearoom serves light lunches and delicious home-baked goods. ⊠*High St.* ☎*01557/814774* ⊕*www. millonthefleet.co.uk* ⊠*£2.50* ⊙*Apr.–Oct., daily 10:30–5.*

> ### GOLF GETAWAYS
>
> There are more than 30 courses in Dumfries and Galloway and 21 in the Borders. The Freedom of the Fairways Pass (five-day pass, £105; three-day pass, £76) allows play on all 21 Borders courses and is available from the Scottish Borders Tourist Board. The Gateway to Golf Pass (six-round pass, £99; three-round pass, £70) is accepted by all clubs in Dumfries and Galloway.

### WHERE TO STAY

££££   **Cally Palace.** Many of the public rooms in this Georgian hotel, built in 1763 as a private mansion, retain their original grandeur, with elaborate plaster ceilings and marble fireplaces. The bedrooms are individually decorated and filled with nice touches like plush robes and complimentary bottles of sherry. Surrounding the house are 150 acres of parkland, with gardens, a loch, and a golf course. In the restaurant, local ingredients star in such dishes as seared medallions of venison. The staff is exceptionally friendly and prepared to spoil you. **Pros:** Beautiful views from balconies, impressive setting, piano music at dinner. **Cons:** Decor is bland, some beds are past their prime. ⊠*Off A75, DG7 2DL* ☎*01557/814341* ⊕*www.mcmillanhotels.co.uk* ↳*56 rooms* △*In-room: no a/c (some). In-hotel: restaurant, bar, golf course, tennis court, pool, bicycles* ▤*AE, MC, V* ⊙*Closed Jan. and Feb.* ⦿*MAP.*

£   **High Auchenlarie Farmhouse.** You're sure to get a hearty breakfast at this 300-year-old working cattle ranch—sausage, bacon, eggs, and grilled tomatoes are on the menu, although lighter options are also available. Set high on a hillside overlooking Wigtown Bay, the B&B provides tremendous views—on a clear day you can see all the way to the Isle of Man. The rooms have solid wood furniture that adds to the country feel. **Pros:** Magnificent views, fun environment, great breakfasts. **Cons:** Owners sometimes close for unannounced periods, no Internet connections. ⊠*DG7 2HB* ☎*01557/840231* ↳*3 rooms* △*In-room: no a/c, no phone. In-hotel: no elevator* ▤*No credit cards* ⊙*Closed Nov.–Feb.* ⦿*BP.*

**SHOPPING**

**Galloway Lodge Preserves** (✉ *24–28 High St.* ☎ *01557/814357*) sells marmalades, mustards, chutneys, jams, and jellies, all made in the village. You can also pick up some Scottish pottery.

**EN ROUTE**

If you want to avoid the A75, take a right by the Anwoth Hotel in Gatehouse of Fleet, where the signpost points to Gatehouse Station. This route eventually leads to Creetown and will provide you with a taste of the Dumfries and Galloway hinterland. Beyond the wooded valley where the Water of Fleet runs (local rivers are often referred to as "Water of" something), dark hills and conifer plantings lend a brooding, empty air to this lonely stretch.

## NEWTON STEWART

*20 mi west of Gatehouse of Fleet, 89 mi southwest of Glasgow, 108 mi southwest of Edinburgh.*

The bustling town of Newton Stewart makes a good touring base for the western region of Galloway.

The A712 heading northeast from town takes you to the **Galloway Forest Park,** where you can walk or bicycle along the paths. At the Clatteringshaws Visitor Centre there are exhibits about the region's wildlife and a reconstruction of an Iron Age dwelling. ✉ *A712, 7 mi northeast of Newton Stewart* ☎ *01644/420285* ⊕ *www.cast.org.uk/ clatteringshaws.htm* ✆ *Free* ⊙ *May–Sept., daily 10:30–5:30; Oct.– Apr., daily 10:30–4:30.*

Birders will love the **Wood of Cree Nature Reserve,** owned and managed by the Royal Society for the Protection of Birds. In the reserve you can see such species as the redstart, pied flycatcher, and wood warbler. To get there, take the minor road that travels north from Newton Stewart alongside the River Cree east of the A714. The entrance is next to a small parking area at the side of the road. ✉ *4 mi north of Newton Stewart* ☎ *01671/402861* ✆ *Donations accepted* ⊙ *Daily 24 hrs.*

The **Creetown Gem Rock Museum,** in the nearby village of Creetown, has an eclectic mineral collection, a dinosaur egg, an erupting volcano, and a crystal cave. There's also an Internet café, a tearoom, and a shop selling stones and crystals—both loose and in settings. ✉ *Chain Rd., off A75, Creetown* ☎ *01671/820357* ⊕ *www.gemrock.net* ✆ *£3.50* ⊙ *Easter– Sept., daily 9:30–5:30; Mar.–Easter, Oct., and Nov., daily 10–4; Dec.– Feb., weekends 10–4; last admission half hr before closing.*

The **Machars** is the name given to the triangular promontory south of Newton Stewart. This is an area of pretty rolling farmlands, yellow-gorse hedgerows, rich grazing for dairy cattle, and stony prehistoric sites. Most of the glossy, green expanse is used for dairy farming. Fields are bordered by dry *stane dykes* (walls) of sharp-edge stones, and small hills and hummocks give the area its characteristic frozen-wave look, a reminder of the glacial activity that shaped the landscape.

## GLEN TROOL

★ *12 mi north of Newton Stewart, 77 mi southwest of Glasgow, 96 mi southwest of Edinburgh.*

Glen Trool, part of Galloway's Forest Park, is one of Scotland's best-kept secrets. With high purple-and-green hilltops shorn rock-bare by glaciers, and with a dark, winding loch and thickets of birch trees sounding with birdcalls, the setting almost looks more highland than the real Highlands. Note **Bruce's Stone,** just above the parking lot, marking the site where in 1307 Scotland's champion Robert the Bruce (King Robert I, 1274–1329) won his first victory in the Scottish Wars of Independence. To get here, follow the A714 north and turn right at the signpost for Glen Trool. This road leads you toward the hills that have thus far been the backdrop for the woodlands. Watch for another sign for Glen Trool. Follow this little road through increasingly wild woodland scenery to its terminus at a parking lot. Only after you have left the car and climbed for a few minutes onto a heathery knoll does the full, rugged panorama become apparent. ⊠*Bargrennan* ☎*01671/840302* ☼*Apr., Sept., and Oct., daily 10:30–4:30; May–Aug., daily 10:30–5:30* ⌨*Free.*

## WIGTOWN

*8 mi south of Newton Stewart, 96 mi southwest of Glasgow, 114 mi southwest of Edinburgh.*

More than 20 bookshops, mostly antiquarian and secondhand stores, have sprung up on the brightly painted main street of Wigtown, voted Scotland's national book town. In an area of grassy marshland near the muddy shores of Wigtown Bay there's a monument to the Wigtown Martyrs, two women who were tied to a stake and left to drown in the incoming tide in 1685, during Covenanting times. Dumfries and Galloway's history is inextricably linked with the ferocity of the so-called Killing Times (roughly 1650–99), when the Covenanters were persecuted for their belief that there should be no bishops in the Church of Scotland, and that the king should not be head of the church.

The 10-day **Wigtown Book Festival** ( ☎*01988/402036* ⊕*www.wigtown-booktown.co.uk*), held in late September and early October, has readings, performances, and other events around town.

The **Bookshop** ( ⊠*17 N. Main St.* ☎*01988/402499*), one of the country's largest secondhand bookstores, offers temptingly full shelves.

Wigtown's **Bladnoch Distillery** is Scotland's southernmost malt-whisky producer. It has a visitor center and a gift shop, and tours are available. Tours are given on the hour between 10 and 4. ⊠*Wigtown* ☎*01988/402605 or 01988/402235* ⊕*www.bladnoch.co.uk* ⌨*Free; tours £3* ☼*Easter–June, Sept., and Oct., weekdays and holidays 9–5; July and Aug., weekdays 9–5, Sat. 11–5, Sun. noon–5.*

# WHITHORN

*11 mi south of Wigtown, 107 mi southwest of Glasgow, 125 mi southwest of Edinburgh.*

The road that is now the A746 was a pilgrims' path that led to the royal burgh of Whithorn, where sat **Whithorn Priory,** one of Scotland's great medieval cathedrals, now an empty shell. It was built in the 12th century and is said to occupy the site of a former stone church, the Candida Casa, built by St. Ninian in the 4th century. As the story goes, the church housed a shrine to Ninian, the earliest of Scotland's saints, and kings and barons sought to visit the shrine at least once in their lives. As you approach the priory, observe the royal arms of pre–1707 Scotland—that is, Scotland before the Union with England—carved and painted above the *pend* (covered walkway).

FISH TALES

The Solway Firth is noted for sea fishing, particularly at the Isle of Whithorn, Port William, Portpatrick, and Stranraer. The wide range of game-fishing opportunities extends from the expensive salmon beats of the River Tweed—sometimes known by its nickname, the Queen of Scottish Rivers—to undiscovered hill *lochans* (small lakes). You must have a fishing permit, available at tourist offices, tackle shops, newsstands, and post offices; and you should obtain permission from a landowner to fish on private property. Many hotels offer on-property fishing, or transportation and equipment so you can fish nearby.

The **Whithorn Story and Visitor Centre** explains the significance of what is claimed to be the site of the earliest Christian community in Scotland. A museum has a collection of early Christian crosses. ⊠ *45–47 George St.* ☏ *01988/500508* ⊕ *www.whithorn.com* 🖃 *£3* ☾ *Apr.–Oct., daily 10:30–5; last tour at 4.*

In the Isle of Whithorn (a small seaport, not an island) are the ruins of **St. Ninian's Chapel,** where pilgrims who came by sea prayed before traveling inland to Whithorn Priory. Some people claim that this, and not Whithorn Priory, is the site of Candida Casa.

# STRANRAER

*34 mi northwest of Whithorn, 89 mi southwest of Glasgow via A77, 133 mi southwest of Edinburgh.*

Stranraer has a lovely garden and is also the main ferry port to Northern Ireland—if you happen to make a purchase in one of its shops, you may wind up with some euro coins from Ireland in your change.

★ The **Castle Kennedy Gardens** surround the shell of the original Castle Kennedy, which was burned in 1716. The current 14th earl of Stair lives on the grounds in Lochinch Castle, built in 1864 (not open to the public). Parks scattered around the property were built by the second earl of Stair in 1733. The earl was a field marshal and used his soldiers to help with the heavy work of constructing banks, ponds, and other major landscape features. When the rhododendrons are in bloom, the effect is kaleidoscopic. There's also a pleasant tearoom. ✉*North of A75, 3 mi east of Stranraer* ☎*01776/702024* ⊕*www.castlekennedy gardens.co.uk* 🎫*£4* ⏱*Easter–Sept., daily 10–5.*

## PORTPATRICK

*8 mi southwest of Stranraer, 97 mi southwest of Glasgow, 143 mi southwest of Edinburgh.*

The holiday town of Portpatrick lies across the Rhinns of Galloway from Stranraer. Once an Irish ferry port, Portpatrick's harbor eventually proved too small for larger vessels.

Today the village is the starting point for Scotland's longest official long-distance footpath, the **Southern Upland Way**, which runs a switch-back course for 212 mi to Cockburnspath, on the east side of the Borders. The path begins on the cliffs just north of the town and follows the coastline for 1½ mi before turning inland.

Just south of Portpatrick are the lichen-yellow ruins of 16th-century **Dunskey Castle**, accessible from a cliff-top path off the B7042.

★ The spectacular **Logan Botanic Gardens**, one of the National Botanic Gardens of Scotland, are a must-see for garden lovers. Displayed here are plants that enjoy the prevailing mild climate, especially tree ferns, cabbage palms, and other Southern Hemisphere exotica. There are free guided walks every second Tuesday of the month at 10:30 AM. ✉*Off B7065 at Port Logan* ☎*01776/860231* 🎫*£3.50* ⏱*Mar. and Oct., daily 10–5; May–Sept., daily 10–6.*

If you wish to visit the southern tip of the Rhinns of Galloway, called the **Mull of Galloway**, follow the B7065/B7041 until you run out of land. The cliffs and seascapes here are rugged, and there's a lighthouse and a bird reserve.

# THE BORDERS & THE SOUTHWEST ESSENTIALS

## TRANSPORTATION

### BY AIR
The nearest Scottish airports are at Edinburgh, Glasgow, and Prestwick (outside of Glasgow).

### BY BOAT & FERRY
P&O European Ferries runs a service from Larne, in Northern Ireland, to Cairnryan, near Stranraer, several times daily. The crossing takes 1 hour on the Superstar Express, 1¾ hours on other ferries. Stena Line operates a ferry service between Stranraer and Belfast.

Information **P&O European Ferries** (☎*0870/2424777* ⊕ *www.poirishsea.com*). **Stena Line** (☎*08705/707070* ⊕ *www.stenaline.com*).

### BY BUS

If you're approaching from the south, contact Scottish Citylink or National Express. For buses from Edinburgh and Glasgow, First and Stagecoach Western are two good choices. Stagecoach Western also serves towns and villages in Dumfries and Galloway.

Information **First** (☎08708/727271 ⊕ www.firstgroup.com). **National Express** (☎08705/808080 ⊕ www.nationalexpress.com). **Scottish Citylink** (☎08705/505050 ⊕ www.citylink.co.uk). **Stagecoach Western** (☎01387/253496 in Dumfries, 01563/525192 in Kilmarnock, 01776/704484 in Stranraer ⊕ www. stagecoachbus.com).

### BY CAR

The main route into both the Borders and Galloway from the south is the M6, which becomes the M74 at the border. Or you can take the scenic and leisurely A7 northeastward through Hawick toward Edinburgh or the A75 and other parallel routes westward into Dumfries and Galloway and to the ferry ports of Stranraer and Cairnryan.

There are, however, several other routes: starting from the east, the A1 brings you from the English city of Newcastle to the border in about an hour. The A1 has the added attraction of Berwick-Upon-Tweed, on the English side of the border, but traffic on the route is heavy. Moving west, the A697, which leaves the A1 north of Morpeth (in England) and crosses the border at Coldstream, is a leisurely back-road option. The A68 is probably the most scenic route to Scotland: after climbing to Carter Bar, it reveals a view of the Borders hills and windy skies before dropping into the ancient town of Jedburgh.

### BY TRAIN

There is no train service in the Borders, apart from the Edinburgh–London King's Cross line. Trains stop at Berwick-Upon-Tweed, just south of the border. First Edinburgh has a bus service linking Hawick, Selkirk, and Galashiels with rail services at Carlisle, Edinburgh, and Berwick.

There is only limited service in the Southwest. Trains from London's Euston to Glasgow stop at Carlisle, just south of the border, and some also stop at Lockerbie. There are direct trains from Carlisle to Dumfries and the Nith Valley, stopping at Gretna Green and Annan. From Glasgow, there are services to Stranraer, the Nith Valley, and Dumfries.

Information **First Edinburgh** (☎0131/663-9233 or 0870/608-2608 ⊕ www. firstgroup.com). **National Rail** (☎08457/484950 ⊕ www.nationalrail.co.uk).

## CONTACTS & RESOURCES

### EMERGENCIES

Dial **999** for an ambulance, the police, or the fire department (no coins are needed for emergency calls from public telephone booths). All towns in the region have at least one pharmacy. Pharmacies are not found in rural areas, where general practitioners often dispense medicine. The police will provide assistance in locating a pharmacist in an emergency.

### TOURS
Tours of the region are primarily conducted by Edinburgh- and Glasgow-based companies. James French runs coach tours in summer. Margot McMurdo arranges custom-tailored, chauffeur-driven tours, as well as golf and fishing packages. Her "Splendour of Scott Country" tour covers the Borders area.

Contact **James French** ( ✉ *French's Garage, Coldingham* ☎ *01890/771283* ⊕ *www.jamesfrenchandson.com*). **Margot McMurdo** ( ✉ *Tweedview Farmhouse, Oliver Farm, Tweedsmuir* ☎📠 *01899/880207* ⊕ *www.aboutscotland.com/tour/guide/margot.html*).

### VISITOR INFORMATION
The Scottish Borders Tourist Board has offices in Jedburgh and Peebles, and the Dumfries and Galloway Tourist Board can be found in Dumfries and Stranraer. Seasonal information centers are at Castle Douglas, Coldstream, Eyemouth, Galashiels, Gatehouse of Fleet, Gretna Green, Hawick, Kelso, Kirkcudbright, Langholm, Melrose, Moffat, Newton Stewart, Sanquhar, and Selkirk.

Information **Scottish Borders Tourist Board** ( ✉ *Murray's Green, Jedburgh TD8 6BE* ☎ *0870/608–0404* 📠 *High St., Peebles EH45 8AG* ☎ *0870/608–0404* ⊕ *www.scot-borders.co.uk*).

Information **Dumfries and Galloway Tourist Board** ( ✉ *64 Whitesands, Dumfries DG1 2RS* ☎ *01387/253862* 📠 *26 Harbour St., Stranraer DG9 7RA* ☎ *01776/702595* ⊕ *www.dumfriesandgalloway.co.uk* 📠 *Murray's Green, Jedburgh TD8 6BE* ☎ *0870/608–0404* 📠 *High St., Peebles EH45 8AG* ☎ *0870/608–0404* ⊕ *www.scot-borders.co.uk*)

# Fife & Angus

**WORD OF MOUTH**

"There is a string of fishing villages along the Fife coast: Crail, Anstruther, Pittenweem, etc. All have their charm and are a short drive from each other . . . Crail has the prettiest harbor, Anstruther has the very interesting fisheries museum, and Pittenweem is still a working fishing harbor. . . . There are beaches around the coast. The biggie is the West Sands in St Andrews (the one where they filmed the famous *Chariots of Fire* sequences)."

—janisj

"A friend recommended that we not miss Glamis Castle. We were there this past June and thought the castle and grounds were beautiful. Suggest you add this to your list of must-see castles."

—AKNIC

www.fodors.com/forums

Updated by
Nick Bruno

**BREEZY CLIFF-TOP WALKWAYS, FISHING VILLAGES,** and open beaches characterize Fife and Angus. They sandwich Scotland's fourth-largest—and often overlooked—city, Dundee. Scotland's east coast has only light rainfall throughout the year; northeastern Fife, in particular, may claim the record for the most sunshine and the least rainfall in Scotland, which all adds to the enjoyment when you're touring the East Neuk (*neuk,* pronounced nyook, is Scots for corner) or exploring the cobbled lanes of the famous golf center of St. Andrews.

Fife proudly styles itself as a "kingdom," and its long history—which really began when the Romans went home in the 4th century and the Picts moved in—lends some substance to the boast. From medieval times its earls were first among Scottish nobility and crowned her kings. For many, however, the most historic event in the region was the birth of golf, in the 15th century, which, legend has it, occurred in St. Andrews, an ancient university town with stone houses and seaside ruins. The Royal & Ancient Golf Club, the ruling body of the game worldwide, still has its headquarters here.

Not surprisingly, fishing and seafaring have also played a role in the history of the East Neuk coastal region. From the 16th through the 19th centuries, a large population lived and worked in the small ports and harbors that form a continuous chain around Fife's coast, which James V once called "a beggar's mantle fringed with gold." Although some fancy it a Scottish equivalent of the Italian Riviera, James V's golden fringe—today a series of waterfront villages darkened by the shrubbery of masts and rigging—is not all that golden in terms of sand or sunshine. The outlook of black rocks and seaweed may seem rather dreary to some, but the house in the villages have character, with brownstone or color-washed fronts, rusty charm, fishy weather vanes, outdoor stone stairways to upper floors, and crude carvings of anchors and lobsters on their lintels. All of the houses are crowded on steep, narrow *wynds* (narrow streets) and hugging pint-size harbors that in the golden era supported village fleets of 100 ships apiece.

North, across the Firth of Tay, lies the region of Angus, whose charm is its variety: in addition to its seacoast and pleasant Lowland market centers, there's also a hinterland of lonely rounded hills with long glens running into the typical Grampian Highland scenery beyond. One of Angus's interesting features, which it shares with the eastern Lowland edge of Perthshire, is its fruit-growing industry, which includes raspberries. The chief fruit-growing area is Strathmore, the broad vale between the northwesterly Grampian Mountains and the small coastal hills of the Sidlaws behind Dundee. Striking out from this valley, you can make a number of day trips to uplands or seacoast.

### ABOUT THE RESTAURANTS

With an affluent population, St. Andrews supports several stylish hotel restaurants. Because it's a university town and popular tourist destination, there are also many good cafés and bistro-style restaurants. In some of the West Fife towns, such as Kirkcaldy and Dunfermline, and in Dundee, restaurants serve not only traditional Scottish fare but also

## TOP REASONS TO GO

**Seeing St. Andrews:** With its medieval streets, ruined cathedral and castle, and peculiarly posh atmosphere, St. Andrews is one of the most incongruous yet beguiling places in Scotland—even without its famous golf course.

**Hitting the links:** If you can't get on the Old Course in St. Andrews by ballot or by other means, Fife and Angus have fabulous fairways aplenty, including the famous links course at Carnoustie ( ⇨ Chapter 11 for the best courses).

**Exploring East Neuk:** As you take in crow-foot gabled fisherman's cottages, winding cobbled lanes, and seaside harbor scenes and lovely beaches, you can almost imagine

the harsh lives of the hard-working Fifers who lived in tiny hamlets such as Crail and Anstruther. Today artists and visitors make it all pleasantly picturesque.

**Discovering Dundee:** This formerly industrial city is becoming better known for its vibrant arts, music, theater, restaurant, and nightlife scenes. It's in a spectacular natural setting by Britain's most powerful river, the Tay.

**Yen for the glens:** The long Angus glens such as Glen Clova that run into the wild Grampian mountains are magical places beloved of outdoors enthusiasts and those just wanting to rediscover nature.

Italian, Indian, and Chinese specialties. Bar lunches are the rule in large and small hotels throughout the region, and in seaside places the carry-*oot* (to-go) meal is an old tradition.

### ABOUT THE HOTELS

If you're staying in Fife, the obvious base is St. Andrews, with ample accommodations of all kinds. Other towns also have a reasonable selection, and you can find good hotels and guesthouses in Dunfermline and Kirkcaldy. Along the coastal strip and in the Howe of Fife between Strathmiglo and Cupar are some excellent country-house hotels, many with their own restaurants.

| WHAT IT COSTS IN POUNDS | | | | | |
|---|---|---|---|---|---|
| | £ | ££ | £££ | ££££ | £££££ |
| RESTAURANTS | under £10 | £10–£14 | £15–£19 | £20–£25 | over £25 |
| HOTELS | under £70 | £70–£120 | £121–£160 | £161–£220 | over £220 |

Restaurant prices are for a main course at dinner. Hotel prices are for two people in a standard double room in high season, generally including the 17.5% V.A.T.

## EXPLORING FIFE & ANGUS

Fife lies north of the Firth of Forth, stretching far up the Forth Valley (which is west and a little north of Edinburgh), with St. Andrews on its eastern coast. Northwest of Fife and across the Firth of Tay, the city of Dundee and its rural hinterland, Angus, stretch still farther north and west toward the foothills of the Grampian Mountains.

## GREAT ITINERARIES

Fife and Angus cover a compact area, so getting around is straightforward. You can visit everything in a series of excursions off the main north–south artery, the A90/M90, which leads from Edinburgh to Aberdeen. From here you can easily make day trips to Edinburgh, Glasgow, or Perthshire. Aberdeenshire and the Central Highlands are not too far away either.

### IF YOU HAVE 2 DAYS

Two days allow you to sample the extremes of the area in every sense. Make your way to 🖼 **St. Andrews** to take in this most attractive of Scottish east-coast Lowland towns. The next day travel north to 🖼 **Dundee** to visit this underrated city's cultural and historic attractions including the RSS *Discovery*, the DCA, the beautifully refurbished McManus Galleries and the curvaceous, Victorian Tay Rail Bridge. Another option is to head to **Kirriemuir**, a typical Angus town, where J. M. Barrie (the author of *Peter Pan*) was born, and to see the castle at **Glamis**—and perhaps to explore the hills via the glens of Angus west of Kirriemuir.

### IF YOU HAVE 5 DAYS

With five days, you can spend two or three days sampling not just 🖼 **St. Andrews** but also the rest of the East Neuk, with its characteristic pantile-roof fishing villages—**Crail, Anstruther** and its Scottish Fisheries Museum, **Pittenweem,** and, just inland, Kellie Castle—all strung along the south-facing coast. Also worth exploring are the inland communities of **Falkland**, with its gorgeous palace; and **Cupar**, close to Hill of Tarvit House and the Fife Folk Museum. For a real treat have a meal and stay overnight at the Peat Inn. If you golf, you could allocate a day on a golf course as well. In Angus you can first take in Dundee's wonderful riverside outlook and West End attractions before taking the breezy coast toward **Arbroath** and **Montrose**, near to which you can find the House of Dun. Staying overnight near 🖼 **Forfar** will bring the inland communities of **Kirriemuir, Glamis,** and **Meigle,** with its outstanding collection of early medieval sculpture, within easy reach the next day.

### TIMING

Spring in the Angus glens can be quite captivating, with the highest mountains still snow-covered. Similarly the moorland colors of autumn are appealing. In fall and winter some hotels in rural Angus fill with foreign sportspeople intent on hunting the local wildfowl. However, Fife and Angus are really spring and summer destinations, when most of the sights are open to visitors.

# ST. ANDREWS & FIFE'S EAST NEUK VILLAGES

In its western parts Fife still bears the scars of heavy industry, especially coal mining, but these signs are less evident as you move east. Northeastern Fife, around the town of St. Andrews, seems to have played no part in the Industrial Revolution; instead, its residents earned a living from the grain fields or from the sea. Fishing has been a major industry, and in the past a string of Fife ports traded across the North

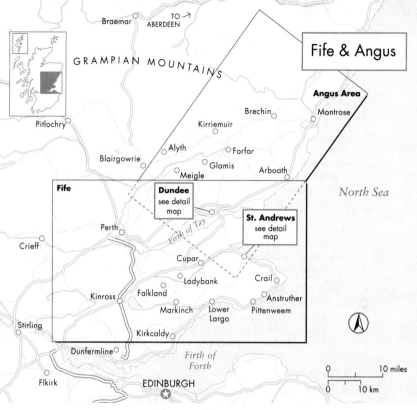

Map: Fife & Angus

Braemar
TO → ABERDEEN

GRAMPIAN MOUNTAINS

**Fife & Angus**

Pitlochry

**Angus Area**

Brechin
Montrose

Kirriemuir

Alyth
Forfar

Blairgowrie
Glamis
Arboath

Meigle

Fife

**Dundee**
see detail map

North Sea

Perth

**St. Andrews**
see detail map

Crieff

Firth of Tay

Cupar

Ladybank
Crail

Kinross
Falkland
Anstruther

Markinch
Lower Largo
Pittenweem

Stirling

Kirkcaldy

Dunfermline

Firth of Forth

Flkirk

EDINBURGH

0          10 miles
0     10 km

---

Sea. Today the legacy of Dutch-influenced architecture—crow-step gables (the stepped effect on the ends of the roofs) and distinctive town houses—gives these East Neuk villages a distinctive character.

St. Andrews is unlike any other Scottish town. Once Scotland's most powerful ecclesiastical center as well as the seat of the country's oldest university and then, much later, the very symbol and spiritual home of golf, the town has a comfortable, well-groomed air, sitting almost smugly apart from the rest of Scotland. This air of superiority has received a huge boost from Prince William's presence as a student here (he graduated in 2005), which has also led to a record number of foreign students enrolling at the university.

## ST. ANDREWS

*52 mi northeast of Edinburgh, 83 mi northeast of Glasgow.*

It may have a ruined cathedral and a grand university—the oldest in Scotland—but the modern claim to fame for St. Andrews is mainly its status as the home of golf. Forget that Scottish kings were crowned here, or that John Knox preached here, or that Reformation reformers were burned at the stake here. Thousands flock to St. Andrews to play at the Old Course, home of the Royal & Ancient Club, and to follow in the footsteps of Hagen, Sarazen, Jones, and Hogan. Of course, non-golfers can tread the city streets to take in historic sights.

The layout is pure Middle Ages: its three main streets—North, Market, and South—converge on the city's earliest religious site, near the cathedral. Like most of the ancient monuments, the cathedral ruins are impressive in their desolation—but this town is no dusty museum. The streets are busy, the shops are stylish, the gray houses sparkle in the sun, and the scene is particularly brightened during the academic year by bicycling students in scarlet gowns. You may want to take a cue from their mode of transport, as parking is notoriously difficult. ■TIP➔ If possible, visit without a car, as the town is small enough to explore on foot or by bicycle.

### MAIN ATTRACTIONS

**⑤ British Golf Museum.** This museum explores the centuries-old relationship between St. Andrews and golf and displays golf memorabilia from the 18th century to the 21st century. It's just opposite the Royal & Ancient Golf Club. ⊠*Bruce Embankment* ☎*01334/460046* ⊕*www.british golfmuseum.co.uk* ⊠*£5.25* ⊗*Mar.–Oct., Mon.–Sat. 9:30–5:30, Sun. 10–5; Nov.–Feb., Mon.–Sat. 10–4.*

**③ St. Andrews Castle.** On the shore north of the cathedral stands ruined St. Andrews Castle, begun at the end of the 13th century. The remains include a rare example of a cold and gruesome bottle-shape dungeon, in which many prisoners spent their last hours. Even more atmospheric is the castle's mine and countermine. The former was a tunnel dug by besieging forces in the 16th century; the latter, a tunnel dug by castle defenders in order to meet and wage battle below ground. You can stoop and crawl into this narrow passageway—an eerie experience, despite the addition of electric light. The visitor center has a good audiovisual presentation on the castle's history. ⊠*N. Castle St.* ☎*01334/477196* ⊕*www.historic-scotland.gov.uk* ⊠*£4; £7 includes admission to St. Rule's Tower and St. Andrews Cathedral* ⊗*Apr.–Sept., daily 9:30–5:30; Oct.–Mar., daily 9:30–4.*

**② St. Andrews Cathedral.** Near St. Rule's Tower, St. Andrews Cathedral is a ruined, poignant fragment of what was once the largest and most magnificent church in Scotland. Work on it began in 1160, and after several delays it was finally consecrated in 1318. The church was subsequently damaged by fire and repaired, but fell into decay during the Reformation. Only ruined gables, parts of the nave's south wall, and other fragments survive. The on-site museum helps you interpret the remains and gives a sense of what the cathedral must once have been like. ⊠*Off Pends Rd.* ☎*01334/477196* ⊕*www.historic-scotland.gov.*

*uk* 📧*£4; £7 includes admission to St. Rule's Tower and St. Andrews
Castle* ⊙*Apr.–Sept., daily 9:30–5:30; Oct.–Mar., daily 9:30–4.*

**❶ St. Rule's Tower.** Local legend has it that St. Andrews was founded by one
St. Regulus, or Rule, who, acting under divine guidance, carried relics
of St. Andrew by sea from Patras in Greece. He was shipwrecked on
this Fife headland and founded a church. The holy man's name survives
in the cylindrical tower, consecrated in 1126 and the oldest surviving
building in St. Andrews. You can enjoy dizzying views of town from
the top of the tower, reached via a steep set of stairs. ✉*Off Pends Rd.*
☎*01334/477196* ⊕*www.historic-scotland.gov.uk* 📧*£4; £7 includes
admission to St. Andrews Cathedral and St. Andrews Castle* ⊙*Apr.–
Sept., daily 9:30–5:30; Oct.–Mar., daily 9:30–4.*

**ALSO WORTH SEEING**

OFF THE
BEATEN
PATH

**Leuchars.** This small town has a 12th-century church with some of the
finest Norman architectural features to be seen anywhere in Scotland.
Note in particular the blind arcading (arch shapes on the wall) and
the beautifully decorated chancel and apse. On the second Saturday of
September, the **Leuchars Air Show** has performances by historic aircraft
and their contemporary counterparts. ✉*A919, 5 mi northwest of St.
Andrews* ☎*08700/130877* ⊕*www.airshow.co.uk.*

**❹ Royal & Ancient Golf Club of St. Andrews.** The ruling house of golf worldwide is the spiritual home of all who play or follow the game. Its
clubhouse on the dunes—a dignified building open to members only—
is adjacent to the famous Old Course. ✉*The Scores* ☎*01334/460000*
⊕*www.randa.org.*

**❼ St. Andrews Aquarium.** Seals, fish, crustaceans, and many other forms
☾ of marine life inhabit aquariums and pool gardens designed to simu-
late their natural habitats. ✉*The Scores, West Sands* ☎*01334/474786*
⊕*www.standrewsaquarium.co.uk* 📧*£6* ⊙*Easter–Oct., daily 10–4;
Nov.–Easter, hrs vary.*

**❻ University of St. Andrews.** St. Andrews is the site of Scotland's oldest
university. Founded in 1411, the university now consists of two stately
old colleges in the middle of town and some modern buildings on the
outskirts. A third, weatherworn college, originally built in 1512, has
become a girls' school. The university leaped into the limelight in 2007,
when the psychology department found that orangutans can commu-
nicate with humans with charadeslike hand gestures. ✉*North St.*
☎*01334/462245* ⊕*www.st-andrews.ac.uk.*

**WHERE TO STAY & EAT**

£££££ ✕**The Seafood Restaurant.** This glass-walled building is perched on the
★ banks of the West Sands. Formerly the site of an open-air theater,
the kitchen, visible to all diners, creates a sense of drama all its own. The
food is adventurous without being flashy: start with lobster in a mango
and chili sauce, then move on to the wild sea bass served with roasted
fennel. ✉*Bruce Embankment* ☎*01334/479475* ▤*AE, MC, V.*

£ ✕**West Port.** In summer while the students are away, it can be easy
to forget that St. Andrews is a university town, but this place seems

# St. Andrews

*North Sea*

*The Scores*

*Gillespie Terrace*

*Golf Pl.*

*Links Rd.*

*Old Station Rd.*

*Old Course*

*College Playing Fields*

*Guardbridge Rd.*

*Kinburn Park*

University of
St. Andrews

*City Rd.*

*Playfair Terrace*

*North St.*

*Market St.*

*South St.*

*St. Mary's Pl.*

*Alfred Pl.*

*Bridge St.*

*Thistle La.*

*Rose La.*

*Bell St.*

*Logies Ln.*

*Church St.*

*Queen's Gardens*

*Westburn La.*

*Abbey St.*

*South Castle St.*

*N. Castle St.*

*Argyle St.*

*Double Dykes Rd.*

*Kennedy Gardens*

*Kinburn Gardens*

← TO STRATHKINESS
LOW ROAD

University
Library

St. Salvator's
College

St. Mary's
College

Byre
Theatre

Queen Mary's
House

Cathedral
Ruins

*Pends Rd.*

**1** ... **2** ... **3** ... **4** ... **5** ... **6** ... **7**

0   1/8 mile
0   1/8 kilometer

British Golf Museum ........ **5**

Royal & Ancient
Golf Club of
St. Andrews ................ **4**

St. Andrews Aquarium .... **7**

St. Andrews Castle ........ **3**

St. Andrews Cathedral .... **2**

St. Rule's Tower ............ **1**

University of
St. Andrews .............. **6**

4

vibrant and youthful year-round. If you want to drink and graze, have a snack at the bar; for something more substantial, such as rib-eye steak with root-vegetable fries or oyster and pea risotto, a table at the restaurant in the back is worth the wait. ✉ *170 South St.* ☎ *01334/473186* ▤ *AE, MC, V.*

££££££ ✕🏨**Old Course Hotel.** It may rely too much on its association with its illustrious golfing neighbor, but the Old Course Hotel's fabulous location and lovely views nearly always impress. It's regularly the host of international golf stars and jet-setters. There are multiple dining choices, but to make the most of your stay here, opt for an aperitif in the Sands Bar followed by dinner in the top-floor Road Hole Grill. **Pros:** Breathtaking views, spectacular spa, golfer's heaven. **Cons:** Indifferent service, patchy air-conditioning. ✉ *Old Station Rd., KY16 9SP* ☎ *01334/474371* ⊕ *www.oldcoursehotel.co.uk* ⇄ *109 rooms, 35 suites* ⌂ *In-room: no a/c, refrigerator. In-hotel: 2 restaurants, bars, pool, gym, spa, laundry service, public Wi-Fi* ▤ *AE, MC, V* ❘❂❘*BP.*

> ## A SWING HISTORY
>
> The town of St. Andrews prospers on golf, golf schools, and golf equipment (the manufacture of golf balls is a local industry). Locals say that the game was first played with a piece of driftwood, a shore pebble, and a rabbit hole on the sandy, coastal turf. Residents of St. Andrews were playing golf on the town links as far back as the 15th century. Rich golfers eventually formed exclusive clubs. The world's first golf club was probably the Honourable Company of Edinburgh Golfers, founded in 1744. The Royal & Ancient Golf Club of St. Andrews was founded in 1754.

**4**

££££££ ✕🏨**Rufflets Country House Hotel.** Ten acres of formal and informal ★ gardens surround this creeper-covered country house just outside St. Andrews. All the rooms are beautifully decorated and have big, comfortable beds and light, well-designed bathrooms. Dinner is served in the roomy Garden Restaurant (£££££), famous for its use of local produce in memorable Scottish dishes. Try the Tay salmon or the pan-seared Rannoch venison. Lighter fare is available at the bar. **Pros:** Attractive gardens, cozy drawing room, memorable meals. **Cons:** Too far to walk to St. Andrews, guest rooms too fussy for some tastes. ✉ *Strathkinness Low Rd., KY16 9TX* ☎ *01334/472594* ⊕ *www.rufflets.co.uk* ⇄ *23 rooms, 4 suites* ⌂ *In-room: no a/c, refrigerator. In-hotel: restaurant, bar, Internet, no-smoking rooms* ▤ *AE, DC, MC, V* ❘❂❘*BP.*

££££–£££££ ✕🏨**Fairmont St Andrews.** Just 2 mi from St. Andrews, this baronial hotel ★ has spectacular views of the bay and superb golf. The rooms eschew swags and frills, opting instead for simple elegance. Look for thoughtful touches like luxurious linens on the beds and heated floors in the ample bathrooms. The restaurants are excellent: the crimson-walled Esperante (££££) offers an inventive menu that draws from the flavors of Tuscany, whereas the more casual Squire (£££) serves Scottish country-style dishes such as rump of lamb with a pea and mint puree. Golfers will find inspiration in the velvety fairways of two cliff-top courses, especially the Torrance Course: 7,037 breathtaking yards designed by the great Scottish player Sam Torrance. **Pros:** Spacious feel, excellent dining options, golf course on doorstep. **Cons:** Lacks character, unattractive mural mars otherwise impressive atrium. ⊠*St. Andrews Bay, KY16 8PN* ☎*01334/837000* ⊕*www.fairmont.com* ⇆*192 rooms, 17 suites* ⚒*In-room: safe, refrigerator, DVD, Wi-Fi. In-hotel: 3 restaurants, room service, bars, golf courses, pool, gym, spa, laundry service* ☰*AE, DC, MC, V* ⑩*BP.*

£–££   ⛉ **Aslar Guest House.** This terraced town house dating from 1865 has large rooms with ornate cornicing and antique reproduction furniture. One room has a four-poster bed, another a fireplace. St. Andrews's historic center is within walking distance. **Pros:** Homey feel, good breakfast. **Cons:** Slightly cluttered feel, gets filled up quickly. ⊠*120 North St., KY16 9AF* ☎*01334/473460* ⊕*www.aslar.com* ⇆*6 rooms* ⚒*In-room: no a/c, no phone, DVD, Wi-Fi. In-hotel: bar, no elevator* ☰*MC, V* ⑩*BP.*

£–££   ⛉ **University of St. Andrews.** For lodgings within walking distance of all the major attractions, it's hard to beat the university for value and convenience. Rooms—mainly singles—vary from merely adequate in New Hall to happily spacious in the older buildings. The newer rooms have private bathrooms. Self-catering accommodations are also available at Albany Park during the summer months. **Pros:** Convenient location, range of accommodations. **Cons:** Institutional feel, closed during school year. ⊠*79 North St., KY16 9AD* ☎*01334/462000* ⊕*www. escapetotranquillity.com* ⇆*120 rooms* ⚒*In-room: no a/c, no phone, no TV. In-hotel: restaurant, bar, laundry facilities, no elevator* ☰*MC, V* ⊙*Closed early Sept.–early June.*

## NIGHTLIFE & THE ARTS

PUBS   The stylish **West Port Bar** ( ⊠*170 South St.* ☎*01334/473186*) has a beer garden and restaurant upstairs that cater to everyone from academics to golfers.

THEATER   The **Byre Theatre** ( ⊠*Abbey St.* ☎*01334/475000* ⊕*www.byretheatre. com*) commissions and produces new works. Experimental and youth theater, small-scale operatic performances, contemporary dance, and Sunday night jazz (in the foyer) are also on the bill. There's an excellent café-bar and bistro.

## GOLF

What serious golfer doesn't dream of playing at world-famous St. Andrews? Six St. Andrews courses, all part of the St. Andrews Trust, are open to visitors, and more than 40 other courses in the region offer golf by the round or by the day. A seventh course, the Castle Course, is planned to open at St. Andrews in summer 2008; David McLay Kidd is the designer.

For information about availability—there's usually a waiting list, which varies according to the time of year—contact **St. Andrews Links Trust** ( ⊠*Pilmour House, St. Andrew* ☎*01334/466666* ⊕*www.standrews. org.uk*). Greens fees range from £64 to £130 for a round on the Old Course and from £8 to £65 for a round on the five other courses.

**Balgove Course.** Redesigned and reopened in 1993, Balgove is a beginner-friendly course at which you can turn up and tee off without prior reservation. *9 holes, 1,520 yds, par 30.*

**Eden Course.** The inland and aptly named Eden, designed in 1914 by Harry S. Colt, has an easy charm compared to the other St. Andrews Links courses. *18 holes, 6,162 yds, par 70.*

**Jubilee Course.** This windswept course, opened in 1897, offers quite a challenge even for experienced golfers. *18 holes, 6,805 yds, par 72.*

★ **New Course.** Not exactly new—it opened in 1895—the New Course is rather overshadowed by the Old Course, but it has a firm following of golfers who appreciate the loop design. *18 holes, 6,604 yds, par 71.*

**Old Course.** Believed to be the oldest golf course in the world, the Old Course was first played in the 15th century. Each year, more than 44,000 rounds are teed off, and no doubt most get stuck in one of its 112 bunkers. A handicap certificate is required. *18 holes, 6,566 yds, par 72.*

**Strathtyrum Course.** Those with a high handicap will enjoy a toddle around this course, opened in 1993, without the worry or embarrassment of holding up more experienced golfers. ■TIP➜**This course is for novices, rather than serious golfers.** *18 holes, 5,094 yds, par 69.*

### SHOPPING

**Bonkers** ( ✉ *80 Market St.* ☎ *01334/473919*) carries a huge selection of books, cards, pottery, and candles. **Renton Oriental Rugs** ( ✉ *72 South St.* ☎ *01334/476334*) is the best place in the region, if not in all Scotland, to buy rugs and carpets of all colors, patterns, and sizes. Many of those on display are antiques and most hail from Afghanistan and Iran. The **St. Andrews Pottery Shop** ( ✉ *Church Sq., between South St. and Market St.* ☎ *01334/477744*) sells decorative domestic stoneware, porcelain, ceramics, enamel jewelry, and terra-cotta pots.

---

## CRAIL

FodorsChoice ★

*10 mi south of St. Andrews via A917.*

The oldest and most aristocratic of East Neuk burghs, pretty Crail is where many fish merchants retired and built cottages. The town landmark is a picturesque Dutch-influenced town house, or *tolbooth,* which contains the oldest bell in Fife, cast in Holland in 1520. Crail is an artists' colony but remains a working harbor; take time to walk the streets and beaches and to sample fish by the harbor. ■TIP➜**As you head into East Neuk from this tiny port, look about for tolbooths, market crosses, and merchant houses and their little** *doocots* **(dovecotes, where pigeons were kept)—typical picturesque touches of this region.**

Full details on the heritage of the region can be found in the **Crail Museum & Heritage Center.** ✉ *62–64 Marketgate* ☎ *01333/450869* ⊕ *www.crail museum.org.uk* ✑ *Free* ☉ *Easter and June–Sept., Mon.–Sat. 10–1 and 2–5, Sun. 2–5; after Easter–May, weekends and holidays 2–5.*

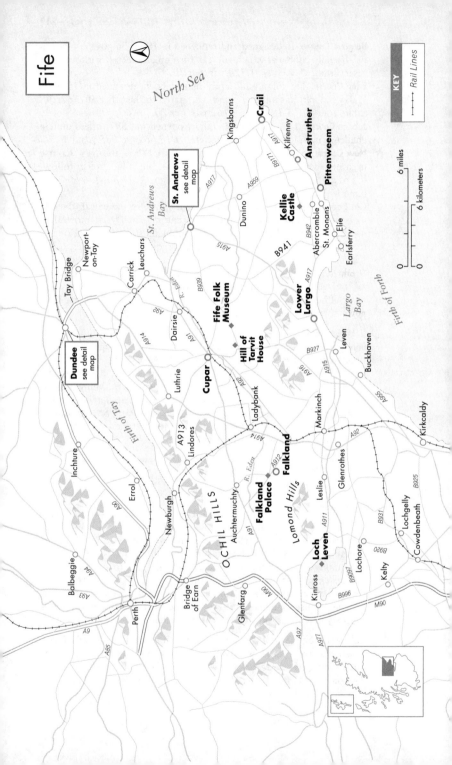

# Fife

North Sea

**KEY**
Rail Lines

6 miles
6 kilometers

Tay Bridge

Newport-on-Tay

**Dundee** see detail map

Inchture

Errol

Balbeggie

Perth

Bridge of Earn

Glenfarg

OCHIL HILLS

Newburgh

Auchtermuchty

Lindores

Luthrie

Dairsie

Carrick

Leuchars

St. Andrews Bay

**St. Andrews** see detail map

Kingsbarns

**Crail**

Kilrenny

**Anstruther**

**Pittenweem**

St. Monans

Abercrombie

Earlsferry

Elie

**Kellie Castle**

Dunino

**Fife Folk Museum**

**Hill of Tarvit House**

**Cupar**

Ladybank

Markinch

Glenrothes

Leslie

Kinross

Kelly

Loch Leven

Lochore

Lochgelly

Cowdenbeath

Lochgelly

Kirkcaldy

Buckhaven

Leven

**Lower Largo**

Largo Bay

Firth of Forth

Firth of Tay

R. Eden

R. Tay

**Falkland Palace**

**Falkland**

Lomond Hills

A917
A959
B9131
A917
B9171
B942
B941
A915
B939
A92
A91
A913
A914
A92
A916
A915
B927
A92
A90
A85
A9
A93
A94
A91
A912
A914
A911
B921
B920
B925
B931
M90
A97
A977
B9097
B996
A90
A961
A985

## ANSTRUTHER

*4 mi southwest of Crail via A917.*

Anstruther, locally called Ainster, has a lovely waterfront with a few shops brightly festooned with children's pails and shovels, a gesture to summer vacationers.

★ Facing Anstruther harbor is the **Scottish Fisheries Museum**, in a colorful cluster of buildings, the earliest of which dates from the 16th century. The museum illustrates the life of Scottish fisherfolk through documents, artifacts, model ships, paintings, and displays (complete with the reek of tarred rope and net). There are also floating exhibits at the quayside. ✉*Anstruther Harbor* ☎*01333/310628* ⊕*www. scotfishmuseum.org* 💷*£5* ⊙*Apr.–Sept., Mon.–Sat. 10–5:30, Sun. 11–5; Oct.–Mar., Mon.–Sat. 10–4:30, Sun. noon–4:30; last admission 1 hr before closing.*

> ### WALKING IN FIFE & ANGUS
>
> Fife's green and undulating landscape includes the Lomond Hills, to the west, which are easy to climb and offer fabulous views of both the Tay and Forth estuaries. The Fife Coastal Path can be bracing or an amble, depending on the stretch and the weather. The Angus Glens are on the cusp of the glorious Grampian mountains, so walkers must research the route and be prepared with map, compass, sturdy boots, and raincoats.

### WHERE TO EAT

££££ ✕ **The Cellar.** Entered through a cobbled courtyard, this unpretentious, old-fashioned restaurant is hugely popular. The low ceiling and exposed beams make for a cozy atmosphere. Specializing in seafood but serving a selection of local beef and lamb as well, the chef serves three-course meals made from top-quality ingredients cooked simply in modern Scottish style. The crayfish bisque gratin is known all over the region, as is the excellent wine list. ✉*24 E. Green* ☎*01333/310378* 🗀*AE, DC, MC, V* ⊙*Closed Sun. and Mon. Nov.–Easter.*

### NIGHTLIFE

The **Dreel Tavern** ( ✉*16 High St. W* ☎*01333/310727*) is a 16th-century coaching inn famous for its hand-drawn ales.

### BICYCLING

The back roads of Fife make pleasant places for biking. You can rent bicycles from **East Neuk Outdoors** ( ✉*Cellardyke Park* ☎*01333/311929*), which also has archery, rappelling, climbing, orienteering, and canoeing equipment.

## PITTENWEEM

*1½ mi southwest of Anstruther via A917.*

Many examples of East Neuk architecture serve as the backdrop for the working harbor at Pittenweem. Look for the crow-step gables, white *harling* (the rough mortar finish on walls), and red pantiles (roof tiles with an S-shape profile). The *weem* part of the town's name comes from the Gaelic *uaime*, meaning cave.

This town's cavern is called **St. Fillan's Cave,** which contains the shrine of St. Fillan, a 6th-century hermit who lived here. It's up a close (alleyway) behind the waterfront. If the cave isn't open, ask locals who is the latest key-holder. ✉ *Cove Wynd* 🎫 *£1* 🕙 *Mon.–Sat. 10–5, Sun. noon–5.*

**Kellie Castle,** dating from the 16th to 17th centuries and restored in Victorian times, stands among the grain fields and woodlands of north-eastern Fife. Four acres of pretty gardens surround the castle, which is in the care of the National Trust for Scotland. ✉ *B9171, 3 mi north-west of Pittenweem* ☎ *01333/720271* ⊕ *www.nts.org.uk* 🎫 *Gardens £3, gardens and castle £8* 🕙 *Castle Apr.–Oct., daily noon–5; garden year-round, daily 9:30–5:30.*

## LOWER LARGO

*10 mi west of Pittenweem via A917 and A915.*

Lower Largo's claim to fame is that it was the birthplace of Alexander Selkirk (1676–1721), the Scottish sailor who inspired Daniel Defoe's *Robinson Crusoe*. Once a juvenile delinquent, he grew up to terror-ize the region and then departed to sail the high seas. In 1704, having quarreled with his captain, Selkirk was put ashore on the isle of Juan Fernandez off the coast of Chile. Four years later a British privateer picked him up; his rescuers found him dressed in goatskins and sur-rounded by tame goats. Piratical adventures on the way home earned him a fortune, and he returned to Largo so richly dressed his mother didn't recognize him. His statue can be seen above the doorway of the house on Main Street where he was born.

### SHOPPING

At nearby Upper Largo, a converted barn is home to **Scotland's Larder** (✉ *Upper Largo* ☎ *01333/360414*), a shop that sells a huge assortment of Scottish preserves, baked goods, and seasonal produce—anything from smoked salmon and oysters to shortbread and Dundee cakes (a rich fruit cake with a distinctive, circular pattern of split almonds on the top). It has tastings, talks, and cooking demonstrations, all of which show off the savory foods of Scotland.

## FALKLAND

Fodor'sChoice   *14 mi northwest of Lower Largo.*
★

One of the loveliest communities in Scotland, Falkland is a royal burgh of twisting streets and crooked stone houses.

★ **Falkland Palace,** a former hunting lodge of the Stuart monarchs, domi-nates the town. The castle is one of the earliest examples in Britain of the French Renaissance style. Overlooking the main street is the palace's most impressive feature—the walls and chambers on its south side, all rich with Renaissance buttresses and stone medallions, built by French masons in the 1530s for King James V (1512–42). He died here, and the palace was a favorite resort of his daughter, Mary, Queen of Scots (1542–87). In the beautiful gardens, overlooked by the palace turret windows, you may easily imagine yourself back at the solemn hour when James on his deathbed pronounced the doom of the house of Stuart: "It cam' wi' a lass and it'll gang wi' a lass." ⊠*Main St.* ☎*01337/857397* ⊕*www.nts.org.*

---

**TENNIS, ANYONE?**

The gardens behind Falkland Palace contain a rare survivor: a royal tennis court, built in 1539. It's not at all like its modern counterpart. Look out for the four *Lunes* (holes in the wall) and the *ais* (a vertical green board), both of which feature in the *jeu quarré* (square-court) version of the game.

---

*uk* ⊠*Gardens £5; gardens and palace £10* ☉*Mar.–Oct., Mon.–Sat. 10–6, Sun. 1–5.*

## LOCH LEVEN

*10 mi southwest of Falkland via A911.*

Scotland's largest Lowland loch, Loch Leven is famed for its fighting trout. The area is also noted for abundant bird life, particularly its wintering wildfowl. Mary, Queen of Scots, was forced to sign the deed of abdication in her island prison in the loch.

On the southern shore overlooking the lock, **Vane Farm Nature Reserve,** a visitor center run by the Royal Society for the Protection of Birds, provides information about Loch Leven's ecology. ⊠*Vane Farm, Rte. B9097, off M90 and B996* ☎*01577/862355* ⊕*www.rspb.org.uk* ⊠*£4* ☉*Daily 10–5.*

## CUPAR

*21 mi northwest of Loch Leven via M90 and A91, 10 mi west of St. Andrews via A91.*

Cupar is a busy market town, with a train station on the Edinburgh–Aberdeen line.

On rising ground near the town stands the National Trust for Scotland's **Hill of Tarvit House.** Originally a 17th-century mansion, the house was altered in the high-Edwardian style in the late 1890s and early 1900s by the Scottish architect Sir Robert Lorimer (1864–1929). Inside the house are fine collections of antique furniture, Chinese porcelain, bronzes, tapestries, and Dutch paintings. Lorimer also designed the formal gardens. A tearoom, open daily noon to 5 between April and October, is on the premises. ⊠*2 mi south of Cupar, off A916* ☎*01334/653127* ⊕*www.nts.org.uk* ⊠*Gardens £4; gardens and house £8* ☉*Gardens daily 9:30–sunset; house Apr.–Oct., daily noon–5.*

To learn more about the history and culture of rural Fife, visit the **Fife Folk Museum.** The life of local rural communities is reflected in artifacts and documents housed in a former weigh house and adjoining weavers' cottages. The museum is 3 mi southeast of Cupar via A916 and B939, and 9 mi southwest of St. Andrews. ⊠*High St., Ceres* ☎*01334/828180* ⤶*£2.50* ⊙*Mid-May–Sept., daily 11:30–4:30.*

At the **Scottish Deer Centre,** red deer can be seen at close quarters on ranger-guided tours. There are also nature trails, falconry displays, an adventure playground (a wood-and-tire fortress suitable for older children), a handful of shops, and a café. ⊠*A91, outside Cupar* ☎*01337/810391* ⤶*£5.50* ⊙*Daily 10–4:30.*

**WHERE TO STAY & EAT**

£££    ✕**Ostlers Close Restaurant.** It's thoroughly unpretentious, but this cottage-style restaurant with plain painted walls and stick-back chairs has earned a well-deserved reputation for top-quality cuisine that is imaginative without trying to be too trendy. The chef's light touch means the flavors are simple, with the shellfish and vegetables especially fresh-tasting. This longtime favorite is tucked away in an alley off the main street. It's a good idea to reserve ahead, particularly for lunch. ⊠*Bonnygate* ☎*01334/655574* ⊟*AE, MC, V* ⊙*Closed Sun. and Mon. No lunch Tues.–Thurs.*

££££    ✕▥**The Peat Inn.** This popular inn is best known for its outstanding
Fodor'sChoice    modern Scottish-style restaurant (£££), generally considered one of
★    the finest in Scotland. Mouthwatering entrées might include Shetland salmon or Gressingham duck breast. Be sure to make room for the mesmerizing desserts, such as warm hazelnut and milk-chocolate fondant with espresso ice cream. A detached building houses eight bright and contemporary two-room suites. **Pros:** Exceptional restaurant, beautiful views, friendly staff. **Cons:** Tired decor, need to book well in advance. ⊠*At B940 and B941, 6 mi southwest of St. Andrews, 3 mi southeast of Ceres* ⌂*Cupar, Fife KY15 5LH* ☎*01334/840206* ⊕*www.thepeatinn. co.uk* ⤶*8 suites* ⌂*In-room: no a/c. In-hotel: restaurant, bar, no elevator, parking (no fee)* ⊟*AE, MC, V* ⊙*Closed Sun. and Mon.* ⫿⦿⫿*CP.*

# DUNDEE & ANGUS

The small city of Dundee sits near the mouth of the river Tay surrounded by the farms and glens of rural Angus and the coastal grassy banks and golf courses of northeastern Fife. A vibrant, industrious city that still isn't part of the main tourist track, Dundee plays a significant role in the biotech and computer-games industries. Dundee has a large student population, a lively arts, music, and nightlife scene, many smart restaurants, and several historical and nautical sights.

Angus combines coastal agriculture on rich, red soils with dramatic inland glens that pierce their way into the foothills of the Grampian mountain ranges to the northwest. ■TIP➔**The main road from Dundee to Aberdeen—the A90—requires drivers to take special care, with its mix of fast cars, trucks, and unexpectedly slow farm traffic.**

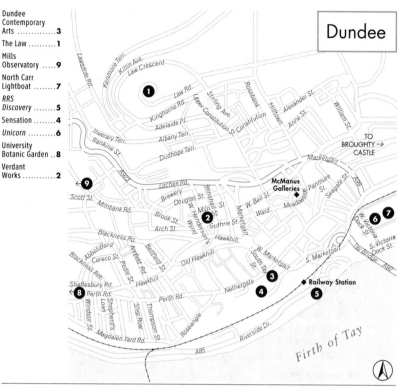

Dundee

4

## DUNDEE

*14 mi northwest of St. Andrews, 58 mi north of Edinburgh, 79 mi northeast of Glasgow.*

Dundee makes an excellent base for exploring Fife and Angus at any time of year. The West End, especially its main thoroughfare Perth Road, has beguiling shops, intimate cafés, and excellent bars. The Dundee Contemporary Arts center has gained the city some attention. As you walk the cobbled streets, you may glimpse the 1888 Tay Rail Bridge, and if you head southwest you can reach Magdalen Green, where landscape artist James McIntosh Patrick (1907–98) found inspiration from the views and ever-changing skyscapes. The popular comic strips *The Beano* and *The Dandy* were first published here in the 1930s, so statues depicting Desperate Dan, Dawg, and a catapult-wielding Minnie the Minx, were erected in the City Square.

### MAIN ATTRACTIONS

**⑤** *Discovery.* Dundee's urban-renewal program—its determination to
**☾** shake off its industrial past—was motivated in part by the arrival of
**★** the RRS (Royal Research Ship) *Discovery,* the vessel used by Captain Robert Scott (1868–1912) on his polar explorations. The steamer was originally built and launched in Dundee; now it's a permanent resident.

An on-board exhibition allows you to sample life as it was aboard the intrepid ship. One exhibit lets you experience life in Antarctica hands-on and heads-in—you can feel the temperature and the wind chill as if you were there. ✉*Discovery Quay* ☎*01382/201245* ⊕*www.rrs discovery.com* 🎫*£7; £11.50 with Verdant Works* ⊙*Apr.–Oct., Mon.–Sat. 10–6, Sun. 11–6; Nov.–Mar., Mon.–Sat. 10–5, Sun. 11–5.*

❸ **Dundee Contemporary Arts.** Between a 17th-century mansion and a cathe-
Ⓒ dral, this strikingly modern building houses one of Britain's most excit-
★ ing artistic venues. There are children's workshops and meet-the-artist events throughout the year. There are also two movie theaters showing mainly independent, revival, and children's films, a craft shop, and a buzzing café-bar called Jute that's open until midnight. ✉*152 Nether-gate* ☎*01382/909252* ⊕*www.dca.org.uk* 🎫*Free* ⊙*Tues., Wed., Fri., and Sat. 10:30–5:30, Thurs. 10:30–8:30, Sun. noon–5:30.*

**McManus Galleries.** Dundee's principal museum and art gallery has dis-plays on local history, trade, and industry. Closed for refurbishment, it's slated to open again in late 2008. ✉*Albert Sq.* ☎*01382/432084* ⊕*www.mcmanus.co.uk* 🎫*Free* ⊙*Mon.–Wed., Fri., and Sat. 10–5, Thurs. 10–7, Sun. 12:30–4.*

❽ **University Botanic Garden.** This renowned botanical garden contains an extensive collection of native and exotic plants outdoors and in tropi-cal and temperate greenhouses. There are some beautiful areas for pic-nicking, as well as a visitor center, an art gallery, and a coffee shop. ✉*Riverside Dr.* ☎*01382/647190* ⊕*www.dundeebotanicgarden.co.uk* 🎫*£3* ⊙*Mar.–Oct., daily 10–4:30; Nov.–Feb., daily 10–3:30.*

❷ **Verdant Works.** In a former jute mill, Verdant Works houses a multi-
Ⓒ faceted exhibit on the story of jute and the town's involvement in the jute trade. Restored machinery, audiovisual displays, and tableaux all bring to life the hard, noisy life of the jute worker. ✉*W. Hendersons Wynd* ☎*01382/225282* ⊕*www.rrsdiscovery.com* 🎫*£6; £11.50 with Discovery* ⊙*Apr.–Oct., Mon.–Sat. 10–6, Sun. 11–6; Nov.–Mar., Wed.–Sat. 10:30–4:30, Sun. 11–4:30.*

**ALSO WORTH SEEING**

OFF THE
BEATEN
PATH

**Broughty Castle.** Originally built to guard the Tay estuary, Broughty Castle is now a museum focusing on fishing, ferries, and the his-tory of the town of Broughty Ferry's whaling industry. There's also a display of arms and armor. ✉*Broughty Ferry* ✛*4 mi east of city center* ☎*01382/436916* ⊕*www.dundeecity.gov.uk* 🎫*Free* ⊙*Apr.–Sept., Mon.–Sat. 10–4, Sun. 12:30–4; Oct.–Mar., Tues.–Sat. 10–4, Sun. 12:30–4.*

❶ **The Law.** For sweeping views of the city, the Angus Glens to the north, and Fife's coastline to the south, head here. This hill (*law* means hill in Scottish) is actually an extinct volcano whose summit reaches 1,640 feet above sea level. A World War II memorial and outdoor viewing area are at the top. ✉*Law Rd.*

❾ **Mills Observatory.** At the top of a thickly forested hill, Mills Observatory is the only full-time public observatory in Britain. There are displays on astronomy, space exploration, scientific instruments, and a 10-inch refracting telescope for night viewing of the stars and planets. ⊠*Balgay Hill, 2 mi west of city center* ☎*01382/435967* 🎫*Free* ☉*Oct.–Mar., weekdays 4–10* PM, *weekends 12:30–4; Apr.–Sept., Tues.–Fri. 11–5, weekends 12:30–4.*

**❼ North Carr Lightboat.** After playing a significant role in World War II, Scotland's only remaining lightship was wrecked on the Fife shore during a storm in 1959 and lost seven crew members. ■**TIP→ The Maritime Volunteer Service, which looks after the North Carr, runs exhilarating trips up the River Tay on its vessels, the *Badger* and *Marigold*. Don't be surprised if dolphins join you.** ⊠*Victoria Dock* ☎*01382/542516* ⊕*www.tayrivertrips.org* 🎫*Free* ☉*Sun. 1–4:30.*

**❹ Sensation.** You can see the world upside down when you're strapped into the gyroscope at this hands-on science center focusing on the five senses. Although the general noise level testifies to the child-friendly nature of the place, enthusiastic staff members persuade visitors of all ages to participate. Among the many experiments and activities, you can "age" yourself on computer screens or practice your balance on wobble boards. ⊠*Greenmarket* ☎*01382/228800* ⊕*www.sensation. org.uk* 🎫*£7* ☉*Daily 10–5; last admission at 4.*

**❻** *Unicorn.* At Victoria Dock is the frigate *Unicorn,* a 46-gun wood warship fronted by a figurehead of a galloping, crested white unicorn. The *Unicorn* has the distinction of being the oldest British-built warship afloat, having been launched in 1824 at Chatham, England. You can clamber right down into the hold, or discuss the models and displays about the Royal Navy's history with the friendly staff. The ship's hours sometimes vary in winter, so call ahead. ⊠*Victoria Dock, east of Tay Rd. bridge* ☎*01382/200900 or 01382/200893* ⊕*www.frigateunicorn. org* 🎫*£4* ☉*Apr.–Oct., daily 10–5; Nov.–Mar., Wed.–Fri. noon–4, weekends 10–4; last admission 20 min before closing.*

## WHERE TO STAY & EAT

££ ✕**Dandilly's.** Heavy wooden tables, large windows, and a quirky staff distinguish this West End eatery, as does the innovative Italian cuisine. Try the signature chicken with apricot and ginger. Make sure to save room for dessert. ⊠*183 Perth Rd.* ☎*01382/669218* ▤*MC, V.*

£ ✕**Het Theatercafe.** At the lively Rep Theatre, you have a choice of the ★ café-bar upstairs, which serves light fare and good coffee, or the restaurant downstairs. The international dishes include chicken *satay* (grilled meat on skewers) and Cajun chicken. Theater posters of past productions and stills of actors decorate the walls. ⊠*Tay Sq.* ☎*01382/206699* ▤*MC, V* ☉*Closed Sun.*

£ ✕**Jute.** Part of Dundee Contemporary Arts, this lively café-bar over-★ looks the town's waterfront. The glass wall between you and the printmaking studio reminds you of the creativity that goes on in the same building. The service is unimposing and the menu stylish but without pretense, with dishes like venison sausages served with creamy mashed potatoes and beet marmalade, or steamed mussels with spring-onion noodles. ⊠*152 Nethergate* ☎*01382/909246* ▤*MC, V.*

4

££–£££   ✕▦**Apex City Quay.** Sleek, Scandinavian-style rooms with easy chairs, satiny pillows, and CD/DVD players to help you unwind at this contemporary quayside hotel. To relax further, or to exercise, head for the Japanese spa and fitness center. The restaurant (££) and brasserie (£), both with views of the harbor, have globally influenced menus with simple Italian and Asian dishes, as well as perfectly cooked steaks. **Pros:** Stylish rooms, excellent brasserie. **Cons:** Not an easy walk into town, often mobbed with conferences. ⊠*1 W. Victoria Dock Rd., DD1 3JP* ☎*01382/202404* ⊕*www.apexhotels.com* ⇆*145 rooms, 8 suites* ⌂*In-room: no a/c, DVD, Wi-Fi. In-hotel: 2 restaurants, bar, pool, gym, spa, laundry service, parking (no fee)* ▤*MC, V* ⦿*CP.*

££   ✕▦**Hotel Broughty Ferry.** The town of Broughty Ferry has now been encircled by Dundee, but it still retains the character of a fishing port. This modern hotel is within walking distance of a surprising variety of restaurants and pubs, but weary travelers can take comfort in knowing that the restaurant on the premises is held in high regard (££). Try the chicken breast stuffed with haggis or something even spicier from the Indian menu. The rooms are pristine, with wooden furniture and quality linens. **Pros:** Good restaurant, quiet location, sparkling pool. **Cons:** Rooms lack character, bar and restaurant have impersonal feel. ⊠*16 W. Queen St., Broughty Ferry, DD5 1AR* ☎*01382/480027* ⊕*www.hotelbroughtyferry.co.uk* ⇆*16 rooms* ⌂*In-room: no a/c. In-hotel: restaurant, bar, pool, gym, no elevator, parking (no fee)* ▤*AE, MC, V* ⦿*BP.*

£–££   ✕▦**Queen's Hotel.** This former railway hotel in the lively West End of Dundee is thoroughly up-to-date inside. Beyond the handsome Victorian facade you can find modern oak furniture filling the spacious rooms. Nosey Parkers Bistro (££), decorated with bright, primary colors, is popular with locals for its international dishes or a quick drink after work. **Pros:** Ideal location, rooms ideal for families. **Cons:** Decor is a hodgepodge of styles, bar lacks atmosphere. ⊠*160 Nethergate, DD1 4DU* ☎*01382/322515* ⊕*www.queenshotel-dundee.com* ⇆*52 rooms, 3 suites* ⌂*In-room: no a/c. In-hotel: restaurant, bar, parking (no fee)* ▤*AE, DC, MC, V* ⦿*BP.*

## NIGHTLIFE & THE ARTS

BARS & PUBS   Dundee's pub scene, centered in the West End–Perth Road area, is one of the liveliest in Scotland. The **Art Bar** ( ⊠*140 Perth Rd.* ☎*01382/227888*) has won a loyal following with its program of live jazz and folk music, as well as its resident DJ, Howard. There's a good chance you may catch a performance by Michael Marra, widely regarded as Scotland's finest poet and songwriter. **Braes** ( ⊠*18 Perth Rd.* ☎*01382/226344*) has a friendly clientele and, like most pubs in the city, is frequented by a diverse crowd. If you find yourself in Broughty Ferry, you can't leave without a tipple in the **Fisherman's Tavern** ( ⊠*10–16 Fort St., Broughty Ferry* ☎*01382/775941*). The **Speedwell Bar** ( ⊠*165–168 Perth Rd.* ☎*01382/667783*), called Mennie's by the locals, is in a mahogany-paneled building brimming with Dundonian character. It's renowned for its superb cask beers and its whale-bone-like Shanks urinals.

**DANCE CLUBS**  **Fat Sam's Disco** ( ⊠*31 S. Ward Rd.* ☎*01382/228181*) attracts clubbers of all ages to its various club nights, which feature DJs spinning everything from Indie to Deep House. It has now become Dundee's premier venue for gigs, hosting the likes of Franz Ferdinand, Pigeon Detectives, Paolo Nutini, and Alabama 3.

**MUSIC**  **Caird Hall** ( ⊠*City Sq.* ☎*01382/434451*) is one of Scotland's finest concert halls, staging a wide range of music.

**THEATER**  The **Dundee Repertory Theatre** ( ⊠*Tay Sq.* ☎*01382/223530*) is home to the nationally respected Dundee Rep Ensemble as well as Scotland's preeminent contemporary-dance group, Scottish Dance Theatre. Popular with locals, the restaurant and bar welcome late-night comedy shows and jazz bands. **Whitehall Theatre** ( ⊠*12 Bellfield St.* ☎*01382/322684*) has mostly musical theater productions, including light opera.

### SHOPPING

**COFFEE & TEA**  **J. Allan Braithwaite** ( ⊠*6 Castle St.* ☎*01382/322693*) carries 13 types of freshly roasted coffees and more than 30 blended teas that you can pop into one of the quaint teapots.

**HOME FURNISHINGS**  Moroccan light fixtures, Asian furnishings, and sumptuous soaps are just some of the largely Eastern-oriented goodies at **Indigo House** ( ⊠*69 Perth Rd.* ☎*01382/206726*). The **Westport Gallery** ( ⊠*44 West Port* ☎*01382/229707*) stocks contemporary designer homeware, including ceramics and glass, plus highly stylized clothing and jewelry.

**JEWELRY**  The **Queen's Gallery** ( ⊠*160 Nethergate* ☎*01382/220600*) has a compelling selection of jewelry, as well as paintings by Scottish artists.

## ARBROATH

*15 mi north of Dundee via A92.*

You can find traditional boatbuilding in the fishing town of Arbroath. It also has several small curers and processors, and shops sell the town's most famous delicacy, "Arbroath smokies"—whole haddock gutted and lightly smoked. A few miles north along the coast is the old fishing village of Auchmithie, with a beautiful little beach that you can walk to via a short path. The jagged, reddish cliffs and caves are home to a flourishing seabird population.

**Arbroath Abbey,** founded in 1178, is an unmistakable presence in the town center; it seems to straddle whole streets, as if the town were simply ignoring the red-stone ruin in its midst. Surviving today are remains of the church, as well as one of the most complete examples in existence of an abbot's residence. From here in 1320 a passionate plea was sent by King Robert the Bruce (1274–1329) and the Scottish Church to Pope John XXII (circa 1245–1334) in far-off Rome. The pope had until then sided with the English kings, who adamantly refused to acknowledge Scottish independence. The Declaration of Arbroath stated firmly, "For as long as but a hundred of us remain alive, never will we on any conditions be brought under English rule. It is in truth not for glory, nor riches, nor honours that we are fighting, but for

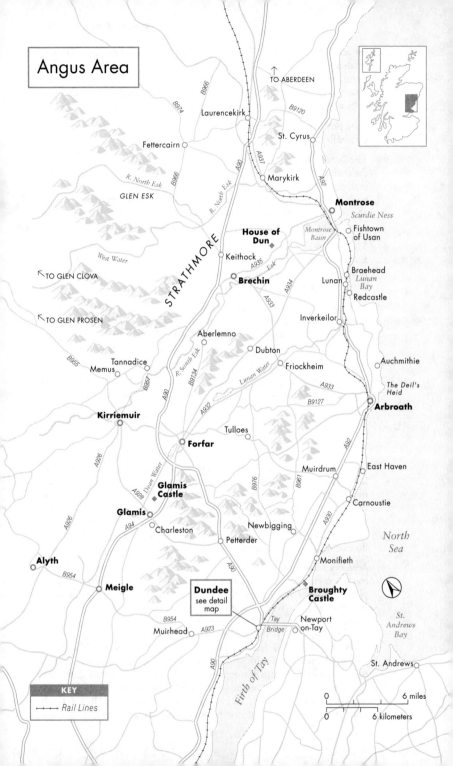

freedom—for that alone, which no honest man gives up but with life itself." Some historians describe this plea, originally drafted in Latin, as the single most important document in Scottish history. The pope advised English king Edward II (1284–1327) to make peace, but warfare was to break out along the border from time to time for the next 200 years. The excellent visitor center recounts this history

**LIGHTHOUSE BUILDERS**

The name Stevenson is strongly associated with the building of lighthouses throughout Scotland. However, the family's most famous son was Robert Louis Stevenson (1850–94), who gravely disappointed his parents by choosing to be a writer instead of an engineer.

in well-planned displays. ⊠*Arbroath town center* ☎*01241/878756* ⊕*www.historic-scotland.gov.uk* ☜*£4.50* ⊙*Apr.–Sept., daily 9:30–5:30; Oct.–Mar., daily 9:30–4:30.*

Arbroath was the base for the construction of the Bell Rock lighthouse on a treacherous, barely exposed rock in the early 19th century. A signal tower was built to facilitate communication with the builders working far from shore. That structure now houses the **Signal Tower Museum,** which tells the story of the lighthouse, built by Robert Stevenson (1772–1850) in 1811. The museum also houses a collection of items related to the history of the town, its customs, and the local fishing industry. ⊠*Ladyloan, west of harbor* ☎*01241/875598* ⊕*www.angus.gov.uk* ☜*Free* ⊙*Sept.–June, Mon.–Sat. 10–5; July and Aug., Mon.–Sat. 10–5, Sun. 2–5.*

### WHERE TO EAT

£ ✕**But 'n' Ben.** This homey restaurant offers a taste of quality Scottish home cooking, including smoked fish pâté and lemon drizzle cake, all at prices that make it an excellent value. After lunch, stroll down to the Auchmithie's lovely, shingle beach. ⊠*Auchmithie* ✥*Near Arbroath, 3 mi off A92* ☎*01241/877223* ▭*MC, V* ⊙*Closed Tues.*

### NIGHTLIFE

For a good pint, seek out the **Foundry Bar** ( ⊠*E. Mary St.* ☎*01241/872524*), a spartan bar frequented by locals and enlivened by impromptu jam sessions on Wednesday and Friday evening. Customers often bring along their fiddles and accordions, and all join in.

## MONTROSE

*14 mi north of Arbroath via A92.*

An unpretentious and attractive town with a museum and a selection of shops, Montrose sits beside a wide estuary known as the Montrose Basin.

The **Montrose Basin Wildlife Centre,** run by the Scottish Wildlife Trust, is a nature reserve with geese, ducks, and swans. Several nature trails can take you up close to the reserve's residents if you're quiet. ⊠*Rossie Braes* ☎*01674/676336* ⊕*www.montrosebasin.org.uk* ☜*£3* ⊙*Visitor center Apr.–Oct., daily 10:30–5; Nov.–Mar., Fri.–Sun. 10:30–4.*

# BEAUTIFUL BEACHES

Scotland's east coast enjoys many hours of sunshine, compared with its west coast, and is blessed with lots of sandy beaches under the ever-changing backdrop of the sky. Take time to explore the beaches and walk along the coast for a change of pace whatever the time of year.

In Fife, Tentsmuir's beach near St. Andrews is popular with kite fly-ers and horseback riders, and the famous and lovely West Sands in St. Andrews is where the movie *Chariots of Fire*'s running sequences were filmed. The small cove beach at Elie, just south of Crail, hosts local cricket matches in summer.

In Angus, the beach at Broughty Ferry, near the city of Dundee, fills with families and children on week-ends and during school holidays—even on the most blustery of days you can find well-wrapped *bairns* (small children) making pictures in the sand.

North of Arbroath lies Auchmithie beach, more shingly (pebbly) than the others and offering a bracing breath of North Sea air. And finally, near the Montrose basin, you can discover the enchanting crescent of Lunan Bay, home to many species of seabirds.

★ The National Trust for Scotland's leading attraction in this area is the **House of Dun,** which overlooks the Montrose Basin. The mansion was built in the 1730s for lawyer David Erskine, otherwise known as Lord Dun (1670–1755). Designed by architect William Adam (1689–1748), the house is particularly noted for its ornate plasterwork and curious Masonic masonry. Some of Lord Dun's heirlooms, including samples from the family's collection of embroidery, tell the story of the Seat of Dun and the eminent family's history. The sprawling grounds have restored workshops, plus an enchanting Victorian walled garden. The house is 4 mi west of Montrose via A935. ⊠*A935* ☎*01674/810264* ⊕*www.nts.org.uk* ✉*Garden £2; garden and house £8* ⊙*House Apr.–June, Sept., and Oct., Fri.–Tues. 12:30–5; July and Aug., Fri.–Tues. 11:30–5. Garden year-round, daily 9–sunset.*

## BRECHIN

*10 mi southwest of Montrose.*

The small market town of Brechin has a cathedral that was founded around 1200 and contains an interesting selection of antiquities, includ-ing the Mary Stone, a Pictish relic.

The town's 10th-century **Round Tower,** next to the cathedral, is one of only two on mainland Scotland (they're more frequently found in Ireland). It was originally built for the local Culdee monks. ✉*Free* ⊙*Daily 9–5.*

The first arrivals in this part of Scotland were the Picts, who came sometime in the first millennium AD. **Pictavia** explores what is known about this race of Celts using actual artifacts, replicas, and interactive exhibits. ⊠*Brechin Castle Centre, off A90* ☎*01307/473785* ⊕*www.*

*pictavia.org.uk* £3.50 ⊙ *Easter–mid-Oct., Mon.–Sat. 9:30–5:30, Sun. 10:30–5:30; mid-Oct.–Easter, Sat. 9–5, Sun. 10–5.*

## THE ANGUS GLENS

*25 mi southwest of Brechin.*

You can rejoin the hurly-burly of the A90 for the return journey south from Montrose or Brechin; the more pleasant route, however, leads southwesterly on minor roads (there are several options) that travel along the face of the Grampians, following the fault line that separates Highland and Lowland. The **Angus Glens** extend north from points on Route A90. Known individually as the glens of Isla, Prosen, Clova, and Esk, these long valleys run into the high hills of the Grampians and some clearly marked walking routes. Those in Glen Clova are especially appealing.

### WHERE TO STAY & EAT

££  ✕ Glen Clova Hotel. Since the 1850s, the hospitality of this hotel has lifted the spirits of many a bone-tired hillwalker. The bedrooms are simply furnished but have comfortable, firm beds. The legendary Climbers Bar pours a fine pint—or glass of wine—and heaves with walkers and climbers, many of whom are staying in the youth hostel or campground a few miles down the road. The restaurant (£) serves good home cooking; try the lamb casserole or the chicken breast stuffed with haggis in a whisky cream sauce. **Pros:** Stunning location, great base for outdoor pursuits, spacious accommodations. **Cons:** Lack of decent public transportation, rooms are booked well in advance. ⊠ *B955, Glen Clova DD8 4QS* ☎ *01575/550350* ⊕ *www.clova.com* 🛏 *10 rooms* In-*room: no a/c. In-hotel: restaurant, bar, no elevator* ═ MC, V ⵊ BP.

## KIRRIEMUIR

*15 mi southeast of Brechin.*

Kirriemuir stands at the heart of Angus's red-sandstone countryside and was the birthplace of the writer J. M. Barrie (1860–1937), best known abroad as the author of *Peter Pan.*

**J. M. Barrie's Birthplace** has the upper floors furnished as they might have been in Barrie's time, complete with manuscripts and personal mementos. The outside washhouse is said to have been Barrie's first theater. Next door, at 11 Brechin Road, is an exhibition about the author. ⊠ *9 Brechin Rd.* ☎ *01575/572646* ⊕ *www.nts.org.uk* £5, *includes Camera Obscura* ⊙ *Apr.–June, Sat. and Mon.–Wed. noon–5, Sun. 1–5; July and Aug., Mon.–Sat. noon–5, Sun. 1–5.*

J. M. Barrie donated the **Camera Obscura,** in a cricket pavilion on Kirriemuir Hill, just northeast of Kirriemuir, to the town. The device—a dark room with a small hole in one wall that projects an image of the outside world onto the opposite wall—is one of only three in the country. It affords magnificent views of the surrounding area on a clear day.

⊠*Kirriemuir Hill* ☎*No phone* ⚏*£5, includes J. M. Barrie's birthplace* ⊙*Apr.–Oct., Mon.–Sat. noon–5, Sun. 1–5.*

**WHERE TO EAT**

££  ✕**Drovers Inn.** Set in the heart of the Angus farmlands, Drovers Inn is a rare find in Scotland, with more the feeling of an English country pub than a Scottish inn. Plain but friendly surroundings, decorated with old farm implements and historic photographs, form the backdrop for simple, top-quality food: savory pies, soups, tasty venison, and Aberdeen Angus steak. Everything from bread to sorbet is made on the premises, and only local produce is used. The inn is popular with locals; weekends it's best to make reservations, even at the bar. ⊠*Off A90, Memus* ✛*Near Kirriemuir* ☎*01307/860322* ⊟*MC, V.*

---

## FORFAR

*7 mi east of Kirriemuir.*

Forfar goes about its business of being the center of a farming hinterland without being preoccupied with tourism. This means it's an everyday, friendly, and pleasant-enough Scottish town, bypassed by the A90 on its way north.

A high point of the town is the **Meffan Museum & Art Gallery,** which displays an impressive collection of Pictish carved stones. Two galleries host frequently changing exhibitions. ⊠*20 W. High St.* ☎*01307/464123* ⚏*Free* ⊙*Mon.–Sat. 10–5.*

**OFF THE BEATEN PATH**

**Aberlemno.** You can see excellent examples of Pictish stone carvings about 5 mi northeast of Forfar alongside the B9134. Carvings of crosses, angels, serpents, and other animals adorn the stones, which date from the 7th to the early 9th centuries. Note the stone in the nearby churchyard—one side is carved with a cross and the other side depicts the only known battle scene in Pictish art, complete with horsemen and foot soldiers.

**WHERE TO STAY**

£  ⌘**Redroofs.** This former cottage hospital, set in the woods near Forfar, is now a hospitable B&B. Rooms are spacious and very comfortable, and the hosts go out of their way to help you plan your sightseeing. Curios collected by the owners on their travels decorate the sitting room. Evening meals can be arranged. **Pros:** Full of character, friendly and helpful owners. **Cons:** Lack of good restaurants nearby, basic facilities. ⊠*Balgavies, Guthrie, DD8 2TH* ☎*01307/830268* ⌂*3 rooms* ⚏*In-room: no a/c, no phone, refrigerator. In-hotel: no-smoking rooms* ⊟*No credit cards* ⦿*BP.*

---

## GLAMIS

*5 mi southwest of Forfar, 6 mi south of Kirriemuir via A928.*

Set in rolling countryside is the little village of Glamis (pronounced Glahms). A row of 19th-century cottages with unusual stone-slab roofs makes up the **Angus Folk Museum,** whose exhibits focus on the tools of domestic and agricultural life in the region during the past 200 years. ✉ *Off A94* ☎ *01307/840288* ⊕ *www.angusahead.com* 🎟 *£5* ⏱ *Apr.–Oct., Sat.–Wed. noon–5.*

FodorsChoice  **Glamis Castle,** one of Scotland's best-known and most beautiful castles,
★  connects Britain's royalty through 10 centuries, from Macbeth ("Thane of Glamis") to the late Princess Margaret—born here in 1930 in the ancestral home of her mother—the first royal princess born in Scotland in 300 years. The property of the earls of Strathmore and Kinghorne since 1372, the castle was largely reconstructed in the late 17th century; the original keep, which is much older, is still intact. One of the most famous rooms in the castle is Duncan's Hall, the legendary setting for Shakespeare's *Macbeth.* Guided tours allow you to see fine collections of china, tapestries, and furniture. Also on the premises are several shops, a produce stall, and a restaurant. ✉ *A94, 1 mi north of Glamis* ☎ *01307/840393* ⊕ *www.glamis-castle.co.uk* 🎟 *Grounds £3.70; castle and grounds £7.50* ⏱ *Mar.–Oct., daily 10–6; Nov. and Dec., daily 11–5.*

## MEIGLE

*7 mi southwest of Glamis, 11 mi northwest of Dundee.*

The town of Meigle, in the wide swath of Strathmore, has one of the most notable medieval collections in western Europe, housed at the **Meigle Museum.** It consists of some 25 sculptured monuments from the Celtic Christian period (8th to 10th centuries), nearly all of which were found in or around the local churchyard. ✉ *A94* ☎ *0131/640612* ⊕ *www.historic-scotland.gov.uk* 🎟 *£3* ⏱ *Apr.–Sept., daily 9:30–5:30; Oct.–Mar. daily 9:30–4:30.*

## ALYTH

*10 mi west of Glamis, 15 mi northwest of Dundee.*

Dating back to the Dark Ages, this market town was completely transformed by the Industrial Revolution, which lined its streets with mills and factories. The 20th century saw the closing of most of these companies, but the town had never forgotten its agricultural heritage. To this day it holds on to its rural appeal.

**Alyth Museum,** a small but intriguing museum about the town's history, displays nearly every type of tool and implement put to use by the resourceful and hardy locals. ✉ *Commercial St.* ☎ *01828/633474* 🎟 *Free* ⏱ *May–Sept., Wed.–Sun. 1–5.*

### WHERE TO STAY

££  🏠 **Tigh Na Leigh.** This grand house, now a B&B, was originally built by the Earl of Airlie for his doctor. Rooms are fresh and airy, with leather, brass or four-poster beds extravagantly dressed in Egyptian cotton. Evening meals can be prepared for guests only and are served in the Scandinavian-style conservatory. **Pros:** Lovingly restored building, luxurious rooms, exceptional food. **Cons:** Only one standard double room, books up quickly. ✉*22–24 Airlie St., PH11 8AJ* ☎*01828/632372* ⊕*www. tighnaleigh.com* ⇔*5 rooms* ⚎*In-room: no a/c. In-hotel: public Internet, no elevator* ▤*MC, V* ⌾⎮*BP.*

# FIFE & ANGUS ESSENTIALS

## TRANSPORTATION

### BY AIR

Dundee Airport is off the A85, 2 mi west of the city center. ScotAirways operates a popular direct flight from London City Airport. Whoosh flies here from Birmingham and Belfast. The Tay estuary and its two bridges make for a stunning view during takeoff or landing.

**Information ScotAirways** ( ☎*0870/6060707* ⊕ *www.scotairways.com*). **Whoosh** ( ☎*0871/2826767* ⊕ *www.flywhoosh.com*).

### BY BUS

Buses connect Edinburgh's St. Andrew Square bus station and Glasgow's Buchanan Street bus station to Fife and Angus. Scottish Citylink operates hourly service to Dundee from both Glasgow and Edinburgh. Stagecoach Fife serves Fife and St. Andrews, and Travel Dundee provides bus service in and around Dundee.

Local service connects St. Andrews and Dundee to many of the smaller towns throughout Fife and Angus. A Day Rover ticket (£6 with Strathtay Scottish or Stagecoach Fife) is a good value. The Strathtay pass covers Dundee and Angus, whereas Stagecoach covers all of Fife. Traveline Scotland is a service that helps you plan all public transport journeys.

**Bus Information Scottish Citylink** ( ☎*08705/505050* ⊕ *www.citylink.co.uk*). **Stagecoach Fife** ( ☎*0871/2002233* ⊕ *www.stagecoachbus.com*). **Strathtay Scottish** ( ☎*01382/228345* ⊕ *www.stagecoachbus.com/strathtay*). **Travel Dundee** ( ☎*08706/082608* ⊕ *www.traveldundee.co.uk*). **Traveline Scotland** ( ☎*08706/082608* ⊕ *www.travelinescotland.com*).

### BY CAR

The M90 motorway from Edinburgh takes you to within a half hour of St. Andrews and Dundee. If you're coming from Fife, you can use the A91 and the A914 and then cross the Tay Bridge to reach Dundee, though the quickest way is to use the fast-paced, less-scenic M90/A90. Travel time from Edinburgh to Dundee is about one hour, from Edinburgh to St. Andrews, 1½ hours.

Fife is easy to get around—although it can be difficult to find a place to park in St. Andrews. Most roads are quiet and uncongested. The most interesting sights are in the east, which is served by a network of cross-country roads. Angus is likewise an easy region to explore because it's serviced by a fast main road, the A90, plus the A92, a gentler road, and rural roads that run between the Grampians and the A90.

### BY TRAIN

First ScotRail stops at Kirkcaldy, Cupar, Leuchars (for St. Andrews), Dundee, Arbroath, and Montrose.

Information **First ScotRail** ( ☎ *08457/484950* ⊕ *www.firstgroup.com/scotrail*).

## CONTACTS & RESOURCES

### EMERGENCIES

Dial ☎**999** in case of an emergency to reach an ambulance, or the fire or police departments (no coins are needed for emergency calls made from public phone booths). Late-night pharmacies are not found outside the larger cities. In St. Andrews, Dundee, and other larger centers, pharmacies use a rotating system for off-hours and Sunday prescription service: your hotel will have details.

### TOURS

Travel Greyhound runs several general orientation bus tours of the main cities and the region from late July to early August. Fishers Tours has bus tours year-round both within and outside the region. Lochs and Glens operates bus tours of Scotland year-round.

Heritage Golf Tours Scotland specializes in golf vacations that include hotel and car rental and course reservations. Links Golf St. Andrews tailors tours to individual requirements.

Bus Tours **Fishers Tours** ( ⊠*16 W. Port, Dundee* ☎*01382/227290* ⊕*www. fisherstours.co.uk*). **Lochs and Glens** ( ⊠*Gartocharn, West Dunbartonshire* ☎*01389/713713* ⊕*www.lochsandglens.com*). **Travel Greyhound** ( ⊠*92 Commercial St., Dundee* ☎*01382/340006*).

Golf Tours **Heritage Golf Tours Scotland** ( ⊠*Swilken House, 21 Loch Dr., Helensburgh* ☎*01436/674630* ⊕*www.golftours-scotland.co.uk*). **Links Golf St. Andrews** ( ⊠*7 Pilmour Links, St. Andrews* ☎*01334/478639* ⊕*www.linksgolf standrews.com*).

### VISITOR INFORMATION

The Arbroath, Dundee, Forth Bridges, Kirkcaldy, and St. Andrews tourist offices are open year-round. Smaller tourist information centers operate seasonally in the following towns: Anstruther, Brechin, Carnoustie, Crail, Forfar, Kirriemuir, and Montrose.

Information **Arbroath** ( ⊠*Market Pl.* ☎*01241/872609*). **Dundee** ( ⊠*21 Castle St.* ☎*01382/527527* ⊕*www.angusanddundee.co.uk*). **Forth Bridges** ( ⊠*St. Margaret's Head* ☎*01383/417759*). **Kirkcaldy** ( ⊠*19 Whytescauseway* ☎*01592/267775*). **St. Andrews** ( ⊠*70 Market St.* ☎*01334/472021* ⊕*www.standrews.com*).

# The Central Highlands

"Stirling Castle overlooks Stirling, with the beautiful panorama and cobblestone courtyards. They have a tearoom with a rooftop eating area. Stirling Castle is said to be haunted, and you could imagine that. The King's and Queen's chambers are well preserved, down to the massive fireplaces."

—Virgogirl

"Pitlochry, a busy Victorian town, is touristy but hey, we were tourists. We'd considered staying someplace smaller and farther north but this was probably a better choice (lots of accommodation and eating options). Driving trips included Scone and Blair castles and a drive along Loch Tay. Edradour distillery was a clear highlight."

—hpl

Updated by
Fiona G.
Parrott

**STAND ON STIRLING CASTLE ROCK** to survey the whole Central Highland region, and you can see Scotland coast to coast. This is where Scotland draws in her waist, from the Clyde in the west to the Forth in the east. You can judge just how near the area is to the well-populated Midland Valley by looking out from the ramparts of Edinburgh Castle: the Highland hills, which meander around the Trossachs region and above Callander, are clearly visible. Similarly, the high-tower blocks of some of Glasgow's peripheral housing developments are noticeable from many of the countryside's higher peaks, particularly Ben Lomond.

Today the old county seats of Perth and Stirling still play important roles as the primary administrative centers of the counties of Perthshire and Stirlingshire, which make up the Central Highlands. Geographically, it's no surprise that this region has been a favorite vacation getaway for Edinburghers and Glaswegians for centuries. So beloved is the area, in fact, that 720 square mi of it were designated part of Scotland's first national park, Loch Lomond and the Trossachs National Park, in 2002. Stirling is a much more beautiful city than Perth, making it a better base for exploring the countryside.

As early as 1794 the local minister in Callander, on the very edge of the Highlands, wrote: "The Trossachs are often visited by persons of taste, who are desirous of seeing nature in her rudest and unpolished state." What these early visitors came to see was a series of lochs and hills, whose crags and slopes were hung harmoniously with shaggy birch, oak, and pinewoods. The tops of the hills are high but not too savage—real wilderness would have been too much for these fledgling nature lovers. The Romantic poets, especially William Wordsworth (1770–1850), sang the praises of such locales. Though Wordsworth is more closely associated with the Lake District in England, his travels through Scotland and the Trossachs inspired several of his poems. But it was Sir Walter Scott (1771–1832) who definitively put this area on the tourist map by setting his 1810 dramatic verse narrative, *The Lady of the Lake,* in the landscape of the Trossachs. Scott's verse was an immediate and huge success, and visitors flooded in to trace the events of the poem across the region. The poem mentions every little bridge and farmhouse and is still the most comprehensive guide to the area. Various engineering schemes of the Glasgow Water Department, however, have rendered some of the topography out of date.

Just as the Trossachs have long attracted those with discriminating tastes, so has Loch Lomond, Scotland's largest loch in terms of surface area. The hard rocks to the north confine it there to a long thin ribbon, and the more yielding Lowlands allow it to spread out and assume a softer, wider form. Here the Lowlands' fields and lush hedgerows quickly give way to dark woods and crags—a half-hour's drive north from Glasgow. The song, "The Banks of Loch Lomond," said to have been written by a Jacobite prisoner incarcerated in Carlisle, England, captures beautifully a particular style of Scottish sentimentality, resulting in the popularity of the "bonnie, bonnie banks" around the world, especially wherever Scots are to be found.

# TOP REASONS TO GO

**Exploring Loch Lomond:** You can see the sparkling waters of Scotland's largest loch by car, by boat, or on foot. A popular option is the network of bicycle tracks that creep over Loch Lomond and the Trossachs National Park, offering every conceivable terrain.

**Take in a castle or two:** Choosing among some of Scotland's most splendid fortresses and mansions is a challenge. Among the highlights are Stirling Castle, with its palace built by James V, and Scone Palace, near Perth, a residence displaying grand aristocratic acquisitions.

**Bag a Munro:** The way to experience the Central Highlands is to head out on foot. The fit and well-kitted-out can "bag a Munro" (hills over 3,000 feet, named after the mountaineer that listed them). The woodland paths and gentle rambles of the Trossachs will stir even the sedentary.

**Whisky, the water of life:** The Scots love their whisky, and what better way to participate in Scottish life and culture than to learn about the land's finest? There are some exceptional distilleries in this region, from the Edradour Distillery to the Famous Grouse.

**Jump on a bike:** This region claims excellent biking trails, ranging from a gentle pedal through Stirling to a wind-in-your-face journey on the Lowland/Highland Trail. Whatever your preference, biking is a beautiful way to tour the countryside.

Scots, in particular, prize the sights of this region, for they are some of the most hallowed in their history. "Scots Wha He Wi' Wallace Bled," a rousing pipe-band tune generally regarded as the Scottish national anthem, is played much here. It deals with William Wallace who, like Robert the Bruce, waged war against England in the 13th and 14th centuries. The most notable battles of Wallace and Bruce were fought at Stirling Bridge and Bannockburn, respectively. In nearby Callander, Rob Roy MacGregor, the Scottish Robin Hood, lived (and looted and terrorized) his way into the storybooks.

Within the region the physical contrast between Lowland and Highland is quite pronounced because of the Highland boundary fault. This geological divide also marked the boundary between Scotland's two languages and cultures, Gaelic and Scots, with the Gaels ensconced northwest behind the mountain barrier. In the Central Highlands the fault runs through Loch Lomond, close to Callander, to the northeast above Perth, and into the old county of Angus. Remember that even though the Central Highlands are easily accessible, there is still much high, rough country in the region. Ben Lawers, near Killin, is the ninth-highest peak in Scotland, and the moor of Rannoch is as bleak and empty a stretch as can be seen anywhere in the northlands. But if the glens and lochs prove to be too lonely or intimidating, it's only a short journey to the softer and less harsh Lowlands.

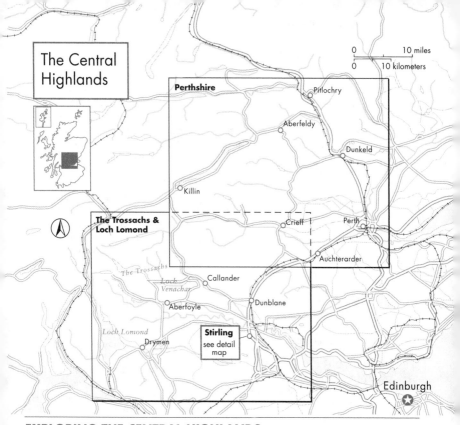

The Central Highlands

Perthshire

Pitlochry

Aberfeldy

Dunkeld

Killin

The Trossachs & Loch Lomond

Crieff

Perth

The Trossachs

Loch Venachar

Callander

Auchterarder

Aberfoyle

Dunblane

Loch Lomond

Drymen

Stirling
see detail map

Edinburgh

0        10 miles
0        10 kilometers

## EXPLORING THE CENTRAL HIGHLANDS

The main towns of Stirling and Perth serve as roadway hubs for the area, making both places natural starting points for tours. Stirling itself is worth covering in some detail on foot. The successive waves of development of this important town can easily be traced—from castle and Old Town architecture to Victorian developments and urban and industrial sprawl.

The Trossachs are a short distance from Stirling, all easily covered in a loop. You can get to Loch Lomond from either Glasgow or Stirling. The main road up the west bank (A82) is not recommended for leisurely touring, as the heavy traffic makes for a hectic drive. Do use this road, however, if you're on your way to Oban, Kintyre, or Argyll.

Loch Lomond is best seen from one of two cul-de-sac roads: by way of Drymen at the south end, up to Rowardennan, or if you're pressed for time, west from Aberfoyle to reach Loch Lomond near its northern end, at Inversnaid. Note that in the Trossachs, the road that some maps show going all the way around Loch Katrine is a private road belonging to the Strathclyde Water Board and is open only to walkers and cyclists. ■TIP➔To save money, try packing a picnic. Local supermarkets

## GREAT ITINERARIES

Scotland's beautiful interior is excellent touring country, though Stirling and Perth are worth your time, too. The glens, in some places, run parallel to the lochs, including those along Lochs Earn, Tay, and Rannoch, making for satisfying loops and round-trips.

### IF YOU HAVE 2 DAYS

There's enough to see in ⛶ **Stirling** to fill up at least a day. The second day, cover the **Trossachs** loop, which includes Loch Venachar, Loch Achray, and Loch Katrine, and the historic towns of **Dunblane** and nearby Doune with Doune Castle, **Callander**, and **Aberfoyle**. Aberfoyle is 27 mi (55 minutes) from Glasgow and 55 mi (1 hour, 22 minutes) from Edinburgh.

### IF YOU HAVE 6 DAYS

Spend a day in ⛶ **Stirling**. If you're shopping for Scottish woolens, wander into Mill Trail country east of Stirling. Then visit **Dunblane** and

Doune Castle, staying overnight at ⛶ **Callander** to explore the fine country northward toward **Balquhidder Glen**. Spend a day in the **Trossachs** around Loch Venachar and Loch Katrine, and take a boat ride to see the landscape at its best. The next day travel to **Drymen** for a morning around **Loch Lomond** before driving into Perthshire. Spend a night at ⛶ **Auchterarder**, with its antiques shops, or travel straight to ⛶ **Perth**, where you should base yourself for two days while exploring Perthshire. Go west for **Crieff** and Drummond Castle Garden or north for Highland resort towns such as **Dunkeld**, with its cathedral, **Pitlochry**, close to the historic Pass of Killiecrankie and impressive Blair Castle, and **Aberfeldy**. Between Pitlochry and Aberfeldy, make time for an escape to the bleak landscapes of Loch Rannoch—a great contrast to the generally pastoral Perthshire countryside.

make delicious and inexpensive sandwiches and salads that are great for outdoor dining. Just remember to pack a blanket and umbrella.

Getting around Perthshire is made interesting by the series of looped tours accessible from the A9, a fast main artery. Exercise caution while driving the A9 itself, however, there have been many accidents in this area. The entire route can be completed in a single day, but if you have time on your hands and are seeking a little spontaneity, you may want to overnight in a village or two along the way.

### ABOUT THE RESTAURANTS

Regional country delicacies—loch trout, river salmon, lamb, and venison—appear regularly on even modest menus in Central Highlands restaurants. In the towns and villages south and southwest of Stirling you can find simple pubs, often crowded and noisy, but serving substantial food at lunchtime (eaten balanced on your knee, perhaps, or at a shared table).

### ABOUT THE HOTELS

In Stirling and Callander, as well as in the small towns and villages throughout the region, you can find a selection of accommodations out of all proportion to the size of the communities (industrial towns are the exceptions). The grand hotels, though few, popped up in the 19th century, when travel in Scotland was the fashion. The level of service at these places has, by and large, not slipped. Alternatively, many country-house inns are a match for the grand hotels in comfort, while adding a personal touch to the service.

| WHAT IT COSTS IN POUNDS | | | | | |
| --- | --- | --- | --- | --- | --- |
| | £ | ££ | £££ | ££££ | £££££ |
| RESTAURANTS | under £10 | £10–£14 | £15–£19 | £20–£25 | over £25 |
| HOTELS | under £70 | £70–£120 | £121–£160 | £161–£220 | over £220 |

Restaurant prices are for a main course at dinner. Hotel prices are for two people in a standard double room in high season and generally include the 17.5% V.A.T.

**TIMING**

The Trossachs and Loch Lomond are always crowded in high summer, so the area makes a good choice for off-season touring. Fall colors are spectacular, and winter brings dramatic Highland light.

# STIRLING

*26 mi northeast of Glasgow, 36 mi northwest of Edinburgh.*

Stirling is one of Britain's great historic towns. An impressive propor-tion of the Old Town walls remain and can be seen from Dumbarton Road, as soon as you step outside the tourist information center. Its castle, built on a steep-sided plug of rock, dominates the landscape, and its esplanade affords views of the surrounding valley plain of the River Forth. In some ways, Stirling is a little Edinburgh with similar "crag-and-tail" foundations and a royal half mile.

Stirling's strategic position, commanding the lowest bridge on the Forth, was appreciated by the Stewart kings, and they spent a lot of time at its castle—a fact that, together with the relics of freedom fight-ers in the neighborhood, has led some Scottish nationalists to declare that Stirling, not Edinburgh, should really be the capital city.

## EXPLORING STIRLING

The historic part of town is tightly nestled around the castle—everything is within easy walking distance. You can either take a taxi or walk—if you're feeling energetic—out to Bannockburn Heritage Centre or the National Wallace Monument, on the town's outskirts. ■ TIP→ **The weather is always changing in this part of the country. Bring sunscreen, a hat, and a waterproof jacket with you wherever you go.**

### MAIN ATTRACTIONS

★ **Bannockburn Heritage Centre.** In 1298, the year after William Wallace's victory, Robert the Bruce (1274–1329) materialized as the nation's champion, and the final bloody phase of the Wars of Independence began. Bruce's rise resulted from the uncertainties and timidity of the great lords of Scotland (ever unsure of which way to jump and whether

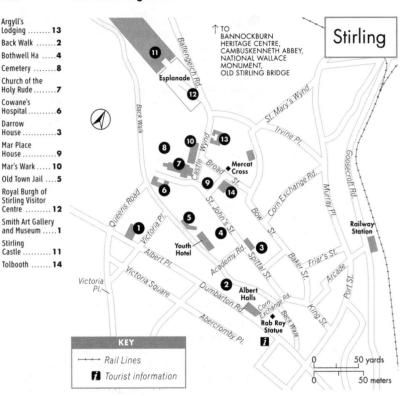

to bow to England's demands). This tale is recounted at the Bannock-burn Heritage Centre, hidden among the sprawl of housing and commercial development on the southern edge of Stirling. This was the site of the famed Battle of Bannockburn in 1314. In Bruce's day the Forth had a shelved and partly wooded floodplain. So he cunningly chose this site, noting the boggy ground on the lower reaches in which the heavy horses of the English would founder. The events of this time have been re-created within the center by means of an audiovisual presentation, models and costumed figures, and an arresting mural depicting the battle in detail. ⊠ *Glasgow Rd., off A80* ☎ *0844/4932139* ⊕ *www.nts. org.uk* 🖅 *£5* ⊙ *Mar., daily 10:30–4; Apr.–Oct., daily 10–5:30.*

**National Wallace Monument.** It was near Old Stirling Bridge that the Scottish freedom fighter William Wallace (circa 1270–1305) and a ragged army of Scots won a major victory in 1297. The movie *Braveheart*, directed by and starring Mel Gibson, was based on Wallace's life. A more accurate version of events is told in an exhibition and audiovisual presentation at this pencil-thin museum on the Abbey Craig. Up close, this Victorian shrine to William Wallace, built between 1856 and 1869, becomes less slim and soaring, revealing itself to be a substantial square tower with a creepy spiral stairway. To reach the monument, follow the Bridge of Allan signs (A9) northward, crossing the River Forth by

Robert Stephenson's (1772–1850) New Bridge of 1832, next to the historic old one. The National Wallace Monument is signposted at the next traffic circle. ⊠*Abbey Craig* ☎*01786/472140* ⊕*www.national wallacemonument.com* ☒*£6.50* ⊙*Mar.–May and Oct., daily 10–5; June, daily 10–6; July and Aug., daily 9–6; Sept., daily 9:30–5:30; Nov.–Feb., daily 10:30–4.*

❺ **Old Town Jail.** The original town jail, now restored, has exhibitions
Ⓒ about life in a 19th-century Scottish prison. Furnished cells, models, and staff—dressed as prisoners, wardens, and prison reformers—bring the gruesome prison regime to life. From October through March, these living-history performances take place only on weekends. ⊠*Access from St. John's St.* ☎*01786/450050* ⊕*www.oldtownjail.com* ☒*£5; £5.95 with a guide* ⊙*Apr. and May, daily 9:30–5:30; June–Sept., daily 9–6; Oct., daily 9:30–5; Nov.–Mar., daily 10–4; last admission 1 hr before closing.*

❶ **Smith Art Gallery and Museum.** This community art gallery, founded in 1874 with the bequest of a local collector, showcases a varied exhibition program of paintings and sculpture. ⊠*Albert Pl., Dumbarton Rd.* ☎*01786/471917* ⊕*www.smithartgallery.demon.co.uk* ☒*Free* ⊙*Tues.–Sat. 10:30–5, Sun. 2–5.*

⓫ **Stirling Castle.** Its magnificent strategic position made Stirling Castle
Fodor'sChoice the grandest prize in the Scots Wars of Independence in the late 13th
★ and early 14th centuries. The Battle of Bannockburn in 1314 was fought within sight of its walls, and the victory by Robert the Bruce yielded both the castle and freedom from English subjugation for almost four centuries.

The daughter of King Robert I (Robert the Bruce), Marjory, married Walter Fitzallan, the high steward of Scotland. Their descendants included the Stewart dynasty of Scottish monarchs (Mary, Queen of Scots, was a Stewart, though she preferred the French spelling, *Stuart*). The Stewarts were responsible for many of the works that survive within the castle walls today. They made Stirling Castle their court and power base, creating fine Renaissance-style buildings that were not completely obliterated, despite subsequent reconstruction for military purposes.

You can enter the castle through its outer defenses, which consist of a great curtain wall and batteries from 1708, built to bulwark earlier defenses by the main gatehouse. From this lower square the most conspicuous feature is the **Palace,** built by King James V (1512–42) between 1538 and 1542. The decorative figures festooning the ornately worked outer walls show the influence of French masons. Work is under way to re-create the furnishings and tapestries of the palace during the reign of James V and his French queen, Mary of Guise. This will transform the empty rooms into the richly adorned living quarters of the kings and queens of Scotland. Overlooking the upper courtyard is the **Great Hall,** built by King James IV (1473–1513) in 1503. Before the Union of Parliaments in 1707, when the Scottish aristocracy sold out to England, this building had been used as one of the seats of the Scottish Parliament. After 1707 it sank into decline, becoming a riding school, then a barracks. It has since been restored to its original splendor.

Among the later works built for regiments stationed here, the **King's Old Building** stands out, it's a 19th-century baronial revival on the site of an earlier building. The oldest building on the site is the **Mint,** or **Coonzie Hoose,** perhaps dating as far back as the 14th century. Below is an arched passageway leading to the westernmost section of the ramparts, the **Nether Bailey.** You'll have the distinct feeling here of being in the bow of a warship sailing up the *carselands* (valley plain) of the Forth Valley, which fans out before the great superstructure of the castle. Among the gun platforms and the crenellations of the ramparts, you may find yourself pondering the strategic significance of Stirling.

To the south lies the hump of the Touch and the Gargunnock hills (part of the Campsie Fells), which diverted potential direct routes from Glasgow and the south. For centuries all roads into the Highlands across the narrow waist of Scotland led to Stirling. If you look carefully northward, you can still see the Old Stirling Bridge, once the lowest and most convenient place to cross the river. For all these geographic reasons, the castle was perhaps the single most important fortress in Scotland. ⊠ *Castlehill* ☎ *01786/450000* ⊕ *www.historic-scotland.gov. uk* ✆ *£8.50, including admission to Argyll's Lodging* ☼ *Apr.–Sept., daily 9:30–6; Oct.–Mar., daily 9:30–5.*

🅭 **Tolbooth.** Built in 1705, the Tolbooth has been many things: courthouse, jail, meeting place. At one time the city's money was kept here. It's undergone much remodeling over the years but has retained its traditional Scottish steeple and gilded weathercock. Today it serves as a popular music and arts venue with a 200-seat auditorium as well as a stylish restaurant and bar. ⊠ *Broad St.*

### ALSO WORTH SEEING

🅭 **Argyll's Lodging.** A nobleman's town house built in three phases from the 16th century onward, this building is actually older than the name it bears—that of Archibald, the ninth earl of Argyll (1629–85), who bought it in 1666. It was for many years a military hospital, then a youth hostel. It has now been refurbished to show how the nobility lived in 17th-century Stirling. Specially commissioned reproduction furniture and fittings are based on the original inventory of the house's contents at that time. ⊠ *Castle Wynd* ☎ *01786/431319* ⊕ *www. historic-scotland.gov.uk* ✆ *£4.50, £8.50 with admission to Stirling Castle* ☼ *Apr.–Sept., daily 9:30–6; Oct.–Mar., daily 9:30–5.*

🅯 **Back Walk.** The upper Back Walk will take you along the outside of the city's walls, past a watchtower and the grimly named Hangman's entry, carved out of the great whinstone boulders that once marked the outer defenses of the town. One of several access areas is off Dumbarton Road, opposite the tourist information center. ⊠ *Runs from Dumbarton Rd. to Castle Rock.*

🅯 **Bothwell Ha.** This 16th-century hall (*ha* in Scots) is said to have been owned by the earl of Bothwell (circa 1535–78), the third husband of

Mary, Queen of Scots (1542–87). Sadly, it's closed to the public. ✉*St. John's St..*

**Cambuskenneth Abbey.** On the south side of the Abbey Craig, the scanty remains of this 13th-century abbey lie in a sweeping bend of the River Forth, with the dramatic outline of Stirling Castle as a backdrop. Important meetings of the Scottish Parliament were once held here, and King Edward I (1239–1307) of England visited in 1304. The abbey was looted and damaged during the Scots Wars of Independence in the late 13th and early 14th centuries. The reconstructed tomb of King James III (1452–88) can be seen near the outline of the high altar. ✉*Ladysneuk Rd.* ☏*01667/460232* ⊕*www.historic-scotland.gov.uk* 🎟*Free* ⊙*May–Sept., daily 9:30–6.*

**❽ Cemetery.** Among the most notable of the many unusual monuments in the cemetery near the Church of the Holy Rude is the **Star Pyramid** of 1858. Also look for the macabre, glass-walled **Martyrs Monument,** erected in memory of two Wigtownshire girls who were drowned in 1685 for their faith. The castle dominates the foreground, and from **Ladies' Rock,** a high perch within the cemetery, there are excellent views of the looming fortress. ✉*Top of St. John's St.*

**❼ Church of the Holy Rude.** The nave of this handsome church survives from the 15th century, and a portion of the original medieval timber roof can also be seen. This is the only Scottish church still in use to have witnessed the coronation of a Scottish monarch—James VI (1566–1625) in 1567. ✉*Top of St. John's St.*

**❻ Cowane's Hospital.** Built in 1639 for *decayed breithers* (unsuccessful merchants), this building has above its entrance a small, cheery statue of the founder himself, John Cowane, which is said to come alive on Hogmanay Night (December 31) to walk the streets with the locals and join in their New Year's revelry. ✉*St. John's St.*

**❸ Darrow House.** Dating from the 17th century, this house displays the characteristic crow-step gables, dormer windows, and projecting turnpike stairs of the period. It's closed to the public. ✉*Spittal St.*

**❾ Mar Place House.** This handsome Georgian building was saved from dereliction and painstakingly restored through the town council's ongoing Old Town renovation program. It's closed to the public. ✉*Mar Pl.*

**❿ Mar's Wark.** These distinctive windowless and roofless ruins are the stark remains of a Renaissance palace built in 1570 by Lord Erskine (died 1572), earl of Mar and Stirling Castle governor. The name means "Mar's work," or building. Look for the armorial carved panels, the gargoyles, and the turrets flanking a railed-off *pend* (archway). During the 1745 Jacobite rebellion, Mar's Wark was laid siege to and severely damaged, but its admirably worn shell survives. The ruins are enclosed by a fence, you may view them from outside only. ✉*Castle Wynd* ☏*01667/460232* ⊕*www.historic-scotland.gov.uk.*

**Old Stirling Bridge.** North of Stirling Castle, on the edge of town, is a narrow, humped 15th-century bridge, now open only to pedestrians. ⊠*Off Drip Rd., A84.*

🔟 **Royal Burgh of Stirling Visitor Centre.** This visitor center at the foot of the Castle Esplanade houses a shop and exhibition hall with an audiovisual presentation on the town and surrounding area. Groups perform Highland dancing on the Esplanade Tuesday evenings from mid-June through August. The dancers wear tartan and step to fiddle or bagpipe music. ☎*01786/479901* ✉*Free* ⊙*Apr.–Oct., daily 9:30–6; Nov.– Mar., daily 9:30–5.*

## WHERE TO STAY & EAT

£££ ✗**Hermann's Brasserie.** Run by Austrian Hermann and his Glaswegian wife, the brasserie makes an arresting marriage of culture and food. The Black-Watch-tartan carpet and alpine murals are as well matched as the *cullen skink* (an archetypal Scottish soup of fish and potato) and Wiener schnitzel. ⊠*58 Broad St.* ☎*01786/450632* ▭*AE, MC, V.*

££ ✗**River House.** At the foot of Stirling Castle, this restaurant sits by its own tranquil loch and is built in the style of a Scottish *crannog* (ancient loch dwelling). Popular with both families and couples, local produce dominates the menu, yet the food reflects Eastern and Mediterranean influences. Try the curried Scottish lamb with lime yogurt. ⊠*The Castle Business Park, Craigforth* ☎*01786/465577* ▭*AE, MC, V.*

£££ ✗🖼**Stirling Highland Hotel.** The impressive 1854 building this hotel
★ occupies was once the Old High School, and many original architectural features remain, including the fully working observatory on the roof. Furnishings are old-fashioned, with solid wood, tartan, florals, and low-key, neutral color schemes. The modern-Scottish Scholars Restaurant (£££££, fixed-price menu) offers outstanding seafood, game, and Aberdeen Angus beef. **Pros:** Near train station, excellent restaurant, some rooms have views the castle. **Cons:** Slightly institutional feel, some pets smells. ⊠*Spittal St., FK8 1DU* ☎*01786/272727* ⊕*www. paramount-hotels.co.uk* ➾*96 rooms* ⌂*In-room: no a/c, dial-up. In-hotel: restaurant, bar, pool, gym, public Wi-Fi, some pets allowed* ▭*AE, DC, MC, V* ℗*BP.*

££ ✗🖼**Park Lodge Hotel.** This elegant 18th-century country-house hotel gives you a taste of French-inspired design and cuisine. It's run by a delightful French family who is only too willing to help. The interior is all fanlights, antique furniture, and candles. Rooms look out over Kings Park and Stirling Castle. The Heritage Restaurant (£££££) serves prix-fixe dinners that typically include French classics such as *filet au poivre* (pepper beef steak) and *magret de canard* (duck breast). **Pros:** Great views of park, homey feel, recently renovated. **Cons:** Too many floral prints, disappointing bathrooms. ⊠*32 Park Terr., FK8 2JS* ☎*01786/474862* ⊕*www.parklodge.net* ➾*9 rooms* ⌂*In-room: no a/c, Ethernet. In-hotel: restaurant, bar, no elevator, some pets allowed* ▭*MC, V* ℗*BP.*

£ 🖼**Castlecroft.** Tucked beneath Stirling Castle, this warm and comfortable modern house is well situated for sightseeing in the Old Town.

It overlooks fine views of the Trossachs and Grampian mountains to the north. People allergic to pets be warned: the owners have a dog and a cat. **Pros**: Great location, lovely views, hearty breakfasts. **Cons**: Some rooms are on the small side, decor needs to be updated. ⊠*Ballengeich Rd., FK8 1TN* ☎*01786/474933* ⊕*www.castlecroft-uk.com* ⤢*6 rooms* ⚡*In-room: no a/c, no phone. In-hotel: bar, no elevator* ⊟*MC, V* ⏺|*BP.*

£ ⛨**Kilronan House.** In Bridge of Allan, close to the Wallace Monument and many shops and restaurants, this granite-walled B&B offers quality accommodation and good value for the money. High ceilings and other details recall the house's genteel Victorian origins, and the well-tended gardens are a pleasant place to relax. **Pros**: Lovely gardens, spacious rooms, close to bus stops. **Cons**: Not all rooms have bathrooms, steep driveway. ⊠*15 Kenilworth Rd., FK9 4DU* ☎*01786/831054* ⊕*www. kilronan.co.uk* ⤢*3 rooms* ⚡*In-room: no a/c, no phone, no TV. In-hotel: bar, no elevator* ⊟*No credit cards* ⏺|*BP.*

£ ⛨**West Plean.** This handsome, rambling, early-Georgian house is part
★ of a working farm, with a walled garden and woodland walks. Well-prepared food and spacious rooms make this B&B an excellent bargain. **Pros**: Beautiful gardens, plenty of peace and quiet, huge and hearty breakfast. **Cons**: Long walk to Stirling, books up quickly. ⊠*Denny Rd., FK7 8HA* ☎*01786/812208* ⊕*www.westpleanhouse.com* ⤢*3 rooms* ⚡*In-room: no a/c. In-hotel: bar, no elevator* ⊟*No credit cards* ⏀*Closed Dec. and Jan.* ⏺|*BP.*

## THE ARTS

The **Macrobert Arts Centre** (⊠*Stirling University* ☎*01786/466666*) has a theater, art gallery, and studio with programs that range from films to pantomime.

## SHOPPING

### CERAMICS & GLASSWARE

South of Stirling, in a farm setting at Larbert (and signposted off A9), is **Barbara Davidson's pottery studio** (⊠*Muirhall Farm* ☎*01324/554430*), run by one of the best-known potters in Scotland. You can make an appointment to paint a pot, which will be glazed, fired, and mailed to you, and in July and August you can even try throwing your own pot. **Village Glass** (⊠*11 Henderson St.* ☎*01786/832137*) sells original glassware handblown on the premises.

### CLOTHING

East of Stirling is **Mill Trail** country, along the foot of the Ochil Hills. A leaflet from any local tourist information center will lead you to the delights of a real mill shop and low mill prices—even on cashmere—at Tillicoultry, Alva, and Alloa.

In Stirling, **House of Henderson** (⊠*6–8 Friars St.* ☎*01786/473681*), a Highland outfitter, sells tartans, woolens, and accessories, and offers a made-to-measure kilt service.

## JEWELRY

**Fotheringham Gallery** ( ✉ *78 Henderson St.* ☎ *01786/832861*) has jewelry and paintings.

# THE TROSSACHS & LOCH LOMOND

Immortalized by Wordsworth and Sir Walter Scott, the Trossachs (the name means "bristly country") may contain some of Scotland's loveliest forest, hills, and glens, well justifying the area's designation as a national park. The Trossachs has a very peculiar charm, for it combines the wildness of the Highlands with the prolific vegetation of an old Lowland forest. Its open ground is a dense mat of bracken and heather, and its woodland is of silver birch, dwarf oak, and hazel—trees that fasten their roots into the crevices of rocks and stop short on the very brink of lochs. There are also quaint towns to visit along the way. Dunblane has a magnificent cathedral; Doune's castle will make you stare in awe and when you step foot inside the Hamilton Toy Shop in Callendar you'll feel like a kid again, marveling with wide eyes at its impressive and extensive collection.

When should you visit the Trossachs? The most colorful season is fall, particularly October, a lovely time when most visitors have departed and the hares, deer, and game birds have taken over. Even in rainy weather the Trossachs of "darksome glens and gleaming lochs" are memorable: the water filtering through the rocks by Loch Lomond comes out so pure and clear that the loch is like a sheet of glass. The best way to explore this area is by car, by bike, or by foot; the latter two depend, of course, on the weather. Keep in mind that roads in this region of the country are narrow and winding, which can make for dangerous conditions in all types of weather.

## DUNBLANE

*7 mi north of Stirling.*

The oldest part of Dunblane—a quaint town with twisting streets and lovely houses—huddles around the square where the partly restored ruins of **Dunblane Cathedral** stand. Bishop Clement oversaw construction of the cathedral in the early 13th century on the site of St. Blane's tiny 8th-century cell. It's contemporary with the Borders abbeys but more mixed in its architecture—part early English and part Norman. Dunblane ceased to be a cathedral, as did most others in Scotland, at the time of the Reformation, in the mid-16th century. ✉ *The Cross* ☎ *01667/460232* ⊕ *www.historic-scotland.gov.uk* 🎟 *Free* ☯ *Apr.–Sept., Mon.–Sat. 9:30–5:30, Sun. 2–5:30; Oct.–Mar., Mon.–Sat. 9:30–4:30, Sun. 2–4:30.*

The Highland-edge community of Doune, 5 mi west of Dunblane, was once a center for pistol making. No self-respecting Highland chief's attire was complete without a prestigious and ornate pair of pistols. Today Doune is more widely known for one of the best-preserved medi-

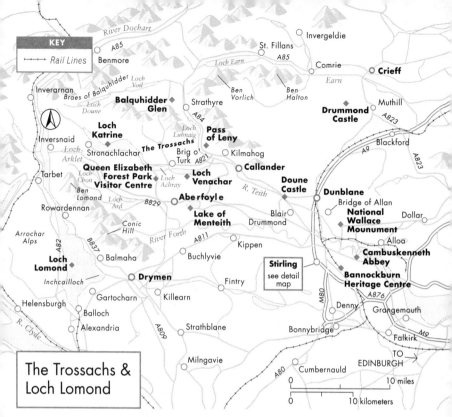


**KEY**

┄┄┼┄┄ Rail Lines

## The Trossachs & Loch Lomond

eval castles in Scotland. It's also a place of pilgrimage for fans of Monty
★ Python's *Holy Grail*, which was filmed here. **Doune Castle** is grim and
high-walled, with echoing, drafty stone vaults. Construction of the fortress began in the early 15th century on a now-peaceful riverside tract.
The best place to photograph this squat, walled fort is from the bridge,
a little way upstream. Be sure to climb up to the curtain-wall walk
for good views. The castle is signposted to the left as you enter the
town from the Dunblane road. ✉ *Off A84, Doune* ☎ *01786/841742*
⊕ *www.historic-scotland.gov.uk* 🎟 *£4* 🕓 *Apr.–Sept., daily 9:30–5:30;
Oct.–Mar., Sat.–Wed. 9:30–4:30.*

### WHERE TO STAY & EAT

££££ ✕ 🏨 **Cromlix House Hotel.** A long, narrow drive leads to this Victorian-
era mansion on a 2,000 acre estate. Inside you can find the original
conservatory and a well-stocked library that enhance the period atmosphere. Meals are served in two elegant, country-house-style dining
rooms with fixed-price menus (£££££). Specialties include game and
lamb from the estate. Try the delicious confit of guinea fowl as a starter,
followed by beef with pickled walnuts. **Pros:** Beautiful and extensive
grounds, gorgeous fireplaces, artwork appropriate for the "old hunting lodge" setting. **Cons:** Some plumbing problems, bedroom decor is
a little stale. ✉ *Kinbuck, FK15 9JT* ⊕ *On B8033, 3 mi northeast of*

*Dunblane* ☎*01786/822125* ⊕*www.cromlixhouse.com* 🛏*6 rooms, 8 suites* ⟳*In-room: no a/c. In-hotel: restaurant, bar, tennis court, public Internet, public Wi-Fi, no-smoking rooms, no elevator* ⊟*AE, DC, MC, V* ❀*BP.*

## CALLANDER

*8 mi northwest of Doune.*

A traditional Highland-edge resort, the wee town of Callander bustles throughout the year, even during off-peak times, simply because it's a gateway to Highland scenery, and Loch Lomond and the Trossachs National Park. As a result, there's plenty of window-shopping here, plus nightlife in pubs and a good selection of accommodations.

☺ The **Hamilton Toy Collection** is one of the most extensive in Britain. Both kids and adults can spend hours amid every conceivable toy from the Victorian age until the 1970s: teddy bears, porcelain dolls, toy soldiers, Matchbox cars, Thunderbirds memorabilia, and a wonderful selection of model railways. ✉*111 Main St.* ☎*01877/330004* 💷*£2* ⏱*Apr.–Oct., Mon.–Sat. 10–4:30, Sun. 12–4:30.*

### WHERE TO STAY & EAT

£  ✕**Pip's Coffee House.** Come to this cheerful little place just off the main street for imaginative soups and salads, as well as exquisite Scottish home baking, including fresh scones. And then, of course, there's great coffee. ✉*Ancaster Sq.* ☎*01877/330470* ⊟*No credit cards.*

£££  ✕⊡**Roman Camp.** This former hunting lodge, dating to 1625, has 20 acres of gardens that give it a secluded feel. You might be surprised that it's within easy walking distance of Callander's town center. The antiques-filled sitting rooms and library are more reminiscent of a stately family home than a hotel. The restaurant (£££££, fixed-price menu) has a good reputation for its salmon, trout, and other fish, all cooked in an imaginative, modern Scottish style. Also delicious is the fillet of Scotch beef with an herb-potato scone and wild-mushroom mousseline. **Pros:** Stunning grounds, decadent rooms, close to shops and restaurants. **Cons:** Service isn't great, some of the rooms could be cleaner. ✉*Main St., FK17 8BG* ☎*01877/330003* ⊕*www.roman-camp-hotel.co.uk* 🛏*11 rooms, 3 suites* ⟳*In-room: no a/c. In-hotel: restaurant, bar, no elevator* ⊟*AE, DC, MC, V* ❀*BP.*

---

### WORD OF MOUTH

"For a short visit and wanting to see an area in some depth, I'd pick somewhere like the Trossachs (near Callander) or Dunkeld/Perth. Both are in the middle of TONS of things to see/do, yet are still a reasonable train to Edinburgh for a day trip. The general Trossachs area would be a good base for Stirling, Loch Lomond, and lots of other lochs/waterfalls and castles—even Glencoe. Perth/Dunkeld would be a good base for Stirling, Blair Atholl, Scone, St. Andrews/Fife, and a bit more mountainous scenery than the Trossachs."
–janisj

## TEEING OFF IN THE TROSSACHS

There are a wealth of beautiful golf courses within the Loch Lomond and the Trossachs National Park. The National Park Golf Pass (£50 for three days, £80 for five days) allows play at Callander, St. Fillans, Aberfoyle, Killin, and Buchanan Castle (£10 supplement).

**Aberfoyle Golf Club** ( ✉ *Braeval, Aberfoyle* ☎ *01877/382493* ⊕ *www.nationalparkgolf.co.uk*).

**Buchanan Castle Golf Club** ( ✉ *A809, Drymen* ☎ *01360/660330*

⊕ *www.buchanancastlegolfclub.co.uk* ).

**Callander Golf Club** ( ✉ *Aveland Rd., Callander* ☎ *01877/330975* ⊕ *www.callandergolfclub.co.uk*).

**Killin Golf Club** ( ✉ *Off A827, Killin* ☎ *01567/820312* ⊕ *www.killingolfclub.co.uk*).

**St. Fillans Golf Club** ( ✉ *S. Loch Earn Rd., St. Fillans* ☎ *01764/685312* ⊕ *www.st-fillansgolf.com*).

### SPORTS & THE OUTDOORS

BICYCLING **Wheels/Trossachs Backpackers** ( ✉ *Invertrossachs Rd.* ☎ *01877/331100* ⊕ *www.scottish-cycling.com*) is a friendly firm that can help you find the best mountain-bike routes around the Trossachs and offers hostel accommodation for cyclists (£15 for a dorm bed).

GOLF **Callander golf course,** designed by Tom Morris in 1890, has fine views and a tricky moorland layout. Keep between the trees on the 15th hole and you may end up with a hole-in-one. ✉ *Aveland Rd.* ☎ *01877/330090* ⊕ *www.callandergolfclub.co.uk* ⚑ *18 holes, 5,151 yds, par 66.*

HIKING Just north of Callander, the mountains squeeze both the road and rocky river into the narrow **Pass of Leny.** An abandoned railway—now a pleasant walking or biking path—also goes through the pass, past Ben Ledi and Loch Lubnaig.

A walk is signposted from the east end of the main street to the **Bracklinn Falls,** over whose lip Sir Walter Scott once rode a pony to win a bet.

It's a 1½-mi walk through the woods up to the **Callander Crags,** with views of the Lowlands as far as the Pentland Hills behind Edinburgh. The walk begins at the west end of the main street.

### SHOPPING

The **Edinburgh Woollen Mill Group** operates three mill shops in and near Callander. All the stores have a vast selection of woolens on display, including luxurious cashmere and striking tartan throws, and will provide overseas mailing and tax-free shopping. *Callander Woollen Mill:* ✉ *12–18 Main St.* ☎ *01877/330612; Kilmahog Woollen Mill:* ✉ *North of town at Trossachs Turning* ☎ *01877/330268; Trossachs Woollen Mill:* ✉ *North of town at Trossachs Turning* ☎ *01877/330178.*

## BALQUHIDDER GLEN

*12 mi north of Callander.*

A 20-minute drive from Callander, through the Pass of Leny and beyond Strathyre, is Balquhidder Glen (pronounced *bal*-whidd-*er*), a typical Highland glen that runs westward. The glen has characteristics seen throughout the north: a flat-bottom U-shape profile, formed by prehistoric glaciers, extensive Forestry-Commission plantings replacing much of the natural woodlands above, a sprinkling of farms, and farther up the glen, hill roads bulldozed into the slopes to provide access for foresters. You may notice a boarded-up look of some of the area's houses, many of which are second homes for affluent residents of the south. The glen is also where Loch Voil and Loch Doune spread out, adding to the stunning vistas.

The area around Balquhidder Glen is known as the Braes (Slopes) of Balquhidder and was the home of the MacLarens and the MacGregors. The **grave of Rob Roy MacGregor,** the 18th-century Scottish outlaw hero and subject of Sir Walter Scott's novel Rob Roy, is signposted beside Balquhidder village. The site of his house, now a private farm, is beyond the parking lot at the end of the road up the glen. The glen has no through road, though there is a right-of-way (on foot) from the churchyard where Rob Roy is buried, through Kirkton Glen and on to open grasslands and a lake.

### WHERE TO STAY & EAT

££££ ✕🔲 **Monachyle Mhor.** Set in 2,000 acres of forests and moorland, this
Fodor'sChoice beautiful lodge has magnificent views across lochs Voil and Doine. The
★ hotel offers complimentary salmon and trout fishing. The rooms are striking with clean, elegant lines and modish luxury, like plush animal-print throws. The bright and airy restaurant (£££££, fixed-price menu) serves expertly prepared and beautiful food that changes daily showing the chef's lightness of touch: try the cream of celeriac, apple, and lime soup, or wild sea bass with new season's pea risotto. **Pros:** Stunning scenery, delicious food. **Cons:** You're pretty isolated, rooms are on the small side. ✉*Balquhidder, FK19 8PQ* ☎*01877/384622* ⊕*www.monachylemhor.com* 🛏*9 rooms, 2 suites* △*In-room: no a/c. In-hotel: restaurant, no elevator, public Wi-Fi* ▭*MC, V* ⦿*BP.*

## THE TROSSACHS

*10 mi west of Callander.*

With its harmonious scenery of hill, loch, and wooded slopes, the Trossachs has been a popular touring region since the late 18th century, at the dawn of the age of the Romantic poets. Influenced by the writings of Sir Walter Scott, early visitors who strayed into the Highlands from the central belt of Scotland admired this as the first "wild" part of Scotland they encountered. Perhaps because the Trossachs represent the very essence of what the Highlands are supposed to be, the whole of this area, including Loch Lomond, is now protected as a national park. Here you can find birch and pine forests, vistas down lochs where the woods creep right to the water's edge, and, in the background, peaks that rise high enough to be called mountains, though they're not as high as those to the north and west. The Trossachs are almost a Scottish visual cliché. They're popular right through the year, drawing not only first-time visitors from all around the world, but also Scots out for a Sunday drive.

The A821 runs west together with the first and gentlest of the Trossachs lochs, **Loch Venachar.** A sturdy gray-stone building, with a small dam at the Callander end, controls the water that feeds into the River Teith (and, hence, into the Forth).

A few minutes after it passes Loch Venachar the A821 becomes muffled in woodlands and twists grad-

> ## SCOTLAND ON TWO WHEELS
>
> The region's big attraction for cyclists is the Lowland/Highland Trail, which stretches over 60 mi and passes through Drymen, Aberfoyle, the Trossachs, Callander, Lochearnhead, and Killin. This route runs along former railroad-track beds, as well as private and minor roads, to reach well into the Central Highlands. Another almost completely traffic-free option is the roadway around Loch Katrine. Mountain bikes can tackle many of the forest roads and trails enjoyed by walkers. Avoid main roads, which can be busy with traffic.

ually down to the village of **Brig o' Turk.** (*Turk* is Gaelic for the Scots *tuirc,* meaning wild boar, a species that has been extinct in this region since about the 16th century.) ✉*On A821.*

**Loch Achray,** stretching west of Brig o' Turk, dutifully fulfills expectations of what a verdant Trossachs loch should be: small, green, reedy meadows backed by dark plantations, rhododendron thickets, and lumpy hills, thickly covered with heather.

The parking lot by Loch Achray is the place to begin the ascent of steep, heathery **Ben An,** which affords some of the best Trossachs' views. The climb requires a couple of hours and good lungs. ✉*On A821.*

★ At the end of Loch Achray, a side road turns right into a narrow pass, leading to **Loch Katrine,** the heart of the Trossachs. Sir Walter Scott traveled here in the early 19th century and was inspired to write *The Lady of the Lake.* At that time, the road here was narrow and almost hidden by the overhanging crags and mossy oaks and birches. Today it ends at a slightly anticlimactic parking lot with a shop, café, and visitor center (there are brochures and restrooms, but don't make special trip). To see the finest of the Trossachs lochs properly, you must—even for just a few minutes—walk a bit farther along the level, paved road beyond the parking lot (open only to Strathclyde Water Board vehicles). Loch Katrine's water is taken by aqueduct and tunnel to Glasgow—a Victorian feat of engineering that has ensured the purity of the supply to Scotland's largest city for more than 100 years. The steamer *Sir Walter Scott* (☎*01877/376316* ✐*£6 one-way, £8 round-trip*) embarks on cruises of Loch Katrine every day between April and late October. The boat leaves from Trossachs Pier at 10:30, 1:15, 2:30, 3:45 and 5. ■TIP➜**Do take the cruise if time permits, as the shores of Katrine**

## A QUEENLY PARK IN THE TROSSACHS

For exquisite nature, drive south from Aberfoyle on the A821 and turn right where signposts read **Queen Elizabeth Forest Park**; here you'll be heading toward higher moorland blanketed with conifers. The conifers hem in the views of Ben Ledi and Ben Venue, which can be seen over the spiky green waves of trees as the road snakes around heathery knolls and hummocks. There's another viewing area, and a small parking lot, at the highest point of the road. Soon the road

swoops off the Highland edge and leads downhill.

Near the start of the descent, the Queen Elizabeth Forest Park Visitor Centre can be seen on the left. The center has displays on the life of the forest, a summer-only café, some fine views over the Lowlands to the south, and a network of footpaths. The Trossachs end here. ⊠ *Off A821* ☎ *01877/382258* ⊕ *www.forestry. gov.uk/qefp* ☉ *Park, daily 24 hrs. Visitor center, Easter–Oct., daily 10–6; Nov.–Dec., weekends 10–6.*

**remain undeveloped and scenic.** ⊠ *Off A821* ☎ *01877/376316* ⊕ *www. lochkatrine.com* ☉ *Visitor center, Apr.–late Oct., daily 9–5.*

## ABERFOYLE

*11 mi south of Loch Katrine, in the Trossachs.*

Aberfoyle has numerous souvenir shops and an attraction that appeals mainly to children.

The **Scottish Wool Centre** tells the story of Scottish wool "from the sheep's back to your back." You can see live specimens of the main breeds in the sheep amphitheater and try your hand at spinning in the textile display area. In the Border collie training area, dogs in training to assist shepherds practice herding ducks. The shop stocks a huge selection of woolen garments and knitwear. ⊠ *Off Main St.* ☎ *01877/382850* 🗐 *£3, free Nov.–Feb.* ☉ *Apr.–Oct., daily 9:30–5:30; Nov., Dec., Feb., and Mar., daily 10–5; Jan., daily 10–4:30.*

The tiny island of **Inchmahome,** on the Lake of Menteith, was a place of refuge in 1547 for the young Mary, Queen of Scots. Between April and September, a ferry takes passengers from the lake's pier to the island (£4.50). ■**TIP→** If the boat is not there when you arrive at the pier, turn the board so that the white side faces the island. The boat will come and collect you. ⊠ *Off A81, 4 mi east of Aberfoyle* ☎ *No phone* 🗐 *Ferry £4.50* ☉ *Apr.–Sept., daily 9:30–4:30.*

**OFF THE BEATEN PATH**

**Along the B829.** From Aberfoyle you can take a trip to see the more enclosed northern portion of **Loch Lomond.** During the off-season the route has an untamed and windswept air when it extends beyond the shelter of trees. Take the B829 (signposted INVERSNAID and STRONACH-LACHAR), which runs west from Aberfoyle and offers outstanding views of Ben Lomond, especially in the vicinity of Loch Ard. The next loch, where the road narrows and bends, is **Loch Chon,** which appears dark and forbidding. Its ominous reputation is further enhanced by the local legend: the presence of a dog-headed monster prone to swallowing passersby. Beyond Loch Chon, the road climbs gently from the plantings to open moor with a breathtaking vista over **Loch Arklet** to the Arrochar Alps, the name given to the high hills west of Loch Lomond. Hidden from sight in a deep trench, Loch Arklet is dammed to feed Loch Katrine. Go left at the road junction (a right will take you to the town of Stronachlachar) and take the open road along Loch Arklet. These deserted green hills were once the rallying grounds of the Clan Gregor. Near the dam on Loch Arklet, on your right, **Garrison Cottage** recalls the days when the government had to billet troops here to keep the MacGregors in order. From Loch Arklet the road zigzags down to **Inversnaid,** where you can see a hotel, house, and parking lot, with **Loch Lomond** stretching out of sight above and below. The only return to Aberfoyle is by retracing the same route.

### WHERE TO STAY

££££   🏨**Macdonald Forest Hills Hotel.** A traditional Scottish-country-house theme pervades this hotel, from the rambling white building itself to the wood-paneled lounges, log fires, and numerous sporting activities. More than 20 acres of gardens and grounds surround the building, which sits on a grassy hillside overlooking Loch Ard. Chintz drapes and reproduction antiques fill the bedrooms. The restaurant (£££££, fixed-price menu) has tartan decor that makes an appropriate backdrop for Scottish game, salmon, beef, and lamb. **Pros:** Stunning views, log fires, good children's programs. **Cons:** Restaurant is pricey and food is average, some of the building looks rundown. ⊠*Kinlochard, FK8 3TL* ☎*01877/387277* ⊕*www.foresthills-hotel.co.uk* ⇌*56 rooms* ⌂*In-room: no a/c. In-hotel: 2 restaurants, tennis court, pool, gym, bicycles, children's programs (ages 5–12), no kids under 5* ⊟*AE, DC, MC, V* ⍩*BP.*

### SPORTS & THE OUTDOORS

BICYCLING **Trossachs Cycle Hire** (⊠*Trossachs Holiday Park* ☎*01877/382614* ⊕*www.trossachsholidays.co.uk*) rents out bicycles from March through October (£5 per hour) and will provide advice on routes.

## DRYMEN

*11 mi southwest of Aberfoyle.*

Drymen is a respectable and cozy town in the Lowland fields, with stores, tea shops, and pubs catering to the well-to-do Scots who have moved here from Glasgow.

For the most outstanding Loch Lomond view from the south end, drive west from Drymen and take a few minutes to clamber up bracken-covered **Duncryne Hill.** At dusk you may be rewarded by a spectacular sunset. You can't miss this distinctive dumpling-shape hill, south of Gartocharn on the Drymen–Balloch road, the A811.

## SHOPPING

**The Rowan Gallery** ( ✉ *36 Main St.* ☎ *01360/660996*) displays original paintings and prints, and specializes in contemporary works by Scottish artists. Also here is a fine selection of ceramics, woodwork, cards, and jewelry.

## LOCH LOMOND

*3 mi west of Drymen via B837, signposted* ROWARDENNAN *and* BALMAHA, *14 mi west of Aberfoyle.*

The upper portion of Loch Lomond, Scotland's largest loch in terms of surface area, is a sparkling ribbon of water snaking into the hills. To the south, the more yielding Lowlands allow the loch to spread out. Wooded islands, some of which can be visited, dot this portion of the loch. As you drive along the B837, you may notice Conic Hill, a wavy ridge of bald, heathery domes behind Balmaha. If you have a regional map, note how Inchcailloch and the other islands line up with Conic Hill. This geographic line is indicative of the Highland boundary fault, which runs through Loch Lomond and the hill.

Before starting your exploration of the loch, take time to visit Loch Lomond Shores on the southern tip of the loch. A castlelike structure here contains the **Loch Lomond and the Trossachs National Park Gateway Centre,** your introduction to Scotland's first national park. A film about the area is shown, and there are shops, restaurants, slipways, and beaches. ✉ *Off A82, near Balloch* ☎ *01389/722199* ⊕ *www.lochlomondshores.com* ⊙ *Weekdays 11–5, weekends 11–6.*

At the little settlement of **Balmaha,** the versatile recreational role filled by Loch Lomond is clear: cruising craft are at the ready, hikers appear out of woodlands on the West Highland Way, and day-trippers stroll at the loch's edge. The heavily wooded offshore islands look alluringly close. One of the best ways to explore them is by taking a cruise or renting a boat. ✉ *On B837.*

The island of **Inchcailloch** (*inch* comes from *innis*, Gaelic for island), just offshore, can be explored in an hour or two. Pleasant pathways thread through oak woods planted in the 18th century, when the bark was used by the tanning industry. ✉ *On B837.*

Loch Lomond is seldom more than a narrow field's length away from the B837 as the road runs northwest to the town of **Rowardennan.** Where the drivable road ends, in a parking lot crunchy with pinecones, you can ramble along one of the marked loch-side footpaths or make your way toward Ben Lomond, 3½ mi away. ✉ *End of B837.*

---

### HIKE THE HIGHLAND WAY

The long-distance walkers' route, the **West Highland Way,** which runs 95 mi from Glasgow to Fort William, follows the bank of Loch Lomond at Inversnaid, which you can reach from the B829. A brief stroll up the path is pleasant, particularly if you're visiting during the spring, when birdsong fills the oak-tree canopy. You may get an inkling of why Scots wax so romantic about the bonnie, bonnie banks of the loch.

## WHERE TO STAY & EAT

**£££££**   ✕🏠**Cameron House.** This beautifully located hotel offers country-club facilities on the shores of Loch Lomond. Pastel shades and antique reproductions decorate the bedrooms. The elegant Georgian Room (£££££, set-price meal) serves excellent Scottish-French cuisine, such as lamb roasted in garlic and fennel, with a millefeuille of wild mushrooms. The Marina Restaurant and Bar (£££££, set-price meal) on the water's edge is informal but stylish and has an open kitchen with a wood-burning oven, perfect for pizzas. **Pros:** Beautiful grounds, good dining. **Cons:** Service leaves something to be desired, spa is several miles from hotel. ✉*Loch Lomond, Alexandria G83 8QZ* ☎*01389/755565* ⊕*www.devere.co.uk* ⤶*96 rooms, 7 suites* ♿*In-room: no a/c. In-hotel: 3 restaurants, bar, golf course, tennis courts, pools, gym, children's programs (ages 5–12)* ▭*AE, DC, MC, V* ⛶*BP.*

**£**   ✕🏠**Balloch House Vintage Inn.** Cute, cozy, and very Scottish, this small hotel offers tasty breakfasts and hearty pub meals like fish-and-chips and local smoked salmon for reasonable prices. The tartan carpet and burning peat fires are nice touches, as are the low ceilings and flickering candles. Rooms upstairs are simple but clean and spacious. Some have great views of the loch. **Pros:** Beautiful building, recently refurbished, near shopping. **Cons:** Noisy pinball machine next to bar, not all rooms have views. ✉*Balloch Rd., Loch Lomond, Balloch, Alexandria G83 8LQ* ☎*01389/752579* ⊕*www.visit-lochlomond.com* ⤶*12 rooms* ♿*In-room: no a/c, cable modems. In-hotel: restaurant, bar* ▭*AE, DC, MC, V* ⛶*BP.*

## SPORTS & THE OUTDOORS

BOAT TOURS   **MacFarlane and Son** ( ✉*Boatyard, Balmaha, Loch Lomond* ☎*01360/870214* ⊕*www.balmahaboatyard.co.uk*) runs cruises on Loch Lomond. The company also rents rowboats and small power-boats so you can explore on your own. From Tarbet, on the western shore, **Cruise Loch Lomond** ( ✉*Boatyard, Tarbet* ☎*01301/702356* ⊕*www.cruiselochlomondltd.com*) runs tours all year.

HIKING   Walking is by far the most popular activity in the **Loch Lomond and the Trossachs National Park** ( ✉*The Old Station, Balloch Rd., Balloch* ☎*01389/722600* ⊕*www.lochlomond-trossachs.org*). There are near-endless possibilities: from carefree meanders on well-kept paths to exhilarating weeklong hikes—like the West Highland way—over vast expanses of mountains, seashore, moors, and forests. You can see and feel the geological variations and enjoy an abundance of Scottish flora and fauna—not to mention the likelihood of experiencing all four seasons in one day.

## SHOPPING

At **Thistle Bagpipe Works** ( ✉*Luss, Dunbartonshire* ☎*01436/860250*), on the western shore of Loch Lomond, you can commission your own made-to-order set of bagpipes. You can also order a complete Highland outfit, including kilt and jacket.

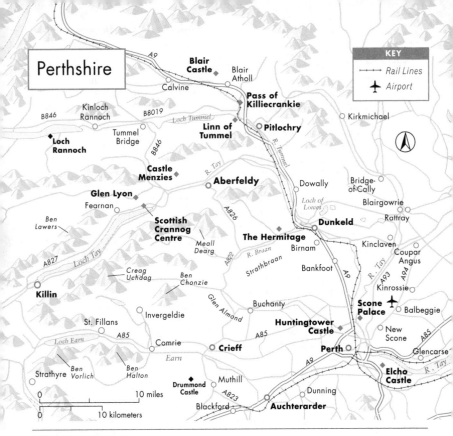

KEY

┼──┼ Rail Lines

✈ Airport

Perthshire

Blair Castle
Blair Atholl
Calvine
Pass of Killiecrankie
Kinloch Rannoch
B846
B8019
Loch Tummel
Tummel Bridge
Linn of Tummel
Pitlochry
Kirkmichael
Loch Rannoch
B846
Castle Menzies
Aberfeldy
Dowally
Bridge-of-Cally
Glen Lyon
Fearnan
R. Tay
Loch of Lowes
Blairgowrie
Ben Lawers
Scottish Crannog Centre
Meall Dearg
The Hermitage
Birnam
Dunkeld
Rattray
A827
A826
A802
R. Braan
Strathbraan
Bankfoot
Kinclaven
Coupar Angus
Loch Tay
Creag Uchdag
Ben Chonzie
A93
A94
Killin
Invergeldie
Glen Almond
Buchanty
Scone Palace
Kinrossie
Balbeggie
St. Fillans
A85
Comrie
Crieff
A85
Huntingtower Castle
Perth
New Scone
A85
Loch Earn
Earn
Glencarse
Strathyre
Ben Vorlich
Ben Halton
Drummond Castle
Muthill
A823
Dunning
A9
Elcho Castle
R. Tay
Blackford
Auchterarder

0 ——————— 10 miles

0 ——————— 10 kilometers

## PERTHSHIRE

Although Perth has an ancient history dating to the Dark Ages, it has been rebuilt and recast innumerable times, and sadly, no trace remains of the pre-Reformation monasteries that once dominated the skyline. In fact, modern Perth has swept much of its colorful history under a grid of busy streets. The town serves a wide rural hinterland and has a well-off air, making it one of Scotland's most interesting shopping towns outside of Edinburgh and Glasgow. Other than that, though, this city is not a big tourist destination.

But Perth's rural hinterland is grand in several senses. On the Highland edge, prosperous-looking farms are scattered across heavily wooded countryside, and even larger properties are screened by trees and parkland. All this changes as the mountain barrier is penetrated, giving rise to grouse moors and deer forest (in this case, *forest* has the Scots meaning of, paradoxically, *open hill*). Parts of Perthshire are quite remote without ever losing their cozy feel.

**PERTH**

*36 mi northeast of Stirling, 43 mi north of Edinburgh, 61 mi northeast of Glasgow.*

Perth has long been a focal point in Scottish history, and several critical events took place here, including the assassination of King James I of Scotland (1394–1437) and John Knox's (1514–72) preaching in St. John's Kirk in 1559. Later, the 17th-century religious wars in Scotland saw the town occupied, first by the marquis of Montrose (1612–50), then later by Oliver Cromwell's (1599–1658) forces. The Jacobites also occupied the town in the 1715 and 1745 rebellions.

Perth's attractions—with the exception of the shops—are scattered and take time to reach on foot. Some, in fact, are far enough away to necessitate the use of a car, bus, or taxi. Scone Palace and a modest selection of castles are within easy reach of Perth.

The cruciform-plan **St. John's Kirk**, dating from the 12th century, was internally divided into three parts at the Reformation, but was restored to something closer to its medieval state by Sir Robert Lorimer in the 1920s. ⊠ *St. John St.* ☎ *01738/626159* ⊕ *www.st-johns-kirk.co.uk* ⌑ *£1 donation* ⊙ *Weekdays 10–4; Sun. services 9:30 and 11.*

The **Perth Art Gallery and Museum** has a wide-ranging collection of natural history, local history, archaeology, and art—including work by the great painter of animals Sir Edwin Landseer and some botanical studies of fungi by Beatrix Potter. ⊠ *78 George St.* ☎ *01738/632488* ⌑ *Free* ⊙ *May–Aug., Mon.–Sat. 10–5, Sun. 1–4:30; Sept.–Apr., Mon.–Sat. 10–5.*

On the North Inch of Perth, look for Balhousie Castle and the **Regimental Museum of the Black Watch.** Some will tell you the Black Watch was a Scottish regiment whose name is a reference to the color of its tartan. An equally plausible explanation, however, is that the regiment was established to keep an undercover watch on rebellious Jacobites. The Gaelic word for black is *dubh,* meaning, in this case, "hidden" or "covert." A wide range of uniforms, weaponry, and marching banners are displayed. The castle is closed on the last Saturday in June. ⊠ *Facing North Inch Park, entrance from Hay St.* ☎ *0131/310–8530* ⊕ *www.theblackwatch.co.uk* ⌑ *Free* ⊙ *May–Sept., Mon.–Sat. 10–4:30; Oct.–Apr., weekdays 10–3:30.*

The Round House, with its magnificent and newly restored dome and rotunda, contains the **Fergusson Gallery,** displaying a selection of 6,000 works—paintings, drawings, and prints—by the Scottish artist J.D. Fergusson (1874–1961). ⊠ *Marshall Pl.* ☎ *01738/441944* ⊕ *www. scottishmuseums.org.uk* ⌑ *Free* ⊙ *Mon.–Sat. 10–5.*

**Huntingtower Castle,** a curious double tower that dates from the 15th century, is associated with an attempt to wrest power from the young James VI in 1582. Some early painted ceilings survive, offering the vaguest hint of the sumptuous interiors, now reduced to bare and drafty rooms. ⊠ *Off A85* ☎ *01738/627231* ⊕ *www.historic-scotland.*

*gov.uk* ✉*£4* ⊙*Apr.–Sept., daily 9:30–5:30; Oct.–Mar., Sat.–Wed. 9:30–4:30.*

**Elcho Castle,** a fortified mansion on the south bank of the River Tay, is the abandoned 15th-century seat of the earls of Wemyss. The internal design, with the grand staircase leading up to the main public rooms, the use of corridors, and the generous number of toilets, shows that this castle was built for comfort as well as defense. ✉*Off A912, close to Rhynd* ☎*01738/639998* ⊕*www.historic-scotland.gov.uk* ✉*£3* ⊙*Apr.–Sept., daily 9:30–5:30.*

⟳
**Fodor'sChoice**
★
About 2 mi from Perth, **Scone Palace** (pronounced *skoon*) is much more cheerful and vibrant than the city's other castles. The palace is the current residence of the earl of Mansfield but is open to visitors. Although it incorporates various earlier works, the palace today has mainly a 19th-century theme, with mock castellations that were fashionable at the time. There's plenty to see if you're interested in the acquisitions of an aristocratic Scottish family: magnificent porcelain, furniture, ivory, clocks, and 16th-century needlework. A coffee shop, restaurant, gift shop, and play area are on-site, and the extensive grounds have a pine plantation. The palace has its own mausoleum nearby, on the site of a long-gone abbey on **Moot Hill,** the ancient coronation place of the Scottish kings. To be crowned, they sat on the Stone of Scone, which was seized in 1296 by Edward I of England, Scotland's greatest enemy, and placed in the coronation chair at Westminster Abbey, in London. It was returned to Scotland in November 1996 and is now on view in Edinburgh Castle. Some Scots hint darkly that Edward was fooled by a substitution and that the real stone is hidden, waiting for Scotland to regain its independence. ✉*Braemar Rd.* ☎*01738/552300* ⊕*www. scone-palace.co.uk* ✉*£7.50* ⊙*Apr.–Oct., daily 9:30–5:30; last admission at 5.*

### WHERE TO STAY & EAT

£££ ✕▥**Parklands.** This stylish Georgian town house overlooks lush woodland. It's perhaps best known for its pair of restaurants, Acanthus and No. 1 The Bank (£££££, set-price dinner), serving Scottish fish, game, and beef. A sense of elegance permeates the low-key, contemporary interior. **Pros:** Flat-screen TV in every room, superb restaurant. **Cons:** Basic decor, some rooms have better views than others. ✉*2 St. Leonard's Bank, PH2 8EB* ☎*01738/622451* ⊕*www.theparklandshotel. com* ⇆*14 rooms* ⚬*In-room: no a/c. In-hotel: 2 restaurants, no elevator, public Wi-Fi* ⊟*AE, DC, MC, V* ⏺*BP.*

££ ✕▥**Sunbank House Hotel.** A lesson in traditional style, this early-Victorian gray-stone mansion sits in a fine residential area near Perth's Branklyn Gardens. The lodging provides solid, unpretentious comforts along with great views over the River Tay and the city. The restaurant (£££££) serves imaginatively prepared prix-fixe dinners that focus on locally raised meats and game. **Pros:** Reasonably priced, friendly staff, delicious local cuisine. **Cons:** Some rooms are very small, you can hear traffic from the main road. ✉*50 Dundee Rd., PH2 7BA* ☎*01738/624882* ⊕*www.sunbankhouse.com* ⇆*9 rooms* ⚬*In-room:*

*no a/c. In-hotel: restaurant, bar, no elevator, public Wi-Fi, no-smoking rooms* ▭*MC, V* ⦶*BP.*

## NIGHTLIFE & THE ARTS

The Victorian **Perth Repertory Theatre** ( ⊠*185 High St.* ☎*0845/612–6324*) stages plays and musicals. **Perth Concert Hall** ( ⊠*King Edward St.* ☎*0845/6126324*) hosts musical performances of all types.

## SHOPPING

CLOTHING  **C & C Proudfoot** ( ⊠*104 South St.* ☎*01738/632483*) sells a comprehensive selection of sheepskins, leather jackets, rugs, slippers, and handbags.

GLASS &  Perth is an especially popular hunting ground for china and glass.
CHINA  **Caithness Glass** ( ⊠*Inveralmond, off A9 at northern town boundary* ☎*01738/492320*) sells all types of silky-smooth glassware in its factory shop. You can watch glassblowers at work, and there's a small museum and a restaurant. **Watson of Perth** ( ⊠*163–167 High St.* ☎*01738/639861*) has sold exquisite bone china and cut crystal since 1900 and can pack your purchase for shipment overseas.

JEWELRY &  Perth proffers an unusual buy: Scottish freshwater pearls from the
ANTIQUES  River Tay, in delicate settings. The Romans coveted these pearls. If you do, too, then you can make your choice at **Cairncross Ltd., Goldsmiths** ( ⊠*18 St. John's St.* ☎*01738/624367*), where you can also admire a display of some of the more unusual shapes and colors of pearls. Some of the settings take their theme from Scottish flowers. Antique jewelry and silver, including a few Scottish items, can be found at **Timothy Hardie** ( ⊠*25 St. John's St.* ☎*01738/633127*). **Whispers of the Past** ( ⊠*15 George St.* ☎*01738/635472*) has a collection of jewelry, linens, and other items.

# DUNKELD

*14 mi north of Perth.*

Thomas Telford's sturdy river bridge of 1809 carries the road into the town of Dunkeld. Here, the National Trust for Scotland not only cares for grand mansions and wildlands but also actively restores smaller properties. The effects of its Little Houses project, where volunteers helped restore rundown areas, can be seen in the square off the main street. All the houses on the square were rebuilt after the 1689 defeat of the Jacobite army here, which occurred after its early victory in the Battle of Killiecrankie.

Across the Tay from Dunkeld lies the village of Birnam. The wood on Birnam Hill, which overlooks the village, is where Macbeth met the three witches who foretold his fate. Altogether less spooky is the **Beatrix Potter Garden,** which celebrates the life and work of this much loved children's writer who spent her childhood holidays in the area. An enchanting garden walk allows you to peep into the homes of Peter Rabbit and Mrs. Tiggywinkle. There's also an exhibition on his life and a shop selling books and toys. ⊠*Birnam, by Dunkeld* ☎*01350/727674*

⊕*www.perthshire.co.uk* ⊘*Garden, daily sunrise–sunset. Exhibition, Apr.–Nov., daily 10–5; Dec.–Mar., Mon.–Sat., 10–5, Sun. 11:30–4.*

At **Loch of Lowes,** a Scottish Wildlife Trust reserve near Dunkeld, the domestic routines of the osprey, one of Scotland's conservation success stories, can be observed in relative comfort. ⊠*Off A923, about 2 mi northeast of Dunkeld* ☎*01350/727337* ⊕*www.swt.org.uk* ⊠*£3* ⊘*Apr.–Sept., daily 10–5.*

★ On the outskirts of Dunkeld, the **Hermitage** is a woodland walk that follows the River Braan. In the 18th century, the dukes of Atholl constructed two follies (a fantasy building) here, **Ossian's cave** and the awesome **Ossian's Hall,** above a spectacular—and noisy—waterfall. You'll also be in the presence of Britain's tallest tree, a Douglas fir measuring 214 feet. ⊠*1 mi west of Dunkeld on A9.*

### SHOPPING

**Dunkeld Antiques** ( ⊠*Tay Terr.* ☎*01350/728832*), facing the river as you cross the bridge, stocks mainly 18th- and 19th-century items, from large furniture to ornaments, books, and prints. At the **Jeremy Law of Scotland's Highland Horn and Deerskin Centre** ( ⊠*City Hall, Atholl St.* ☎*01350/727569*), you can purchase stag antlers and cow horns shaped into walking sticks, cutlery, and tableware. Deerskin shoes and moccasins, small leather goods made from deerskin, and a specialty malt-whisky collection of more than 200 different malts are also sold. The center has a worldwide postal service and a tax-free shop.

## PITLOCHRY

*15 mi north of Dunkeld.*

A typical central Highland resort, always full of hustle and bustle, Pitlochry has wall-to-wall gift shops, large hotels, and a mountainous golf course. It's very picturesque, but also a little over the top on the souvenir front.

Most Scottish dams have salmon passes or ladders of some kind, enabling the fish to swim upstream to their spawning grounds. In Pitlochry, the **Pitlochry Dam and Fish Ladder,** just behind the main street, leads into a glass-paneled pipe that allows the fish to observe the visitors. ⊠*Off A9 at Pitlochry* ☎*01796/473152* ⊠*£3* ⊘*Apr.–Oct., weekdays 10–5:30.*

If you have a whisky-tasting bent, visit **Edradour Distillery,** which claims to be the smallest single-malt distillery in Scotland (but then, so do others). There's a fun, informative tour of the distillery where you get to see how the whisky is made; you also get to savor a free dram at the end of the tour. ⊠*2½ mi east of Pitlochry* ☎*01796/472095* ⊕*www. edradour.co.uk* ⊠*Free* ⊘*Tours Mar.–Oct., Mon.–Sat. 9:30–5, Sun. noon–5; Nov. and Dec., Mon.–Sat. 10–4.*

The **Linn of Tummel,** a series of marked walks along the river and through tall, mature woodlands, is a little north of Pitlochry. Above the Linn, the A9 rises on stilts and gives an exciting view of the valley.

★ The **Pass of Killiecrankie**, set among the oak woods and rocky river just north of the Linn of Tummel, was the site of a famous battle won by the Jacobites in 1689. The National Trust for Scotland's **visitor center** at Killiecrankie explains the significance of this battle, which was the first attempt to restore the Stewart monarchy. The battle was noted for the death of the central Jacobite leader, John Graham of Claverhouse (1649–89), also known as Bonnie Dundee, who was hit by a stray bullet. The rebellion fizzled after Claverhouse's death. ✉ *Off A9, 4 mi north of Pitlochry* ☎🏠 *01796/473233* ⊕ *www.nts. org.uk* ⊗ *Site year-round, daily 24 hrs, visitor center Apr.–Oct., daily 10–5:30.*

> ## LOCH RANNOCH
>
> With its shoreline of birch trees framed by dark pines, Loch Rannoch is the quintessential Highland loch. Fans of Robert Louis Stevenson (1850–94), especially of *Kidnapped* (1886), will not want to miss the last, lonely section of road. Stevenson describes the setting: "The mist rose and died away, and showed us that country lying as waste as the sea, only the moorfowl and the peewees crying upon it, and far over to the east a herd of deer, moving like dots." Loch Rannoch is off B846, 20 mi west of Pitlochry.

### NIGHTLIFE & THE ARTS

**Pitlochry Festival Theatre** ( ☎ *01796/484626 box office, 01796/484600 general inquiries* ⊗ *Apr.–Sept., daily 10–8; Oct.–Mar., daily 10–6*) presents six plays each season, hosts eight Sunday concerts, and holds art exhibitions.

## BLAIR CASTLE

Fodor'sChoice
★

*10 mi north of Pitlochry.*

Thanks to its historic contents and war-torn past, Blair Castle is one of Scotland's most highly rated sights. The turreted white castle was home to successive dukes of Atholl and their families, the Murrays, until the death of the 10th duke. One of the castle's fascinating details is a preserved piece of floor still bearing marks of the red-hot shot fired through the roof during the 1745 Jacobite rebellion—the last occasion in Scottish history that a castle was besieged. The castle holds not only military artifacts—historically, the duke was allowed to keep a private army, the Atholl Highlanders—but also a collection of furniture and paintings. Outside is a Victorian walled garden. ✉ *From Pitlochry take A9 to Blair Atholl and follow signs* ☎ *01796/481207* ⊕ *www. blair-castle.co.uk* 💷 *£7.50* ⊗ *Apr.–Oct., daily 9:30–4:30; last admission at 3:30.*

### SHOPPING

The **House of Bruar** ( ✉ *A9, just north of Blair Atholl* ☎ *01796/483236*) is an Aladdin's cave for shopaholics who love top-quality Scottish clothing, blown glass, and sweets and condiments. Take a walk up the path that crosses the Bruar Falls, accessed at the back of the shopping complex. There are two bridges with waterfalls, pools, rock formations, and indigenous trees at either side.

## ABERFELDY

*15 mi southwest of Pitlochry, 25 mi southwest of Blair Castle.*

The sleepy town of Aberfeldy is a popular base for people exploring the region. It's Scotland's first fair-trade town and has a water mill that produces delicious stone-ground oatmeal. There's also a whisky distillery and plenty of local golf courses nearby. Aberfeldy Bridge (1733), with five arches and a humpback, was designed by William Adam (1689–1748).

**Castle Menzies,** a 16th-century fortified tower house, contains the **Clan Menzies Museum,** which displays many relics of the clan's history. The castle stands west of Aberfeldy, on the opposite bank of the River Tay. ⊠ *Off B846* ☎ *01887/820982* 💷 *£4* ⊙ *Apr.–Oct., Mon. 10:30–5, Sun. 2–5.*

**Glen Lyon,** just a few miles away from Aberfeldy, is one of central Scotland's most attractive glens. It has a rushing river, thick forests, and the typical *big hoose* (big house) hidden on private grounds. There's a dam at the head of the loch, a reminder that little of Scotland's scenic beauty is unadulterated. You can reach the glen by a high road from Loch Tay: take the A827 to Fearnan, then turn north to Fortingall. The **Fortingall yew,** in the churchyard near the Fortingall Hotel, wearily rests its great limbs on the ground. This tree is thought to be more than 3,000 years old. Legend has it that Pontius Pilate was born beside it, during the time his father was serving as a Roman legionnaire in Scotland. After viewing the yew, turn west into Glen Lyon. ⊠ *Off A827, 15 mi from Aberfeldy via Fortingall and Fearnan.*

**OFF THE BEATEN PATH**

**Scottish Crannog Centre.** Here's your chance to travel back 5,000 years to a time when the local inhabitants of this area, in common with others across Scotland and Ireland, started building defensive homesteads, known as *crannogs,* on wooden piles standing in lochs. They were approachable only by narrow bridges that could be easily defended. This practice continued until as late as the 17th century. Archaeologists have found many remains of crannogs in lochs throughout Scotland. One of the best-preserved was found several feet under the surface of Loch Tay, off the north shore at Fearnan, and it's now possible to visit an accurate replica built on the south shore. An exhibition gives details about crannog construction and the way of life in and around crannogs. The Crannog Centre is just west of Aberfeldy, on the southern shore of Loch Tay. ⊠ *Kenmore, South Loch Tay* ☎ *01887/830583* ⊕ *www.crannog.co.uk* 💷 *£4.95* ⊙ *Mid-Mar.–Oct., daily 10–5:30; Nov., weekends 10–4; last entry 1 hr before closing.*

### BOATING

**Loch Tay Boating Centre** ( ⊠ *Pier Rd., Kenmore* ☎ *01887/830291*) rents cabin cruisers, speedboats, fishing boats, and canoes. It's open from April through mid-October daily from 9 to 7 PM.

## KILLIN

*24 mi southwest of Aberfeldy, 39 mi north of Stirling, 45 mi west of Perth.*

A village with an almost alpine flavor, known for its modest but surprisingly diverse selection of crafts and woolen wares, Killin is also noted for its scenery.

The **Falls of Dochart,** white-water rapids overlooked by a pine-clad islet, are at the west end of the village. ✉ *Off A827.*

The **Breadalbane Folklore Centre,** by the Falls of Dochart, focuses on the area's heritage and folk tales. The most curious of these are the "Healing Stones of St. Fillan"—water-worn stones that have been looked after lovingly for centuries for their supposed curative powers. ✉ *Off A827* ☎ *01567/820254* ✉ *£2.75* ⊘ *Apr.–June, Sept., and Oct., daily 10–5; July and Aug., daily 10–5:30.*

Across the River Dochart and near the golf course sit the ruins of **Finlarig Castle,** built by Black Duncan of the Cowl, a notorious Campbell laird. The castle grounds can be visited at any time. ✉ *Off A827.*

### WHERE TO STAY

£  ⊡ **Lodge House.** Few other guesthouses in Scotland can match the mountain views from this 100-year-old property, it's certainly worth the short drive 15 mi west from Killin to Crianlarich. Informal and cozy, the bedrooms are plain and unfussy, but more than adequate. The breakfast is good Scots fare, and evening meals can be arranged on request. You may wish to walk along the riverbank after dinner, or have a wee dram in the tiny bar instead. **Pros:** Epic views, cozy setting, peaceful. **Cons:** Long drive to the nearest town, some rooms are dated. ✉ *Crianlarich, FK20 8RU* ☎ *01838/300276* ⊕ *www.lodgehouse.co.uk* ⇩ *6 rooms* ⌂ *In-room: no a/c, no phone. In-hotel: no elevator, public Wi-Fi* ⊟ *MC, V* ⊙ *BP.*

### BICYCLING

If you want to explore the north end of the Glasgow–Killin cycleway, rent a mountain bike from **Killin Outdoor Centre and Mountain Shop** (✉ *Main St.* ☎ *01567/820652*). Also available are canoes, crampons, skis, and ice axes.

**EN ROUTE** Southwest of Killin the A827 joins the main A85. By turning south over the watershed, you will see fine views of the hill ridges behind Killin. The road leads into **Glen Ogle,** "amid the wildest and finest scenery we had yet seen…putting one in mind of prints of the Khyber Pass," as Queen Victoria (1819–1901) recorded in her diary when she traveled this way in 1842.

## CRIEFF

*25 mi southeast of Killin.*

The hilly town of Crieff offers walks with Highland views from **Knock Hill** above the town. Signs point the way there from Crieff's center.

If you wish to discover the delights of whisky distilling, sign up for the **Famous Grouse Experience** at the Glenturret Distillery. A guide takes you through the distillery and to the Pavilion Bar where you can have a glass of Famous Grouse Finest (a blended, not a single-malt whisky) and try your skill at "nosing." Here you learn how whisky is made and why time, water, soil, and air are so important to the taste. You might cap your tour with lunch or dinner at either of the two Scottish restaurants. Signs lead to the distillery on the west side of the town. ⊠ *The Hosh, off A822* ☏ *01764/656565* ⊕ *www.famousgrouse.co.uk/experience* 🎫 *£7.50* ⏰ *Mar.–Dec., daily 9–6, last tour at 4:30; Jan. and Feb., daily 10–4:30, last tour at 3.*

**Drummond Castle Garden** is a very large, formal Victorian parterre celebrating family and Scottish heraldry. The flower beds are planted and trimmed in the shapes of various heraldic symbols, such as a lion rampant and a checkerboard, associated with the coat of arms of the family that owns the castle and the Scottish Royal Coat of Arms. It's regarded as one of the finest of its kind in Europe, and it even made an appearance in the film *Rob Roy.* ⊠ *Off A822, 6 mi southwest of Crieff* ☏ *01764/681433* ⊕ *www.drummondcastlegardens.co.uk* 🎫 *£4* ⏰ *Easter weekend and May–Oct., daily 1–6; last admission at 5.*

### SHOPPING

Crieff is a center for china and glassware. **Stuart Crystal** ( ⊠ *Muthill Rd.* ☏ *01764/654004*), a factory shop, sells not only its own Stuart crystal but also Waterford, Dartington, and Wedgwood wares.

# AUCHTERARDER

*11 mi southeast of Crieff.*

Famous for the Gleneagles Hotel and nearby golf courses, Auchterarder also has a flock of tony antiques shops to amuse Gleneagles's golf widows and widowers.

### WHERE TO STAY & EAT

££££ | Fodor's Choice ★    ✕▥ **Gleneagles Hotel.** One of Britain's most famous hotels, Gleneagles is the very essence of modern grandeur. Like a vast, secret palace, it stands hidden in breathtaking countryside amid its world-famous golf courses. The rooms are elegant, hung with indulgent draperies and filled with soft leather furniture. All the details are here, from fluffy bathrobes hanging behind the door to freshly cut flowers in every room. For the most celebrated Scottish dining experience, enjoy Andrew Fairlie's signature dishes of lobster smoked over whisky barrels, and black truffle gnocchi (£££££). Recreation facilities are nearly endless: a shopping arcade, a spa, an equestrian center, a falconry center, and more. **Pros:** Numerous amenities add up to an unforgettable experience for all, three courses are a golfer's paradise. **Cons:** Luxury comes at steep price, you may not want to leave. ⊠ *Auchterarder PH3 1NF* ☏ *01764/662231* ⊕ *www.gleneagles.com* 🛏 *216 rooms, 13 suites* ⚿ *In-room: no a/c, refrigerator, Wi-Fi. In-hotel: 4 restaurants, room service, golf courses,* *tennis courts, pools, gym, spa, bicycles, concierge, children's programs (ages 4–10)* ⊟AE, DC, MC, V ⟨◎⟩BP.

# THE CENTRAL HIGHLANDS ESSENTIALS

## TRANSPORTATION

### BY AIR

Perth and Stirling can be reached easily from the Edinburgh, Dundee, and Glasgow airports by train, car, or bus.

### BY BUS

A good network of buses connects with the central belt via Edinburgh and Glasgow. For more information contact Scottish Citylink or National Express. The Perth and Kinross Council supplies a map showing all public transport routes in Perthshire, marked with nearby attractions. This map can be obtained from any tourist information center in Perthshire.

The following companies organize reliable service on routes throughout the Central Highlands: First, Scottish Citylink, and Stagecoach.

**Information** **First** ( ⊠ *Goosecroft Rd. bus station, Stirling* ☎ *08708/727271* ⊕ *www.firstgroup.com*). **National Express** ( ☎ *08705/808080* ⊕ *www.nationalexpress.com*). **Scottish Citylink** ( ⊠ *Leonard St. bus station, Perth* ☎ *08705/505050* ⊕ *www.citylink.co.uk*). **Stagecoach** ( ⊠ *Ruthvenfield Rd., Inveralmond Industrial Estate, Perth* ☎ *01738/629339* ⊕ *www.stagecoachbus.com*).

### BY CAR

You'll find easy access to the area from the central belt of Scotland via the motorway network. The M9 runs within sight of the walls of Stirling Castle, and Perth can be reached via the M90 over the Forth Bridge. Two signed touring routes are useful: the Perthshire Tourist Route, and the Deeside Tourist Route, with a spectacular journey via Blairgowrie and Glenshee to Deeside and Aberdeen. Local tourist information centers can supply maps of these routes.

### BY TRAIN

The Central Highlands are linked to Edinburgh and Glasgow by rail, with through routes to England (some direct-service routes from London take fewer than five hours). Several Savers ticket options are available, although in some cases on the ScotRail system, the discount fares must be purchased before your arrival in the United Kingdom. Contact National Rail or ScotRail for details.

The West Highland Line runs through the western portion of the area. Services also run to Stirling, Dunblane, Perth, and Gleneagles, stops on the Inverness–Perth line include Dunkeld, Pitlochry, and Blair Atholl.

**Information** **First ScotRail** ( ☎ *08457/550033* ⊕ *www.firstgroup.com/scotrail*). **National Rail Enquiries** ( ☎ *08457/484950* ⊕ *www.nationalrail.co.uk*).

## CONTACTS & RESOURCES

### EMERGENCIES

In case of an emergency, dial **999** to reach an ambulance or the police or fire departments (no coins are needed for emergency calls from phone booths). If you need to see a doctor or dentist, ask for recommendations from the nearest tourist information center, your hotel receptionist, or B&B host. Late-night pharmacies are found only in the larger towns and cities. In an emergency the police will help you find a pharmacist.

Hospitals **Perth Royal Infirmary** ( ⊠ *Taymount Terr., Perth* ☎ *01738/623311*). **Stirling Royal Infirmary** ( ⊠ *Livilands Gate, Stirling* ☎ *01786/434000*). **Vale of Leven Hospital** ( ⊠ *Main St., Alexandria* ☎ *01389/754121*).

### TOURS

The nearest visitor center is your best source for tour routes and reservations. Don't miss the opportunity to take a boat trip on a loch, especially in the Trossachs (Loch Katrine) and Loch Lomond; consult a visitor center for details.

### VISITOR INFORMATION

The tourist offices listed below are open year-round. Seasonal tourist information centers are also open (generally from April to October) in the following towns: Aberfoyle, Balloch, Callander, Drymen, Dunblane, Helensburgh, Killin, Pirnhall, Tarbet, and Tyndrum.

Information **Aberfeldy** ( ⊠ *The Sq.* ☎ *01887/820276* ⊕ *www.perthshire.co.uk*). **Alva** ( ⊠ *Mill Trail Visitor Centre, W. Stirling St.* ☎ *01259/769696* ⊕ *www.stirling. co.uk*). **Auchterarder** ( ⊠ *90 High St.* ☎ *01764/663450* ⊕ *www.perthshire.co.uk*). **Blairgowrie** ( ⊠ *26 Wellmeadow* ☎ *01250/872960* ⊕ *www.perthshire.co.uk*). **Crieff** ( ⊠ *Town Hall, High St.* ☎ *01764/652578* ⊕ *www.perthshire.co.uk*). **Dunbarton** ( ⊠ *A82 northbound* ☎ *08707/200612*). **Dunkeld** ( ⊠ *The Cross* ☎ *01350/727688* ⊕ *www.perthshire.co.uk*). **Falkirk** ( ⊠ *2/4 Glebe St.* ☎ *01324/620244*). **Kinross** ( ⊠ *Heart of Scotland Visitor Centre, Service Area Junction 6 M90* ☎ *01577/863680* ⊕ *www.perthshire.co.uk*). **Loch Lomond & the Trossachs National Park Gateway Centre** ( ⊠ *Loch Lomond Shores, near Balloch* ☎ *08707/200631* ⊕ *www.incallander. co.uk*). **Perth** ( ⊠ *Lower City Mills, W. Mill St.* ☎ *01738/450600* ⊕ *www.perthshire. co.uk*). **Pitlochry** ( ⊠ *22 Atholl Rd.* ☎ *01796/472215* ⊕ *www.perthshire.co.uk*). **Stirling** ( ⊠ *41 Dumbarton Rd.* ☎ *01786/479901* ⊠ *Royal Burgh of Stirling Visitor Centre, Castle Esplanade* ☎ *01786/475019* ⊕ *www.stirling.co.uk*).

# Aberdeen & the Northeast

**WORD OF MOUTH**

"The setting of Dunnottar Castle is one of the high-lights of Scotland. It is on a steep hill jutting out into the coastline. The best views of the castle are from the hillsides surrounding it. There are several areas where you can walk to view it and take photos. What a sight!"

—gopack

"We took the Glenfiddich tour, and were fascinated by their extraordinary commitment to detail and quality control. I still like the Macallan whisky better, but you could definitely do worse for a tour."

—mr_go

Updated by
Shona Main

**HERE, IN THIS GRANITE SHOULDER** of Grampian, are Royal Deeside, the countryside that Queen Victoria made her own; the Castle Country route, where fortresses stand hard against the hills; and the Malt Whisky Trail, where peaty streams embrace the country's greatest concentration of distilleries. The region's gateway is the city of Aberdeen, constructed of granite and now aglitter with new wealth and new blood drawn together by North Sea oil.

Because of its isolation, Aberdeen has historically been a fairly autonomous place. Even now it's perceived by many U.K. inhabitants as lying almost out of reach in the northeast. In reality, it's 90- minutes flying time from London or a little more than two hours by car from Edinburgh. Its magnificent, confident 18th- and early-19th-century city center amply rewards exploration. Yet even if this popular base for travelers vanished from the map, an extensive portion of the northeast would still remain at the top of many travelers' wish lists, studded as it is with some of Scotland's most enduring travel icons.

Some credit Sir Walter Scott with having opened up Scotland for tourism through his poems and novels. Others say General Wade did it when he built the Highland roads. But it was probably Queen Victoria who gave Scottish tourism its real momentum when, in 1842, she first came to Scotland and when, in 1847—on orders of a doctor, who thought the relatively dry climate of upper Deeside would suit her—she bought Balmoral. The pretty little castle was knocked down to make room for a much grander house in full-flown Scottish baronial style, designed, in fact, by her husband, Prince Albert. Before long the entire Deeside and the region north were dotted with country houses and mock-baronial châteaux. The locals, bless 'em, took it all in stride. To this day, the hundreds who line the road when the queen and her family arrive for services at the family's parish church at Crathie are invariably visitors to Deeside—one of Balmoral's attractions for the monarch has always been the villagers' respect for royal privacy.

Balmoral is merely the most famous castle in the area. There are so many others that in one part of the region a Castle Trail has been established, leading you to such fortresses as the ruined medieval Kildrummy Castle, which once controlled the strategic routes through the valley of the River Don. In later structures, such as Castle Fraser, you can trace the changing styles and tastes of each of its owners over the centuries. Grand mansions such as Haddo House, with its symmetrical facade and elegant interior, surrender any defensive role entirely.

A trail leading to a more ephemeral kind of pleasure can be found south of Elgin and Banff, where the glens embrace Scotland's greatest concentration of malt-whisky distilleries. With so many in Morayshire, where the distilling is centered in the valley of the River Spey and its tributaries, there's now a Whisky Trail. Follow it to experience a surprising wealth of flavors, considering that whisky is made of three basic ingredients.

The northeast's chief attraction lies in the gradual transition from high mountain plateau—by a series of gentle steps through hill, forest, and farmland—to the Moray Firth and North Sea coast, where

## TOP REASONS TO GO

**Exploring castles:** With more than 75 castles, some Victorian and others dating back to the 13th century, this area has everything from ravaged ruins like Dunnottar to opulent Fyvie Castle. They still evoke the power, grandeur, and sometimes the cruelty of Scotland's past.

**Hit the whisky trail:** The valley of the River Spey is famous for its single-malt distilleries, nine of which are connected by the signposted Malt Whisky Trail. You can choose from bigger operations such as Glenfiddich to the iconic Strathisla.

**See the seaside:** The fishing industry may be in decline, but the big-city port of Abberdeen and the colorful smaller fishing towns of Stonehaven and Cullen in the northeast are great (and very different) places to soak up the seagoing atmosphere—and some seafood.

**Go fish:** With major rivers, including the Dee and Don, loch and estuary fishing at the Spey, the northeast is one of Scotland's leading game-fishing areas. It's big business, though, so make sure you have a permit.

**Practice your swing:** The northeast has more than 50 golf clubs, some of which have championship courses. Less-famous clubs have some amazing courses as well.

**6**

the word "unadulterated" is redefined. Here you'll find some of the United Kingdom's most perfect wild shorelines, both sandy and sheer cliff, and breezy fishing villages like Cullen on the Banffshire coat and Stonehaven, south of Aberdeen. The Grampian Mountains, to the west, contain some of the highest ground in the nation, in the area of the Cairngorms. In recognition of this area's very special nature, Cairngorms National Park (Scotland's second, after Loch Lomond and the Trossachs National Park) was created in early 2003. The Grampian hills also have shaped the character of the folk who live in the northeast. In earlier times the massif made communication with the south somewhat difficult. As a result, native northeasterners still speak the richest Lowland Scottish.

## EXPLORING ABERDEEN & THE NORTHEAST

Start, as most people do, in Aberdeen. Once you have spent time there, you may be inclined to venture west into Deeside, with its royal connections and looming mountain backdrop, and then pass over the hills into the Castle Country to the north. You might head farther west to touch on Speyside and the Whisky Trail, before meandering back east and south along the pristine coastline at Scotland's northeasternmost tip.

### ABOUT THE RESTAURANTS & HOTELS

The northeast has some splendid country hotels with log fires and old Victorian furnishings, where you can also be sure of eating well. Many hotels in Aberdeen are in older homes that have a baronial feel. Beware, as others with grand-sounding names are in modern buildings with little charm. Some offer competitive rates on weekends. Partly in response to the demands of spendthrift workers in the oil industry,

## GREAT ITINERARIES

Although the Grampian area isn't huge, it has many different terrains. To get a real flavor of this most authentic of Scottish regions, sample both the coastline and the mountains. Near Angus and the Cairngorms, it's the most popular and populated route to the north of Scotland.

### IF YOU HAVE 3 DAYS

Setting out from **Aberdeen**, follow in the footsteps of Queen Victoria and tour the castles and glens of Royal Deeside. Head southward to the fishing town of **Stonehaven** and the breathtaking clifftop fortress of Dunnottar. After lunch take the A957/A93 to **Crathes Castle** before continuing west along the A93 for ▣ **Ballater**. The next morning visit Her Majesty's **Balmoral Castle** (note that it's open only April to July)—explore the ballroom and grounds, take a pony ride, and then treat yourself to a walk in nearby Glen Muick. Here you can find the famous climb of Lochnagar, so beloved by

Victoria. End the day at **Kildrummy Castle**, and stay overnight. The next morning set off for Castle Country and some serious castle-hopping—**Corgarff Castle, Cragievar, Castle Fraser**—and a little castle relief at the Grampian Transport Museum before returning to Aberdeen.

### IF YOU HAVE 5 DAYS

Downtown ▣ **Aberdeen's** silver granite certainly deserves two days. Then travel into Speyside to visit distilleries in **Dufftown, Craigellachie, Aberlour**, and **Glenlivet**. Spend the morning exploring Elgin's religious sites before moving east along the coast to stay overnight in ▣**Cullen**. Visit the magnificent Duff House gallery in **Banff** before returning to Aberdeen. On the last day see a castle or two: **Crathes** in Deeside or **Dunnottar** by Stonehaven; **Haddo House** or **Fyvie Castle**, northwest of **Ellon**; or loop northwest for **Corgarff**, the ruined castle at ▣ **Kildrummy**, or **Castle Fraser**.

restaurants have cropped up all over Aberdeen, and the quality of the food improves yearly.

| WHAT IT COSTS IN POUNDS | | | | | |
|---|---|---|---|---|---|
| | £ | ££ | £££ | ££££ | £££££ |
| RESTAURANTS | under £10 | £10–£14 | £15–£19 | £20–£25 | over £25 |
| HOTELS | under £70 | £70–£120 | £120–£160 | £160–£220 | over £220 |

Restaurant prices are for a main course at dinner. Hotel prices are for two people in a standard double room in high season, generally including the 17.5% V.A.T.

### TIMING

May and June are probably the loveliest times to visit, but many travelers arrive from late spring to early fall. Because the National Trust for Scotland tends to close its properties in winter, many of the northeast's castles are not suitable for off-season travel, though you can always see them from the outside. Duff House, Macduff Marine Aquarium, and some of the distilleries are open much of the year.

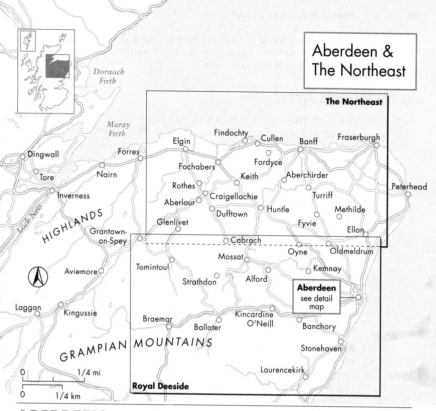

Aberdeen & The Northeast

**The Northeast**

Dornoch Firth

Moray Firth

Dingwall

Tore

Inverness

HIGHLANDS

Loch Ness

Forres

Nairn

Grantown-on-Spey

Aviemore

Laggan

Kingussie

Elgin

Findochty

Cullen

Banff

Fraserburgh

Fochabers

Fordyce

Keith

Aberchirder

Peterhead

Rothes

Craigellachie

Turriff

Aberlour

Dufftown

Huntle

Methilde

Glenlivet

Fyvie

Ellon

Cabrach

Oyne

Oldmeldrum

Mossat

Kemnay

Tomintoul

Strathdon

Alford

**Aberdeen**
see detail map

Braemar

Kincardine O'Neill

Banchory

Ballater

GRAMPIAN MOUNTAINS

Stonehaven

Laurencekirk

0        1/4 mi

0        1/4 km

**Royal Deeside**

# ABERDEEN

As the gateway to Royal Deeside and the Malt Whisky Trail, Aberdeen attracts many visitors, and few leave without a sense of the city's grand past and prosperous present. Distinctive architecture, some fine museums, universities, and good restaurants, nightlife, and shopping add to the appeal of Scotland's third-largest city (population 202,000). Still, many people will be eager to get out into the countryside.

In the 18th century, local granite quarrying produced a durable silver stone that would be used boldly in the glittering blocks, spires, columns, and parapets of Victorian-era Aberdonian structures. The city remains one of the United Kingdom's most distinctive, although some would say it depends on the weather and the brightness of the day. The mica chips embedded in the rock look like a million mirrors in the sunshine. In rain (and there is a fair amount of driving rain from the North Sea) and heavy clouds, however, their sparkle is snuffed out.

The city lies between the Dee and Don rivers, with a working harbor that has access to the sea; it has been a major fishing port and is the main commercial port in northern Scotland. The North Sea has always been important to Aberdeen. In the 1850s the city was famed for its sleek, fast clippers that sailed to India for cargoes of tea. In the late

1960s the course of Aberdeen's history was unequivocally altered when oil and gas were discovered offshore, sparking rapid growth, prosperity, and further industrialization.

## AROUND UNION STREET

Aberdeen centers on Union Street, with its many fine survivors of the Victorian and Edwardian streetscape. Marischal College, dating from the late 16th century, has many grand buildings that are worth exploring. You can explore the center of Aberdeen in half a day, but you'll probably want to devote a full day to poking around its interesting old buildings.

### MAIN ATTRACTIONS

**7** **Aberdeen Art Gallery.** The museum contains diverse paintings, prints, and drawings, sculpture, porcelain, costumes, and much else—from 18th-century art to major contemporary works by Lucien Freud and Henry Moore. Local marble has been used in interior walls, pillars, and the central fountain, designed by the acclaimed British sculptor Barbara Hepworth. ■TIP→ **Look out for the unique collection of Abderdeen silver on the ground floor.** The museum also hosts frequent temporary exhibitions and has a bustling café. ⊠*Schoolhill* ☎*01224/523700* ⊕*www. aagm.co.uk* ☞*Free* ⊗*Mon.–Sat. 10–5, Sun. 2–5.*

**13** **Aberdeen Maritime Museum.** This excellent museum, which incorporates the 1593 Provost Ross's House, tells the story of the city's involvement with the sea, from early inshore fisheries to tea clippers and the North Sea oil boom. It's a fascinating place for kids and adults, with its ship models, paintings, and equipment associated with the fishing, shipbuilding, and oil and gas industries. ⊠*Ship Row* ☎*01224/337701* ⊕*www.aagm.co.uk* ☞*Free* ⊗*Mon.–Sat. 10–5, Sun. noon–3.*

**4** **Marischal College.** Founded in 1593 by the Earl Marischal (the earls Marischal held hereditary office as keepers of the king's mares), Marischal College was a Protestant alternative to the Catholic King's College in Old Aberdeen. The two joined to form the University of Aberdeen in 1860. The original university building has undergone extensive renovations, and the current facade was built in 1891. The spectacularly ornate work is set off by the gilded flags, and this turn-of-the-20th-century creation is still the world's second-largest granite building. Only El Escorial, outside Madrid, is larger. The main part of the building, no longer needed by the university, is slated to become the new headquarters for the city council. The fascinating main galleries of the **Marischal Museum** hold two exhibits: the "Encyclopaedia of the North East" displays artifacts and photographs relating to the region's heritage; "Collecting the World" explores what local collectors gathered on their world travels and displays Egyptian and 19th-century ethnographic material. ⊠*Broad St.* ☎*01224/274301* ⊕*www.abdn.ac.uk* ☞*Free* ⊗*Museum weekdays 10–5, Sun. 2–5.*

**5** **Provost Skene's House.** Now a museum portraying civic life, the house has restored, furnished period rooms and a painted chapel. Steeply

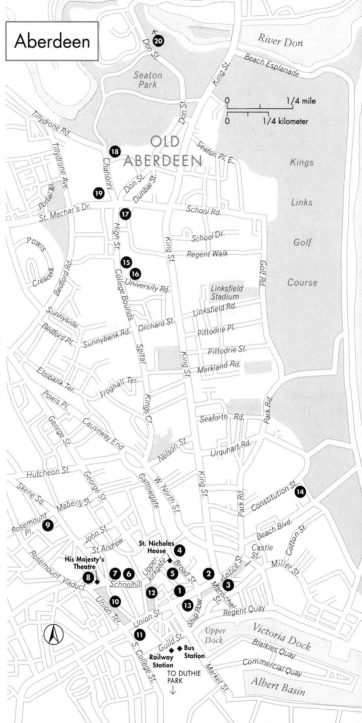

# Aberdeen

gabled and built from rubble, it dates in part from 1545. The house was originally a mayor's domestic dwelling (provost is Scottish for "mayor"). Its costume gallery displays colorful exhibitions of fashions from different centuries. ⊠*Guestrow off Broad St.* ☎*01224/641086* ⊕*www.aagm. co.uk* ⊠*Free* ⊗*Mon.–Sat. 10–5, Sun. 1–4.*

**GETTING AROUND ABERDEEN**

You can find taxi stands throughout the center of Aberdeen: along Union Street, at the railway station at Guild Street, at Back Wynd, and at Regent Quay. The taxis have meters and are mostly black, though some are beige, maroon, or white. They are great ways to travel between neighborhoods.

⓬ **St. Nicholas Kirk.** The original burgh church, the Mither Kirk, as this edifice is known, is curiously not within the bounds of the early town settlement; that was to the east, near the end of present-day Union Street. During the 12th century the port of Aberdeen flourished, and there wasn't room for the church within the settlement. Its earliest features are its pillars—supporting a tower built much later—and its clerestory windows: both date from the 12th century. St. Nicholas was divided into east and west kirks at the Reformation, followed by a substantial amount of renovation from 1741 on. ■TIP➜ In the chapel, look for two books: one contains the names of the victims of an oil-rig disaster in 1989; the second is empty, a reminder the many others who have lost their lives in the oil industry in the North Sea. ⊠*Union St.* ⊗*Weekdays 10–1, Sun. for services.*

**ALSO WORTH SEEING**

**OFF THE BEATEN PATH**

**Duthie Park and Winter Gardens.** A great place to feed the ducks, Duthie Park also has a boating pond and trampolines, carved wooden animals, and playgrounds. In the very attractive (and warm!) Winter Gardens are fish in ponds, free-flying birds, and turtles and terrapins among the luxuriant foliage and flowers. The park lies close beside Aberdeen's other river, the Dee. ⊠*Polmuir Rd., Riverside Dr., about 1 mi south of city center* ⊠*Free* ⊗*Gardens daily 10–sunset.*

❸ **Mercat Cross.** Built in 1686 and restored in 1820, the Mercat Cross (the term stems from "marketplace"), always the symbolic center of a Scottish medieval burgh, stands just beyond King Street. Along its parapet are 12 portrait panels of the Stewart monarchs.

❻ **Robert Gordon University.** When it was built in 1731, this institution was used to educate poor boys. Adjacent is the independent Robert Gordon School. It's closed to the public. ⊠*Schoolhill.*

❽ **Rosemount Viaduct.** Three silvery, handsome buildings on this bridge are collectively known by all Aberdonians as Education, Salvation, and Damnation. The **Central Library** and **St. Mark's Church** date from the last decade of the 19th century, and **His Majesty's Theatre** (1904–08) has been restored inside to its full Edwardian splendor. If you're taking photographs, you can choose an angle that includes the statue of

## A GOOD WALK

For a lovely stroll near Marischal College, start at the east end of Union Street, east of Marischal Street. Here within the original old town is a square called Castlegate. The actual castle once stood somewhere behind the Salvation Army Citadel (1896), an imposing baronial granite tower whose design was inspired by Balmoral Castle. On the north side of Castle Street stands the 17th-century Tolbooth, a reminder of Aberdeen's earliest days. The impressive Mercat Cross is near King Street. Turn north down Broad Street to reach Marischal College, whose sparkling granite frontage dominates the top end of the street.

A survivor from an earlier Aberdeen can be found opposite Marischal College, beyond the concrete supports of St. Nicholas House (which houses the tourist information center): Provost Skene's House was once part of a closely packed area of town houses and is now a museum portraying civic life. Just around the corner on Upperkirkgate, at the lowest point, are two modern shopping malls—the St. Nicholas Centre on the left, the Bon-Accord Centre on the right.

**6**

Scotland's first freedom fighter, Sir William Wallace (1270–1305), in the foreground pointing majestically to Damnation.

**⑭ Satrosphere.** The hands-on exhibits at Satrosphere bring science and technology to life. Children (and adults) of even the most unscientific bent love displays such as the see-through sheep that eats grass, digests it, then produces pellets from its bottom. ⊠ *179 Constitution St.* ☎ *01224/640340* ⊕ *www.satrosphere.net* 🎟 *£5.75* ⊘ *Daily 10–5.*

**❷ Tolbooth.** The city was governed from this 17th-century building for 200 years. It was also the burgh court and jail. You can see it from the outside only. ⊠ *Castle St.*

**⑪ Union Bridge.** Built in the early 19th century, as was much of Union Street, this bridge has a gentle rise—or descent, if you're traveling east. The north side of Union Bridge is the most obvious reminder of the artificial raising of the grand thoroughfare's levels (despite appearances, you'll discover you're not at ground level). Much of the original work remains. ⊠ *Union St.*

**❶ Union Street.** This great thoroughfare is to Aberdeen what Princes Street is to Edinburgh: the central pivot of the city plan and the product of a wave of enthusiasm to rebuild the city in a contemporary style in the early 19th century.

**⑩ Union Terrace.** In the 19th-century development of Union Terrace stands a statue of Robert Burns (1759–96) addressing a daisy. Behind Burns are the **Union Terrace Gardens**, faintly echoing Edinburgh's Princes Street Gardens in that both separate the older part of the city, to the east, from the 19th-century development to the west. Most buildings around the grand-looking Caledonian Hotel are late Victorian.

**⑨ The Village.** This museum and educational center has interactive displays
that show you what life was like in a village 2,000 years ago. You can
dress up in period costumes, put together jigsaw puzzles, watch puppet
shows, and try your hand at spinning, weaving, and mosaic making.
⊠ *Rosemount Pl.* ☎ *01224/648041* 💷 *£3* ⊙ *Mon., Wed., Fri., and
Sat. 10–noon, Sun. 2:30–4:30.*

## OLD ABERDEEN

Old Aberdeen is very much a separate area of the city, north of the modern center and clustered around St. Machar's Cathedral and the many fine buildings of the University of Aberdeen. The neighborhood is north of the center of town, easily reachable by bus. It's a compact area, and will take you no more than a few hours to explore.

### MAIN ATTRACTIONS

**⑲ Cruickshank Botanic Gardens.** Built on land bequeathed by Miss Anne Crickshank in memory of her beloved brother Alexander, the small Cruickshank Botanic Garden has a peaceful water garden and lush greens ideal for lounging around on—when the weather allows—and beautifully tended subtropical and alpine collections. ⊠ *St. Machar Dr. at The Chanonry* ☎ *01224/272704* 💷 *Free* ⊙ *Daily 9–5.*

> **WORD OF MOUTH**
>
> "I would explore the city of Aberdeen, shopping on Union Street and seeing Provost Skene's House; Duthie Park and Winter Gardens have spectacular rose gardens, or check out the beach. Stonehaven is also excellent. Dunnottar Castle is really amazing and should not be missed ... with the backdrop of the sea and it being on a cliff."
> –amelie

**⑯ King's College.** Founded in 1494, King's College is now part of the University of Aberdeen. Its **chapel**, which was built around 1500, has an unmistakable flying (or crown) spire. That it has survived at all was because of the zeal of the principal, who defended his church against the destructive fanaticism that swept through Scotland during the Reformation, when the building was less than a century old. Today the renovated chapel plays an important role in university life. ■ TIP→ **Don't miss the tall oak screen that separates the nave from the choir, the ribbed wooden ceiling, and the stalls, as it constitutes the finest medieval wood carvings found anywhere in Scotland.** The **King's College Centre** will tell you more about the university. ⊠ *High St.* ☎ *01224/272660* ⊙ *Weekdays 9:30–5, Sat. 11–4.*

Fodor'sChoice
★

**NEED A BREAK?**

St. Machar Bar ( ⊠ *97 High St.* ☎ *01224/483079*) is a small, vibrant pub in the middle of the university campus, selling not just pints but also *stovies* (a hot potato-based stew). This is a great place to warm up or pass away the time with a newspaper if the weather is unbecoming.

**⑱ St. Machar's Cathedral.** It's said that St. Machar was sent by St. Columba to build a church on a grassy platform near the sea, where a river flowed in the shape of a shepherd's crook. This spot fit the bill. Although it was founded in AD 580, most of the existing building dates from the 15th and 16th centuries. The central tower collapsed in 1688, reducing the building to half its original length. The nave is thought to have been rebuilt in red sandstone in 1370, but the final renovation was completed in granite by the middle of the 15th century. Along with the nave ceiling, the twin octagonal spires were finished in time to take a battering in the Reformation, when the barons of the Mearns stripped the lead off the roof of St. Machar's and stole the bells. The cathedral suffered further mistreatment—including the removal of stone by Oliver Cromwell's English garrison in the 1650s—until it was fully restored in the 19th century. ⊠ *Chanonry* ☎ *01224/485988* ⊗ *Daily 9–5.*

**⑰ Town House.** This Georgian work, plain and handsome, incorporates parts of an earlier building from 1720. It's not open to the public. ⊠ *High St., Old Aberdeen.*

### ALSO WORTH SEEING

**⑳ Brig o'Balgownie.** Until 1827 the only way out of Aberdeen going north was over the River Don on this single-arch bridge. It dates from 1314 and is thought to have been built by Richard Cementarius, Aberdeen's first provost. ⊠ *Seaton Park.*

**⑮ College Bounds.** Handsome 18th- and 19th-century houses line this cobbled street (which has paved sidewalks) in the oldest part of the city. ⊠ *Old Aberdeen.*

## WHERE TO STAY & EAT

££££
Fodor's Choice
★

✕ **Silver Darling.** Huge windows overlook the harbor at this quayside favorite, one of Aberdeen's most acclaimed restaurants. It specializes, as its name suggests, in fish (a silver darling is a herring). Try the ravioli with langoustine, mushrooms, samphire, and vanilla or the pan-fried halibut with crab gnocchi. Stark white tablecloths add a hint of sophistication; flowers throw in a dash of color. ⊠ *Pocra Quay, Footdee* ☎ *01224/576229* ⚐ *Reservations essential* ▤ *AE, DC, MC, V* ⊗ *Closed Sun. No lunch Sat.*

££
★

✕ **Blue Moon.** Devoid of the usual posters of the Taj Mahal, Aberdeen's favorite Indian restaurant is refreshingly light and modern. Soothing shades of blue defy the fieriness of the curries. The menu is simple: you pick the type of curry you prefer, then the main ingredient. There's a choice of prawn, chicken, lamb, vegetables, or Quorn—a low-fat meat substitute popular among British vegetarians. There's a second location on Alford Lane. ⊠ *11 Holburn St.* ☎ *01224/589977* ⊠ *1 Alford La.* ☎ *01224/593000* ▤ *MC, V.*

£

✕ **Ashvale.** Ask anyone about this long-established place and the response will probably be overwhelmingly positive. Fish-and-chips are undoubtedly the specialty here. Attempt the "Whale"—a gigantic 1-pound fillet of battered cod—and you'll be rewarded with a free dessert. This will be the priciest fish-and-chips you've ever ordered, but the fresh fish and secret-recipe batter is now the stuff of legend. ⊠ *42–48 Great Western Rd.* ☎ *01224/596981* ▤ *AE, MC, V.*

£

✕ **Howie's.** As do its sister restaurants in St. Andrews and Edinburgh, Howie's maintains a consistently high standards for food and service.

Inside you can find sleek tables and chairs occupied by the attractive clientele. You can see why they remain that way: healthy dishes such as steamed breast of chicken and bok choi with ginger and spring onion ooze flavor and fragrance, but are light on the calories. This allows you to indulge in the blueberry crème brûlée with a crumbly topping. The staff bends over backward to accommodate children. ⊠ *50 Chapel St.* ☎ *01224/639500* ⊟ *AE, DC, MC, V.*

££££  
Fodor's Choice  
★  
✕🖫 **Marcliffe at Pitfodels.** This spacious country-house hotel on 11 wooded acres combines old and new to impressive effect. Some of the individually decorated rooms have reproduction antique furnishings, whereas others are more modern. The restaurant (££££) serves the freshest local seafood and top-quality Aberdeen Angus beef, and you can choose from more than 400 wines to go with your meal. Since it opened in 1993, this faux château has hosted such dignitaries as Prince Charles, Prime Minister Tony Blair, the Sultan of Brunei, and actor Charlton Heston. **Pros:** Lush gardens, a gentle pace. **Cons:** A little out of town, restaurant is pricey. ⊠ *N. Deeside Rd., Pitfodels, AB15 9YA* ☎ *01224/861000* ⊕ *www.marcliffe.com* ⌖ *35 rooms, 7 suites* ⚷ *In-room: no a/c, refrigerator. In-hotel: restaurant, room service, bar, spa, laundry service, no-smoking rooms* ⊟ *AE, DC, MC, V* ⱺ*BP.*

££££  
🖫 **Holiday Inn Aberdeen West.** Ten minutes from the city center, this chain hotel built in 2006 has already established a reputation for service and good looks, at least on the inside. Its newness means it feels fresh and unsullied with rooms that, while not large, have funky flat-screen TVs and other nice touches. With a decent Italian restaurant and two friendly bars, this hotel really is an all-rounder. **Pros:** Spotlessly clean, nice room amenities. **Cons:** A taxi ride from the city center, not an architectural gem. ⊠ *Westhill Dr., AB32 6TT* ☎ *01224/270300* ⊕ *www.ichotels-group.com* ⌖ *86 rooms, 1 suite* ⚷ *In-room: Wi-Fi. In-hotel: restaurant, bar, gym, no-smoking rooms* ⊟ *AE, DC, MC, V* ⱺ*BP.*

££  
🖫 **Atholl Hotel.** With its many turrets and gables, this granite hotel recalls a bygone era but has modern amenities. It's in the middle of a leafy residential area about five minutes west of the city center. Rooms are done in rich, dark colors; if space is more important than a view, opt for a room on the 1st floor. The restaurant prepares such traditional Scottish dishes as lamb cutlets and roasted rib of beef. ⊠ *54 Kings Gate, AB15 4YN* ☎ *01224/323505* ⊕ *www.atholl-aberdeen.com* ⌖ *35 rooms* ⚷ *In-room: no a/c, Ethernet. In-hotel: restaurant, bar, laundry service, no-smoking rooms* ⊟ *AE, DC, MC, V* ⱺ*BP.*

££  
🖫 **Craighaar Hotel.** Perhaps because it's five minutes to the airport, the Craighaar is popular with business executives. A rustic cinnamon and terra-cotta color scheme and modern teak furnishings decorate the hotel. The gallery suites—split-level rooms—give you plenty of room to spread out. They have nice touches like flat-screen TVs and DVD players. The restaurant's menu has a Scottish slant, with dishes such as lamb with an herb crust, whisky-and-mint sauce, and *skirlie* (oatmeal-stuffed) tomato. **Pros:** The best breakfast in town, well-kept rooms and public spaces. **Cons:** Some drab rooms, modern building lacks atmosphere. ⊠ *Waterton Rd., Bankhead AB21 9HS* ☎ *01224/712275* ⊕ *www.craighaarhotel.com* ⌖ *55 rooms, 6 suites* ⚷ *In-room: no a/c,*

*Wi-Fi. In-hotel: restaurant, bar, no elevator, laundry service, no-smoking rooms* ⊟*AE, DC, MC, V* ⏀*BP.*

££  ⚏ **The Jays Guest House.** Alice Jennings or her husband George will greet you at the front door of this cozy granite home. The warmth and friendliness of your hosts, who are pleased to recommend local restaurants or help plan trips out of town, will make your stay memorable. The spacious rooms are impeccably clean. Breakfasts may include scrumptious oatcakes, savory omelets, or your own special request. **Pros:** Immaculate rooms, expert advice on city's sites, near shops and restaurants. **Cons:** No public areas, not all rooms have en-suite bathrooms. ⊠*422 King St., AB24 3BR* ☎*01224/638295* ⊕*www.jaysguesthouse.co.uk* ⇱*10 rooms, 2 with shared bath* ♿*In-room: no a/c, no phone, Wi-Fi. In-hotel: public Internet, no-smoking rooms* ⊟*MC, V* ⏀*BP.*

## NIGHTLIFE & THE ARTS

Aberdeen has a fairly lively nightlife scene revolving around pubs and clubs. Theaters, concert halls, arts centers, and cinemas are also well represented. The principal newspapers—the *Press and Journal* and the *Evening Express*—and *Aberdeen Leopard* magazine can fill you in on what's going on anywhere in the northeast. Aberdeen's tourist information center has a monthly publication with an events calendar.

6

### THE ARTS
Aberdeen is a rich city, both financially and culturally. August sees the world-renowned **Aberdeen International Youth Festival** (*Box office* ⊠*Music Hall, Union St.* ☎*01224/213800* ⊕*www.aiyf.org*), which attracts youth orchestras, choirs, dance troupes, and theater companies from many countries. During the festival some companies take their productions to other venues in the northeast.

ARTS CENTERS  **Aberdeen Arts Centre** (⊠*33 King St.* ☎*01224/635208*) hosts experi-
★  mental plays, poetry readings, and exhibitions by local and Scottish artists. The **Lemon Tree** (⊠*5 W. North St.* ☎*01224/642230*) has an innovative and international program of dance, stand-up comedy, puppet theater, and folk, jazz, and rock-and-roll music. **Peacock Visual Arts** (⊠*21 Castle St.* ☎*01224/639539*) displays photographic, video, and slide exhibits of contemporary art and architecture. About 20 mi north of Aberdeen, **Haddo House** (⊠*Off B999 near Methlick* ☎*01651/851440*) offers a mixed-bag of events, from opera and ballet to Shakespeare, Scots-language plays, and puppetry.

CONCERT  The Edwardian **His Majesty's Theatre** (⊠*Rosemount Viaduct*
HALLS  ☎*01224/641122*) hosts performances on par with those in some of the world's biggest cities. It's a regular venue for musicals and operas, as well as classical and modern dance. The **Music Hall** (⊠*Union St.* ☎*01224/641122*) presents seasonal programs of concerts by the Scottish National Orchestra, the Scottish Chamber Orchestra, and other major groups. Events also include folk concerts, crafts fairs, and exhibitions.

FILM  **The Belmont** ( ⊠ *49 Belmont St.* ☎*01224/343536*) screens independent and classic films. **UGC Cinemas** ( ⊠ *Queen's Link Leisure Park, Links Rd.* ☎*0871/200–2000*) shows recent releases.

**NIGHTLIFE**

With a greater club-to-clubber ratio than either Edinburgh or Glasgow, loud music and dancing dominate a night out in Aberdeen. There are also plenty of pubs and pool halls for those with two left feet. Pubs close at midnight on weekdays and 1 AM on weekends; clubs go until 2 or 3 AM.

BARS & PUBS  Union Street is lined with bars of all sorts. **Archibald Simpson** ( ⊠ *5 Castle St.* ☎*01224/621365*) has cheap drinks and a typical pub menu, so patrons range from families who stop by for a meal early in the evening to groups of young people guzzling drinks before heading to the clubs. The old-fashioned **Illicit Still** ( ⊠ *Guest Row, Broad St.* ☎*01224/623123*) is named after the 18th-century practice of brewing your own beer to avoid the malt tax. A beautifully kitted-out drinking establishment, it serves up hearty pub grub. Drawing a slightly older crowd, the traditional **Old Blackfriars** ( ⊠ *52 Castle St.* ☎*01224/581922*) enjoys a nice location at the end of Union Street. The lighting is dim and the big fireplace warms things up on a chilly evening. This cask ale pub has a great selection—Belhaven St. Andrews Ale and Caledonian 80 top the list.

Fodor'sChoice  Dating from 1850, **The Prince of Wales** ( ⊠ *7 St. Nicholas La.* ★  ☎*01224/640597*) has retained its paneled walls and wooden tables. Here you can belly up to the longest bar in Aberdeen. Good-quality food and reasonable prices draw lunchtime crowds. For billiards, **Riley's** ( ⊠ *74–78 Chapel St.* ☎*01224/561894*) has a number of tables that can be had at £5 for an hour or £6 for the day. **Soul** ( ⊠ *333 Union St.* ☎*01224/211150*), in a converted church, has private booths with stained-glass windows and ecclesiastical furnishings. The eclectic menu includes everything from chicken satay and mussels. It's the most interesting of the Union Street hangouts.

DANCE CLUBS  People tend to dress up a bit to go clubbing, and jeans or sneakers might get you turned away at the door. Clubs are open until 2 AM during the week and until 3 AM on Friday and Saturday nights.

The Moroccan-style **Kef** ( ⊠ *9 Belmont St.* ☎*01224/648000*) entices those who'd prefer to lounge on floor cushions and sip cocktails than work up a sweat on the dance floor. Pop and dance music take the floor at **Liquid** ( ⊠ *5 Bridge Pl.* ☎*01224/595239*), which attracts students and young professionals. On weekends a strict dress code—dress to kill—is enforced. **Ministry** ( ⊠ *16 Dee St.* ☎*01224/594585*) one of the few permanent fixtures in the city's volatile club scene, hosts theme nights for collegiate crowds.

MUSIC CLUBS  The **Lemon Tree** ( ⊠ *5 W. North St.* ☎*01224/642230*), with a wide-ranging music program, is the main rock venue and stages frequent jazz concerts.

## SPORTS & THE OUTDOORS

### BICYCLING

**Alpine Bikes** (✉ *64–70 Holburn St.* ☎ *01224/211455*) rents mountain bikes from June to August. The staff will give you good advice on scenic routes.

### GOLF

Northeast Scotland is known for good golf; you can expect to pay £15 to £80 per round at the golf courses in and around Aberdeen. Make reservations at least 24 hours in advance. Some private courses restrict tee times for visiting golfers to certain days or hours during the week, so be sure to check that the course you wish to play is open when you want to play it.

★ **Murcar.** Sea views and a variety of rugged terrain—from sand dunes to tinkling burns—are the highlights of this course, founded in 1909. It's most famous for breathtaking vistas at the 7th hole, appropriately called the Serpentine. Designer Archibald Simpson considered this course to be one of his finest. ✉ *Bridge of Don* ☎ *01224/704354* ⚑ *18 holes, 6,314 yds, SSS 72.*

**Royal Aberdeen Golf Club, Balgownie.** Founded in 1780, this club is the sixth oldest in the world, and there are fine views of Aberdeen from its fairways. ✉ *Bridge of Don* ☎ *01224/702571* ⚑ *18 holes, 6,415 yds, SSS 73.*

**Westhill.** This parkland course, founded in 1977, overlooks Royal Deeside. It's the most inexpensive in the area, charging £20 to £30 per day. ✉ *Westhill Heights* ☎ *01224/740159* ⚑ *18 holes, 5,849 yds, SSS 69.*

## SHOPPING

### DEPARTMENT STORES

You can find most of the large national department stores in the Bon Accord, St. Nicholas, and Trinity shopping malls or along Union Street.

**Debenhams** (✉ *Trinity Center, Union St.* ☎ *01224/578510*) is a well-stocked department store with excellent men's and women's fashion as well as jewelry and housewares. The spacious **John Lewis** (✉ *George St., reached via Bon Accord Centre* ☎ *01224/625000*) resembles a double-decker sandwich with its filling illuminated. You can find clothing, household items, giftware, and much more.

### SPECIALTY SHOPS

There are clusters of small specialty shops in the Chapel Street–Thistle Street area at the west end of Union Street. At the **Aberdeen Family History Society Shop** (✉ *158–164 King St.* ☎ *01224/646323*) you can browse through publications related to local history and genealogical research. For a small fee the Aberdeen & North East Family History Society will undertake some research on your behalf. For Scottish kilts, tartans, crests, and other traditionally Scottish clothes, a good place to start is **Alex Scott & Co** (✉ *43 Schoolhill* ☎ *01224/643924*). The **Books and Beans** (✉ *22 Belmont St.* ☎ *01224/646438*) is a secondhand bookshop with its own little café. You're welcome to browse and sip at the same time. **Colin Wood** (⊠*25 Rose St.* ☎*01224/643019*) is the place to go for small antiques, prints, and regional maps. **Nova** (⊠*18–20 Chapel St.* ☎*01224/641270*), where the locals go for gifts, stocks Scottish silver jewelry. You can also find major U.K. brand names, such as Neal's Yard, Dartington Glass, and Crabtree and Evelyn. The **Toy Bazaar** (⊠*45 Schoolhill* ☎*01224/640021*) stocks toys for children preschool age and up.

# ROYAL DEESIDE & CASTLE COUNTRY

Deeside, the valley running west from Aberdeen down which the River Dee flows, earned its "royal" appellation when discovered by Queen Victoria. To this day, where royalty goes, lesser aristocracy and freshly minted millionaires follow. It's still the aspiration of many to own a grand shooting estate in Deeside. In a sense this yearning is understandable because the piney hill slope, purple moor, and blue river intermingle tastefully here. Royal Deeside's gradual scenic change adds a growing sense of excitement as you travel deeper into the Grampians.

There are castles along the Dee as well as to the north in Castle Country, a region that also illustrates the gradual geological change in the northeast: uplands lapped by a tide of farms. All the Donside and Deeside castles are picturesquely sited, with most fitted out with tall slender turrets, winding stairs, and crooked chambers that epitomize Scottish baronial style. All have tales of ghosts and bloodshed, siege and torture. Many were tidied up and "domesticated" during the 19th century. Although best toured by car, much of this area is accessible either by public transportation or on tours from Aberdeen.

## STONEHAVEN

*15 mi south of Aberdeen.*

This historic town near splendid Dunnotrar Castle was once a popular holiday destination, with Robert Burns enjoying walks along the golden sands. The surrounding red-clay fields were made famous by Lewis Grassic Gibbon (real name James Leslie Mitchell) who attended school in the town and who wrote the seminal Scottish trilogy, *A Scots Quair,* about the people, the land, and the impact of World War I. The decline of the fishing industry emptied the harbor, but the town, being so close to Aberdeen, has begun to thrive again. It's now famous for its Hogmany (New Year) celebrations, where local men swing huge balls of fire on chains before tossing them into the harbor.

FodorśChoice
★

It's hard to beat the magnificent, cliff-top ruins of **Dunnottar Castle,** which straddles a headland overlooking Stonehaven and the North Sea. Building began in the 14th century, when Sir William Keith, Marischal of Scotland (keeper of the king's mares and one of the king's right-hand men), decided to build a tower house to demonstrate his power. Subsequent generations added on to the structure over the centuries, and

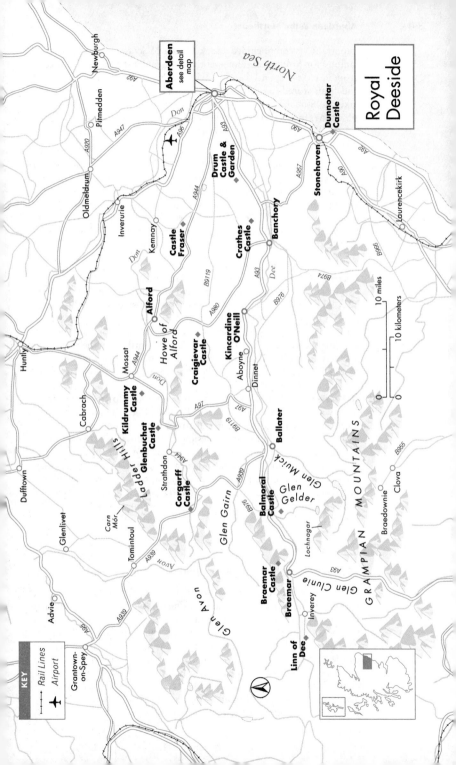

# Royal Deeside

KEY

Rail Lines
Airport

North Sea

Aberdeen
see detail
map

Newburgh
Pitmedden
Oldmeldrum
Inverurie
Kemnay
Castle Fraser
Drum Castle & Garden
Crathes Castle
Banchory
Dunnottar Castle
Stonehaven
Laurencekirk

Don

Huntly
Cabrach
Dufftown
Glenlivet
Advie
Grantown-on-Spey
Mossat
Strathdon
Tomintoul
Kildrummy Castle
Glenbuchat Castle
Corgarff Castle
Carn Mór
Ladder Hills
Howe of Alford
Alford
Craigievar Castle
Kincardine O'Neill
Aboyne
Dinnet
Ballater

Dee

Balmoral Castle
Glen Gelder
Braemar Castle
Braemar
Inverey
Linn of Dee
Lochnagar
Glen Muick
Glen Gairn
Glen Clunie
Glen Avon

GRAMPIAN MOUNTAINS

Braedownie
Clova

10 miles
10 kilometers

important visitors included Mary, Queen of Scots. The castle is most famous for holding out for eight months against Oliver Cromwell's army in 1651–52, and thereby saving the Scottish crown jewels, which had been stored here for safekeeping. Reach the castle via the A90; take the Stonehaven turnoff and follow the signs. ■ TIP→ **Wear sensible shoes to investigate the ruins; allow about two hours.** ⊠*Stonehaven* ☎*01569/860223* ⊕*www.dunnottarcastle.co.uk* ☑*£5* ♥*Easter–Oct., Mon.–Sat. 9–6, Sun. 2–5; Nov.–Easter, Fri.–Mon. 9–sunset.*

Ⓒ They were extremely popular in the 1930s, but the **Stonehaven Open-Air Swimming Pool,** an art-deco gem, is one of only a few remaining outdoor heated pools in Scotland. Salty water from the North Sea is pumped in and heated to a toasty 29°C (84°F). Run by a local trust, this place is perfect for families. ■ TIP→ **Ask about Wednesday's midnight swims, when you can float under the stars.** ⊠*Queen Elizabeth Park* ☎*01569/762134* ☑*£3.50* ♥*June–Sept., weekdays 1–1:30, weekends 10–6.*

### WHERE TO STAY & EAT

£££ ✕ **Carron Art Deco Restaurant.** For an outstanding meal of classic Scottish dishes served in the most splendid surroundings, try the Carron. ★ This longtime favorite evokes the style and class of the 1930s, making it a must for both architecture and food lovers. Look out for the rather risqué figure of a woman etched onto a mirror between two dazzlingly tiled columns. The food is not diminished by the surroundings: try the grilled North Sea haddock on blanched white asparagus or the Aberdeen Angus beef fillet on braised leeks. ⊠*Cameron St.* ☎*01569/760460* ⊟*AE, MC, V.*

££ 🏠 **Bayview B&B.** Sitting right on the beach but just down the lane from ★ the town square, this newly built B&B couldn't be in a more convenient location—or have better views. The rooms are all on the lower level and each room is individually designed with original artwork, fascinating knickknacks, and lovely furnishings. The huge, healthy breakfasts will fortify you against the northeast winds. **Pros:** Spick-and-span rooms, eccentric design. **Cons:** Smallish rooms, no view from breakfast room. ⊠*Beachgate La., AB39 2BD* ☎*01569/766933* ⊕*www. bayviewbandb.co.uk* ⤴*3 rooms* ☖*In-room: no a/c, Wi-Fi. In hotel: Internet* ⊟*AE, MC, V* ⦿*BP.*

## DRUM CASTLE & GARDEN

*15 mi northwest of Stonehaven, 11 mi west of Aberdeen.*

Drum Castle is a foursquare tower that dates from the 13th century, with later additions up to Victorian times. Note the tower's rounded corners, said to make battering-ram attacks more difficult. Nearby, fragments of the ancient Forest of Drum still stand, dating from the days when Scotland was covered by great stands of oak and pine. The Garden of Historic Roses, open from April to October, lays claim to some old-fashioned roses not commonly seen today. ⊠*Off A93* ☎*01330/811204* ⊕*www.nts.org.uk* ☑*Garden £2.50; castle and garden £8* ♥*Castle Apr., May, and Sept., daily 12:30–5; June–Aug., daily 10–5. Grounds daily 9:30–sunset.*

## Which Castle Is Right for You?

We admit it—there are almost too many castles in this part of Scotland. Since it's nearly impossible to see all of them, we've noted the prime characteristics of each to help you decide which you'd most like to visit.

■ **Balmoral:** The Queen's home has the royals' seal of approval and baronial largesse, though you don't see much inside.

■ **Balvenie:** This ruined castle is known for its indomitable bearing and verdant surroundings.

■ **Braemar:** Stop here, and you may see a restoration in progress; the interior is closed at this writing.

■ **Corgarff:** You'll find a sober solitude out on the moorland, as well as 18th-century graffiti and a defensive wall.

■ **Craigievar:** Highlights of this 17th-century castle are fairytale turrets and untouched splendor. It's closed at this writing for exterior renovations.

■ **Crathes:** Expect tight quarters, notable family portraits, and a network of walled gardens.

■ **Dunnottar:** The dramatic, scene-stealing clifftop location of these ruins by the sea is unbeatable.

■ **Drum:** A fusion of architectural styles and some historic roses are notable at this castle.

■ **Fraser:** Opulent period furnishings and woodland walks make for a rewarding day.

■ **Fyvie:** Come here for an awesome art collection, rich interiors, and a haunting magnificence.

■ **Kildrummy:** This is the place for evocative ruins, some from the 13th century, and tales of a treacherous past. Nearby gardens were built in the castle quarry.

6

## BANCHORY

*8 mi west of Drum Castle & Garden, 19 mi west of Aberdeen via A93.*

Banchory is an immaculate town filled with pinkish granite buildings. It's usually bustling with ice-cream-eating strollers, out on a day trip from Aberdeen.

If you visit in autumn and have time to spare, drive for a mile along the B974 south of Banchory to the **Brig o'Feuch** (pronounced fyooch, the *ch* as in loch). The area around this bridge is very pleasant: salmon leap in season, and the fall colors and foaming waters make for an attractive scene.

**Crathes Castle,** 16 mi west of Aberdeen, was once the home of the Burnett family. Keepers of the Forest of Drum for generations, the family acquired lands here by marriage and later built a castle, completed in 1596. The National Trust for Scotland cares for the castle, furnished with many original pieces and family portraits. Outside are grand gardens with calculated symmetry and clipped yew hedges. Make sure to sample the tasty home baking in the tearoom. ⊠ *Off A93, 3½ mi east of Banchory* ☎ *0844/4932166* ⊕ *www.nts.org.uk* ⚑ *Garden £8; cas-*

*tle and garden £10* ⊘ *Apr.–Sept., daily 10–5:30; Oct., daily 10–4:30; last admission 45 min before closing; Nov.–Mar., guided tours only, Thurs.–Sun. 10–3:45.*

## WHERE TO STAY & EAT

££££   ✕🏠**Banchory Lodge.** With the River Dee flowing a few yards beyond the garden, tranquil Banchory Lodge is an ideal spot for anglers. The house was built in the 17th century and it retains its period charm. Rooms are individually decorated, though all have bold color schemes and tartan or floral fabrics. The restaurant (£££) serves Scottish cuisine with French overtones; try the pork grilled with Stilton cheese or the smoked hake in a creamy white-wine sauce. **Pros:** Fabulous river setting, great for outdoors enthusiasts. **Cons:** Some decor needs sprucing up, restaurant closes fairly early. ⊠*Dee St., AB31 5HS* ☎*01330/822625* ⊕*www.banchorylodge.co.uk* ⬅*22 rooms* ♿*In-room: no a/c. In-hotel: restaurant, bar, bicycles, no elevator* ⊟*AE, DC, MC, V* ⦿*BP.*

## KINCARDINE O'NEILL

*9 mi west of Banchory.*

The ruined kirk in the little village of Kincardine O'Neill was built in 1233 and once sheltered travelers: it was the last hospice before the Mounth, the name given to the massif that shuts off the south side of the Dee Valley. Beyond Banchory (and the B974), no motor roads run south until you reach Braemar (A93), though the Mounth is crossed by a network of tracks once used by Scottish soldiers, invading armies (including the Romans), and cattle drovers. Photography buffs won't want to miss the bridge at Potarch, just to the east.

OFF THE
BEATEN
PATH

**Queen's View.** To reach one of the most spectacular vistas in northeast Scotland—stretching across the Howe of Cromar to Lochnagar—take the B9094 due north from Aboyne, then turn left onto the B9119 for 6 mi.

## BALLATER

*22mi west of Kincardine O'Neill, 43 mi west of Aberdeen.*

The handsome holiday resort of Ballater, once noted for the curative properties of its waters, has profited from the proximity of the royals, nearby at Balmoral. You might be amused by the array of BY ROYAL APPOINTMENT signs proudly hanging from many of its various shops (even monarchs need bakers and butchers). Take time to stroll around this well-laid-out community. The railway station houses the tourist information center and a display on the glories of the Great North of Scotland branch railway line, closed in the 1960s along with so many others in this country.

As long as you have your own car, you can capture the feel of the eastern Highlands yet still be close to town. Start your expedition into

★  **Glen Muick** (Gaelic for pig, pronounced mick) by crossing the River Dee and heading west on the B976. When the road forks, you'll take the

**CLOSE UP**

# Do ye ken fitehm sayin', laddie?

"Much," said Doctor Johnson, "may be made of a Scotchman if he be caught young." This quote sums up, even today, the attitude of some English people—confident in their English, the language of parliament and much of the media—to the Scots language. The Scots have long been made to feel uncomfortable about their mother tongue, and until the 1970s (and in some private schools, even today) they were actively encouraged to ape the dialect of the Thames Valley ("standard English") in order to "get on" in life.

The Scots language (that is, Lowland Scots, not Gaelic) was a northern form of Middle English and in its day was the language used in the court and in literature. It borrowed from Scandinavian, Dutch, French, and Gaelic. After a series of historical blows—such as the decamping of the Scottish court to England after 1603 and the printing of the King James Bible in English but not in Scots—it declined as a literary or official language. It survives in various forms but is virtually an underground language, spoken among ordinary folk, especially in its heartland, in the northeast.

You may even find yourself exporting a few useful words, such as *dreich* (gloomy), *glaikit* (acting and looking foolish), or *dinna fash* (don't worry), all of which are much more expressive than their English equivalents.

Some Scottish words are used and understood across the entire country (and world), such as *wee* (small), *aye* (yes), *lassie* (girl), and *bonny* (pretty). Regional variations are evident even in the simplest of greetings. When you meet someone in the Borders, *Whit fettle?* (What state are you in?) or *Hou*

*ye lestin?* (How are you lasting?) may throw you for a loop; elsewhere you could hear *Hou's yer dous?* (How are your pigeons?). If a group of Scots take a fancy to you at the pub, you may be asked to *Come intil the body o the kirk*, and if all goes well, your departure may be met with a jovial farewell, *haste ye back* (return soon).

Scottish Gaelic, an entirely different language, is still spoken across the Highlands and Hebrides. There's also a large Gaelic-speaking population in Glasgow as a result of the Celtic diaspora—islanders migrating to Glasgow in search of jobs in the 19th century. Speakers of Gaelic in Scotland were once persecuted, after the failure of the 18th-century Jacobite rebellions. Official persecution has now turned to guilt-tinged support, as the promoters of Gaelic now lobby for substantial public funds to underwrite television programming and language classes for new learners.

One of the joys of Scottish television is watching Gaelic news programs to see how the ancient language copes with such topics as nuclear energy, the Internet, and the latest band to hit the charts. A number of Gaelic words have been absorbed into English: *banshee* (a wailing female spirit), *galore* (plenty), *slob* (a slovenly person), and *brat* (a spoiled or unruly child).

To experience Gaelic language and culture in all its unfettered glory, you can attend the Royal National Mod—a competition-based festival with speeches, drama, and music, all in Gaelic—which is held in a different location every year.

6

unnamed single-track road that runs along the River Muick. The native red deer are quite common throughout the Scottish Highlands, but the flat valley floor here is one of the very best places to see them. Beyond the lower glen, the prospect opens to reveal fine views of the battlement of cliffs edging the mountain called Lochnagar.

## WHERE TO STAY & EAT

£££  ✕⌨ **Raemoir House Hotel.** With portions dating from the 16th to 19th centuries, this baronial former home evokes the past but offers today's comforts. Guest rooms—a number of which have four-poster beds—have a genteel period charm and large, modern bathrooms. The restaurant (£££££; fixed-price menu), in an oval ballroom, has a solid reputation based on exquisite Scottish fare created with seasonal local produce. And the morning room, despite its name, is the perfect place to nurse a wee nip of whisky before bed. You can take some lovely walks on the estate's 3,500 acres of hillock and woodland. **Pros:** Perfect mix of old-fashioned and modern luxury, staff is informal and efficient. **Cons:** Pricey, some rooms are better than others. ⊠ *Off A980, Raemoir, AB31 4ED* ☎ *01330/824884* ⊕ *www.raemoir.com* ⟳ *17 rooms, 3 suites* ⌂ *In-room: no a/c. In-hotel: restaurant, bar, no elevator* ⊟ *AE, DC, MC, V* ❀*BP.*

£    ✕⌨ **The Green Inn.** A family affair, this hotel is run by a couple who
★    take great pleasure in looking after their guests. Their son—trained by the great celebrity chef Raymond Blanc—serves what is considered by many to be the best food in the northeast. In the dining room (££££; fixed-price menu), the tables are laid with heavy china and polished cutlery. The prix-fixe dinner might include partridge with caramelized apple. The à la carte breakfast (add £10) can be whatever you like, from kippers to kedgeree. The bedrooms are large and plain, yet elegantly furnished with king-size beds and creature comforts like super-soft duvets, fluffy towels, and cocoonlike dressing gowns. There's excellent fishing in the nearby Dee. **Pros:** Amazing value for the money, discreet and efficient service. **Cons:** Books up quickly, restaurant serves rather petite portions. ⊠ *Victoria Rd., AB35 5QQ* ☎ *01339/55701* ⊕ *www. green-inn.com* ⟳ *3 rooms* ⌂ *In-room: no a/c. In-hotel: restaurant, bar, no elevator* ⊟ *AE, DC, MC, V* ❀*CP.*

££££  ⌨ **Hilton Craigendarroch Hotel.** This magnificent country-house hotel, just outside Ballater on a hillside overlooking the River Dee, manages to keep everyone happy. Choose between a classically furnished room in the main house and a private, less-expensive pine lodge set among the trees. Fitted with labor-saving appliances, the lodges are perfect for families. The hotel's restaurants include the Oaks, for modern Scottish food, and the Club House brasserie, for lighter fare. Anglers should inquire in advance about day fishing permits. **Pros:** Grounds are great for walks, lovely pool area, relaxing spa. **Cons:** Feels understaffed, food can be erratic. ⊠ *Braemar Rd., AB35 5XA* ☎ *013397/55858* ⊕ *www. hilton.com* ⟳ *39 rooms, 6 suites* ⌂ *In-room: no a/c, kitchen (some), refrigerator (some). In-hotel: 2 restaurants, room service, bars, tennis court, pools, gym, laundry facilities, laundry service, no-smoking rooms, some pets allowed* ⊟ *AE, DC, MC, V.*

## SHOPPING

Head to the **Clothes Shop** (⊠*1 Braemar Rd.* ☎*013397/55947*) for fleeces and waterproofs to keep you dry on the hills. At either location of **Countrywear** (⊠*15 and 35 Bridge St.* ☎*013397/55453*), you can find everything you need for Highland country living, including fishing tackle, natty tweeds, and that flexible garment popular in Scotland between seasons: the body warmer. For a low-cost gift you could always see what's being boiled up at **Dee Valley Confectioners** (⊠*Station Sq.* ☎*013397/55499*). The **McEwan Gallery** (⊠*On A939, 1 mi west of Ballater* ☎*013397/55429*) displays fine paintings, watercolors, prints, and books (many with a Scottish or golf theme) in an unusual house built by the Swiss artist Rudolphe Christen in 1902.

# BALMORAL CASTLE

★ *7 mi west of Ballater.*

The enormous parking lot is indicative of the popularity of Balmoral Castle, one of Queen Elizabeth II's favorite family retreats. Balmoral's visiting hours depend on whether the royals are in residence. In truth, there are more interesting and historic buildings to explore, as the only part of the castle on view is the ballroom, with an exhibition of royal artifacts. The Carriage Hall has displays of commemorative china, carriages, and native wildlife. Perhaps it's just as well that most of the house is closed to the public, for Balmoral suffers from a bad rash of tartanitis. Thanks to Victoria and Albert, stags' heads abounded, the bagpipes wailed incessantly, and the garish Stuart tartan was used for every item of furnishings, from carpets to chair covers. A more somber Duff tartan, black and green to blend with the environment, was later adopted, and from the brief glimpse you may get of Balmoral's interior, it's clear that royal taste is now more restrained. Queen Elizabeth II, however, follows her predecessors' routine in spending a holiday of about six weeks in Deeside, usually from mid-August to the end of September. During this time Balmoral is closed to visitors.

Around and about Balmoral are some notable spots—Cairn O'Mount, Cambus O'May, and the Cairngorms from the Linn of Dee—and some of them may be seen on pony-trekking expeditions, which use Balmoral stalking ponies and go around the grounds and estate. When the royals are in residence, even the grounds are closed to the public. ⊠*A93* ☎*013397/42534* ⊕*www.balmoralcastle.com* ⊠*£7* ⊙*Apr.–July, daily 10–5; last admission 1 hr before closing.*

**EN ROUTE** As you continue west into Highland scenery, further pine-framed glimpses appear of the "steep frowning glories of dark Lochnagar," as it was described by the poet Lord Byron (1788–1824). Lochnagar (3,786 feet) was made known to an audience wider than hill walkers by the Prince of Wales, who published a children's story, *The Old Man of Lochnagar.*

## CLOSE UP

## Around Queen Victoria's Retreat

Balmoral is a Victorian fantasy, designed for Queen Victoria (1819–1901) by her consort, Prince Albert (1819–61), in 1855. "It seems like a dream to be here in our dear Highland Home again," Queen Victoria wrote. "Every year my heart becomes more fixed in this dear Paradise."

Victoria loved Balmoral more for its setting than its house, so be sure to take in its pleasant gardens. Year by year Victoria and Albert added to the estate, taking over neighboring houses, securing the forest and moorland around it, and developing deer stalking and grouse shooting here. In consequence, Balmoral is now a large property, as the grounds run 12 mi along the Deeside road. Its privacy is protected by belts of pinewood, and the only view of the castle from the A93 is a partial one, from a point near Inver, 2 mi west of the gates.

There's an excellent bird's-eye view of Balmoral from an old military road, now the A939, which climbs out of Crathie, northbound for Cockbridge and the Don Valley. This view embraces the summit of Lochnagar, in whose *corries* (hollows) the snow lies year-round and whose boulder fields the current Prince of Wales, Charles Windsor, so fondly and so frequently treads.

## BRAEMAR

*17 mi west of Ballater, 60 mi west of Aberdeen, 51 mi north of Perth via A93.*

The village of Braemar is associated with the **Braemar Highland Gathering,** held every September. Although there are many such gatherings celebrated throughout Scotland, this one is distinguished by the presence of the royal family. Competitions and events include hammer throwing, caber tossing, running races, Highland dancing, and bagpipe playing. You can find out more at the **Braemar Highland Heritage Centre,** in a converted stable block in the middle of town. It tells the history of the village with displays and a film, and it also has a gift shop. ✉ *The Mews, Mar Rd.* ☎ *013397/41944* ✆ *Free* ⏱ *Apr.–Sept., daily 9–6; Oct., daily 9–5; Nov.–Mar., daily 10–noon and 1–5.*

Braemar is dominated by **Braemar Castle** on its outskirts. The castle dates from the 17th century, although its defensive walls, in the shape of a pointed star, came later. At Braemar (the *braes*, or slopes, of the district of Mar) the standard, or rebel flag, was first raised at the start of the spectacularly unsuccessful Jacobite Rebellion of 1715. Thirty years later, during the last rebellion, Braemar Castle was strengthened and garrisoned by Hanoverian (government) troops. At the time of this writing, the interior castle was closed. It was slated to reopen in 2008, but call ahead to make certain. In the meantime, you're free to tour the grounds. ✉ *A93* ☎ *013397/41219* ⏺ *www.braemarcastle.co.uk.*

**OFF THE BEATEN PATH**

**Linn of Dee.** Although the main A93 slinks off to the south from Braemar, a little unmarked road will take you farther west into the hilly heartland. In fact, even if you do not have your own car, you can still explore this area by catching the post bus that leaves from the Braemar post office once a day. The road offers views over the winding River Dee and the blue hills before passing through the tiny hamlet of Inverey and crossing a bridge at the Linn of Dee. *Linn* is a Scots word meaning "rocky narrows," and the river's gash here is deep and roaring. Park beyond the bridge and walk back to admire the sylvan setting.

### WHERE TO STAY

£ ⌂**Callater Lodge.** The owners of this B&B, a Victorian-era granite house with pleasant grounds, extend a warm welcome to those seeking a comfortable place to rest in the center of the village. The rooms are homey and modern, and the lounge and well-stocked library, both with fireplaces, are pleasant spots to while away the hours. You can easily walk to number of places to dine. **Pros:** Staff's knowledge of the area cannot be beaten, pleasant public rooms. **Cons:** Decor in the rooms can be a bit twee, breakfast options are limited. ✉*9 Glenshee Rd., AB35 5YQ* ☎*013397/41275* ⊕*www.hotel-braemar.co.uk* ⇆*6 rooms* ↻*In-room: no a/c. In-hotel: bar* ▱*AE, DC, MC, V* ⊘*Closed Nov. and Dec.* ✸*BP.*

### GOLF

The tricky 18-hole **Braemar Golf Course,** founded in 1902, is laden with foaming waters. Erratic duffers take note: the compassionate course managers have installed, near the water, poles with little nets on the end for those occasional shots that may go awry. The cost for a round is £20 during the week, £25 on weekends. ✉*Cluny Bank Rd.* ☎*013397/41618* ⚐*18 holes, 4,916 yds, SSS 64.*

## CORGARFF CASTLE

*23 mi northeast of Braemar, 14 mi northwest of Ballater.*

Eighteenth-century soldiers paved a military highway, now the A939, north from Ballater to Corgarff Castle, an isolated tower house on the moorland with a star-shape defensive wall—a curious replica of Braemar Castle. Corgarff was built as a hunting lodge for the earls of Mar in the 16th century. After an eventful history that included the wife of a later laird being burned alive in a family dispute, the castle ended its career as a garrison for Hanoverian troops. The troops were responsible for preventing illegal whisky distilling. ✉*Signposted off A939* ☎*01975/651460* ⊕*www.historic-scotland.gov.uk* ▱*£4.50* ⊘*Apr.–Sept., daily 9:30–6:30; Oct.–Mar., weekends 9:30–4:30; last admission half hr before closing.*

**EN ROUTE** If you return east from Corgarff Castle to the A939/A944 junction and make a left onto the A944, the thorough castle signposting indicates you're on the **Castle Trail.** The A944 meanders along the River Don to the village of Strathdon, where a great mound by the roadside—on the left—turns out to be a *motte,* or the base of a wooden castle, built in the late 12th century. Although it takes considerable imagination to become enthusiastic about a great grass-covered heap, surviving mottes have contributed greatly to the understanding of the history of Scottish castles. The A944 then joins the A97 (go left), and a few minutes later a sign points to Glenbuchat Castle, a plain Z-plan tower house. ⊕*www. agtb.org/castletrail.htm.*

## KILDRUMMY CASTLE

★ *18 mi northeast of Corgarff, 23 mi north of Ballater, 22 mi north of Aboyne.*

Kildrummy Castle is significant because of its age—it dates to the 13th century—and because it has ties to the mainstream medieval traditions of European castle building. It shares features with Harlech and Caernarfon, in Wales, as well as with Château de Coucy, near Laon, France. Kildrummy underwent several expansions at the hands of England's King Edward I (1239–1307); the castle was back in Scottish hands in 1306, when it was besieged by King Edward I's son. The defenders were betrayed by Osbarn the Smith, who was promised a large amount of gold by the English forces. They gave it to him after the castle fell, pouring it molten down his throat, or so the ghoulish story goes. Kildrummy's prominence ended after the collapse of the 1715 Jacobite uprising. It had been the rebel headquarters and was consequently dismantled. ⊠*A97* ☎*019755/71331* ⊕*www.www.historic-scotland.gov. uk* ⊡*£3.50* ⊗*Apr.–Sept., daily 9:30–5:30.*

The **Kildrummy Castle Gardens,** behind the castle and with a separate entrance from the main road, are built in what was the original quarry for the castle. This sheltered bowl within the woodlands has a broad range of shrubs and alpine plants and a notable water garden. ⊠*A97* ☎*019755/71203 or 019755/71277* ⊕*www.kildrummy-castle-gardens. co.uk* ⊡*£3.50* ⊗*Apr.–Sept., daily 9:30–5:30; call to confirm opening times late in season.*

### WHERE TO STAY & EAT

££££  ✕⌂ **Kildrummy Castle Hotel.** A grand late-Victorian country house, this elegant lodging offers a peaceful stay and attentive service. Hand-carved oak paneling, elaborate plasterwork, and gentle color schemes create a serene environment, enhanced by the views of nearby Kildrummy Castle Gardens. The Scottish cuisine served in the excellent restaurant (£££££) uses local game as well as seafood. **Pros:** Fabulous old hunting lodge, great views. **Cons:** Rather pricey, some common areas are musty. ⊠*A97, Kildrummy AB33 8RA* ☎*019755/71288* ⊕*www.kildrummy-castlehotel.co.uk* ➦*16 rooms* ⌂*In-room: no a/c. In-hotel: restaurant, bar, laundry service, no-smoking rooms, some pets allowed, no elevator* ▤*MC, V* ⊗*Closed Jan.* ⵑ⋈*BP.*

## ALFORD

*9 mi east of Kildrummy, 28 mi west of Aberdeen.*

A plain and sturdy settlement in the Howe (Hollow) of Alford, this town gives those who have grown somewhat weary of castle-hopping a break: it has a museum instead.

The **Grampian Transport Museum** specializes in road-based means of locomotion, backed up by an archives and library. One of its more unusual exhibits is the *Craigievar Express*, a steam-driven creation invented by the local postman to deliver mail more efficiently. ⊠ *Alford* ☏ *019755/62292* ⊕ *www.gtm.org.uk* ✉ *£5.40* ⊘ *Apr.–Sept., daily 10–5; Oct., daily 10–4.*

## CRAIGIEVAR CASTLE

*5 mi south of Alford.*

Craigievar Castle is much as the stonemasons left it in 1626, with its pepper-pot turrets and towers. It was built in relatively peaceful times by William Forbes, a successful merchant in trade with the Baltic Sea ports (he was also known as Danzig Willie). The castle is scheduled to be closed throughout 2008 for exterior work, though the grounds may be open; call ahead to check. ⊠ *5 mi south of Alford on A980* ☏ *013398/83635* ⊕ *www.nts.org.uk* ✉ *£10* ⊘ *Apr.–June, Fri.–Tues. 10–5; July and Aug., daily 10–5; last admission 45 min before closing.*

## CASTLE FRASER

*8 mi southeast of Alford.*

The massive Castle Fraser, southeast of Alford, is the largest of the castles of Mar. Although it shows a variety of styles reflecting the taste of its owners from the 15th through the 19th centuries, its design is typical of the cavalcade of castles that exist here in the northeast, and for good reason, as this—along with many other of the region's castles, including Midmar, Craigievar, Crathes, and Glenbuchat—was designed by a family of master masons called Bell. The walled garden includes a 19th-century knot garden, with colorful flowerbeds, box hedging, gravel paths, and splendid herbaceous borders. Have lunch in the tearoom or the picnic area. ⊠ *8 mi southeast of Alford off A944* ☏ *01330/833463* ⊕ *www.nts.org.uk* ✉ *£8* ⊘ *Castle Easter–June, Sept., and Oct., Wed.–Sun. 11–5; July and Aug., daily 11–5; last admission 45 min before closing.*

# THE NORTHEAST & THE MALT WHISKY TRAIL

This route starts inland, traveling toward Speyside—the valley, or strath, of the River Spey—famed for its whisky distilleries, which it promotes in yet another signposted trail. Distilling scotch is not an intrinsically spectacular process. It involves pure water, malted barley, and sometimes peat smoke, then a lot of bubbling and fermentation, all of which cause a number of odd smells. The result is a prestigious product with a fascinating range of flavors that you either enjoy immensely or not at all.

Instead of closely following the Malt Whisky Trail, just dip into it and blend it with some other aspects of the lower end of Speyside—the county of Moray. Whisky notwithstanding, Moray's scenic qualities, low rainfall, and other reassuring weather statistics are also worth remembering. The suggested route then allows you to sample the northeastern seaboard, including some of the best but least-known coastal scenery in Scotland.

## DUFFTOWN

★ *54 mi from Aberdeen via A96 and A920, turn west at Huntly.*

On one of the Spey tributaries, Dufftown was planned in 1817 by the earl of Fife.

In the center of town, the conspicuous battlemented **clock tower**—the centerpiece of the planned town and a former jail—houses the local tourist information center. ⊠ *The Square* ☎ *01340/820501* ⊙ *Apr.–Oct., daily 9–5.*

Many make **Glenfiddich Distillery**, ½ mi north of Dufftown, their first stop on the Malt Whisky Trail. The independent company of William Grant and Sons Limited was the first to realize the tourist potential of the distilling process. The company began offering tours and subsequently built an entertaining visitor center. The audiovisual show and displays are as worthwhile as the two-hour in-depth tour (£12; reserve ahead in summer), and the traditional stone-walled premises with the typical pagoda-roof malting buildings are pleasant. Check out the Glenfiddich Distillery Art Gallery shows the work of international artists who have completed a residency at the distillery. It's open Thursday to Sunday 12:30 to 5:30. ⊠ *North of Dufftown on A941* ☎ *01340/820373* ⊕ *www.glenfiddich.com* ⊠ *Free, tour £12* ⊙ *Easter–mid-Oct., Mon.–Sat. 9:30–4:30, Sun. noon–4:30; mid-Oct.–Easter, weekdays 9:30–4:30.*

On a mound just above the Glenfiddich Distillery is a grim, gray, and squat curtain-walled castle, **Balvenie.** This ruined fortress, which dates from the 13th century, once commanded the glens and passes toward Speyside and Elgin. The Balvenie distillery is next to the castle. ⊠ *A941* ☎ *01340/820121* ⊕ *www.historic-scotland.gov.uk* ⊠ *£3.50* ⊙ *Apr.–Sept., daily 9:30–6:30; last entry half hr before closing.*

**Mortlach Church,** set in a hollow by the Dullan Water, is thought to be one of Scotland's oldest Christian sites, perhaps founded by St. Moluag, a contemporary of St. Columba, as early as AD 566. Note the weathered Pictish cross in the churchyard and the even older stone under cover in the vestibule, with a strange Pictish elephantlike beast carved on it. Though much of the church was rebuilt after 1876, some early work survives, including three lancet windows from the 13th century and a leper's squint (a hole extended to the outside of the church so that lepers could hear the service but be kept away from the rest of the congregation).

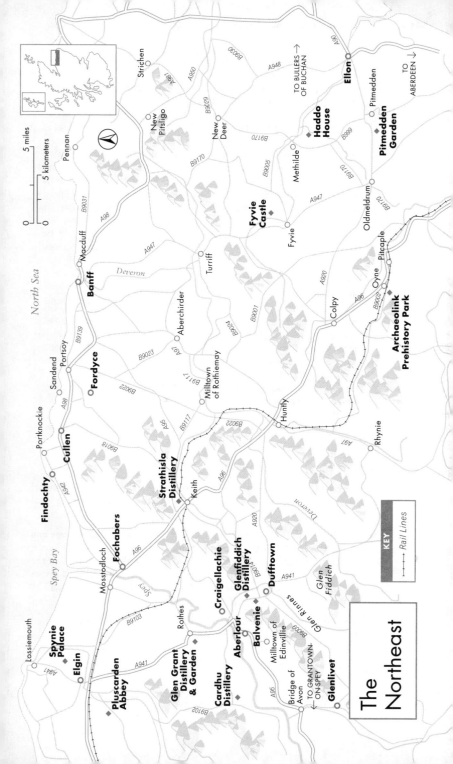

The Northeast

KEY
→ Rail Lines

5 miles
5 kilometers

North Sea

Strichen
New Pitsligo
New Deer
Ellon
Pitmedden
Haddo House
Pitmedden Garden
TO BULLERS OF BUCHAN →
TO ABERDEEN ↓
Methilde
Oldmeldrum
Fyvie Castle
Fyvie
Pitcaple
Oyne
Colpy
Archaeolink Prehistory Park
Pennan
Macduff
Banff
Deveron
Turriff
Aberchirder
Milltown of Rothiemay
Huntly
Rhynie
Portsoy
Sandend
Fordyce
Portknockie
Cullen
Strathisla Distillery
Keith
Findochty
Fochabers
Craigellachie
Glenfiddich Distillery
Dufftown
Glen Fiddich
Mosstodloch
Spey Bay
Spey
Rothes
Aberlour
Balvenie
Milltown of Edinville
Glen Rinnes
Deveron
Lossiemouth
Spynie Palace
Elgin
Plusgarden Abbey
Glen Grant Distillery & Garden
Cardhu Distillery
Bridge of Avon
TO GRANTOWN-ON-SPEY →
Glenlivet

A90
B9030
A948
B9029
B9170
B9170
B9005
B9999
A947
B9170
A920
A96
B9002
A920
A96
A97
A947
B9037
A98
A947
B9139
B9023
A97
B9001
B9024
B9117
B9022
A95
B9117
B9902
A96
B9018
A98
A942
A96
A920
B9014
A941
B9009
A95
A941
B9103
B9102
A95
B9014

## CLOSE UP

# Whisky, the Water of Life

Conjured from an innocuous mix of malted barley, water, and yeast, malt whisky is for many synonymous with Scotland. Clans produced whisky for hundreds of years before it emerged as Scotland's national drink and major export. Today those centuries of expertise result in a sublimely subtle drink with many different layers of flavor. Each distillery produces a malt with—to the expert—instantly identifiable, predominant notes peculiarly its own.

There are two types of whisky: malt and grain. Malt whisky, generally acknowledged to have a more sophisticated bouquet and flavor, is made with malted barley—barley that is soaked in water until the grains germinate and then dried to halt the germination, all of which adds extra flavor and a touch of sweetness to the brew. Grain whisky also contains malted barley, but with the addition of unmalted barley and maize.

Blended whiskies, which make up many of the leading brands, usually balance malt- and grain-whisky distillations; deluxe blends contain a higher percentage of malts. Blends that contain several malt whiskies are called "vatted malts." Whisky connoisseurs often prefer to taste the single malts: the unblended whisky from a single distillery. In simple terms, malt whiskies may be classified into "eastern" and "western" in style, with the whisky made in the east of Scotland, for example in Speyside, being lighter and sweeter than the products of the western isles, which often have a taste of peat smoke or even iodine.

The production process is, by comparison, relatively straightforward: just malt your barley, mash it, ferment it and distill it, then mature to perfection. To find out the details, join a distillery tour, and be rewarded with a dram.

## CRAIGELLACHIE

*4 mi northwest of Dufftown via A941.*

Renowned as an angling resort, Craigellachie, like so many settlements on the River Spey, is sometimes enveloped in the malty reek of the local industry.

★ Just before the village you'll notice the huge **Speyside Cooperage and Visitor Centre,** a major stop on the Malt Whisky Trail. Inside you can watch highly skilled coopers make and repair oak barrels used in the local whisky industry. The "Acorn to Cask" exhibit tells all about the ancient craft of coopering. ✉*Dufftown Rd.* ☎*01340/871108* 💷*£3.20* ⊙ *Weekdays 9:30–4.*

The Spey itself is crossed by a handsome **suspension bridge,** designed by Thomas Telford (1757–1834) in 1814 and now bypassed by the modern road.

## ABERLOUR

*2 mi southwest of Craigellachie via A95.*

Aberlour, often listed as Charlestown of Aberlour on maps, is a handsome little burgh, essentially Victorian in style, though actually founded in 1812 by the local landowner.

The names of the noted local whisky stills are Cragganmore, Aberlour, and **Glenfarclas**, just 5 mi south of town. Unlike other tours, the Glenfarclas one takes you to the room where the whisky casks are filled. The tours end with tastings in the superlative Ship Room, the intact lounge of an ocean liner called the *Empress of Australia.* ⊠ *Off A95, Ballindalloch* ☎ *01807/500257* ⊕ *www.glenfarclas.co.uk* 🖃 *£3.50* 🕒 *Apr. and May, weekdays 10–5; June–Sept., Mon.–Sat. 10–4; Oct.–Mar., weekdays 10–4.*

> **FISH TALE**
>
> The Spey is one of Scotland's most popular rivers for anglers. **Ballindalloch Castle** ( ⊠ *Off A95, between Craigellachie and Grant-own on Spey* ☎ *01807/500–205* ⊕ *www.ballindallochcastle.co.uk*), the family home of the Macpherson-Grants since 1546, offers a limited number of permits for fishing on the banks of the Spey and the Avon. It's 10 mi southwest of Craigellachie.

### WHERE TO EAT

£ ✕**Old Pantry.** This pleasant corner restaurant and gift shop overlook Aberlour's tree-shaded central square. The kitchen serves everything from a cup of coffee with a sticky cake to a three-course spread of soup, roast meat, and traditional pudding. ⊠ *The Square* ☎ *01340/871617* 🖃 *MC, V.*

### SHOPPING

A couple of miles west of Aberlour, look for **Speyside Pottery** ( ⊠ *Ballindalloch* ☎ *01807/500338*), where Thomas and Anne Gough produce domestic stoneware in satisfying, traditional shapes. Call ahead for opening hours in winter.

## GLENLIVET

★ *10 mi southwest of Aberlour via A95 and B9008.*

Glenlivet is a very small village with a very famous distillery by the same name. The first licensed distillery in the highlands, was founded in 1824 by George Smith. Today Glenlivet Distillery produces one of the best-known 12-year-old single malts in the world. Take the free distillery tour for a chance to see inside the huge bonded warehouse where the whisky steeps in oak casks. The River Livet runs through the glen and past the distillery in an area renowned for its birdlife. ⊠ *Glenlivet, Ballindalloch* ☎ *01340/821720* ⊕ *www.glenlivet.com* 🖃 *Free* 🕒 *Apr.–Oct., Mon.–Sat. 10–4, Sun. 12:30–4.*

**WHERE TO STAY & EAT**

£££ ⊠🍴 **Minmore House.** With the dis-
★ tinctive feel of a private home, the
Minmore House has faded chintz in
the drawing room (where afternoon
tea is served) and a paneled library.
An eclectic mix of antique furnishings and old paintings decorate the
guest rooms. Don't be alarmed if
these seem to move around—it's
just the resident ghost. The restaurant (£££££) serves a prix-fixe dinner of exceptional contemporary
Scottish cuisine that may include
Aberdeen Angus beef. After dinner, enjoy one of more than 100
malt whiskies in the library bar.
The Speyside Way long-distance

> **HOW TO TASTE WHISKY**
>
> When tasting whisky, follow these
> simple steps. First, pour a dram.
> Turn and tilt the glass to coat the
> sides. Smell the whisky, "nosing"
> to inhale the heady aromas. If
> you want, you can add a little
> water and turn the glass gently to
> watch it "marry" with the whisky,
> nosing as you go. Take a wee sip
> and swirl it over your tongue and
> sense what connossiers call the
> "mouthfeel." Swallow and admire
> the finish. Repeat until convinced
> it's a good malt!

footpath passes below the house, and the area is famous for bird-
watching. **Pros:** Homemade jam with breakfast, good-humored staff.
**Cons:** Hard to diet here, bathrooms can be chilly at night. ⊠ *Glenlivet,
Ballindalloch, Banffshire AB37 9DB* 🕾 *01807/590378* ⊕ *www.min-
morehousehotel.com* 🛏 *9 rooms* ⚷ *In-room: no a/c, no TV. In-hotel:
restaurant, bar, no kids under 7, some pets allowed* ▤ *AE, MC, V*
⊗ *Closed Feb.* 🅾*BP.*

## CARDHU DISTILLERY

*10 mi north of Glenlivet via B9008, A95, and B9102.*

Cardhu Distillery was established by John and Helen Cumming in 1811,
though it was officially founded in 1824, after distilling was made legal
by the Excise Act of 1823. Today its product lies at the heart of John-
nie Walker Blends. Guided tours take you to the mashing, ferment-
ing, and distilling halls. You may even taste the remarkably smooth
single malt before it gets near any blending vats. ⊠ *B1902 , Knockando*
🕾 *01340/872555* ⊕ *www.scotchwhisky.net* 🎫 *£4* ⊗ *Dec.–Feb., weekdays 11–3; Mar.–June and Nov., weekdays 10–5; July–Sept., Mon.–Sat.
10–5, Sun. noon–4; last tour 1 hr before closing.*

## GLEN GRANT DISTILLERY & GARDEN

*12 mi northeast of Cardhu via B9102 and A941.*

James Grant founded the distillery in 1840 when he was only 25, and
it was the first in the country to be electrically powered. Glen Grant
will come as a welcome relief to less-than-enthusiastic companions of
dedicated Malt Whisky Trail followers, because in addition to the distillery there's a large and beautiful garden. The gardens are planted and
tended as Grant planned them, with orchards and woodland walks,
log bridges over waterfalls, a magnificent lily pond, and azaleas and

rhododendrons in profusion. Now owned by Chivas Regal, Glen Grant produces a distinctive pale-gold, clear whisky, with an almost floral or fruity finish, using peculiarly tall stills and special purifiers. ⊠*A941, Rothes* ☎*01542/783318* ⊕*www.chivas.com* ⊟*Free* ☾*Apr.–Oct., Mon.–Sat. 10–4, Sun. 12:30–4.*

## ELGIN

*10 mi north of Rothes via A941, 69 mi northwest of Aberdeen, 41 mi east of Inverness via A96.*

As the center of the fertile Laigh (low-lying lands) of Moray, Elgin has been of local importance for centuries. Like Aberdeen, it's self-supporting and previously remote, sheltered by great hills to the south and lying between two major rivers, the Spey and the Findhorn. Beginning in the 13th century, Elgin became an important religious center, a cathedral city with a walled town growing up around the cathedral and adjacent to the original settlement.

Elgin prospered, and by the early 18th century it became a mini-Edinburgh of the north and a place where country gentlemen spent their winters. It even echoed Edinburgh in carrying out wide-scale reconstruction in the early part of the 18th century. Many fine neoclassical buildings survive today despite much misguided demolition in the late 20th century for better traffic flow. However, the central main-street plan and some of the older little streets and *wynds* (alleyways) remain. You can also see Elgin's past in the arcaded shop fronts—some of which date from the late-17th century—on the main shopping street.

At the center of Elgin, the most conspicuous structure is **St. Giles Church,** which divides High Street. The grand foursquare building constructed in 1828 exhibits the Greek-revival style: note the columns, the pilasters, and the top of the spire, surmounted by a representation of the Lysicrates Monument.

Cooper Park contains a magnificent ruin, the **Elgin Cathedral,** consecrated in 1224. Its eventful story included devastation by fire: a 1390 act of retaliation by Alexander Stewart (circa 1343–1405), the Wolf of Badenoch. The illegitimate-son-turned-bandit of King David II (1324–71) had sought revenge for his excommunication by the bishop of Moray. The cathedral was rebuilt but finally fell into disuse after the Reformation in 1560. By 1567 the highest authority in the land, the regent earl of Moray, had stripped the lead from the roof to pay for his army. Thus ended the career of the religious seat known as the Lamp of the North. Some traces of the cathedral settlement survive—the gateway Pann's Port and the Bishop's Palace—although they've been drastically altered. Cooper Park is a five-minute walk northeast of Elgin Museum, across the bypass road. ⊠*Cooper Park* ☎*01343/547171* ⊕*www. historic-scotland.gov.uk* ⊟*£4.50; £6 with Spynie Palace* ☾*Apr.–Sept., daily 9:30–6:30; Oct.–Mar., Sat.–Wed. 9:30–4:30; last admission half hr before closing.*

Just north of Elgin is **Spynie Palace,** the impressive 15th-century former headquarters of the bishops of Moray. It has now fallen into ruin, though the top of the tower has good views over the Laigh of Moray. Find it by turning right off the main A941 Elgin–Lossiemouth road. ☎01343/546358 ⊕www.historic-scotland.gov.uk ✉£3.50; £6 with Elgin Cathedral ⊙Apr.–Sept., daily 9:30–6:30; Oct.–Mar., weekends 9:30–4:30; last admission half hr before closing.

**OFF THE BEATEN PATH**

**Pluscarden Abbey.** Given the general destruction caused by the 16th-century upheaval of the Reformation, abbeys in Scotland tend to be ruinous and deserted, but at Pluscarden Abbey the monks' way of life continues. Originally a 13th-century structure, the abbey was abandoned by the religious community after the Reformation. Monks from Prinknash Abbey near Gloucester, England, returned here in 1948, and the abbey is now a Benedictine community. ⊠Off B9010, 6 mi southwest of Elgin ⊕www.pluscardenabbey.org ✉Free ⊙Daily 9–5.

### SHOPPING

**Gordon and MacPhail** ( ⊠58–60 South St. ☎01343/545110), an outstanding delicatessen and wine merchant, also stocks rare malt whiskies. This is a good place to shop for gifts for those foodies among your friends. **Johnstons of Elgin** ( ⊠Newmill ☎01343/554099) is a woolen mill with a worldwide reputation for its luxury fabrics, especially cashmere. The bold color range is particularly appealing. The large shop stocks not only the firm's own products but also top-quality Scottish crafts and giftware. There's also a coffee shop on the premises.

## FOCHABERS

*9 mi east of Elgin.*

Just before reaching the center of Fochabers, you can see the works of a major local employer, Baxters of Fochabers. From Tokyo to New York, upmarket stores stock the company's soups, jams, chutneys, and other gourmet products—all of which are made here, close to the River Spey. Take home a can of Royal Game Soup, a favorite of the late Queen Mum. The **Baxters Highland Village** presents a video, *Baxters Experience,* about the history of the business, plus interactive exhibits and cooking demonstrations. You can have a look at a re-creation of the Baxters' first grocery shop, a real shop that stocks Baxters' goods, and a shop called the Best of Scotland, specializing all kinds of Scottish products. A restaurant serves up an assortment of delectables. ⊠1 mi west of Fochabers on A96 ☎01343/820666 ⊕www.baxters.com ✉Free ⊙Jan.–Mar., daily 10–5; Apr.–Dec., daily 9–5:30.

Once over the Spey Bridge and past the cricket ground (a very unusual sight in Scotland), you can find the symmetrical, 18th-century Fochabers village square lined with antiques dealers. Through one of these shops, Pringle Antiques, you can enter the **Fochabers Folk Museum,** a converted church that has a fine collection of items relating to past life in the village and surrounding area. Exhibits include carts and carriages, farm implements, and Victorian toys. ⊠*Behind Pringle Antiques* ☎*01343/821204* *⊠Free* ☉*Easter–Oct., Tues.–Fri. 11–4, weekends 2–4.*

One of the village's lesser-known treasures is the **Gordon Chapel** ( ⊠*Duke St., just off the Square*), which has an exceptional set of stained-glass windows by Pre-Raphaelite artist Sir Edward Burne-Jones.

★ Whisky lovers should take the A96 a few minutes southeast from Fochabers to see one of Scotland's most iconic distilleries, the **Strathisla Distillery.** Strathisla Distillery was built in 1786 and now produces the main component of the Chivas Regal blend. Guided tours take you to the mash house, tun room, and still house—all pretty much the same as they were when production began. The tour ends with a tasting session. ⊠*Seafield Ave., Keith* ☎*01542/783044* ⊕*www.chivas.com* ☎*£5* ☉*Apr.–Oct., Mon.–Sat. 10–4, Sun. 12:30–4.*

### SHOPPING

**Art and Antiques** ( ⊠*33–35 High St.* ☎*01343/829104*) combines an unusual mix of original art by the owners with ceramic, glassware, and small pieces of furniture. **Watts Antiques** ( ⊠*45 High St.* ☎*01343/820077*) has small collectibles, jewelry, ornaments, and china.

If you're interested in works by local artists, head to **Just Art** ( ⊠*64 High St.* ☎*01343/820500*), a fine gallery with high-quality ceramics and paintings. At **the Quaich** ( ⊠*85 High St.* ☎*01343/820981*) you can stock up on cards and small gifts, then sit with a cup of tea and a homebaked snack.

## FINDOCHTY

*10 mi east of Fochabers on A942.*

The residents of Findochty are known for their fastidiousness and creativity in painting their houses, taking the art of house painting to a new level. Some residents even paint the mortar between the stonework a different color from the exterior. The harbor, with many colorful small sailing boats tied up to the quay, has a faint echo of the Mediterranean about it. A 15-minute stroll about the older part of the village will take you past several blocks of painted homes.

### WHERE TO EAT

££££ ★ ✕**Old Monastery.** On a broad, wooded slope set back from the coast near Buckie, with westward views as far as the hills of Wester Ross, sits the Old Monastery, once a Victorian religious establishment. The monastic theme carries through to the restrained interior of the Cloisters Bar and the Chapel Restaurant, where the creamy walls are hand-stenciled in shades of terra–cotta and green. Local specialties—fresh fish, venison, and Aberdeen Angus beef—make up the Scottish prix-fixe menu. The restaurant is on an unclassified road off the A98. Follow signs to Drybridge, but instead of turning into the village, continue up the hill for 1½ mi. ⊠*Drybridge, Buckie* ☎*01542/832660* ⊟*AE, MC, V* ☉*Closed Mon. and Tues. No dinner Sun.*

**EN ROUTE** Driving east from Findochty you'll pass a string of salty little fishing villages. They paint a colorful scene with their gabled houses and fishing nets set out to dry amid the rocky shoreline.

## CULLEN

*3 mi east of Findochty.*

Look for some wonderfully painted homes at Cullen, in the old fishermen's town below the railway viaduct. The real attractions of this little resort, however, are its white-sand beach and the fine view west toward the aptly named Bowfiddle Rock. A stroll along the beach reveals the shape of the fishing settlement below and the 18th-century town above. Most unusual for a town of its size, Cullen has numerous specialty shops—antiques and gift stores, butchers, an ironmonger, a baker, a pharmacy, and a locally famous ice-cream shop among them—as well as several hotels and cafés.

### WHERE TO STAY & EAT

££ ✕◫ **The Seafield Hotel.** A former coaching inn built in 1822, this hotel has retained its high standards. Deep, rich colors prevail, and comfort and friendliness are key. The restaurant (£££), with its golden walls and tartan carpet, has an extensive à la carte Scottish menu that includes seafood, game, beef, and lamb and a stock of more than 200 malt whiskies. **Pros:** Bucketloads of character, local seafood is expertly prepared. **Cons:** Some rooms need refurbishing, wine list can be pricey. ⊠*Seafield St., AB56 4SG* ☎*01542/840791* ⊕*www.theseafieldarms.co.uk* ⇨*21 rooms* ⬙*In-room: no a/c. In-hotel: restaurant, room service, bar, no elevator, laundry service, no-smoking rooms, public Internet* ⊟*AE, MC, V* ⎟◉⎟*BP.*

## FORDYCE

*5 mi east of Cullen.*

The historic village of Fordyce lies among the barley fields of Banffshire like a small slice of rural England gone far adrift. It's a quaint little place where the maze of narrow streets still follows a medieval plan. You can stroll by the churchyard, picnic on the old bleaching green (a notice board explains everything), or visit a restored 19th-century carpenter's workshop, where musical instruments are made.

## BANFF

*36 mi east of Elgin, 47 mi north of Aberdeen.*

Midway along the northeast coast, overlooking Moray Firth and the estuary of the River Deveron, Banff is a fishing town of considerable elegance that feels as though it's a million miles from tartan-clad Scotland. Part Georgian, like Edinburgh's New Town, and part 16th-century small burgh, like Culross, Banff is an exemplary east-coast salty town, with a tiny harbor and fine architecture. It's also within easy reach of plenty of unspoiled coastline—cliff and rock to the east, at Gardenstown (known as Gamrie) and Pennan, or beautiful little sandy beaches westward toward Sandend and Cullen.

The jewel in Banff's crown is the grand mansion of **Duff House**, a splendid William Adam–designed (1689–1748) baroque mansion that has been restored as an outstation of the National Galleries of Scotland. Many fine paintings are displayed in rooms furnished to reflect the days when the house was occupied by the dukes of Fife. A good tearoom and a shop are found in the basement. ⊠ *Off A98* ☎ *01261/818181* ⊕ *www.duffhouse.com* 🎫 *£6* ⊙ *Daily 11–5.*

Across the river in Banff's twin town, Macduff, on the shore east of the harbor, stands **Macduff Marine Aquarium.** A 250,000-gallon central tank and many smaller display areas and touch pools show the sea life of the Moray Firth and North Atlantic. On Wednesday and weekends at 2 PM you can watch divers descend into the tank to feed the hungry fish. ⊠ *11 High Shore* ☎ *01261/833369* ⊕ *www.marine-aquarium. com* 🎫 *£5.20* ⊙ *Daily 10–5.*

## FYVIE CASTLE

*18 mi south of Banff, 18 mi northwest of Ellon.*

In an area rich with castles, Fyvie Castle stands out as the most complex. Five great towers built by five successive powerful families turned a 13th-century foursquare castle into an opulent Edwardian statement of wealth. There are some superb paintings on view, including 12 Raeburns, as well as myriad sumptuous interiors and many walks on the castle grounds. A former lady of the house, Lillia Drummond, was apparently starved to death by her husband, who entombed her body inside the walls of a secret room. In the 1920s when the bones were disrupted during renovations, a string of such terrible misfortune followed that they were quickly returned and the room sealed off. Her name is carved into the windowsill of the Drummond Room. ⊠ *Off A947, between Oldmeldrum and Turriff* ☎ *0844/4932182* ⊕ *www. nts.org.uk* 🎫 *£8* ⊙ *Apr.–June and Sept., Sat.–Wed., noon–5; July and Aug., daily 11–5; last admission 45 min before closing.*

## HADDO HOUSE

★ *12 mi southeast of Fyvie Castle.*

Created as the home of the Gordon family, earls and marquesses of Aberdeen, Haddo House—designed by William Adam—is now cared for by the National Trust for Scotland. Built in 1732, the elegant mansion has a light and graceful Georgian design, with curving wings on either side of a harmonious, symmetrical facade. The interior is late-Victorian ornate, filled with magnificent paintings (including works by Pompeo Batoni and Sir Thomas Lawrence) and plenty of objets d'art. Pre-Raphaelite stained-glass windows by Sir Edward Burne-Jones grace the chapel. Outside is a terrace garden with a fountain, and few yards farther is Haddo Country Park, which has walking trails leading to memorials about the Gordon family. ☒ *Off B999, 8 mi northwest of Ellon* ☎ *01651/851888* ⊕ *www.nts.org.uk* 🎫 *£8* ⊙ *Easter, May, June, Sept., and Oct., Fri.–Mon. 11–5; July and Aug., daily 11–5.*

## ELLON

*8 mi southeast of Haddo House, 32 mi southwest of Banff.*

Formerly a market center on what was then the lowest bridging point of the River Ythan, Ellon, a bedroom suburb of Aberdeen, is a small town at the center of a rural hinterland. It's also well placed for visiting Fyvie Castle and Haddo House.

Five miles west of Ellon, at Pitmedden, is a unique re-creation by the National Trust for Scotland of a 17th-century garden. **Pitmedden Garden** is best visited in high summer, from July onward, when annual bedding plants form intricate formal patterns. The 100-acre estate also has woodland and farmland walks, as well as the Museum of Farming Life. ☎ *0844/4932177* ⊕ *www.nts.org.uk* 🎫 *£5* ⊙ *Garden, shop, museum, and tearoom May–Sept., daily 10–5:30; grounds daily 10–5:30; last entry half hr before closing.*

**OFF THE BEATEN PATH**

**Archaeolink Prehistory Park.** A strange grass-covered dome rises from the hillside halfway between Insch and Inverurie. This example of modern architecture houses an exhibition about far older structures: the many stone circles, symbol stones, and other prehistoric monuments scattered all over this part of the northeast. Dedicated to the "exploration of life before history," Archaeolink also includes open-air exhibits, such as a replica of an Iron Age farm. ☒ *Off A96 at Oyne, 20 mi west of Ellon* ☎ *01464/851500* ⊕ *www.archaeolink.co.uk* 🎫 *£5.50* ⊙ *Apr.– Oct., daily 10–5; Nov.–Mar., daily 11–4.*

# ABERDEEN & THE NORTHEAST ESSENTIALS

## TRANSPORTATION

### BY AIR

CARRIERS Aberdeen is easy to reach from other parts of the United Kingdom, as well as Europe. British Airways flies London and Shetland, and Air France flies to Paris.

British Airways, bmi/British Midland, easyJet, and KLM provide service between Aberdeen and most major U.K. airports.

Contacts **Air France** ( ☎ *0870/142-4343* ⊕ *www.airfrance.com*). **bmi/ British Midland** ( ☎ *0870/607-0555* ⊕ *www.flybmi.com*). **British Airways** ( ☎ *0870/850-9850* ⊕ *www.ba.com*). **easyJet** ( ☎ *0870/600-0000* ⊕ *www.easy jet.com*). **KLM** ( ☎ *0870/507-4074* ⊕ *www.klmuk.com*). **SAS** ( ☎ *0870/6072-7727* ⊕ *www.scandinavian.net*).

AIRPORTS Aberdeen Airport—serving both international and domestic flights—is in Dyce, 7 mi west of the city center on the A96 (Inverness).

Information **Aberdeen Airport** (☎ *0870/040-0006* ⊕ *www.baa.co.uk*).

AIRPORT First Aberdeen Bus 27 operates between the airport terminal and Union
TRANSFERS Street in the center of Aberdeen. Buses (£1.80) run frequently at peak times, less often at midday and in the evening; the journey time is approximately 40 minutes.

The drive to the center of Aberdeen is easy via the A96 (which can be busy during rush hour).

Dyce is on First ScotRail's Inverness–Aberdeen route. The rail station is a short taxi ride from the terminal building. The ride takes 12 minutes, and trains run approximately every two hours. If you intend to visit the western region first, you can travel northwest, from Aberdeen, by rail, direct to Elgin via Inverurie, Insch, Huntly, and Keith.

Information **First Aberdeen** (☎ *01224/650000* ⊕ *www.firstaberdeen.co.uk*). **First ScotRail** (☎ *08457/550033* ⊕ *www.firstgroup.com/scotrail*).

### BY BOAT & FERRY

There's ferry service between Aberdeen, Lerwick (Shetland), and Kirkwall (Orkney) operated by Northlink Ferries.

Information **Northlink Ferries** (✉ *Ferry Rd., Stromness, Orkney* ☎ *0845/600-0449* ⊕ *www.northlinkferries.co.uk*).

### BY BUS

Long-distance buses run to Aberdeen and from most parts of Scotland, England, and Wales. Contact National Express for bus connections with English towns. Contact Scottish Citylink for bus connections with Scottish towns.

There's a network of buses throughout the northeast, but they take a long time and connections are not always well timed. First Aberdeen operates services within the city of Aberdeen. Timetables are available from the tourist information center at St. Nicholas House.

Information **First Aberdeen** (☎ *01224/650000* ⊕ *www.firstaberdeen.co.uk*). **National Express** (☎ *08705/808080* ⊕ *www.nationalexpress.com*). **Scottish Citylink** (☎ *08705/505050* ⊕ *www.citylink.co.uk*).

### BY CAR

A car is the best way to see the northeast. You can travel from Glasgow and Edinburgh to Aberdeen on a continuous stretch of the A90/M90, a fairly scenic route that runs up Strathmore, with a fine hill view to the west. The coastal route, the A92, is a more leisurely alternative, with its interesting resorts and fishing villages. The most scenic route, however, is the A93 from Perth, north to Blairgowrie and into Glen Shee. The A93 then goes over the Cairnwell Pass, the highest main road in the United Kingdom. (This route isn't recommended in winter, when snow can make driving difficult.)

Aberdeen is a compact city with good signage. Its center is Union Street, the main thoroughfare running east–west, which tends to get crowded with traffic. Anderson Drive is an efficient ring road on the city's west side; be extra careful on its many traffic circles. It's best to leave your car in one of the parking garages (arrive early to get a space) and walk around, or use the convenient park-and-ride stop at the Bridge of Don, north of the city. Street maps are available from the tourist information center, newsdealers, and booksellers.

Around the northeast roads are generally not busy, but speeding and erratic driving can be a problem on the main A roads. The rural side roads are a pleasure to drive.

### BY TRAIN
You can reach Aberdeen directly from Edinburgh (2½ hours), Glasgow (3 hours), and Inverness (2½ hours). Get a First ScotRail timetable for full details. There are also London–Aberdeen routes that go through Edinburgh and the east-coast main line.

Information **First ScotRail** (☎ 08457/550033 ⊕ www.firstgroup.com/scotrail).

## CONTACTS & RESOURCES

### EMERGENCIES
Dial ☎999 in case of an emergency to reach an ambulance, or the fire, coast guard, or police departments (no coins are needed for emergency calls made from public phone booths). For a doctor or dentist, consult your hotel receptionist, B&B proprietor, or the yellow pages.

There's a lost-property office at the Grampian Police headquarters.

Notices on pharmacy doors will guide you to the nearest open pharmacy at any given time. Anderson Pharmacy and Boots the Chemists Ltd., both in Aberdeen, keep longer hours than most. There's an in-store pharmacist at Safeway Food Store, also in Aberdeen.

Emergency Contact **Grampian Police** ( ⊠ Force Headquarters, Queen St., Aberdeen ☎ 0845/600–5700).

Hospitals **Aberdeen Royal Infirmary** ( ⊠ Accident and Emergency Department, Foresterhill, Aberdeen ☎ 01224/681818). **Dr. Gray's Hospital, Elgin** ( ⊠ Accident and Emergency Department, at end of High St. on A96 ☎ 01343/543131).

Pharmacies **Anderson Pharmacy** ( ⊠ 34 Holburn St., Aberdeen ☎ 01224/587148). **Boots the Chemists Ltd** ( ⊠ Bon Accord Centre, George St., Aberdeen ☎ 01224/626080). **Safeway Food Store** ( ⊠ 215 King St., Aberdeen ☎ 01224/624398).

### TOURS
BUS TOURS  First Bus conducts city tours of Aberdeen, available on most days between July and mid-September. Grampian Coaches offers daily tours encompassing the Castle Trail, Malt Whisky Trail, and Royal Deeside (£12 to £14).

Contacts **First Bus** (☎ *01224/650000* ⊕ *www.firstgroup.com*). **Grampian Coaches** (☎ *01224/650024* ⊕ *www.firstgroup.com/grampian*).

PRIVATE
GUIDES
The Scottish Tourist Guides Association can supply experienced personal guides, including foreign-language-speaking guides if necessary.

Contact **Scottish Tourist Guides Association** ( ✉ *The Old Town Jail, St. John's St., Stirling* ☎ *01786/447784* ⊕ *www.stga.co.uk*).

## VISITOR INFORMATION
The tourist information center in Aberdeen has a currency exchange and supplies information on all of Scotland's northeast. There are also year-round tourist information offices in Braemar and Elgin. In summer, also look for tourist information centers in Alford, Banchory, Banff, Crathie, Dufftown, Forres, Fraserburgh, Huntly, Stonehaven, and Tomintoul.

Tourist Information **Aberdeen** ( ✉ *23 Union St.* ☎ *01224/288828* ⊕ *www.agtb. org*). **Ballater** ( ✉ *The Old Royal Station, Station Sq.* ☎ *013397/55306*). **Braemar** ( ✉ *The Mews, Mar Rd.* ☎ *013397/41600* ⊕ *www.braemarscotland.co.uk*). **Elgin** ( ✉ *17 High St.* ☎ *01343/542666*).

6

# Argyll & the Isles

Updated by
Fiona G.
Parrott

**DIVIDED IN TWO BY THE** long peninsula of Kintyre, western Scotland is characterized by a complicated, splintered seaboard. The west is an aesthetic delight, though it does catch those moist (yes, that's a euphemism) Atlantic weather systems. But the occasional wet foray is a small price to pay for the glittering freshness of oak woods and bracken-covered hillsides and for the bright interplay of sea, loch, and rugged green peninsula. Only a few decades ago the Clyde estuary was a coastal playground for people living in Glasgow and along Clydeside: their annual holiday was a steamer trip to any one of a number of resorts, known as going *doon the watter*. From the faded resort of Dunoon, Loch Lomond and the Trossachs, Scotland's first national park stretches to the north. A quarter of the park is in Argyll, mostly consisting of the Argyll Forest. Signs and visitor centers lead you into an exploration of the park's natural attractions.

Some impressive castles gaze out over this luxuriant landscape. Ruined Dunstaffnage and Kilchurn castles once guarded the western seaboard; turreted Inveraray Castle and magnificent Brodick, on the Isle of Arran, now guard their own historic interiors, with hundreds of antiques and portraits. The Kilmartin area has stone circles, carved stones, and burial mounds from the Bronze Age and earlier, taking imaginative travelers thousands of years back in time. Gardens are another Argyll specialty thanks to the temperate west-coast climate—Crarae Gardens, south of Inveraray, invites you down winding paths through plantings of magnolias and azaleas that reach their colorful peaks in late spring. The Brodick Castle grounds have fine azalea plantings, and Ardkinglas Woodland Garden adds an outstanding conifer collection.

Western Scotland's tiny islands are essentially microcosms of Scotland: each has its jagged cliffs or tongues of rock, its smiling sands and fertile pastures, its grim and ghostly fortress, and its tale of clan outrage or mythical beast. The pace of life is gentle out here, and the roads narrow and tortuous—not designed for heavy vehicles (beware pilgrim buses to Iona in summer, as they can cause major delays on the south-side routes). Arran is the place for hill walking on Goat Fell, the mountain that gives the island its distinctive profile. On Islay you can hunt down peaty, iodine-scented malt whisky. The process of choosing your favorite whisky makes for a pleasant evening in the island's friendly pubs and hotels. Mull has yet more castles, a short stretch of narrow-gauge railway, and the pretty port of Tobermory, with its brightly painted houses. Iona (just off Mull's western tip) is famous as an early seat of Christianity in Scotland and the burial place of Scottish kings in the Dark Ages. You could spend all your time touring these larger islands, but plenty of small islands are just as lovely, and they're blissfully uncrowded.

## EXPLORING ARGYLL & THE ISLES

With long sea lochs carved into its hilly, wooded interior, Argyll is a beguiling interweaving of water and land. The Kintyre Peninsula stretches between the islands of the Firth of Clyde (including Arran)

## TOP REASONS TO GO

**Whisky, whisky, whisky:** This is whisky country. Take the "whisky trail" in Port Ellen on the Isle of Islay; it's a leisurely 3-mi stroll passing Ardbeg, Laphroaig, and Lagavulin distilleries. Here the whiskies share the distinct flavors of peat, seaweed, and iodine. Arran, Oban, and Jura have their own unique distilleries. All have plenty of local character and provide an intimate visiting experience.

**Seaside biking:** Oban and Arran are two great cycling destinations. Biking along the coast provides breathtaking scenery; just keep in mind that it rains a lot in this part of the country, so bring rain gear.

**Iona and its abbey:** Maybe it's the remoteness—especially if you explore beyond the abbey—that adds to the almost mystical sense of history here, but a visit to this early center of Scottish Christianity is a magical experience. This was also the burial place of Scottish kings until the 11th century.

**Fantastic fishing and golf:** The largest skate in Britain are found in the waters off the Isle of Mull. There are 20 coastal settlements suited to sea angling where charter-boat companies offer trips. If it's loch and river sites you're after, there are 50 for game fishing that yield salmon, trout, and other fish. Prefer to tee off? Western Scotland has about two dozen golf courses, notably some fine coastal links. Machrihanish, near Campbeltown, is the best known.

**Glorious gardens:** Plants flourish in the mild Gulf Steam that brushes against this broken, western coastline. For vivid flowers, trees, birds and butterflies, visit Crarae Gardens, southwest of Inveraray. The Achamore House Gardens on the Isle of Gigha is another colorful extravaganza.

and the islands of the Inner Hebrides. Loch Fyne tends to get in the way of a breezy mainland tour: it's a long haul around the end of this fjordlike sea loch to Inveraray. Ferry services allow all kinds of interisland tours and can shorten mainland trips as well.

### ABOUT THE RESTAURANTS

This part of Scotland has a few restaurants of distinction, and local ingredients are high in quality: the seafood, fresh from the sparkling lochs and sea, could hardly be better. Beef, lamb, and game are also common. In rural districts it's prudent to choose a hotel or guesthouse that serves a decent evening meal as well as breakfast. Restaurants can be few and far here, and the weather is often wet or windy or cold (or all three). You don't want to travel far for an evening meal if you don't have to.

### ABOUT THE HOTELS

Accommodations in Argyll and on the isles range from châteaulike hotels to modest inns. Many traditional provincial hotels and hotels in small coastal resorts have been equipped with modern conveniences yet retain their personalized service and historic charm. Apart from these, however, your choices are limited; the best overnight option is usually a simple guesthouse offering bed, breakfast, and an evening meal.

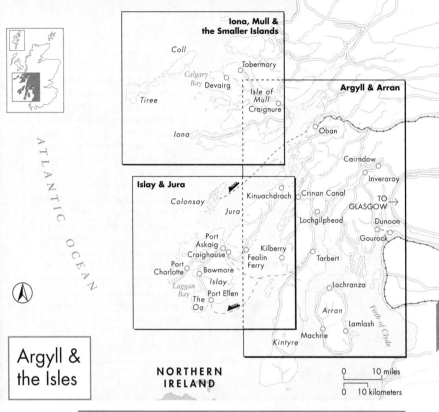

## TIMING

This part of the mainland is close enough to Glasgow that it's convenient to reach year-round. Oban is just over two hours by car or three hours by bus from the city, but getting to the isles (which require ferries) will take longer. You can take advantage of quiet roads and plentiful accommodations in early spring and late autumn. The summer months of July and August can get very busy indeed. Book accommodations and restaurants in advance, or you'll miss out. In winter short daylight hours and strong winds can make island stays rather bleak.

## GREAT ITINERARIES

You could easily spend a week exploring the islands alone, so consider spending at least a few nights in this region. Argyll and some island excursions make pleasant and easy side trips from Glasgow or Loch Lomond.

### IF YOU HAVE 2 DAYS

From Glasgow make your way to **Inveraray** via Loch Lomond (A82) and the Rest and Be Thankful Pass (A83). Continue south via the **Crarae Gardens,** then south to Lochgilphead, where you take A816 north to the **Crinan Canal.** Continue north on A816 and stay overnight in ⛴ **Oban.** The next day follow A85 east to see **Dunstaffnage Castle** and **Kilchurn Castle** before returning to the Loch Lomond/ Glasgow area.

### IF YOU HAVE 4 DAYS

Starting from Ardrossan, in Ayrshire, take the ferry to ⛴ **Brodick** and stay overnight on the island of Arran, visiting **Brodick Castle.** Cross to Kintyre Peninsula by taking the ferry from **Lochranza** for Claonaig; then cross the peninsula itself to Kennacraig. For a lovely day trip head south to the Isle of Gigha and its **Achamore House Gardens;** then return north to the ⛴ **Crinan** area. The next day go up to **Oban** and make an excursion to Mull for **Iona,** ⛴ **Tobermory,** and **Torosay Castle.** Finally, return to Oban or leave Mull via Fishnish Pier, where you can take a ferry to Lochaline and travel north on the mainland from there.

# AROUND ARGYLL

Topographical grandeur and rocky shores are what make Argyll special. Try to take to the water at least once, even if your time is limited. The sea and the sea lochs have played a vital role in the history of western Scotland since the time of the war galleys of the clans. Oban is the major ferry gateway and transport hub, with a main road leading south into the Kintyre Peninsula.

## OBAN

*96 mi northwest of Glasgow, 125 mi northwest of Edinburgh, 50 mi south of Fort William, 118 mi southwest of Inverness.*

It's almost impossible to avoid Oban when touring the west. Luckily it has a waterfront with some character and serves as a launch point for several ferry excursions. A traditional Scottish resort town, Oban has *ceilidhs* (song, music, and dance festivals) and tartan kitsch as well as late-night revelry in pubs and hotel bars. There's an inescapable sense, however, that just over the horizon, on the islands or down Kintyre, lie more peaceful and traditional environs.

Four miles north of Oban stands **Dunstaffnage Castle,** once an important stronghold of the MacDougall clan in the 13th century. From the ramparts you have outstanding views across the **Sound of Mull** and the **Firth of Lorne,** a nautical crossroads of sorts, once watched over by

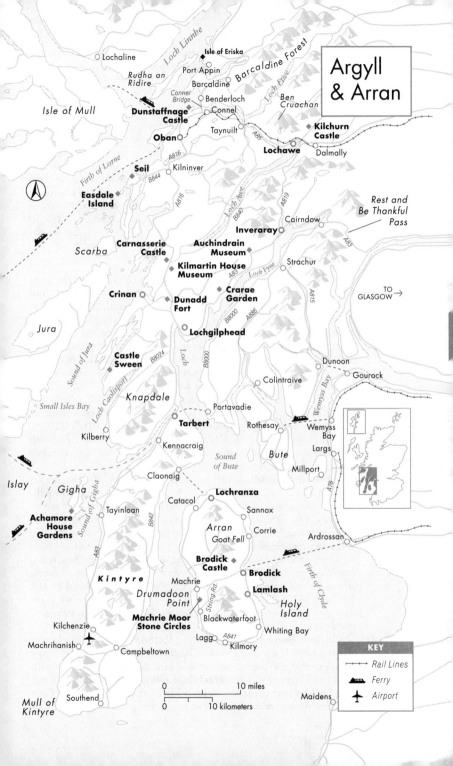

# Argyll & Arran

Lochaline
Isle of Eriska
Loch Linnhe
Port Appin
Barcaldine Forest
Rudha an Ridire
Barcaldine
Loch Etive
Connel Bridge
Benderloch
Ben Cruachan
Isle of Mull
**Dunstaffnage Castle**
Connel
**Kilchurn Castle**
**Oban**
Taynuilt
A85
**Lochawe**
Dalmally
Firth of Lorne
A816
Kilninver
Rest and Be Thankful Pass
**Seil**
B844
Cairndow
A819
Loch Awe
A83
Scarba
B840
**Easdale Island**
A816
**Inveraray**
Strachur
**Carnasserie Castle**
**Auchindrain Museum**
Loch Fyne
TO GLASGOW →
**Kilmartin House Museum**
A83
A815
**Crinan**
**Dunadd Fort**
**Crarae Garden**
Jura
B8000
A886
**Lochgilphead**
Dunoon
**Castle Sween**
B8024
Loch
B8000
Gourock
Loch Caolisport
Colintraive
Wemyss Bay
Knapdale
Small Isles Bay
Portavadie
**Tarbert**
Rothesay
Wemyss Bay
Kilberry
Kennacraig
Bute
Largs
Sound of Bute
Islay
Gigha
Claonaig
Millport
Sound of Gigha
**Lochranza**
Catacol
Sannox
**Achamore House Gardens**
Tayinloan
B842
Corrie
Ardrossan
Arran
Goat Fell
A83
**Brodick Castle**
Firth of Clyde
**Kintyre**
**Brodick**
Machrie
**Lamlash**
Drumadoon Point
Strad Rd.
Holy Island
**Machrie Moor Stone Circles**
Blackwaterfoot
Kilchenzie
A841
Whiting Bay
Machrihanish
Lagg
Kilmory
Campbeltown

Mull of Kintyre
Southend
Maidens

0 _____ 10 miles
0 _____ 10 kilometers

### KEY

Rail Lines
Ferry
Airport

Dunstaffnage Castle and commanded by the galleys (*birlinn* in Gaelic) of the Lords of the Isles. ⊠ *Off A85* ☎ *01631/562465* ⊕ *www.historic-scotland.gov.uk* 🎟 *£3.50* ⊘ *Apr.–Sept., daily 9:30–5:30; Oct.–Mar., Sat.–Wed. 9:30–4:30.*

☼ At the **Scottish Sealife Sanctuary** kids and adults love the outstanding display of marine life, including shoals of herring, sharks, rays, catfish, otters, and seals. Many of the animals at the sanctuary have been rescued, and this is where they receive rehabilitation before being released into the wild. There is also a beautiful aquarium. Kids will appreciate the adventure playground and gift shop. The restaurant serves morning coffee with homemade scones, plus a full lunch menu, and afternoon tea. To get here drive north from Oban for 10 mi on A828. ⊠ *Barcaldine, Connel* ☎ *01631/720386* ⊕ *www.sealsanctuary.co.uk* 🎟 *£9.50* ⊘ *Jan.–mid-Feb., weekends 10–4; Mar.–Oct., daily 10–5; last admission 1 hr before closing.*

## WHERE TO STAY & EAT

**£££££** ✕🏠 **Isle of Eriska.** A severe, baronial-style granite facade belies the luxurious welcome within this hotel, set on its own island 10 mi north of Oban and accessible by a bridge from the mainland. Every detail in the spacious rooms has been carefully chosen for your comfort, and there are plenty of outdoors activities as well as a few spa rooms for treatments. The restaurant serves innovative Scottish cuisine made with local ingredients: try the scallop and zucchini timbale with lobster, artichoke, and champagne butter sauce. Take a stroll to watch seals and otters offshore or herons and badgers on the grounds. **Pros:** Exceptional food, service, and peace and quiet. **Cons:** You're in the middle of nowhere so you don't have a lot of choice when it comes to dining out. ⊠ *Ledaig, by Oban, Argyll PA37 1SD* ☎ *01631/720371* ⊕ *www.eriska-hotel.co.uk* 🛏 *22 rooms* ⬧ *In-room: no a/c. In-hotel: restaurant, golf course, tennis court, spa, pool, gym, Wi-Fi, no elevator* ▭ *AE, MC, V* ⊘ *Closed Jan.* ⧖*MAP.*

**££££** ✕🏠 **Manor House Hotel.** On the coast near Oban, this 1780 stone house, once the home of the duke of Argyll, has wonderful sea views. The public areas are furnished with antiques, the bedrooms with lovely reproductions. The restaurant (£££££) serves a five-course prix-fixe dinner of Scottish and French dishes, including lots of local seafood and game in season, complemented by a carefully selected wine list. The house is within walking distance of the center of the city and the bus, train, and ferry terminals. **Pros:** Excellent restaurant, location near all necessary amenities. **Con:** Smallish bedrooms. ⊠ *Gallanach Rd., PA34 4LS* ☎ *01631/562087* ⊕ *www.manorhouseoban.com* 🛏 *11 rooms* ⬧ *In-room: no a/c. In-hotel: restaurant, bar, no kids under 12, no elevator* ▭ *AE, MC, V* ⧖*MAP.*

**££** 🏠 **Kilchrenan House.** A fully refurbished Victorian-era stone house, this bed-and-breakfast is a few minutes' walk from the town center. Many of the comfortable rooms, individually furnished in netural tones with clean-lined, light-wood pieces and some antiques, overlook the sea and the islands. **Pros:** Great sea views, tasteful attention to detail. **Con:** Some bedrooms on the top floor have a slanting roof that can be irri-

tating. ✉*Corran Esplanade, PA34 5AQ* ☎01631/562663 ⊕*www.
kilchrenanhouse.co.uk* ⤳*10 rooms* ⏃*In-room: no a/c. In-hotel: bar,
no elevator* ▭*MC, V* ⊘*Closed Dec. and Jan.* †○|*BP.*

£ 🏠**Dungrianach.** Meaning "the sunny house on the hill," Dungrianach
★ is a late Victorian house set high in a wooded area with superb views
of the islands. Although it feels quite isolated, it's only a few minutes'
walk from the center of Oban and the ferry piers. Antique and reproduction furniture fill the guest rooms. **Pros:** Plenty of space for your car,
great views. **Cons:** No credit cards, closed throughout winter. ✉*Pulpit
Hill, PA34 4LU* ☎01631/562840 ⊕*www.dungrianach.com* ⤳*2
rooms* ⏃*In-room: no a/c, no phone. In-hotel: bar, no elevator* ▭*No
credit cards* ⊘*Closed Oct.–Mar.* †○|*BP.*

£ 🏠**Ronebhal Guest House.** You can see Loch Etive and the mountains
beyond from this stone house 5 mi east of Oban, set back within its own
lovely grounds. Rooms are light and modern, and some have expansive bay windows. The front bedrooms have the best views of the loch.
**Pros:** Nice library, good breakfast. **Cons:** Some slightly worn decor, not
good for families with young children. ✉*A85, Connel, Argyll PA37
1PJ* ☎01631/710310 ⊕*www.ronebhal.co.uk* ⤳*6 rooms, 4 with bath*
⏃*In-room: no a/c, no phone. In-hotel: bar, no kids under 7, no-smoking
rooms, no elevator* ▭*MC, V* ⊘*Closed Dec. and Jan.* †○|*BP.*

### SPORTS & THE OUTDOORS

BICYCLING You can rent bicycles from **Oban Cycles** ( ✉*29 Lochside St.*
☎01631/566996), whose shopkeepers will give you advice on waterside routes as far out as Ganavan Bay and Dunstaffnage Castle.

FISHING **The Gannet** ( ✉*3 Kiel Croft, Benderloch* ☎01631/720262), a char-
ter-fishing company run by Adrian Lauder, offers full-day sea-angling
trips for £500 a day for up to 10 passengers (so that would be £50
per person); a light lunch is included. Fishing parties are limited to 10
people (8 for skate-fishing).

## LOCHAWE

*18 mi east of Oban.*

Lochawe is a loch-side community squeezed between the broad shoulder of Ben Cruachan and Loch Awe itself. The road gets busy in peak
season, filled with people trying to park near Lochawe Station.

★ **Kilchurn Castle,** a ruined fortress at the east end of Loch Awe, was built
in the 15th century by Sir Colin Campbell (d. 1493) of Glenorchy, and
rebuilt in the 17th century. Airy vantage points amid the towers have
fine panoramas of the surrounding highlands and loch. It's only accessible by boat from the pier, but worth the trip. ✉*A85, 1 mi northeast
of Lochawe* ☎01866/833333 ⊕*www.historic-scotland.gov.uk* ▱*Free*
⊘*Daily 24 hrs.*

The **Duncan Ban Macintyre Monument** was erected in honor of this Gaelic
poet (1724–1812), sometimes referred to as the Robert Burns of the
Highlands. ■**TIP**→The view from here is one of the finest in Argyll, taking in Ben Cruachan and the other peaks nearby, as well as Loch Awe and

its scattering of islands. To find the monument from Dalmally, just east of Loch Awe, follow an old road running southwest toward the banks of the loch. You can see the round, granite structure from the road's highest point, often called Monument Hill.

**EN ROUTE**

The A819 south to Inveraray initially runs alongside Loch Awe, the longest loch in Scotland, but soon leaves these pleasant banks to turn east and join the A83, which carries traffic from Glasgow and Loch Lomond by way of the high **Rest and Be Thankful** pass. This quasi-alpine pass, set among high green slopes and gray rocks, is one of the most scenic points along the road.

## INVERARAY

★ *21 mi south of Lochawe, 61 mi north of Glasgow, 29 mi west of Loch Lomond.*

On the approaches to Inveraray, note the ornate 18th-century bridge-work that carries the road along the loch side. This is your first sign that Inveraray is not just a jumble of houses; in fact, much of it was designed as a planned town for the third duke of Argyll in the mid-18th century. The town is a sparkling fishing village with cute shops, attractions, and the haunted Campbell Castle all within walking distance. There are lovely views of the water and plenty of fishing boats to watch. Several worthwhile gardens and museums are nearby, too.

The current seat of the Campbell duke is **Inveraray Castle,** a smart, grayish-green turreted stone house with a self-satisfied air, visible through trees from the town itself. Spires on the four corner turrets give it a vaguely French look. Like the town, the castle was begun around 1743. Tours of the interior convey the history of the powerful Campbell family. You can hike around the estate grounds, but wear sturdy footwear. ⊠*Off A83* ☎*01499/302203* ⊕*www.inveraray-castle.com* ⊠*£6.30* ⊙*Apr.–Oct., Mon.–Sat. 10–5:45, Sun. noon–5:45; last admission 5.*

The **Inveraray Jail** houses realistic courtroom scenes, carefully re-created cells, and other paraphernalia that give you a glimpse of life behind bars in Victorian times—and today. The site includes a Scottish crafts shop. ⊠*Inveraray* ☎*01499/302381* ⊕*www.inverarayjail. co.uk* ⊠*£6.50* ⊙*Apr.–Oct., daily 9:30–6; Nov.–Mar., daily 10–5; last admission 1 hr before closing.*

The 1911 lightship *Arctic Penguin* is a rare example of a riveted iron vessel. It now houses exhibits on the maritime heritage of the River Clyde and the rest of Scotland's west coast. Beside it sits the "puffer" *Eilean Eisdeal,* a tiny interisland freight boat. ⊠*Inveraray Pier* ☎*01499/302213* ⊕*www.inveraraypier.com* ⊠*£3.80* ⊙*Apr.–Oct., daily 10–5.*

**Ardkinglas Woodland Garden** has one of Britain's finest collections of conifers, set off by rhododendron blossoms in early summer. You'll find it around the head of Loch Fyne, about 10 mi east of Inveraray.

✉ *A83, Cairndow* ☎ *01499/600261* ⊕ *www.ardkinglas.com* ✉ *£3.50* ✆ *Daily sunrise–sunset.*

At **Loch Fyne Oysters,** about 10 mi northeast of Inveraray, you can stop at the shop to purchase these delicious shellfish to go, or order them to be shipped. You can also consume a dozen with a glass of wine at the restaurant and bar. ✉ *A83, Clachan Farm, Cairndow* ☎ *01499/600236* ⊕ *www.loch-fyne.com* ✆ *Daily 9–7.*

★ Step a few centuries back in time at the open-air **Auchindrain Museum,** a rare surviving example of an 18th-century communal tenancy farm. The old bracken-thatch and iron-roof buildings, about 20 in all, give you a feel for early farming life in the Highlands, and the interpretation center explains it all. Among the furnished buildings are cottages, longhouses, and barns. The museum is 5 mi south of Inveraray. ✉ *A83* ☎ *01499/500235* ⊕ *www.auchindrainmuseum.org.uk* ✉ *£4.50* ✆ *Apr.–Oct., daily 10–5; last admission 4.*

★ Well worth a visit for plant lovers is 100-acre **Crarae Garden,** where magnolias, azaleas, and rhododendrons flourish in the moist, lush environment around Crarae Burn (a small stream). A rocky gorge and waterfalls add appeal, and the flowers and trees attract several different species of birds and butterflies. The gardens are 10 mi southwest of Inveraray. ✉ *Off A83* ☎ *01546/886614* ⊕ *www.nts.org.uk* ✉ *£5* ✆ *Gardens daily 9:30–sunset; visitor center Apr.–Sept., daily 10–5.*

### WHERE TO STAY & EAT

££  ✕☐ **The George Hotel.** The Clark family has run this 18th-century for-
Fodor'sChoice  mer coaching inn at the heart of town for six generations, and the
★  warmth of the welcome reflects the benefit of continuity. Roaring log fires invite repose in the common rooms, and antiques and oil paintings in the individually decorated rooms make you feel as though you were in another, slower-paced era. Room vary in price substantially based on size and amenities; the most expensive have whirlpool tubs. Locals fill the restaurant to sample the excellent food, such as king scallop and bacon kebabs with lemon basil and shallots. **Pros:** Excellent restaurant, atmospheric stone-floored bars, hotel Scottish in every way. **Cons:** Too much tartan for some; small, unattractive reception area; some old mattresses. ✉ *Main St. E, PA32 8TT* ☎ *01499/302111* ⊕ *www.the-georgehotel.co.uk* ✆ *15 rooms* ☐ *In-room: no a/c. In-hotel: restaurant, 2 bars, no elevator* ☐ *MC, V* ❏ *BP.*

## LOCHGILPHEAD

*26 mi south of Inveraray.*

Lochgilphead, the largest town in this region, looks best when the tide is in, as Loch Gilp (really a bite out of Loch Fyne) reveals a muddy shoreline at low tide. With a series of well-kept, colorful buildings along its main street, this neat little town is worth a look.

### HORSEBACK RIDING

**Castle Riding Centre and Argyll Trail Riding** ( ⊠*Brenfield Farm, Ardrishaig* ☎*01546/603274*), south of Lochgilphead, offers guided rides along routes throughout Argyll and the West Highlands.

### SHOPPING

The factory shop at the **Highbank Collection** ( ⊠*Highbank Industrial Estate* ☎*01546/602044*) sells hand-painted pottery and glassware, colorful ceramics, and model wooden boats.

## CRINAN

*1 mi north of Lochgilphead.*

Crinan is synonymous with its canal, the reason for this tiny community's existence and its mainstay. The narrow road beside the Crinan Hotel bustles with yachting types waiting to pass through the locks, bringing a surprisingly cosmopolitan feel to such an out-of-the-way corner of Scotland. Also accessible from Crinan are the worthwhile Kilmartin House Museum and some castles. To reach Crinan, take the A816 Oban road north from Lochgilphead for about a mile, then turn left.

The **Crinan Canal** opened in 1801 to let fishing vessels reach Hebridean fishing grounds without making the long haul south around the Kintyre Peninsula. At its western end the canal drops to the sea in a series of locks.

★ For an exceptional encounter with early Scottish history, visit the **Kilmartin House Museum,** about 8 mi north of Crinan. The museum explores more than 300 ancient monuments, all within a 6-mi radius of the village of Kilmartin. Learn about the stone circles and avenues, burial mounds, and carved stones dating from the Bronze Age and earlier that are scattered thickly around this neighborhood, and then go out and explore them. Nearby **Dunadd Fort,** a rocky hump rising out of the level ground between Crinan and Kilmartin, was once the capital of the early kingdom of Dalriada, founded by the first wave of Scots who migrated from Ireland around AD 500. Clamber up the rock to see a basin, a footprint, and an outline of a boar carved on the smooth upper face of the knoll. ⊠*At Kilmartin, on A816* ☎*01546/510278* ⊕*www.kilmartin.org* ☎*£4.60* ☉*Mar.–Oct., daily 10–5:30.*

The tower house of **Carnasserie Castle,** 8 mi north of Crinan, has the distinction of having belonged to the writer of the first book printed in Gaelic. The writer, John Carswell, bishop of the isles, translated a text by the Scottish reformer John Knox into Gaelic and published it in 1567. ⊠*Off A816, 2 mi north of Kilmartin* ☎*0131/668–8800* ⊕*www.historic-scotland.gov.uk* ☎*Free* ☉*Daily 24 hrs.*

**OFF THE BEATEN PATH**

**Castle Sween.** The oldest stone castle on the Scottish mainland, dating from the 12th century, sits on a rocky bit of coast about 12 mi south of Crinan. You can reach it by an unclassified road from Crinan that grants outstanding views of the Paps of Jura (the mountains on

Jura), across the sound. There are some temptingly deserted white-sand beaches here.

## WHERE TO STAY & EAT

££ ✗🏠 **Allt-Na-Craig.** This large stone Victorian house, 4 mi south of Loch-
★ gilphead, is set in lovely gardens overlooking Loch Fyne on the edge of the village. It was once the home of *Wind in the Willows* author Kenneth Graham. Nearby is the yacht-filled eastern basin of the Crinan Canal. Charlotte Nicol's hearty home cooking (£££) using local ingredients is well worth a stay, whether you are a meat lover or a vegetarian. The cottage has a kitchen and can be rented by the week. **Pros:** Atmospheric, good food, and views. **Cons:** You're pretty isolated, so it helps to have a car. ✉ *Tarbert Rd., Ardrishaig PA30 8EP* ☎ *01546/603245* ⊕ *www.allt-na-craig.co.uk* 🛏 *5 rooms, 1 cottage* 🔑 *In-room: no a/c. In-hotel: restaurant, public Wi-Fi, no elevator* ☰*MC, V* �‖*BP.*

# KINTYRE PENINSULA

*52 mi (to Campbeltown) south of Lochgilphead.*

Rivers and streams crisscross this long, narrow strip of green pasturelands and hills stretching south from Lochgilphead.

**Tarbert,** a name that appears throughout the Highlands, is the Gaelic word for "place of portage," and a glance at the map tells you why it was given to this little town with a workaday waterfront: Tarbert sits on the narrow neck of land between East and West Loch Tarbert, where long ago boats were actually carried across the land to avoid looping all the way around the peninsula.

The **Isle of Gigha,** barely 5 mi long, is sheltered in a frost-free, seawarmed climate between Kintyre and Islay. The island was long favored by British aristocrats as a summer destination.

One relic of the Isle of Gigha's aristocratic legacy is the **Achamore House Gardens,** which produce lush shrubberies with spectacular azalea displays in late spring. For a nimble day trip, take the 20-minute ferry to Gigha from Tayinloan and walk right over to the gardens. You may not want to take your car, as the walk is fairly easy. ☎ *01583/505267* ⊕ *www.isle-of-gigha.co.uk* ✉ *Gardens £2; ferry £4.50 per person plus £15.80 per car* ⊙ *Gardens daily sunrise–sunset. Ferry Mon.–Sat. 9–5, Sun. at 11, 2, and 3.*

## GOLF

You can play **Machrihanish Golf Club's** perfectly manicured 18 holes warmed by Gulf Stream breezes. U.S. Navy Seal teams-in-training have been known to drop from the air into a chilly nearby loch. ✉ *Campbeltown* ☎ *01586/810213* ⊕ *www.machgolf.com* ⛳ *18 holes, 6,228 yds, par 70.*

# ARRAN

Many Scots, especially those from Glasgow and the west, are well disposed toward Arran, as it reminds them of unhurried childhood holidays. Called "Scotland in Miniature" by the tourist board, Arran really does have it all: mountains, glens, beaches, waterfalls, standing stone circles, Viking forts, castles, and a malt-whisky distillery (in Lochranza).

To get to Arran, take the ferry from Ardrossan, on the mainland. (It's also possible to take the ferry from Claonaig on the Kintyre Peninsula in summer.) You can see a number of fellow travelers wearing hiking boots: they're ready for the delights of Goat Fell, the impressive peak (2,868 feet) that gives Arran one of the most distinctive profiles of any island in Scotland. As the ferry approaches Brodick, you can see Goat Fell's cone. Arran's southern half is less mountainous; the Highland Boundary Fault crosses just to the north of Brodick Bay. Exploring the island is easy, as the A841 road neatly circles it.

## BRODICK

*1 hr by ferry from Ardrossan.*

The largest township on Arran, Brodick is really a village, its frontage lined by a number of Victorian hotels, set spaciously back from a promenade and beach.

The **Isle of Arran Heritage Museum** documents life on the island from ancient times to the present. Several buildings, including a cottage and *smiddy* (smithy), have period furnishings as well as displays on prehistoric life, farming, fishing, and other aspects of the island's social history. ⊠ *Rosaburn, Brodick* ☎ *01770/302636* ⊕ *www.arranmuseum. co.uk* ≤ *£3* ⊘ *Apr.–Oct., daily 10:30–4:30.*

In **Glen Rosa** you can stroll through a long glen glimpsing the wild ridges that beckon so many outdoors enthusiasts. To get here from Brodick, pass the Isle of Arran Heritage Museum and find the junction where the String Road cuts across the island. Drive a short way up the String Road and turn right at the signpost into the glen. The road soon becomes undrivable; park the car and wander on foot.

★ Arran's biggest cultural draw is **Brodick Castle,** on the north side of Brodick Bay. The red-sandstone structure, parts of which date back to the 13th century, is cosseted by trees and parkland; several rooms are open to the public. The castle's furniture, paintings, and silver are opulent in their own right—try counting the number of deer heads on the hall walls—but the real attraction is the garden, where brilliantly colored rhododendrons bloom, particularly in late spring and early summer. There are many unusual varieties of azalea, though the ordinary yellow kind is unmatched for its scent. Your first encounter with these is like hitting a wall of perfume. Save time to visit the Servants' Hall, where an excellent restaurant serves morning coffee (with hot scones—try the date-and-walnut variety), lunch with a daily-changing menu, and afternoon teas with home-baked goods. ✉*1 mi north of Brodick Pier* ☎*01770/302202* ⊕*www.nts.org.uk* ☎*Castle and gardens £10* ☉*Castle and restaurant Easter–Oct., daily 11–4:30. Reception center, shop, and walled garden Easter–Oct., daily 10–4:30; Nov.–Dec. 21, Fri.–Sun. 10–3:30.*

### WHERE TO STAY & EAT

££  ✕**The Brodick Bar.** Local beef, lamb, and game, plus the most succulent scallops you'll ever taste, are what keeps the locals (and visitors) coming back to this casual, friendly, small-town spot, which includes a pub and a brasserie. Among the good selection of malt whiskies is Arran malt, made on the island. Light wood and tartan help keep the mood casual. There's another outpost, the Wine Port, near Brodick Castle. ✉*Alma Rd.* ☎*01770/302169* ⊟*MC, V.*

£  ⊡**Glencloy Farmhouse.** Surrounded by colorful gardens, this 19th-century sandstone house nestles in a peaceful valley. Brodick and views of the hills and sea are a few minutes' walk away. Breakfast is a treat, with organic eggs, homemade jam, and fresh-baked bread and muffins. **Pros:** Outstanding breakfast; lovely location. **Cons:** Plenty of the owners' personal decorations all around; access road has many potholes. ✉*Brodick, Isle of Arran KA26 8DA* ☎*01770/302251* ⤺*5 rooms, 2 with bath* ⚒*In-room: no a/c, no phone. In-hotel: no elevator* ⊟*MC, V* ☉*Closed Nov.–Feb.* ⍓*BP.*

### SHOPPING

Arran's shops are well stocked with locally produced goods. The Home Farm is a popular shopping area with several shops and a small restaurant. The **Duchess Court Shops** ( ✉*The Home Farm* ☎*01770/302831*) include Bear Necessities, with everything bearly; the Nature Shop, with nature-oriented books and gifts; and Arran Aromatics, one of Scotland's top makers of toiletries. **The Island Cheese Company** ( ✉*The Home Farm* ☎*01770/302788*) stocks Arran blue cheese among other handmade Scottish cheeses.

## LAMLASH

*4 mi south of Brodick.*

With views offshore to Holy Island, which is now a Buddhist retreat, Lamlash has a breezy seaside-holiday atmosphere. To reach the highest point accessible by car, go through the village and turn right beside the bridge onto Ross Road, which climbs steeply from a thickly planted valley, **Glen Scorrodale,** and yields fine views of Lamlash Bay. From Lamlash you can explore the southern part of Arran: 10 mi southwest is the little community of **Lagg,** sitting peacefully by the banks of the

Kilmory Water, and **Whiting Bay** has a waterfront string of hotels and well-kept properties.

### WHERE TO STAY & EAT

££
★ ✕⊡**Lagg Hotel.** Arran's oldest inn is an 18th-century lodge with fireplaces in the common rooms and 11 acres of gardens and grounds that meander down to the river. Each room is quiet and bright, if a little flowery in its decor, and many overlook the riverside flower beds or woodland. Hearty but elegant home cooking in the restaurant (£££) focuses on entrées such as lemon tagliatelle with butternut squash and pan-seared duck breast with potatoes. The friendly locals in the bar help make a stay here a fine evening. The inn is 12 mi southwest of Lamlash. **Pros:** Beautiful gardens, warming fireplaces, good-size rooms. **Con:** Floral designs everywhere. ⊠*Kilmory, Isle of Arran KA278PQ* ☎*01770/870255* ⊕*www.lagghotel.com* ⇨*9 rooms* ⌂*In-room: no a/c. In-hotel: restaurant, bars, no-smoking rooms, no elevator* ⊟*MC, V* ⦿*BP.*

### BICYCLING

You can rent bicycles at **Whiting Bay Cycle Hire** ( ⊠*Elim, Silverhill, Whiting Bay* ☎*01770/700382*), open May through September.

### SHOPPING

**Patterson Arran** ( ⊠*The Old Mill, Lamlash* ☎*01770/600606*) is famous for its preserves and marmalades, as well as its mustards.

---

## MACHRIE

*11 mi north of Lagg.*

The area surrounding Machrie, home to a popular beach, is littered with prehistoric sites: chambered cairns, hut circles, and standing stones dating from the Bronze Age.

★ From Machrie, a well-surfaced track takes you to a grassy moor by a ruined farm, where you can see the **Machrie Moor Stone Circles:** small, rounded granite-boulder circles and much taller, eerie red-sandstone monoliths. Out on the bare moor, the lost and lonely stones are very evocative, well worth a walk to see if you like the feeling of solitude. The stones are about 1 mi outside of Machrie; just follow the HISTORIC SCOTLAND sign pointing the way.

### HORSEBACK RIDING

Even novices can enjoy a guided ride on a mount from **Cairnhouse Riding Centre** ( ⊠*On A84, 2 mi south of Machrie* ☎*01770/860466*). The stables are in Blackwaterfoot.

### SHOPPING

The **Old Byre Showroom** ( ⊠*On A841, 2 mi north of Machrie* ☎*01770/840227*) sells sheepskin goods, hand-knit sweaters, designer knitwear, leather goods, and rugs. The store is at Auchencar Farm.

EN
ROUTE
Continuing south to Blackwaterfoot, you can return to Brodick via the String Road: from the Kinloch Hotel, head up the hill. As you drive, there are more fine views of the granite complexities of Arran's hills:

gray notched ridges beyond brown moors and, past the watershed, a vista of Brodick Bay.

## LOCHRANZA

*14 mi north of Brodick.*

North of Brodick is Lochranza, a community sheltered by the Bay of Loch Ranza, which spills into the flat-bottom glacial glen. The only distillery on Arran, the Isle of Arran Distillery, is here; it opened in 1995 and is in the mountains overlooking Lochranza Bay.

The village is set off by a picturesque ruin, **Lochranza Castle,** set on a low sand spit. This is said to have been the landing place of Robert the Bruce when he returned from Rathlin Island in 1307 to start the campaign that won Scotland's independence. A sign indicates where you can pick up the key to get in. ⊠*Off A841* ☎*0131/668–8800* ⊕*www. historic-scotland.gov.uk* 🎫*Free* ⊙*Apr.–Sept., daily 9:30–5:30; Oct.– Mar., daily 9:30–4:30.*

# ISLAY & JURA

Islay has a character distinct from that of the rest of the islands that make up the Hebrides. In contrast to areas where most residents live on crofts (small plots generally worked by people in their spare time), Islay's western half in particular has large, self-sustaining farms. Many of the island's best beaches, wildlife preserves, and historical sites are also on its western half, whereas the southeast is mainly an extension of the island of Jura's inhospitable quartzite hills. Islay is particularly known for its birds, including the rare chough (a crow with red legs and beak) and, in winter, its barnacle geese. Several distilleries produce delectable malt whiskies. A peaty taste characterizes many of the island's malt whiskies, which are available in local pubs, off-license shops, and distillery shops. Though not all have shops, most distilleries welcome visitors by appointment; some charge a small fee for a tour, which you can redeem against a purchase of whisky.

Although it's possible to meet an Islay native in a local pub, such an event is less likely on Jura, given the island's one road, one distillery, one hotel, and six sporting estates. In fact, you have a better chance of bumping into one of the island's red deer, which outnumber the human population by at least 20 to 1. The island has a much more rug-

## THE WHISKY COAST

Scotland likes trails for travelers, whether castles or whisky are being pursued. The country's dramatic west coast, from the Isle of Skye in the north to Islay and Arran in the south, has plenty of distinguished distilleries. The Whisky Coast (www.whiskycoast. co.uk) is a consortium of distilleries, hotels, restaurants, golf courses, and tour operators created to make planning a trip around the area. easier The Web site is one starting point if you're dreaming of touring this part of the country in search of the perfect dram.

ged look than Islay, with its profiles of the Paps of Jura, a hill range at its most impressive when basking in the rays of a west-coast sunset.

## BOWMORE

*11 mi north of Port Ellen on Islay.*

Compact Bowmore is about the same size (population 1,000) as Port Ellen, but it works slightly better as a base for touring because it's central to Islay's main routes. Sharing its name with the whisky made in the distillery by the shore, Bowmore is a tidy town, its grid pattern having been laid out in 1768 by the local landowner Daniel Campbell, of Shawfield. Main Street stretches from the pier head to the command-ing parish church, built in 1767 in an unusual circular design—so the devil could not hide in a corner.

You can purchase whisky and take a tour at **Bowmore Distillery** ( ⊠*School St.* ☎*01496/810671*). The facility was founded 1779.

★ The **Islay Woollen Mill,** set in a wooded hollow by the river, has a fas-cinating array of working machinery; the proud owner will take you around. The shop here sells high-quality products that were woven on-site. Beyond the usual tweed there's a distinctive selection of hats, caps, and clothing made from the mill's own cloth. All the tartans and tweeds worn in the film *Braveheart* were woven here. Look for the sign for the mill 3 mi north of Bowmore, on the main road about a mile east beyond the tiny community of Bridgend. ⊠*Off A846* ☎*01496/810563* ⊕*www.islaywoollenmill.co.uk* ⊠*Free* ⊗*Mon.–Sat. 10–5.*

### WHERE TO STAY & EAT

££ ✕⽥ **Harbour Inn.** The cheerfully noisy bar of this harborside inn is fre-quented by off-duty distillery workers who are happy to rub elbows with travelers and exchange island gossip. The superb restaurant (£££), which has expansive views over the water, serves morning coffee, lunch, and dinner. Menus highlight local lobster, crab, and prawns, as well as island lamb and beef. The bedrooms are bright and contemporary, with simple wood or velvet-upholstered furniture; some have water views. **Pros:** Great location and restaurant. **Con:** Restaurant service slow; bedroom linens poor for the price. ⊠*The Square, PA43 7JR* ☎*01496/810330* ⊕*www.harbour-inn.com* ⟿*7 rooms* ⟨In-room: no a/c. In-hotel: restaurant, bar, no elevator* ⊟*MC, V* ��*BP.*

## PORT CHARLOTTE

*11 mi west of Bowmore via A846/A847, on Islay.*

Port Charlotte has a local museum and is the start of a scenic drive.

Above the road on the north side in a converted kirk (church) is the **Museum of Islay Life,** a haphazard but authentic and informative dis-play of times past. ⊠*A847* ☎*01496/850358* ⊕*www.islaymuseum. freeserve.co.uk* ⊠*£3* ⊗*Apr.–Oct., Mon.–Sat. 10–5.*

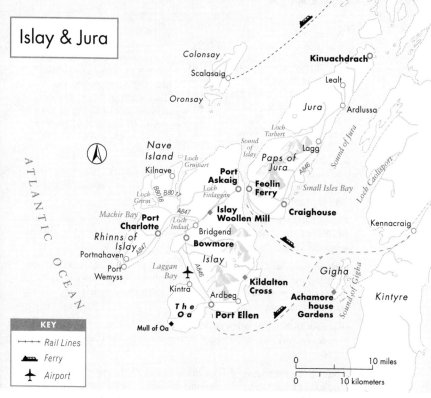

# Islay & Jura

Colonsay

Scalasaig

Oronsay

Kinuachdrach

Lealt

Jura

Ardlussa

Loch
Tarbert

Sound
of
Islay

Lagg

Paps of
Jura

Nave
Island

Loch
Gruinart

A846

Kilnave

Port
Askaig

Feolin
Ferry

Loch
Finlaggan

Small Isles Bay

Craighouse

Sound of Jura

Loch Caolisport

Kennacraig

ATLANTIC OCEAN

Loch
Gorm

B801

B8017

Port
Charlotte

A847

Islay
Woollen Mill

Machir Bay

Loch
Indaal

Bridgend

Rhinns of
Islay

Bowmore

A847

Islay

Portnahaven

Port
Wemyss

Laggan
Bay

A846

Gigha

Kintyre

Kintra

Kildalton
Cross

Ardbeg

Achamore
house
Gardens

Sound of Gigha

The
Oa

Port Ellen

Mull of Oa

### KEY

- Rail Lines
- Ferry
- Airport

0 _____ 10 miles

0 _____ 10 kilometers

South of Port Charlotte, a loop road lets you explore the wild land-scapes of the **Rhinns of Islay**. At the south end of the Rhinns are the scattered cottages of **Portnahaven** and its twin, **Port Wemyss**. Take the A847 to the villages, then return by the bleak, unclassified road that loops north and east, passing by the recumbent stone circle at Coultoon and the chapel at Kilchiaran. The strange whooping sound you may hear as you turn away from Portnahaven comes from Scotland's first wave-powered generator, sucking and blowing as it supplies electricity for both villages. It's well worth the climb down to the shore to see it in action.

## THE OA

*13 mi south of Bowmore on Islay.*

The southern Oa peninsula is a region of caves that's rich in smuggling lore. At its tip, the Mull of Oa, is a monument recalling the 650 men who lost their lives in 1918 when the British ships *Tuscania* and *Otranto* sank nearby. To get here, drive south on the A846: before you reach Port Ellen, go straight ahead; when the A846 turns to a minor road to Imeraval, make a right at the junction, then a left. Bring good strong shoes for walking.

## PORT ELLEN

*11 mi south of Bowmore on Islay.*

The sturdy community of Port Ellen was founded in the 1820s, and much of its architecture dates from the following decades. It has a harbor (ferries stop here), a few shops, and a handful of inns. The road traveling east from Port Ellen for 3 mi passes three top distilleries

and makes a very pleasant afternoon's "whisky walk." Tours are free at all three distilleries, but you must call ahead for an appointment; there may be no tours on weekends at times.

**Ardbeg Distillery** (☎01496/302244 ⊕www.ardbeg.com) is the farthest from Port Ellen. It closed in 1981, but whisky aficionados cheered when the malt flowed again in 1997.

**Laphroaig Distillery** (☎01496/302418 ⊕www.laphroaig.com) is a little less than 1 mi from Port Ellen toward Ardberg. The whisky it produces is one of the most distinctive in the Western Isles, with a tangy, peaty seaweed-and-iodine flavor.

**Lagavulin Distillery** (☎01496/302400 ⊕www.discovering-distilleries.com/lagavulin) has the whisky with the strongest iodine scent of all the island malts.

★ About 8 mi northeast of Port Ellen is one of the highlights of Scotland's Celtic heritage. After passing through a pleasantly rolling, partly wooded landscape, take a narrow road (it's signposted KILDALTON CROSS) from Ardbeg. This leads to a ruined chapel with surrounding kirkyard, in which stands the finest carved cross anywhere in Scotland: the 8th-century **Kildalton Cross.** Carved from a single slab of epidiorite rock, the ringed cross is encrusted on both sides with elaborate designs in the style of the Iona school. The surrounding grave slabs date as far back as the 12th and 13th centuries. ⊕www.historic-scotland.gov.uk.

### SPORTS & THE OUTDOORS

GOLF **Machrie Golf Links** would be a lot more crowded if it were a little more accessible. The course was designed in 1891, and except for minor changes in the 1970s, has changed little. Watch out for the sand dunes! ⊠1 mi from airport, 4 mi from Port Ellen ☎01496/302310 ⊕www.machrie.com ⚑18 holes, 5,894 yds, par 71.

HORSEBACK **Ballivicar Pony Trekking** (⊠Ballivicar Farm ☎01496/302251) leads trips RIDING on nearby beaches and into the surrounding countryside.

## PORT ASKAIG

*3 mi northeast of Loch Finlaggan via A846, on Islay.*

Serving as the ferry port for Jura, Port Askaig is a mere cluster of cottages. Uphill, just outside the village, a side road travels along the coast, giving impressive views of Jura on the way. There are distilleries near here, too; make appointments for tours.

At road's end, the **Bunnahabhain Distillery** (☎01496/840646 ⊕*www.bunnahabhain.com*) sits on the shore. It was established in 1881.

You can also purchase whisky at the **Caol Ila Distillery** (☎01496/840207 ⊕*www.islayinfo.com/islay_caolila_distillery.html*), which filled its first bottle in 1846.

### WHERE TO STAY & EAT

££ ✕🖼 **Port Askaig Hotel.** The hotel grounds extend all the way to the shore at this modern roadside inn overlooking the Sound of Islay and the island of Jura. Accommodations are comfortable without being luxurious, and the traditional Scottish food (££) is well prepared, using homegrown produce, fish, and meats. **Pros:** Staff bilingual in Gaelic, adorable setting and bar. **Cons:** Some rooms are too plain and worn. ⊠*Port Askaig PA46 7RD* ☎01496/840245 ⊕*www.portaskaig.co.uk* ➾*8 rooms, 6 with bath* ⚴*In-room: no a/c, no phone. In-hotel: restaurant, bars, no elevator* ▤*MC, V* ⦿*BP.*

## JURA

*5 min by ferry from Port Askaig.*

The rugged, mountainous landscape of the island of Jura, home to only about 200 people, looms immediately east of Port Askaig. Having crossed the Sound of Islay from Port Askaig, you'll find it easy to choose which road to take—Jura has only one, starting at Feolin, the ferry pier. Apart from the initial stretch it's all single-lane. The A846 starts off below one of the many raised beaches, then climbs across moorland, providing scenic views across the Sound of Jura. The Paps (mountains) of Jura are a striking feature of the island. The ruined Claig Castle, on an island just offshore, was built by the Lords of the Isles to control the sound.

Beyond the farm buildings of Ardfin, and Jura House (with gardens that are occasionally open to the public), the road turns northward across open moorland with scattered forestry blocks and the faint evidence, in the shape of parallel ridges, of the original inhabitants' "lazy beds," or narrow fields separated by furrows to drain away the excess water. The original settlements were cleared with the other parts of the Highlands when the island became more of a sheep pasture and deer forest.

The community of Craighouse has the island's only distillery, the **Isle of Jura Distillery** (⊠*A846* ☎01496/820240 ⊕*www.isleofjura.com*), producing malt whisky since 1810. Phone ahead to reserve your place on a tour.

The settlement of **Kinuachdrach** once served as a crossing point to Scarba and the mainland. To get to Kinuachdrach after crossing the river at Lealt, follow the track beyond the surface road for 5 mi. The coastal footpath to Corryvreckan lies beyond, over the bare moors. This area has two enticements: the first, for fans of George Orwell (1903–50), is the house of **Barnhill** (not open to the public), where the author wrote *1984*; the second, for wilderness enthusiasts, is the whirlpool of the **Gulf of Corryvreckan** and the unspoiled coastal scenery.

### WHERE TO STAY & EAT

££  ✕▣ **Jura Hotel.** In spite of its monopoly, this hotel in pleasant gardens can be relied on for adequate accommodations. Rooms are simple and a bit old-fashioned. The restaurant serves good, satisfying food prepared with local ingredients. **Pro:** Good views across the bay, spacious rooms, next door to distillery. **Cons:** Room decor is tired, to say the least; you may have to share a bathroom. ⊠ *Craighouse, PA60 7XU* ☎ *01496/820243* ⊕ *www.jurahotel.co.uk* ⟿ *18 rooms, 11 with bath* ♿ *In-room: no a/c, no phone, no TV. In-hotel: restaurant, bar, no elevator* ⊟ *AE, DC, MC, V* ⧖ *BP.*

# IONA & THE ISLE OF MULL

Though Mull certainly has an indigenous population, the island is often called the Officers' Mess because of its popularity with retired military personnel. Across from the Ross of Mull is the island of Iona, cradle of Scottish Christianity and ancient burial site of the kings of Scotland.

## CRAIGNURE

*40-min ferry crossing to Mull from Oban, 15-min ferry crossing to Fishnish (5 mi northwest of Craignure) from Lochaline.*

Craignure, little more than a pier and some houses, is close to the Isle of Mull's two best-known castles, Torosay and Duart. Reservations for the year-round ferries that travel from Oban to Craignure are advisable in summer. The ferry from Lochaline to Fishnish, just northwest of Craignure, does not accept reservations and does not run on Sunday.

★  A trip to **Torosay Castle** can include the novelty of steam-and-diesel service on a narrow-gauge railway, which takes 20 minutes to run from the pier at Craignure to the grounds of Torosay (about ½ mi). Scottish baronial in style, the turreted mid-19th-century castle has a friendly air. You're free to wander round the principal rooms, which include the front hall dominated by a collection of red deer-stag antlers. The castle's gardens are home to blue poppies and many other rare plants. ⊠ *Off A849, about 1 mi southeast of Craignure* ☎ *01680/812421* ▣ *01680/812470* ⊕ *www.torosay.com* ⧈ *Castle, garden, play park, tearoom/gallery £5.50, garden, playpark, tearoom/gallery £4.75* ⊗ *Castle: Easter–Oct., daily 10:30–5; last admission at 4:30. Gardens: daily 9–sunset.*

The 13th-century **Duart Castle,** ancient seat of the Macleans, was ruined by the Campbells in 1691 but purchased and restored by Sir Fitzroy Maclean in 1911. It stands dramatically on a clifftop overlooking the Sound of Mull. Inside, one display depicts the wreck of the *Swan,* a Cromwellian vessel sunk offshore in 1653 and excavated in the 1990s

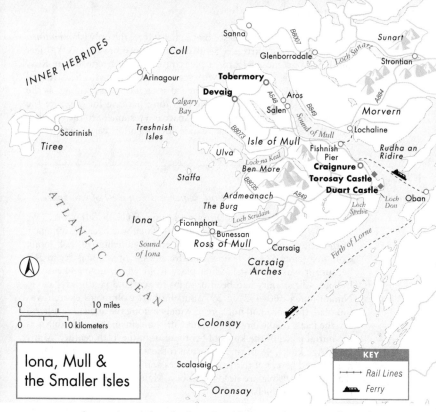

Iona, Mull &
the Smaller Isles

**KEY**

| | Rail Lines |
| ---- | ---- |
| | Ferry |

by marine archaeologists. Outside you can visit nearby **Millennium Wood,** planted with groups of Mull's indigenous trees. You can walk 4 mi along the shore from Torosay to Duart Castle; if you have less energy, you can drive from Craignure. To reach Duart by car, take the A849 and turn left around the shore of Duart Bay. ⊠ *3 mi southeast of Craignure* ☎ *01680/812309* ⊕ *www.duartcastle.com* ⊡ *£5* ⊙ *Apr., Sun.–Thurs. 11–4; May–mid-Oct., daily 10:30–5:30.*

### WHERE TO STAY & EAT

££   ✕⌷ **Craignure Inn.** This 18th-century whitewashed drover's inn, a short walk from the ferry pier, has a lively bar that often hosts local musicians. Hearty, home-cooked meals (£) include staples such as shepherd's pie and fish-and-chips. The rooms are warm and snug, with polished-wood furniture, exposed beams, and views of the Sound of Mull. **Pros:** Exciting bar scene, hearty local foods. **Con:** Live music can get loud. ⊠ *Craignure PA65 6AY* ☎ *01680/812305* ⊕ *www.craignure-inn.co.uk* ⇆ *3 rooms* ⌖ *In-room: no a/c. In-hotel: restaurant, bar, no elevator* ⊟ *MC, V* ⦿ *BP.*

EN
ROUTE

Between Craignure and Fionnphort at the end of the Ross of Mull, the double-lane road narrows as it heads southwest, touched by sea inlets at Lochs Don and Spelve. Inland, vivid grass and high rock faces in Glen More make gray and green the prevalent hues. These stepped-rock faces reach their highest point in Ben More, the only island *munro* outside Skye (a munro is a Scottish mountain more than 3,000 feet high). Stay on the A849 for a pleasant drive the length of the Ross of Mull, a wide promontory with scattered settlements. The National Trust for Scotland cares for the rugged stretch of coast, known as the Burg. The A849 eventually ends in a long parking lot opposite the houses of Fionnphort. The parking space is a testament to the popularity of the nearby island of Iona, which does not allow cars. Ferry service is frequent in summer.

## IONA

Fodor'sChoice *5 min by ferry from Fionnphort, which is 36 mi west of Craignure.*
★

No less a travel writer than Dr. Samuel Johnson (1709–84) wrote, "We were now treading that illustrious Island which was once the luminary of the Caledonian regions." The fiery and argumentative Irish monk Columba (circa 521–97) chose Iona for the site of a monastery in 563 because it was the first landing place from which he could *not* see Ireland. Christianity had been brought to Scotland (Galloway) by St. Ninian (circa 360–432) in 397, but until St. Columba's church was founded, the word had not spread widely among the ancient northerners, the Picts. As the most important Christian site in the land, Iona was the burial place of the kings of Scotland until the 11th century. Many Dark Age kings, 48 of them Scottish (others were Pictish and Celtic), are interred here, not to mention princes and bishops. The tombstones that are still visible are near the abbey. Many carved slabs also commemorate clan chiefs.

Beyond the ancient cloisters, the island's most delightful aspect is its almost mystical tranquillity—enhanced by the fact that most visitors make only the short walk from the ferry pier to the abbey (by way of the nunnery), rather than press on to the island's farther reaches.

**Iona Abbey** survived repeated Norse sackings but finally fell into disuse around the time of the Reformation. Restoration work began at the turn of the 20th century. In 1938 the Iona Community (☎*01681/700404* ⊕*www.iona.org.uk*), an ecumenical religious group, was founded. It was involved in rebuilding the abbey and now offers multiday programs at several buildings on the island. Today the restored buildings, including the abbey, serve as a spiritual center under the jurisdiction of the Church of Scotland. Guided tours, run by the Iona Community, are every half hour in summer and on demand in winter. ☎*01681/700793* ⊕*www.historic-scotland.gov.uk* ▧*£4.50* ☉*Apr.–Sept., daily 9:30– 5:30; Oct.–Mar., daily 9:30–4:30.*

### WHERE TO STAY & EAT

£££ ✕▦ **St. Columba Hotel.** An 1846 former manse, St. Columba stands next to the cathedral about ¼ mi from the ferry pier. Rooms are very simple, but all front rooms have glorious views across the Sound of Iona to Mull. Chefs in the restaurant (£££) serve exceptional three-course meals using organic ingredients. **Pros:** Ecominded; this place is all about what's good for the earth and soul; nice log fires. **Con:** No TV in hotel, rooms minimal in style. ⊠ *Isle of Iona PA76 6SL* ☎ *01681/700304* ⊕ *www.stcolumba-hotel.co.uk* 🛏 *27 rooms* ♿ *In-room: no a/c, no TV. In-hotel: restaurant, bar, public Wi-Fi* ▤ *MC, V* ⊙ *Closed mid-Oct.–Easter* ¶ *BP.*

### SHOPPING

Iona has a few pleasant surprises for shoppers, the biggest of which is the **Old Printing Press Bookshop** (⊠ *Beside St. Columba Hotel* ☎ *01681/700699*), an excellent antiquarian bookstore. The **Iona Community Shop** (⊠ *Across from Iona Abbey* ☎ *01681/700404*) carries Celtic-inspired gift items, as well as sheet music and songbooks, and CDs and tapes.

## DERVAIG

*60 mi north of Fionnphort, 27 mi northwest of Craignure, on the Isle of Mull.*

A pretty riverside village, Dervaig has a circular, pointed church tower that is reminiscent of the Irish-Celtic style of the 8th and 9th centuries. The Bellart is a good trout- and salmon-fishing river, and Calgary Bay, 5 mi away, offers one of the best beaches on Mull.

At the **Old Byre Heritage Centre,** an audiovisual presentation on the history of the region plays hourly. The tearoom's wholesome fare, particularly the homemade soup, is a boon to travelers. There's also a craft shop. On B8073 you can see signs for the center just before the village of Dervaig. ⊠ *Dervaig* ☎ *01688/400229* ⊕ *www.old-byre.co.uk* 💷 *£4* ⊙ *Easter–Oct., Wed.–Sun. 10:30–6:30; last admission at 5:30.*

### WHERE TO STAY & EAT

££ ✕🏨 **Calgary Hotel.** In a small wooded valley overlooking the beautiful sandy bay, this former farmhouse feels quite secluded. Rooms have colorful quilts and drapes, and some have views over the woods to Calgary Bay. The hotel also rents several apartments by the week. The restaurant (£25 for three courses), in a converted dovecote, serves sophisticated Scottish fare. Try the organic salmon with new potatoes or the pheasant breast with traditional black pudding. **Pros:** Excellent staff, south-facing rooms have lovely bay views, lots of polished wood. **Con:** Not for those who want a remote location. ⊠ *Calgary, by Dervaig, PA75 6QW* ☎ *01688/400256* ⊕ *www.calgary.co.uk* 🛏 *9 rooms, 2 apartments* ♿ *In-room: no a/c. In-hotel: restaurant, bar, no elevator* ▤ *MC, V* ⊙ *Closed Dec.–Feb.* ¶ *BP.*

## TOBERMORY

*5 mi northeast of Dervaig on the Isle of Mull.*

Founded as a fishing station, Tobermory gradually declined, hastened by the arrival of railroad service in Oban. Still, the brightly painted crescent of 18th-century buildings around the harbor—now a popular mooring for yacht captains—gives Tobermory a Mediterranean look.

### WHERE TO STAY & EAT

££ ✕⊡ **Tobermory Hotel.** Made up of a row of former fishermen's cottages, this lodging on Tobermory's waterfront has many rooms with views of the bay. Some have nice touches like a four-poster bed, but all are modest in size and have minimal furniture. Using local produce, the restaurant (£££££) prepares traditional dishes with a twist: for example, the spiced-salmon fillet is served over a haddock-and-prawn roll and topped with lemon-and-coriander cream. **Pros:** Adorable cottage setting with fireplace, toys for children. **Con:** Small rooms and bathrooms. ⊠ *Main St., PA75 6NT* ☏ *01688/302091* ⊕ *www.thetobermoryhotel. com* ↪ *16 rooms* ⚐ *In-room: no a/c. In-hotel: restaurant, bar, no elevator* ☰ *MC, V* ⓘⓄⓘ *BP.*

### THE ARTS

The renown **Mull Theatre** ( ⊠ *Druimfin* ☏ *01688/302673* ⊕ *www.mull theatre.com*) will reopen at this new location in spring 2008; call or check the Web for updates. This theater has the not-insignificant distinction of being the smallest professional theater in the United Kingdom, and it stages a varied program of plays throughout the summer.

# THE SMALLER ISLANDS

Caledonian MacBrayne ferries travel from Oban to three other fairly sizeable islands, Tiree, Coll, and Colonsay, with populations of about 800, 150, and 100, respectively. The islands have pristine beaches and prehistoric artifacts much as other Scottish islands do, but their remoteness means you'll likely be exploring all by yourself.

## TIREE

*4 hr sail from Oban, via Coll.*

A fertile, low-lying island with its own microclimate, Tiree is windswept, but it has more hours of sunshine per year than any other part of the British Isles. Long, rolling Atlantic swells attract surfers, and summer visitors can raise the population to the nearly 4,500 it supported in the 1830s. Among Tiree's several archaeological sites are a large boulder near Vaul covered with more than 50 Bronze Age–cup marks, and an excavated *broch* (stone tower) at Dun Mor Vaul.

## COLL

*3-hr sail from Oban.*

Near Tiree, Coll is even lower lying but also rockier and less fertile. The island is rich in archaeology, with standing stones at Totronald, a cairn at Annagour, and the remains of several Iron Age forts around the island.

The keep of **Breachacha Castle,** on the south end of the island, dates to 1450. A former stronghold of the Maclean clan, the castle is very similar to Kisimul Castle on the Isle of Barra. Today the castle is privately owned, but you may view it from the road near Uig.

## COLONSAY & ORONSAY

*2½-hr sail from Oban.*

**Colonsay** is one of Scotland's quietest, most unspoiled, and least populous islands. The beautiful beach at Kiloran Bay is an utterly peaceful place even at the height of summer. The standing stones at Kilchattan Farm are known as Fingal's Limpet Hammers. Fingal, or Finn, Mac-Coul is a warrior of massive size and strength in Celtic mythology. Standing before the stones, you can imagine Fingal wielding them like hammers to cull equally large limpets from Scotland's rocky coast. The island's social life revolves around the bar at the 19th-century Colonsay Hotel, 100 yards from the ferry pier. The adjacent island of Oronsay can be reached at low tide in a 1½ -mi wade across a sandy sound; there's a ruined cloister.

# ARGYLL & THE ISLES ESSENTIALS

## TRANSPORTATION

7

### BY AIR

British Airways Express flies from Glasgow to Campbeltown (on the Kintyre Peninsula) and the islands of Islay and Tiree.

Information **British Airways Express** (☎ *0870/850–9850* ⊕ *www.ba.com*). **Campbeltown Airport** (☎ *01667/462445* ⊕ *www.hial.co.uk*). **Islay Airport** (☎ *01667/462445* ⊕ *www.hial.co.uk*). **Tiree Airport** (☎ *01667/462445* ⊕ *www. hial.co.uk*).

### BY BOAT & FERRY

Caledonian MacBrayne (CalMac) operates car-ferry service to and from the main islands. ■TIP➔**An Island Hopscotch ticket reduces the cost of island-hopping.** Western Ferries operates between Dunoon, in Argyll, and Gourock, west of Glasgow. The ferry passage between Dunoon and Gourock is one frequented by locals. It saves a lot of traveling time, and you can take your car across as well.

Ferry reservations are needed if you have a car; foot passengers do not need to make reservations. Pay for reservations online or by phone.

Information **Caledonian MacBrayne** (✉ *Ferry Terminal, Gourock* ☎ *08705/650000* ⊕ *www.calmac.co.uk*). **Western Ferries** (✉ *Hunter's Quay, Dunoon* ☎ *01369/704452* ⊕ *www.western-ferries.co.uk*).

### BY BUS

You can travel on buses throughout these regions; however, buses are nowhere near as frequent or reliable as they are on the mainland. Buses are cheaper than traveling by car, but they will take you longer and hinder your flexibility.

Scottish Citylink runs daily bus service from Glasgow's Buchanan Street station to the mid-Argyll region and Kintyre. The trip to Oban takes about 3 hours. The other companies listed below provide local service within the region.

**Information** **B. Mundell Ltd** ( ✉ *Islay* ☎ *01496/840273*). **Bowmans Coaches** ( ✉ *Mull* ☎ *01631/563221* ⊕ *www.bowmanscoaches.co.uk*). **Scottish Citylink** ( ☎ *08705/505050* ⊕ *www.citylink.co.uk*). **Stagecoach Western Buses** ( ✉ *Arran* ☎ *08712/002233* ⊕ *www.stagecoachbus.com/western*). **West Coast Motor Service** ( ✉ *Mid-Argyll and Kintyre* ☎ *01586/552319* ⊕ *www.westcoastmotors.co.uk*).

### BY CAR

Negotiating this area is easy except in July and August, when the roads around Oban may be congested. There are some single-lane roads, especially on the east side of the Kintyre Peninsula and on the islands.

You'll probably have to board a ferry at some point; all ferries take cars as well as pedestrians. The A85 takes you to Oban (just over 2 hours by car from Glasgow), the main ferry terminal for Mull. The A83 rounds Loch Fyne and heads down Kintyre to Kennacraig, the ferry terminal for Islay. Farther down the A83 is Tayinloan, the ferry port for Gigha. You can reach Brodick on Arran by ferry from Ardrossan, on the Clyde coast (A8/A78 from Glasgow), or, in summer, you can travel to Lochranza from Claonaig on the Kintyre Peninsula.

### BY TRAIN

Oban and Ardrossan are the main rail stations; it's a three-hour trip from Glasgow to Oban. For information call First ScotRail. All trains connect with ferries. A narrow-gauge railway takes ferry passengers from the pier head at Craignure (Mull) to Torosay Castle, a distance of about half a mile.

**Information** **First ScotRail** ( ☎ *08456/015929* ⊕ *www.firstgroup.com/scotrail*).

## CONTACTS & RESOURCES

### EMERGENCIES

Dial **999** in case of an emergency to reach an ambulance, coast guard, or the fire or police departments (no coins are needed for emergency calls made from public phone booths). Lorne and Islands District General Hospital has an emergency room.

**Hospital** **Lorne and Islands District General Hospital** ( ✉ *Glengallen Rd., Oban* ☎ *01631/567500*).

### TOURS

BOAT TOURS   Gordon Grant Tours leads an excursion to Mull, Iona, and Staffa and leaves Mull on other trips to Treshnish Isles and Staffa. From Taynuilt, near Oban, boat trips are available from Loch Etive Cruises. Sea Life Surveys offers four- and six-hour whale-watching and wildlife day trips from Tobermory, on the Isle of Mull. Turas Mara runs daily excursions in summer from Oban and Mull to Staffa, Iona, and the Treshnish Isles and specializes in wildlife tours.

Contact **Gordon Grant Tours** ( ✉ *Waterfront, Railway Pier, Oban* ☎ *01631/562842* ⊕ *www.fingals-cave-staffa.co.uk*). **Loch Etive Cruises** ( ✉ *Taynuilt* ☎ *01866/822430*). **Sea Life Surveys** ( ✉ *Torrbreac, Dervaig, Mull* ☎ *01688/400223*). **Turas Mara** ( ✉ *Penmore Mill, Dervaig, Mull* ☎☎ *01688/400242* ⊕ *www.turasmara.com*).

BUS TOURS  *Many of the bus companies listed in By Bus, above, arrange sightseeing tours.* Bowmans Tours runs trips from Oban to Mull, Staffa, and Iona between March and October.

Contact **Bowmans Tours** ( ✉ *Waterfront, Railway Pier Oban* ☎ *01631/563221* ⊕ *www.bowmanstours.co.uk*).

## VISITOR INFORMATION

The tourist offices in Lochgilphead, Tarbert, and Tobermory (Mull) are open April through October only; the rest are open year-round. Visitscottishheartlands.com is a regional Web site.

Information **Argyll** ( ⊕ *www.visitscottishheartlands.com*). **Bowmore, Islay** ( ✉ *The Square* ☎ *01496/810254*). **Brodick, Arran** ( ✉ *The Pier* ☎ *01770/303776*). **Campbeltown** ( ✉ *Mackinnon House, The Pier* ☎ *01586/552056*). **Craignure, Mull** ( ✉ *The Pierhead* ☎ *01680/812377*). **Dunoon** ( ✉ *7 Alexandra Parade* ☎ *01369/703785*). **Inveraray** ( ✉ *Front St.* ☎ *01499/302063*). **Lochgilphead** ( ✉ *Lochnell St.* ☎ *01546/602344*). **Oban** ( ✉ *Argyll Sq.* ☎ *01631/563122*). **Tarbert, Loch Fyne** ( ✉ *Harbour St.* ☎ *08452/255121*). **Tobermory, Mull** ( ✉ *Main St.* ☎ *01688/302182*).

7

# Around the Great Glen

"I think a one-way trip on the Jacobite Steam Train would still be a lot of fun. Our kids enjoyed the trip both ways (and we noticed scenery coming back that we did not see on the way up), but I think they would have gotten a huge kick out of it even if we had only taken a one-way trip. If you are just taking the train from Mallaig to Fort William, sit on the righthand side for the best views of Glenfinnan Viaduct."

—Barbara_in_FL

"There are four trains a day from Fort William to Mallaig in addition to the Jacobite steam train. The scenery is just as beautiful whether you're on the diesel or steam train."

—GeoffHamer

Updated by
Nick Bruno

**THE ANCIENT RIFT VALLEY OF** the Great Glen is a dramatic feature on the map of Scotland, giving the impression that the top half of the country has slid southwest. Geologists confirm that this actually occurred, after matching granite from Strontian, in Morvern, west of Fort William, with the same type of rock found at Foyers, on the east side of Loch Ness, some 65 mi away. The Great Glen, with its sense of openness, lacks the grandeur of Glencoe or the mountains of the Torridons, but the highest mountain in the United Kingdom, Ben Nevis (4,406 feet), looms over its southern portals, and spectacular scenery lies within a short distance of the main glen.

A map of Scotland gives a hint of the grandeur and beauty to be found in this valley: fingers of inland lochs, craggy and steep-sided mountains, rugged promontories, and deep inlets. But no map can convey the area's brilliant purple and emerald moorland, its forests and astonishingly varied wildlife (mountain hares, red deer, golden eagles, ospreys), or the courtesy of its soft-spoken inhabitants and their sense of history.

Though it's the capital of the Highlands, Inverness has the flavor of a Lowland town, its winds blowing in a sea-salt air from the Moray Firth. Inverness is also home to one of the world's most famous monster myths: in 1933, during a quiet news week, the editor of a local paper decided to run a story about a strange sighting of something splashing about in Loch Ness. The story lives on, and the dubious Loch Ness phenomenon continues to keep cameras trained on the deep waters.

Fort William, without a monster on its doorstep, makes do with Ben Nevis and the Road to the Isles, a title sometimes applied to the breathtaking scenic route to Mallaig. This is best seen by rail, since the road to Mallaig is still narrow, winding, and single track in places, and meeting an oncoming bus can be alarming—especially if you're distracted by the view. On the way, road and rail routes pass Loch Morar, the country's deepest body of water, which lays claim to its own monster, Morag. Away from the Great Glen to the north lie the heartlands of Scotland, a bare backbone of remote mountains.

The great hills that loom to the southeast form the border of Strathspey, the broad valley of the fast-flowing River Spey. This area, commonly called Speyside, is known as one of Scotland's main whisky-distilling areas and is traversed by the Malt Whisky Trail.

Impressive castles are also on the agenda in the Great Glen, perhaps one of the best known of which is ruined Urquhart Castle, a favorite haunt of Nessie-watchers because of its location halfway down Loch Ness. To the east are two top-of-the-list castles that are still inhabited: Cawdor Castle, with its happy marriage of different furnishings—modern and ancient, mellow and brightly colored—and Brodie Castle, with its magnificent library and a collection of paintings that extend well into the 20th century.

## TOP REASONS TO GO

**Castles, fortresses, and battlefields:** Hear stories of the Highland people and famous figures like Bonnie Prince Charlie, and absorb the atmosphere of castles and battlefields, at Culloden Moor, Cawdor and Brodie castles, Fort George, and Glencoe.

**Hill walking and outdoor activities:** The Great Glen area is renowned for its hill walking. Some of the best routes are around Glen Nevis, Glencoe, and on Ben Nevis, the highest mountain in Great Britain. It's not just hiking country: Glenmore Lodge in Aviemore offers everything from kayaking to ice climbing.

**Wild landscapes and rare wildlife:** Spot rare plants and beasts including tiny least willow trees and golden eagles in the near-arctic tundra of Cairngorms National Park. You can even get up close to the mightiest of

nonindigenous animals at the Cairngorm Reindeer Centre.

**Whisky Trail:** The two westernmost distilleries on the Malt Whisky Trail are in Forres. Benromach is the smallest distillery in Moray, while Dallas Dhu is preserved as a museum. You can strike out from here to nearby distilleries in Speyside (see Chapter 6).

**Stunning beaches:** The west coast may not have tropical temperatures, but it has untouched white-sand beaches with limpid waters. The coastline between Morar and Arisaig is lined with miles upon miles of them.

**Boat trips:** There are many ferries to the small isles (or to Skye) from Arisaig and Mallaig, or just go watching for sealife. You can also go Nessie-watching on Loch Ness—or just enjoy the views.

## EXPLORING THE GREAT GLEN

The first possible route originates in Fort William and heads west to Mallaig, taking in the unique qualities of the birch-knoll and blue-island West Highland views. The second route centers on Inverness, moving east into Speyside, then west down the Great Glen. There are many romantic and historic associations with this area. It was here that the rash adventurer Prince Charles Edward Stuart (1720–88) arrived for the final Jacobite Rebellion, of 1745–46, and it was from here that he departed after the last battle.

### ABOUT THE RESTAURANTS & HOTELS

Inverness, Fort William, and Aviemore have plenty of hotels, B&Bs, cafés, and restaurants in all price ranges. Fort William has a particularly good seafood restaurant. Outside of the towns, there are many country-house hotels serving superb meals. Because this is an established vacation area, you should have no trouble finding a room for a night; however, the area is quite busy in the peak season.

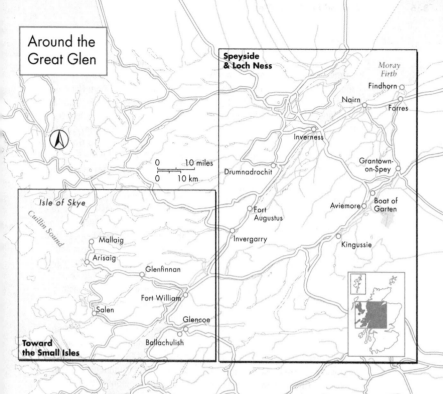

Around the Great Glen

**Speyside & Loch Ness**

Moray Firth

Findhorn
Nairn
Forres
Inverness
Grantown-on-Spey
Drumnadrochit
Fort Augustus
Aviemore
Boat of Garten
Invergarry
Kingussie

Isle of Skye
Cuillin Sound
Mallaig
Arisaig
Glenfinnan
Fort William
Salen
Glencoe
Ballachulish

**Toward the Small Isles**

0    10 miles
0    10 km

| | £ | ££ | £££ | ££££ | £££££ |
|---|---|---|---|---|---|
| **WHAT IT COSTS IN POUNDS** | | | | | |
| RESTAURANTS | Under £10 | £10–£14 | £15–£19 | £20–£25 | over £25 |
| HOTELS | Under £70 | £70–£120 | £121–£160 | £161–£220 | over £220 |

Restaurant prices are for a main course at dinner. Hotel prices are for two people in a standard double room in high season, generally including the 17.5% V.A.T.

**TIMING**

This is a spring and autumn kind of area—summer contends with pesky midges, and winter brings raw chill. However, in summer, if the weather is settled, it can be very pleasant in the far west, perhaps on the Road to the Isles, toward Mallaig. Early spring can be a good time to sample Scottish skiing at Nevis Range or Glencoe—however, declining snowfall means there are fewer opportunities to ski these days.

# SPEYSIDE & LOCH NESS

Because Jacobite tales are interwoven with landmarks throughout this entire area, you should first learn something about this thorny but colorful period of Scottish history in which the Jacobites tried to restore

## GREAT ITINERARIES

The road (A830) from Fort William northwest to Mallaig, though narrow and winding, is one of the classic routes of Scottish touring and is popularly known as the Road to the Isles. Similarly, the Great Glen road (A82), from Fort William northeast to Inverness, is a vital coast-to-coast link.

If you are heading to Mallaig, you'll definitely want to venture over to the Isle of Skye *(see Chapter 9)* or perhaps to the Small Isles. For those with more time, a trip around the Great Glen could be combined with forays north into the Northern Highlands, east toward Aberdeen and the Malt Whisky Trail, southeastward to the Central Highlands, or south to Argyll.

### IF YOU HAVE 2 DAYS

Base yourself at ⊡**Fort William** so that you can take in the spectacular scenery of **Glencoe** and Glen Nevis and also get a glimpse of the western seaboard toward **Mallaig**.

### IF YOU HAVE 4 DAYS

Spend two days each at one of two bases at each end of the Great Glen, say ⊡**Inverness** or ⊡**Nairn**, at the north end, and ⊡**Fort William** or ⊡**Ballachulish** at the south end. On the first day travel to Nairn from Inverness, and from Nairn go eastward to take a quick glance at Findhorn and/or Forres before traveling southward via **Cawdor Castle** and/or **Brodie Castle** to Grantown-on-Spey. Then follow the Spey as far as you like via **Boat of Garten**, with its ospreys in spring and early summer; **Aviemore** and its mountain scenery; and **Kingussie,** where the Highland Folk Museum does a good job of explaining what life was really like before modern domestic and agricultural equipment made things easy. The next day explore **Loch Ness,** traveling down the eastern bank as far as **Fort Augustus** and returning up the western bank via **Drumnadrochit**; if you have time on a long summer evening, divert northward at Drumnadrochit to discover the beautiful glens Affric and Cannich, before returning to Inverness. On the third day travel south to Fort William or Ballachulish, taking in the **Caledonian Canal.** Explore Glencoe. Spend a day doing the trip to **Mallaig** through **Glenfinnan,** or stop in **Arisaig** and take an unforgettable day cruise among the Small Isles.

the exiled Stuarts to the British monarchy. One of the best places to do this is at Culloden, just east of Inverness, where a major battle ended in final, catastrophic defeat for the Jacobites. Inverness itself is not really a town in which to linger, unless you need to do some shopping. Other areas to concentrate on are the inner Moray Firth moving down into Speyside, with its famous distilleries and great salmon fishing, before moving west into the Great Glen. Loch Ness is just one of the attractions hereabouts. In the Great Glen and Speyside, the best sights are often hidden from the main road, an excellent reason to favor peaceful rural byways and to avoid as far as possible the busy A82 (down Loch Ness's western shore), as well as the A96 and A9, which carry much of the eastern traffic in the area.

## INVERNESS

*176 mi north of Glasgow, 109 mi northwest of Aberdeen, 161 mi northwest of Edinburgh.*

Inverness seems designed for the tourist, with its banks, souvenirs, high-quality woolens, and well-equipped visitor center. Compared with other Scottish towns, however, Inverness has less to offer visitors who have a keen interest in Scottish history. Throughout its past, Inverness was burned and ravaged by the restive Highland clans competing for dominance in the region. Thus, a decorative wall panel here and a fragment of tower there are all that remain amid the modern shopping facilities and 19th-century downtown developments. The town does make a convenient base, however, for exploring the northern end of the Great Glen.

One of Inverness's few historic landmarks is the **castle** (the local Sheriff Court), nestled above the river. The current structure is Victorian, built after a former fort was blown up by the Jacobites in the 1745 campaign.

☾ The excellent, although small, **Inverness Museum and Art Gallery** covers archaeology, art, local history, and the natural environment in its lively displays. ✉ *Castle Wynd* ☎ *01463/237114* ⊕ *www.invernessmuseum. com* ☛ *Free* ☾ *Mon.–Sat. 10–5.*

**Inverness Dolphin Cruises** (☎ *01463/717900*) provides trips by boat from Inverness harbor into the Moray Firth, offering you the chance to see dolphins in their breeding area. An unusual option from Inverness is a day trip to Orkney: **John o'Groats Ferries** (☎ *01955/611353*) runs day tours from Inverness to Orkney, daily from May through August.

**8**

### WHERE TO STAY & EAT

££££ ✕⊞**Dunain Park Hotel.** It's not difficult to relax at this atmospheric 18th-century mansion amid 6 acres of wooded gardens. An open fire awaits you in the living room, a good place to sip a drink and browse through books and magazines. Antiques and traditional touches make the bedrooms equally cozy and attractive. The restaurant serves French-influenced Scottish dishes including upscale fish-and-chips: marinated scallops and butternut squash chips. The hotel is 2½ mi southwest of Inverness on A82. **Pros:** Attractive Victorian gardens, lounges full of country-house charm. **Cons:** Quality of service can be inconsistent, not ideal for families with young children. ✉ *A82, Dunain IV3 8JN* ☎ *01463/230512* ⊕ *www.dunainparkhotel.co.uk* ➳ *5 rooms, 6 suites, 2 cottages* ⅋ *In-room: no a/c. In-hotel: restaurant, laundry service, public Internet, no elevator* ⊟ *AE, MC, V* ⋈ *BP.*

££££ ✕⊞**Glenmoriston Town House.** Great food and excellent fishing distin-
★ guish this stylish hotel with exclusive rights to a stretch of the River Nairn. Most of the guest rooms are decorated in unfussy and calming hues, a good choice because they're generally on the small side. However, it's the restaurant (£££££; fixed-price menu), Abstract, that wins the plaudits: chef Gordon Ramsey helped transform it into one of the best in the region. The French-influenced cuisine, including dishes such

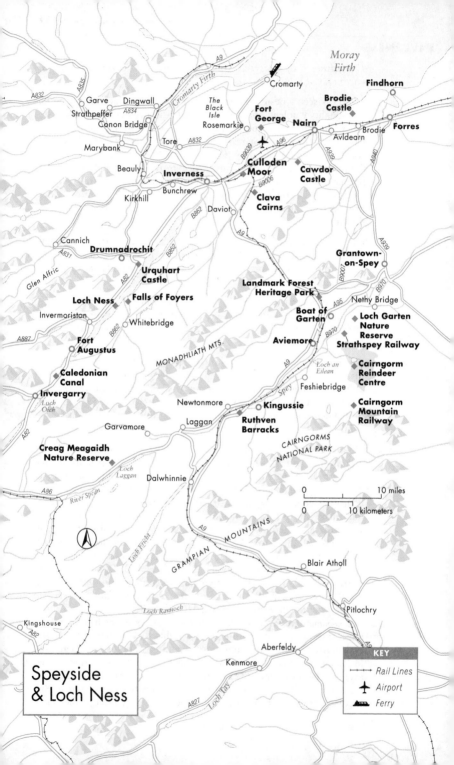

*Moray Firth*

Cromarty

A9

A832
Garve · Dingwall
Strathpeffer · A834
Conon Bridge

A835

*Cromarty Firth*

*The Black Isle*
Rosemarkie

**Brodie Castle**
Findhorn

**Fort George**
Nairn
Brodie
Forres

A96
Avldearn

A832
Tore

A99
A940

Marybank

B9009

Beauly
**Inverness**
Bunchrew
**Culloden Moor**
B9006
**Cawdor Castle**

Kirkhill

B862
Daviot

**Clava Cairns**

Cannich
A831

**Drumnadrochit**

B862

A9

**Grantown-on-Spey**

A939

Glen Affric

**Urquhart Castle**

A82

B9007

A95
**Landmark Forest Heritage Park**

**Loch Ness** · **Falls of Foyers**

Nethy Bridge

Invermoriston

B862
Whitebridge

**Boat of Garten**

A970

**Loch Garten Nature Reserve**
**Strathspey Railway**

A887

**Fort Augustus**

**Aviemore**

*Loch an Eilean*

**Cairngorm Reindeer Centre**

**Caledonian Canal**

MONADHLIATH MTS.

A9

Feshiebridge

*Spey*

**Invergarry**
*Loch Oich*

Newtonmore

**Kingussie**

**Cairngorm Mountain Railway**

A82

Garvamore

Laggan

**Ruthven Barracks**

CAIRNGORMS NATIONAL PARK

**Creag Meagaidh Nature Reserve**
*Loch Laggan*

Dalwhinnie

A86
*River Spean*

0    10 miles
0    10 kilometers

A9

GRAMPIAN MOUNTAINS

Blair Atholl

Kingshouse

*Loch Ericht*

A82

*Loch Rannoch*

Pitlochry

Aberfeldy

Kenmore

A827
*Loch Tay*

## Speyside & Loch Ness

as roasted scallops on a pea puree and sea bream with an oyster-and-citrus tartar, has garnered numerous awards. The bar may be the most sophisticated-looking place in town to sample a malt or two—indeed, there are nearly 200 to choose from and a decent cocktail list to boot. **Pros:** Fabulous restaurant, comfortable beds. **Cons:** Cramped rooms, lacks decent soundproofing. ⊠*Ness Bank, IV2 4SF* ☎*01463/223777* ⊕*www.glenmoristontownhouse.com* ⇨*30 rooms* &*In-room: no a/c, Wi-Fi. In-hotel: restaurant, room service, bar, laundry service* ▤*AE, DC, MC, V* ¶◯*BP.*

£££ 🏠**Glendruidh House Hotel.** This former dower house (a dwelling given to the widow on an estate) 2 mi south of the heart of the city exudes character from its turreted exterior to its circular drawing room warmed by open fires. Guest rooms have antique furnishings and look onto tranquil, mature gardens frequented by birds and badgers. Book in advance to sample fine food featuring local produce in the intimate dining room (for guests only). **Pros:** Quiet location, peaceful gardens. **Cons:** Brief breakfast hours, outside city center. ⊠*Old Edinburgh Rd. S, IV2 6AR* ☎*01463/226499* ⊕*www.cozzee-nessie-bed.co.uk* ⇨*5 rooms* &*In-room: no a/c. In-hotel: bar, public Internet, laundry service, no elevator* ▤*AE, DC, MC, V* ¶◯*BP.*

££ 🏠**Ballifeary House.** The particularly helpful proprietors at this well-
★ maintained bed-and-breakfast, in a pretty 19th-century villa, offer high standards of comfort and service. Common areas are decorated with Victorian-style furnishings, and guest rooms are comfortable, bright, and immaculate. It's a short stroll from your room to several good restaurants in downtown Inverness. **Pros:** Outstanding hosts, neutrally furnished rooms, cozy lounge; fabulous breakfast choice. **Cons:** The 15-minute walk into town might be inconvenient for some, not good for families with younger children. ⊠*10 Ballifeary Rd., IV3 5PJ* ☎*01463/235572* ⊕*www.ballifearyhousehotel.co.uk* ⇨*6 rooms* &*In-room: Wi-Fi (some), DVD, no a/c, no phone. In-hotel: bar, public Wi-Fi, no kids under 15, no elevator* ▤*MC, V* ¶◯*BP.*

££ 🏠**Clach Mhuilinn.** Pleasantly modern, this home 1 mi south of the city
★ center sits amid a lush garden in a residential area. At this long-established B&B, the Culloden Room has calming, neutral hues, and the Tartan Suite has understated tartan touches and its own sitting room. Both have pampering contemporary bathrooms with large showers. The substantial breakfast is served before a view of the pristine lawn and abundant plant life. **Pros:** Immaculately maintained, spacious guest rooms; helpful hosts; part of Green Tourism program. **Cons:** No young children, popularity means you often need to book well in advance. ⊠*7 Harris Rd., IV2 3LS* ☎*01463/237059* ⊕*www.ness.co.uk* ⇨*1 room, 1 suite* &*In-room: refrigerator, no a/c, no phone. In-hotel: bar, public Wi-Fi, no kids under 16, no elevator* ▤*MC, V* ⊗*Closed Nov.–Mar.* ¶◯*BP.*

££ 🏠**Lodge at Daviot Mains.** Built in Highland-lodge style, this B&B is filled with the comforts of home; expect special treats on your arrival. Rooms are decorated in bold colors and have vibrant artwork. The master bedroom has a four-poster canopy bed and bay windows that overlook verdant pastures. The Lodge at Daviot Mains is 5 mi south of Inverness on the A9. **Pros:** Excellent value, surrounding pastureland grazed by cows and sheep, some wheelchair access. **Cons:** Decor a little dated for some tastes. ⊠*A9, Daviot IV2 5ER* ☏*01463/772215* ⊕*www.thelodgeatdaviotmains.co.uk* ⋑*7 rooms* ♿*In-room: no a/c. In-hotel: public Internet* ▭*MC, V* ⓄⒾ*BP.*

££   🏨**Moyness House.** Scottish author Neil M. Gunn (1891–1973), known for short stories and novels that evoke images of the Highlands, such as *Morning Tide, Highland River,* and *Butcher's Broom,* once lived in this lovely Victorian villa. It sits beyond well-trimmed hedges on a quiet residential street, a few minutes' walk from downtown Inverness. Careful decorative touches grace each colorful room. The friendly owners provide excellent service and sound sightseeing advice. **Pros:** Relaxing interiors and garden, great location near the river. **Cons:** Decor a bit flowery and fussy for some, you need to book early as it's popular. ⊠*6 Bruce Gardens, IV3 5EN* ☏*01463/233836* ⊕*www.moyness.co.uk* ⋑*7 rooms* ♿*In-room: Wi-Fi, no a/c. In-hotel: bar, public Wi-Fi, no elevator* ▭*AE, MC, V* ⓄⒾ*BP.*

£   🏨**Atholdene House.** This family-run stone villa dating from 1879
★ extends a warm welcome with a roaring fire, parlor games, and drinks in the common room. Rooms are simply decorated, with a mix of contemporary and antique furnishings. Downtown Inverness is a short walk away. **Pros:** Reasonably priced, child's play area, quality produce at breakfast. **Cons:** Basic guest rooms lack fancy facilities, can get a little noisy due to soundproofing. ⊠*20 Southside Rd., IV2 3BG* ☏*01463/233565* ⊕*www.atholdenehouse.com* ⋑*11 rooms, 2 with shared bath* ♿*In-room: no a/c, no phone. In-hotel: bar, public Internet* ▭*MC, V* ⓄⒾ*BP, CP.*

### NIGHTLIFE & THE ARTS

BARS &   **Blackfriars Pub** (⊠*Academy St.* ☏*01463/233881*) prides itself on its
LOUNGES   cask-conditioned ales. You can enjoy one to the accompaniment of regular live entertainment including jazz nights and *ceilidhs* (a mix of country dancing, music, and song; pronounced *kay*-lees) and poetry readings. The **Gellion's Bar** (⊠*14 Bridge St.* ☏*01463/233648*) claims to be Inverness's oldest pub, dating from 1841. It hosts live music nightly, with ceilidhs on Saturday and the occasional Wednesday from 5 to 8 PM. There's live music at the **Harlequin** (⊠*1 View Pl.* ☏*01463/718178*), which has castle and river views. The kitchen turns out Scottish fare.

CABARET   June through September, **Scottish Showtime** (⊠*Church St.* ☏*01349/830930*), at the Ramada Inverness, presents Scottish cabaret of the tartan-clad-dancer and bagpipe–accordion variety.

THEATER   There's plenty of drama at the **Eden Court Theatre** (⊠*Bishops Rd.*
★   ☏*01463/234234* ⊕*www.eden-court.co.uk*), but the varied program includes movies, music, comedy, ballet, pantomime, and musicals. You can also check out the art gallery and the excellent café.

### GOLF

**Inverness Golf Club,** established in 1883, welcomes visitors to its parkland course 1 mi from downtown. ⊠*Culcabock Rd.* ☏*01463/239882* ⊕*www.invernessgolfclub.co.uk* 🏌*18 holes, 6,256 yds, par 69.*

**Torvean Golf Course** is a municipal course with one of the longest par-5s (565 yards) in the north of Scotland. ✉*Glenurquhart Rd.* ☎*01463/711434* ⊕*www.torveangolfclub.co.uk* ⚹*.18 holes, 5,784 yds, par 68.*

### SHOPPING

Although Inverness has the usual indoor shopping malls and department stores—including Marks and Spencer—the most interesting goods are in the specialty outlets in and around town. Don't miss the atmospheric indoor **Victorian Market** ( ✉*Academy St.*), built in 1870, which houses more than 40 privately owned specialty shops.

BOOKSTORES **Leakey's Secondhand Bookshop** ( ✉*Greyfriars Hall, Church St.* ☎*01463/239947*)
★ claims to be the biggest secondhand bookstore in Scotland. When you get tired of leafing through some of the 100,000 or so titles and maps, climb to the mezzanine café and study the cavernous church interiors.

CLOTHING **Duncan Chisholm and Sons** ( ✉*47–51 Castle St.* ☎*01463/234599*) specializes in Highland dress and tartans. Mail-order and made-to-measure services are available. **James Pringle Ltd.** ( ✉*Dores Rd.* ☎*01463/223311*) stocks a vast selection of cashmere, lambswool, tartans, and tweeds, as well as furniture and Scottish gifts. A profesional weaver gives demonstrations on the loom, and you can have lunch in the on-site coffee shop.

GALLERIES The **Castle Gallery** ( ✉*43 Castle St.* ☎*01463/729512*) displays contemporary painting, sculpture, prints, and crafts by British artists. The
★ **Riverside Gallery** ( ✉*11 Bank St.* ☎*01463/224781*) sells paintings, etchings, and prints of Highland landscapes, as well as abstract and representational contemporary work by Highland artists.

LOCAL **Highland Wineries** ( ✉*Moniack Castle, 7 mi west of Inverness on A862*
SPECIALTIES *toward Beauly, Kirkhill* ☎*01463/831283*) creates wines from Scottish ingredients, such as birch sap, and also makes jams, marmalade, and
★ other preserves. Gourmets should head to the **Pork, Cheese and Pie Shop** ( ✉*36 Eastgate* ☎*01463/237776*) for the pungent and mouthwatering displays of food and drink from Scotland and overseas.

## CULLODEN MOOR

*5 mi east of Inverness via B9006.*

Culloden Moor was the scene of the last major battle fought on British soil—to this day considered one of the most infamous and tragic in all of warfare. Here, on a cold April day in 1746, the outnumbered Jacobite forces of Bonnie Prince Charlie were destroyed by the superior firepower of George II's army. The victorious commander, the duke of Cumberland (George II's son), earned the name of "Butcher" Cumberland for the bloody reprisals carried out by his men on Highland families, Jacobite or not, caught in the vicinity. In the battle itself, the duke's army—greatly outnumbering the Scots—killed more than 1,000 soldiers. The National Trust for Scotland has re-created a slightly eerie

8

CLOSE UP

## Bonnie Prince Charlie

His life became the stuff of legends. Charles Edward Louis John Casimir Silvester Maria Stuart, better known as Bonnie Prince Charlie or the Young Pretender, was born in Rome in 1720. The grandson of ousted King James II of England, Scotland, and Ireland (King James VII of Scotland) and son of James Stuart, the Old Pretender, he was the focus of Jacobite hopes to reclaim the throne of Scotland. Charles was charming and attractive, and he enjoyed more than the occasional drink.

In 1745 Charles led a Scottish uprising to restore his father to the throne. He sailed to the Outer Hebrides with only a few men but with promised support from France. When that support failed to arrive, he sought help from the Jacobite supporters, many from the Highland clans, who were faithful to his family. With 6,000 men behind him, Charles saw victory in Prestonpans and Falkirk, but the tide turned when he lied to his men about additional Jacobite troops waiting south of the border. When these fictitious troops did not materialize, his army retreated to Culloden where, on the April 16, 1746, they were massacred.

Charles escaped to the Isle of Benbecula where he met and fell in love with Flora MacDonald. After James had hidden there for a week, Flora dressed him as her maid and brought him to sympathizers on the Isle of Skye. They helped him escape to France.

Scotland endured harsh reprisals from the government after the rebellion. As for Charles, he spent the rest of his life in drunken exile, taking the title count of Albany. In 1772 he married Princess Louise of Stolberg-Gedern, only to separate from her eight years later. He died a broken man in Rome in 1788.

—by Fiona G. Parrott

version of the battlefield as it looked in 1746. An innovative visitor center enables you to get closer to the sights and sounds of the infamous battle and to interact with the characters involved. Academic research and technology have helped re-create the Gaelic dialect, song, and music of the time. ⊠B9006 ☎01463/790607 ⊕www.nts.org. uk/Culloden ☑£8 ⊙ Visitor center Nov.–Mar., daily 10–4; Apr.–Oct., daily 9–6; last entry half hr before closing.

Not far from Culloden, on a narrow road southeast of the battlefield, are the **Clava Cairns,** dating from the Bronze Age. In a cluster among the trees, these stones and monuments form a large ring with passage graves, which consist of a central chamber below a cairn, reached via a tunnel. Placards explain the graves' significance. ⊠B851.

## NAIRN

*12 mi east of Culloden Moor, 17 mi east of Inverness via B9006/B9091, 92 mi west of Aberdeen.*

Although Nairn has the air of a Lowland town, it's actually part of the Highlands. This once-prosperous fishing village has something of a split personality. King James VI (1566–1625) once boasted of a town so large the residents in either end spoke different languages. This was a reference to Nairn, whose fisherfolk, living by the sea, spoke Lowland Scots, whereas its uptown farmers and crofters spoke Gaelic. Nearby is Nairn Castle, loaded with history.

The fishing boats have moved to larger ports, but Nairn's historic flavor has been preserved at the **Nairn Museum,** in a handsome Georgian building in the center of town. Exhibits emphasize artifacts, photographs, and model boats relating to the town's fishing past. A genealogy service is also offered, and there are occasional craft demonstrations. A library in the same building has a strong local-history section. ⊠ *Viewfield House, Viewfield Dr.* ☎ *01667/456791* ⊕ *www.nairnmuseum.co.uk* 🖃 *£3.50* ⊙ *Apr.–Oct., Mon.–Sat. 10–4:30; Nov., Sat. 10–4:30.*

> **WORD OF MOUTH**
>
> "At Cawdor Castle, as we entered the courtyard and started talking about the drawbridge, a beautiful and elegant woman who had entered in front of us turned and explained how the drawbridge worked. We thanked her and she continued on her way. When we were looking at some photos on display in the castle that we realized that the woman was Lady Cawdor! This was a very interesting house, and many of the room descriptions were very funny."
> –theatrelover

Ⓒ
Fodor'sChoice
★
Shakespeare's (1564–1616) Macbeth was Thane of Cawdor, but the sense of history that exists within the turreted walls of **Cawdor Castle** is more than fictional. Cawdor is a lived-in castle, not an abandoned, decaying structure. The earliest part of the castle is the 14th-century central tower; the rooms contain family portraits, tapestries, fine furniture, and paraphernalia reflecting 600 years of history. Outside the castle walls are sheltered gardens and woodland walks. Children will have a ball exploring the lush and mysterious Big Wood, with its wild flowers and varied wildlife. There are lots of creepy stories and fantastic tales amid the dank dungeons and drawbridges. ■ **TIP→ The Cawdor estate has cottages to rent on the property.** ⊠ *Cawdor* ✛ *Off B9090, 5 mi southwest of Nairn* ☎ *01667/404401* ⊕ *www.cawdorcastle.com* 🖃 *Grounds £4; castle £8* ⊙ *May–mid-Oct., daily 10–5.*

**WHERE TO STAY & EAT**

££££online ✕🍴 **Boath House.** An elegant Regency survivor, this stunning 1820s manor house is surrounded by 20 manicured acres of gardens, lawns, and woodland that you're welcome to explore. The spacious rooms have handsome 19th-century furniture and contemporary Scottish art. An Aveda spa on the lower level provides rest and relaxation. The restaurant's chef uses local produce, seasonal game, and fresh fish and seafood delivered straight off the boat. You can choose to add dinner as part of the room rate. **Pros:** Beautiful grounds include a lake; exceptional dining experience and period atmosphere. **Cons:** The quality of the spa treatments could be improved; some older mattresses; some bathrooms not consistent with the price. ⊠ *Off A96, Auldearn IV12 5TE* ☎ *01667/454896* ⊕ *www.boath-house.com* ➷ *7 rooms, 1* *cottage* ♿*In-room: no a/c. In-hotel: restaurant, spa, public Internet* ⊟*AE, MC, V* ¶⊙∣*BP.*

### GOLF

Nairn's courses are highly regarded by golfers and are very popular, so book far in advance. **Nairn Dunbar Golf Club,** founded in 1899, is a difficult course with gorse-lined fairways and lovely sea views. ⊠*Lochloy Rd.* ☎*01667/452741* ⊕*www.nairndunbar.com* ⚲*18 holes, 6,765 yds, par 72.*

★ **Nairn Golf Club,** founded in 1887, hosted the 1999 Walker Cup on its Championship Course, a traditional Scottish coastal golf links with what are claimed to be the finest greens in Scotland. ⊠*Seabank Rd.* ☎*01667/453208* ⊕*www.nairngolfclub.co.uk* ⚲*18 holes, 6,721 yds, par 79.*

### SHOPPING

At **Auldearn Antiques** ( ⊠*Dalmore Manse, Lethen Rd., Auldearn* ✛*East of Nairn* ☎*01667/453087*) it's easy to spend an hour or more wandering around the old church, filled with furniture, fireplaces, architectural antiques, and linens, and the converted farmsteads, with their tempting antique (or just old) chinaware and textiles. Visit **Brodie Country Fare** ( ⊠*Brodie* ✛*East of Nairn off A96* ☎*01309/641555*) only if you're feeling flush: you may covet the unusual knitwear, quality designer clothing and shoes, gifts, and toys, but they are *not* cheap. The excellent restaurant, on the other hand, is quite inexpensive. **Nairn Antiques** ( ⊠*St. Ninian Pl., near traffic circle* ☎*01667/453303*) carries a wide selection of antique jewelry, silver, and glassware, as well as pottery and prints.

## FORT GEORGE

★ *10 mi west of Nairn.*

As a direct result of the battle at Culloden, the nervous government in London ordered the construction of a large fort on a promontory reaching into the Moray Firth: Fort George was started in 1748 and completed some 20 years later. It's perhaps the best-preserved 18th-century military fortification in Europe. A visitor center and tableaux at the fort portray the 18th-century Scottish soldier's way of life, as does the **Regimental Museum of the Queen's Own Highlanders.** To get here take the B9092 north from A96 west of Nairn. ⊠*Ardersier* ☎*01667/460232* ⊕*www.historic-scotland.gov.uk* 🎫*£6.50* ⊙*Apr.– Sept., daily 9:30–5:30; Oct.–Mar., daily 9:30–4:30; last admission 45 min before closing.*

## FORRES

*10 mi east of Nairn via A96.*

The burgh of Forres is everything a Scottish medieval town should be, with a handsome tolbooth (the former courthouse and prison) as its centerpiece. It's remarkable how well the old buildings have adapted to their modern retail uses. With two distilleries—one still operating, the other preserved as a museum—Forres is a key point on the Malt Whisky Trail; Brodie Castle is also nearby.

At the eastern end of town, don't miss **Sueno's Stone,** a soaring pillar of stone carved with ranks of cavalry, foot soldiers, and dying victims. The stone is said to commemorate a 10th-century victory.

**Benromach Distillery** is the smallest distillery in Moray and was founded in 1898. It's now owned by whisky specialists Gordon and MacPhail, whose shop in Elgin stocks a vast range of malts. The firm's history is outlined in a video, which also explains the production process at Benromach. Tutored nosing and tasting is one of the special features of a tour here. ⊠ *Invererne Rd.* ☎ *01309/675968* ⊕ *www.benromach.com* 🎫 *£3* ☾ *Oct.–Apr., weekdays 10–4; May and Sept., Mon.–Sat. 9:30–5; June–Aug., Mon.–Sat. 9:30, Sun. noon–4.*

**Dallas Dhu Historic Distillery,** the last port of call on the Malt Whisky Trail, was the last distillery built in the 19th century. No longer a working distillery, the entire structure is open to visitors. An audio-visual presentation tells the story of Scotch whisky. ⊠ *Mannachie Rd.* ☎ *01309/676548* 🎫 *£5* ☾ *Apr.–Sept., daily 9:30–6:30; Oct.–Mar., Sat.–Wed. 9:30–4:30.*

At **Brodie Castle,** 2 mi west of Forres, the original medieval castle was rebuilt and extended in the 17th and 19th centuries. Fine examples of late-17th-century plasterwork are preserved in the Dining Room and Blue Sitting Room; an impressive library and a superb collection of pictures extend into the 20th century. Brodie Castle is in the care of the National Trust for Scotland. ⊠ *Off A96, Brodie* ✛ *Between Nairn and Forres* ☎ *0844/493–2156* ⊕ *www.nts.org.uk* 🎫 *Grounds £2; castle £8* ☾ *Grounds daily 10:30–sunset; castle, Apr., July, and Aug., daily 10:30–5; May, June, Sept., and Oct., Sun.–Thurs. 10:30–5.*

## FINDHORN

*6 mi north of Forres via A96 and B9011.*

Findhorn stretches along the edge of the semienclosed Findhorn Bay, which provides excellent bird-watching territory.

At the southern end of the tiny town is the **Findhorn Foundation ecovillage,** a community dedicated to developing "new ways of living infused with spiritual values." Village inhabitants farm and garden to sustain themselves through direct connection with the earth. A visit—check in at Visitor Reception for information—affords a thought-provoking glimpse into the lives of the ultra-independent villagers, homes made out of whisky barrels, and the Universal Hall, made of wood and beautiful engraved glass. The **Phoenix Shop** sells organic foodstuffs and handmade crafts. ⊠ *The Park* ☎ *01309/690311* ⊕ *www.findhorn.org* 🎫 *Free; tour £3* ☾ *Dec.–Feb., weekdays 10–5; Mar., Apr., Oct., and Nov., weekdays 10–5, Sat. 1–4; May–Sept., weekdays 10–5, weekends 1–4.*

## GRANTOWN-ON-SPEY

*24 mi south of Forres via A940 and A939.*

The sturdy settlement of Grantown-on-Spey, set amid tall pines that flank the River Spey, is a classic Scottish planned town. The community was planned and laid out by the local landowner, in this case Sir James Grant, in 1776. It has handsome buildings in silver granite and some good shopping for locally made crafts.

### WHERE TO STAY & EAT

£££   ✕🖥 **The Pines Hotel.** Grantown's elegant and relaxing 19th-century ★   atmosphere is encapsulated at this well-run small hotel within walking distance of the center as well as woodlands. Flower borders and immaculate lawns surround the handsome country house, which is full of interesting antiques, artwork, and curios. After a day's outdoor pursuits, guests can unwind with a malt whisky in the cozy lounges or play genteel parlor games. The rooms have character and comfort, with well-chosen artworks and quality bed linens. The fine restaurant (£££££; fixed-price dinner) serves innovative Scots fare in dishes such as Scottish salmon with pistachio served on a bed of olive oil mashed potatoes with red pepper and corn salsa. **Pros:** gardens with a pond and resident red squirrels, library. **Con:** Meals are quite pricey. ⊠ *Woodside Ave., PH26 3JR* ☎ *01479/872092* ⊕ *www.thepinesgrantown.co.uk* ⟋ *8 rooms* ⚅ *In-room: no a/c. In-hotel: restaurant, no elevator* ⊟ *AE, DC, MC, V* ⊘ *Closed Nov.–Mar.* ⦿ *BP, MAP.*

### SHOPPING

**Ewe and Me** ( ⊠ *82 High St.* ☎ *01479/872911*) is a well-stocked gift shop with silver jewelry, glassware, Highland Stoneware platters and jugs, stuffed toys, and greeting cards. **Speyside Heather Centre** ( ⊠ *Skye of Curr* ☎ *01479/851359*) has 200 to 300 varieties of heather for sale. Of course there's a demonstration about the uses of heather. Should you need sustenance, head to the center's Clootie Dumpling restaurant.

## BOAT OF GARTEN

*11 mi southwest of Grantown via B970.*

In the peaceful village of Boat of Garten, the scent of pine trees mingles with an equally evocative smell—that of steam trains. Other nearby diversions include a theme park for kids and a nature reserve.

☉   Boat of Garten is the terminus of the **Strathspey Steam Railway** ( ☎ *01479/810725* ⊕ *www.strathspeyrailway.co.uk*), and the oily scent of smoke and steam hangs faintly in the air near the authentically preserved train station. From here you can take a 5-mi train trip to Aviemore, a chance to wallow in nostalgia and enjoy superb views of the high and often white domes of the Cairngorm Mountains. Breakfasts, lunches, and special dinners are served on board from March to mid-September.

☉   **Landmark Forest Theme Park** has entertainments such as a Timber Trail with a fire tower you can climb, a steam-powered sawmill, and a

Clydesdale horse that hauls the logs. At the forestry workshop, you can try out crosscut sawing. Kids will want to check out the Wild Forest Maze, terrifyingly steep waterslides, a climbing wall, miniature cars and trucks, and an adventure playground. ■ TIP→ **Plan on spending about three to five hours here.** Reach Carrbridge on the quiet B9153—keep off the A9. ✉ *On B9153, Carrbridge ✛3 mi north of Boat of Garten* ☎ *01479/841613* ⊕ *www.landmark-centre.co.uk* 🎫 *£3.50–£10* ☉ *Apr.–mid-July, daily 10–6; mid-July and Aug., daily 10–7; Sept.–Mar., daily 10–5; last admission 1 hr before closing.*

The **Loch Garten Nature Reserve** achieved fame when the osprey, a large bird that was facing extinction in the early part of the 20th century, returned to breed here. Instead of cordoning off the nest site, conservation officials encouraged visitors by constructing a blind for bird-watching. Now thousands of people visit annually to glimpse the domestic arrangements of this fish-eating bird, which has since bred in many other parts of the Highlands. The sanctuary, which is about 1 mi east of Boat of Garten via the B970, is administered by the Royal Society for the Protection of Birds. ☎ *01479/831476* ⊕ *www.rspb.org.uk* 🎫 *£3.50* ☉ *Osprey observation post late Apr.–mid-Aug., daily 10–6; other areas of reserve year-round, daily 24 hrs.*

## AVIEMORE

*6 mi southwest of Boat of Garten via B970, 30 mi south of Inverness.*

Once a quiet junction on the Highland Railway, Aviemore now has all the brashness and concrete boxiness of a year-round holiday resort; the A9 is the main road from Inverness. It's near some lovely country, though. The Aviemore area is a versatile walking base, but you must be dressed properly and carry emergency safety gear for high-level excursions onto the near-arctic plateau.

★ For skiing and rugged hiking follow the B970 south to **Cairngorms National Park.** Past Loch Morlich at the high parking lots on the exposed shoulders of the Cairngorm Mountains are dozens of trails for hiking and cycling. The park is especially popular with birding enthusiasts, as it's the best place to see the Scottish Crossbill, the only bird unique to Britain. Cairngorm became Scotland's second national park in March 2003. ✉ *Aviemore* ☎ *01479/873535* ⊕ *www.cairngorms.co.uk.*

The **CairnGorm Mountain Railway,** a funicular railway to the top of Cairn Gorm (the mountain that gives its name to the Cairngorms) at this ski area, operates both during and after the ski season and affords extensive views of the broad valley of the Spey. At the top is a visitor center and restaurant. ■ TIP→ **Be forewarned: it can get very cold above 3,000 feet, and weather conditions can change rapidly, even in the middle of summer.** Prebooking is recommended. ✉ *Off B9152* ☎ *01479/861336* ⊕ *www.cairngormmountain.com* 🎫 *£8.95* ☉ *Daily 10–4:30.*

On the high slopes of the Cairngorms, you may see the reindeer herd ☾ that was introduced here in the 1950s. Inquire at the **Cairngorm Reindeer**

## CLOSE UP

# Cairngorms National Park

Britain's newest national park is also its largest, covering nearly 1,400 square mi of countryside. At its heart is a wild arctic landscape that sits on a granite plateau. Five of Scotland's 9 4,000-feet-high mountains are found in this range, and there are 13 more over 3,000 feet. These rounded mountains, including Cairn Gorm (meaning "blue hill" in Gaelic) and Ben Macdui, the second highest in Britain at 4, 295 feet, were formed at the end of the last Ice Age. The Larig Ghru pass, a stunning U-shaped glen, was formed by the retreating glacier.

Hikers underestimate this landscape at your peril: the fierce conditions often found on the Cairngorms plateau have claimed many lives. If you venture out into it, make sure you are well-prepared and have informed someone of your planned route and estimated return time.

The environment supports rare arctic-alpine and tundra plant and animal species (a quarter of Britain's threatened species) including flora such as the least willow and alpine blue-sow thistle, and birds such as the ptarmigan, Scottish crossbill and dotterel. Lower down the slopes, terrain that was once filled with woodland is now characterized by heather, cotton grass, and sphagnum moss. This open expanse allows visitors to glimpse wild animals such as the golden eagle, roe deer, or red deer.

Fragments of the ancient Caledonian forest (largely Scots pine, birch, and rowan) remain and are home to pine martins, red squirrels, and capercaillie (a large grouse). Studding these forests are dramatic glens and the rivers Spey, Don, and Dee, which are home to Atlantic salmon, otters, and freshwater pearl mussels.

**Centre,** 6 mi east of Aviemore by Loch Morlich, about accompanying the herders on their daily rounds. Daily visits depart at 11, with additional departures in summer. The reindeer are docile creatures and seem to enjoy human company. Be sure to wear waterproof gear, as conditions can be wet and muddy. ⊠ *Off B970, Loch Morlich, Glen More Forest Park* ☎ *01479/861228* ⊕ *www.reindeer-company.demon.co.uk* ⊑ *£8* ⊙ *Feb.–Dec., daily 10–5.*

The place that best sums up Speyside's piney ambience is probably a
★ nature reserve called **Loch an Eilean** (signs guide you there from Aviemore). On the **Rothiemurchus Estate** ( ⊠ *B970* ☎ *01479/810858* ⊕ *www. rothiemurchus.net*), a converted cottage beside Loch an Eilean serves as a visitor center. The estate also offers several diversions, including stalking, fly-fishing for salmon and trout, guided walks, safari tours, dog sledding, off-road driving, clay-pigeon shooting, and farm-shop tastings of estate-produced beef, venison, and trout.

### SPORTS & THE OUTDOORS

★ Scotland's National Outdoor Training Centre, **Glenmore Lodge** ( ⊠ *Off B970* ☎ *01479/861256*), 6 mi east of Aviemore in Cairngorms National Park, is your best bet for trying a new activity or enhancing your outdoor skills. Take your pick from the impressive courses (many are multiday) on rock and ice climbing, hiking, kayaking, open boating, ski touring, mountain biking, and more. Some classes are for kids over 14.

There's basic accommodation and equipment rental at the center, along with superb facilities such as an indoor climbing wall.

## KINGUSSIE

*13 mi southwest of Aviemore, via A9 and A86.*

The village of Kingussie (pronounced Kin-*yoo*-see) is of interest primarily for its **Highland Folk Museum.** The interior exhibits are in what was an 18th-century shooting lodge, its paneled and varnished ambience still apparent. Displays include 18th-century furniture, clothing, and implements. Outside, Highland buildings have been reconstructed, among them a smokehouse, blackhouse (dwelling typical of the Western Isles), and the Norse-type Clackmill. The museum also maintains a "living museum" with a Victorian-era schoolhouse and tailors, clockmakers, and joiners demonstrating their trades in nearby Newtownmore. ✉*Duke St.* ☎*01540/661307* ⊕*www.highlandfolk.com* ✉*Highland Folk Museum £3; Newtonmore Museum £5* ☉*Highland Folk Museum, Apr.–Aug., Mon.–Sat. 10–5; Sept. and Oct., weekdays 10–4; Nov.–Mar., by appointment only. Newtonmore Museum, Apr.–Aug., daily 10:30–5:30; Sept., daily 11–4:30; Oct., weekdays 11–4:30.*

**Ruthven Barracks,** which from a distance looks like a ruined castle on a mound, is redolent with tales of the '45 (as the last Jacobite Rebellion is often called). The defeated Jacobite forces rallied here after the battle at Culloden, but then abandoned and blew up the government outpost they had earlier captured. You'll see its crumbling yet imposing stone outline as you approach Kingussie. ✉*B970, ½ mi south of Kingussie* ☎*01667/460232* ⊕*www.historic-scotland.gov.uk* ✉*Free* ☉*Daily 24 hrs.*

### WHERE TO STAY & EAT

££££
★ ✕🏠 **The Cross.** Meals are superb and the wine list extensive at this noted "restaurant with rooms" on 4 acres of grounds. The fixed-price dinner (£41), which could include Scrabster sea bass, local venison, or Scotch beef, draws foodies from near and far, but you can dine here even if you're not an overnight guest. Bedrooms—many with queen-size or king-size mattresses—are individually decorated and may have a balcony, canopy bed, or antique dressing table. The former tweed-mill building retains many interesting features and sits next to a babbling burn. **Pros:** Oustanding food, CD cubes in each room with contemporary Scottish artists, have champagne on the terrace or a whisky in the cozy lounge. **Cons:** No children under 10 in the dining room, rooms are not quite up to the standard of the restaurant. ✉*Tweed Mill Brae, Ardbroilach Rd., PH21 1LB* ☎*01540/661166* ⊕*www.thecross.co.uk* 🛏*8 rooms* ⚫*In-room: no a/c. In-hotel: restaurant, no elevator* ▭*AE, MC, V* ☉*Closed Jan. No dinner Sun. and Mon.* ❑*BP, MAP.*

£ 🏠**Osprey Hotel.** The basic rooms at this characterful stone house are filled with eclectic and well-worn furniture. Woodlands surround the hotel, which is adjacent to a nature reserve and overlooks flower-filled memorial gardens. This is not the plushest of hotels inside, but it's certainly a good-value base for outdoorsy types. Some decent restaurants are nearby, and the owners arrange meals on request. **Pros:** Great budget value, good for pet owners. **Cons:** Bedrooms are very simple, lack of good soundproofing. ⊠*Ruthven Rd., Inverness-shire PH21 1EN* 🕿*01540/661510* ⊕*www.ospreyhotel.co.uk* 🛏*8 rooms* ⚙*In-room: no a/c, no phone, Ethernet. In-hotel: bar, some pets allowed, no elevator* ▭*MC, V.*

**EN ROUTE**   A stretch of the **A86,** quite narrow in some places, hugs the western shore of Loch Laggan. It has superb views of the mountainous heartlands to the north, and, over the silvery spine of hills known as the Grey Corries, culminates with views of Ben Nevis to the south. Halfway along the loch is the Creag Meagaidh Nature Reserve, a sublime picnic spot and a good base for walks into the restored woodland below the spectacular ice-carved crags of Coire Ardair.

## INVERGARRY & THE CALEDONIAN CANAL

*40 mi west of Kingussie.*

Traveling north up the Great Glen takes you parallel to Loch Lochy (on the eastern shore) and over the Caledonian Canal at Laggan Locks, north of Invergarry. From this beautiful spot, which offers stunning vistas of lochs, mountains, and glens in all directions, you can look back on the impressive profile of Ben Nevis. The canal, which links the lochs of the Great Glen—Loch Lochy, Loch Oich, and Loch Ness—owes its origins to a combination of military as well as political pressures that emerged at the time of the Napoleonic Wars with France: for the most part, the British needed a better and faster way to get naval vessels from one side of Scotland to the other. The great Scottish engineer Thomas Telford (1757–1834) surveyed the route in 1803. The canal, which took 19 years to complete, has 29 locks and 42 gates. Telford ingeniously took advantage of the three lochs that lie in the Great Glen, which have a combined length of 45 mi, so that only 22 mi of canal had to be constructed to connect the lochs and complete the waterway from coast to coast.

### WHERE TO STAY & EAT

££  ✕▦ **Glengarry Castle Hotel.** This rambling Victorian baronial mansion, ★  tucked away in Invergarry, makes a good base for touring the area; the village is just south of Loch Ness and within easy reach of the Great Glen's most popular sights. The alluringly old-fashioned rooms have traditional Victorian decor; some more expensive rooms have superb views over Loch Oich. The restaurant (£28 for four courses) serves classic Scottish fare with a contemporary twist, such as fillet of Angus beef with whisky and tarragon sauce or oak-smoked salmon parcels filled with chive-scented scrambled eggs. The grounds include the ruins of Invergarry Castle, a seat of the MacDonnell clan. The hotel entrance is south of the A82–A87 road junction. **Pros:** Atmospheric building and gardens, good-value takeout lunches, family rooms available. **Cons:** showers not always piping hot, not good for people using wheelchairs as there is no elevator or ground-floor guest rooms. ⊠*Off A82, Inver-*

*garry PH35 4HW* ☎*01809/501254* ⊕*www.glengarry.net* ⇆*26 rooms* ⌂*In-room: no a/c. In-hotel: restaurant, water sports, tennis court, no elevator, public Wi-Fi* ▤*MC, V* ⊗*Closed Nov.–Mar.* ⟡*BP.*

## FORT AUGUSTUS & LOCH NESS

*7 mi north of Invergarry.*

The best place to see the locks of the Caledonian Canal in action is at **Fort Augustus,** at the southern tip of Loch Ness. In the village center considerable canal activity takes place at a series of locks that rise from Loch Ness. Fort Augustus itself was captured by the Jacobite clans during the 1745 Rebellion. Later the fort was rebuilt as a Benedictine abbey, but the monks no longer live here. The **Caledonian Canal Heritage Centre** (✉*Ardchattan House, Canalside* ☎*01320/366493*), in a converted lockkeeper's cottage, gives the history of the canal and its uses over the years.

The **Clansman Centre** (✉*Canalside* ☎*01320/366444* ⊕*www.scottish-swords.com*) in Fort Augustus, in a handsome Victorian canalside building, re-creates the atmosphere of a 17th-century turf house and has exhibits and a show that allows visitors to learn about the harsh way of life and hear some stirring tales. The gift shop sells Celtic jewelery, traditional Highland garb, and ceremonial armor.

From the B862, just east of Fort Augustus, you can get your first good long view of the formidable and famous **Loch Ness,** which has a greater volume of water than any other Scottish loch, a maximum depth of more than 800 feet, and its own monster—at least according to popular myth. Early travelers who passed this way included English lexicographer Dr. Samuel Johnson (1709–84) and his guide and biographer, James Boswell (1740–95), who were on their way to the Hebrides in 1783. They remarked at the time about the poor condition of the population and the squalor of their homes. Another early travel writer and naturalist, Thomas Pennant (1726–98), noted that the loch kept the locality frost-free in winter. Even General Wade came here, his troops blasting and digging a road up much of the eastern shore. None of these observant early travelers ever made mention of a monster. Clearly, they had not read the local guidebooks.

**Jacobite Cruises** (☎*01463/233999* ⊕*www.jacobite.co.uk*) runs morning and afternoon cruises on Loch Ness to Urquhart Castle as well as various boat and coach excursions throughout the region. The starting point is in Clansman Harbour, 8 mi south of Inverness and 5 mi northeast of Drumnadochit on A82.

**EN ROUTE** A more leisurely alternative to the fast-moving traffic on the busy A82 to Inverness, and one that combines monster-watching with peaceful road touring, is to take the B862 from Fort Augustus and follow the east bank of Loch Ness; join the B852 just beyond Whitebridge and take the opportunity to view the waterfalls at Foyers. The B862 runs around the end of Loch Ness, then climbs into moorland and forestry plantation. The half-hidden track beside the road is a remnant of the military road built by General Wade. Loch Ness quickly drops out of sight but is soon replaced by the peaceful, reedy Loch Tarff.

## DRUMNADROCHIT

*21 mi north of Fort Augustus via A82.*

If you're in search of the infamous beast Nessie, head to Drumnadrochit and the **Loch Ness Exhibition Centre,** which explores the facts and the fakes, the photographs, the unexplained sonar contacts, and the sincere testimony of eyewitnesses. You can take a cruise of the loch from the center, too. You'll have to make up your own mind on Nessie. All that's really known is that Loch Ness's huge volume of water has a warming effect on the local weather, making the lake conducive to mirages in still, warm conditions. These are often the circumstances in which the "monster" appears. Whether or not the *bestia aquatilis* lurks in the depths—more than ever in doubt since 1994, when the man who took one of the most convincing photos of Nessie confessed on his deathbed that it was a fake—plenty of camera-toting, sonar-wielding, and submarine-traveling scientists and curiosity seekers haunt the lake. ⊠*Off A82* ☎*01456/450573* ⊕*www.loch-ness-scotland.com* 🎫*£5.95* ⊘*Easter–May, daily 9:30–5; June and Sept., daily 9–6; July and Aug., daily 9–8; Oct., daily 9:30–5:30; Nov.–Easter, daily 10–3:30; last admission half hr before closing.*

**Urquhart Castle,** 2 mi southeast of Drumnadrochit, is a favorite Loch Ness monster–watching spot. This weary fortress stands on a promontory overlooking the loch, as it has since the Middle Ages. Because of its central and strategic position in the Great Glen line of communication, the castle has a complex history involving military offense and defense, as well as its own destruction and renovation. The castle was begun in the 13th century and was destroyed before the end of the 17th century to prevent its use by the Jacobites. The ruins of what was one of the largest castles in Scotland were then plundered for building material. A visitor center relates these events and gives an idea of what life was like here in medieval times. ⊠*On A82* ☎*01456/450551* ⊕*www.historic-scotland.gov.uk* 🎫*£6.50* ⊘*Apr.–Oct., daily 9:30–6; Nov.–Mar., daily 9:30–5; last admission 45 min before closing.*

### WHERE TO STAY & EAT

£££–££££    ✕🏨 **Polmaily House.** This country-house hotel amid 18 acres of lovely parkland sits on the northern edge of Loch Ness. Books, log fires, and a helpful staff contribute to an atmosphere that can be warmer than that found at grander, more expensive hotels. Families are sincerely welcomed, and there are plenty of activities for youngsters. Some guest rooms could use refurbishing, and there may be maintenance issues. The restaurant (£35 fixed-price menu) serves traditional British cuisine using fresh Highland produce. **Pros:** Friendly staff, area has lots of outdoor activities. **Con:** Hotel may be understaffed at times. ⊠*A831, 1½ mi northwest of Urquhart Castle, IV63 6XT* ☎*01456/450343* ⊕*www.polmaily.co.uk* 🛏*12 rooms, 2 suites* ⚙*In-room: no a/c. In-hotel: restaurant, bar, pool, no elevator* ═*MC, V* ❙⊙❙*BP, MAP.*

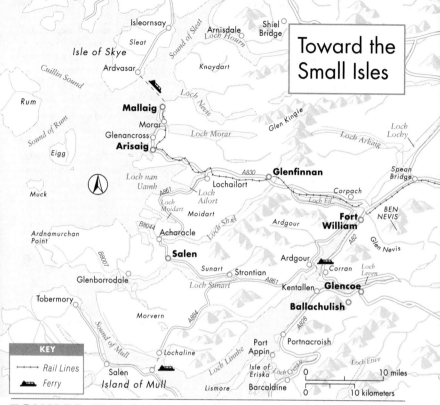

Toward the
Small Isles

## TOWARD THE SMALL ISLES

Fort William has enough points of interest—a museum, exhibits, and shopping—to compensate for its less-than-picturesque setting. The town's primary purpose is to serve the west Highland hinterland; its role as a tourist stop is secondary. Because this is a relatively wet part of Scotland and because Fort William itself can always be explored if it rains, head west on A830 toward the coast if the weather looks clear: on a sunny day the Small Isles—Rum, Eigg, Canna, and Muck—look as blue as the sea and sky together. From here you can also visit Skye via the ferry at Mallaig, or take a day cruise from Arisaig to the Small Isles for a glimpse of traffic-free island life. South of Fort William, scenic Ballachulish and Glencoe are within easy striking distance.

## GLENCOE

★ *92 mi north of Glasgow, 44 mi northwest of Edinburgh.*

Glencoe is both a small town and a region of awesome beauty, with high peaks and secluded glens. The area, where wild, craggy buttresses loom darkly over the road, has a special place in the folk memory of Scotland: the glen was the site of an infamous massacre in 1692, still remembered in the Highlands for the treachery with which soldiers of the Campbell clan, acting as a government militia, treated their hosts, the MacDonalds. According to Highland code, in his own home a clansman should give shelter even to his sworn enemy. In the face of bitter weather, the Campbells were accepted as guests by the MacDonalds. Apparently acting on orders from the British government, the Campbells turned on their hosts, committing murder "under trust."

The National Trust for Scotland's **Visitor Center** at Glencoe (at the west end of the glen, 1 mi east of Glencoe village) tells the story of the MacDonald massacre and has an excellent display on mountaineering. You can also get advice about walking. ⌧*A82* ☎*01855/811307* ⊕*www.glencoe-nts. org.uk* 🎫*£5 for exhibition* ⊙*Jan., Feb., and Nov.–mid-Dec., Thurs.–Sun. 10–4; Mar., and mid-Dec.–early Jan., daily 10–4; Apr.–Aug., daily 9:30– 5:30; Sept.and Oct., daily 10–5.*

### SKIING

The **Glencoe Ski Centre** ( ⌧*Kingshouse, Glencoe* ☎*01855/851226* ⊕*www.glencoemountain.com*), at the east end of the glen, has challenging black runs, well-maintained beginner and intermediate runs on the lower plateau, and snowboarding facilities.

## BALLACHULISH

*1 mi west of Glencoe, 15 mi south of Fort William, 39 mi north of Oban.*

Ballachulish, once a slate-quarrying community, serves as a gateway to the western approaches to Glencoe (though there's a Glencoe village as well).

### WHERE TO STAY & EAT

££££££   ✕🏠 **Airds Hotel.** This charming former ferry inn, dating to the 17th
★    century, has a great restaurant and some of the finest views in all of Scotland. Set in a peaceful village midway between Ballachulish and Oban, the long white building, backed by trees, has a congenial air. Quilted bedspreads, cozy lounges, and family mementos make you feel at home. The staff is happy to arrange fishing trips. The restaurant (£50 fixed-price menu; note that dinner is included for guests) serves excellent Scottish cuisine, including venison and grouse. **Pros:** Fabulous views from breakfast room, nice touches like spare Wellingtons (boots) for the unprepared. **Cons:** You pay a pretty penny. ⌧*Off A828, Port Appin PA38 4DF* ☎*01631/730236* ⊕*www.airds-hotel.com* 📞*11 rooms, 1 suite, 1 cottage* ⚐*In-room: no a/c, DVD. In-hotel: restaurant, bar, bicycles, public Internet, no elevator* ☰*MC, V* ⍟❘*MAP.*

££££   ✕🏠 **Ballachulish House and Golf Course.** In a building from 1640, this inti-
★    mate, lovely, country-house hotel with a library and garden lies near the shore of Loch Linnhe, in the shadows of Glencoe. The Georgian-style bedrooms have luxurious Egyptian linens; some have four-poster beds. The pretty, challenging golf course that surrounds the hotel has fine greens and majestic mountain scenery, but the restaurant (£45 fixed-price menu) is what makes the hotel outstanding. Allan Donald, one of the country's best chefs, is known for sophisticated Scottish fare,

including braised Perthshire beef and seared fillet of sea bass. **Pros:** Beautiful grounds, cozy library and lounge. **Cons:** Regimented dining times, not suitable for families with younger children. ✉*Ballachulish PH49 4JX* ☎*01855/811266* ⊕*www.ballachulishhouse.com* ⏍*8 rooms* ⚲*In-room: no TV. In-hotel: restaurant, bar, golf course, no kids under 10, no elevator* ⊟*AE, MC, V* ❍❘*BP.*

## FORT WILLIAM

*15 mi north of Ballachulish, 69 mi southwest of Inverness, 108 mi northwest of Glasgow, 138 mi northwest of Edinburgh.*

As its name suggests, Fort William originated as a military outpost, first established by Oliver Cromwell's General Monk in 1655 and refortified by George I (1660–1727) in 1715 to help combat an uprising by the turbulent Jacobite clans. It remains the southern gateway to the Great Glen and the far west, and it's a busy, tourist-oriented place.

The **West Highland Museum,** in the town center, explores the history of Prince Charles Edward Stuart and the 1745 Rebellion. Included in the museum's folk exhibits are a costume and tartan display and a famous collection of Jacobite relics. ✉*Cameron Sq.* ☎*01397/702169* ⊕*www.westhighlandmuseum.org. uk* ⏍*£3* ⊙*June and Sept., Mon.–Sat. 10–5; July and Aug., Mon.–Sat. 10–5, Sun. 2–5; Oct.–May, Mon.–Sat. 10–4.*

Great Britain's highest mountain, the 4,406-foot **Ben Nevis,** looms over Fort William less than 4 mi from Loch Linnhe, an inlet of the sea. A trek to its summit is a rewarding experience, but you should be fit and well prepared—food and water, map and compass, first-aid kit, whistle, hat, gloves, and warm clothing (yes, even in summer) for starters—as the unpredictable weather can make it a hazardous hike. Ask for advice at the local tourist office before you begin.

The most relaxing way to take in the landscape of birch- and bracken-covered wild slopes is by rail. The best ride is on the **Jacobite Steam Train** (☎*01524/737751* ⊕*www.westcoastrailway.co.uk*), a famously scenic 84-mi round-trip that runs between Fort William and Mallaig from mid-May through mid-October; cost is £29. You'll see mountains, lochs, beaches, and islands along the way.

**First Scotrail** (☎*08457/484950* ⊕*www.firstgroup.com/scotrail/*) operates a diesel train on the line between Fort William and Mallaig.

A huge collection of gemstones, crystals, and fossils, including a 26-pound uncut emerald, are displayed at **Treasures of the Earth,** in a converted church near Fort William. ✉*A830, Corpach* ☎*01397/772283* ⏍*£3.95* ⊙*July–Sept., daily 9:30–7; Oct.–Dec. and Feb.–June, daily 10–5.*

### WHERE TO STAY & EAT

££ ✕**Crannog Seafood Restaurant.** With its reputation for quality and sim-
★ plicity, this restaurant on the town pier has single-handedly transformed the local dining scene. The sight of a fishing boat drawing up on the

shores of Loch Linnhe to take its catch straight to the kitchen says it all about the freshness of the fish. The chef's capable touch ensures the fresh flavors are not overwhelmed. From the window seats you can watch the sun setting on the far side of the loch. ⊠*The Waterfront at the Underwater Centre* ☎*01397/705589* ▤*MC, V.*

££££ ✕⌂**Inverlochy Castle Hotel.** A red-granite Victorian mansion, Inverlochy Castle stands on 50 acres of woodlands in the shadow of Ben Nevis, with striking Highland landscape visible on every side. Dating from 1863, the hotel retains all the splendor of its period, with a fine fresco ceiling, crystal chandeliers, and a handsome staircase in the Great Hall. The bedrooms, traditional in style, are plush and comfortable. An excellent restaurant serves local specialties including Isle of Skye crab and venison. **Pros:** Relaxing public rooms have sublime views, snooker (a kind of pool) room, flexible kitchen will cater for children. **Cons:** Not for those who must have modern decor, bathrooms do not have the wow factor. ⊠*Torlundy PH33 6SN* ✛*3 mi northeast of Fort William on A82* ☎*01397/702177* ⊕*www.inverlochycastlehotel.com* ⇗*14 rooms, 3 suites* ♿*In-room: no a/c, Wi-Fi. In-hotel: restaurant, tennis court, no elevator* ▤*AE, MC, V* ⊗*Closed Jan. and Feb.* ⦿*BP.*

££–£££ ⌂**Crolinnhe.** An elegant Victorian house with colorful gardens, this exceptionally comfortable B&B overlooks Loch Linnhe yet is only a 10-minute walk from town. Antique and reproduction furniture in the rooms is set off by pastel walls and boldly colored drapes. Ask for the Superior Room, which has its own hot tub. The cooked-to-order breakfasts are first-rate. **Pros:** Stunning loch views; helpful host. **Cons:** Furnishings may be a bit fussy for some. ⊠*Grange Rd., PH33 6JF* ☎*01397/702709* ⊕*www.crolinnhe.co.uk* ⇗*3 rooms* ♿*In-room: no a/c, no phone. In-hotel: bar, public Internet, no elevator* ▤*MC, V* ⊗*Closed Nov.–Easter* ⦿*BP.*

££ ⌂**The Grange.** A delightful, white-frosted confection of a Victorian villa
**Fodor's**Choice stands in pretty gardens a 10-minute walk from downtown. Interest-
★ ing antiques in each room, fresh flowers, log fires, and views of Loch Linnhe make this B&B quite special. The owners delight in giving sight-seeing advice, and the bountiful breakfasts are first-rate. **Pros:** Lots of little extras and great attention to detail, elegant lounge with plenty of books. **Con:** Not suitable for families with younger children. ⊠*Grange Rd., Fort William PH33 6JF* ☎*01397/705516* ⊕*www.thegrange-scotland.co.uk* ⇗*4 rooms* ♿*In-room: no a/c, no phone. In-hotel: bar, no elevator, no kids under 12* ▤*MC, V* ⊗*Closed Oct.–Mar.* ⦿*BP.*

## SPORTS & THE OUTDOORS

BICYCLING For a thrilling ride down Ben Nevis, take the gondola up to the beginning of the **Nevis Range Mountain Bike Track** ( ⊠*Off A82* ☎*01397/705825*) and then shoot off on a 2,000-foot descent. The track, host of the 2007 Mountain Bike World Championships, is 7 mi north of Fort William. It's open May to September, weather permitting; an adult multitrip pass costs £20. Rent mountain and road bikes from **Off Beat Bikes** ( ⊠*117 High St.* ☎*01397/704008*).

GOLF  The **Fort William Golf Course** has spectacular views of Ben Nevis and
★  welcomes visitors. ⊠*Torlundy, Fort William* ☎*01397/704464* 🏌*18
holes, 6,217 yds, par 70.*

HIKING  This area—especially around Glen Nevis, Glencoe, and Ben Nevis—is
popular with hikers; however, routes are not well-marked, so contact
the Fort William tourist information center before you go. The center
will provide you with route advice based on your interests, level of fitness, and hiking experience. **Ben Nevis** is a large and dangerous mountain, where snow can fall on the summit plateau any time of the year.
Several excellent guides are available locally; they should be consulted
for high-altitude routes.

For a walk in **Glen Nevis,** drive north from Fort William on the A82
toward Fort Augustus. On the outskirts of town, just before the bridge
over the River Nevis, turn right up the unclassified road signposted
Glen Nevis. Drive about 6 mi, past a youth hostel, a campground, and
a few houses, and cross the River Nevis over the bridge at Achriabhach
(Lower Falls). Notice the southern flanks of Ben Nevis rising steeply
to the east and the Mamores mountains to the west. Park at a parking lot about 2½ mi from the bridge. Starting here, a footpath leads to
waterfalls and a steel-cabled bridge (1 mi), and then to Steall, a ruined
croft beside a boulder-strewn stream (a good picnic place). You can
continue up the glen for some distance without danger of becoming
lost, so long as you stay on the path and keep the river to your right.
Watch your step going through the tree-lined gorge. The return route
is back the way you came.

SKIING  **Nevis Range** (☎*01397/705825*), a modern development on the flanks of
Aonach Mor, 7 mi north of Fort William, has good and varied skiing,
as well as views of Ben Nevis. There's a gondola system and runs for
all skill levels. Skiing gets under way, adequate snowfall permitting, at
the end of December. The season normally continues until early April.
Daily ski passes are £24.

### SHOPPING

★  The majority of shops here are along High Street, which in summer
attracts bustling crowds intent on stocking up for excursions to the west.
The **Granite House** ( ⊠*74 High St.* ☎*01397/703651*) stocks contemporary jewelry, china, and crystal, regional crafts and clothing, music and
musical instruments, and toys and collectibles. **Nevisport** ( ⊠*High St.*
☎*01397/704921*) has been selling outdoor supplies, maps, and travel
books for more than 30 years from its flagship store. The **Scottish Crafts
and Whisky Centre** ( ⊠*135–139 High St.* ☎*01397/704406*) has lots of
crafts and souvenirs, as well as homemade chocolates and a vast range
of malt whiskies, including miniatures and limited-edition bottlings.
**Treasures of the Earth** ( ⊠*Corpach* ☎*01397/772283*) stocks an Aladdin's
cave assortment of gemstone jewelry, crystal ornaments, mineral specimens, polished stones, fossils, and books on related subjects. The shop
is closed in January.

8

## ACHARACLE

*3 mi north of Salen.*

On the way north to Acharacle (pronounced ach-*ar*-ra-kle with a Scots *ch*), you'll pass through deep-green plantations and moorland lily ponds. This spread-out settlement, backed by the hills of Moidart, lies at the shallow and reedy west end of **Loch Shiel**; the north end is more dramatic and sits deep within the rugged hills.

## GLENFINNAN

*10 mi west of Fort William, 26 mi southeast of Mallaig.*

Perhaps the most visitor-oriented stop on the route between Arisaig or Mallaig and Fort William, Glenfinnan has much to offer if you're interested in Scottish history. Here the National Trust for Scotland has capitalized on the romance surrounding the story of the Jacobites and their intention of returning a Stuart monarch and the Roman Catholic religion to a country that had become staunchly Protestant. In Glenfinnan in 1745, the sometimes-reluctant clans joined forces and rallied to Prince Charles Edward Stuart's cause.

The raising of the prince's standard is commemorated by the **Glenfinnan Monument,** an unusual tower on the banks of Loch Shiel; the story of his campaign is told in the nearby visitor center. Note that the figure at the top of the monument is of a Highlander, not the prince. ■ TIP➡ **The view down Loch Shiel from the Glenfinnan Monument is one of the most photographed in Scotland.** ✉*A830* ☎*01397/722250* ⊕*www.nts.org. uk* 🎫*£3* ⊙*Monument year-round, daily 24 hrs; visitor center Apr.– June, Sept., and Oct., daily 10–5; July and Aug., daily 9:30–5:30.*

As impressive as the Glenfinnan Monument (especially if you've tired of the Jacobite "Will He No Come Back Again" sentiment) is the curving railway viaduct that stretches across the green slopes behind the monument. The **Glenfinnan Viaduct,** 21 spans and 1,248 feet long, was in its time the wonder of the Highlands. The railway's contractor, Robert MacAlpine, known as Concrete Bob by the locals, pioneered the use of concrete for bridges when his company built the Mallaig extension, which opened in 1901. The viaduct is famous again, this time for its appearance in the *Harry Potter* films. *See Fort William, above, for information about the Jacobite Steam Train that uses this viaduct on its run between Fort William and Mallaig.*

### WHERE TO STAY & EAT

££–£££ ✕🏨 **Glenfinnan House.** This high-ceilinged hotel was built in the 18th
★ century as the home of Alexander MacDonald VII of Glenaladale, who was wounded fighting for Bonnie Prince Charlie, and transformed into an even grander mansion in the mid-19th century. Today you can discover the dark-wood interiors from this period in the simply furnished, serene guest rooms. From many rooms there are stunning lochside views of Ben Nevis. Scottish fare with a contemporary twist is served in the stately dining room (£30 for fixed-price menu). Expect top-notch ser-

vice from the cosmopolitan staff. **Pros:** Fabulous setting, atmospheric dining experience. **Cons:** Driveway not well maintained, some guest rooms look a little tired. ⊠ *Off A830, PH37 4LT* ☎ *01397/722235* ⊕ *www.glenfinnanhouse.com* ↩ *13 rooms* ♿ *In-room: no a/c, no TV. In-hotel: restaurant, bar, public Wi-Fi, no elevator* ⊟ *MC, V* ☉ *Closed mid-Nov.–mid-Mar.* ¶⊙ *BP.*

**EN ROUTE**

As you get closer to Arisaig along A830, you'll be able to spot Eigg, a low island marked by the dramatic black peak of An Sgurr. Beyond Eigg is the larger Rum, with its range of hills and the Norse-named, cloud-capped Rum Coullin looming over the island. The breathtaking seaward views should continue to distract you from the road beside Loch nan Uamh (from Gaelic, meaning "cave" and pronounced *oo*-am). This loch is associated with Prince Charles Edward Stuart's nine-month stay on the mainland, during which he gathered a small army, marched as far south as Derby in England, alarmed the king, retreated to unavoidable defeat at Culloden in the spring, and then spent a few months as a fugitive in the Highlands. A cairn by the shore marks the spot where the prince was picked up by a French ship; he never returned to Scotland.

## ARISAIG

*15 mi west of Glenfinnan.*

Considering its small size, Arisaig, gateway to the **Small Isles,** offers a surprising choice of high-quality options for dining and lodging. To the north of Arisaig, the road cuts across a headland to reach a stretch of coastline where silver sands glitter with the mica in the local rock; clear water, blue sky, and white sand lend a tropical flavor to the beaches—when the sun is shining.

From Arisaig try to visit a couple of the Small Isles: **Rum, Eigg, Muck,** and **Canna,** each tiny and with few or no inhabitants. Rum serves as a wildlife reserve.

**Arisaig Marine Ltd.** ( ⊠ *Arisaig Harbour* ☎ *01687/450224* ⊕ *www.arisaig.co.uk*) runs a boat service from the harbor at Arisaig to the islands at Easter and from May to September, daily at 11. The MV *Sheerwater* delivers supplies and sometimes visitors to the tiny island communities. Arisaig Marine also operates day cruises for whale-, seal-, and bird-watching. Available for charter from Arisaig Marine is a fast twin-engine motor yacht, which can take up to 12 passengers around the Small Isles and farther afield.

### WHERE TO STAY & EAT

££ ✕⊡ **Arisaig Hotel.** A 1720 former coaching inn, this hotel is close to the water and has magnificent views of the Small Isles. The inn has retained its provinciality with simple furnishings, and its restaurant is renowned for its home cooking. High-quality local ingredients are used to good advantage: haddock, salmon, and scallops are specialties, as are "proper" puds, such as sticky ginger pudding. **Pros:** Good-value restaurant, lots of life and music in the bar. **Cons:** Dated furnishings, the main bar may be noisy for some. ⌧*Arisaig PH39 4NH* ☎*01687/450210* ⊕*www.arisaighotel.co.uk* ⌁*13 rooms* ⌂*In-room: no a/c. In-hotel: restaurant, bar, no elevator* ⊟*MC, V* ⦿*BP.*

££    ⨉▦ **Old Library Lodge and Restaurant.** On the waterfront, this converted 1722 barn has cozy rooms with contemporary furnishings. Ask for a room with jaw-dropping views of the sea and harbor. A plus is the fine, reasonably priced restaurant (£27 fixed-price dinner); local fish and other fare is prepared in a French-bistro style and served in the whitewashed, airy dining room. **Pros:** Sea views and bracing air, dining for seafood lovers. **Con:** Some small rooms. ⌧*Arisaig PH39 4NH* ☎*01687/450651* ⊕*www.oldlibrary.co.uk* ⌁*6 rooms* ⌂*In-room: no a/c. In-hotel: restaurant, no kids under 18, no elevator* ⊟*AE, MC, V* ⊘*Closed Nov.* ⦿*BP.*

---

## MALLAIG

*8 mi north of Arisaig, 44 mi northwest of Fort William.*

After the approach along the coast, the workaday fishing port of Mallaig itself is anticlimactic. It has a few shops, and there's some bustle by the quayside when fishing boats unload or the Skye ferry departs: this is the departure point for the southern ferry connection to the Isle of Skye, the largest island of the Inner Hebrides. Mallaig is also the starting point for day cruises up the Sound of Sleat, which separates Skye from the mainland. The sound offers views into the rugged Knoydart region and its long, fjordlike sea lochs, Lochs Nevis and Hourn. The area to the immediate north and west beyond Loch Nevis, one of the most remote in Scotland, is often referred to as the Rough Bounds of Knoydart.

★    For year-round cruises to Loch Nevis, Inverie, and Tarbet, contact **Bruce Watt Sea Cruises** ( ☎*01687/462320* ⊕*www.road-to-the-isles.org.uk*).

**Caledonian MacBrayne** ( ☎*01475/650100* ⊕*www.calmac.co.uk*) runs scheduled service and cruises from Mallaig to Skye, the Small Isles, and Mull.

The town's **Heritage Centre** has exhibits, films, photographs, and models on all aspects of the local history. ⌧*Station Rd.* ☎*01687/462085* ⊕*www.mallaigheritage.org.uk* ▨*£2* ⊘*Apr.–Oct., Mon.–Sat. 9:30–4:30, Sun. 12:30–4:30; Nov.–Mar., Wed.–Sat. noon–5.*

A small, unnamed side road just south of Mallaig leads east to an even smaller road that will bring you to **Loch Morar,** the deepest of all the Scottish lochs (more than 1,000 feet); the next deepest point is miles out into the Atlantic, beyond the continental shelf. The loch is said to have a resident monster, Morag, which undoubtedly gets less recognition than its famous cousin Nessie.

### BIKING

Explore the lochside road and the scenic coastal routes south of Mallaig, with views of white-sand beaches and limpid waters, by hiring a bike with **Cycles2U** ( ☎*01687/461021 or 07800/956913* ⊕*www.road-*

*to-the-isles.org.uk*). Choose from mountain bikes, kids' wheels, and tandems, and use a network of rental spots and pick-up areas (so you can drop your bike off when the muscles give up). In Mallaig, stop at the Springbank Guesthouse in East Bay.

# AROUND THE GREAT GLEN ESSENTIALS

## TRANSPORTATION

### BY AIR

Inverness Airport has flights from London, Edinburgh, and Glasgow. Domestic flights covering the Highlands and islands are operated by British Airways, Servisair, easyJet, Eastern Airways, and Highland Airways. Fort William has bus and train connections with Glasgow, so Glasgow Airport can be an appropriate access point.

Contact **British Airways** (☎ *0870/850–9850* ⊕ *www.britishairways.com*). **Eastern Airways** (☎ *08703/669100* ⊕ *www.easternairways.com*). **easyJet** (☎ *0870/600– 0000* ⊕ *www.easyjet.com*). **Highland Airways** (☎ *0845/4502245* ⊕ *www.highland airways.co.uk*). **Servisair** (☎ *01667/464040* ⊕ *www.servisair.com*).

Information **Glasgow Airport** (☎ *0870/040–0008* ⊕ *www.glasgowairport.com*). **Inverness Airport** (⌧ *Dalcross* ☎ *01667/462445* ⊕ *www.hial.co.uk*).

### BY BUS

A long-distance Scottish Citylink service connects Glasgow and Fort William. Inverness is also well served from the central belt of Scotland; for information call the Inverness Coach Station. For bargain-priced coach transport between the main cities of Glasgow, Edinburgh, Perth, Dundee, Aberdeen, and Inverness, contact Megabus (book on the Web site).

There's limited service available within the Great Glen area and some local service running from Fort William. Highland Country Buses operates buses down the Great Glen and around Fort William. A number of postbus services will help get you to the more remote corners of the area. A timetable is available from Royal Mail Post Buses.

Information **Highland Country Buses** (⌧ *Fort William Bus Station, Ardgour Rd., Fort William* ☎ *01397/702373* ⊕ *www.rapsons.com*). **Inverness Coach Station** (⌧ *Off Academy St., Inverness* ☎ *01463/233371*). **Megabus** (⊕ *www.megabus. com*). **Royal Mail Post Buses** (☎ *01463/256273* ⊕ *www.royalmail.com*). **Scottish Citylink** (☎ *08705/505050* ⊕ *www.citylink.co.uk*).

### BY CAR

The fast A9 brings you to Inverness in roughly three hours from Glasgow or Edinburgh, even if you take your time.

As in all areas of rural Scotland, a car is a great asset for exploring the Great Glen and Speyside, especially since the best of the area is away from the main roads. You can use the main A82 from Inverness to Fort William, or use the smaller B862/B852 roads (former military roads) to explore the much quieter east side of Loch Ness. The same applies to Speyside, where several options open up away from the A9, especially through the pinewoods by Coylumbridge and Feshiebridge, east of the main road. Mallaig, west of Fort William, has improving road connections, but the road is still narrow and winding in many places, and rail remains the most enjoyable way to experience the rugged hills and loch scenery between these two places. In Morvern, the area across Loch Linnhe southwest of Fort William, you may encounter single-lane roads, which require slower speeds and concentration.

### BY TRAIN

There are connections from London to Inverness and Fort William (including overnight sleeper service), as well as reliable links from Glasgow and Edinburgh. For information call First Scotrail.

Though there's no rail connection among towns within the Great Glen, this area has the West Highland line, which links Fort William to Mallaig; a trip on this scenic line is recommended. The Jacobite Steam Train is an exciting summer (mid-May to mid-October) option on the same route. There's train service between Glasgow (Queen Street) and Inverness, via Aviemore, which gives access to the heart of Speyside.

Information **First Scotrail** ( ☎ 08457/484950  ⊕ www.firstgroup.com/scotrail). **Jacobite Steam Train** ( ☎ 01524/737751  ⊕ www.westcoastrailway.co.uk).

## CONTACTS & RESOURCES

### EMERGENCIES

In case of any emergency, dial **999** for an ambulance, the police, the coast guard, or the fire department (no coins are needed for emergency calls from phone booths). Pharmacies are not common away from the larger towns, and doctors often dispense medicines in rural areas. In an emergency, the police will assist you in locating a pharmacist. In Fort William, Boots the Chemist is open weekdays from 8:45 to 6, Saturday from 8:45 to 5:30. In Inverness, Kinmylies Pharmacy is open weekdays until 6 and Saturday until 5:30.

Hospitals **Belford Hospital** ( ⊠ Belford Rd., Fort William  ☎ 01397/702481). **Raigmore Hospital** ( ⊠ Old Perth Rd., Inverness  ☎ 01463/704000). **Town and County Hospital** ( ⊠ Cawdor Rd., Nairn  ☎ 01667/452101).

Pharmacies **Boots the Chemist** ( ⊠ High St., Fort William  ☎ 01397/705143). **Kinmylies Pharmacy** ( ⊠ 1 Charleston Ct., Kinmylies, Inverness  ☎ 01463/221094).

### FISHING

The Great Glen is laced with rivers and lochs where you can fly-fish for salmon and trout. The fishing seasons are as follows: salmon, from early February through September or early October (depending on the area); brown trout, from March 15 to September 30; sea trout, from May through September or early October; rainbow trout, no statutory-close season. Sea angling from shore or boat is also possible. Tourist centers can provide information on locations, permits, and fishing rights.

## TOURS

Inverness Tours runs the occasional boat cruise but is mainly known for tours around the Highlands in well-equipped vehicles, which are led by expert guides and heritage enthusiasts. James Johnstone, a personal guide, is based in Inverness but will drive you anywhere; he has a particularly good knowledge of the Highlands and islands, including the Outer Isles.

Information **Inverness Tours** (☎ *01456/450168* ⊕ *www.invernesstours.com*). **James Johnstone** (☎ *01463/798372* ⊕ *www.jajcd.com*).

## VISITOR INFORMATION

Aviemore, Fort William, and Inverness have year-round tourist offices. Other tourist centers, open seasonally, include those at Ballachulish, Fort Augustus, Grantown-on-Spey, Kingussie, Mallaig, and Nairn. A regional Web site for the Highlands, www.visithighlands.com, covers this whole area.

Information **Aviemore** (✉ *Grampian Rd.* ☎ *01479/810363*). **Fort William** (✉ *Cameron Centre, Cameron Sq.* ☎ *01397/703781*). **Inverness** (✉ *Castle Wynd* ☎ *01463/234353* ⊕ *www.inverness-scotland.com*).

8

# The Northern Highlands & the Western Isles

Updated by
Nick Bruno

**MUCH OF THE ROMANCE OF** "Caledonia stern and wild"—the splendid and tranquil landscape, the Highland clans, red deer and golden eagles, Celtic mists and legends—is concentrated in this region. This is where you can find Eilean Donan, the most romantic of Scottish castles; the land's end at John OO'Groats; and Skye, the mysterious island immortalized by the exploits of Bonnie Prince Charlie. The old counties of Ross and Cromarty (sometimes called Easter and Wester Ross), Sutherland, and Caithness constitute the most northern portion of mainland Scotland. The population is sparse, mountains and moorland limit the choice of touring routes, and distances are less important than whether the winding, hilly roads you sometimes encounter are two lanes or one. Although the Isle of Skye is a very popular destination in the summer months, it's hardly overrun with tourists. Throughout the region you'll have plenty of room to enjoy the desolate landscapes, dramatic coastlines, and expansive skies.

Much of Sutherland and Wester Ross is made up of a rocky platform of Lewisian gneiss, certainly the oldest rocks in Britain, scoured and hollowed by glacial action into numerous lochs. On top of this rolling, wet moorland landscape sit strangely shaped quartzite-capped sandstone mountains, eroded and pinnacled. Take a walk here, and the Ice Age doesn't seem so far away. One of the region's leitmotifs is the sea lochs that thrust salty fingers into the loneliest landscapes in Scotland, carrying the Atlantic's salty tang among the moors and deep forests. Strange, solitary peaks rear up out of the heather, and if you're lucky, you may sight a golden eagle soaring overhead in search of rabbits.

Many place-names in this region reflect its early links with Scandinavia. Sutherland was once the southernmost land belonging to the Vikings. Cape Wrath got its name from the Viking word *hvarth* (turning point), and Laxford, Suilven, and dozens of other names in the area have Norse rather than Gaelic derivations.

The island of Skye and the Outer Hebrides, which are now often referred to as the Western Isles, are the stronghold of the Gaelic language. Skye, famous for its misty mountains, called the Cuillins, has a surprisingly wide variety of landscape, considering its relatively small size. The south of the island is generally flatter; its coastline is the place to hunt out hidden beaches, perhaps overlooked by a ruined castle, and its interior moorlands are dotted with lochans (small lakes). As you travel northward, however, the landscape becomes increasingly mountainous, with green pastures surrounding the scattered crofting (farming) communities and sea inlets strewn with jewel-like islets, miniature versions of Skye itself.

## EXPLORING THE NORTHERN HIGHLANDS & THE WESTERN ISLES

From Inverness, the gateway to the Northern Highlands, roads fan out like the spokes of a wheel to join the coastal route around the rim of mainland Scotland. Many roads here are single lane, requiring you to pause at passing places to allow ongoing traffic to pass: do not underestimate driving times, especially when driving on minor roads or on the

## TOP REASONS TO GO

**Explore Skye, the misty island:** The landscape ranges from the lush, undulating hills and coastal tracks of Sleat in the Garden of Skye to the deep glens that cut into the saw-toothed peaks of the Cuillins. Farther north are stunning geological features like the Old Man of Storr and Kilt Rock.

**Tuck into some seafood:** Amazing regional specialties abound. Sample Bracadale crab, Dunvegan Bay langoustines, and Sconser king prawns, as well as the local smoked salmon, lobster, scallops, and oysters. Finish up with Stornoway black pudding.

**Walk the coast in the Outer Hebrides:** There are no wilder places in Britain to enjoy an invigorating coastal walk than on Lewis and the Uists. Expect vast swaths of golden sand set against blue bays, or—when the weather is rough—giant waves crashing against the rocks.

**Get close to nature:** Seals, deer, small mammals like weasels and stoats, otters, as well as an abundance of birdlife can be seen throughout the Northern Highlands and Western Isles. Don't miss a boating foray to the Handa Island bird reserve, off Scourie.

**Drive a single-track road:** In the Northern Highlands, take a drive on single-track roads like Destitution Road, north of Gairloch, which lead through the most dramatic scenery in Britain. The area is a primeval landscape where strange craggy mountains, with Gaelic and Nordic names like An Teallach, Suilven, and Stac Polly, jut out of vast, desolate bog lands dotted with lochans.

islands. There are simply no roads into the wilder areas, and few roads at all—so you're bound to be sharing the roads with heavy trucks and buses. Ferry services are generally very reliable, weather permitting.

On a map, this area may seem far from major urban centers, but it's easy to reach. Inverness has an airport with direct links to London, Edinburgh, Glasgow, and even Amsterdam.

### ABOUT THE RESTAURANTS & HOTELS

Charming, earthy, inexpensive inns and a few good modern hotels will welcome you with warmth and vivacity as you come in after a day of touring in the cool, moist Highlands air. Several restaurants of very high standard dot the region, especially on Skye. Most country-house inns serve reliable, hearty, seafood, and meat-and-potatoes meals.

| WHAT IT COSTS IN POUNDS | | | | | |
|---|---|---|---|---|---|
| | £ | ££ | £££ | ££££ | £££££ |
| RESTAURANTS | under £10 | £10–£14 | £15–£19 | £20–£25 | over £25 |
| HOTELS | under £70 | £70–£120 | £121–£160 | £161–£220 | over £220 |

Restaurant prices are for a main course at dinner. Hotel prices are for two people in a standard double room in high season, generally including the 17.5% V.A.T.

## GREAT ITINERARIES

The quality of the northern light and the sheer beauty of the landscapes add to the adventure. Above all, don't rush things. Multiple-journey ferry tickets—the Island Hopscotch, for example—can help you stay flexible. You could easily combine the itineraries below with forays into the Great Glen (including Inverness and Loch Ness) or even up to Orkney and the Shetland Islands.

### IF YOU HAVE 2 DAYS

If you only have two days, head to the fabled isle of Skye, whose mists shroud so many legends. Stay in towns with remarkable hotels, such as 🚢 **Broadford** or 🚢 **Armadale,** then tour the spectacular countryside, including the celebrated Cuillin Ridge near **Glen Brittle**. Be sure to detour to see **Eilean Donan Castle** once you're back on the mainland.

### IF YOU HAVE 5 DAYS

If the weather looks settled, head for Skye, and base yourself at 🚢 **Portree.** The next day, visit **Glen Brittle** and the Cuillin Ridge. On your third day, take the ferry from Uig, in the north of Skye, to 🚢 **Tarbert,** in the Western Isles, and visit the **Calanais Standing Stones,** the **Arnol**

**Black House,** and some deserted beaches. The next day, travel to 🚢 **Stornoway** and catch the ferry to 🚢 **Ullapool** on the mainland. On your fifth day, return to Inverness by way of the **Corrieshalloch Gorge** and **Strathpeffer.**

### IF YOU HAVE 8 DAYS

Tackle the coastal loop of the north of Scotland counterclockwise. Start at 🚢 **Ullapool,** then take the ferry for 🚢 **Stornoway** and the Western Isles. Spend your second day visiting Stornoway's harbor and museum, and on your third day, drive north to visit **Port of Ness,** the **Butt of Lewis Lighthouse,** the **Arnol Black House,** and the **Calanais Standing Stones.** The fourth day, drive to 🚢 **Tarbert** and then **Northton** for a visit to the **Seallam! Visitor Centre and Co Leis Thu? Genealogical Research Centre.** The next day, take the ferry to North Uist, returning to Tarbert in the evening. On your sixth day, take the ferry to Uig on Skye and travel to 🚢 **Portree.** Spend your seventh day visiting **Glen Brittle,** then move on to 🚢 **Broadford.** On your last day, cross the Skye Bridge and return to Inverness.

**9**

### TIMING

The Northern Highlands and islands are best seen from late May to early September. The earlier in the spring or later in the autumn you go, the greater the chances of your encountering the elements in their extreme form, and the fewer attractions and accommodations you will find open; even tourist-friendly Skye closes down almost completely by the end of October. As a final deciding factor, you may not want to take a western sea passage in a gale, a frequent occurrence in the winter months.

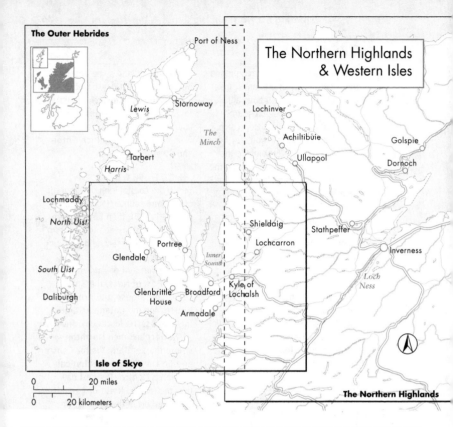

**The Outer Hebrides**

Port of Ness

Lewis
Stornoway

*The Minch*

Tarbert

Harris

Lochmaddy

North Uist

Glendale

Portree

South Uist

Daliburgh

Glenbrittle House
Broadford

Armadale

*Inner Sound*

Kyle of Lochalsh

Shieldaig

Lochcarron

Lochinver

Achiltibuie

Ullapool

Golspie

Dornoch

Stathpeffer

Inverness

*Loch Ness*

**Isle of Skye**

| 0 | 20 miles |
| 0 | 20 kilometers |

# THE NORTHERN LANDSCAPES

Wester Ross and Sutherland have some of the most distinctive mountain profiles and coastal stretches in all of Scotland. The rim roads around the wilds of Durness overlooking rocky shores and beaches are as dramatic as the awe-inspring and desolate cross-country routes like Destitution Road in Wester Ross. The essence of Caithness, the area at the top of Scotland, is space, big skies, and distant blue hills beyond endless rolling moors (although "tax-break" conifer planting has encroached on the views in some areas). There's a surprising amount to see and do on the east coast beyond Inverness—try to allow enough time to take in the visitor centers and croft houses squat farm buildings.

## STRATHPEFFER

*19 mi northwest of Inverness via A9, A835, and A834.*

At the spa town of Strathpeffer you can take a walk to admire Victorian "holiday houses" and the Eagle Stone, a boulder carved with Pictish signs in the 7th century, now perched on a hill just outside the town.

The Highland Museum of Childhood displays early Highlands toys in the former railway station.

The **Strathpeffer Spa Pavilion** ( ✉ *The Square* ☎ *01957/420124* ⊕ *www. strathpefferpavilion.org*) has been spruced up and now serves as a venue for artistic events including classical concerts, cabaret, and period-costume dancing.

Not far from Strathpeffer are the tumbling **Falls of Rogie** (signposted off the A835), where an interestingly bouncy suspension bridge presents you with a fine view of the splashing waters below.

### WHERE TO STAY

££ **Craigvar.** Host Margaret Scott is a delight and stocks plenty of tour-★ ist leaflets to keep you busy at this pretty Georgian bed-and-breakfast. Idiosyncratic pictures—from 18th-century portraits to Japanese-style still lifes—hang on the walls. The Blue Room has a four-poster bed and Victorian bath. **Pros:** Good location on town square, friendly owner. **Cons:** Impractical carpets in the bathrooms, rooms get booked up early. ✉ *The Square, Strathpeffer, Ross-shire IV14 9DL* ☎ *01997/421622* ⊕ *www.craigvar.com* ⇨ *3 rooms* ♿ *In-room: no a/c. In-hotel: bar, no elevator* ☰ *MC, V* ⦿ *BP.*

## CORRIESHALLOCH GORGE

★ *39 mi northwest of Strathpeffer.*

For a thrilling touch of vertigo, don't miss Corrieshalloch Gorge. A river draining the high moors plunges 150 feet into a 200-foot-deep, thickly wooded gorge. There's a suspension-bridge viewpoint and a heady atmosphere of romantic grandeur, like an old Scottish print come to life. A short walk leads from a parking area to the viewpoint.

**9**

## ULLAPOOL

*12 mi northwest of Corrieshalloch Gorge, 238 mi north of Glasgow.*

By the shores of salty Loch Broom, Ullapool was founded in 1788 as a fishing station to exploit the local herring stocks. There's still a smattering of fishing vessels, as well as visting yachts and foreign ships. When their crews fill the pubs, the town has a cosmopolitan feel. The harbor area comes to life when the Lewis ferry arrives and departs. Ullapool is an ideal base for hiking and taking wildlife and nature cruises, especially to the Summer Isles.

In the **Ullapool Museum,** films, photographs, and audiovisual displays tell the story of the area from the ice age to modern times. ✉ *7–8 W. Argyle St.* ☎ *01854/612987* ⊕ *www.ullapoolmuseum.co.uk* ⤢ *£3* ⊙ *Apr.– Oct., Mon.–Sat. 10–5.*

### WHERE TO STAY

££ **The Royal Hotel.** Sitting atop a hill above Ullapool, the Royal Hotel ★ has fabulous views over the harbor and Loch Broom. The curvy 1960s facade was added to a 19th-century coaching inn. Guest rooms are

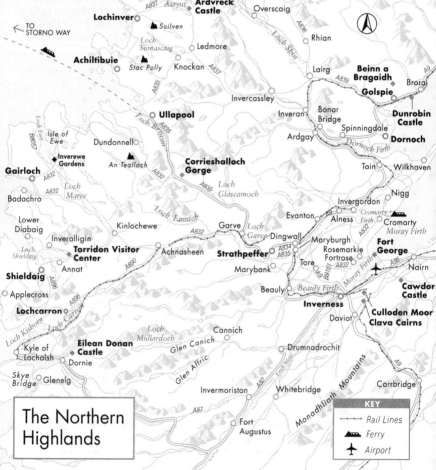

## The Northern Highlands

AREA SHOWN IN INSERT ↑

KEY
- Rail Lines
- Ferry
- Airport

bright and spacious. The clientele is diverse, especially during late September's Loopulu music festival, when the likes of the Stanglers have been known to walk on the nearby beaches and appreciate the breakfast peaches. ■TIP➜ **Ask for a room with balcony and views of the loch.** Pros: Stunning views from balconies, a short walk to Ullapool, good breakfasts. Cons: Restaurant is uneven, some rooms have older mattresses. ⊠*Garve Rd., IV26 2SY* ☎*01854/612181* ⊕*www.royalhotel-ullapool.com* ↩*50 rooms* ⌂*In-room: no a/c. In-hotel: restaurant, bar* ⊟*AE, DC, V* ⊺⊙*BP.*

> **GET HOOKED IN THE HIGHLANDS**
>
> The possibilities for fishing are endless in Sutherland, as a glance at the loch-covered map suggests. Brown trout and salmon are abundant. You can fish from the banks of Loch Garve, 4 mi west of Strathpeffer, or Loch Assynt, 5 mi east of Lochinver, from March to October. Boat fishing is popular on Loch Maree, southeast of Gairloch and north of Poolewe, from May to October. Fishing permits are available at local post offices, shops, and hotels.

**EN ROUTE** Drive north of Ullapool on the A835 into **Coigach and Assynt,** and you can enter a different kind of landscape. Here you won't find the broad flanks of great hills that hem you in, as you would in the Great Glen or Glen Coe. Instead, in Wester Ross the mountains rear out of the hummocky terrain and seem to shift their position, hiding behind one another in bewitching ways. Even their names seem different from those of the *bens* (mountain peaks or high hills) elsewhere: Cul Mor, Cul Beag, Stac Polly, Canisp, Suilven. Some owe their origins to Norse words rather than to Gaelic—a reminder that Vikings used to sail this northern seaboard. Much of this area lies within the Inverpolly National Nature Reserve.

## ACHILTIBUIE

*25 mi northwest of Ullapool.*

Achiltibuie is a small farming community set in magnificent mountain and coastal scenery. Offshore are the attractive **Summer Isles,** whose history dates back to Viking raids. Cruises from Ullapool visit the largest and only inhabited island, Tanera Mhor, where you can buy special Summer Isle stamps—Tanera Mhor is the only Scottish island to have a private postal service. Achiltibuie has become a bit of a foodie haven thanks to businesses like the Achiltibuie Smokehouse and the Hydropondicum, which continues to grow in weird and wonderful ways.

At the **Achiltibuie Smokehouse,** Summer Isles Foods smokes all sorts of fish—salmon, haddock, eel, and trout—which can be purchased in the small shop; mail order is available. ⊠*Altandhu* ☎*01854/622353* ⊕*www.summerislesfoods.com* ⊙*Easter–mid-Oct., weekdays 9:30–5.*

☉ Fodor'sChoice ★ The **Hydroponicum** produces luscious fruit and vegetables throughout the year. The plants are suspended above nutrient-filled pools from which their roots draw required sustenance by means of a wick. You can sample tomatoes, beans, lettuce, pears, figs, and more in the Lily-pond Café, and buy perishable and nonperishable items in the shop. The ever-developing Eco Centre showcases ingenious and amusing green technologies—ever seen solar-powered bagpipes? ⊠ *Achiltibuie* ☎ *01854/622202* ⊕ *www.thehydroponicum.com* ☒ *£4.50 for guided tour* ⊙ *Apr.–Sept., daily 11–4; Oct. weekdays 11–4.*

## LOCHINVER

*18 mi north of Achiltibuie via unclassified road, 38 mi north of Ullapool via A835/A837.*

Lochinver is a bustling shoreside community of whitewashed cottages, with a busy harbor used by the west-coast-fishing fleet, and a couple of dining and lodging options. Behind the town the mountain Suilven rises abruptly. This unusual monolith is best seen from across the water, however. Take the cul-de-sac, **Baddidarroch Road,** for the finest photo opportunity.

Bold souls spending time at Lochinver may enjoy the interesting single-lane B869 **Drumbeg Loop** to the north of Lochinver—it has several challenging hairpin turns along with breathtaking views. (The junction is on the north side of the River Inver bridge on the outskirts of the village, signposted as STOER and CLASHNESSIE.) Just beyond the scattered community of Stoer, a road leads west to **Stoer Point Lighthouse.** If you're an energetic walker, you can hike across the short turf and heather along the cliff top for fine views east toward the profiles of the northwest mountains. There's also a red-sandstone sea stack: the **Old Man of Stoer.** This makes a pleasant excursion on a long summer evening. If you stay on the Drumbeg section, there's a particularly tricky hairpin turn in a steep dip, which may force you to take your eyes off the fine view of Quinag, yet another of Sutherland's shapely mountains.

### WHERE TO STAY & EAT

££££ ╳⌂ **Inver Lodge Hotel.** On a hillside above Lochinver, this modern hotel has stunning views of the sea. Floral fabrics and traditional mahogany furniture decorate the smart guest rooms. The restaurant (£££££) makes the most of fresh, local seafood on its Scottish menu; try the lobster, straight from the sea the day you dine. Anglers feel especially at home here, with three salmon rivers and many trout lochs within easy reach. **Pros:** Cozy public room with a fireplace, refreshing sauna, wonderful fishing nearby. **Cons:** Drab exterior, not good for families with children. ⊠ *Iolaire Rd., Sutherland IV27 4LU* ☎ *01571/844496* ⊕ *www.inverlodge.com* ⇆ *20 rooms* ⚿ *In-room: no a/c, Wi-Fi. In-hotel: restaurant, room service, sauna, no kids under 10* ⊟ *AE, DC, MC, V* ⊙ *Closed Nov.–Easter* |⊙|*BP.*

£ ⌂ **Davar.** The light-filled rooms at this modern, comfortable B&B have views over Lochinver Bay. Green carpets set off pastel walls, and the bedrooms are simple but spacious. **Pros:** Lounge filled with books and games, wonderful mountain views. **Cons:** Decor is a little busy, too small for some travelers. ⊠ *Lochinver, Sutherland IV27 4LJ* ☎ *01571/844501*

⊕*www.davar-lochinver.co.uk* ⟳3 *rooms* ♿*In-room: no a/c, no phone. In-hotel: no elevator* ⊟*No credit cards* ⊘*Closed Dec.–Mar.* ⦿❘*BP.*

£ ▦**Polcraig Guest House.** This quiet detached house with views toward Lochinver Bay has high-quality accommodations. Rooms in this B&B are pretty and uncluttered with pine furniture, floral prints, and a green, blue, or pink color scheme. **Pros:** Amiable hosts, great breakfasts, fishing trips can be

> ## RULE OF THREE
>
> Scourie has a trio of attractions not found together anywhere else on the globe: Highland cattle, red- and black-throated divers, and palm trees. There is reputedly a reward for anyone who can capture all three in a photograph. Your best bet to do so is from the shore of Scourie Bay.

arranged. **Cons:** Bland exterior, on a very steep road. ⊠*Lochinver, Sutherland, IV27 4LD* ☎*01571/844429* ✉*cathelmac@aol.com* ⟳*5 rooms* ♿*In-room: no a/c, no phone. In-hotel: no elevator* ⊟*No credit cards* ⦿❘*BP.*

### SHOPPING

**Highland Stoneware** ( ⊠*Baddidarroch* ☎*01571/844376*) manufactures tableware and decorative items with hand-painted designs of Highland wildflowers, animals, and landscapes. In the showroom you can browse and purchase wares.

At Inverkirkaig, just south of Lochinver, don't miss **Achins Book & Craft Shop** ( ⊠*Inverkirkaig* ☎*01571/844262*). The shop is a great place for Scottish books on natural history, hill walking, and trout fishing. It also sells well-chosen craft items—knitwear, tweeds, and pottery—along with works by local artists and recordings of traditional music. The shop is open daily from 9:30 to 6 between Easter and October (phone ahead in winter to check opening times), and its pleasant coffee shop is open from Easter through October, daily 10 to 5.

9

## SCOURIE

*28 mi north of Lochinver.*

Scourie is a small settlement catering to visitors—fisherfolk especially—with a range of accommodations. The bayside town makes a good base for a trip to the bird sanctuary on the island of Handa.

★ Just off the coast of Scourie is **Handa Island,** a bird sanctuary that shelters huge seabird colonies, especially impressive at nesting time in spring and early summer. Visitors can gaze upon over 200,000 birds nesting on spectacular cliffs, including guillemots, razorbills, great skuas, kittiwakes, and even the odd puffin from the towering sandstone vantage point of Stack an Seabhaig (Hawk's Stack). This remarkable park, administered by the Scottish Wildlife Trust, is open only in spring and summer. It can be reached by a small open boat from Tarbet; contact the tourist information center in Lochinver or Durness for details.
■**TIP→** Sturdy boots, a sturdy jacket, and a degree of fitness are needed to walk the path around the island.

### WHERE TO STAY & EAT

££  ✕⛺**Eddrachilles Hotel.** This longtime favorite has one of the best views of any lodging in Scotland—across the islands of Eddrachilles Bay. (If you're entranced, you can explore them by boat.) The hotel sits on 320 acres of private moorland and is just south of the Handa Island bird sanctuary. The bedrooms are modern and comfortable, with chandeliers hanging above and photographs on the walls. In the restaurant, the chef uses local produce to prepare meals in straightforward Scottish style, with the emphasis on fish and game; try the poached salmon or the saddle of venison. **Pros:** Attractive garden, stunning shoreline nearby, close to bird sanctuary. **Cons:** Restaurant's quality can vary, service sometimes disappoints. ✉*Badcall Bay, IV27 4TH* ☎*01971/502080* ⊕*www.eddrachilles.com* ⇨*11 rooms* ♨*In-room: no a/c. In-hotel: restaurant, bar, no elevator* ═*MC, V* ☉*Closed Nov.–Feb.* ¶⦿*BP.*

---

## DURNESS

*27 mi north of Scourie, 55 mi north of Lochinver.*

The sudden patches of green surrounding the village of Durness, on the north coast, are caused by the richer limestone outcrops among the acid moorlands.

The limestone's most spectacular feature is **Smoo Cave,** hollowed out of the limestone by rushing water. Access is via a steep cliff path. Also worth exploring are the wonderful near white-sand beaches, especially the one at Sango Bay. The village of Durness has handy shops and facilities, and the ever-intriguing Balnakeil Craft Village. Boat tours around the Kyle of Durness run daily from April through September; reservations are advised because there's a limit of six per 20-minute tour. The seasonal **tourist information center** ( ✉*Durine* ☎*01971/511259*) has information on this and other local attractions.

★  Artisans sell pottery, leather, weavings, paintings, and more from their studios at **Balnakeil Craft Village** ( ☎*01971/511777*). The complex, on an unnamed road but clearly signed from Durness, is open April through October. Hours at the studios vary, but most shops stay open daily from 10 to 5, and even later on summer evenings.

If you've made it this far north, you'll probably want to go all the way to **Cape Wrath,** a rugged headland at the northwest tip of Scotland. The white-sand beaches, impressive dunes covered in marram grass, and crashing seas of nearby Balnakeil Bay make it an exhilarating place to visit. You can't drive your own vehicle, however. From May through September, a small boat ( ☎*01971/511376*) ferries people here from Keoldale; once you're across the sea inlet called the Kyle of Durness, a minibus ( ☎*01971/511287*) will then take you to the lighthouse.

The highest mainland cliffs in Scotland, including **Clo Mor,** at 920 feet, lie between the Kyle and Cape Wrath.

**EN ROUTE**  The north-coast road along the top of Scotland is both attractive and severe. It runs, for example, around the head of Loch Eriboll, which was a World War II convoy assembly point and was usually referred to as "Loch 'orrible" by the crews. Yet it has its own desolate charm. There are lots of interesting landmarks including croft dwellings, crumbling lime kiln structures and a pebbly beach that reaches out to a mound of land, Ard Neakie.

## THURSO

*74 mi east of Durness.*

The town of Thurso is quite substantial for a community so far north. In town are the Thurso Heritage Museum and Old St. Peter's Kirk, which dates back to the 12th century. There are also fine beaches, particularly to the east, at Dunnet Bay. And with several restaurants and hotels, Thurso is one of the few towns that makes a good starting point for exploring the far north. Don't expect the landscape to be unspoiled, however; the town was the site of Britain's first nuclear-power plant. It's now in the process of being decommissioned.

Many people make the trip to the northernmost point of mainland Britain, which is at **Dunnet Head,** with its fine views to Orkney.

### WHERE TO STAY & EAT

££ ✕⌂ **Forss Country House Hotel.** Don't be fooled by the stark exterior, as this house dating from 1810 is a charming place to stay. It's surrounded by woodland and plenty of places to fish (guide service and instruction provided). Spare, dark-wood antique and reproduction furniture fill the simple rooms. Log fires and sturdy Scottish cuisine make for a charming place to stay. Prix-fixe meals at the restaurant (£££££) might include haggis-stuffed sirloin with Glenmorangie whisky sauce. **Pros:** Large guest rooms, lots of outdoor activities, hearty meals. **Cons:** Shutters on windows lack some privacy, heavy old doors make a racket. ✉*Forss, KW14 7XY* ✛*About 4 mi west of Thurso* ☎*01847/861201* ⊕*www.forsshousehotel.co.uk* ⟲*8 rooms, 5 suites* ⌕*In-room: no a/c, DVD. In-hotel: restaurant, bar, no elevator* ▭*AE, DC, MC, V.*

£ ⌂ **Murray House.** In the center of Thurso, this Victorian town house is convenient to the Orkney ferry. Floral wallpaper and bedding decorate the rooms. You may sit in the garden or watch a film in the lounge. **Pros:** Near the railway station and the ferry, evening meals can be arranged. **Cons:** Smallish rooms, dated decor. ✉*1 Campbell St., Thurso KW14 7HD* ☎*01847/895759* ⊕*www.murrayhousebb.com* ⟲*5 rooms* ⌕*In-room: no a/c. In-hotel: bar, no elevator* ▭*No credit cards* ⏺*BP.*

### BICYCLING

At the **Wheels Cycle Shop** ( ✉*35 High St.* ☎*01847/896124*), the staff rents bikes and gives advice on the best routes.

## JOHN O'GROATS

*21 mi east of Thurso via A836.*

The windswept little outpost of John o'Groats is usually taken to be the most northern community on the Scottish mainland, though that is not strictly accurate, as an exploration of the little network of roads between Dunnet Head and John o'Groats will confirm. A crafts center has a few high-quality shops selling knitwear, candles, and gifts.

Head east to **Duncansby Head** for spectacular views of cliffs and sea stacks by the lighthouse—and puffins, too.

**John o'Groats Ferries** ( ☎*01955/611353* ⊕*www.jogferry.co.uk*) operates wildlife cruises from John o'Groats Harbor. The 1½-hour trip takes you past spectacular cliff scenery and bird life into the Pentland Firth, to Duncansby Stacks, and to the island of Stroma. Cruises cost £15 and are available daily at 2:30 between June and August.

### THE ARTS

The **Lyth Arts Centre** ( ⊠*Lyth* ✛*4 mi off A9* ☎*01955/641270*), between Wick and John o'Groats, is housed in a Victorian-era school building. From April through November each year, it hosts performances by professional touring music and theater companies, as well as exhibitions of contemporary fine art. Check local papers or tourist information centers for opening times, schedules, and fees.

## WICK

*17 mi south of John o'Groats, 22 mi southeast of Thurso via A882.*

Wick is a substantial town that was built on its fishing industry. The town itself is not very appealing, but it does have the gaunt, bleak ruins of **Castle Sinclair** and **Castle Girnigoe** teetering on a cliff top 3 mi north of the town.

To learn how this town grew, visit the **Wick Heritage Centre**—it's run by local people in part for the local community, and they're real enthusiasts. The center is the largest museum in the Northern Highlands and has on display a restored fisherman's house, a fish kiln, and a blacksmith's shop, as well as collections of everything from fossils to 19th-century toys. An art gallery and terraced gardens overlooking the town round out the offerings. ⊠*19 Bank Row* ☎*01955/605393* ⊕*www. wickheritage.org* ⊇*£3* ⊙*Easter–Oct., Mon.–Sat. 10–3:45.*

The **Northlands Viking Centre,** which highlights the role of Scandinavian settlers in this area, has models of the Viking settlement at Freswick and of a Viking longship, as well as coins and other artifacts. ⊠*The Old School, Auckengill* ✛*Near Keiss, 10 mi north of Wick via A9* ☎*01955/607771* ⊇*£2* ⊙*June–Sept., daily 10–4.*

**EN ROUTE** — Signposted west off the A9 about 10 mi south of Wick are the extraordinary **Grey Cairns of Camster,** two Neolithic chambered cairns, dating from 4000 BC to 3000 BC, that are among the best preserved in Britain. **Camster Round Cairn** is 20 yards in diameter and 13 yards high, and

**Camster Long Cairn** reaches nearly 77 yards in length. Nineteenth-century excavations revealed skeletons, pottery, and flint tools in the round cairn's internal chamber. If you don't mind dirty knees, you can crawl into the chambers in both cairns.

## DUNBEATH

*21 mi south of Wick.*

The moors of Caithness roll down to the sea at Dunbeath, where you find the **Dunbeath Heritage Centre** in a former school. Inside are photographs and domestic and crofting artifacts that relay the area's history from the Bronze Age to the oil age. It's particularly helpful to those researching family histories. ⊠ *Off A9* ☎ *01593/731233* ⊕ *www. dunbeath-heritage.org.uk* 🎫 *£2* ⊙ *Easter–Oct., daily 10–5; phone for winter hrs.*

The **Laidhay Croft Museum**, just north of Dunbeath, feels more like a private home than a museum. It was built in the 18th century, comprises a longhouse and barn—animals and people lived under the same long roof—and is furnished as it would have been during its working life. ⊠ *Off A9* ☎ *01593/731233* 🎫 *£2* ⊙ *Easter–Oct., daily 10–5.*

## HELMSDALE

*15 mi south of Dunbeath.*

Helmsdale is a fascinating fishing village with a checkered past. It was a busy Viking settlement and then the scene of an aristocratic poisoning plot before it was transformed into a 19th-century village to house some of the people removed from their land to make way for sheep. These "clearances," perpetrated by the Duke of Sutherland, were among the area's most inhumane.

☪ The **Timespan Heritage Centre**, a thought-provoking mix of displays,
★ artifacts, and audiovisual materials, portrays the history of the area from the Stone Age to the 1869 gold rush in the Strath of Kildonan. The complex also includes a café and an art gallery with changing exhibitions. ⊠ *Helmsdale* ☎ *01431/821327* ⊕ *www.timespan.org.uk* 🎫 *£4.50* ⊙ *Easter–Oct., Mon.–Sat. 10–5, Sun. 2–5; last admission 1 hr before closing.*

## GOLSPIE

*18 mi south of Helmsdale.*

Although it has a number of shops and accommodations, the little coastal town of Golspie seems like a place that visitors merely pass through.

The Scottish home of the dukes of Sutherland is flamboyant **Dunrobin Castle,** an ancient seat developed by the first duke into a 19th-century white-turreted behemoth. As well as lavish interiors, there are Versailles-inspired gardens and falconry demonstrations. Trains so fascinated the duke that he built his own railroad in the park and staffed it with his servants. ✉*A9* ☎*01408/633177* 🎫*£7* 🕐*Mar.–May, Sept., and early Oct., daily 10:30–4:30; June–Aug., daily 10:30–5:30; last entry 30 min before closing.*

### SHOPPING

The **Orcadian Stone Company** ( ✉*Main St.* ☎*01408/633483*) makes stone products (including giftware crafted from local Caithness slate), incised plaques, and prepared mineral specimens. There's also a geological exhibition. The shop is open from Easter to October and for three weeks before Christmas, Monday to Saturday, 9 to 5:30.

> **A BRUTAL DUKE**
>
> Traveling south on the A9 from Helmsdale to Golspie, you can see the controversial statue of the first Duke of Sutherland, looking like some Eastern Bloc despot. He's perched on Beinn a Bragaidh (Ben Braggie), the hilltop to the west. Many people want to remove it, as the "improvement" policies of the duke were ultimately responsible for the brutality of the Sutherland Clearances of 1810–20, which removed people from their farms in favor of sheep farming.

## DORNOCH

*10 mi south of Golspie, 40 mi north of Inverness.*

A town of sandstone houses, tiny rose-filled gardens, and a 13th-century cathedral with stunning traditional and modern stained-glass windows, Dornoch is well worth a visit. It's noted for its links: you may hear it referred to as the St. Andrews of the North, but because of the town's location so far north, the golf courses here are delightfully uncrowded. Royal Dornoch is the jewel in its crown, praised by the world's top golfers.

### WHERE TO STAY & EAT

££ ✕🏨 **Dornoch Castle Hotel.** A genuine late-15th-century castle, once sheltering the bishops of Caithness, this hotel blends the quite old and the more modern. The lounge is a relaxing room of soft green and cream, and bedrooms wear pastel stripes and floral fabrics. This is not a luxury hotel, but it's clean and comfortable, with a friendly staff and satisfying, well-cooked Scottish food in the restaurant (£££). Try the steak rolled in crushed peppercorns and wrapped in Parma ham. **Pros:** Grand exterior, lovely gardens, friendly hotel staff. **Cons:** Some rooms need refurbishing, interior lacks the atmosphere that the outside promises. ✉*Dornoch IV25 3SD* ☎*01862/810216* ⊕*www.dornochcastlehotel. com* 🛏*22 rooms, 2 suites* 🛇*In-room: no a/c. In-hotel: restaurant, room service, no elevator* 🖃*AE, MC, V* 🍽*BP.*

££ 🏨 **Highfield House.** On its own grounds on the edge of town, this B&B has accommodations in a modern family home. Rooms are light and airy, with pastel colors and natural-wood furnishings. Your morning meal, served in the pretty breakfast room, includes local sausages and black pudding. **Pros:** Spacious rooms, good location, hearty breakfasts. **Con:** Not for families with young children. ⊠*Evelix Rd., IV25 3HR* ☎*01862/810909* ⊕*www.highfieldhouse.co.uk* ⤢*3 rooms* ⚘*In-room: no a/c, no phone. In-hotel: bicycles, no kids under 14, no elevator* ⊟*No credit cards* ⦿*BP.*

### GOLF

★ Were it not for its remote northern location, **Royal Dornoch** would undoubtedly be a candidate for the British Open Championship. It's a superb, breezy, and challenging links course. ⊠*Golf Rd* ☎*01862/810219* ⊕*www.royaldornoch.com* ⚲*18 holes, 6,200 yds, par 70.*

**EN ROUTE** If you're driving south toward Inverness on the A9, consider detouring first to Tain (look for signs to the town) for a visit to its excellent heritage center **Tain through Time.** The complex consists of a museum, the Collegiate Church, and the Pilgrimage Centre, all inviting you to explore Tain's history as an important pilgrimage site, thanks to the shrine of St. Duthus. In the late 15th century King James IV (1473–1513) was a frequent pilgrim here. ⊠*Tower St.* ☎*01862/894089* ⊕*www.tainmuseum.org.uk* ⛁*£3.50* ⊙*Apr.–Oct., Mon.–Sat. 10–5; by appointment only in other months.*

# TORRIDON

Torridon has a grand, rugged, and wild air that feels especially remote, yet it doesn't take much more than an hour's drive west from Inverness before you reach Kinlochewe, near the east end of Glen Torridon. The western side is equally spectacular. Walking trails and mountain panoramas abound. Torridon is a wonderful place to visit if you want to tackle one of the legendary peaks here—Beinn Alligin, Liathach, and Beinn Eighe—or if you enjoy outdoor activities like kayaking, climbing, or mountain biking. The A890, which runs from the A832 into the heart of Torridon, is a single-lane road in some stretches, with plenty of open vistas across the deserted heart of northern Scotland.

9

## LOCHCARRON

*66 mi west of Inverness via A9/A835/A832/A890.*

Strung along the shore, the village of Lochcarron has some attractive croft buildings, a couple of churches (one an 18th-century ruin set in a graveyard), a golf club, and some handy shops. **The Smithy Heritage Centre,** in a restored blacksmith's forge, provides visitor information about the area and arranges woodland walks. ⊠*Ribhuachan, by Lochcarron* ☎*01520/722246* ⊙*Apr.–Oct., Mon.–Sat. 10–5:30.*

### SHOPPING

At **Lochcarron Weavers** (⊠*Mid Strome* ☎*01520/722212*) you can observe a weaver at work, producing pure-wool worsted tartans that can be bought here or at the firm's other outlets in the area.

## SHIELDAIG

*16 mi northwest of Lochcarron.*

Just west of the southern coast of Upper Loch Torridon is Shieldaig, a village that sits in an attractive crescent overlooking a loch of its own, **Loch Shieldaig.** For an atmospheric evening foray, walk north toward Loch Torridon, at the northern end of the village by the church. The path—fairly well made, though hiking shoes are recommended—leads to exquisite views and tiny rocky beaches.

★ The scenic spectacle of **Glen Torridon** lies east of Shieldaig. Some say that Glen Torridon has the finest mountain scenery in Scotland. It consists mainly of the long gray quartzite flanks of **Beinn Eighe** (rhymes with *say*) and **Liathach** (*leea-*gach), with its distinct ridge profile that looks like the keel of an upturned boat. At the end of the glen the National Trust for Scotland operates a **visitor center** that explains the ecology and geology of the area. A small deer museum has displays on these quintessentially Scottish beasts. ☎*01445/791368* ⊕*www.nts.org.uk* ☞*£3* ⊙ *Visitor center Easter–Sept., daily 10–6; deer museum year-round, daily 9–5.*

**OFF THE BEATEN PATH**

**Applecross.** The tame way to reach this small community facing Skye is by a coastal road from near Shieldaig; the exciting route turns west off the A896 a few miles farther south. A series of hairpin turns corkscrews up the steep wall at the head of a corrie (a glacier-cut mountain valley), over the **Bealach na Ba** (Pass of the Cattle). There are spectacular views of Skye from the bare plateau on top, and you can brag afterward that you've been on what is probably Scotland's highest drivable road.

### WHERE TO STAY & EAT

£££ ✕▥**The Torridon and Torridon Inn.** The Victorian Gothic turrets of this former hunting lodge promise atmosphere and grandeur. Log fires, handsome plasterwork ceilings, mounted stag heads, and traditional furnishings set the mood downstairs, and bedrooms are decorated in restrained pastel shades with antique mahogany furniture. Their Torridon Inn annex offers more modest contemporary-style accommodation. The four-course dinner (£££££) may include seafood, beef, lamb, and game, and the cellar has many fine wines. ■TIP➜Ask for a room with loch views. Pros: Breathtaking location, center for outdoor activities, bar has more than 300 malts. Cons: Isolated location, modern wing lacks character, rather pricey. ⊠*A896, Annat IV22 2EY* ⊹*By Achnasheen, Wester Ross* ☎*01445/791242* ⊕*www.thetorridon.com* ⇨*18 rooms, 1 suite* ♿*In-room: no a/c. In-hotel: restaurant, bar, laundry service* ▤*AE, DC, MC, V* � †◎*BP.*

## GAIRLOCH

*38 mi north of Shieldaig.*

Aside from its restaurants and lodgings, Gairloch has one further advantage: lying just a short way from the mountains of the interior, this small oasis often escapes the rain clouds that can cling to the high summits. You can enjoy a round of golf here and perhaps stay dry, even when the nearby Torridon hills are deluged.

In the village is the **Gairloch Heritage Museum,** with exhibitions covering prehistoric times to the present. ✉ *Junction of A832 and B8031* ☎ *01445/712287* ⊕ *www.gairlochheritagemuseum.org.uk* 🖅 *£3* ⊙ *Easter–Sept., Mon.–Sat. 10–5; Oct., weekdays 10–1:30; Nov.–Mar. by appointment.*

**Fodor'sChoice** Southeast of Gairloch stretches one of Scotland's most scenic lochs, **Loch** ★ **Maree.** Its harmonious environs, with tall Scots pines and the mountain Slioch looming as a backdrop, witnessed the destruction of much of the tree cover in the 18th century. Iron ore was shipped in and smelted using local oak to feed the furnaces. Oak now grows here only on the northern limits of the range. Scottish Natural Heritage has an **information center** and nature trails by the loch and in the Beinn Eighe Nature Reserve. Red-deer sightings are virtually guaranteed; locals say the best place to spot another local denizen, the endangered pine marten (a member of the weasel family), is around the trash containers in the parking turnoffs.

★ The highlight of this area is **Inverewe Gardens,** 6 mi northeast of Gairloch. The main attraction lies in the contrast between the bleak coastal headlands and thin-soiled moors, and the lush plantings of the garden behind its dense shelterbelts. These are proof of the efficacy of the warm North Atlantic Drift, part of the Gulf Stream, which takes the edge off winter frosts. Inverewe is sometimes described as subtropical, but this inaccuracy irritates the head gardener; do not expect coconuts and palm trees here. Instead, look for rarities like the blue Himalayan poppy. ✉ *A832, Poolewe* ☎ *01445/781200* ⊕ *www.nts.org.uk* 🖅 *£8* ⊙ *Easter–Oct., daily 9:30–9; Jan.–Easter, daily 9:30–4.*

### WHERE TO STAY & EAT

££ ✕🏨 **Dundonnell Hotel.** This excellent family-run hotel, set on the roadside by Little Loch Broom, northeast of Gairloch, has cultivated a solid reputation for its hospitality and cuisine. Light floral curtains and bedspreads and contemporary furnishings fill the fresh, modern bedrooms. Many of the guest rooms and public rooms have stunning views of pristine hills and lochs. The restaurant serves homemade soups and fresh seafood, including sea bass, monk fish, and salmon. ■ TIP→ **Ask for a room with loch views. Pros:** Fabulous scenery, plenty of outdoor activities, good dining options. **Cons:** bland exterior, chintzy '70s decor. ✉ *Dundonnell IV23 2QR* ☎ *01854/633204* ⊕ *www.dundonnellhotel. com* 🛏 *32 rooms* ♿ *In-room: no a/c. In-hotel: restaurant, bar* ▭ *AE, MC, V* ⧦ *BP.*

£ 🏨 **The Mountain Restaurant and Lodge.** A café, lodge, and book shop all rolled into one, this property is a center of activity in Gairloch. Guest rooms are cozy, and one even has a four-poster bed. The café has a conservatory with a sweeping view over the sea. Huge, fresh-baked scones, both savory and sweet, are excellent for breakfast and lunch. Books of all subjects are everywhere, spilling over from the shop into the restaurant. Mountaineering memorabilia decorate the walls. **Pros:**

Good dining options, great for spotting wildlife like porpoises and seals. **Cons:** Dated decor, gets booked up quickly. ⊠*Strath Sq., IV21 2BX* ☎*01445/712316* ⤴*3 rooms* ⌂*In-room: no a/c. In-hotel: restaurant, no elevator* ⊟*MC, V* ⊘*Closed Jan.–Mar.* ⦿*CP.*

### GOLF

**Gairloch Golf Club** is one of the few on this stretch of coast. ☎*01445/712407* ⊕*www.gairlochgolfclub.com* ⚑*18 holes, 2,072 yds, SSS par 62.*

**EN ROUTE**  The road between Gairloch and the Corrieshalloch Gorge initially heads north and passes coastal scenery with views of Gruinard Bay and its white beaches, then woodlands around Dundonnell and Loch Broom. Soon the route traverses wild country: the toothed ramparts of the mountain An Teallach (pronounced *tyel*-lack) are visible on the horizon. The moorland route you travel is known chillingly as **Destitution Road.** It was built in the 1840s to give the local folk (long vanished from the area) some way of earning a living after the failure of the potato crop. It's said the workers were paid only in food. At Corrieshalloch the road, A832, joins the A835 for Inverness.

# ISLE OF SKYE

Skye ranks near the top of most visitors' must-see lists: the romance of Prince Charles Edward Stuart (1720–88), known as Bonnie Prince Charlie, combined with the misty Cuillin Hills and their proximity to the mainland all contribute to its popularity. Today Skye remains fey, mysterious, and mountainous, an island of sunsets that linger brilliantly until late at night and of beautiful, magical mists. Much photographed are the really old crofts, one or two of which are still inhabited, with their thick stone walls and thatch roofs. Much written about is the story known as the Adventure—the sad history of the "prince in the heather" and pretender to the British throne, Bonnie Prince Charlie.

From the gentle, lush terrain of the Garden of Skye in the south to the wild Cuillin Mountains in the north, Skye has abundant beauty and memorable vistas aplenty. As well as a good range of accommodation in small villages like Broadford and Glendale, the island now has some very fine restauarants that show off the best in the island's produce and culinary talent.

To reach Skye these days, you can cross over the bridge spanning the narrow channel of Kyle Akin, between Kyle of Lochalsh and Kyleakin, or take the (more romantic) ferry options between Mallaig and Armadale or between Glenelg and Kylerea. You can tour comfortably around the island in two or three days. Orientation is easy: follow the only roads around the loops on the northern part of the island and enjoy the road running the length of the Sleat Peninsula in southern Skye, taking the loop roads that exit to the north and south as you please. There are some stretches of single-lane road, but none poses a problem.

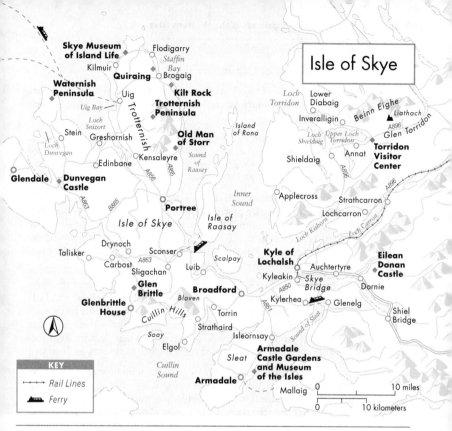

Isle of Skye

## KEY

⊢•••⊣ Rail Lines

🚢 Ferry

---

## KYLE OF LOCHALSH

*55 mi west of Inverness, 120 mi northwest of Glasgow.*

This little town is the mainland gateway to Skye. The area has seen great changes since the Skye Bridge, opened in 1995, transformed not only travel to Skye but the very seascape itself. The most noticeable attraction, though (in fact, almost a cliché), is not in Kyle at all, but 8 mi farther east at Dornie—Eilean Donan Castle.

**Fodor's Choice** Guarding the confluence of lochs Long, Alsh, and Duich stands that
★ most picturesque of all Scottish castles, **Eilean Donan Castle,** perched on an islet connected to the mainland by a stone-arched bridge. Dating from the 14th century, this romantic icon has all the massive stone walls, timber ceilings, and winding stairs that you could ask for. Empty and neglected for years after being bombarded by frigates of the Royal Navy during an abortive Spanish-Jacobite landing in 1719, it was almost entirely rebuilt from a ruin in the early 20th century. The kitchen re-creates the busy scene before a grand banquet. Now the hero of travel brochures, Eilean Donan has appeared in many Hollywood movies and TV shows. ⊠ *Off A97, Dornie* ☎ *01599/555202* ⊕ *www.eileandonancastle.com* ≦ *£5* ⊙ *Apr.–Oct., daily 10–6; last admission at 5.*

## BROADFORD

*8 mi west of Kyle of Lochalsh via Skye Bridge.*

One of the larger of Skye's settlements, Broadford lies along the shore of Broadford Bay, which has on occasion welcomed whales to its sheltered waters.

You can observe and handle snakes, frogs, lizards, and tortoises at the **Serpentarium**, in the town center. ⊠*The Old Mill, Harrapool* ☎*01471/822209* ⊕*www.skyeserpentarium.org.uk* 🎫*£3* ⊙*Easter–May and Sept. and Oct., Mon.–Sat. 10–5; July and Aug., daily 10–5.*

For fantastic views of the Cuillins, seabirds, abundant sealife and the Inner Hebrides, book a place onboard one of the **Misty Island Boat Trips** ( ⊠*Elgol* ☎*01471/866288* ⊕*www.mistyisleboattrips.co.uk*). The expansive scenery around Loch Coruisk is some of the most spectacular in Scotland. Round-trip journeys depart from the nearby town of Elgol Monday to Saturday at 11:15 and 2:15.

**OFF THE BEATEN PATH**

**The Road to Elgol.** The B8083 leads from Broadford to one of the finest views in Scotland. This road passes through **Strath Suardal** and little **Loch Cill Chriosd** (Kilchrist) by a ruined church. If there are cattle wading in the loch and the light is soft—typical of Skye—then this place takes on the air of a romantic oil painting. Skye marble, with its attractive green veining, was produced from the marble quarry at **Torrin.**

You can appreciate breathtaking views of the mountain called **Bla Bheinn** (*Blaven*) as the A881 continues to Elgol, a gathering of crofts along this road that descends to a pier. Admire the heart-stopping profile of the Cuillin peaks from the shore, or, at a point about halfway down the hill, you can find the path that goes toward them across the rough grasslands. For even better views, take a boat trip on the **Bella Jane** ( ⊠*Elgol Jetty* ☎*0800/731–3089* ⊕*www.bellajane.co.uk*) from Elgol jetty toward Loch Coruisk; you'll be able to land and walk up to the loch itself, as well as see seals during your boat trip. The boat excursion is available from April through October, daily, and advance booking is essential (tickets are £18).

### WHERE TO STAY & EAT

£££   ✕🏠 **Broadford Hotel.** Extensive renovations have transformed the interior of this imposing 17th-century building into a stylish hotel. The owners cleverly play on its association with the Drambuie whisky recipe bequeathed to a previous owner by Bonnie Prince Charlie. Guest rooms are done up in the strong Drambuie tartan colors, softened a bit by more relaxing hues. Expect well-crafted dishes in the restaurant like fettuccine in a wild–woodland-mushroom cream sauce, and locally caught langoustines served with a summer fruit salad. **Pros:** Excellent restaurant, innovative drinks in the bar. **Cons:** No real public spaces, noise from ongoing renovations. ⊠*Torrin Rd., IV49 9AB* ☎*01471/822204* ⊕*www.broadfordhotel.co.uk* 🛏*30 rooms* ⚒*In-room: no a/c, Wi-Fi. In-hotel: restaurant, bar* ☐*AE, MC, V* ⊚*BP.*

### BICYCLING

If you want to explore the country roads **Fairwinds Bicycle Hire** ( ✉ *Fairwinds, Elgol Rd.* ☎01471/822270) rents bicycles year-round.

### SHOPPING

**Craft Encounters** ( ✉*A850* ☎*01471/822754*) stocks local crafts, including pottery and jewelry.

## ARMADALE

*17 mi south of Broadford, 43 mi south of Portree, 5 mi (ferry crossing) west of Mallaig.*

Rolling moorlands, scattered with rivers and lochans, give way to enchanting hidden coves and scattered waterside communities here in **Sleat,** the southernmost part of Skye. Sleat well rewards a day or two spent exploring its side roads and its many craft outlets. For most visitors, Armadale is the first town to visit.

The popular **Armadale Castle Gardens and the Museum of the Isles,** including the Clan Donald Centre, tell the story of the Macdonalds and their proud title—the Lords of the Isles—with the help of an excellent audio-visual presentation. In the 15th century the clan was powerful enough to threaten the authority of the Stuart monarchs of Scotland. There are extensive gardens and nature trails, plus a gift shop, restaurant, library, and archive facility. Also on the grounds are high-quality accommodations in seven cottages with kitchen facilities. ✉*½ mi north of Armadale Pier* ☎*01471/844305 or 01471/844275* ⊕*www.clandonald.com* 💷*£5* ☉*Apr.–Oct., daily 9:30–5:30; last entry 30 min before closing.*

### WHERE TO STAY & EAT

££££–£££££ ╳⊡**Kinloch Lodge.** This country house, run as a lodging by Lord and Lady Macdonald with flair and professionalism, provides your bed, breakfast, and dinner for one price. Bookcases filled with interesting volumes and family photographs fill the warm, restful lounges, and the elegant bedrooms are individually decorated with antiques, chintz fabrics, and quilted bedspreads. The restaurant menu (£40 fixed-price dinner) might include lamb with a peppercorn and pinhead-oatmeal crust and "dark-chocolate nemesis" for dessert. Like the food? You can take cookery courses with Lady Macdonald. **Pros:** Historic property, interior full of character, renowned formal restaurant. **Cons:** Guest rooms near the kitchen can be noisy, some rooms need refurbishing. ✉*Off A851, Sleat IV43 8QY* ☎*01471/833214* ⊕*www.kinloch-lodge.co.uk* ↩*16 rooms* ⚙*In-room: no a/c. In-hotel: restaurant, bars, no elevator* 🟰*AE, MC, V* 🍴*MAP.*

£££ ╳⊡**Hotel Eilean Iarmain.** The Isle Ornsay Hotel (as it's sometimes known) has an enchanting collection of wood paneling, chintz fab-

> ### WORD OF MOUTH
>
> "If you are going to visit Skye, spend at least one night on the island. Go onto Skye via the bridge (beautiful drive along the Five Sisters) and leave Skye via the ferry (the Road to the Isles is also beautiful), or vice versa."
> —noe847

rics, and country-style antiques. Each room at the lodging, which sits beside the shore, is individual decorated. Try the Tower Room, with its nooks and crannies, or the room with the canopy bed from Armadale Castle. The menu in the restaurant (£££££) changes daily, but might include such dishes as seared venison with juniper, or steamed mussels with cream and whisky. **Pros:** Wonderful waterfront location, plenty of sporting activities, superb wine list in restaurant. **Cons:** Service is not as good as it could be, some rooms updating, furnishings a little careworn. ☒*Isleornsay, Sleat IV43 8QR* ☎*01471/833332* ⊕*www. eileaniarmain.co.uk* ➴*12 rooms, 4 suites* ⚙*In-room: no a/c, no TV (some). In-hotel: restaurant, bar* ⊟*AE, MC, V* ⫿⊙*BP.*

### SHOPPING

★ **Ragamuffin** ( ☒*Armadale Pier* ☎*01471/844217*) specializes in designer knitwear. The friendly staff will make you a cup of coffee while you browse, then mail your purchases back home for you.

The wee **Skye Ferry Filling Station** ( ☒*Ardvasar* ☎*01471/844249*) is a photogenic filling station and shop near the ferry port selling general supplies and knickknacks.

## PORTREE

*43 mi north of Armadale.*

Portree, the population center of the island, is a pleasant place clustered around a small and sheltered bay. Although not overburdened by historical features, it's a good touring base.

☾ On the outskirts of town is **Tigh na Coille: Aros** (*Tigh na Coille* is Gaelic for "house of the forest," and *Aros* means "home" or "homestead"), which provides an excellent account of Skye's often turbulent history over the centuries. It's also a great place to peep at the island's abundant wildlife. Park rangers regularly enthrall visitors by revealing the lives of Skye's sea eagles and sparrow hawks by way of nifty nest cams. You can find a gift shop, restaurant, and theater, which hosts musical events. ☒*Viewfield Rd.* ☎*01478/613649* ⊕*www.aros.co.uk* ☒*£4 for exhibition* ⊙*Daily 10–5.*

### WHERE TO STAY & EAT

££££ ✕▦ **Cuillin Hills Hotel.** Just outside Portree, this Victorian-era hunting lodge has many rooms with views over Portree Bay toward the Cuillin Hills. Bold floral patterns enliven the bedrooms. The seafood dishes in the restaurant (£££££) are especially good: try the local prawns, lobster, or scallops. ■**TIP**➔ **Ask for a room with views of the harbor and Cuillins beyond.** **Pros:** Portree is a short stroll away, good breakfast menu, attentive service. **Cons:** Restaurant can get very busy, food is pricey, some rooms could do with refurbishment. ☒*Portree IV51 9QU* ☎*01478/612003* ⊕*www. cuillinhills-hotel-skye.co.uk* ➴*27 rooms* ⚙*In-room: no a/c, Wi-Fi. In-hotel: restaurant, bar, laundry service, no elevator* ⊟*AE, MC, V* ⫿⊙*BP.*

£££ ✕▦ **Bosville Hotel.** Wood furniture and tartan fabrics fill the traditional guest rooms at this comfortable, family-run hotel. Make sure to ask for a room with harbor views. You have an excellent choice of eating

# CLANS & TARTANS

Whatever the origins of the clans—some with Norman roots, intermarried into Celtic society; some of Norse origin, the product of Viking raids on Scotland; others traceable to the monastic system; yet others possibly descended from Pictish tribes—by the 13th century the clan system was at the heart of Gaelic tribal culture. By the 15th century the clan chiefs of the Scottish Highlands were a threat even to the authority of the Stewart monarchs.

The word *clann* means "family" or "children" in Gaelic, and it was the custom for clan chiefs to board out their sons among nearby families, a practice that helped to bond the clan unit and create strong allegiances: the chief became "father" of the tribe and was owed loyalty by lesser chiefs and ordinary clansmen.

The clan chiefs' need for strong men-at-arms, fast-running messengers, and bards for entertainment and the preservation of clan genealogy was the probable origin of the Highland Games, still celebrated in many Highland communities each year, and which are an otherwise rather inexplicable mix of sports, music, and dance.

Gradually, by the 18th century, increasing knowledge of Lowland agricultural improvements, and better roads into the Highlands that improved communication of ideas and "southern" ways, began to weaken the clan system. After Culloden, as more modern economic influences took hold, those on the "wrong" side lost all; many chiefs lost their lands, tartan was banned, and clan culture withered.

Tartan's own origins as a part of the clan system are disputed; the Gaelic word for striped cloth is *breacan*—piebald or spotted—so even the word itself is not Highland. However, when cloth was locally spun, woven, and dyed using plant derivatives, each neighborhood would have different dyestuffs. In this way, particular combinations of colors and favorite patterns of the local weavers could become associated with a particular area and therefore clan.

Between 1746 and 1782 the wearing of tartan was generally prohibited. By the time the ban was lifted, many recipes for dyes and weaving patterns had been forgotten.

It took the influence of Sir Walter Scott, with his romantic, and fashionable, view of Highland history, to create the "modern myth" of clans and tartan. Sir Walter engineered George IV's visit to Scotland in 1822, which turned into a tartan extravaganza. The idea of one tartan or group of tartans "belonging" to one particular clan was created at this time—literally created, with new patterns and color ways dreamed up and "assigned" to particular clans. Queen Victoria and Prince Albert reinforced the tartan culture later in the century.

It's considered "proper" in some circles to wear the "right" tartan, that is, that of your clan. You may be able to find a clan connection with the expertise such as that available at **Scotland's Clan Tartan Centre** (⊠ *70–74 Bangor Rd., Leith, Edinburgh* ☎ *0131/553–5161*).

9

options: fine cuisine in the Chandlery Seafood Restaurant (££), or a more homey supper of Scottish fare in the bar (£). **Pros:** Cozy bar, fabulous views. **Cons:** Some rooms need refurbishment, tired decor in bistro. ⊠ *Bosville Terr., IV51 9DG* ☎ *01478/612846* ⊕ *www.macleodhotels. co.uk* ⊅ *19 rooms* ⌂ *In-room: no a/c. In-hotel: restaurant, bar* ⊟ *AE, DC, MC, V* ⊚ *BP.*

££–£££  ✕⊡ **Rosedale Hotel.** The higgledy-piggledy 19th-century buildings that make up this harbor-front hotel contain clean and comfortable rooms are done in pastels and florals. There's a superb restaurant serving delicious Scottish cooking. The menu (££) might include breast of duck with cranberries and parsnip puree, or pasta rolls with smoked haddock and lemon butter. Ask for a room at the front for views of the water. **Pros:** Friendly staff, first-class location, all-round great value—especially the restaurant. **Cons:** Dated decor in many rooms, tricky parking. ⊠ *The Harbour, IV51 9DB* ☎ *01478/613131* ⊕ *www. rosedalehotelskye.co.uk* ⊅ *19 rooms* ⌂ *In-room: no a/c. In-hotel: restaurant, bar, no elevator* ⊟ *MC, V* ⊗ *Closed Dec.–Mar.* ⊚ *BP.*

### SHOPPING

★ **An Tuireann Arts Centre** ( ⊠ *Struan Rd.* ☎ *01478/613306*) is a showcase for locally made crafts. It's a good place to look for unusual gifts or greetings cards. **Croft Comforts** ( ⊠ *2 Wentworth St.* ☎ *01478/613762*) has a wonderful selection of silver, antique and modern jewelry, porcelain, and pottery, as well as larger items. In addition, the staff provides a wealth of information about Skye: just ask David or Fiona Middleton for advice on places to eat, attractions to visit, or hidden coves to enjoy, and you won't be disappointed. **Skye Batiks** ( ⊠ *The Green* ☎ *01478/613331*) stocks unique Celtic-influenced batik clothing, cushion covers, and wall hangings; chunky handwoven cotton smocks, jackets, and skirts; silver jewelry; wood carvings; and much more. **Skye Original Prints** ( ⊠ *1 Wentworth St.* ☎ *01478/612544*) sells works by local artist Tom Mackenzie.

## TROTTERNISH PENINSULA

*16 mi north of Portree via A855.*

As A855, the main road, goes north from Portree, cliffs rise to the left. They're actually the edge of an ancient lava flow, set back from the road and running for miles as your rugged companion.

In some places the hardened lava has created spectacular features, including a curious pinnacle called the **Old Man of Storr.**

The A855 travels past neat white croft houses and forestry plantings to **Kilt Rock.** Everyone on the Skye tour circuit stops here to peep over the cliffs (there's a safe viewing platform) for a look at the geology of the cliff edge: columns of two types (and colors) of rock create a folded, pleated effect, just like a kilt.

The spectacular **Quiraing** dominates the horizon 5 mi past Kilt Rock. For a closer view of the strange pinnacles and rock forms, make a left onto a small road at Brogaig by Staffin Bay. There's a parking lot near the point where this road breaches the ever-present cliff line, though you have to walk back toward the Quiraing itself, where the rock formations and cliffs are most dramatic. The trail is on uneven, stony ground, and it's a steep scramble up to the rock formations. In ages past, stolen cattle were hidden deep within the Quiraing's rocky jaws.

The main A855 reaches around the top end of Trotternish, to the **Skye Museum of Island Life** at Kilmuir, where you can see the old crofting ways brought to life. Included in the displays and exhibits are documents and photographs, reconstructed interiors, and implements. Flora Macdonald, helpmate of Bonnie Prince Charlie, is buried nearby. ⊠ *Kilmuir* 🕾🕾 *01470/552206* ⊕ *www.skyemuseum.co.uk* 🖃 *£2.50* ⊗ *Easter–Oct., daily 9–5.*

### WHERE TO STAY & EAT

£££   ✕🖻 **Flodigarry Country House Hotel.** Close links with Flora Macdonald, Prince Charles Edward Stuart's helpmate, are not the least of the attractions at this country-house hotel, which is well placed for exploring the north and west of Skye. Yes, you can actually have a room in Flora's own cottage, adjacent to the hotel, where six of her children were born. The main hotel is a bit grander, and serves excellent seafood in the restaurant (£££££). There are no TVs in the rooms, but you can ask to borrow a portable. **Pros:** The chance to stay within historic walls, stunning views of the Quiraing. **Cons:** Some beds are on the small side, erratic customer service. ⊠ *Staffin, Isle of Skye IV51 9HZ* 🕾 *01470/552203* ⊕ *www.flodigarry.co.uk* 🛏 *18 rooms* ♨ *In-room: no a/c, no TV. In-hotel: restaurant, bar, no elevator* ▭ *MC, V* ⦿ *BP.*

## WATERNISH PENINSULA

*20 mi northwest of Portree via A850.*

The northwest corner of Skye has scattered crofting communities, magnificent coastal views, and a few good restaurants well worth the trip in themselves. In the Hallin area look westward for an islet-scattered sea loch with small cliffs rising from the water—and looking like miniature models of full-size islands. Just above the village of Stein, on the left side of the road, is a restored and inhabited "black house"—a thatched cottage blackened over time because a hole in its roof stood in for a chimney—today a rare sight on Skye and, in any event, now painted white.

Stoneware pottery is fired in a wood-fired kiln at the **Edinbane Pottery Workshop and Gallery,** in southern Waternish. You can watch the potters work, then buy from the showroom. ⊠ *Edinbane* 🕾 *01470/582234* ⊕ *www.edinbane-pottery.co.uk* ⊗ *Easter–Oct., daily 9–6; Nov.–Easter, weekdays 9–6.*

### WHERE TO STAY & EAT

££££   ✕ **Loch Bay Seafood Restaurant.** On the waterfront in the village of Stein
★   stands this distinctive black-and-white restaurant. The relaxed place is where the island's top chefs relax on their nights off, so you know the food must be good. The seafood is freshly caught and simply pre-

pared, the goal being to enhance the natural flavors of the ingredients rather than overwhelm the senses with extraneous sauces. ⊠ *Near fishing jetty, Stein* ☎ *01470/592235* ▭ *MC, V* ⊙ *Closed Nov.–Easter and weekends except Sat. July–Oct.*

£££–££££ ✕▣ **Greshornish House.** Apart from the splendid isolation of the lochside location, this hotel's best feature is its restaurant, where mahogany tables are laid with damask, crystal, and candelabras. The menu (£££££) might include scallops poached in white wine, local lobster or king prawns grilled with wild garlic butter, or Skye lamb cutlets flavored with heather honey and ginger. Greshornish is a quirky hotel with spacious, if rather eclectically furnished, public rooms and bedrooms of all shapes and sizes. **Pros:** Exceptional food, homey atmosphere, verdant grounds with lots of sheep as neighbors. **Cons:** Furnishings are a tad dated, need a vehicle to get around. ⊠ *Greshornish IV51 9PN* ☎ *01470/582266* 🖷 *01470/582345* ⊕ *www.greshornishhouse. com* ⇝ *9 rooms* ⌂ *In-room: no a/c. In-hotel: restaurant, tennis court, no elevator* ▭ *AE, MC, V* ¶◎¶ *MAP.*

---

## DUNVEGAN CASTLE

*22 mi west of Portree.*

In a commanding position above a sea loch, Dunvegan Castle has been the seat of the chiefs of Clan MacLeod for more than 700 years. Though the structure has been greatly changed over the centuries, a gloomy ambience prevails, and there's plenty of family history on display, notably the Fairy Flag—a silk banner, thought to be originally from Rhodes or Syria and believed to have magically saved the clan from danger. The banner's powers are said to suffice for only one more use. Make time to visit the gardens, with their water garden and falls, fern house, a walled garden, and various viewing points. Dunvegan Sea Cruises runs a boat trip from the castle to the nearby seal colony for £6.50 per person. ⊠ *At junction of A850 and A863, Dunvegan* ☎ *01470/521206* ⊕ *www.dunvegancastle.com* 🖾 *Garden £5; castle and garden £7.50* ⊙ *Mid-Mar.–Oct., daily 10–5; Nov.–mid-Mar., daily 11–4; last entry 30 min before closing.*

### WHERE TO STAY

££ ▣ **Roskhill House.** A 19th-century croft house that once housed the ★ local post office in its dining room, this pretty white hotel feels like a home away from home. Bold colors decorate the bedrooms, and the lounge is filled with books and games. Stone walls, stick-back chairs, and a scarlet carpet lend the dining room a publike air. In the morning, the breakfast options are a change from the usual heavy fare. There are even vegetarian choices. **Pros:** Great breakfasts, genuinely friendly and helpful hosts, cozy lounge with fireplace. **Cons:** Very small place, booked up well in advance. ⊠ *Roskhill, by Dunvegan, IV55 8ZD* ☎ *01470/521317* ⊕ *www.roskhillhouse.co.uk* ⇝ *4 rooms* ⌂ *In-room: no a/c, no phone, no TV. In-hotel: public Internet, no elevator* ▭ *MC, V* ¶◎¶ *BP.*

## GLENDALE

*5 mi south of Dunvegan.*

The Glendale Visitor Route, a signed driving trail off the A863 through the westernmost area of northwest Skye, leads past crafts outlets, museums, and other attractions.

The **Toy Museum,** has a remarkable collection of dolls, trains, games, puzzles, and books that transports visitors back to their childhoods. ⊠*Glendale* 🕾*01470/511240* ⊕*www.toy-museum.co.uk* 🖃*£3* 🕓*Mon.–Sat. 10–6.*

**Borreraig Park** has a fascinating museum of island life—rightly described by the owner as "a unique gallimaufry for your delight and edification"—that includes a detailed series of panels on the making of bagpipes and on the history of the MacCrimmons, hereditary pipers to the Clan MacLeod. A superb gift shop stocks unique island-made sweaters (the exact sheep can be named), bagpipes, silver and gold jewelry in Celtic designs, and recordings of traditional music. ⊠*Borreraig Park* 🕾*01470/511311* 🖃*£2.50* 🕓*Daily 10–6.*

### WHERE TO STAY & EAT

££££££
Fodor'sChoice
★

✕🖾 **Three Chimneys Restaurant with Rooms.** One of Skye's top-notch restaurants (£50 fixed-price menu), Shirley and Eddie Spear's shoreside cottage might be small on space, but it's big on flavor: fresh local seafood, beef, lamb, and game are transformed into dishes such as prawn and lobster bisque, or grilled loin of lamb with honey-roasted root vegetables and sherried button-mushroom sauce. Skye soft fruits—raspberries, strawberries, black currants—may follow for dessert. Adjacent to the restaurant are luxury accommodations in a courtyard wing, with magnificent sea views from all the rooms. **Pros:** Exceptional restaurant, friendly and professional service, wonderful location with lots of walking trails. **Cons:** Expensive rates, no children's menu at restaurant. ⊠*B884, Colbost, by Dunvegan, IV55 8ZT* 🕾*01470/511258* ⊕*www. threechimneys.co.uk* 🛏*6 rooms* 🕭*In-room: no a/c, DVD. In-hotel: no elevator* 🖃*AE, MC, V* 🕓*No lunch Sun.* 🍴*BP.*

### SHOPPING

**Skye Silver** ( ⊠*The Old School, Colbost, Glendale* 🕾*01470/511263*), west of Dunvegan, designs gold and silver jewelry with Celtic themes. More unusual pieces that reflect the natural forms of the seashore and countryside: silver-coral earrings, silver-leaf pendants, and starfish and cockleshell earrings.

## GLEN BRITTLE & THE CUILLINS

★ *28 mi southeast of Glendale.*

You can safely enjoy spectacular mountain scenery in Glen Brittle, with some fine views of the Cuillin Ridge (which is not for the casual walker, as there are many steep and dangerous cliff faces). Glen Brittle extends off the A863/B8009 on the west side of the island. The drive from Carbost along a single-track road is one of the most dramatic in Scotland

and draws outdoorsy types from throughout the world. At the southern end of the glen is a murky-color beach, a campground, and the chance for a gentle stroll amid the foothills of the Cuillins.

# THE OUTER HEBRIDES

The Outer Hebrides—the Western Isles in common parlance—stretch about 130 mi from end to end and lie about 50 mi from the Scottish mainland. This splintered archipelago extends from the Butt of Lewis in the north to the 600-foot Barra Head on Berneray in the south, whose lighthouse has the greatest arc of visibility in the world. The Isle of Lewis and Harris is the northernmost and largest of the group. The island's only major town, Stornoway, is on a nearly landlocked harbor on the east coast of Lewis; it's probably the most convenient starting point for a driving tour of the islands if you're approaching the Western Isles from the Northern Highlands. Lewis has some fine historic attractions, including the Calanais standing stones—a truly magical place. Both Lewis and Harris have beautiful white-sand beaches, whereas the Uists are known for their prehistoric sites and rare wildlife.

Just south of the Sound of Harris is North Uist, rich in monoliths, chambered cairns, and other reminders of a prehistoric past. Though it's one of the smaller islands in the chain, Benbecula, sandwiched between North and South Uist and sometimes referred to as the Hill of the Fords, is in fact less bare and neglected looking than its bigger neighbors to the north. South Uist, once a refuge of the old Catholic faith, is dotted with ruined forts and chapels; in summer its wild gardens burst with alpine and rock plants. Eriskay and a scattering of islets almost block the 6-mi strait between South Uist and Barra, an isle you can walk across in an hour.

Harris tweed is available at many outlets on the islands, including some of the weavers' homes; keep an eye out for signs directing you to weavers' workshops. Sunday on the islands is strictly observed as a day of rest, and nearly all shops and visitor attractions are closed.

## STORNOWAY

*2½-hr ferry trip from Ullapool, on Lewis.*

The port capital for the Outer Hebrides is Stornoway, the only major town on Lewis.

★ The fabulous **An Lanntair Arts Centre,** opened in 2006, has exhibitions of contemporary and traditional art, as well as a cinema, a gift shop, and a restaurant serving international and Scottish fare. There are frequent traditional musical and theatrical events in the impressive auditorium. ⌧*Kenneth St.* ☎*01851/703307* ⊕*www.lanntair.com* ☑*Free* ☺*Mon.–Sat. 10* AM*–11* PM.

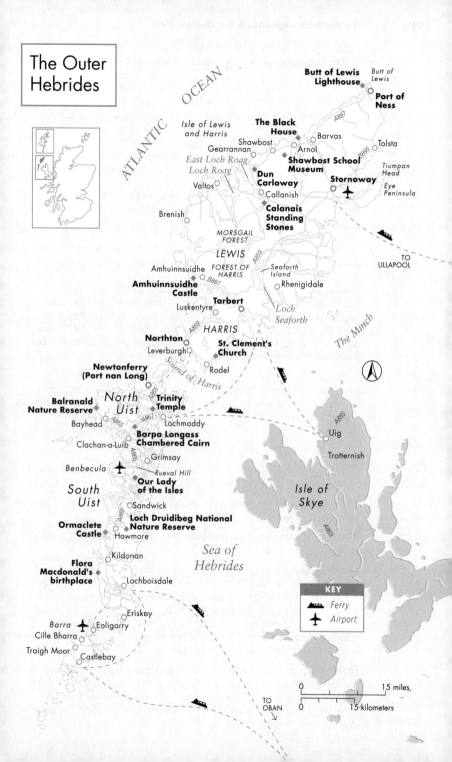

### WHERE TO STAY & EAT

££   ✕⊡**Park Guest House and Restaurant.** This handsome Victorian-era house and has retained many of its original features, including the grand fireplaces. Most of the guest rooms were refurbished in 2007, so along with old-fashioned touches like brass beds they have up-to-date bathrooms. Expect an interesting mix of tourists and people traveling for business. The quality of the food is a cut above most places on Lewis. For breakfast you have unusual choices like Stornoway kippers and black pudding. The restaurant's innovative menu (£££) includes lamb, game, and seafood dishes. ■ TIP➔ Cooks should look into the on-site cooking classes. **Pros:** Excellent restaurant and on-site cookery courses. **Cons:** Rooms facing the main road can be noisy and service indifferent. ✉ *30 James St., HS1 2QN* ☏*01851/702485* ⊕*www. theparkguesthouse.co.uk* ⇆*8 rooms* ⌂*In-room: no a/c. In-hotel: restaurant, bar, no elevator* ▤*AE, MC, V* ⫶○⫶*BP.*

£   ⊡**27 Springfield Road.** A quiet residential area backing onto open fields is the setting for this detached house with comfortable accommodations. Sleek furniture fills the rooms: one is done in blue and pink florals; another has navy and beige geometric prints. Immaculate gardens surround the house, which is just a short walk from downtown. **Pro:** Helpful hosts, good value. **Cons:** Unremarkable modern house, busy decor. ✉ *27 Springfield Rd., HS1 2PS* ☏*01851/703254* ⊕*www. davinamacdonald.co.uk* ⇆*3 rooms* ⌂*In-room: no a/c, no phone. In-hotel: no elevator* ▤*No credit cards* ⫶○⫶*BP.*

### BICYCLING

**Alex Dan Cycle Centre** ( ✉*67 Kenneth St.* ☏*01851/704025*) rents bicycles and can give you advice on where to ride, including a route to Tolsta that takes in five stunning beaches before reaching the edge of moorland.

## PORT OF NESS

*30 mi north of Stornoway via the A857, on Lewis.*

The stark, windswept community of Port of Ness cradles a small harbor squeezed in among the rocks.

The port is overlooked by **Harbour View** ( ☏*01851/810735*), a small gallery with its own café.

At the northernmost point of Lewis stands the **Butt of Lewis Lighthouse,** designed by David and Thomas Stevenson (of the prominent engineering family whose best-known member was not an engineer at all: the novelist Robert Louis Stevenson). The lighthouse was first lighted in 1862. The adjacent cliffs provide a good vantage point for viewing seabirds, whales, and porpoises. The lighthouse is a few minutes northwest of Port of Ness along the B8014.

In the small community of Arnol, 21 mi southwest of Port of Ness, look for signs off the A858 for the **Black House,** a well-preserved example of an increasingly rare type of traditional Hebridean home. Once common throughout the islands—even into the 1950s—these dwellings were built without mortar and thatched on a timber framework without eaves. Other characteristic features include an open central peat hearth and the absence of a chimney—hence the soot and the designation *black*. On display inside are many of the house's original furnishings. To reach Arnol from Port of Ness, go back south on the A857 and pick up the A858 at Barvas. ⊠ *Off A858, Arnol* ☎ *01851/710395* ⊕ *www.historic-scotland.gov.uk* ☜ *£5* ⊙ *Apr.–Sept., Mon.–Sat. 9:30–5:30; Oct.–Mar., Mon.–Sat. 9:30–4.*

### SHOPPING

At **Borgh Pottery** (⊠ *Fivepenny House, Borve, on road to Ness* ☎ *01851/850345*), open from Monday to Saturday 9:30 to 6, you can buy attractive hand-thrown studio pottery made on the premises, including lamps, vases, mugs, and dishes.

**EN ROUTE** The journey along the A857 to the Calanais Standing Stones takes you past several interesting sights.

**Dun Carloway** (⊠ *Off A857*), one of the best-preserved Iron Age *brochs* (circular stone towers) in Scotland, dominates the scattered community of Carloway. The mysterious tower was probably built around 2,000 years ago as protection against seaborne raiders. The interpretive center explains more about the broch and its setting.

Up a side road north from Carloway at the community of **Gearrannan** (☎ *01851/643416* ⊕ *www.gearrannan.com*) an old black-house village has been brought back to life with a museum and guided tours explaining the old island way of life.

## CALANAIS STANDING STONES

★ *22 mi southeast of Arnol on Lewis.*

At Calanais (Callanish) are the Calanais Standing Stones, lines of megaliths reminiscent of those in Stonehenge, in England. Probably positioned in several stages between 3000 BC and 1500 BC, this grouping consists of an avenue of 19 monoliths extending northward from a circle of 13 stones, with other rows leading south, east, and west. Researchers believe they may have been used for astronomical observations. The site itself is accessible at any time. The **visitor center** has an exhibit on the stones, a gift shop, and a tearoom. ⊠ *Off A858, Calanais* ☎ *01851/621422* ☜ *£3* ⊙ *Visitor center Apr.–Sept., Mon.–Sat. 10–6; Oct.–Mar., Wed.–Sat. 10–4.*

The restored black house next to the gate leading to the Calanais Standing Stones is the site of the **Callanish Stones Tearoom** (☎ *01851/621373*), an interesting spot in which to take refreshment or browse among the crafts on display.

## TARBERT

*47 mi south of Calanais on Harris.*

Tarbert, the main port of Harris, has a few worthwhile sights. **Traigh Luskentyre**, roughly 5 mi southwest of Tarbert, is a spectacular example of Harris's tidy selection of beaches—2 mi of yellow sands adjacent to **Traigh Seilebost** beach, with superb views northward to the hills of the Forest of Harris.

Turreted **Amhuinnsuidhe Castle** (pronounced avun-*shooee*) was built in the 1860s by the earls of Dunmore as a base for fishing and hunting in the North Harris deer forest. The castle stands about 10 mi northwest of Tarbert on the B887, and you can view it from the outside only.

> ### THE BONNIE PRINCE
>
> At the Battle of Culloden, George II's army outnumbered that of Prince Charles Edward Stuart. After the battle, Bonnie Prince Charlie wandered over the Highlands. He escaped to the isles of Harris and South Uist, where he met Flora Macdonald (1722–90), the woman who took him, disguised as her maid, "over the sea to Skye." *Will ye nO' come back again...Speed, bonnie boat...Charlie is my darling...*the tunes and lyrics of Lady Nairn, jaunty or mournful, composed long after the events, are as good an epitaph as any adventurer could wish for.

**Caledonian MacBrayne** (☎08705/650000 ⊕*www.calmac.co.uk*) runs a twice-daily ferry service beween Tarbert and Uig on Skye.

## NORTHTON

*16 mi south of Tarbert on Harris.*

The little community of Northton, near Leverburgh and the ferry to North Uist, has two attractions.

The **McGillivray Centre** focuses on the life and work of William McGillivray (1796–1852), a noted naturalist with strong links to Harris. McGillivray authored the five-volume *History of British Birds*. Some of his original drawings are on display in the center (others can be seen in London at the British Museum of Natural History). ⊠*Off A859* ☎*01859/502011* 🖂*Donations accepted* ⊙*Mon.–Sat. 9–9.*

The **Seallam! Visitor Centre and Co Leis Thu? Genealogical Research Centre** is where you can trace your Western Isles ancestry. Photographs and interpretive signs describe the history of Harris and its people. The owners organize guided walks and cultural evenings weekly between May and September. ⊠*Off A859* ☎*01859/520258* ⊕*www.seallam. com* 🖂*£3* ⊙*Mon.–Sat. 9–5.*

At the southernmost point of Harris is the community of Rodel, where you can find **St. Clement's Church**, a cruciform church standing on a hillock. This is the most impressive pre-Reformation church in the Outer Hebrides; it was built around 1500 and contains the magnificently sculptured tomb (1528) of the church's builder, Alasdair Crotach,

MacLeod chief of Dunvegan Castle. Rodel is 4 mi south of Northon and 20 mi south of Tarbert.

## NORTH UIST

*8 mi south of Rodel via ferry from Leverburgh, Harris.*

The island of North Uist is particularly known for its prehistoric remains.

At **Newtonferry (Port nan Long),** by Otternish and the ferry pier for the Leverburgh (Harris) ferry service, stand the remains of what was reputed to be the last inhabited broch in North Uist, **Dun an Sticar.** This defensive tower, reached by a causeway over the loch, was home to Hugh Macdonald, a descendant of MacDonald of Sleat, until 1602.

You can explore the ruins of **Trinity Temple (Teampull na Trionaid),** a medieval college and monastery said to have been founded in the 13th century by Beathag, daughter of Somerled, the progenitor of the Clan Donald. The ruins stand 8 mi southwest of Lochmaddy, off the A865.

The **Barpa Langass Chambered Cairn,** dating from the 3rd millennium BC, is the only chambered cairn in the Western Isles known to have retained its inner chamber fully intact. You can peek inside, but don't venture too far without a light. It sits very close to the A867 between Lochmaddy and Clachen.

The **Balranald Nature Reserve,** administered by the Royal Society for the Protection of Birds, shelters large numbers of waders and seabirds. It's on the west side of North Uist. Ask for information at the Goular visitor center. ✉ *Off A865, 3 mi northwest of Bayhead* ☎ *01876/560287* ⊕ *www.rspb.org* ✉ *Free* ⊗ *Daily 24 hrs.*

## SOUTH UIST

*34 mi south of Newtonferry via Grimsay, Benbecula, and 3 causeways.*

Carpets of wildflowers in spring and early summer, superb deserted beaches, and historical connections to Flora Macdonald and Bonnie Prince Charlie head the list of reasons to visit the island of South Uist. You can travel the length of South Uist along Route A865, making short treks off this main road on your way to Lochboisdale, on the southeast coast of the island. At Lochboisdale you can catch ferries to Barra, the southernmost principal island of the Outer Hebrides, or to Oban, on the mainland.

A few miles south of Howmore, just west of A865, stand the ruins of **Ormaclete Castle,** built in 1708 for the chief of the Clan Ranald but destroyed by fire in 1715 on the eve of the Battle of Sheriffmuir.

The **Kildonan Museum and Heritage Centre** houses South Uist artifacts collected in the 1950s and 1960s by Father John Morrison, a local priest. There are also archaeological displays that explain what South Uist was like from the Bronze Age until the Viking raids. You can shop for gifts in the crafts shop and have a bite in the tearoom. ✉ *A865, Kildonan* ☎ *01878/710343* 💷 *£2* ⊙ *Easter–Oct., Mon.–Sat. 10–5, Sun. 2–5.*

At Gearraidh Bhailteas, you can see the ruins that mark **Flora Macdonald's birthplace.** South Uist's most famous daughter, Flora helped the Young Pretender, Prince Charles Edward Stuart, avoid capture and was feted as a heroine afterward. Legend has it that Flora helped the fugitive prince escape from South Uist in a rowboat with the prince disguised as Flora's maid. ✉ *¼ mi west of A865, ½ mi north of Milton.*

### SHOPPING

**Hebridean Jewellery** ( ✉ *Garrieganichy, Iochdar* ☎ *01870/610288*) sells lovely jewelry based on Celtic and Pictish designs, as well as some modern styles; the owners also run a crafts shop on the premises.

# NORTHERN HIGHLANDS & WESTERN ISLES ESSENTIALS

## TRANSPORTATION

### BY AIR

The main airports for the Northern Highlands are Inverness and Wick (both on the mainland). Loganair has direct air service from Edinburgh and Glasgow to Inverness and from Edinburgh to Wick. You can fly from London Gatwick, Luton Airport (near London) or Bristol to Inverness on one of the daily easyJet flights. British Airways also has a service from Gatwick. Loganair operates flights among the islands of Barra, Benbecula, and Lewis in the Outer Hebrides (weekdays only). Highland Airways operates flights from Inverness to Stornoway and Benbecula.

**Information British Airways** ( ☎ *0870/850–9850* ⊕ *www.britishairways. com*). **easyJet** ( ☎ *0870/600–0000* ⊕ *www.easyjet.com*). **Highland Airways** ( ☎ *0845/450–2245* ⊕ *www.highlandairways.co.uk*). **Loganair** ( ☎ *01856/872494* ⊕ *www.loganair.co.uk*).

**Information Inverness Airport** ( ☎ *01667/462445* ⊕ *www.hial.co.uk/inverness-airport.html*). **Stornoway Airport** ( ☎ *01851/702256* ⊕ *www.hial.co.uk/stornoway-airport.html*).

### BY BOAT & FERRY

Ferries run from Ullapool to Stornoway, from Oban to Castlebay and Lochboisdale, and from Uig (on the Isle of Skye) to Tarbert and Lochmaddy. Causeways link North Uist, Benbecula, and South Uist. The Island Hopscotch planned-route ticket and the Island Rover pass, both offered by Caledonian MacBrayne (called CalMac) give considerable reductions on interisland ferry fares. Various tickets are available, including the Hopscotch 12 (connecting Skye, Harris, Lewis, and the Uists), which costs £36 per person.

**Information Caledonian MacBrayne** ( ⊠ *Ferry Terminal, Gourock* ☎*01475/650100* ⊕*www.calmac.co.uk*). **Oban to Castlebay and Lochboisdale ferry** (☎*01631/566688*). **Ullapool to Stornoway ferry** (☎*01854/612358*). **Uig to Tarbert and Lochmaddy ferry** (☎*01470/542219*).

## BY BUS

Scottish Citylink and National Express run buses to Inverness, Ullapool, Thurso, Scrabster, and Wick. There are also coach connections between the ferry ports of Tarbert and Stornoway; consult the local tourist information center for details. Buses are a reliable way to see this region, but they often don't run frequently.

Highland Country Buses provides bus service in the Highlands area. On the Outer Hebrides several small operators run regular routes to most towns and villages. The post-bus service—which also delivers mail—becomes increasingly important in remote areas; it supplements the regular bus service, which runs only a few times per week. A full timetable of services for the Northern Highlands (and the rest of Scotland) is available from the Royal Mail.

**Information Highland Country Buses** ( ☎*01463/710555* ⊕*www.rapsons.com*). **National Express** ( ☎*08705/808080* ⊕*www.nationalexpress.co.uk*). **Royal Mail Post Buses** ( ☎*0845/7740740* ⊕*www.royalmail.com/postbus*). **Scottish Citylink** ( ☎*08705/505050* ⊕*www.citylink.co.uk*).

## BY CAR

Because of the infrequent bus services and sparse railway stations, a car is definitely the best way to explore this region. The twisting, winding single-lane roads demand a degree of driving dexterity, however. Local rules of the road require that when two cars meet, whichever driver reaches a passing place first must stop in it or opposite it and allow the oncoming car to continue. Small cars tend to yield to large commercial vehicles. Never park in passing places, and remember that these sections of the road can also allow traffic behind you to pass. Note that in this sparsely populated area, distances between gas stations can be considerable.

## BY TRAIN

Main railway stations in the area include Oban (for Barra and the Uists) and Kyle of Lochalsh (for Skye), on the west coast, or Inverness (for points north to Thurso and Wick). There's direct service from London to Inverness and connecting service from Edinburgh and Glasgow. For information contact National Rail or First ScotRail.

Stops on the northern lines (Inverness to Thurso–Wick and Inverness to Kyle of Lochalsh) include Beauly, Muir of Ord, and Dingwall; on the Thurso–Wick line, Alness, Invergordon, Fearn, Tain, Ardgay, Culrain, Invershin, Lairg, Rogart, Golspie, Brora, Helmsdale, Kildonan, Kinbrace, Forsinard, Altnabreac, Scotscalder, and Georgemas Junction; and on the Kyle line, Garve, Lochluichart, Achanalt, Achnasheen, Achnashellach, Strathcarron, Attadale, Stromeferry, Duncraig, Plockton, and Duirinish.

Information **National Rail** ( ☎ *08457/484950* ⊕ *www.nationalrail.co.uk*). **First ScotRail** ( ☎ *08457/550033* ⊕ *www.firstgroup.com/scotrail*).

## CONTACTS & RESOURCES

### EMERGENCIES

Dial **999** in an emergency for an ambulance, the police, the fire department, or the coast guard (no coins are needed for emergency calls from public phone booths). Pharmacies are not found in rural areas. Pharmacies in the main towns—Thurso, Wick, Stornoway—keep normal shop hours. In an emergency the police will provide assistance in locating a pharmacist. General practitioners may also dispense medicine in rural areas.

### TOURS

J. A. Johnstone Chauffeur Drive will escort you anywhere and gives a lot of information about the Highlands and islands, including the Outer Hebrides. Puffin Express runs unusual "Wildlife and Stone Age" day tours from Inverness between Easter and October, with limited tours in winter (when the owner goes wolf-watching in Poland). Raasay Outdoor Centre organizes courses in kayaking, sailing, windsurfing, climbing, rappeling, archery, walking, and navigation skills.

Contact **J. A. Johnstone Chauffeur Drive** ( ☎ *01463/798372*). **Puffin Express** ( ☎ *01463/717181* ⊕ *www.puffinexpress.co.uk*). **Raasay Outdoor Centre** ( ☎ *01478/660266* ⊕ *www.raasayoutdoorcentre.co.uk*).

### VISITOR INFORMATION

The tourist information centers at Dornoch, Dunvegan, Durness, Portree, Stornoway, Tarbert, and Ullapool are open year-round, with limited winter hours at Dunvegan, Durness, and Ullapool.

Seasonal tourist information centers are at Bettyhill, Broadford (Skye), Castlebay (Barra, Outer Hebrides), Gairloch, Helmsdale, John O'Groats, Kyle of Lochalsh, Lairg, Lochboisdale (South Uist, Outer Hebrides), Lochcarron, Lochinver, Lochmaddy (North Uist, Outer Hebrides), North Kessock, Shiel Bridge, Strathpeffer, Thurso, and Uig.

Information **Dornoch** ( ✉ *The Square* ☎ *01862/810555*). **Dunvegan, Skye** ( ✉ *2 Lochside* ☎ *01470/521581*). **Durness** ( ✉ *Sango* ☎ *01971/511259*). **Portree, Skye** ( ✉ *Bayfield House, Bayfield Rd.* ☎ *01478/612137*). **Stornoway, Isle of Lewis and Harris** ( ✉ *26 Cromwell St.* ☎ *01851/703088* ⊕ *www.visithebrides.com*). **Tarbert, Isle of Lewis and Harris** ( ✉ *Pier Rd.* ☎ *01859/502011*). **Ullapool** ( ✉ *Argyll St. R* ☎ *01854/612135*).

# Orkney & Shetland

**WORD OF MOUTH**

"I love Shetland and prefer it to Orkney. It is so different from anywhere else, whereas Orkney feels more like a detached part of Scotland. Scenically, I also think Shetland has the edge of the two. However, in terms of monuments Orkney has a lot more to offer than Shetland (although Jarlshof is superb). In Orkney on Mainland, both Maes Howe and Skara Brae are musts. Ferries between islands in Shetland are more convenient/frequent and cheaper than Orkney, so driving is easy."

—wasleys

"Highland Park—the northernmost distillery in Scotland—is located on Orkney. My favorite Scotch and reason enough for me to want to visit."

—DanM

Updated by
Shona Main
and Nick
Bruno

**A SCANDINAVIAN HERITAGE GIVES THE** 200 islets that make up Orkney and Shetland an ambience different from that of any other region of Scotland. For mainland Scots, visiting this archipelago off the northernmost tip of the country is a little like traveling abroad without having to worry about a different language or currency. Both Orkney and Shetland are essentially bleak and austere, but have awe-inspiring seascapes and genuinely warm, friendly people. Neither has yet been overrun by tourism. Both support communities of artists and craftspeople who find inspiration in the islands' landscapes and history.

An Orcadian has been defined as a farmer with a boat, whereas a Shetlander has been called a fisherman with a croft (small farm). Orkney, the southern archipelago, is greener and is rich with artifacts that testify to the many centuries of continuous settlement here: stone circles, burial chambers, ancient settlements, and fortifications. North of Orkney, Shetland, with its ocean views and sparse landscapes—trees are a rarity because of ever-present wind—seems even more remote. However, don't let Shetland's desolate countryside fool you: it has a wealth of historic interest and is far from being a backwater island. Oil money from its mineral resources and its position as a crossroads in the northern seas for centuries have helped make Shetland a cosmopolitan place.

## EXPLORING ORKNEY & SHETLAND

Both Orkney and Shetland require at least a couple of days if you're to do more than just scratch the surface. Since getting to Shetland isn't easy, you may want to spend three or four days here. In any case, the isles generate their own laid-back approach to life, and once here, you may want to take it slowly.

### ABOUT THE RESTAURANTS
The seafood is first class on the islands, and so is Orkney's malt whisky. Meals are usually of the stick-to-your-ribs variety, as vegetable gardeners do face some extra challenges from the northerly latitude. For local tastes, try the seaweed-fed lamb, local Orkney cheeses, Shetlandic heather, *bere bannocks* (barley-and-oat cakes), and ales from both islands (such as the well-named Skullsplitter and the mellower Simmer Dim).

### ABOUT THE HOTELS
Accommodations in Orkney and Shetland are on par with mainland Scotland. However, to experience a simpler lifestyle, check out the unique "camping bods" in Shetland—old cottages providing inexpensive, basic lodging (log fires, cold water, and sometimes no electricity). For details, contact the Shetland Tourist Information Centre.

| WHAT IT COSTS IN POUNDS | | | | |
|---|---|---|---|---|
| £ | ££ | £££ | ££££ | £££££ |
| RESTAURANTS under £10 | £10–£14 | £15–£19 | £20–£25 | over £25 |

Restaurant prices are for a main course at dinner. Hotel prices are for two people in a standard double room in high season, generally including the 17.5% V.A.T.

## TOP REASONS TO GO

**Standing stones and ancient sites:** Among the many Neolithic treasures in Orkney are the Ring of Brogar, 3,000-year old clusters of standing stones, and Skara Brae, the remarkable remains of a village. In Shetland, Jarlshof has been the home to different societies since the Bronze Age. Don't miss Mousa Broch and Clickimin Broch in Shetland, two Iron Age towers.

**Music and arts festivals:** The Shetland Folk Festival in May is a fiddly-diddly shindig that attracts musicians and revelers from around the world. Orkney's St. Magnus Festival is less of a pub-crawl and more of a high-brow celebration of classical music, poetry, and performance.

**Seabirds, seals, and more:** These islands have some of the planet's most important colonies of seabirds,

with millions clinging to colossal cliffs. You're guaranteed to see seals and mayspot dolphins, orcas, or porpoises. In Shetland, Noss and Eshaness nature reserves are prime spots, or you can check out the puffins by Sumburgh Head.

**Pure relaxation:** There's a much more laid-back approach to life on these islands than on the mainland. Shetlanders are particularly renowned for their hospitality and are often happy to share stories and tips that will enrich your adventure.

**Explore the coast and ocean:** The rugged landscapes, beautiful beaches, and unspoiled waters make a perfect backdrop for outdoor pursuits, be they an invigorating stroll, seafishing, diving, or exploring the coastline and sea lochs by boat.

| WHAT IT COSTS IN POUNDS | | | | | |
|---|---|---|---|---|---|
| HOTELS | under £70 | £70–£120 | £121–£160 | £161–£220 | over £220 |

Restaurant prices are for a main course at dinner. Hotel prices are for two people in a standard double room in high season, generally including the 17.5% V.A.T.

### TIMING

The bird colonies are at their most lively in early summer, which is also when the long northern daylight hours allow you plenty of sightseeing time. The summer season starts in late May and runs until September, but beware the changeable weather at any time: it could be 75°F one day and then hail the next.

# AROUND ORKNEY

Most of Orkney's many prehistoric sites are open to view, providing an insight into the life of bygone eras. At Maes Howe, for example, it becomes evident that graffiti is not solely an expression of today's youths: the Vikings left their marks here way back in the 12th century. ■TIP→ **You can purchase the Historic Scotland joint-entry ticket at the first site you visit; the ticket costs less than paying separately for entry into each site.**

## GREAT ITINERARIES

Getting around is quite straightforward—the roads are good on both Shetland and Orkney. A fast and frequent interisland passenger and car ferry service makes island-hopping perfectly practical.

### IF YOU HAVE 1 DAY

From Inverness take a day trip to Orkney—though it will be a long one—via the bus and ferry. Start by visiting the historic sites in ☷ **Kirkwall**, then visit **Skara Brae, Maes Howe,** and the **Ring of Brogar.**

### IF YOU HAVE 5 DAYS

Get a good taste of Orkney by taking in the main sights—St. Magnus Cathedral, Earl Patrick's Palace, and the Bishop's Palace in ☷ **Kirkwall**—then go out to **Skara Brae, Maes Howe,** and the **Ring of Brogar.** You could also see a bit of Shetland in this length of time. Don't miss **Mousa Broch,** the **Shetland Croft House Museum, Old Scatness, Jarlshof** and **Sumburgh Head,** and **St. Ninian's Isle.** Stay overnight in ☷ **Lerwick** and make a quick exploration of Lerwick itself and **Scalloway;** then make a trip up to Eshaness to get a flavor of the north of Mainland. If you have enough time on your fifth day, you might visit the **Hermaness National Nature Reserve.**

## STROMNESS & THE NEOLITHIC SITES

*1¾ hrs north of Thurso via ferry from Scrabster.*

Stromness, with its ferry connections, makes a good base for visiting the northern and western parts of Orkney, and the town holds two points of interest. Nearby are three spectacular ancient sites, the Ring of Brogar, Maes Howe, and Skara Brae.

The **Pier Arts Centre** is a former merchant's house and adjoining buildings that now serve as a gallery with a superb permanent collection of more than 100 20th-century paintings and sculptures, including works by Barbara Hepworth and Ben Nicholson. ⊠ *28–30 Victoria St.* ☎ *01856/850209* ⊕ *www.pierartscentre.com* ⊡ *Free* ☉ *Sept.–May, Mon.–Sat. 10:30–5; June–Aug., Tues.–Sat. 10:30–5, Sun. 1–5.*

The **Stromness Museum** has exhibits on fishing, shipping, and whaling. Also here are model ships and displays on the German fleet that was scuttled on Scapa Flow in 1919 and the Hudson Bay Company, which recruited workers in Stromness between the late 18th and 19th centuries. ⊠ *52 Alfred St.* ☎ *01856/850025* ⊡ *£2.50* ☉ *Oct.–Apr., Mon.–Sat. 10–5; May–Sept., Mon.–Sat. 10–5, Sun. 10–12:30 and 1:30–5.*

Fodor'sChoice The **Ring of Brogar,** 5 mi northeast of Stromness, is a magnificent circle ★ of 36 neolithic stones (originally 60) surrounded by a deep ditch. When the fog descends over the stones—a frequent occurrence—their looming shapes seem to come alive. Though their original use is uncertain, it's not hard to imagine strange rituals taking place here in the misty past. The stones stand between Loch of Harray and Loch of Stenness. ⊠ *On B9055* ☎ *01856/841815* ⊕ *www.historic-scotland.gov.uk* ⊡ *Free* ☉ *Year-round.*

# The Orkney Islands

ATLANTIC OCEAN

Seal Skerry

North Ronaldsay

Hollandstoun

*Papa Westray*

Holland

*The North Sound*

North Ronaldsay Firth

Pierowall

Northwall

*Westray*

Burness

*Sanday*

Kettletoft

Rapness

Calfsound

Braeswick

*Westray Firth*

Sanday Sound

*Rousay*

Wasbister

*Eday*

Whitehall

Brough Head

Brinyan

Backaland

Aith

**Birsay**

*Stronsay*

**Marwick Head Nature Reserve**

**Gurness Broch**

*Stronsay Firth*

Dounby

*Marwick Bay*

**Unstan Chambered Tomb**

*Shapinsay*

**Skara Brae**

*Mainland*

Balfour

Finstown

TO → SCALLOWAY

**Ring of Brogar**

**Maes Howe**

**Kirkwall**

Skaill

**Stromness**

**Orphir Church**

Moness

Orphir

St. Mary's

*Scapa Flow*

*Copinsay*

Rackwick

**Italian Chapel**

**Scapa Flow Visitor Centre**

Lamburgh

Lyness

*Hoy*

St. Margaret's Hope

*South Ronaldsay*

Burwick

*Old Head*

*Pentland Firth*

*Pentland Skerries*

Scrabster

Gills

John o' Groats

Thurso

| 0 | | | 10 miles |
| 0 | | | 10 kilometers |

**KEY**

Ferry

Airport

**Fodor'sChoice**
★    The huge burial mound of **Maes Howe** (circa 2500 BC) measures 115 feet in diameter and contains an enormous burial chamber. It was raided by Vikings in the 12th century, and Norse crusaders found shelter here, leaving a rich collection of runic inscriptions. It's 6 mi northeast of Stromness and 1 mi from the Ring of Brogar. ✉️*On A965* ☎️*01856/761606* ⊕*www.historic-scotland.gov.uk* 🎫*£5* 🕐*Apr.–Sept., daily 9:30–5; Oct.–Mar., daily 9:30–4.*

★    At the Neolithic village of **Skara Brae,** 8 mi north of Stromness, are houses containing stone beds, fireplaces, and cupboards that have survived since the village was first occupied around 3000 BC. These structures, joined by covered passages, were preserved in sand until they were uncovered in 1850. ✉️*On B9056* ☎️*01856/841815* ⊕*www.historic-scotland.gov.uk* 🎫*£6.50 Apr.–Sept. Skara Brae and Skail House; £5.50 Oct.–Mar. Skara Brae only* 🕐*Apr.–Sept., daily 9:30–5:30; Oct.–Mar., daily 9:30–4:30.*

**WHERE TO STAY**

££    🏨**Mill of Eyrland.** White-painted stone walls, country antiques, and the rippling sound of a stream running beneath the windows make for a pleasant stay at this former mill dating from 1861. The old machinery can still be seen, and attractive gardens surround the house. Evening meals are available on request. This makes a good base for visiting nearby archaeological sites. **Pros:** Lovely original features in public rooms, beautiful views out to Scapa Flow. **Cons:** Some areas need maintenance; breakfast is served at one big table, so be prepared to be sociable. ✉️*Stenness KW16 3HA* ☎️*01856/850136* ⊕*www.millofeyrland. co.uk* 🛏️*4 rooms, 2 with bath* 🏠*In-room: no a/c, no phone. In-hotel: bar, no elevator, no-smoking rooms* 💳*No credit cards* 🍽️*BP.*

## MARWICK HEAD NATURE RESERVE

*5 mi north of Skara Brae, 14 mi north of Stromness.*

The Royal Society for the Protection of Birds tends this nature reserve, whose cliffs are home to thousands of seabirds, including cormorants and guillemots. The Kitchener Memorial, which recalls the 1916 sinking of the cruiser HMS *Hampshire* with Lord Kitchener aboard, sits atop a cliff. Access to the reserve, which is unstaffed, is along a path north from Marwick Bay. Take care near cliff edges. ✉️*Off B9056* ☎️*01856/850176* ⊕*www.rspb.org.uk* 🎫*Free* 🕐*Daily.*

## BIRSAY

*12 mi north of Stromness, 25 mi northwest of Kirkwall.*

A Romanesque church can be seen at the **Brough of Birsay,** a tidal island with the remains of an early Pictish and then Norse settlement. (*Brough* is another word for burgh.) The collection of roofless stone structures on the tiny island, close to Birsay, are accessible only at low tide. ■**TIP→**To ensure you won't be swept away, check the tides with the tourism office before setting out.

**Gurness Broch** is an Iron Age tower standing more than 10 feet high, surrounded by stone huts. Built between 500 BC and 200 BC, its foundations and dimensions suggest that it was one of the biggest brochs in Scotland. It's along the coast about 8 mi from Birsay. ⊠ *On A966, Aikerness* ☎ *01856/751414* ⊕ *www.historic-scotland.gov.uk* ⬛ *£4.50* ⊘ *Apr.–Sept., daily 9:30–5:30.*

## KIRKWALL

*16 mi east of Stromness.*

In bustling Kirkwall, the main town on Orkney and a ferry port, there's plenty to see in the narrow, winding streets extending from the harbor.

The **Earl's Palace,** built in 1607, is perhaps the best surviving example of Renaissance architecture in Scotland. There are no tours, so you can explore the palace ruins at your own pace. ⊠ *Palace Rd.* ☎ *01856/871918* ⬛ *£2.20, includes Bishop's Palace* ⊘ *Apr.–Sept., daily 9:30–6.*

Many of the buildings in Kirkwall retain a strong medieval feel. The **Bishop's Palace,** near the Earl's Palace, dates to the 12th century. It was rebuilt in the late 15th century, and its round tower was added in the 16th century. ⊠ *Palace Rd.* ☎ *01856/871918* ⬛ *£2.20, includes Earl's Palace* ⊘ *Apr.–Sept., daily 9:30–6.*

★ Founded by Jarl Rognvald in 1137 and named for his uncle, **St. Magnus Cathedral** was mostly finished by 1200, although more work was carried out during the following 300 years. The cathedral is still in use and contains some fine examples of Norman architecture, although traces of later styles are found here and there. The ornamentation on some of the tombstones is particularly striking. ⊠ *Broad St.* ☎ *01856/874894* ⊘ *Mon.–Sat. 9–6, Sun. 2–6.*

The **Orkney Wireless Museum** tells the story of wartime communications at Scapa Flow. Thousands of servicemen and servicewomen were stationed here and used the equipment displayed in the museum to protect the Home Fleet. The museum also contains many handsome 1930s wireless radios and examples of the handicrafts produced by Italian prisoners of war. ⊠ *Kiln Corner, Junction Rd.* ☎ *01856/871400* ⊕ *www.owm.org.uk* ⬛ *£2* ⊘ *Apr.–Sept., Mon.–Sat. 1–4:30, Sun. 2–4.30.*

After shopping and exploring Kirkwall, you'll have earned a dram of the local single malt at the **Highland Park Distillery** ( ⊠ *Holm Rd.* ☎ *01856/874619* ⊕ *www.highlandpark.co.uk*). Highland Park is a mellow whisky, less sweet than the Speyside malts, yet without the peat or iodine tinge of the western malts. It can be purchased all over Orkney (and farther afield), as well as from the distillery itself, which has a gift shop.

The intriguing **Unstan Chambered Tomb** is a burial chamber that lies within a 5,000-year-old cairn. Access to the tomb can be awkward for those with mobility problems. ✉ *On A964, 7½ mi west of Kirkwall* ☎ *01856/841815* 🌐 *www.historic-scotland.gov.uk* 🎫 *Free* ⏲ *Apr.–Sept., daily 9:30–5:30; Oct.–Mar., daily 9:30–4:30.*

> **NORDIC TRAILS**
>
> The Orkneyinga Saga, an oral history first written down in the 13th century, tells of the Norse conquest of Orkney. There are murders and battles galore. Panels at the Orkneyinga Saga Centre discuss the saga and Viking life. There's an Orkneyinga Trail with other panels around the island at Viking sites associated with the saga.

OFF THE BEATEN PATH

**Italian Chapel.** During World War II, 550 Italian prisoners of war were captured in North Africa and sent to Orkney to assist with the building of the Churchill Barriers, four causeways that blocked entry into Scapa Flow. Using two corrugated-iron military structures they constructed this beautiful, inspiring chapel. The elaborate interior frescoes were painted with whatever came to hand—bits of metal, colorful stones, leftover paints. It's 7 mi south of Kirkwall and just across from the first of the Churchill Barriers. ✉ *On A961, Lambholm* 🎫 *Free* ⏲ *Apr.–Sept., daily 9 AM–10 PM; Oct.–Mar., daily 9–4:30.*

**Orkneyinga Saga Centre.** This makes a good starting point for an exploration of Orkney's Norse heritage. Exhibits include the remains of the 12th-century Orphir Church, Scotland's only circular medieval church, and also the outline of a Viking drinking hall. The center is 8 mi southwest of Kirkwall. ✉ *Off A964, Orphir* ☎ *01856/811319* 🎫 *Free* ⏲ *Daily 9–5.*

### WHERE TO STAY & EAT

££ ★ ✕🏨 **Creel Inn.** This outstanding "restaurant with rooms" sits right on the waterfront 13 mi south of Kirkwall, on the island of South Ronaldsay; it's well worth the drive. All the guest rooms, decorated in a simple country style, overlook St. Margaret's Hope Bay. The charm of the restaurant (£££) lies partly in the fuss-free decor that makes everyone, from the local farmer to a visiting business executive, feel welcome. Imaginative modern Scottish cuisine uses the freshest Orcadian seafood, seaweed-fed lamb, and locally grown vegetables. **Pros:** Food deserves its glowing reputation, quaint harbor setting. **Con:** Not food for families with younger children. ✉ *Front Rd., St. Margaret's Hope, South Ronaldsay KW17 2SL* ☎ *01856/831311* 🌐 *www.thecreel.co.uk* *3 rooms* *In-room: no a/c, no phone. In-hotel: restaurant, no kids under 5, no elevator* ▭ *MC, V* ⏲ *Closed Oct.–Mar.* *BP.*

££ ✕🏨 **Foveran Hotel.** Thirty-four acres of grounds surround this modern, ranch-style hotel overlooking Scapa Flow. The Foveran has an attractive light-wood, Scandinavian-style dining room, as well as a sitting room with a fireplace. The restaurant (££) serves homemade soups, fresh seafood, and an achingly sweet Orkney Fudge cheesecake. The rooms are simply furnished, with firm beds and well-maintained baths. **Pros:** Friendly, efficient service, local produce simply cooked to perfection. **Cons:** Building a bit bland, you must book the popular restaurant ahead. ✉ *Off A964, St. Ola KW15 1SF* ☎ *01856/872389* 🌐 *www.*

*foveranhotel.co.uk* ⤥*8 rooms* &*In-room: no a/c. In-hotel: restaurant, bar, Internet, no elevator* ⊟*MC, V* ¶⊙|*BP.*

££ 🖼️**Merkister Hotel.** On the edge of Loch Harray, this hotel is an angler's dream. Experienced ghillies (guides) lead experts to the choicest spots and provide instruction for novices. Left your rod at home? You can rent all the equipment you need, including boats. The comfortable, traditional-style rooms encourage a good night's sleep after a hard day on the water. Skerries, the hotel's restaurant, serves Scottish cuisine. Halfway between Kirkwall and Stromness, the Merkister makes a good base for touring the region. **Pros:** Great lochside location, "trust bar" where you tell them what you drank and then pay for it. **Cons:** Some small rooms, decor a bit dated. ⊠*On A965, Harray Loch, Harray KW17 2LF* ☎*01856/771366* ⊕*www.merkister.com* ⤥*16 rooms* &*In-room: no a/c. In-hotel: restaurant, Internet, no elevator* ⊟*AE, MC, V* ¶⊙|*BP.*

£ 🖼️**Miller's House and Harbourside Guest House.** Built by a naval lieutenant, James Miller, this old house dates to before 1660. The rooms are fresh, simple, and spotless, with an understated style. The highpoint of a stay here is the breakfast, with the kippers, Orkney salmon, homemade bread and smooth creamy porridge all worth trying. **Pros:** Great value for the money, near the ferry. **Cons:** Not easy to find, in winter the heating can be too hot or too cold. ⊠*13 John St., KW16 3AD* ☎*01856/851969* ✉*millershouse@orkney.com* ⤥*6 rooms* &*In-room: no a/c. In-hotel: no elevator* ⊟*MC, V* ¶⊙|*CP or BP.*

### THE ARTS

The region's cultural highlight is Kirkwall's **St. Magnus Festival** (☎*01856/871445* ⊕*www.stmagnusfestival.com*), usually held the third week in June. Its impressive program includes distinguished orchestral, operatic, and choral artists. Orkney also hosts an annual folk festival at the end of May.

### SPORTS & THE OUTDOORS

BICYCLING Bicycles can be rented from **Bobby's Cycle Centre** (⊠*Tankerness La.* ☎ *01856/875777*), open year-round.

DIVING The cool, clear waters of Scapa Flow and eight sunken ships that were part of Germany's fleet during World War I make for an unparalleled diving experience. Several companies organize trips to Scapa Flow and other nearby dive sites, including **Orkney Divers** (⊠*St. Margaret's Hope Pier, St. Margaret's Hope, South Ronaldsay* ☎*01856/831225*).

FISHING The **Merkister Hotel** (⊠*Harray Loch, Harray* ☎*01856/771366*) arranges fishing packages, with all equipment, including boats, available to rent.

### SHOPPING

Kirkwall is Orkney's main shopping hub. At **Judith Glue** (⊠*25 Broad St.* ☎*01856/874225*) you can purchase designer knitwear with traditional patterns, as well as handmade crafts and hampers of local produce. Don't miss **Ola Gorrie Jewellery** (⊠*11 Broad St.* ☎*01856/873251*), which sells a huge array of gold and silver jewelry with Celtic and Norse themes, including a delightful representation of a dragon origi-

## Island Festivals

Islanders know how to celebrate their unique heritage and the performing arts. Joining one of the island festivals can be a memorable part of any trip.

Shetland has quite a strong cultural identity, thanks to its Scandinavian heritage. There are, for instance, books of local dialect verse, a whole folklore contained in knitting patterns, and a strong tradition of fiddle playing. In the middle of the long winter, at the end of January, the Shetlanders celebrate their Viking culture with the Up Helly Aa Festival, which involves much merrymaking, dressing up, and the burning of a replica of a Viking

longship. The Shetland Folk Festival, held in April, and October's Shetland Accordion and Fiddle Festival both attract large numbers of visitors.

Orkney's St. Magnus Festival, a celebration focusing on classical music, is based in Kirkwall and is usually held the third week in June. Orkney also hosts a jazz festival in April, an annual folk festival at the end of May, the unique Boys' Ploughing Match in mid-August, and The Ba' (ball; street rugby-football played by the Uppies and Doonies residents of Kirkwall) on Christmas and New Year's Day.

nally drawn on the wall of the burial chamber at Maes Howe. **Ortak** (⊠*Albert St.* ☎*01856/873536*) stocks Celtic-theme jewelry and has exhibits and jewelry-making demonstrations.

### SCAPA FLOW VISITOR CENTRE

*On Hoy, 14 mi southwest of Kirkwall, 6 mi south of Stromness via ferry.*

On the island of Hoy, Scapa Flow Visitor Centre explores the strategic role that this sheltered anchorage played in two world wars. ■**TIP→ If you want to take your car over to Hoy, book well in advance with Orkney Ferries, as this is a popular route.** The visitor center is a short walk from the ferry terminal. ⊠*Off B9047, Lyness* ☎*01856/791300 center, 01856/872044 ferry* ⊠*Free* ☉*June–Sept., Mon.–Sat. 9–4, Sun. 10–4; Oct.–May, weekdays 9–4.*

# AROUND SHETLAND

The Shetland coastline is an incredible 900 mi because of all the indentations, and there isn't a point on the island farther than 3 mi from the sea. Settlements away from Lerwick, the primary town, are small and scattered.

### LERWICK

*14 hrs by ferry from Aberdeen.*

Lerwick was founded by Dutch fishermen in the 17th century. Handsome stone buildings—known as *lodberries*—line the harbor and pro-

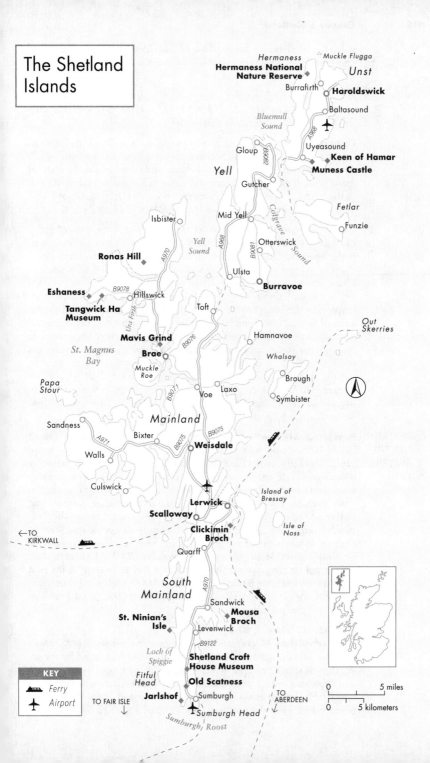

# The Shetland
# Islands

Muckle Flugga

Hermaness

**Hermaness National
Nature Reserve**

*Unst*

Burrafirth

**Haroldswick**

Baltasound

*Bluemull
Sound*

A968

Gloup

B9082

Uyeasound

**Keen of Hamar**

**Muness Castle**

*Yell*

Gutcher

*Fetlar*

Isbister

Mid Yell

Funzie

*Yell
Sound*

A968

B9081

Otterswick

**Ronas Hill**

A970

Ulsta

**Burravoe**

**Eshaness**

B9078

Hillswick

Toft

*Out
Skerries*

**Tangwick Ha
Museum**

Hamnavoe

*Whalsay*

*Ura Firth*

**Mavis Grind**

B9076

*St. Magnus
Bay*

**Brae**

**Brough**

*Muckle
Roe*

*Papa
Stour*

B9071

Voe

Laxo

Symbister

*Mainland*

Sandness

A971

Bixter

B9075

B9075

Walls

**Weisdale**

Culswick

*Island of
Bressay*

**Lerwick**

**Scalloway**

*Isle of
Noss*

**Clickimin
Broch**

←TO
KIRKWALL

Quarff

*South
Mainland*

A970

Sandwick

**Mousa
Broch**

**St. Ninian's
Isle**

Levenwick

*Loch of
Spiggie*

B9122

**Shetland Croft
House Museum**

*Fitful
Head*

**Old Scatness**

**Jarlshof**

Sumburgh

TO FAIR ISLE
↓

TO
ABERDEEN
↓

*Sumburgh Head*

*Sumburgh Roost*

**KEY**

🛳 *Ferry*

✈ *Airport*

0          5 miles

0          5 kilometers

vided loading bays for goods, some of them illegal. The town's twisting flagstone lanes and harbor once heaved with activity and it's still an active port today.

**Fort Charlotte,** a 17th-century stronghold, was built to protect the Sound of Bressay. ⊠*Market St.* ☎*01856/841815* ⌂*Free* ⊙*Apr.–Sept., daily 9:30–6:30; Oct.–Mar., daily 9:30–4:30.*

**Clickimin Broch,** on the site of what was originally an Iron Age fortification, makes a good introduction to these mysterious Pictish buildings. It was possibly intended as a place of retreat and protection in the event of attack. South of the broch are vivid views of the cliffs at the south end of the island of Bressay, which shelters Lerwick Harbor. ⊠*Off A970, 1 mi south of Lerwick* ☎*01856/841815* ⌂*Free* ⊙*Daily 24 hrs.*

⟳ On the last remaining stretch of the old waterfront at the restored Hay's ★ Dock, the striking **Shetland Museum** building, with its sail-like tower, is the Shetlands' fabulous new cultural hub and a stimulating introduction to local culture. The impressive spaces are filled with displays about archaeology, art and textiles, island culture, and contemporary art. Standout exhibits include the magical, cavelike "Trowie Knowe" (exploring the local trows, or trolls), the last remaining *sixareen* (a kind of fishing boat), and the Monk's Stone, a carving depicting the Irish monks who introduced Christianity to the people of Shetland. The museum is also a wonderful place to hang out; look for vintage vessels moored in the dock and seals that pop up to observe everyone checking out the sparkling scene from the stylish, glass-fronted café-restaurant terrace. ⊠*Hay's Dock* ☎*01595/695057* ⊕*www.shetland-museum. org.uk* ⌂*Free* ⊙*Mon.–Wed., Fri., and Sat. 10–5, Thurs. 10–7, Sun. noon–5.*

OFF THE BEATEN PATH
**Noss National Nature Reserve.** The island of Noss (which means "nose" in old Norse) rises to a point called the Noup. The smell and noise of the birds that make their homes on the vertiginous cliffs make for a violent assault on the senses. The residents nest in orderly fashion: black and white guillemots (45,000 pairs) and razorbills at the bottom; gulls, gannets, cormorants, and kittiwake in the middle; fulmars and puffins at the top. If you get too close to their chicks, some will dive-bomb from above. To get here, take a ferry from Lerwick to Bressay, then an inflatable boat to Noss; call the reserve office, managed by Scottish Natural Heritage, for boat schedules. ∎**TIP➔ Be sure to wear waterproof clothing and sensible shoes; mid-May to mid-July is the best time to view breeding birds.** ⊠*Bressay* ☎*01595/693345* ⊕*www.nnr-scotland.org.uk* ⌂*£3* ⊙*Mid-May–Aug., Tues., Wed., and Fri.–Sun. 10–5, weather permitting.*

**WHERE TO STAY & EAT**

££ ✕▦ **Shetland Hotel.** Modern and decently appointed—a result of the area's oil boom and the needs of high-flying executives—the Shetland is friendlier than its somber exterior would suggest. All the rooms are a good size and decorated in rich tones. Restaurant favorites include Shetland lamb and freshly landed seafood, and the fish soup and bannocks—savory scones—help keep the northern winds at bay. **Pro:** Well located opposite the ferry and Lerwick town center. **Cons:** Ugly exterior, interior needs refurbishment. ✉*Holmsgarth Rd., ZE1 0PW* ☎*01595/695515* 🖷*01595/695828* ⊕*www.shetland-hotels.com* 🛏*64 rooms, 1 suite* ♿*In-room: no a/c, Wi-Fi. In-hotel: 2 restaurants, room service, bars* ▭*AE, DC, MC, V* ⏹|*BP.*

£ 🏨**Alder Lodge.** Occupying a solid, 1830s-built former bank building, this guesthouse is on a quiet street within easy reach of Lerwick's harbor, shops, pubs, and attractions. The spacious guest rooms have orthopedic beds and well-looked-after bathrooms. The lounge is a cozy place to unwind in the evenings, and there's an eccentrically adorned patio to relax in when the weather is fine. **Pros:** Comfortable beds, superb location, child friendly. **Con:** Breakfasts may be too greasy for some tastes. ✉*8 Clairmont Pl., ZE1 0BR* ☎*01595/695705* 🛏*8 rooms* ♿*In-room: refrigerator, no a/c. In-hotel: laundry service, no elevator* ▭*No credit cards* ⏹|*BP.*

£ 🏨**Lerwick Youth Hostel.** In the center of Lerwick, this lodging offers very affordable double-, family-, and group-size rooms with white-painted walls, pine furniture, and colorful curtains and bedding. The turn-of-the-20th-century house has pretty architectural features, like big windows, pine shutters, and handsome fireplaces. The café serves healthy meals using whole foods and fresh vegetables. **Pros:** Superb value, a sociable set-up. **Cons:** Only basic facilities, can be noisy when groups are staying. ✉*King Harald St., ZE1 0EQ* ☎*01595/692114* ⊕*www.islesburgh.org.uk* 🛏*60 beds* ♿*In-room: no a/c, no TV. In-hotel: laundry facilities, no kids under 5, Internet, no elevator* ▭*MC, V* ⊘*Closed Oct.–Mar.*

### BICYCLING

Bicycles can be rented from **Eric Brown Cycles** (✉*Grantfield Garage, North Rd.* ☎*01595/692709*), open year-round.

### SHOPPING

**Anderson & Co.** (✉*60–62 Commercial St.* ☎*01595/693714*) carries handmade knitwear and souvenirs. **Ninian** (✉*110 Commercial St.* ☎*01595/696655*) sells traditional and funky handmade scarves, clothing, and throws, all using Shetland wool.

**Hjaltasteyn** (✉*161 Commercial St.* ☎*01595/696224*) sells handcrafted gold and silver jewelry set with precious gems. **J.G. Rae Limited** (✉*92 Commercial St.* ☎*01595/693686*) stocks gold and silver jewelry with Norse and Celtic motifs. Browse around the colorful mix of goods

---

**TROWS & TALES**

The Shetlands have a long tradition of folk tales, many with Norse origins. Speak to Elma Johnson, a storyteller and spellbinding tour guide, and you may believe the place is teeming with trows, the cousins of Scandinavian trolls. If you don't see the "little people," there's a cavelike dwelling in the new Shetland Museum—the Trowie Knowe—and a fantastical device—the Trowie Detector—that may help track down these elusive characters. To enter this magical world of Shetlandic history and folklore, book a trip with **Island Trails** (☎*01950/422408* ⊕*www.island-trails.co.uk*).

in the **Peerie Shop** ( ✉ *Esplanade* ☎ *01595/692816*); then enjoy some baked goods or soup and the best Italian coffee on the island at the stylish café, which doubles as an art gallery.

**Shetland Times** ( ✉ *Commercial St.* ☎ *01595/695531* ) is the best book-shop within a radius of about 250 mi, stocking a good selection of travel guides and local history titles.

## THE SOUTH MAINLAND

*14 to 25 mi south of Lerwick via A970.*

The narrow 3- or 4-mi-wide stretch of land that reaches south from Lerwick to Sumburgh Head has a number of fascinating ancient sites (and an airport) as well as farmland, wild landscapes, and dramatic ocean views.

★ Sandwick, 14 mi south of Lerwick via A970, is the departure point for the passenger ferry to the tiny isle of Mousa, where you can see **Mousa Broch,** a fortified Iron Age stone tower about 40 feet high. The mas-sive walls give a real sense of security, which must have been reassur-ing for islanders subject to attacks from ship-borne raiders. Exploring this beautifully preserved, curved-stone structure, standing on what still feels like an untouched island, makes you feel as if you're back in 100 BC. From May to July the ferry also takes bookings for night trips (£12) to see the bewitching sight of thousands of storm petrels return-ing to their home after a day at sea. ✉ *Mousa* ☎ *01856/841815 Mousa Broch, 01950/431367 ferry* ⊕ *www.mousaboattrips.co.uk* ✉ *Site free; ferry round-trip £10* ☉ *Site daily; ferry Apr.–Sept., once or twice daily in afternoon.*

☾ The **Shetland Croft House Museum,** a 19th-century thatched house, takes
★ you back to the way of life of the rural Shetlander, which the tradition-ally attired attendant will be delighted to discuss with you. The peat fire casts a glow on the box bed, the resting chair, and the wealth of domestic implements, including a handmill for preparing meal and a willow basket for carrying peat. There's also period clothing, such as shawls both thick and lacy. The upturned boat in the field outside is used for storing and drying fish and mutton. Huts like this inspired the design of the new Scottish Parliament. The museum is 7 mi south of Sandwick. ✉ *East of A970, on unmarked road, South Voe, Dun-rossness* ☎ *01595/695057* ⊕ *www.shetland-museum.org.uk* ✉ *Free* ☉ *May–Sept., daily 10–1 and 2–5.*

☾ Ongoing excavations at **Old Scatness** have uncovered the remains of an
★ Iron Age village, including one building that still has a roof. Enthusias-tic and entertaining guides tell stories that breathe life into the stones and the middens. They also show how the former residents made their clothes and cooked their food, including their staple dish: seaweed porridge. Call ahead for hours. ✉ *Off A970, Virkie, Dunrossness* ☎ *01595/694688* ⊕ *www.shetland-heritage.co.uk/amenitytrust* ✉ *£3* ☉ *June–Sept., hrs vary.*

**Jarlshof** is one of Shetland's archaeological highlights. In 1897 a huge storm blew away 4,000 years of sand to expose the extensive remains of Norse buildings, prehistoric wheelhouses, and earth houses that represented thousands of years of continuous settlement. It's a large and complex site, and you can roam the remains freely. The small visitor center is packed with facts and figures and illustrates Jarlshof's more recent history as a medieval farmstead and home of the 16th-century Earl of Orkney and Shetland, "cruel" Patrick Stewart, who enslaved the men of Scalloway to build Scalloway Castle. ✉ *Sumburgh Head* ☎ *01950/460112* ⊕ *www.historic-scotland.gov.uk* 🎫 *£4.50* 🕐 *Apr.– Sept., daily 9:30–5:30.*

### PUFFINS & MORE

Every summer more than a million birds alight on the Shetlands' cliff faces to nest, feeding on the fish in the North Atlantic. Birdwatchers can spot more than 20 species, from tiny storm petrels to gannets with 6-foot wing spans. Popular with visitors are the puffins, with their short necks, striped beaks, and comical orange feet. Look for them on the cliffs at Sumburgh Head near the lighthouse, 2 mi south of Sumburgh Airport. It's a steep climb to the viewing areas and not for those who suffer from vertigo. The visitor center in Lerwick has leaflets about nesting sites.

It was on **St. Ninian's Isle** that a schoolboy helping archaeologists excavate the ruins of a 12th-century church discovered the St. Ninian treasure, a collection of 28 silver objects dating from the 8th century. This Celtic silver is housed in the Museum of Scotland in Edinburgh, but good replicas are in the Shetland Museum in Lerwick. Although you can't see the silver, walking over the causeway of golden sand (called a *tombolo*) that joins St. Ninian's Isle to the mainland and hearing the sound of the sea lapping—or crashing—at either side of it is an unforgettable experience. The island is 8 mi north of Sumburgh via A970 and B9122; then turn left at Skelberry.

### SHOPPING

**Lawrence J. Smith Ltd.** ( ✉ *Hoswick, 2 mi west of Sandwick* ☎ *01950/431215*) sells Shetland knitwear—made by hand and machine—in a wide selection of colors.

## SCALLOWAY

*21 mi north of St. Ninian's Isle, 6 mi west of Lerwick.*

On the west coast of Mainland Island is Scalloway, which preceded Lerwick as the capital of the region. During World War II, Scalloway was the port for the "Shetland Bus," a secret fleet of boats that carried British agents to Norway to perform acts of sabotage against the Germans, who were occupying the country. On the return trips, the boats would carry refugees back to Shetland. Look for the information board just off A970, which overlooks the settlement and its castle.

**Scalloway Castle,** on the harbor, was built in 1600 by Patrick Stewart, Earl of Orkney and Shetland. He was hanged in 1615 for his cruelty and misdeeds, and the castle was never used again. To enter the castle, you must retrieve the key from the shopkeeper at Shetland Woollen Company, or, on Sunday, from the host at the Royal Hotel. You may explore the castle ruins to your heart's content; unsafe areas are fenced off. ⊠*On A970* ☎*01856/841815* ⊕*www.historic-scotland.gov.uk* ⊠*Free* ⊗*Daily.*

### SHOPPING

The **Shetland Woollen Company** ( ⊠*Castle St.* ☎*01595/880243*), open Monday to Saturday 9:30 to 5, is one of many purveyors in Scalloway with a selection of Shetland knitwear.

## WEISDALE

*9 mi north of Lerwick.*

Built using stones from the Kergord estate's "cleared" (forcibly evicted) crofts, Weisdale Mill redeemed itself in 1940 when it became the administrative headquarters for the "Shetland Bus." Now the **Bonhoga Gallery,** it has been beautifully remodeled into a contemporary art gallery, showing quirky exhibitions by local, national, and international artists. Downstairs is the **Shetland Textile Working Museum,** which has inventive exhibitions on the history of textiles and knitting in the Islands, including the famous Fair Isle technique. Both attractions share a café that looks over the Weisdale burn and serves excellent coffee and snacks. ⊠*On B9075* ☎*01595/830400 gallery, 01595/830419 museum* ⊗*Tues.–Sat. 10:30–4:30, Sun. noon–4:30.*

### SHOPPING

**Shetland Jewelry** ( ⊠*Sound Side* ☎*01595/830275*) sells gold and silver Celtic-inspired jewelry.

## BRAE

*24 mi north of Scalloway.*

The rugged moorland and tranquil *voes* (inlets) of Brae are the home of Busta House, one of the best hotels on the island.

Beyond Brae the main road meanders past **Mavis Grind,** a strip of land so narrow you can throw a stone—if you're strong—from the Atlantic, in one inlet, to the North Sea, in another.

**OFF THE BEATEN PATH**

**Eshaness and Ronas Hill.** About 15 mi from Brae are the rugged, forbidding cliffs around Eshaness; drive north and then turn left onto B9078. On the way, look for the sandstone stacks in the bay that resemble a Viking galley under sail. After viewing the cliffs at Eshaness and calling in at **Tangwick Haa Museum** ( ⊠*Off B9078, Tangwick* ☎*01806/503389*), a former laird's house filled with a collection of photographs from the turn of the last century, return to join the A970 at Hillswick and follow an ancillary road from the head of Ura Firth.

This road provides vistas of rounded, bare **Ronas Hill,** the highest hill in Shetland. Though only 1,468 feet high, it's noted for its arctic-alpine flora growing at low levels.

### WHERE TO STAY & EAT

£ ✕ **Braewick Cafe.** The café's stunning position overlooking Eshaness's ★ seastacks (columns of rock in the sea), the Drongs, and the wholesome fare that uses the owners' produce attract Shetlanders and visitors by word of mouth. Browse the inventive local craft creations in the shop while waiting for a deliciously crispy battered-fish supper, or just sit back in the sofas by the huge picture window and watch the dramatic sea and sky. Don't pass up the many tempting home-baked desserts like sponges, cheesecakes, and giant scones. ⊠*Eshaness* ☎*01806/503345* ⊟*AE, MC, V.*

£££ ✕⌷ **Busta House.** Surrounded by terraced grounds, Busta House dates ★ in part from the 16th century and has a restrained, austere elegance that tells you something of the Gifford family that lived here in the 18th century—ask the current owners about the Gifford family's ill-starred history. All the rooms are different (ask about size, location, and possible noise when you book) and are prettily furnished, many with antique headboards. The 16th-century Long Room is a delightful place to sample a selection of malt whiskies beside a peat fire. The restaurant serves four-course dinners (£32 prix-fixe), and the bar has a less expensive (around £9 for main courses) à la carte menu. Try the peppered-mackerel pâté and the scallops in basil sauce. This is a good place to get away from it all. **Pros:** Truly haunting atmosphere, whisky and after-dinner ghost stories in the drawing room. **Cons:** Easy to get lost in the maze of corridors, noisy plumbing, lack of soundproofing. ⊠*Off A970, ZE2 9QN* ☎*01806/522506* ⊕*www.bustahouse.com* ↷*22 rooms* ⌂*In-room: no a/c. In-hotel: restaurant, bar, Internet, no elevator* ⊟*AE, DC, MC, V* ⍿*BP.*

## YELL

*11 mi northeast of Brae, 31 mi north of Lerwick via A970, A968, or B9076, and ferry from Toft.*

A desolate-looking blanket bog cloaks two-thirds of the island of Yell, creating an atmospheric landscape to pass through on the way to Unst to the north. To get here, catch the ferry from Toft to Ulsta and take the B9081 east to Burravoe.

Burravoe's **Old Haa** *(hall),* the oldest building on the island, is known for its crow-stepped gables (the stepped effect on the ends of the roofs), typical of an early-18th-century Shetland-merchant's house. One of the displays in the upstairs museum tells the story of the wrecking of the German ship, the *Bohus,* in 1924. A copy of the ship's figurehead is displayed outside the Old Haa; the original remains at the shipwreck, overlooking Otterswick along the coast on the B9081. The Old Haa serves light meals with home-baked buns, cakes, and other goodies and also acts as a kind of unofficial information center. The staff is friendly and gives advice to sightseers. There's also a crafts shop on the prem-

*ises. ⊠Burravoe ☎01957/722339
🎫Free ⊘Late Apr.–Sept., Tues.–
Thurs. and Sat. 10–4, Sun. 2–5.*

## UNST

*49 mi north of Lerwick via ferry
from Gutcher.*

A ferry (take the A968 at Mid Yell
to Gutcher) crosses the Bluemull
Sound to Unst, the northernmost
inhabited island in Scotland. On a
long summer evening, views north
to Muckle Flugga, with only the
ocean beyond, are incomparable.
If you're a bird-watcher, head to
the Hermaness and Keen of Hamar
nature reserves.

**Muness Castle,** Scotland's northernmost castle, was built just before
the end of the 16th century and has

circular corner towers. Admission is free. To get here from the A968,
turn right onto the B9084. ⊠B9084 ⊕www.historic-scotland.gov.uk.

Just to the north of Muness Castle is the **Keen of Hamar National Nature
Reserve,** off A968, with subarctic flora and arctic terns.

In the far north of Unst is **Haroldswick,** with its post office, proud of its
status as the most northerly one, and heritage center. Named after King
Harold of Norway, it was at this sheltered bay that the Norwegians
landed in AD 875 to claim the islands. Also here is **Unst Boat Haven,**
displaying a collection of traditional small fishing and sailing boats
reflecting Shetland's maritime heritage. ☎01957/711528 ⊕www.unst.
org 🎫£2 ⊘May–Sept., daily 2–5.

★ The **Hermaness National Nature Reserve,** a bleak moorland ending in
rocky cliffs, is prime bird-watching territory. About half the world's
population (6,000 pairs) of great skuas, called "bonxies" by locals,
are found here. ■TIP➜ **These sky pirates attack anything that strays
near their nests, including humans, so keep to the paths.** Thousands of
other seabirds, including more than 50,000 puffins, nest in spectacular profusion on the cliffs, about one hour's walk from the reserve
entrance. Hermaness is not just about birds—gray seals gather in caves
at the foot of the cliffs in fall, and offshore, dolphins and occasionally
whales (including orcas) can be seen on calm days. The flora includes
the insect-eating butterwort and sundew, purple field gentians, orchids,
and red campion. The visitor center at the lighthouse has leaflets that
outline a walk; mid-May to mid-July is the best time to visit. To get here
from Haroldswick, follow the B9086 around the head of Burra Firth, a
sea inlet. ⊠Shore Station, Burra Firth ☎01957/711278 ⊕www.nnr-
scotland.org.uk 🎫Free ⊘Mid-Apr.–mid-Sept., daily 9–5.

A path in the Hermaness National Nature Reserve meanders across moorland and climbs up a gentle hill, from which you can see, to the north, a series of tilting offshore rocks; the largest of these sea-battered protrusions is **Muckle Flugga,** meaning "big, steep-sided island," on which stands a lighthouse. This is the northernmost point in Scotland—the sea rolls out on three sides, and no land lies beyond.

# ORKNEY & SHETLAND ESSENTIALS

## TRANSPORTATION

### BY AIR

British Airways provides regular service to Lerwick in Shetland and Kirkwall in Orkney from Edinburgh, Glasgow, Aberdeen, and Inverness. Because of the isolation of Orkney and Shetland, there's also a network of interisland flights, through Loganair (contact British Airways).

**Contact British Airways** (☎ 0870/850–9850 ⊕ www.britishairways.com).

### BY BOAT & FERRY

To get to Lerwick and Shetland, take the ferry from the port in Aberdeen. To reach Stromness on Orkney, take the ferry from the port in Scrabster. Contact Northlink Ferries for reservations. Northlink also runs longer sea voyages from Aberdeen to Kirkwall. If you're arriving in Aberdeen on Sunday morning and plan on meeting a train, note that the station does not open until 9:30 AM. Northlink allows you to stay in your cabin or the restaurant until 10 AM.

An alternate way of reaching Orkney is the ferry from John o'Groats to Burwick, operated by John o'Groats Ferries. There are up to four daily departures May through September. The ferry from Gill's Bay, Caithness, to St. Margaret's Hope on Orkney, operated by Pentland Ferries, has three daily departures.

In Orkney, Orkney Ferries has service between the islands. To get to Orkney from Shetland (or vice versa), Northlink Ferries has service between Lerwick and Kirkwall. ■ TIP→ **Always book ferry tickets in advance.**

**Information** **John o'Groats Ferries** (☎ 01955/611353 ⊕ www.jogferry.co.uk). **Orkney Ferries** (☎ 01856/872044 ⊕ www.orkneyferries.co.uk). **Northlink Ferries** (☎ 0845/6000449 ⊕ www.northlinkferries.co.uk). **Pentland Ferries** (☎ 01856/831226 ⊕ www.pentlandferries.co.uk).

### BY BUS

On the mainland, Aberdeen and Thurso have two reliable bus companies with destinations all over Scotland and the rest of Britain: Scottish Citylink and National Express. John o'Groats Ferries operates the Orkney Bus, a direct express coach from Inverness to Kirkwall (via ferry) that runs daily from May to early September.

The main bus service on Orkney is operated by Orkney Coaches and on Shetland, by J. Leask. Shetland Islands Council provides information on all bus routes and timetables on its Web site.

Information **John o'Groats Ferries** ( ☎ *01955/611353* ⊕ *www.jogferry.co.uk*). **J. Leask** ( ☎ *01595/693162* ⊕ *www.leaskstravel.co.uk*). **National Express** ( ☎ *08705/808080* ⊕ *www.nationalexpress.co.uk*). **Orkney Coaches** ( ☎ *01856/870555* ⊕ *www.rapsons. co.uk*). **Scottish Citylink** ( ☎ *08705/505050* ⊕ *www.citylink.co.uk*). **Shetland Islands Council** ( ⊕ *www.shetland.gov.uk/transport*).

### BY CAR
The most convenient way of getting around these islands is by car, especially if your time is limited. The roads are well maintained and traffic is nearly nonexistent. Orkney has causeways connecting some of the islands, but in some cases using these roads will take you on fairly roundabout routes.

You can transport your rental car from Aberdeen, but for fewer than five days it's usually cheaper to rent a car from one of Shetland's many agencies. Most are based in Lerwick, Shetland, and Kirkwall, Orkney.

Local Agencies **Bolts Car and Minibus Hire** ( ✉ *26 North Rd., Lerwick* ☎ *01595/693636* ⊕ *www.boltscarhire.co.uk*). **James D. Peace & Co.** ( ✉ *Junction Rd., Kirkwall* ☎ *01856/872866* ⊕ *www.orkneycarhire.co.uk*). **Star Rent-a-Car** ( ✉ *22 Commercial Rd., Lerwick* ☎ *01595/692075* ⊕ *www.starrentacar.co.uk*). **W. R. Tullock** ( ✉ *Terminal Bldg., Kirkwall Airport, Kirkwall* ☎ *01856/875500* ⊕ *www. orkneycarrental.co.uk*).

### BY TRAIN
There are no trains on Orkney or Shetland, but you can take the train to Aberdeen or Thurso and then take a ferry to the islands. For information, contact First ScotRail.

Information **First ScotRail** ( ☎ *08457/484950* ⊕ *www.firstgroup.com/scotrail*).

## CONTACTS & RESOURCES

### EMERGENCIES
Dial ☎ **999** for the police, fire department, or an ambulance (no coins are needed for emergency calls from public phone booths).

Hospitals **Balfour Hospital** ( ✉ *New Scapa Rd., Kirkwall, Orkney* ☎ *01856/885400*). **Gilbert Bain Hospital** ( ✉ *South Rd., Lerwick, Shetland* ☎ *01595/743000*).

### TOURS
Orkney Coaches runs general tours of Orkney, and J. Leask arranges tours of Shetland and Orkney. These companies can also tailor tours to your interests. Michael Hartley, an accredited tour guide in Orkney, runs Wildabout; call for details on minibus tours that combine sightseeing of archaeological sites and the folklore, flora, and fauna of the islands. In Shetland, Island Trails offers excellent tours enriched by the many myths, customs, and folklore of the islanders, as told by Shetland storyteller Elma Johnson. To visit the outlying islands of Shetland,

such as the mist-capped Foula and the once-inhabited Hildasay, take a Cycharters day or afternoon trip on their boat, the Cyfish: the company also offers private charters. Several companies tour the spectacular Noss Bird Sanctuary on Shetland, a national nature reserve, in summer, weather permitting. The tourist information center has details.

Information **Cycharters** ( ☎ *01595/696598* ⊕ *www.cycharters.co.uk*). **Island Trails** ( ☎ *01950/422408* ⊕ *www.island-trails.co.uk*). **J. Leask** ( ☎ *01595/693162* ⊕ *www.leaskstravel.co.uk*). **Orkney Coaches** ( ☎ *01856/870555* ⊕ *www.rapsons. co.uk*). **Wildabout** ( ☎ *01856/851011* ⊕ *www.wildaboutorkney.com*).

## VISITOR INFORMATION

The Orkney visitor centers in Kirkwall and Stromness, and the Shetland visitor center, in Lerwick, are open year-round.

Information **Kirkwall, Orkney** ( ✉ *6 Broad St., Kirkwall, Orkney* ☎ *01856/872856* ⊕ *www.visitorkney.com*). **Lerwick, Shetland** ( ✉ *Market Cross, Lerwick, Shetland* ☎ *08701/999440* ⊕ *www.visitshetland.com*). **Stromness, Orkney** ( ✉ *Pier Head, Stromness, Orkney* ☎ *01856/850716* ⊕ *www.visitorkney.com*).

# A Golfer's Country

**WORD OF MOUTH**

"I am compelled to put in a strong word for the birthplace of golf. Scotland offers the very best of the linksland—scenic, interesting, challenging, tougher'n hell when the 'conditions' hit, venues that one never tires of, even after many tries. It is a combination of the land, the people, yes, the climate that makes a round on Royal Dornoch or Cruden Bay or Machrihanish or Southerness or THE HOME—St. Andrews—a moment to be treasured. MAGIC! Haste ye back!"

—jinx

Updated by
Nick Bruno

**11**

**THERE ARE SOME 550 GOLF** courses in Scotland and only 5 million residents, so the country has probably the highest ratio of courses to people anywhere in the world. If you're a golfer coming to Scotland, you'll probably want to play the "famous names" sometime in your career. Telling your friends in the clubhouse back home that you got a birdie at the Road Hole on the Old Course in St. Andrews somehow conveys more prestige than an excellent round at a delightful but obscure course.

So, by all means, play the championship courses and impress your friends, but remember they *are* championship courses; you may enjoy the game itself much more at a less challenging, albeit lesser known, course. Remember, too, that everyone else wants to play them, so booking can be a problem at peak times in summer. Book early, or if you're staying in a hotel attached to a course, get them to book for you.

Happily, golf has always had a peculiar classlessness in Scotland. It's a game for everyone, and for centuries Scottish towns and cities have maintained golf courses for the enjoyment of their citizens. Admittedly, there are a few clubs that have always been noted for their exclusive air, and newer golf courses are emerging as part of exclusive leisure complexes, but these are exceptions to the tradition of recreation for all. Golf here is usually a democratic game, played by ordinary folk as well as the wealthy. Indeed, signs saying NO GOLF can be seen on grassy areas around the public housing projects in parts of Edinburgh and Glasgow; some children prefer a golf club and ball even to a soccer ball.

**TIPS ABOUT PLAYING IN SCOTLAND**
Golf courses are everywhere in Scotland except for in the far northern Highlands and some islands. Most courses welcome visitors with a minimum of formalities, and some at surprisingly low cost.

Be aware of the topography of a course. Scotland is where the distinction between "links" and "parkland" courses was first made. Links courses are by the sea and are subject to the attendant sea breezes and mists, which can make them trickier to play. The natural topography of sand dunes and long, coarse grasses can add to the challenge of playing, too. Invariably, a parkland course is in a wooded area and its terrain is more obviously landscaped. A "moorland" course is found in an upland area.

Here are three pieces of advice, particularly for North Americans: 1) in Scotland the game is usually played fairly quickly, so don't dawdle if others are waiting; 2) caddy carts are hand-pulled carts for your clubs; driven golf carts are rarely available; and 3) when they say "rough," they really mean "rough."

Unless specified otherwise below, course-playing hours are generally 9 AM to sundown, which in June can be as late as 10 PM. Note that some courses advertise the *SSS*, "standard scratch score," instead of par (which may be different); this is the score a scratch golfer could achieve under perfect conditions. *For more information about regional courses, see Sports & the Outdoors in individual chapters*. For a complete list of courses, contact local tourist offices or www.golf.visitscotland.com.

Clubs, balls, and other golfing gear are generally for rent from clubhouses, except at the most basic municipal courses. Don't get caught by the dress codes enforced at many golfing establishments: in general, untailored shorts, roundneck shirts, jeans, and sneakers are frowned upon. The prestigious courses may ask for evidence of your golf skills by way of a handicap certificate; check in advance and always carry this with you. ■ TIP➡ Some areas offer regional golf passes that are a great way to save money. Check with the local tourist board.

Run by Scotland's national tourist board, ⊕*http://golf.visitscotland. com* is a comprehensive Web site with information about the golf courses in the country. A course search, links to golf course and regional golf Web sites, lists of special golfing events and tour operators, and information on accommodations convenient to the courses are available. Another site, ⊕*www.uk-golfguide.com*, has a handy feature that allows you to see the courses via Google Earth.

### THE STEWARTRY

At the very southern border, the Stewartry is a delightful part of Scotland set in the rich farmlands around Dumfries, a golfing vacation area since Victorian times. There are also several fine 9-hole courses in the area.

**Powfoot.** A pleasant mix of links and parkland holes (nine of each) and views south over the Solway Firth to distract you make this lesser-known British Championship course a pleasure to play. ⊠*Powfoot Golf Club, Cummertrees, Annan* ☎☎*01461/207521* ⊕*www.powfootgolfclub.com* ⳋ*18 holes, 6,255 yds, SSS 71* ⊠*Weekdays £37 per round, £48 per day; weekends £43 per round, £60 per day* ⊙*Weekdays and Sun. after 1.*

**Southerness.** Mackenzie Ross designed this course, the first built in Scotland after World War II, in 1947. Southerness is a long course, played over extensive links with fine views southward over the Solway Firth. The greens are hard and fast, and the frequent winds make for some testing golf. ⊠*Southerness Golf Club, Southerness* ☎*01387/880677* ⊕*www.southernessgolfclub.com* ⳋ*Reservations essential* ⳋ*18 holes, 6,566 yds, par 69* ⊠*Weekdays £45 per round, £60 per day; weekends £55 per round, £70 per day* ⊙*Daily.*

### AYRSHIRE & THE CLYDE COAST

An hour south of Glasgow, Ayrshire and the Clyde Coast have been a holiday area for Glaswegians for generations. Few golfers need an introduction to the names of Turnberry, Royal Troon, Prestwick, or Western Gailes—all challenging links courses along this coast. There are at least 20 other courses in the area within an hour's drive.

**Girvan.** This is an old, established course with play along a narrow coastal strip and a more lush inland section next to the Water of Girvan—a river that constitutes a particular hazard at the 15th, unless you're a big hitter. The course is scenic, with good views of

Ailsa Craig and the Clyde Estuary. ⊠*40 Golf Course Rd., Girvan* ☎*01465/714346* ⊕*www.golfsouthayrshire.com* ⅄*.18 holes, 5,064 yds, par 64* ⚑*Weekdays £14 per round, £25 per day; weekends £18 per round, £33 per day* ⊙*Daily.*

**Prestwick.** Tom Morris was involved in designing this challenging Ayrshire coastal links course, which saw the birth of the British Open Championship in 1860. Prestwick has excellent, fast rail links with Glasgow. ⊠*2 Links Rd., Prestwick* ☎*01292/477404* ⊕*www.prestwickgc. co.uk* ⅄*.18 holes, 6,544 yds, par 71* ⚑*Weekdays £115 per round, £170 per day; Sun. £145 per round* ⊙*Sun.–Fri.*

**Royal Troon.** Of the two courses at Royal Troon, it's the Old Course—a traditional links course with superb sea views—that is used for the British Open Championship. You can buy a day ticket for one round on each course, which is a good value, as the ticket includes an excellent lunch. ⊠*Craigend Rd., Troon* ☎*01292/311555* ⊕*www.royaltroon. com* ⅄*.Old Course: 18 holes, 7,150 yds, SSS 74. Portland Course: 18 holes, 6,289, yds, SSS 70* ⚑*£220 per day (one round on each course), lunch included* ⊙*Mon., Tues., and Thurs.*

**Turnberry.** The Ailsa Course at Turnberry is perhaps the most famous links course in Scotland. Right on the seashore, the course is open to the elements, and the ninth hole requires you to hit the ball over the open sea. The British Open was staged here in 1977, 1986, and 1994. A second course, the Kintyre, is more compact than the Ailsa, with tricky sloped greens. Five of the holes have sea views, the rest are more inland. ⊠*Turnberry Hotel, Golf Courses and Spa, Turnberry* ☎*01655/331000* ⊕*www.turnberry.co.uk* ⅄*.Ailsa Course: 18 holes, 6,976 yds, SSS 72. Kintyre Course: 18 holes, 6,853 yds, SSS 72* ⚑*Ailsa Course: weekdays £140 per round for hotel guests, £1,560 per round for nonguests; weekends £140 per round for hotel guests, £200 per round for nonguests. Kintyre Course: daily £90 per round for hotel guests, £120 per round for nonguests* ⊙*Daily.*

★ **Western Gailes.** Known as the finest natural links course in Scotland, Western Gailes is entirely nature-made, and the greens are kept in truly magnificent condition. This is the final qualifying course when the British Open is held at Troon or Turnberry. Tom Watson lists the par-5 sixth as one of his favorite holes. ⊠*Gailes, Irvine* ☎*01294/311649* ⊕*www.westerngailes.com* ⅄*.18 holes, 6,700 yds, par 71* ⚑*Mon., Wed., Fri. £115 per round, £165 double round (lunch included); Sun. afternoon £125 per round* ⊙*Mon., Wed., Fri., and Sun. afternoon.*

## GLASGOW

Most of Glasgow's old golf clubs have moved out to the suburbs—you can tee off from at least 30 different courses less than an hour from the city center. Remember: in addition to these, all the Ayrshire courses are just down the road.

**Douglas Park.** North of the city near Milngavie (pronounced mul-*gai*), Douglas Park is a long, attractive course set among birch and pine trees with masses of rhododendrons blooming in early summer. The Campsie Fells form a pleasant backdrop. ⊠*Hillfoot, Bearsden* ☎*0141/942–0985* ⊕*www.douglasparkgolfclub.co.uk* ⚑*18 holes, 5,962 yds, par 69* ⛳*£30 per round* ⊙ *Wed. and Thurs., by appointment only.*

**Gailes.** The Glasgow Golf Club originally played on Glasgow Green in the heart of the ancient city center, but as the pressure for space grew, the club moved north to the leafy suburb of Bearsden, on the road to Loch Lomond. Killermont, the club's home course, is not open to visitors, but you can play the club's other course at Gailes, near Irvine on the Firth of Clyde. The Glasgow Club's Tennant Cup, in June, is the oldest open amateur tournament in the world. ⊠*Gailes* ✛*Near Irvine* ☎*0141/942–2011* ⊕*www.glasgowgailes-golf.com* ⚑*18 holes, 6,537 yds, SSS 72* ⛳*Weekdays £60 per round, £75 per day; weekends £70 per round* ⊙ *Weekdays 9:30–4:30, weekends after 2:30.*

## EAST LOTHIAN

The sand dunes that stretch eastward from Edinburgh along the southern shore of the Firth of Forth made an ideal location for some of the world's earliest golf courses. Muirfield is perhaps the most famous course in the area, but around it are more than a dozen others. All are links courses, many with views to the islands of the Firth of Forth and northward to Fife. If you weary of the East Lothian courses, try one of the nearly 30 courses within the city of Edinburgh, 20 mi or so to the west.

**Dunbar.** This ancient golfing site by the sea was founded in 1794 and has a lighthouse at the ninth hole. It's a good choice for experiencing a typical east-coast links course in a seaside town but within easy reach of Edinburgh. There are stunning views of the Firth of Forth and May Island. ⊠*East Links, Dunbar* ☎*01368/862086* ⊕*www.dunbar-golf-club.co.uk* ⚑*Reservations essential* ⚑*18 holes, 6,404 yds, par 71* ⛳*Weekdays £50 per round, £65 per day; weekends £60 per round, £85 per day* ⊙*Daily.*

**Muirfield.** The championship course at Muirfield is one of the best-known links courses in the world, so be prepared to pay the price of fame with expensive greens fees and severe limitations on when you can play. This exclusivity also means you should be prepared for a degree of curtness toward visitors. But it may be worth the expense and hassle to be able to walk in the footsteps of some of the greatest names in golf. A handicap certificate may be required. ⊠*Muirfield, Gullane* ☎*01620/842123* ⊕*www.muirfield.org.uk* ⚑*Reservations essential* ⚑*18 holes, 6,601 yds, par 70* ⛳*£160 per round, £220 per day* ⊙ *Visitors Tues. and Thurs., tee off between 8:30 and 9:50.*

## EDINBURGH

Scotland's capital has nearly 30 golf courses within its boundaries. Most are parkland courses, though along the shores of the Firth of Forth they take on the characteristics of traditional links. Some are used by private clubs and offer visitors limited access; others that belong to the city are more accessible and have much lower fees.

**Barnton, Royal Burgess Golfing Society.** Dating to 1735 this is one of the world's oldest golf clubs. Its members originally played on Bruntsfield Links; now they and their guests play on elegantly manicured parkland in the city's northwestern suburbs. It's a long course with fine greens. ✉ *181 Whitehouse Rd., Barnton* ☎ *0131/339–2075* ⊕ *www.royal-burgess.co.uk* ⛳ *Reservations essential* ⛳ *18 holes, 6,111 yds, par 68* 💳 *Weekdays £60 per day; weekends £75 per day* ☼ *Daily.*

**Braids.** Braids (no connection with James Braid) is beautifully laid out over a rugged range of small hills in the southern suburbs. The views to the south and the Pentland Hills and north toward the Edinburgh skyline are worth a visit in themselves. The city built this course at the turn of the 20th century after urban development forced golfers out of the city center. The 9-hole Princes Course was completed in 2003. Reservations are recommended for weekend play. ✉ *The Braids, Braids Hill Approach* ☎ *0131/447–6666 for Braids, 0131/447–3568 for Princes* ⊕ *www.edinburghleisure.co.uk/* ⛳ *Braids: 18 holes, 5,865 yds, par 70. Princes: 9 holes* 💳 *Braids: weekdays £19 per round, weekends £23 per round; Princes: weekdays £7 per round, weekends £9 per round* ☼ *Daily.*

**Bruntsfield Links.** The British Seniors and several other championship games are held at this Willie Park–designed 1898 course 3 mi west of the city. The course meanders among 155 acres of mature parkland and has fine views over the Firth of Forth to Fife. Bruntsfield takes its name from one of the oldest golf links in Scotland, in the center of Edinburgh—now just a 9-hole pitch-and-putt course—where the club used to play. ✉ *32 Barnton Ave., Davidson's Mains* ☎ *0131/336–1479* ⊕ *www.sol.co.uk/b/bruntsfieldlinks* ⛳ *Reservations essential* ⛳ *18 holes, 6,407 yds, par 71* 💳 *Weekdays £55 per round, £80 per day; weekends £65 per round, £85 per day* ☼ *Daily.*

## FIFE

The presence of St. Andrews makes this an important area—a pilgrimage center, even—for fans of the sport, but Fife has other courses, too. Along the north shores of the Firth of Forth is a string of ancient villages, each with its harbor, ancient red-roof buildings, and golf course. In all, there are about 30 courses in the area.

**Ladybank.** Fife is known for its coastal courses, but this one is an interesting inland contrast: although Ladybank, designed by Tom Morris in 1876, is laid out on fairly level ground, the fir woods, birches, and heathery rough give it a Highland flavor among the gentle Lowland fields. Qualifying rounds of the British Open are played here when the main championship is played at St. Andrews. ✉ *Annsmuir, Ladybank* ☎ *01337/830814* ⊕ *www.ladybankgolf.co.uk* ⛳ *Reservations essential* ⛳ *18 holes, 6,580 yds, par 71* 💳 *May–Sept., weekdays £47 per round, £67 per day; weekends £57 per round. Oct. and Apr., weekdays £37 per round, £57 per day; weekends £47 per round. Nov.–Mar., weekdays £20 for a round; weekends £25 (Sun. by arrangement with the Secretary)* ☼ *Daily.*

**Leven.** A fine Fife course used as a British Open qualifier, this links course feels like the more famous St. Andrews, with hummocky terrain and a tang of salt in the air. The 1st and 18th share the same fairway, and the 18th green has a creek running by it. ⊠ *The Promenade, Leven* ☎ *01333/428859* ⊕ *www.leven-links.com* ⌕ *Reservations essential* ⛳ *18 holes, 6,450 yds, par 71* ▣ *Weekdays £45 per round, £55 per day; Sun. £60 per round, £70 per day* ⊘ *Sun.–Fri.*

**St. Andrews.** Few would dispute the claim of St. Andrews to be the home of golf, holding as it does the Royal & Ancient, the organization that governs the sport worldwide. Golf has been played here since the 15th century, and to play in Fife is for most golfers a cherished ambition. St. Andrews itself has five other 18-hole courses (a sixth will open in summer 2008) besides the famous 15th-century Old Course. *For full details, see St. Andrews in Chapter 4.*

**St. Michael's.** Established in 1903, this undulating parkland course may have humbler origins than its exalted neighbor, but it's just as enjoyable. The back nine have wide, generous fairways, yet there are plenty of hazards and golfing tests on the way. The legendary par-3 15th (St. Mike's), next to the railway line, requires much subtlety and skill. ⊠ *Gallowhill, Leuchars* ☎ *01334/838666* ⊕ *www.stmichaelsgolfclub. co.uk* ⛳ *18 holes, 5,563 yards, par 70* ▣ *Weekdays £27 per round, £35 per day; weekends £35 per round by appointment* ⊘ *Daily.*

## PERTHSHIRE

Perthshire has several attractive country courses developed specifically for visiting golfers. Gleneagles Hotel *(see Chapter 5)* is, with its outstanding facilities, the most famous of these golf resorts. But several courses in the area, set on the edges of beautiful Highland scenery, will delight any golfer.

**Callander.** Callander was designed by Tom Morris in 1913 and has a scenic upland feel in a town well prepared for visitors. Pine and birch woods and hilly fairways afford fine views, especially toward Ben Ledi, and the tricky moorland layout demands accurate hitting off the tee. ⊠ *Callander Golf Club, Aveland Rd., Callander* ☎ *01877/330090* ⊕ *www.callandergolfclub.co.uk* ⛳ *18 holes, 4,431 yds, par 63* ▣ *Weekdays £22 per round, £30 per day; weekends £30 per round, £40 per day* ⊘ *Daily.*

**Killin.** A scenic course, Killin is typically Highland, with a roaring river, woodland birdsong, and a backdrop of high green hills. There are a few surprises, including two blind shots to reach the green at the fourth. The attractive village of Killin has an almost alpine feel, especially in spring, when the hilltops may still be white. ⊠ *Killin Golf Club, Aberfeldy Rd., Killin* ☎ *01567/820312* ⊕ *www.killingolfclub.co.uk* ⛳ *9 holes, 2,338 yds, par 66* ▣ *£18 per round, £24 per day* ⊘ *Apr.–Oct., daily.*

★ **Rosemount, Blairgowrie Golf Club.** Well-known to native golfers looking for a challenge, Rosemount's 18 (James Braid, 1934) are laid out on rolling land in the pine, birch, and fir woods, which bring a wild air to the scene. You may encounter a browsing roe deer if you stray too far.

There are, however, wide fairways and at least some large greens. The club is open daily, but visitor play may be restricted depending on tournament and match schedules. If you can't manage a game on Rosemount itself, you can play on Lansdowne, another 18-hole course, or Wee, a 9-hole course. A handicap certificate may be required to play here. ⊠ *Golf Course Rd., Blairgowrie* ☎ *01250/872622* ⊕ *www.theblairgowriegolf club.co.uk* ⚑ *Rosemount: 18 holes, 6,590 yds, par 72. Lansdowne: 18 holes, 6,802 yds, par 72. Wee: 9 holes, 2,352 yds, par 32* ▧ *Rosemount: £75 per round; Lansdowne: £50 per round; Wee: £30 per round. £80 per day (includes 1 round on Rosemount and 1 on Lansdowne)* ⊘ *Daily.*

## ANGUS

East of Perthshire, north of the city of Dundee, lies a string of demanding courses along the shores of the North Sea and inland into the foothills of the Grampian Mountains. The most famous course in Angus is probably Carnoustie, one of several British Open Championship venues in Scotland. Golfers who excel in windy conditions particularly enjoy the breezes blowing eastward from the sea. Inland Edzell, Forfar, Brechin, and Kirriemuir all have courses nestling in the Strathmore farmlands.

**Camperdown Park.** For an alternative to the famously wild and windy east-coast links courses, try this magnificent municipal parkland golf challenge on the outskirts of Dundee. You can enjoy a game amid handsome tree-lined fairways near the imposing Camperdown House and wildlife park. ⊠ *Camperdown Park, Angus Rd., Dundee* ☎ *01382/623398* ⊕ *www.dundeecity.gov.uk/golf* ⚑ *18 holes, 6,548 yards, par 71* ▧ *Weekdays £25 per round; weekends £30 per day* ⊘ *Daily.*

**Carnoustie.** The venue for the British Open Championship in 1999 and 2007, the extensive coastal links around Carnoustie have been played since at least 1527. Open winners here have included Armour, Hogan, Cotton, Player, and Watson. Carnoustie was also once a training ground for coaches, many of whom went to the United States. The choice Burnside course is full of historical snippets and local color, as well as being tough and interesting. The Buddon course, designed by Peter Allis and Davis Thomas, is recommended for links novices. ⊠ *Links Parade, Carnoustie* ☎ *01241/802270* ⊕ *www.carnoustie golflinks.co.uk* ⚑ *Reservations essential* ⚑ *Championship course: 18 holes, 6,941 yds, par 75; Burnside: 18 holes, 6,028 yds, par 68; Buddon: 18 holes, 5,420 yds, par 66* ▧ *Championship: Apr.–Oct., £125 per round; Burnside: £34 per round; Buddon: £29 per round; combined ticket for all 3 courses: £145* ⊘ *Weekdays 9–3:50, Sat. after 2, Sun. after 12:30.*

**Panmure.** Down the road from the famous Carnoustie club, this traditional links course offers an excellent challenge with its seaside climate, undulating greens, and sometimes excruciating—but always entertaining—burrows. The signature sixth is named after Open Championship winner Ben Hogan, who practiced here prior to his triumphant tournament at Carnoustie in 1953. ⊠ *Station Rd., Car-*

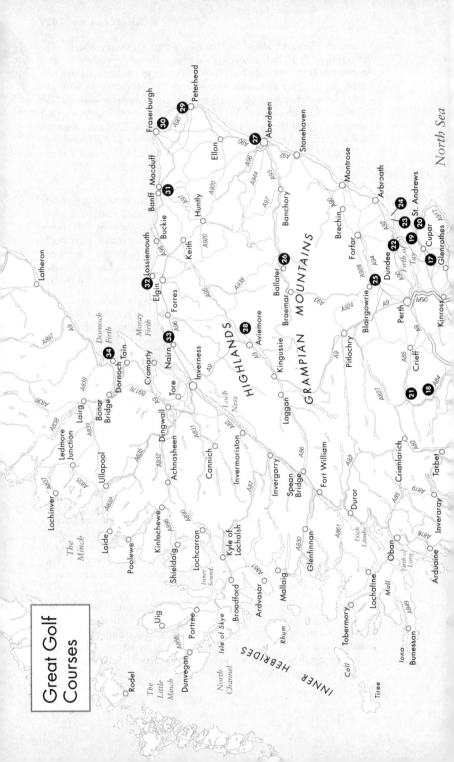

Great Golf
Courses

North Sea

The Minch

The Little Minch

North Channel

INNER HEBRIDES

Dornoch Firth

Moray Firth

HIGHLANDS

GRAMPIAN MOUNTAINS

Firth of Tay

Firth of Lorn

Loch Ness

Laheron

Peterhead
Fraserburgh
29
30
Aberdeen
Stonehaven
Ellon
Macduff
Banff
31
Buckie
Huntly
Keith
Montrose
Brechin
Arbroath
24
St. Andrews
23
20
Cupar
22
19
Glenrothes
17
Dundee
25
Perth
Blairgowrie
Pitlochry
Kinross
Lossiemouth
32
Elgin
Forres
Ballater
26
Braemar
Banchory
Forfar
Aviemore
28
Kingussie
Nairn
33
Inverness
Tain
Dornoch
34
Bonar Bridge
Lairg
Ledmore Junction
Cromarty
Tore
Dingwall
Crieff
21
18
Laggan
Achnasheen
Cannich
Invermoriston
Ullapool
Lochinver
Laide
Poolewe
Kinlochewe
Lochcarron
Shieldaig
Kyle of Lochalsh
Invergarry
Spean Bridge
Fort William
Duror
Crianlarich
Tarbet
Glenfinnan
Mallaig
Ardvasar
Broadford
Isle of Skye
Portree
Dunvegan
Uig
Rodel
Rhum
Loch Linnhe
Lochaline
Oban
Inveraray
Arduaine
Mull
Tobermory
Iona
Bunessan
Coll
Tiree

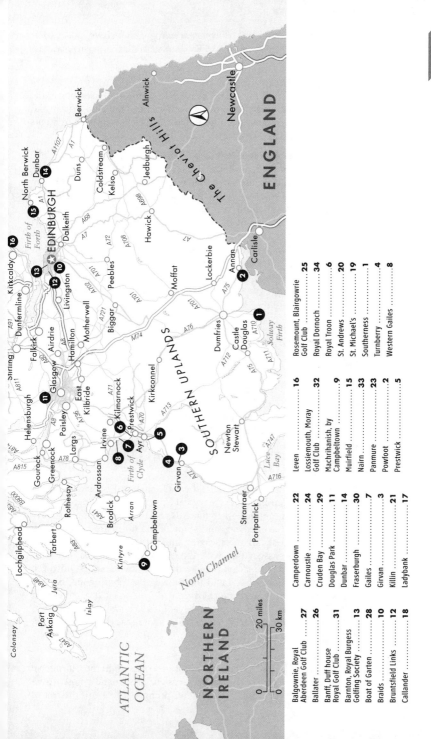

Balgownie, Royal
Aberdeen Golf Club ...... **27**
Ballater .................. **26**
Banff, Duff house
Royal Golf Club ........ **31**
Barnton, Royal Burgess
Golfing Society ........ **13**
Boat of Garten .......... **28**
Braids .................. **10**
Bruntsfield Links ........ **12**
Callander ................ **18**

Camperdown ............ **22**
Carnoustie .............. **24**
Cruden Bay ............. **29**
Douglas Park ........... **11**
Dunbar ................. **14**
Fraserburgh ............ **30**
Gailes .................. **7**
Girvan ................. **3**
Killin .................. **21**
Ladybank ............... **17**

Leven .................. **22**
Lossiemouth, Moray
Golf Club ............. **32**
Machrihanish, by
Campbeltown .......... **9**
Muirfield .............. **15**
Nairn .................. **33**
Panmure ............... **23**
Powfoot ............... **2**
Prestwick .............. **5**

Rosemount, Blairgowrie
Golf Club ............. **25**
Royal Dornoch ......... **34**
Royal Troon ........... **6**
St. Andrews ........... **20**
St. Michael's .......... **19**
Southerness ........... **1**
Turnberry ............. **4**
Western Gailes ........ **8**

*noustie* ☎*01241/855120* ⊕*www.panmuregolfclub.co.uk* ⚐*Reservations essential* ⚑*18 holes, 6,085 yards, par 70* ⊟*£65 per round, £85 per day* ⊙*Daily.*

## ABERDEENSHIRE

Aberdeen, Scotland's third-largest city, is known for its sparkling granite buildings and amazing displays of roses each summer. Within the city, there are six courses, and to the north, as far as Fraserburgh and Peterhead, there are five others, including the popular Cruden Bay.

**Balgownie, Royal Aberdeen Golf Club.** This old club, founded in 1780, is the archetypal Scottish links course: long and testing over uneven ground, with the frequently added hazard of a sea breeze. Prickly gorse is inclined to close in and form an additional hurdle. The two courses are tucked behind the rough, grassy sand dunes, and there are surprisingly few views of the sea. One historical note: in 1783 this club originated the five-minute-search rule for a lost ball. A handicap certificate or letter of introduction may be required. ⊠*Links Rd., Bridge of Don, Aberdeen* ☎*01224/702571* ⊕*www.royalaberdeen golf.com* ⚐*Reservations essential* ⚑*Balgownie: 18 holes, 6,415 yds, par 70; Silverburn: 18 holes, 4,021 yds, SSS 61* ⊟*Balgownie: weekdays £100 per round, £150 per day, weekends £120 per round; Silverburn: weekdays £50 per round, £75 per day, weekends £60 per round* ⊙*Balgownie: tee off weekdays 10–11:30 and 2–3:30, weekends after 3:30; Silverburn: daily.*

**Ballater.** The mountains of Royal Deeside surround this course laid out along the sandy flats of the River Dee. Ideal for a relaxing round of golf, the course makes maximum use of the fine setting between river and woods. The club, originally opened in 1906, has a holiday atmosphere, and the shops and pleasant walks in nearby Ballater make this a good place for nongolfing partners. Reservations are advised. ⊠*Victoria Rd., Ballater* ☎*013397/55567* ⊕*www.ballatergolfclub.co.uk* ⚑*18 holes, 6,059 yds, par 70* ⊟*Weekdays £24 per round, £34 per day; weekends £28 per round, £45 per day* ⊙*Daily.*

**Cruden Bay.** An east-coast Lowland course sheltered behind extensive sand hills, Cruden Bay offers a typical Scottish golf experience. Runnels and valleys, among other hazards, on the challenging fairways ensure plenty of excitement, and some of the holes are rated among the country's finest. Like Gleneagles and Turnberry, this course owes its origins to an association with the grand railway hotels that were built in the heyday of steam. Unlike the other two courses, however, Cruden Bay's railway hotel and the railway itself have gone, but the course remains in fine shape. ⊠*Aulton Rd., Cruden Bay, Peterhead* ☎*01779/812285* ⊕*www.crudenbaygolfclub.co.uk* ⚐*Reservations essential* ⚑*18 holes, 6,287 yds, par 70* ⊟*Weekdays £60 per round, £80 per day; weekends £70 per round* ⊙*Daily.*

## SPEYSIDE

On the main A9 road an hour south of Inverness amid the Cairngorm Mountains, the valley of the River Spey is one of Scotland's most attractive all-year sports centers, with winter skiing and fine golf the rest of

**CLOSE UP**

# The Evolution of "Gowf"

**11**

The matter of who invented golf has been long debated, but there's no doubt that its development into one of the most popular games in the world stems from Scotland.

The first written reference to golf, variously spelled as "gowf" or "goff," was in 1457, when James II (1430–60) of Scotland declared that both golf and football (soccer) should be "*utterly cryit doune and nocht usit*" (publicly criticized and prohibited) because they distracted his subjects from archery practice. Mary, Queen of Scots (1542–87), was fond of golf. When in Edinburgh in 1567, she played on Leith Links and on Bruntsfield Links. When in Fife, she played at Falkland and at St. Andrews itself.

Golf clubs (i.e., organizations) arose in the middle of the 18th century. The Honourable Company of Edinburgh Golfers, now residing at Muirfield, was founded in 1744. From then on, clubs sprang up all over Scotland: Royal Aberdeen (1780), Crail Golfing Society (1786), Dunbar (1794), and the Royal Perth Golfing Society (1824). By the early 19th century, clubs had been set up in England, and the game was being carried all over the world by enthusiastic Scots. These golf missionaries spread their knowledge not only of the sport, but also of the courses. Large parts of the Scottish coast are natural golf courses; indeed, the origins of bunkers and the word *links* (courses) are found in the sand dunes of Scotland's shores. Willie Park of Musselburgh, James Braid, and C. K. Hutchison are some of the best known of Scotland's golf-course architects.

Many of the important changes in the design and construction of balls and clubs were pioneered by the players who lived and worked around the town courses. The original balls, called *featheries*, were leather bags stuffed with boiled feathers and often lasted only one round. In 1848, the gutta-percha ball, called a *guttie*, was introduced. It proved superior and was in general use until the invention of the rubber-core ball in 1901. Clubs were traditionally made of wood with shafts of ash (later hickory), and heads of thorn, apple, or pear. Heads were spliced, then bound to the shaft with twine.

Caddies—the word comes from the French *cadet* (young boy)—carried the players' clubs, usually under the arm. Golf carts didn't come into fashion in Britain until the 1950s, and some people still consider them to be potentially injurious to the national health and moral fiber. The technology of golf continues to change, but its addictive qualities are timeless.

the year. The area's main courses are Newtonmore, Grantown-on-Spey, and Boat of Garten, all fine inland courses with wonderful views of the surrounding mountains and challenging golf provided by the springy turf and the heather.

**Boat of Garten.** This is possibly one of Scotland's greatest "undiscovered" courses. Boat of Garten, which dates to the late 19th century, was redesigned and extended by famous golf architect James Braid in 1932, and each of its 18 holes is individual: some cut through birch wood and heathery rough; most have long views to the Cairngorms and a strong Highland air. An unusual feature is the preserved steam railway that runs along part of the course. ✉ *Boat of Garten* ✦ *Village center* ☎ *01479/831282* ⊕ *www.boatgolf.com* ⬦ *Reservations essential* ⛳ *18 holes, 5,876 yds, par 70* 🏌 *Weekdays £32 per round, £42 per day; weekends £37 per round, £47 per day* ☉ *Daily.*

## MORAY COAST

No one can say that the Lowlands have a monopoly on Scotland's fine seaside golf courses. The Moray Coast, stretching eastward from Inverness, has some spectacular sand dunes that have been adapted to create stimulating and exciting links courses. The two courses at Nairn have long been known to golfers both famous and unknown.

**Banff, Duff House Royal Golf Club.** Just moments away from the sea, this club combines a coastal course with a parkland setting. It lies only minutes from Banff center, within the parkland grounds of Duff House, a country-house art gallery in a William Adam–designed mansion. The club has inherited the ancient traditions of seaside play (golf records here go back to the 17th century). Mature trees and gentle slopes create a pleasant playing environment. ✉ *The Barnyards, Banff* ☎ *01261/812075* ⊕ *www.theduffhouseroyalgolfclub.co.uk* ⬦ *Reservations essential* ⛳ *18 holes, 6,161 yds, par 70* 🏌 *Apr.–Sept. weekdays £52 per round, £65 per day; weekends £65 per round, £75 per day. Oct.–Mar. weekdays £28 per round, £33 per day; weekends £33 per round, £39 per day* ☉ *Daily.*

**Fraserburgh.** This northeast fishing town has extensive links and dunes that seem to have grown up around the course rather than the other way around. Be prepared for a hill climb and a tough finish. You can warm up on the extra nine holes. ✉ *Philorth, Fraserburgh* ✦ *At eastern end of town* ☎ *01346/516616* ⊕ *www.golffraserburgh.com* ⛳ *18 holes, 6,200 yds, par 70* 🏌 *Weekdays £30 per round, £40 per day; weekends £35 per round, £45 per day* ☉ *Daily.*

**Lossiemouth, Moray Golf Club.** Discover the mild airs of what's called the Moray Riviera, as Tom Morris did in 1889 when he was inspired by the lay of the natural links. There are two courses plus a six-hole minicourse. There's lots of history here, with golfing memorabilia in the clubhouse, as well as the tale of the pre–World War I British prime minister Asquith, who managed to be attacked by suffragettes at the 17th hole. All other hazards on these testing courses are entirely natural, with the 18th hole providing a memorable finish. ✉ *Stotfield Rd., Lossiemouth* ☎ *01343/812018* ⊕ *www.moraygolf.co.uk* ⛳ *Old Course: 18 holes, 6,572 yds, par 71; New Course: 18 holes, 6,008 yds, par 69* 🏌 *Old Course: weekdays £45 per round, £65 per day; weekends £55 per round, £70 per day. New Course: weekdays £35 per round, £45 per day; weekends £40 per round, £50 per day. Joint ticket (1 round on each course) £60 weekdays, £70 weekends* ☉ *Daily.*

★ **Nairn.** Well regarded in golfing circles, Nairn dates from 1887 and is the regular home of Scotland's Northern Open. Huge greens, aggressive gorse, a beach hazard for five of the holes, a steady prevailing wind, and distracting views across the Moray Firth to the northern hills make play here unforgettable. The adjoining 9-hole Newton Course is ideal for a warm-up or a fun round for the family. ⊠*Seabank Rd., Nairn* ☎*01667/453208* ⊕*www.nairngolfclub.co.uk* ⚑*Reservations essential* ⚓*Championship: 18 holes, 6,721 yds, par 72; Newton: 9 holes, 3,542 yds, par 58* 🏌*Championship: £80 per round, £110 per day; Newton: £16 per round* ☉*Daily.*

### DORNOCH FIRTH

The east coast north of Inverness is deeply indented with firths (the word is linked to the Norwegian *fjord*) that border some excellent, relatively unknown golf courses. Knowledgeable golfers have been making the northern pilgrimage to these courses for well over 100 years. There are half a dozen enjoyable links courses around Dornoch and Strathpeffer, an inland Victorian golfing holiday center.

Fodor's Choice
★
**Royal Dornoch.** This course, laid out by Tom Morris in 1886 on a sort of coastal shelf behind the shore, has matured to become one of the world's finest. Its location in the north of Scotland, though less than an hour's drive from Inverness Airport, means it's far from overrun even in peak season. The little town of Dornoch is sleepy and timeless. A handicap certificate may be required. The Royal Dornoch's Struie is a historic course that has been modified over the years. It's a challenging course with wonderful views of the Dornoch Firth and the mountains to the west. ⊠*Golf Rd., Dornoch* ☎*01862/810219* ⊕*www.royaldornoch.com* ⚑*Reservations essential* ⚓*Chamionship Course: 18 holes, 6,514 yds, par 70. Struie Course: 18 holes, 6,276 yds, par 70* 🏌*Championship Course: weekdays £82 per round; weekends £92 per round. Struie Course: single round £35, day ticket £45. Combined ticket: weekdays £93, weekends £103* ☉*Daily.*

### ARGYLL

The lochs and glens of Argyll in the west of Scotland have provided the scenic backdrop for family outings for generations. The string of courses north from the Mull of Kintyre all offer golf in a relaxed environment, with sea, beach, and hills not far away.

**Machrihanish, by Campbeltown.** Many enthusiasts discuss this course in hushed tones—it's a kind of out-of-the-way golfers' Shangri-la, though developments are now being built around it, as well as another course. It was laid out in 1876 by Tom Morris on the links around the sandy Machrihanish Bay. The drive off the first tee is across the beach to reach the green—an intimidating start to a memorable series of individual holes. Consider flying from Glasgow to nearby Campbeltown if time is short. The new Machrihanish Dunes course, adjacent to this course, is set to open in 2008. ⊠*Machrihanish, near Campbeltown* ☎*01586/810277* ⊕*www.machgolf.com* ⚑*Reservations essential* ⚓*18 holes, 6,225 yds, par 70* 🏌*Weekdays and Sun. £40 per round, £60 per day; Sat. £50 per round, £75 per day* ☉*Daily.*

# UNDERSTANDING SCOTLAND

# SCOTLAND AT A GLANCE

## FAST FACTS

**Capital:** Edinburgh

**National anthem:** "God Save the Queen"

**Type of government:** Scotland is part of the United Kingdom, which is a constitutional monarchy. It also has its own Parliament.

**Administrative divisions:** 32 council areas

**Independence:** April 6, 1320; the Declaration of Arbroath. Scottish nobles wrote Pope John XXII during the War of Independence and asked him to persuade the English king to stop his hostility toward the Scottish.

**Constitution:** There is no one document; it's a centuries-old accumulation of statutes as well as common law and practice.

**Legal system:** Scotland's system is organized separately from that of the rest of the United Kingdom. The two highest courts are the High Court of Justiciary (criminal) and the Court of Session (civil). Appeals to the British House of Lords may be made only from the Court of Session. The sheriff courts deal with less important civil and criminal cases.

**Suffrage:** 18 years of age

**Legislature:** Governed as an integral part of the United Kingdom's constitutional monarchy, Scotland is represented by 59 Members of Parliament in the House of Commons in London. On May 6, 1999, Scotland gained its own Parliament, located in Edinburgh, for the first time in nearly 300 years. Parliament has the power to pass Scottish laws; it's responsible for managing agriculture, education, health, and justice, and it can impose certain taxes within Scotland.

**Population:** 5,116,900

**Population density:** 65 persons per sq km (168.35 persons per sq mi)

**Median age:** Male 37, female 39

**Life expectancy:** Male 73.4, female 78.7

**Literacy:** 99%

**Language:** Predominantly English (fewer than 1,000 people speak only Gaelic, and fewer than 60,000 speak Gaelic in addition to English)

**Ethnic groups:** 98% of the population is Caucasian (88% of this is Scottish and 7.5% other British); Indian, Pakistani, Bangladeshi, and other South Asian groups are the largest ethnic minorities.

**Religion:** Residents identified their religion as follows: 42.4% Church of Scotland, 27.55% none, 15.88% Roman Catholic, 6.81% other Christian, 0.13% Buddhist, 0.11% Hindu, 0.13% Jewish, 0.84% Muslim, 0.13% Sikh, 0.53% another religion, 5.49% not answered

**Discoveries & Inventions:** Steam engine (1765), postage stamp (1834), telephone (1876), television (1924), penicillin (1928), radar (1935)

*We look to Scotland for all our ideas of civilization.*
*—Voltaire*

## GEOGRAPHY & ENVIRONMENT

**Land area:** 78,722 sq km (30,414 sq mi)

**Coastline:** 3,680 km (2,280 mi)

**Terrain:** Scotland is divided into three distinct regions, roughly from north to south: the Highlands (characterized by mountains with deep ravines, valleys, cliffs, lakes, and sea lochs); the Central Lowlands (mainly hills and rivers); and the Southern Uplands (moorland plateaus, rolling valleys, and mountainous outcrops).

**Islands:** 790, of which 10% are inhabited. The largest groups are Shetland and Orkney to the north, and the Hebrides, including Lewis, Harris, Barra, Skye, and Mull, to the west.

**Natural resources:** Coal, petroleum, natural gas, zinc, iron ore, limestone, clay, silica, gold

**Natural hazards:** Winter windstorms, floods

**Flora:** Dominant flora: rowan (tree belonging to the rose family), oak, fir, pine, and larch trees; heather, ferns, mosses, grasses, saxifrage, and mountain willow

**Fauna:** Principal fauna: deer, hare, rabbit, otter, ermine, pine marten, wildcat, grouse, blackcock, ptarmigan, waterfowl, kite, osprey, golden eagle, salmon, trout, cod, haddock, herring, various types of shellfish

**Environmental issues:** Climate change, air pollution, wind farms, recycling, nuclear power

*There are two seasons in Scotland: June and winter.*
*—Billy Connolly*

## ECONOMY

**Currency:** British pound (GBP)
**Exchange rate:** £1 = $2.05
**GDP:** £86 billion ($176 billion)
**Per-capita income:** £16,944 ($34,735)
**Inflation:** 1.8% in the United Kingdom
**Unemployment:** 4.8%
**Workforce:** 2,667,000 (services 79.1%; agriculture 1.4%; industry 19.5%)
**Major industries:** Aerospace, chemicals, construction, digital media and creative industries, energy, financial services, food and drink, life sciences, microelectronics and optoelectronics, textiles, and tourism
**Agricultural products:** Barley, wheat, oats, potatoes, livestock (sheep and cattle)
**Exports:** £17.5 billion ($35.9 billion)
**Major export products:** Office machinery, radio/TV/communication equipment, whisky, chemicals, manufactured machinery/equipment and transport equipment
**Export partners:** United States, Germany, France, Ireland, Netherlands
**Imports:** £57 billion ($117 billion)

*We'll never know the worth of water till the well go dry.*
*—18th-century Scottish proverb*

## DID YOU KNOW?

■ **Christmas was not celebrated as a festival in Scotland for about 250 years (from the end of the 17th century up to the 1950s) because the Protestant church believed Christmas to be a Catholic holiday and therefore banned it.** Many Scots worked over Christmas and their winter solstice holiday took place at New Year or "hogmanay."

■ **Kilts are not native to Scotland.** They originated in France.

■ **The first woman to play golf at St. Andrew's Golf Club was Mary, Queen of Scots, in 1552. She was the club's founder.**

■ **More redheads are born in Scotland than in any other country: 11% of the population has red hair.**

■ **Homer Simpson's catchphrase "Doh!" was based on the catchphrase of actor James Finlayson, who was born in Falkirk in 1887 and starred alongside Laurel and Hardy in many of their films.**

# BEYOND THE TARTAN PLAID

On some old recordings of Scottish songs still in circulation, you may run across "Roamin' in the Gloamin'" or "I Love a Lassie" or one of the other comic ditties of Harry Lauder, a star of the music halls of the 1920s. With his garish kilt, short crooked walking stick, rich rolling Rs, and *pawky* (cheerfully impudent) humor—chiefly based on the alleged meanness (stinginess) of the Scots—he impressed a Scottish character on the world. But his was, needless to say, a false impression and one the Scots have been trying to stamp out ever since.

How, then, do you characterize the Scots? Temperamentally, they're a mass of contradictions. They've been likened to a soft-boiled egg: a dour, hard shell, a mushy middle. Historically, fortitude and resilience have been their hallmarks, with streaks of both resignation and ferocity warring with sentimentality and love of family.

The Scots are in general suspicious of the go-getter, respecting success only when it has been a few hundred years in the making. But they're by no means plodders. This is the nation that built commerce throughout the British Empire, opened unexplored territories, and was responsible for much of humankind's scientific and technological advancement; a nation boastful about things it's not too good at and modest about genuine achievements. Consider the following extract from a handout about the Edinburgh School of Medicine: "If one excepts a few discoveries such as that of 'fixed air' by Black, of the diverse functions of the nerve-roots by Bell, of the anesthetic properties of chloroform by Simpson, of the invention of certain powerful drugs by Christison, and of the importance of antiseptic procedures by Lister, the influence of Edinburgh medicine has been of a steady constructive rather than a revolutionary type."

Among things that strike most newcomers to Scotland are the generosity of the Scots; their obsession with respectability; their satisfaction with themselves and their desire to stay as they are; and, above all, their passionate love of Scotland. An obstinate refusal to go along with English ideas has led to accusations that the nation has a head-in-the-sand attitude toward progress. But the Scots have their own ideas of progress, and they jealously guard the institutions that remain unique to them. The return of a parliament to Scottish soil in 1999, albeit one with limited powers, has generated a surge of pride in national identity.

## EDUCATION & LEGAL SYSTEM
When it comes to education, Scotland has a proud record. The nation had four universities—St. Andrews, Aberdeen, Glasgow, and Edinburgh—when England had only two: Oxford and Cambridge. A phenomenon of Scottish social history is the *lad o' pairts* (lad from the countryside)—the poor child of a feckless father and a fiercely self-sacrificing mother, sternly tutored by the village *dominie* (schoolmaster) and turned loose at the age of 13 with so firm a base of learning that he rose to the top of his profession. "Meal Monday," the midsemester holiday at a Scottish university, is a survivor of the long weekend that once enabled students to return to their distant homes—on foot—and replenish the sack of "meal" (oatmeal) that was their only sustenance.

Just as the Scots have their own traditions in education, so is their legal system distinct from England's. In England the police both investigate crime and prosecute suspects. In Scotland there's a public prosecutor directly responsible to the lord advocate (equivalent to England's attorney general), who is in turn accountable to parliament. For the most part, however, you'll notice few practical differences, except in terminology. The barrister in England becomes an advocate in Scotland. Cases for prosecution go before the "procurator fiscal" and are tried by the "sheriff" or "sheriff-substitute." In criminal cases Scotland adds to "guilty" and "not guilty" a third verdict: "not proven." This, say the cynics, signifies "We know you did it—but not enough evidence has been presented to prove it."

## RELIGION

The Presbyterian Church of Scotland—the Kirk—is entirely independent of the Church of England. Until the 20th century it was a power in the land and did much to shape Scottish character. There are still those who can remember when the minister visited houses like an inquisitor and put members of the families through their catechism. On Sunday morning the elders patrolled the streets, ordering people into church and rebuking those who sat at home in their gardens.

Religion in Scotland, as elsewhere, has lost much of its grip, so much so that a fair number of old metropolitan churches have been converted to theaters, restaurants, and pubs. But the Kirk remains influential in rural districts, where Kirk officials are pillars of local society. Ministers and their spouses are seen in all their somber glory in Edinburgh in springtime, when the General Assembly of the Kirk takes place, and for a week or more Scottish newspapers devote several column inches daily to the deliberations. The Episcopal Church of Scotland has bishops, as its name implies (unlike the Kirk, where the ministers are all equal), and a more colorful ritual. Considered genteel, Episcopalianism in Scotland has been described rather sourly by the Scottish novelist Lewis Grassie Gibbon as "more a matter of social status than theological conviction...a grateful bourgeois acknowledgment of anglicisation."

Of the various nonconformist offshoots of the established Kirk, the Free Kirk of Scotland is the largest. It remains faithful to the monolithic unity of its forefathers, adhering to the grim discipline that John Knox promoted long ago. The Free Kirk is strong in parts of the Outer Hebrides—Lewis, Harris, and North Uist. On Sunday in these areas no buses run, and all the shops are shut. Among the fishing communities, especially those of the northeast from Buckie to Peterhead, evangelical movements, such as the Jehovah's Witnesses, have made impressive inroads.

## SCOTCH OR SCOTS?

A word is needed on the vexed subject of nomenclature. A "scotchman" is not a native of Scotland but a nautical device for "scotching," or clamping, a running rope. Though you may find that some of those who are more conservative refer to themselves as Scotchmen and consider themselves Scotch, most prefer Scot or Scotsman and call themselves Scottish or Scots. You may include the Scots in the broader term *British,* but they dislike the word *Brits,* and nothing infuriates them more than being called English. Nonetheless, there are a lot of Anglo-Scots, that is, people of Scottish birth who live in England or are the offspring of marriages between Scottish and English people. The term Anglo-Scots is not to be confused with Sassenachs, the Gaelic word for "Saxon," which is applied facetiously or disdainfully to all the English. But at the same time, English people who live in Scotland remain English to their dying day, and their children after them.

# BOOKS & MOVIES

## BOOKS

Scotland has always had a love and respect for books and learning, for poetry and song. From the poems of Robert Burns, which reflect his Ayrshire roots, to the "bothy ballads" of the northeast, with which the farmhands entertained each other after a hard day's work, from Sir Walter Scott's Borders sagas to Mairi Hedderwick's Katie Morag children's stories set in the Western Isles—all share the strong visual thread of their own Scottish landscapes. Whether written 200 or 2 years ago, these books and poems have much to tell visitors about the character of Scotland's hugely varied countryside and of the resilient, soft-hearted, yet sometimes dour Scottish people. Wherever you intend to travel in Scotland, there are books to read to set the scene beforehand. Dipping into some nonfiction, whether it's a guide to history or the landscape, can also enhance your visit.

### FICTION

Edinburgh has inspired many writers. Muriel Spark's *The Prime of Miss Jean Brodie* was written in 1961 yet still has much to say about the importance of the city's private schools to the financial success and social life of Edinburgh's prim middle classes. Laura Hird's novel *Born Free* paints a more modern portrait of life in the Scottish capital through the various points of view of a very dysfunctional working-class family. Ian Rankin's famous Inspector Rebus crime thrillers cunningly contrast the architecture and wealth of Edinburgh's Old and New towns and the poverty of public-housing occupants. Among his best works are *Let It Bleed, Mortal Causes,* and *Black and Blue.* On the lighter side, Alexander McCall Smith's Isabel Dalhousie mysteries, including *The Sunday Philosophy Club,* are set in modern Edinburgh.

Glasgow, too, has its dark side, chronicled in Denise Mina's trilogy of con-temporary detective novels: *Garnethill, Exile,* and *Resolution,* where the criminal underbelly of the city comes to life through reluctant detective Maureen O'Donnell. Mina's sharp eye for detail provides vivid views of the cityscape. Louise Welsh's protagonist, Rilke, travels around Glasgow's trendy West End district solving the mystery of some disturbing old photographs in Welsh's literary crime novel *The Cutting Room.* Christopher Brookmyre's Glasgow-based novels fall under the popular Scottish subgenre "tartan noir" they involve murder, mystery, and plenty of sharp Scottish wit. The protagonist in five of his novels (*Quite Ugly One Morning, Country of the Blind, Boiling a Frog, Be My Enemy,* and *Attack of the Unsinkable Rubber Ducks),* is investigative journalist Jack Parlablane, who picks on local white-collar criminals. James Kelman's deep, brooding characters, coupled with his use of urban Scots dialect, resonate Glasgow from beginning to end. His best book, *A Disaffection* (1989), was nominated for the prestigious Booker Prize. Like Kelman, Anne Donovan also writes in Scots; however, her characters and stories have a lighter, softer tone. Her debut novel, *Buddha Da,* unravels the story of Jimmy, a painter whose decision to become a Buddhist changes his family forever.

The novels of Lewis Grassic Gibbon (pseudonym of James Leslie Mitchell, 1901–35) are set in the bleak farmlands of Kincardineshire, in an area known as the Howe of Mearns, south of Stonehaven, where he grew up. *A Scots Quair, Sunset Song, Cloud Howe,* and *Grey Granite* incorporate the rhythms and cadences of speech in the northeast, which you can still hear today. The unremitting harshness of farming life, described in *A Scots Quair,* is still to some extent valid, despite the advent of modern machinery and farming practices. Nonetheless, the spare beauty of the landscape—with its patchwork of fields rising to higher ground and a spectacular coastline with towering cliffs and white-sand beaches—rewards those who visit the area.

Another writer and poet whose work is intimately related to his environment is George Mackay Brown (1921–96), born in Stromness, Orkney. His work reflects Orkney's rich heritage of prehistoric sites, its farming and fishing communities, and its religious history. *Greenvoe* vividly describes life in an imaginary Orkney village; you may also want to read *Fishermen with Ploughs* or his other books of poems.

Scotland's most famous poet and champion of the underdog was Robert Burns (1759–96), who found inspiration in the landscapes of his native Ayrshire in southwest Scotland. His poems and songs will never be far away during your visit, and indeed he has been translated into more languages than any other poet writing in English, including Shakespeare. The Burns Heritage Trail takes you to Alloway, where you can visit his birthplace; to Auld Alloway Kirk, where Tam o'Shanter saw the witches; and to the Tam o' Shanter Experience, a tourist attraction that brings the poem to life. Burns Night (January 25) is still a fixture on the Scottish calendar, with readings of "To a Haggis" and "The Selkirk Grace" being the highlights.

For a taste of life in the Scottish Hebridean islands before you arrive, read Mairi Hedderwick's delightful Katie Morag stories, set on a Hebridean island. Children's stories they may be, but for insights into life on the islands—positive and negative—they are hard to equal. Many teenagers on the islands still dream of their eventual escape to Glasgow or Edinburgh, just as they did 50 or 100 years ago, and Katie Morag's day-to-day life perhaps shows why: the islands are not rich in dance clubs, sports and entertainment centers, fashion boutiques, or Internet cafés. But they are rich in community spirit, tradition and music, and beauty of land and seascape, all of which comes across vividly both in Mairi Hedderwick's text and in the superb, amusingly detailed illustrations. *Katie Morag and the Big Boy Cousins* is a good title to start with.

Historical novels are a painless way to absorb some of Scotland's history. Mollie Hunter's work is geared toward teenagers; *Escape from Loch Leven* deals with Mary, Queen of Scots, and *The Ghosts of Glencoe* covers the Glencoe massacre. Eric Linklater's *The Prince in the Heather* tells of Bonnie Prince Charlie's efforts to escape after the failure of the 1745 Jacobite rebellion. D.K. Broster's *The Flight of the Heron* and its sequel, *The Dark Mile*, deal with the changes to the clan system effected by the defeat of the Jacobites at Culloden in the mid-18th century.

And then there are those quintessentially Scottish books that you're told to read. The novels and narrative poems of Sir Walter Scott (1771–1832) don't seem very accessible these days, and with their lengthy introductions, melodramatic plots, overpowering wealth of historical detail, and stately language, they offer no instant gratification. Still, Scott not only tells a great story, he is also historically accurate, and his settings among the hills and river valleys of southern Scotland are not so very different today. Try reading *Rob Roy* or *The Lady of the Lake* when traveling in the Trossachs, or *Redgauntlet* if you're in Dumfries and Galloway.

Another top storyteller, Robert Louis Stevenson (1850–94), was born in Edinburgh though destined to spend much of his life outside Scotland. Read *Kidnapped* and shiver amid the bleak expanse of Rannoch Moor. Then go and gaze across that very moor—its gray, brown, and watery wastes so accurately described by Stevenson—and imagine being a fugitive among its hummocks and pools.

The *Oxford Literary Guide to the British Isles,* edited by Dorothy Eagle and Hilary Carnell, *A Reader's Guide to Writers' Britain* by Sally Varlow, and *Scotland: A Literary Guide,* by Alan Bold, can direct you to other literary landscapes in addition to those mentioned above. Edinburgh has been named the first UNESCO World City of Literature; Allan Foster's *Literary Traveler in Edinburgh* is an illustrated sightseeing guide to literary hot spots, including writers' homes and the settings for famous works.

## NONFICTION

Scottish history is both extensive and absorbing. The most accessible book on the subject to date, Tom Devine's *The Scottish Nation,* examines the last three centuries from the Act of Union to the reestablishment of the Scottish Parliament. Another pivotal historical book is Neal Ascherson's *Stone Voices: The Search for Scotland,* in which archaeology, geology, myth, and travel combine to create an impressive image of Scotland as a nation. George Rosie's *Curious Scotland: Tales from a Hidden History* explores a more marginal historical timeline. If you're interested in facts such as why a Hebridean island was deliberately infested with anthrax, then it's the book to read. John Prebble's *The Highland Clearances* is an excellent commentary on the aftermath of the Battle of Culloden. For raw urban historical narrative, try Alexander McArthur and Herbert Kingsley Long's *No Mean City: A Story of the Glasgow Slum.*

For books on Scottish art and architecture, Duncan MacMillan's *Scottish Art in the 20th Century, 1890–2001* is a comprehensive guide to artists from Charles Rennie Mackintosh to Ken Currie. Jude Burkhauser's *Glasgow Girls: Women in Art and Design 1880–1920* is more narrow in scope but equally intriguing. Bella Bathurst's *The Lighthouse Stevensons* uniquely catalogs the engineering revolution of lighthouse building through the work of four generations of writer Robert Louis Stevenson's family. For good background information on castles, look for Damien Noonan's *Castles and Ancient Monuments of Scotland* and John G. Dunbar's *Scottish Royal Palaces.*

Football in Scotland is, in many respects, a religion. To find out more on the subject, read David Ross's passionate *The Roar of the Crowd: Following Scottish Football Down the Years.* Another important sport in Scotland is the game invented there: golf. A popular book on the subject, Malcolm Campbell's *Scottish Golf Book* will not only tell you where to putt but also will give you a thorough background on the game itself. Curtis Gillespie's memoir *Playing Through: A Year of Life and Links Along the Scottish Coast* takes a more personal approach to golf and its past through the year he spent with his family in Gullane, as does Lorne Rubenstein's *A Season in Dornoch: Golf and Life in the Scottish Highlands.*

Travel and landscape books on Scotland are almost as plentiful as the country's native thistle. Although initially published in 1779, the reflections and descriptions in Samuel Johnson and James Boswell's *Journey to the Hebrides* (reprinted in 1996) are just as relevant today. Kathleen Jamie's poetically told *Findings* will wet your taste buds for Scotland's picturesque countryside like no other. Cameron McNeish has written some excellent books; *The Munros: Scotland's Highest Mountains* (out of print) is a carefully crafted guide to climbing those peaks. Colin Prior's impressive photography collection *Highland Wilderness* gives stunning panoramic views of the wild but wonderful north.

## MOVIES

The quintessential "kilt movies" are *Rob Roy* (1995), with Liam Neeson and Jessica Lange—shot at and around Glen Nevis and Glencoe, the gardens of Drummond Castle, and Crichton Castle—and Mel Gibson's *Braveheart* (1995), the story of Scotland's first freedom fighter, Sir William Wallace (circa 1270–1305), which also uses the spectacular craggy scenery of Glen Nevis. Both films are great on atmosphere though not so hot on accurate historical detail; they do give a fine preview of Scotland's varied scenery. *Highlander* (1986), with Christopher Lambert and Sean Connery, also uses the spectacular crags of Glencoe, along with the prototypical Scottish castle Eilean Donan—almost a visual cliché in Scottish terms.

The movie of the Scottish classic tale by Muriel Spark, *The Prime of Miss Jean Brodie* (1969), starring Maggie Smith, was filmed in several locations around Edinburgh, as well as in London. In stark contrast *Trainspotting* (1996), directed by Danny Boyle and starring Ewan McGregor, is a commentary (based on the book by Irvine Welsh) on heroin addicts in a depressed Edinburgh housing project; however, filming took place in both Glasgow and Edinburgh. Danny Boyle's first feature film, *Shallow Grave* (1994), which also stars Ewan McGregor, is a highly entertaining suspense thriller about money, friends, and murder. Because the film was shot almost entirely in Edinburgh, it gives viewers a much better sense of the city. *Festival*, a 2005 film written and directed by Annie Griffin, takes a humorous look behind the scenes of Edinburgh's Festival Fringe.

Award-winning director Ken Loach has set several films in Glasgow. His gritty portrayals of extreme Glaswegian life are captured in the unofficial trilogy *My Name Is Joe* (1998), *Sweet Sixteen* (2002), and *Ae Fond Kiss* (2004). Because of the strong local dialects used, all three films have English subtitles. On a more uplifting note, the well-received, must-see *American Cousins* (2003) tells the warmhearted story of two American mafiosi taking refuge with their Scottish cousin in his Glasgow fish-and-chips shop. The well-received *Red Road*

(2006) stars Kate Dickie in a dark drama about a CCTV operator who becomes obsessed with a man she sees on one of her screens.

To get a good sense of the Scottish landscape, watch *Restless Natives* (1985), a road-trip comedy about two guys from Edinburgh who travel the countryside holding up tour buses. For a hilarious peek into island life, see *Whisky Galore!* (1949), set on the Outer Hebridean island of Todday. The cult film *The Wicker Man* (1973), starring Christopher Lee, is shot in various locations from Skye to Culzean Castle. Its chilling plot of a secret island society, wanton lust, and pagan blasphemy has inspired an annual musical festival.

For English films set in Scotland, *Her Majesty, Mrs Brown* (1997), known in Scotland as *Mrs Brown,* and starring Dame Judi Dench and Billy Connolly, tells the tender story of Queen Victoria and John Brown, her favorite gillie (servant). It was filmed at locations in the Borders and the Highlands, with the Ardverikie Estate near Dalwhinnie standing in for Balmoral. Another entertaining, albeit extremely different kind of film, is *Monty Python and the Holy Grail* (1975). Glencoe, Rannoch Moor, Doune Castle, Arnhall Castle, Duke's Pass, Loch Tay, Sheriffmuir, and Castle Stalker all make magnificent appearances.

For more information on movies filmed in Scotland, you can buy *The Pocket Scottish Movie Book* by Brian Pendreigh, or you can visit the Scotland the Movie Guide Web site ( *www.scotlandthemovie.com*).

# CHRONOLOGY

**7000 BC** Hunter-gatherers move north into Scotland after the ice sheets of the last Ice Age recede; these travelers leave arrowheads and bone implements as testimony to their passing.

**ca. 6000 BC** First settlers arrive, bringing farming methods with them.

**ca. 3000 BC** Neolithic migration from Mediterranean: "chambered cairn" people in north (such as the Grey Cairns of Camster), "beaker people" in southeast.

**ca. 300 BC** Iron Age: infusion of Celtic peoples from the south and from Ireland; "Gallic forts" and "brochs" (towers) built.

**AD 79–89** Julius Agricola (AD 40–93), Roman governor of Britain, invades Scotland; Scots tribes defeated at the battle of Mons Graupius (thought to be somewhere in the Grampians). Roman forts built at Inchtuthil and Ardoch.

**142** Emperor Antoninus Pius (86–161) orders the defensive Antonine Wall built between the Firths of Forth and Clyde.

**185** Antonine Wall abandoned.

**392** St. Ninian's (ca. 360–432) mission to the Picts sets out from the first Christian chapel at Whitehorn.

**400–500** Tribes of Celtic origin, including the Scotti, emigrate from Ireland to present-day Argyllshire and establish the kingdom of Dalriada.

**400–843** Four kingdoms exist in Scotland: Dalriada (Argyllshire), the kingdom of the Picts (Aberdeenshire down to Fife and the Highlands excepting Argyllshire), Strathclyde (southwest Scotland), and the Lothians (Edinburgh and the Borders).

**563** Columba (ca. 521–97) establishes monastery at Iona.

**843** Kenneth MacAlpin, king of Dalriada, unites with the Picts while remaining king. In this way the embryonic Kingdom of Scotland is born, with its capital at Scone.

**780–1065** Scandinavian invasions; Hebrides remain Norse until 1263, Orkney and Shetland until 1472.

**1018** Malcolm II (ca. 953–1034) brings the Lothians into the Kingdom of Scotland and (temporarily) repels the English.

**1034** Duncan (d. 1040), king of Strathclyde, ascends the throne of Scotland and unification is complete.

**1040** Duncan is slain by his rival, Macbeth (d. 1057), whose wife has a claim to the throne.

---

## HOUSE OF CANMORE

**1057** Malcolm III (ca. 1031–93), known as Canmore (Big Head), murders Macbeth and assumes the throne.

1093    Death of Malcolm's queen, St. Margaret (1046–93), who brought Roman Catholicism to Scotland.

1099    Donald III becomes the last king of Scots to be buried on the island of Iona.

1124–53    David I (ca. 1082–1153), *sair sanct* (sore saint), builds the abbeys of Jedburgh (1118), Kelso (1128), Melrose (1136), and Dryburgh (1150) and brings Norman culture to Scotland.

1250    Queen Margaret, wife of Malcolm III, is canonized, becoming Scotland's first (and only) royal saint.

1290    Death of Alexander III, great-great-grandson of David I. The heir is his granddaughter, Margaret, Maid of Norway (1283–90). She dies at sea on her way from Norway to claim the Scottish throne and marry the future Edward II (1284–1327), son of Edward I of England (1239–1307). The Scots naively ask Edward I, subsequently known as the Hammer of the Scots, to arbitrate between the remaining 13 claimants to the throne. Edward's choice, John Balliol (1249–1315), is known as Toom Tabard (Empty Coat).

1295    Under continued threat from England, Scotland signs its first treaty of the "auld alliance" with France. Wine trade flourishes.

1297    Revolutionary William Wallace (ca. 1270–1305), immortalized by Burns, leads the Scots against the English.

1305    Wallace captured by the English and executed.

1306–29    Reign of Robert the Bruce (1274–1329), later to become King Robert I. Defeats Edward II (1284–1327) at Bannockburn, 1314; Treaty of Northampton, 1328, recognizes Scottish sovereignty.

1349    The first cases of the Black Death are recorded in Scotland.

## HOUSE OF STEWART

1371    Robert II (1316–90), the first Stewart monarch and son of Robert the Bruce's daughter Marjorie and Walter the Steward, is crowned. Struggle (dramatized in Scott's novels) between the crown and Scottish barons over control of the barons' land ensues for the next century, punctuated by sporadic warfare with England.

1383    Bishop Wardlaw of Glasgow is the first Scot to be made a cardinal.

1411    University of St. Andrews founded.

1451    University of Glasgow founded.

1488–1513    Reign of James IV (1473–1513). The Renaissance reaches Scotland. The Golden Age of Scots poetry includes Robert Henryson (ca. 1425–1508), William Dunbar (ca. 1460–1530), Gavin Douglas (1474–1522), and the king himself.

1495    University of Aberdeen founded.

1507   Andrew Myllar and Walter Chapman set up first Scots printing press in Edinburgh.

1513   After invading England in support of the French, James IV is slain at Flodden.

1542   Henry VIII (1491–1547) defeats James V (1512–42) at Solway Moss; the dying James, hearing of the birth of his daughter, Mary, declares: "It came with a lass [Marjorie Bruce] and it will pass with a lass."

1542–67   Reign of Mary, Queen of Scots (1542–87); Mary's mother is appointed regent. Romantic, Catholic, and with an excellent claim to the English throne, Mary proved to be no match for her barons, John Knox (1513–72), or her cousin Elizabeth I (1533–1603) of England.

1560   Mary returns to Scotland from France after the death of her husband, Francis II of France, at the same time that Catholicism is abolished in favor of Protestantism. The spelling "Stuart" adopted instead of "Stewart."

1565   Mary marries Lord Darnley (1545–67), a Catholic.

1567   Darnley is murdered at Kirk o' Field; Mary marries one of the conspirators, the earl of Bothwell (ca. 1535–78). Driven from Scotland, she appeals to Elizabeth, who imprisons her. Mary's son, James (1566–1625), is crowned James VI of Scotland.

1582   University of Edinburgh is founded.

1587   Elizabeth orders the execution of Mary.

1600   Charles I is born in Scotland.

1603   Elizabeth dies without issue; James VI is crowned James I of England. Parliaments remain separate for another century.

1638   National Covenant challenges Charles I's personal rule.

1639–41   Crisis. The Scots and then the English parliaments revolt against Charles I (1600–49).

1643   Solemn League and Covenant establishes Presbyterianism as the Church of Scotland (the Kirk). Civil War in England.

1649   Charles I beheaded. Oliver Cromwell (1599–1658) made Protector.

1650–52   Cromwell roots out Scots royalists.

1658   The first Edinburgh–London coach is established. The journey takes two weeks.

1660   Restoration of Charles II (1630–85). Episcopalianism reestablished in Scotland; Covenanters persecuted.

1688   The unpopular James VII of Scotland (and II of England, Scotland, and Ireland) flees to France.

1688–89   Glorious Revolution; James VII and II (1633–1701), a Catholic, deposed in favor of his daughter Mary (1662–94) and her husband, William of Orange (1650–1702). Supporters of James (known as Jacobites) defeated at Killiecrankie. Presbyterianism reestablished.

1692   Highlanders who were late in taking oath to William and Mary massacred at Glencoe.

1695   The first bank in Scotland, the Bank of Scotland, is founded.

1698–1700   Attempted Scottish colony at Darien (on the Isthmus of Panama) fails. Many of the Scottish nobility face bankruptcy, and are therefore open to overtures from an English government anxious to unite the Scottish and English parliaments.

1707   Union of English and Scots parliaments under Queen Anne (1665–1714), the last Stuart monarch; deprived of French wine trade, Scots turn to whisky.

## HOUSE OF HANOVER

1714   Queen Anne dies; George I (1660–1727) of Hanover, descended from a daughter of James VI and I, crowned.

1715   First Jacobite Rebellion. James II's son, James Edward Stuart, agrees to undertake an invasion of England. His supporter, the earl of Mar (1675–1732), is defeated.

1730–90   Scottish Enlightenment. The Edinburgh Medical School is the best in Europe; David Hume (1711–76) and Adam Smith (1723–90) redefine philosophy and economics. In the arts, Allan Ramsay the elder (1686–1758) and Robert Burns (1759–96) refine Scottish poetry; Allan Ramsay the younger (1713–84) and Henry Raeburn (1756–1823) rank among the finest painters of the era. Edinburgh's New Town, begun in the 1770s by the brothers Adam (Robert, 1728–92; brother James, 1730–94; father William 1689–1748), provides a fitting setting.

1736   The first public theater in Scotland is opened in Carruber's Close in Edinburgh.

1745–46   Last Jacobite Rebellion. Bonnie Prince Charlie (1720–88), grandson of James II, is defeated at Culloden and eventually escapes back to France; wearing of the kilt is forbidden until 1782. James Watt (1736–1819), born in Greenock, is granted a patent for his steam engine.

1760   Thomas Braidwood (1715–1806), opens the first school for the deaf and dumb in Great Britain, in Edinburgh.

1771   Birth of Walter Scott (1771–1832), Romantic novelist.

1778   First cotton mill, at Rothesay.

1788   Death of Bonnie Prince Charlie in Rome.

1790   Forth and Clyde Canal opened.

1800–50   Highland Clearances: increased rents, and conversion of farms to sheep pasture lead to mass migration, sometimes forced, to North America and elsewhere. Meanwhile, the Lowlands industrialize; Catholic Irish immigrate to factories of Glasgow and the southwest.

1807   The first museum in Scotland, the Hunterian Museum, is founded.

1822   Visit of George IV to Scotland, the first British monarch to make such a trip since Charles I. Sir Walter Scott orchestrates the visit, and almost single-handedly invents Scotland's national costume: the formal kilt, tartan plaid, and jacket.

1831   The first passenger rail service in Scotland opens on the line between Glasgow and Garnkirk.

1832   Parliamentary Reform Act expands the franchise, redistributes seats.

1837   Victoria (1819–1901) ascends to the British throne.

1842   Edinburgh–Glasgow railroad opened.

1846   Edinburgh–London railroad opened.

1848   Queen Victoria buys estate at Balmoral as her Scottish residence. Andrew Carnegie emigrates from Dunfermline to Pittsburgh.

1860   The first British Open golf championship is held in Scotland, at St. Andrews.

1884–85   Gladstone's Reform Act gives the majority of men 21 and older the right to vote. Office of Secretary for Scotland authorized.

1886   Scottish Home Rule Association founded.

1890   Forth Rail Bridge opened.

1901   Death of Queen Victoria.

---

## HOUSE OF WINDSOR

1928   Equal Franchise Act gives the vote to women. Scottish Office established as governmental department in Edinburgh. Scottish National Party founded.

1931   Depression hits industrialized Scotland severely.

1939   The first German air raids of World War II on Scotland are made on the Forth Estuary.

1945   Two Scottish Nationalists elected to parliament.

1947   The Edinburgh International Festival, with events in all the performing arts, is launched.

1959   Finnart Oil Terminal, Chapelcross Nuclear Power Station, and Dounreay Fast Breeder Reactor opened.

1964   Forth Road Bridge opened.

1970   British Petroleum strikes oil in the North Sea; revives economy of northeast.

1973   Britain becomes a member of the European Economic Community (formerly known as the Common Market).

1974   Eleven Scottish Nationalists elected as members of Parliament. Old counties reorganized and renamed as new regions and districts.

1979   Referendum on devolution—the creation of a separate Scotland: 33% in favor, 31% against; 36% don't vote.

1981   Europe's largest oil terminal opens at Sullom Voe, Shetland.

1992   Increasing attention focused on Scotland's dissatisfaction with rule from London. Poll shows 50% of Scots want independence.

1995   In the face of a Tory government that looks increasingly like a lame duck, Scotland continues to argue its own way forward. The Labour Party, if elected in the 1997 general election, promises a Scottish parliament but wants to keep Scotland within the United Kingdom; the Scottish National Party still wants independence and sees Labour's Scottish parliament as a stepping-stone to full autonomy.

1997   The Labour Party wins the general election in May. A referendum in Scotland votes in favor of the establishment of a Scottish parliament (with restricted powers). The first successful cloning of an animal in the world is achieved with the birth of Dolly the Sheep at the Roslin Institute in Edinburgh.

1999   Scotland elects its first parliament in 300 years. A coalition is formed between the Labour Party and the Liberal Democrats to run the country.

2000   Death of Scotland's first, and much respected, first minister, Donald Dewar. Henry McLeish becomes first minister.

2001   Henry McLeish resigns amid scandal. Jack McConnel becomes first minister.

2002   The Millennium Link—the restoration of the canal link between Glasgow and Edinburgh—is completed at a cost of £78 million. It includes the Falkirk Wheel, the world's only rotating boat lift.

2004   The Scottish Parliament Building opens for business.

2007   Alex Salmond, leader of the Scottish National Party, becomes the First Minister of Scotland heading a minority government.

# Scotland Essentials

PLANNING TOOLS, EXPERT INSIGHT,
GREAT CONTACTS

There are planners and there are those who,
excuse the pun, fly by the seat of their pants.
We happily place ourselves among the planners.
Our writers and editors try to anticipate all the
issues you may face before and during any journey, and then they do their research. This section
is the product of their efforts. Use it to get excited
about your trip to Scotland, to inform your travel
planning, or to guide you on the road should the
seat of your pants start to feel threadbare.

# GETTING STARTED

We're really proud of our Web site: Fodors.com is a great place to begin any journey. Scan "Travel News" for suggested itineraries, travel deals, restaurant and hotel openings, and other up-to-the-minute info. Check out "Book It" to research prices and book plane tickets, hotel rooms, rental cars, and vacation packages. Head to "Talk" for on-the-ground pointers from travelers who frequent our message boards. You can also link to loads of other travel-related resources.

## ▌ RESOURCES

### ONLINE TRAVEL TOOLS

**All About Scotland VisitScotland** (⊕www.visitscotland.com) is Scotland's official Web site and includes a number of special-interest sites on topics from golf to genealogy. **VisitBritain** (⊕www.visitbritain.com), Great Britain's official site, has ample information on Scotland's sights, accommodations, and more.

**Currency Conversion Google** (⊕www.google.com) does currency conversion. **Oanda.com** (⊕www.oanda.com) also allows you to print out a handy table with the current day's conversion rates. **XE.com** (⊕www.xe.com) is a good currency-conversion Web site.

**Historic Sites National Trust for Scotland** (⊕www.nts.org.uk) has information about stately homes, gardens, and castles. **Historic Scotland** (⊕www.historic-scotland.gov.uk) cares for the more than 300 historic properties described on its site; it offers an Explorer pass.

**Safety Transportation Security Administration** (TSA ⊕www.tsa.gov).

**Time Zones Timeanddate.com** (⊕www.timeanddate.com/worldclock) can help you figure out the correct time anywhere.

**Weather Accuweather.com** (⊕www.accuweather.com) is an independent weather-forecasting service with good coverage of hurricanes. **Weather.com** (⊕www.weather.com) is the Web site for the Weather Channel.

**Other Resources CIA World Factbook** (⊕www.odci.gov/cia/publications/factbook/index.html) has profiles of every country in the world.

### VISITOR INFORMATION

The "Essentials" section at the end of each chapter lists locations for local and regional tourist information centers; many have Web sites.

**In Britain VisitScotland** (✉Ocean Point One, 94 Ocean Dr., Edinburgh ☎0845/225–5121 ⊕www.visitscotland.com Drop-in visits only ✉19 Cockspur St., off Trafalgar Sq., London). **The Scotland Desk, Britain and London Visitor Centre** (Drop-in visits ✉1 Regent St., Piccadilly Circus, London; mail inquiries only ⌂Thames Tower, Black's Rd., London W6 9EL).

**In the U.S. VisitBritain** (In U.S. ✉551 5th Ave., 7th fl., New York, NY ☎212/986–2200 or 800/462–2748 Drop-in visits only ✉625 N. Michigan Ave., Suite 1510, Chicago, IL ⊕www.visitbritain.com).

## ▌ THINGS TO CONSIDER

### GOVERNMENT ADVISORIES

As different countries have different worldviews, look at travel advisories from a range of governments to get more of a sense of what's going on out there. And be sure to parse the language carefully. For example, a warning to "avoid all travel" carries more weight than one urging you to "avoid nonessential travel," and both are much stronger than a plea to "exercise caution." A U.S. government travel warning is more permanent (though not necessarily more serious) than a so-called public announcement, which carries an expiration date.

■ **TIP→** Consider registering online with the State Department (https://travelregistration.state.gov/ibrs/), so the government will know to look for you should a crisis occur in the country you're visiting.

The U.S. Department of State's Web site has more than just travel warnings and advisories. The consular information sheets issued for every country have general safety tips, entry requirements (though be sure to verify these with the country's embassy), and other useful details.

**General Information & Warnings U.K. Foreign & Commonwealth Office** (⊕www. fco.gov.uk/travel). **U.S. Department of State** (⊕www.travel.state.gov).

### GEAR

Travel light. Porters are more or less extinct these days (and very expensive where you can find them). Also, if you're traveling around the country by car, train, or bus, large, heavy luggage is more of a burden than anything else. Save a little packing space for things you might buy while traveling.

In Scotland casual clothes are the norm, and very few hotels or restaurants insist on jackets and ties for men in the evening. It is, however, handy to have something semi-dressy for going out to dinner or the theater. For summer, lightweight clothing is usually adequate, except in the evening, when you'll need a jacket or sweater. A waterproof coat or parka and an umbrella are essential. You can't go wrong with comfortable walking shoes, especially when you're climbing Edinburgh's steep urban hills or visiting Glasgow's massive museums. Drip-dry and wrinkle-resistant fabrics are a good bet since only the most prestigious hotels have speedy laundering or dry-cleaning service. Bring insect repellent if you plan to hike.

Some visitors to Scotland appear to think it necessary to adopt Scottish dress. It's not unless you've been invited to a wedding, and even then it's optional. Scots themselves do not wear tartan ties or Balmoral "bunnets" (caps), and only an enthusiastic minority prefers the kilt for everyday wear.

### PASSPORTS & VISAS

U.S. citizens need only a valid passport to enter Great Britain for stays of up to six months. Travelers should be prepared to show sufficient funds to support and accommodate themselves while in Britain and to show a return or onward ticket. If only one parent is traveling with a child under 17 and his or her last name differs from the child's, then he or she will need a signed and notarized letter from the parent with the same last name as the child authorizing permission to travel. Airlines, ferries, and trains have different policies for children traveling alone, so if your child must travel alone, make sure to check with the carrier prior to purchasing your child's ticket. Health certificates are not required for travel in Scotland.

### PASSPORTS

U.S. passports are valid for 10 years. You must apply in person if you're getting a passport for the first time; if your previous passport was lost, stolen, or damaged; or if your previous passport has expired and was issued more than 15 years ago or when you were under 16. All children under 18 must appear in person to apply for or renew a passport. Both parents must accompany any child under 14 (or send a notarized statement with their permission) and provide proof of their relationship to the child.

■ **TIP→** Before your trip, make two copies of your passport's data page (one for someone at home and another for you to carry separately). Or scan the page and e-mail it to someone at home and/or yourself.

There are 13 regional passport offices, as well as 7,000 passport-acceptance facilities in post offices, public libraries, and other governmental offices. If you're renewing a passport, you can do so by mail. Forms are available at passport-acceptance facilities and online.

The cost to apply for a new passport is $97 for adults, $82 for children under 16; renewals are $67. Allow six weeks for processing, both for first-time passports and renewals. For an expediting fee of $60 you can reduce this time to about two weeks. If your trip is less than two weeks away, you can get a passport even more rapidly by going to a passport office with the necessary documentation. Private expediters can get things done in as little as 48 hours, but charge hefty fees for their services.

## VISAS

U.S. citizens are not required to obtain a visa prior to traveling in Great Britain for stays of less than six months.

**U.S. Passport Information** **U.S. Department of State** (☎877/487–2778 ⊕http://travel.state.gov/passport).

**U.S. Passport & Visa Expediters** **A. Briggs Passport & Visa Expeditors** (☎800/806–0581 or 202/338–0111 ⊕www.abriggs.com). **American Passport Express** (☎603/559–9888 ⊕www.americanpassport.com). **Passport Express** (☎800/362–8196 ⊕www.passportexpress.com). **Travel Document Systems** (☎800/874–5100 or 202/638–3800 ⊕www.traveldocs.com). **Travel the World Visas** (☎866/886–8472 or 202/223–8822 ⊕www.world-visa.com).

## SHOTS & MEDICATIONS

No particular shots are necessary for visiting Scotland from the United States. *For more information see Health under On the Ground in Scotland, below.*

**Health Warnings** **National Centers for Disease Control & Prevention** (CDC ☎877/394–8747 international travelers'

health line ⊕wwwn.cdc.gov/travel). **World Health Organization** (WHO ⊕www.who.int).

## TRIP INSURANCE

This type of insurance is handy if you're using low-cost airlines to fly in and around the United Kingdom or Europe, as cancellations and luggage mishaps are commonplace.

We believe that comprehensive trip insurance is especially valuable if you're booking a very expensive or complicated trip (particularly to an isolated region) or if you're booking far in advance. But whether you get insurance has more to do with how comfortable you are assuming all that risk yourself.

Comprehensive travel policies typically cover trip-cancellation and interruption, letting you cancel or cut your trip short because of a personal emergency, illness, or, in some cases, acts of terrorism in your destination. Such policies also cover evacuation and medical care. Some also cover you for trip delays because of bad weather or mechanical problems as well as for lost or delayed baggage. Another type of coverage to look for is financial default—that is, when your trip is disrupted because a tour operator, airline, or cruise line goes out of business. Generally you must buy this when you book your trip or shortly thereafter, and it's only available to you if your operator isn't on a list of excluded companies. Be sure to read the fine print!

If you're going abroad, consider buying medical-only coverage at the very least. Neither Medicare nor some private insurers cover medical expenses anywhere outside of the United States (including time aboard a cruise ship, even if it leaves from a U.S. port). Medical-only policies typically reimburse you for medical care (excluding that related to preexisting conditions) and hospitalization abroad, and provide for evacuation. You still have to pay the bills and await reimbursement from the insurer, though.

## Trip-Insurance Resources

| INSURANCE-COMPARISON SITES | | |
|---|---|---|
| Insure My Trip.com | 800/487–4722 | www.insuremytrip.com. |
| Square Mouth.com | 727/490–5803 or 800/240–0369 | www.squaremouth.com. |
| COMPREHENSIVE TRAVEL INSURERS | | |
| Access America | 800/284–8300 | www.accessamerica.com. |
| CSA Travel Protection | 800/873–9855 | www.csatravelprotection.com. |
| HTH Worldwide | 610/254–8700 or 888/243–2358 | www.hthworldwide.com. |
| Travelex Insurance | 800/228–9792 | www.travelex-insurance.com. |
| Travel Guard International | 715/345–0505 or 800/826–4919 | www.travelguard.com. |
| Travel Insured International | 800/243–3174 | www.travelinsured.com. |
| MEDICAL-ONLY INSURERS | | |
| International Medical Group | 800/628–4664 | www.imglobal.com. |
| International SOS | | www.internationalsos.com. |
| Wallach & Company | 540/687–3166 or 800/237–6615 | www.wallach.com. |

Expect comprehensive travel-insurance policies to cost about 4% to 7% or 8% of the total price of your trip (it's more like 8% to 12% if you're over age 70). A medical-only policy may be cheaper than a comprehensive policy. Always read the fine print of your policy to make sure that you're covered for the risks that are of most concern to you. Compare several policies to make sure you're getting the best price and range of coverage available.

Although Britain has a subsidized national Health Service, free at the point of service to British citizens, foreign visitors are expected to pay for any treatment they receive. Expect to receive a bill after you return home. Check with your health-insurance company to make sure you are covered at all times—even while abroad.

# BOOKING YOUR TRIP

## ▌ ONLINE

Unless your cousin is a travel agent, you're probably among the millions of people who make most of their travel arrangements online. But is it truly better to book directly on an airline or hotel Web site? And when does a real live travel agent come in handy?

Also, with discounters and wholesalers you must generally prepay, and everything is nonrefundable. And before you fork over the dough, be sure to check the terms and conditions, so you know what a given company will do for you if there's a problem and what you'll have to deal with on your own.

▌TIP➔ **To be absolutely sure everything was processed correctly, confirm reservations made through online travel agents, discounters, and wholesalers directly with your hotel before leaving home.**

Booking engines like Expedia, Travelocity, and Orbitz are actually travel agents, albeit high-volume, online ones. And airline travel packagers like American Airlines Vacations and Virgin Vacations—well, they're travel agents, too. But they may still not work with all the world's hotels.

An aggregator site will search many sites and pull the best prices for airfares, hotels, and rental cars from them. Most aggregators compare the major travel-booking sites such as Expedia, Travelocity, and Orbitz; some also look at airline Web sites, though rarely the sites of smaller budget airlines. Some aggregators also compare other travel products, including complex packages—a good thing, as you can sometimes get the best overall deal by booking an air-and-hotel package.

## ▌ WITH A TRAVEL AGENT

If you use an agent—brick-and-mortar or virtual—you'll pay a fee for the service. And know that the service you get from some online agents isn't comprehensive. For example Expedia and Travelocity don't search for prices on budget airlines like easyJet, Ryanair, or other small foreign carriers. That said, some agents (online or not) *do* have access to fares that are difficult to find otherwise, and the savings can more than make up for any surcharge. That and your tickets are often protected by the agents' insurance company when it comes to cancellations, etc.

A knowledgeable brick-and-mortar travel agent can be a godsend if you're booking a cruise, a package trip that's not available to you directly, an air pass, or a complicated itinerary including several overseas flights. What's more, travel agents that specialize in a destination may have exclusive access to certain deals and insider information on things such as charter flights. Agents who specialize in types of travelers (senior citizens, gays and lesbians, naturists) or types of trips (cruises, luxury travel, safaris) can also be invaluable.

▌TIP➔ **Remember that Expedia, Travelocity, and Orbitz are travel agents, not just booking engines. To resolve any problems with a reservation made through these companies, contact them first.**

**Agent Resources American Society of Travel Agents** ( ☎ 703/739–2782 ⊕ www. travelsense.org).

## ▌ ACCOMMODATIONS

Your choices in Scotland range from small, local B&Bs to large, elegant hotels—some of the chain variety. Bed-and-breakfasts, the backbone of British low-cost travel,

# Online-Booking Resources

| AGGREGATORS | | |
|---|---|---|
| Kayak | www.kayak.com | looks at cruises and vacation packages. |
| Mobissimo | www.mobissimo.com | examines airfare, hotels, cars, and tons of activities. |
| Qixo | www.qixo.com | compares cruises, vacation packages, and even travel insurance. |
| Sidestep | www.sidestep.com | compares vacation packages, and lists travel deals and some activities. |
| Travelgrove | www.travelgrove.com | compares cruises and vacation packages and lets you search by themes. |
| **BOOKING ENGINES** | | |
| Cheap Tickets | www.cheaptickets.com | discounter. |
| Expedia | www.expedia.com | large online agency that charges a booking fee for airline tickets. |
| Hotwire | www.hotwire.com | discounter. |
| lastminute.com | www.lastminute.com | specializes in last-minute travel; the main site is for the U.K., but it has a link to a U.S. site. |
| Luxury Link | www.luxurylink.com | has auctions (surprisingly good deals) as well as offers on the high-end side of travel. |
| Onetravel.com | www.onetravel.com | discounter for hotels, car rentals, airfares, and packages. |
| Orbitz | www.orbitz.com | charges a booking fee for airline tickets, but gives a clear breakdown of fees and taxes before you book. |
| Priceline.com | www.priceline.com | discounter that also allows bidding. |
| Travel.com | www.travel.com | allows you to compare its rates with those of other booking engines. |
| Travelocity | www.travelocity.com | charges a booking fee for airline tickets but promises good problem resolution. |
| **ONLINE ACCOMMODATIONS** | | |
| Hotelbook.com | www.hotelbook.com | focuses on independent hotels worldwide. |
| Hotel Club | www.hotelclub.net | good for major cities and some resort areas. |
| Hotels.com | www.hotels.com | big Expedia-owned wholesaler that offers rooms in hotels all over the world. |
| **OTHER RESOURCES** | | |
| Bidding For Travel | www.biddingfortravel.com | good place to figure out what you can get and for how much before you start bidding on, say, Priceline. |

tend to be less expensive than large hotels because many are spare rooms in spacious homes; proprietors keep costs down and guests get something with a more personal, Scottish touch. Large hotels vary in style and price. In Scotland many lean toward Scottish themes when it comes to decoration, but you can expect the same quality and service from a chain hotel wherever you are in the world. Accommodation is expensive, especially because the pound is so strong against the dollar. Keep in mind that hotel rooms in Scotland are smaller than what you'd find in the United States.

VisitScotland publishes two annually updated *Where to Stay* guides, *Hotels & Guest Houses* (£8.99) and *Bed & Breakfast* (£5.99), which give detailed information on facilities provided and classify and grade the accommodation using simple star (for hotels) and diamond (for guesthouses, inns, and B&Bs) systems. The greater the number of stars or diamonds, the greater the number of facilities and the more luxurious they are. The various area tourist boards also annually publish separate accommodation listings, which can be obtained either from VisitScotland or from the individual tourist authority.

The lodgings we list are the cream of the crop in each price category. Properties are assigned price categories based on the range from their least-expensive standard double room at high season (excluding holidays) to the most expensive. Properties marked ✕🖼 are lodging establishments whose restaurants warrant a special trip. Unless otherwise noted, all lodgings listed have an elevator, a private bathroom, air-conditioning, a room phone, and a television. Price charts appear at the start of each chapter or, for Edinburgh and Glasgow, in the "Where to Stay" section.

We always list the facilities that are available, but we don't specify whether they cost extra; when pricing accommodations, always ask what's included. Many hotels and most guesthouses and B&Bs include a breakfast within the basic room rate. Meal-plan symbols appear at the end of a review.

Some hotels, B&Bs and guesthouses offer discounted rates for stays of two nights or longer.

Most hotels and other lodgings require you to give your credit-card details before they will confirm your reservation. If you don't feel comfortable e-mailing this information, ask if you can fax it (some places prefer faxes). However you book, get confirmation in writing and have a copy of it handy when you check in.

Be sure you understand the hotel's cancellation policy. Some places allow you to cancel without any kind of penalty— even if you prepaid to secure a discounted rate—if you cancel at least 24 hours in advance. Others require you to cancel a week in advance or penalize you the cost of one night. Small inns and B&Bs are most likely to require you to cancel far in advance.

Most hotels allow children under a certain age to stay in their parents' room at no extra charge, but others charge for them as extra adults; find out the cutoff age for discounts.

■TIP→ Assume that hotels operate on the European Plan (EP, no meals) unless we specify that they use the Breakfast Plan (BP, with full breakfast), Continental Plan (CP, continental breakfast), Full American Plan (FAP, all meals), or Modified American Plan (MAP breakfast and dinner).

### APARTMENT & HOUSE RENTALS

Rental houses and flats (apartments) are becoming more popular lodging choices for travelers visiting Scotland, particularly for those staying in one place for more than a few days. Some places may rent only by the week. Prices can work out to be cheaper than a hotel (though perhaps not than a B&B; this will depend on the number in your group), and the space and comfort are much better than what you'd find in a hotel or B&B.

In the country, your chances of finding a small house to rent are good; in the city

# Online-Booking Resources

CONTACTS

| | | |
|---|---|---|
| At Home Abroad | 212/421–9165 | www.athomeabroadinc.com. |
| Barclay International Group | 516/364–0064 or 800/845–6636 | www.barclayweb.com. |
| Home Away | 512/493–0382 | www.homeaway.com |
| Hometours International | 865/690–8484 | thor.he.net/~hometour. |
| Interhome | 954/791–8282 or 800/882–6864 | www.interhome.us. |
| National Trust for Scotland | 0131/243–9331 | www.nts.org.uk. |
| Vacation Home Rentals Worldwide | 201/767–9393 or 800/633–3284 | www.vhrww.com. |
| Villas & Apartments Abroad | 212/213–6435 or 800/433–3020 | www.vaanyc.com. |
| Villas International | 415/499–9490 or 800/221–2260 | www.villasintl.com. |
| Villas of Distinction | 707/778–1800 or 800/289–0900 | www.villasofdistinction.com. |

you're more likely to find a flat (apartment) to let (rent). Either way, your best bet for finding these rentals is online. Individuals and large consortiums can own these properties, so it just depends on what you're looking for. The White House is a good, central place for rentals in Glasgow, and Scottish Apartment is a good source for apartments in Edinburgh. The National Trust for Scotland has many unique properties, from island cottages to castles, for rent.

Contacts **Scottish Apartment** (☎0131/240–0080 ⊕www.scottishapartment.com). **White House** (☎0141/339–9375 ⊕www. whitehouse-apartments.com).

## BED-AND-BREAKFASTS

B&Bs, common throughout Scotland, are a special British tradition and the backbone of budget travel, with an average price of £40 to £85 per night, depending on the region, time of year, and particular accommodation. They're usually in a family home, don't often have private bathrooms, and usually offer only breakfast. Guesthouses are a slightly larger,

somewhat more luxurious version. More upscale B&Bs, along the line of American B&Bs or small inns, can be found in Edinburgh and Glasgow especially, but in other parts of Scotland as well. All provide a glimpse of everyday British life. Note that local tourist offices can book a B&B for you; there may be a small charge for this service.

Reservation Services **Bed & Breakfast. com** (☎512/322–2710 or 800/462–2632 ⊕www.bedandbreakfast.com) also sends out an online newsletter. **Bed & Breakfast Inns Online** (☎615/868–1946 or 800/215–7365 ⊕www.bbonline.com). **Bed & Breakfast Scotland** (⊕www.bedandbreakfastscotland.co.uk). **UK Bed and Breakfast Accommodation** (⊕www.bedandbreakfasts.co.uk).

## FARMHOUSE & CROFTING HOLIDAYS

A popular option for families with children is a farmhouse holiday, combining the freedom of B&B accommodations with the hospitality of Scottish family life. You need a car if you're deep in the country, though. Information is available from VisitBritain or VisitScotland (⇨ *Resources in Getting Started, above*), from Scottish Farmhouse Holidays, and from the Farm Stay UK.

**Contacts Farm Stay UK** (☎024/7669–6909 ⊕www.farmstayuk.co.uk). **Scottish Farmhouse Holidays** (☎01890/751830 ⊕www.scotfarmhols.co.uk).

**HOME EXCHANGES**
With a direct home exchange you stay in someone else's home while they stay in yours. Some outfits also deal with vacation homes, so you're not actually staying in someone's full-time residence, just their vacant weekend place.

**Exchange Clubs Home Exchange.com** (☎800/877-8723 ⊕www.homeexchange.com); $99.95 for a 1-year online listing. **HomeLink International** (☎800/638-3841 ⊕www.homelink.org); $90 yearly for Web-only membership; $140 includes Web access and two catalogs. **Intervac U.S.** (☎800/756-4663 ⊕www.intervacus.com); has various online packages ranging from $65 to $155.

**HOTELS**
If you're touring around, you're not likely to be stranded: even in the height of the season—July and August—hotel occupancy has run at about 80%. On the other hand, if you arrive in Edinburgh at festival time or some place where a big Highland Gathering or golf tournament is in progress, you'll have an extremely limited choice of accommodations, and your best bet will be to try for a room in a nearby village. To secure your first choice, reserve in advance, either directly with the facility, or through local information centers (⇨ *individual city or regional chapters*), making use of their "Book-a-Bed-Ahead" services. Telephone bookings made from home should be confirmed by e-mail or letter. Country hotels expect you to turn up by about 6 PM.

Scotland has a national star-grading scheme (1 to 5 stars) to take some of the guesswork out of booking hotels (⇨ *Accommodations, above*).

# ▌AIRLINE TICKETS

Most domestic airline tickets are electronic; international tickets may be either electronic or paper. With an e-ticket the only thing you receive is an e-mailed receipt citing your itinerary and reservation and ticket numbers.

The greatest advantage of an e-ticket is that if you lose your receipt, you can simply print out another copy or ask the airline to do it for you at check-in. You usually pay a surcharge (up to $50) to get a paper ticket, if you can get one at all.

The sole advantage of a paper ticket is that it may be easier to endorse over to another airline if your flight is canceled and the airline with which you booked can't accommodate you on another flight.

▌**TIP→** Discount air passes that let you travel economically in a country or region must often be purchased before you leave home. In some cases you can only get them through a travel agent.

The least expensive airfares to Scotland are often priced for round-trip travel and must usually be purchased in advance. Airlines generally allow you to change your return date for a fee; most low-fare tickets, however, are nonrefundable. The Discover Europe Airpass from bmi is available on the airline's British and European flights. The pass is valid for up to 90 days and allows passengers to travel to a combination of European cities for reduced fares. The Europe Pass from British Airways offers travelers a way to choose from the airline's and its partners' networks.

In Britain the best place to search for consolidator, or so-called bucket shop, tickets is through Cheap Flights, a Web site that pools all flights available and then directs you to a phone number or site to purchase tickets.

If you intend to fly to Scotland from London, take advantage of the current fare wars on internal routes—notably between London's four airports and Glasgow–Edinburgh. Among the cheapest are Ryanair between London Stansted (with its excellent rail links from London's Liverpool Street Station) and Glasgow Prestwick; easyJet offers bargain fares from London Luton/Gatwick/Stansted (all with good rail links from central London) to Glasgow, Edinburgh, Aberdeen, and Inverness. Even British Airways now offers competitive fares on some flights.

Air Pass Info **bmi** (☎800/788-0555, 020/8745-7321 in U.K. ⊕www.flybmi. com). **British Airways** (☎800/247-9297, 0870/850-9850 in U.K ⊕www.britishairways. com). **DER Travel Services** (☎800/782-2424 ⊕www.der.com). **easyJet** (☎0870/600-0000 ⊕www.easyjet.com). **FlightPass** (EuropebyAir ☎888/387-2479 ⊕www.europebyair.com). **Ryanair** (☎0871/246-0000 ⊕www.ryanair. com). **Zoom** (☎0870/240-0055 ⊕www. flyzoom.com).

# ▮ RENTAL CARS

If you're going beyond the major cities, having a car makes traveling much easier in Scotland. Public transportation is good but you need your own vehicle to reach the more isolated areas. You can rent any type of car you desire; however, in Scotland cars tend to be on the smaller side. Many roads are narrow, and a smaller car saves money on gas. Common models are the Nissan Micra, Renault Clio,

Ford Focus, and Peugeot 407 SW. Four-wheel-drive vehicles aren't a necessity. Most cars are manual (not automatic) and come with air-conditioning, although you rarely need it in Scotland. The cars are in very good condition and must pass a series of inspections and tests before they are rented out. When you're returning the car, allow an extra hour to drop it off and sort out any paperwork.

When you reserve a car, ask about cancellation penalties, taxes, drop-off charges (if you're planning to pick up the car in one city and leave it in another), and surcharges (for being under or over a certain age, for additional drivers, or for driving across state or country borders or beyond a specific distance from your point of rental). All these things can add substantially to your costs. Request car seats and extras such as GPS when you book.

Rates are sometimes—but not always—better if you book in advance or reserve through a rental agency's Web site. There are other reasons to book ahead, though: for popular destinations, during busy times of the year, or to ensure that you get certain types of cars (vans, SUVs).

▮TIP→ **Make sure that a confirmed reservation guarantees you a car. Agencies sometimes overbook, particularly for busy weekends and holiday periods.**

If you're traveling to more than one country, make sure your rental contract permits you to take the car across borders and that the insurance policy covers you in every country you visit. British cars have the steering wheel on the right, so you may want to leave your rented car in Britain and pick up a left-side drive when you cross the Channel.

Rates in Glasgow begin at £25 a day and £140 a week for an economy car with a manual transmission and unlimited mileage. This does not include tax on car rentals, which is 17.5%. The busiest months are June through August, when rates may

# Car-Rental Resources

| AUTOMOBILE ASSOCIATIONS | | |
|---|---|---|
| U.S.: American Automobile Association (AAA) | 315/797–5000 | www.aaa.com; most contact with the organization is through state and regional members. |
| National Automobile Club | 650/294–7000 | www.thenac.com; membership is open to California residents only. |
| Automobile Association (AA) | 0870/600–0371 | www.theaa.co.uk |
| Royal Automobile Club | 0800/731–1104 | www.rac.co.uk. |
| **LOCAL AGENCIES** | | |
| Arnold Clark | 0131/333–0124 | www.arnoldclarkrental.co.uk. |
| **MAJOR AGENCIES** | | |
| Alamo | 800/462–5266 | www.alamo.com. |
| Avis | 800/331–1084 | www.avis.com. |
| Budget | 800/472–3325 | www.budget.com. |
| Hertz | 800/654–3001 | www.hertz.com. |
| National Car Rental | 800/227–7368 | www.nationalcar.com. |
| **WHOLESALERS** | | |
| Auto Europe | 888/223–5555 | www.autoeurope.com. |
| Europe by Car | 212/581–3040 in New York, 800/223–1516 | www.europebycar.com. |
| Eurovacations | 877/471–3876 | www.eurovacations.com. |
| Kemwel | 877/820–0668 | www.kemwel.com. |

go up 30%. During this time, book at least two to four weeks in advance.

Companies frequently restrict rentals to people over age 23 and under age 75. If you are over 70, some companies require you to have your own insurance. If you are under 25, a surcharge of £11 per day plus V.A.T. will apply

Child car seats usually cost about £24 extra; you must ask for a car seat when you book, at least 48 hours in advance. Adding one extra driver is usually included in the original rental price.

## CAR-RENTAL INSURANCE

If you own a car, your personal auto insurance may cover a rental to some degree, though not all policies protect you abroad; always read your policy's fine print. If you don't have auto insurance, then seriously consider buying the collision- or loss-damage waiver (CDW or LDW) from the car-rental company, which eliminates your liability for damage to the car.

Some credit cards offer CDW coverage, but it's usually supplemental to your own insurance and rarely covers SUVs, minivans, luxury models, and the like. If your coverage is secondary, you may still be liable for loss-of-use costs from the car-rental company. But no credit-card insurance is valid unless you use that card for *all* transactions, from reserving to paying the final bill. All companies exclude car rental in some countries, so be sure to find out about the destination to which you are traveling.

■ TIP→ Diners Club offers primary CDW coverage on all rentals reserved and paid for with the card. This means that Diners Club's company—not your own car insurance—pays in case of an accident. It *doesn't* mean your car-insurance company won't raise your rates once it discovers you had an accident.

Some rental agencies require you to purchase CDW coverage; many will even include it in quoted rates. All will strongly encourage you to buy CDW— possibly implying that it's required—so be sure to ask about such things before renting. In most cases it's cheaper to add a supplemental CDW plan to your comprehensive travel-insurance policy (⇨ *Trip Insurance under Things to Consider in Getting Started, above*) than to purchase it from a rental company. That said, you don't want to pay for a supplement if you're required to buy insurance from the rental company.

■ TIP→ You can decline the insurance from the rental company and purchase it through a third-party provider such as Travel Guard (www.travelguard.com)—$9 per day for $35,000 of coverage. That's sometimes just under half the price of the CDW offered by some car-rental companies.

## ▌ TRAIN PASSES

To save money, look into rail passes. But be aware that if you don't plan to cover many miles, you may come out ahead by buying individual tickets. If you plan to travel by train in Scotland, consider purchasing a BritRail Pass, which also allows travel in England and Wales. All BritRail passes must be purchased in your home country; they're sold by travel agents as well as BritRail or Rail Europe. Rail passes do not guarantee seats on the trains, so be sure to reserve ahead. Remember that EurailPasses aren't honored in Great Britain.

The cost of an unlimited BritRail adult pass for 4 days is $232/$349 (standard/first class); for 8 days, $332/$499; for 15 days, $499/$748; for 22 days, $631/$950; and for a month, $748/$1,124. The Youth Pass, for ages 16 to 25, costs $185/$279 for 4 days, $265/$400 for 8 days, $400/$599 for 15 days, $505/$760 for 22 days, and $599/$899 for one month. The Senior Pass, for passengers over 60, costs $209/$296 for 4 days, $299/$425 for 8 days, $449/$636 for 15 days, $575/$808 for 22 days, and $679/$956 for one month. Another option is a Flexipass, which allows a particular number of days of travel within a given period: for example, 4 days in 2 months for $293.

The Scottish Freedom Pass allows transportation on all Caledonian MacBrayne and Strathclyde ferries in addition to major bus links and the Glasgow underground. You can travel any 4 days in an 8-day period for $217 or any 8 days in a 15-day period for $292.

**Information** ACP Rail International (⊕www.acprail.com). BritRail Travel (☎886/274-8724 ⊕www.britrail.com). DER Travel Services (☎800/782-2424 ⊕www.der.com). Rail Europe (☎877/257-2887 ⊕www.raileurope.com).

## ▌ TRAIN TICKETS

Train tickets for long-distance travel (versus commuter trains) in Britain are much cheaper if purchased in advance. Prices for the same journey can vary by hundreds of pounds depending upon whether you buy the ticket on the day of your journey or two weeks ahead. For more information about how to purchase your tickets, *see* By Train *in* Transportation, *below.*

## ▌ VACATION PACKAGES

Packages *are not* guided excursions. Packages combine airfare, accommodations, and perhaps a rental car or other extras (theater tickets, guided excursions, boat trips, reserved entry to popular museums, transit passes), but they let you do your own thing. During busy periods packages may be your only option, as flights and rooms may be sold out otherwise.

Packages will definitely save you time. They can also save you money, particularly in peak seasons, but—and this is a really big "but"—you should price each part of the package separately to be sure. And be aware that prices advertised on Web sites and in newspapers rarely include service charges or taxes, which can up your costs by hundreds of dollars.

■TIP➜ **Some packages and cruises are sold only through travel agents. Don't always assume that you can get the best deal by booking everything yourself.**

Each year consumers are stranded or lose their money when packagers—even large ones with excellent reputations—go out of business. How can you protect yourself?

First, always pay with a credit card; if you have a problem, your credit-card company may help you resolve it. Second, buy trip insurance that covers default. Third, choose a company that belongs to the United States Tour Operators Association, whose members must set aside funds to cover defaults. Finally, choose a company that also participates in the Tour Operator Program of the American Society of Travel Agents (ASTA), which will act as mediator in any disputes.

**Organizations American Society of Travel Agents** (ASTA ☎703/739–2782 or 800/965–2782 ⊕www.astanet.com). **United States Tour Operators Association** (USTOA ☎212/599–6599 ⊕www.ustoa.com).

■TIP➜ **Local tourism boards can provide information about lesser-known and small-niche operators that sell packages to only a few destinations.**

# ▌GUIDED TOURS

Guided tours are a good option when you don't want to do it all yourself. You travel along with a group (sometimes large, sometimes small), stay in prebooked hotels, eat with your fellow travelers (the cost of meals sometimes included in the price of your tour, sometimes not), and follow a schedule.

Whenever you book a guided tour, find out what's included and what isn't. A "land-only" tour includes all your travel (by bus, in most cases) in the destination, but not necessarily your flights to and from or even within it. Also, in most cases prices in tour brochures don't include fees and taxes. And remember that you'll be expected to tip your guide (in cash) at the end of the tour.

## SIGHTSEEING GUIDES

The Scottish Tourist Guides Association has members throughout Scotland who are fully qualified professional guides able to conduct walking tours in the major cities, half- or full-day tours or extended tours throughout Scotland, driving tours, and special study tours. Many guides speak at least one language in addition to English. Fees are negotiable with individual guides.

**Tourist Guides Association Scottish Tourist Guides Association** (☎01786/451953 ⊕www.stga.co.uk).

# TRANSPORTATION

The country's main hubs are Glasgow, Prestwick (near Glasgow), Edinburgh, Inverness, and Aberdeen, as they are the Scottish cities with major airports. Glasgow and Prestwick are the gateways to the west and southwest, Edinburgh the east and southeast, Aberdeen and Inverness the north. All of these cities have excellent bus and train transportation services and well-maintained roads that link them with each other and other cities within Scotland.

## ▌ BY AIR

Flying time to Glasgow is 6½ hours from New York, 7½ hours from Chicago, 9½ hours from Dallas, 10 hours from Los Angeles, and 21½ hours from Sydney.

Smoking policies vary from carrier to carrier. Most airlines prohibit smoking on all of their flights; others allow smoking only on certain routes or certain departures. Ask your carrier about its policy.

**Airlines & Airports Airline and Airport Links.com** (⊕www.airlineandairportlinks. com) has links to many of the world's airlines and airports.

**Airline-Security Issues Transportation Security Administration** (⊕www.tsa.gov) has answers for almost every question that might come up.

### AIRPORTS

The major international gateway to Scotland is Glasgow Airport (GLA), about 7 mi outside Glasgow. Edinburgh Airport (EDI), 7 mi from the city, has extremely limited transatlantic flights (Continental has service from New York, and there's service to Toronto), but does offer connections for dozens of European cities and hourly flights to London's Gatwick (LGW) and Heathrow (LHR) airports. It's also possible to fly into Glasgow and then take bus or train service to Edinburgh in less than two hours. Aberdeen Airport

(ABZ) has direct flights from Amsterdam. Refer to chapter "Essentials" sections for information on airport transfers.

All Scottish airports offer typical modern amenities: restaurants, cafés, shopping (from clothes to music to tourist trinkets), sandwich and salad bars, pubs, pharmacies, book shops, and newsstands; some even have relaxation centers with spas and hair salons. Glasgow is the largest, most interesting airport when it comes to a delayed flight. There are plenty of hotels near all airports, so you always have a place to rest your head for the day or night. All airports also have Internet access.

**Airport Information Aberdeen Airport** (☎0870/040–0006 ⊕www.aberdeenairport. com). **Edinburgh Airport** (☎0870/040–0007 ⊕www.edinburghairport.com). **Glasgow Airport** (☎0870/040–0008 ⊕www. glasgowairport.com). **Glasgow Prestwick Airport** (☎0871/223–0700 ⊕www.gpia. co.uk). **Inverness Airport** (☎01667/464000 ⊕www.hial.co.uk).

### GROUND TRANSPORTATION
Refer to chapter "Essentials" sections for information on airport transfers.

### FLIGHTS
Although a small country, Scotland has a significant air network. Contact British Airways or British Airways Express for details on flights from London's Heathrow Airport or from Glasgow, Edinburgh, Aberdeen, and Inverness to the farthest corners of the Scottish mainland and to the islands. *See individual chapters for information on flying to various islands.*

Among the low-cost carriers, Ryanair flies from London Stansted to Prestwick, south of Glasgow; bmibaby has service from Heathrow; and easyJet flies from London Luton/Gatwick/Stansted to and between Glasgow, Edinburgh, Aberdeen, and Inverness, plus to and from Belfast. At this writing, Flybe (www.flybe.com) is starting service to Inverness from Bristol, Exeter, Manchester, and Southampton in spring 2008.

**Airline Contacts American Airlines** (☎800/433–7300 ⊕www.aa.com). **British Airways** (☎800/247–9297 ⊕www.britishairways.com). **Continental Airlines** (☎800/523–3273 for U.S. and Mexico reservations, 800/231–0856 for international reservations ⊕www.continental.com). **Delta Airlines** (☎800/221–1212 for U.S. reservations, 800/241–4141 for international reservations ⊕www.delta.com). **Northwest Airlines** (☎800/225–2525 ⊕www.nwa.com). **United Airlines** (☎800/864–8331 for U.S. reservations, 800/538–2929 for international reservations ⊕www.united.com). **USAirways** (☎800/428–4322 for U.S. and Canada reservations, 800/622–1015 for international reservations ⊕www.usairways.com). **Virgin Atlantic** (☎800/821–5438 ⊕www.virginatlantic.com).

**From London to Edinburgh & Glasgow bmibaby/British Midland** (☎0870/264–2229 in U.K. ⊕www.bmibaby.com). **British Airways** (☎0870/850–9850 in U.K. ⊕www.britishairways.com). **easyJet** (☎0871/244–2366 or 0905/821–0905 ⊕www.easyjet.com). **Ryanair** (☎353/1249–7791 ⊕www.ryanair.com).

**Within Scotland British Airways** (☎0870/850–9850 in U.K. ⊕www.britishairways.com). **easyJet** (☎0871/244–2366 or 0905/821–0905 ⊕www.easyjet.com).

# ▮ BY BIKE

The best months for cycling in Scotland are May, June, and September, when the roads are often quieter and the weather is usually better. Winds are predominantly from the southwest, so plan your route accordingly.

Because Scotland's main roads are continually being upgraded, bicyclists can easily reach the network of quieter rural roads in southern and much of eastern Scotland, especially Grampian. Still, care must be taken in getting from some town centers to rural riding areas, so if in doubt, ask a local. In a few areas of the Highlands, notably in northwestern Scotland, the rugged terrain and limited population have resulted in the lack of side roads, making it more difficult—sometimes impossible—to plan a minor-road route in these areas.

Several agencies now promote "safe routes" for recreational cyclists. These routes are signposted, and agencies have produced maps or leaflets showing where they run. Perhaps best known is the Glasgow–Loch Lomond–Killin Cycleway, which uses former railway track beds, forest trails, quiet rural side roads, and some main roads. VisitScotland's has advice on its dedicated Web site: cycling.visitscotland.com.

## TRANSPORTING BIKES
Although some rural bus services will transport cycles if space is available, don't count on getting your bike on a bus. Be sure to check well in advance with the appropriate bus company.

You can take bicycles on car and passenger ferries in Scotland, and it's not generally necessary to book in advance. Check cycles on car ferries early so that they can be loaded through the car entrance.

ScotRail strongly advises that you make a train reservation for you and your bike at least one month in advance. On several trains reservations are compulsory.

## BIKING ORGANIZATIONS
The Cyclists' Touring Club publishes a members' magazine, route maps, and guides. Sustrans Ltd. is a nonprofit organization dedicated to providing environmentally friendly routes for cyclists, notably in and around cities.

**Bike Maps & Information Cyclists' Touring Club** (☎0870/873–0060 ⊕www.ctc.org.uk). **Sustrans Ltd.** (☎0131/539–8122 ⊕www.

sustrans.org.uk). **VisitScotland** (⊕cycling. visitscotland.com).

# ❚ BY BOAT

Because Scotland has so many islands, plus the great Firth of Clyde waterway, ferry services are of paramount importance. Most ferries transport vehicles as well as foot passengers, although a few smaller ones are for passengers only.

The main operator is Caledonian MacBrayne Ltd., known generally as CalMac. Services extend from the Firth of Clyde in the south, where there's an extremely extensive network, right up to the northwest of Scotland and all of the Hebrides. CalMac sells an Island Rover runabout ticket, which is ideal for touring holidays in the islands, as well as an island-hopping scheme called Island Hopscotch. Fares can range from £4 for a short trip to almost £50 for a longer trip with several legs.

The Dunoon–Gourock route on the Clyde is served by Western Ferries; the Islay–Jura service is operated by Serco Denholm.

The Falkirk Wheel in Tamfourhill, about halfway between Glasgow and Edinburgh, is an attraction as much as a form of transportation. The only rotating boat lift in the world, it carries tour boats from the Forth and Clyde Canal over to the Union Canal, and back again.

Northlink Ferries operates a car ferry for Orkney between Scrabster, near Thurso, and Stromness, on the main island of Orkney; and between Aberdeen and Kirkwall, which is also on Mainland, Orkney. Northlink also runs ferries for Shetland between Aberdeen and Lerwick.

The "Essentials" sections of each chapter have details about ferry services.

For fares and schedules, contact ferry companies directly. Traveler's checks (in pounds), cash, and major credit cards are accepted for payment.

**Information Caledonian MacBrayne** (☎01475/650100, 08705/650000 reservations, 01475/650288 brochure hotline ⊕www.calmac.co.uk). **The Falkirk Wheel** (✉Lime Rd., Tamfourhill ☎01324/619888, 08700/500208 reservations ⊕www.thefalkirkwheel.co.uk). **Northlink Ferries** (☎0845/600–0449 ⊕www.northlinkferries.co.uk). **Serco Denholm** (☎01475/731540). **Western Ferries** (☎01369/704452 ⊕www.western-ferries.co.uk).

# ❚ BY BUS

The country's bus (short-haul) and coach (long-distance) network is extensive. Bus service is comprehensive in cities, less so in country districts—something to consider if you want to explore really rural areas. Express service links main cities and towns, connecting, for example, Glasgow and Edinburgh to Inverness, Aberdeen, Perth, Skye, Ayr, Dumfries, and Carlisle; or Inverness with Aberdeen, Wick, Thurso, and Fort William. These express services are very fast, and fares are reasonable. Scottish Citylink, National Express, and Megabus are some of the main operators; there are about 20 in all. There is one class of service, and all buses are nonsmoking.

On Scottish Citylink, the Explorer Passes offer complete freedom of travel on all services throughout Scotland. Three permutations give either three days of consecutive travel, any 5 days of travel out of 10, or any 8 days of travel in a 16-day period. They're available from Scottish Citylink offices, and cost £35 to £79.

National Express offers some highly discounted seats on buses from London to more than 50 cities in the United Kingdom, including Glasgow and Aberdeen. Tickets range from £1 to £10, but only when purchased online. Megabus (order tickets online), a discount service, has competitive prices between major cities throughout Scotland, including Aberdeen, Dundee, Glasgow, Inverness, and Perth.

Those travelers ages 16 to 25 are eligible for 30% reductions with the National Express NX2 Card (£10).

Contact Traveline Scotland for information on all public transportation and timetables.

For town, suburban, or short-distance journeys, you normally buy your ticket on the bus, from a pay box, or from the driver. Sometimes you need exact change. For longer journeys—for example, Glasgow–Inverness—it's usual (and a good idea; busy routes and times can book up) to reserve a seat and pay at the bus station booking office. Credit cards and traveler's checks are accepted at most bus stations.

Long-distance buses usually provide the cheapest way to travel between England and Scotland; fares may be as little as a third of the rail fares for comparable trips. However, the trip is not as comfortable as by train (no dining cart or carriage, smaller bathrooms, less specious seats), and it takes longer. Glasgow to London by bus (nonstop) takes 8 hours, 45 minutes; by train it takes 5 hours, 30 minutes.

The London terminal is Victoria Coach Station for National Express and the London Victoria Greenline Coach Station for Megabus.

**Bus Information Traveline Scotland** (☎0870/608–2608 ⊕www.traveline scotland.com).

**Bus Lines Megabus** (⊕www.megabus.com). **National Express** (☎08705/808080 ⊕www. nationalexpress.com). **Scottish Citylink** (☎08705/505050 ⊕www.citylink.co.uk).

# ▌BY CAR

If you plan to stick mostly to the cities, you will not need a car. All cities here are either so compact that all attrac-

tions are within easy walking distance of each other (Aberdeen, Dundee, Edinburgh, Inverness, and Stirling) or have an excellent local public transport system (Glasgow). And there is often good train and/or bus service from major cities to nearby day-trip destinations. Bus tours are also a good option for a day trip out of town; from Inverness, you can even catch a (quick) glance at the isles of Orkney this way.

Once you leave Edinburgh, Glasgow, and the other major cities, a car will make journeys faster and much more enjoyable than trying to work out public-transportation connections to the farther-flung reaches of Scotland (though it's possible to see much of the country by public transportation). A car allows you to set your own pace and visit off-the-beaten-path towns and sights most easily.

In Scotland your own driver's license is acceptable. International driving permits (IDPs) are available from the American Automobile Association and, in the United Kingdom, from the Automobile Association and Royal Automobile Club. These international permits, valid only in conjunction with your regular driver's license, are universally recognized; having one may save you a problem with local authorities.

## GASOLINE

Expect to pay a lot more for gasoline, about £4.37 a gallon (97p a liter) for unleaded—up to 10p a gallon higher in remote rural locations. The British imperial gallon is about 20% more in volume than the U.S. gallon—approximately 4.5 liters. Pumps dispense in liters, not gallons. Most gas stations are self-service and stock unleaded, super unleaded, and LRP (replacing four-star) plus diesel; most also accept major credit cards.

## PARKING

On-street parking is a bit of a lottery in Scotland. Depending on the location and time of day, the streets can be packed or empty of cars. In the cities, you must pay for your on-street parking by getting a sticker from a parking machine; these machines are clearly marked with a large p. Make sure you have the exact change; it's normally around £2 for four hours but can vary. Put the parking sticker on the inside of your front windshield and make sure the time expiration is clearly visible for parking attendants. Parking lots are scattered throughout urban areas and tend to be more or less the same price as on-street parking. Most parking lots are near shopping malls or busy financial districts.

The local penalty for illegally parked cars is £25, and parking regulations are strictly enforced.

## ROAD CONDITIONS

A good network of superhighways, known as motorways, and divided highways, known as dual carriageways, extends throughout Britain. In the remoter areas of Scotland where the motorway hasn't penetrated, travel is noticeably slower. Motorways shown with the prefix M are mainly two or three lanes in each direction, without any right-hand turns. These are the roads to use to cover long distances, though inevitably you'll see less of the countryside. Service areas are at most about an hour apart. Dual carriageways, usually shown on a map as a thick red line (often with a black line in the center) and the prefix A followed by a number perhaps with a bracketed T (for example, A304[T]), are similar to motorways, except that right turns are sometimes permitted, and you'll find both traffic lights and traffic circles on them.

The vast network of other main roads, which typical maps show as either single red a roads, or narrower brown b roads, also numbered, are for the most part the old coach and turnpike roads built originally for horses and carriages. Travel along these roads is slower than on motorways, and passing is more difficult.

On the other hand, you'll see much more of Scotland.

Minor roads (shown as yellow or white on most maps, unlettered and unnumbered) are the ancient lanes and byways of Britain, roads that are not only living history but a superb way of discovering hidden parts of Scotland. You have to drive along them slowly and carefully. On single-track roads, found in the north and west of Scotland, there's no room for two vehicles to pass, and you must use a passing place if you meet an oncoming car or tractor, or if a car behind wishes to overtake you. Never hold up traffic on single-track roads.

| FROM | TO | DRIVING TIME |
|------|-----|--------------|
| Edinburgh | Glasgow | 1 hour |
| Glasgow | Stirling | ½ hour |
| Stirling | Dundee | 1 hour |
| Dundee | Aberdeen | 1¼ hours |
| Aberdeen | Inverness | 2½ hours |
| Inverness | Glasgow | 3 hours |
| Edinburgh | Inverness | 3½ hours |
| Glasgow | Dundee | 1½ hours |

## ROADSIDE EMERGENCIES

For aid if your car breaks down, contact the 24-hour rescue numbers of either the Automobile Association or the Royal Automobile Club. If you're a member of the AAA (American Automobile Association) or another association, check your membership details before you travel; reciprocal agreements may give you free roadside aid.

### EMERGENCY SERVICES

In the U.K. **Automobile Association** (AA ☎08705/500600 ⊕www.theaa.co.uk). **Royal Automobile Club** (RAC ☎08705/722722 ⊕www.rac.co.uk).

In the U.S. **American Automobile Association** (AAA ☎800/564–6222 ⊕www.aaa.com).

## RULES OF THE ROAD

The most noticeable difference for most visitors is that when in Britain, you drive on the left and steer the car on the right. Give yourself time to adjust to driving on the left—especially if you pick up your car at the airport.

One of the most complicated questions facing visitors to Britain is that of speed limits. In urban areas, except for certain freeways, it's generally 30 mph, but it's 40 mph on some main roads, as indicated by circular red-rimmed signs. In rural areas the official limit is 60 mph on ordinary roads and 70 mph on divided highways and motorways—and traffic police can be hard on speeders, especially in urban areas. Driving while using a cell phone is illegal, and the use of seat belts is mandatory for passengers in front and back seats. Service stations and newsstands sell copies of the Highway Code (£1.99), which lists driving rules and has pictures of signs. It's also online at www.highway-code.gov.uk.

Drunk-driving laws are strictly enforced. It's safer to avoid alcohol if you're driving.

## ▌ BY TAXI

In Edinburgh, Glasgow, and the larger cities, taxis with their TAXI sign illuminated can be hailed on the street, or booked by phone (expect a charge). Elsewhere, most communities of any size at all have a taxi service; your hotel will be able to supply telephone numbers. Very often you can find an advertisement for the local taxi service in public phone booths.

## ▌ BY TRAIN

Train service within Scotland is generally run by ScotRail, one of the most efficient of Britain's service providers. Trains are modern, clean, and comfortable. Scotland's rail network extends all the way to Thurso and Wick, the most northerly stations in the British Isles. Low-land services, most of which originate in Glasgow or Edinburgh, are generally fast and reliable. A shuttle makes the 50-minute trip between the cities every half hour. Long-distance services carry buffet and refreshment cars. One word of caution: there are very few trains in the Highlands on Sunday.

*For information about money-saving BritRail passes that must be purchased before your trip, see Train Passes in Booking Your Trip, above.*

## CLASSES

Most trains have first-class and standard-class coaches. First-class coaches are always less crowded; they have wider seats and are often cleaner and less well-worn than standard-class cars, and they're a lot more expensive. However, on weekends you can often upgrade from standard to first class for a small fee (often £5 to £10)—ask at the time of booking.

## FARES & SCHEDULES

The best way to find out which train to take, which station to catch it at, and what times trains travel to your destination is to call National Rail Enquiries. It's a helpful, comprehensive, free service that covers all Britain's rail lines. National Rail will help you choose the best train to take, and then connect you with the ticket office for that train company so that you can buy tickets.

Train fares vary according to class of ticket purchased and distance traveled. Before you buy your ticket, stop at the Information Office/Travel Centre and request the lowest fare to your destination and information about any special offers. There's often little difference between the cost of a one-way and round-trip ticket. So if you're planning on departing from and returning to the same destination, buy a round-trip fare upon your departure, rather than purchasing two separate one-way tickets. It's also much cheaper to buy a one-way or round-trip ticket in advance than on the day of your trip (except for commuter services); the closer to the date of travel, the more expensive the ticket will be.

■**TIP→** Ask the local tourist board about hotel and local transportation packages that include tickets to major museum exhibits or other special events.

**Information National Rail Enquiries** ( ☎08457/484950, 020/7278–5240 outside Britain ⊕www.nationalrail.co.uk). **ScotRail** ( ☎0845/601–5929 ⊕www.firstscotrail.com).

## PAYING
All major credit cards and cash are accepted for train fares paid both in person and by phone.

## RESERVATIONS
Reserving your ticket in advance is always recommended.

Tickets and rail passes do not guarantee seats on the trains. For that you need a seat reservation, which if made at the time of ticket purchase is usually included in the ticket price, or if booked separately, must be paid for at a cost of £1 *per train* on your itinerary. You also need a reservation if you purchase overnight sleeping accommodations.

## FROM ENGLAND
There are two main rail routes to Scotland from the south of England. The first, the west-coast main line, runs from London Euston to Glasgow Central; it takes 5½ hours to make the 400-mi trip to central Scotland, and service is frequent and reliable. Useful for daytime travel to the Scottish Highlands is the direct train to Stirling and Aviemore, terminating at Inverness. For a restful route to the Scottish Highlands, take the overnight sleeper service, with soundproof sleeping carriages. It runs from London Euston, departing in late evening, to Perth, Stirling, Aviemore, and Inverness, where it arrives the following morning.

The east-coast main line from London King's Cross to Edinburgh provides the quickest trip to the Scottish capital. Between 8 AM and 6 PM there are 16 trains to Edinburgh, 3 of them through to Aberdeen. Limited-stop expresses like the *Flying Scotsman* make the 393-mi London-to-Edinburgh journey in around four hours. Connecting services to most parts of Scotland—particularly the Western Highlands—are often better from Edinburgh than from Glasgow.

Trains from elsewhere in England are good: regular service connects Birmingham, Manchester, Liverpool, and Bristol with Glasgow and Edinburgh. From Harwich (the port of call for ships from Holland, Germany, and Denmark), you can travel to Glasgow via Manchester. But it's faster to change at Peterborough for the east-coast main line to Edinburgh.

## SCENIC ROUTES
Although many routes in Scotland run through extremely attractive countryside, several stand out: from Glasgow to Oban via Loch Lomond; to Fort William and Mallaig via Rannoch (ferry connection to Skye); from Edinburgh to Inverness via the Forth Bridge and Perth; from Inverness to Kyle of Lochalsh and to Wick; and from Inverness to Aberdeen.

A private train, the *Royal Scotsman,* does all-inclusive scenic tours, partly under steam power, with banquets en route. This is a luxury experience: some evenings require formal wear. You can customize the length of your trip from two nights (£1,740) to seven nights (£5,140) per person.

**Train Tours The Royal Scotsman** ( ☎0845/077–2222 or 800/524–2420 ⊕www. royalscotsman.com).

# ON THE GROUND

## ■ COMMUNICATIONS

### INTERNET

Make sure your laptop is dual-voltage; most, but not all, laptops operate equally well on 110 and 220 volts and so require only an adapter. Never plug your computer into any socket without first asking about surge protection: although Scotland is computer-friendly, few hotels and B&Bs outside the major cities have built-in current stabilizers. Electrical fluctuations and surges can short your adapter or even destroy your computer, so it's worthwhile to purchase a surge protector in the United Kingdom that plugs into the socket.

All hotels and many B&Bs have facilities for computer users, such as a dedicated PC room or broadband and Wi-Fi services for Internet access.

**Contacts Cybercafes** ( ⊕ www.cybercafes. com) lists over 4,000 Internet cafés worldwide.

### PHONES

The good news is that you can now make a direct-dial telephone call from virtually any point on earth. The bad news? You can't always do so cheaply. Calling from a hotel is almost always the most expensive option; hotels usually add huge surcharges to all calls, particularly international ones. In some countries you can phone from call centers or even the post office. Calling cards usually keep costs to a minimum, but only if you purchase them locally. And then there are mobile phones *(⇨below)*, which are sometimes more prevalent—particularly in the developing world—than land lines; as expensive as mobile-phone calls can be, they are still usually a much cheaper option than calling from your hotel.

When you're calling anywhere in Great Britain from the United States, the country code is 44. When dialing a Scottish or British number from abroad, drop the initial 0 from the local area code. For instance, if you're calling Edinburgh Castle from New York City, dial 011 (the international code), 44 (the Great Britain country code), 131 (the Edinburgh city code), and then 225–9846 (the number proper). In Scotland cellular-phone numbers, the 0800 toll-free code, and local-rate 0345 numbers do not have a 1 after the initial 0, nor do many premium-rate numbers, for example 0891, and special-rate numbers, for example 08705.

Freephone (toll-free) numbers start with 0800 or 0808; national information numbers start with 0845. A word of warning: 0870 numbers are *not* toll-free numbers; in fact, numbers beginning with 0871 or the 0900 prefix are premium-rate numbers, and it costs extra to call them. The amount varies and is usually relatively small when dialed from within the country but can be excessive when dialed from outside the United Kingdom.

### CALLING WITHIN SCOTLAND

Cell phones are popular, but there are three types of public pay phones: those that accept only coins, those that accept only phone cards, and those that take British Telecom (BT) phone cards and credit cards. For coin-only phones, insert coins *before* dialing (minimum charge is 10p). Sometimes phones have a "press on answer" (POA) button, which you press when the caller answers.

All calls are charged according to the time of day. Standard rate is weekdays 8 AM TO 6 PM; cheap rate is weekdays 6 PM TO 8 AM and all day on weekends, when it's even cheaper. A local call from a pay phone before 6 PM costs 30p for three minutes. A daytime call to the United States will cost 24p a minute on a regular phone (weekends are cheaper), 80p on a pay phone.

To call a number with the same area code as the number from which you are dial-

# LOCAL DO'S & TABOOS

### CUSTOMS OF THE COUNTRY

In Scotland it's rude to walk away from conversation, even if it's with someone you don't know. If you're at a pub, keep in mind that it's very important to buy a round of drinks if you're socializing with a group of people. You don't simply buy your own drink; you buy a drink for all of the people you're there with, and those people do the same. It can make for a very foggy evening.

Conversational topics that are considered taboo are money matters; the Scots are quite private about their finances.

### GREETINGS

Although many Scots are fantastic talkers, they're less enthusiastic with greetings on the physical front. If you're in less familiar company, a handshake is more appreciated than a kiss or hug.

### SIGHTSEEING

When you are visiting houses of worship, modest attire is appreciated, though you will see shorts and even bared midriffs. Photographs are welcome in churches, outside of services.

Shorts and other close-fitting attire are allowed just about anywhere at any time, weather permitting; these days locals tend not to cover up as much as they used to.

It's the same with food; Scots eat and drink just about anywhere, and much of the time they do it standing up or even walking.

Local etiquette is strong; you should give up your seats for elderly people or pregnant women without a second thought. Polite driving etiquette is carefully observed; allow people to pass and be courteous. Jaywalking isn't rude or illegal, but it's much safer to cross with the lights, especially if traffic is coming from a direction you might not be used to.

As for waiting in lines and moving through crowds, be courteous. The Scots are very polite and you'll be noticed (and not in a good way) if you're not polite in return.

### OUT ON THE TOWN

People may dress up for a special restaurant or for clubbing, but other people will be casual. Some clubs frown on sneakers.

If you're visiting a family home, a simple bouquet of flowers is a welcome gift. If you're invited for a meal, bringing a bottle of wine is appropriate, if you wish, as is some candy for the children. To thank a host for hospitality, either a phone call or thank-you card is always appreciated.

### DOING BUSINESS

Punctuality is of prime importance, so call ahead if you anticipate a late arrival. Spouses do not generally attend business dinners, unless specifically invited.

If you invite someone to dine, it's usually assumed that you'll pick up the tab. However, if you're the visitor, your host may insist on paying.

### LANGUAGE

The Lowland Scots language, which borrows from Scandinavian, Dutch, French, and Gaelic, survives in various forms but is virtually an underground language, spoken at home among ordinary folk, especially in its heartland, in northeast Scotland. Gaelic, too, hangs on in spite of the Highlands depopulation.

Otherwise, Scots speak English with only an accent (which may be hard for Americans to understand), and virtually all will "modulate" either unconsciously or out of politeness into more understandable English when conversing with a non-Scots speaker.

ing, omit the area-code digits when you dial. A local call before 6 PM costs 15p, 30p from a pay phone.

For long-distance calls within Britain, dial the area code (which usually begins with 01), followed by the telephone number. The area-code prefix is used only when you're dialing from outside the city. In provincial areas the dialing codes for nearby towns are often posted in the booth.

To call the operator, dial 100; directory inquiries (information), 118–500; international directory inquiries, 118–505.

### CALLING OUTSIDE SCOTLAND
The country code for the United States is 1.

To make international calls *from* Scotland, dial 00 + the country code + area code + number. For the international operator, credit card, or collect calls, dial 155.

**Access Codes AT&T Direct** (☎0500/890011 for cable and wireless, 0800/890011 for British Telecom, 0800/0130011 for AT&T, 800/435–0812 for other areas). **MCI World-Phone** (In U.K. ☎0800/890222 to call U.S. via MCI, 800/444–4141 for other areas). **Sprint International Access** (☎0500/890877 cable and wireless, 0800/890877 British Telecom, 800/877–4646 for other areas).

### CALLING CARDS
You can purchase BT (British Telecom) phone cards for use on public phones from shops, post offices, and newsstands. They're ideal for longer calls, are composed of units of 20p, and come in values of £2, £5, £10, and £20. An indicator panel on the phone shows the number of units you've used; at the end of your call the card is returned. Where credit cards are taken, slide the card through, as indicated. Beware of buying cards that require you to dial a free phone number; some of these are not legitimate. It's better to get a BT card.

### MOBILE PHONES
If you have a multiband phone (some countries use different frequencies than what's used in the United States) and your service provider uses the world-standard GSM network (as do T-Mobile, Cingular, and Verizon), you can probably use your phone abroad. Roaming fees can be steep, however: 99¢ a minute is considered reasonable. And overseas you normally pay the toll charges for incoming calls. It's almost always cheaper to send a text message than to make a call, since text messages have a very low set fee (often less than 5¢).

If you just want to make local calls, consider buying a new SIM card (note that your provider may have to unlock your phone for you to use a different SIM card) and a prepaid-service plan in the destination. You'll then have a local number and can make local calls at local rates. If your trip is extensive, you could also simply buy a new cell phone in your destination, as the initial cost will be offset over time.

■TIP→ **If you travel internationally frequently, save one of your old mobile phones or buy a cheap one on the Internet; ask your cell-phone company to unlock it for you, and take it with you as a travel phone, buying a new SIM card with pay-as-you-go service in each destination.**

Cell phones are getting less and less expensive to buy; so much so that it's now cheaper to buy a new cell phone while abroad than it is to rent one. Rates run from as low as £20 a month for unlimited calls with a pay-as-you-go card. Visit or contact one of the cell-phone providers below for more information.

**Contacts Cellular Abroad** (☎800/287–5072 ⊕www.cellularabroad.com) rents and sells GMS phones and sells SIM cards that work in many countries. **Mobal** (☎888/888–9162 ⊕www.mobalrental.com) rents mobiles and sells GSM phones (starting at $49) that will operate in 140 countries. Per-call rates vary throughout the world. **Planet Fone**

(☎888/988–4777 ⊕www.planetfone.com) rents cell phones, but the per-minute rates are expensive.

# ▌CUSTOMS & DUTIES

You're always allowed to bring goods of a certain value back home without having to pay any duty or import tax. But there's a limit on the amount of tobacco and liquor you can bring back duty-free, and some countries have separate limits for perfumes; for exact figures, check with your customs department. The values of so-called "duty-free" goods are included in these amounts. When you shop abroad, save all your receipts, as customs inspectors may ask to see them as well as the items you purchased. If the total value of your goods is more than the duty-free limit, you'll have to pay a tax (most often a flat percentage) on the value of everything beyond that limit.

**Information in Scotland HM Customs and Excise** (☎0845/010–9000, 020/8929–0152 advice service, 020/8929–6731, 020/8910–3602 complaints ⊕www.hmce.gov.uk).

**U.S. Information U.S. Customs and Border Protection** (⊕www.cbp.gov).

# ▌EATING OUT

The restaurants we review in this book are the cream of the crop in each price category. The Scottish food scene has changed dramatically since 2000. Today the traditional Scottish restaurant offers more than fish-and-chips, fried sausage, and black pudding; you'll find the freshest of scallops, organic salmon, wild duck, and free-range Angus beef as well as locally grown vegetables and fruits. Scottish soil produces the fluffiest potatoes, sweetest carrots, and plumpest raspberries you may ever eat. Whether you want to try traditional haggis (usually ground-up sheep's organs cooked with onions, suet, and spices in the animal's stomach) is up to you. But you don't need to limit yourself to Scottish food; some of the Chinese, Greek, Indian, Italian, Japanese, Mexican, Mongolian and Russian restaurants (to name but a few) are superb.

It's not just the urban areas that will spoil you for choice; fabulous restaurants are popping up in the smaller villages as well. Dining in Scotland can be an experience for all the senses, but it is not always cheap; don't forget your credit card. City Scots usually take their midday meals in a pub, wine bar, bistro, or department-store restaurant (which might not serve alcohol). When traveling, Scots generally eat inexpensively and quickly at a country pub or village tearoom. Places like Glasgow, Edinburgh, and Aberdeen have restaurants of cosmopolitan character and various price levels; of these, the more notable tend to open only in the evening.

Note that most pubs do not have any waitstaff, and you're expected to go to the bar and order a beverage and your meal—this can be particularly disconcerting when you're seated in a "restaurant" upstairs but are still expected to go downstairs and get your own drinks and food. You're not expected to tip the bartender, but you are expected to tip restaurant waitstaff, by leaving 10% to 15% of the tab on the table, *only* if SERVICE NOT INCLUDED is stamped on your bill.

Since 2007, smoking has been banned in pubs, clubs, and restaurants throughout Britain.

## MEALS & MEALTIMES

To start the day with a full stomach, try a traditional Scottish breakfast of bacon and fried eggs served with sausage, fried mushrooms and tomatoes, and usually fried bread or potato scones. Most places also serve kippers (smoked herring). All this is in addition to juice, porridge, cereal, toast, and other bread products.

"All-day" meal places are becoming prevalent. The normal lunch period, however, is 12:30 to 2:30. A few places serve high tea—one hot dish and masses of cakes, bread and butter, and jam, served with tea only, around 5:30 to 6:30. Typical dinner times are fairly early, around 5 to 8.

Familiar fast-food chains are often more expensive than a good home-cooked meal in a local café or pub, where large servings of British comfort food—fish-and-chips, stuffed baked potatoes, and sandwiches—are served. In more upscale restaurants, cutting costs can be as simple as requesting *tap* water; "water" means a bottle of mineral water that could cost up to £5.

Unless otherwise noted, the restaurants listed in this guide are open daily for lunch and dinner.

### PAYING

Many restaurants exclude service charges from the printed menu (which the law obliges them to display outside), then add 10% to 15% to the check, or else stamp SERVICE NOT INCLUDED along the bottom, in which case you should add the 10% to 15%. Just don't pay twice for service—unscrupulous restaurateurs have been known to add service but leave the total on the credit-card slip blank.

Credit cards are widely accepted at most types of restaurants.

*For guidelines on tipping, see Tipping below.*

Price charts appear at the start of each chapter or, for Edinburgh and Glasgow, in the "Where to Eat" section.

### RESERVATIONS & DRESS

Regardless of where you are, it's a good idea to make a reservation if you can. We only mention them specifically when reservations are essential (there's no other way you'll ever get a table) or when they are not accepted. For popular restaurants, book as far ahead as you can (often 30 days), and reconfirm as soon as you arrive. (Large parties should always call ahead to check the reservations policy.) We mention dress only when men

---

### WORD OF MOUTH

Was the service stellar or not up to snuff? Did the food give you shivers of delight or leave you cold? Did the prices and portions make you happy or sad? Rate restaurants and write your own reviews in "Travel Ratings" or start a discussion about your favorite places in "Travel Talk" on www.fodors.com. Your comments might even appear in our books. Yes, you, too, can be a correspondent!

---

are required to wear a jacket or a jacket and tie.

Online-reservation services make it easy to book a table before you even leave home. Toptable has listings in many Scottish cities.

**Contacts Toptable** ( ⊕ www.toptable.co.uk).

### WINES, BEER & SPIRITS

Bars and pubs typically sell two kinds of beer: lager is light in color, very carbonated, and served cold, and ale is dark, semicarbonated, and served just below room temperature. You may also come across a pub serving "real ales," which are hand-drawn, very flavorful beers from smaller breweries. These traditionally produced real ales have a fervent following; check out the Campaign for Real Ale's Web site, www.camra.org.uk.

You can order Scotland's most famous beverage—whisky (here, most definitely spelled without an *e*)—at any local pub. All pubs serve any number of single-malt and blended whiskies. It's also possible to tour numerous distilleries, where you can sample a dram and purchase a bottle for the trip home. Most distilleries are concentrated in Speyside (on the Malt Whisky Trail) and Islay.

The legal drinking age in Scotland is 18.

# ELECTRICITY

The electrical current in Scotland, as in the rest of Great Britain, is 240 volts (in line with the rest of Europe), 50 cycles alternating current (AC); wall outlets take three-pin plugs, and shaver sockets take two round, oversize prongs.

Consider making a small investment in a universal adapter, which has several types of plugs in one lightweight, compact unit. Most laptops and mobile-phone chargers are dual voltage (i.e., they operate equally well on 110 and 220 volts), so require only an adapter. These days the same is true of small appliances such as hair dryers. Always check labels and manufacturer instructions to be sure. Don't use 110-volt outlets marked FOR SHAVERS ONLY for high-wattage appliances such as hair dryers.

**Contacts Steve Kropla's Help for World Traveler's** ( ⊕ www.kropla.com) has information on electrical and telephone plugs around the world. **Walkabout Travel Gear** ( ⊕ www.walkabouttravelgear.com) has a good coverage of electricity under "adapters."

# EMERGENCIES

If you need to report an emergency, dial 999 for police, fire, or ambulance. Be prepared to give the telephone number you're calling from. You can get 24-hour treatment in Accident and Emergency at British hospitals, although you should expect to wait hours for treatment. Treatment from the National Health Service is free to British citizens, but as a foreigner, you will be billed after the fact for your care. *See Trip Insurance in Getting Started, above, for more about this subject.* Prescriptions are valid only if made out by doctors registered in the United Kingdom. For additional information, also see the "Essentials" sections at the end of each chapter.

**General Emergency Contacts Ambulance, fire, police** ( ☎ 999).

**U.S. Embassies American Consulate General** ( ✉ 3 Regent Terr., Calton, Edinburgh ☎ 0131/556–8315). **U.S. Embassy** ( ✉ 24 Grosvenor Sq., London ☎ 020/7499–9000); for passports go to the **U.S. Passport Unit** ( ✉ 55 Upper Brook St., London ☎ 020/7499–9000 ⊕ www.usembassy.org.uk).

# HEALTH

*For information on travel insurance, shots and medications, and medical-assistance companies see Things to Consider in Getting Started, above.*

## SPECIFIC ISSUES IN SCOTLAND

If you take prescription drugs, keep a supply in your carry-on luggage and make a list of all your prescriptions to keep on file at home while you are abroad. You will not be able to renew a U.S. prescription at a pharmacy in Britain. Prescriptions are accepted only if issued by a U.K.–registered physician.

If you're traveling in the Highlands and islands in summer, pack some midge repellent and antihistamine cream to reduce swelling: the Highland midge is a force to be reckoned with. Check ⊕ *www.midgeforecast.co.uk* for updates on these biting pests.

## OVER-THE-COUNTER REMEDIES

Over-the-counter medications in England are similar to those in the United States, with a few significant differences. Medications are sold in boxes rather than bottles, and are sold in very small amounts—usually no more than 12 pills per package. There are also fewer brands than you're likely to be used to—you can, for example, find aspirin, but usually only one kind in a store. You can buy generic ibuprofen or a popular European brand of ibuprofen, Nurofen, which is sold everywhere. Tylenol is not sold in the United Kingdom, but its main ingredient, acetaminophen, is—although, confusingly, it's called paracetomol.

Drugstores are generally called pharmacies, but sometimes referred to as chemists' shops. The biggest drugstore chain in the country is Boots, which has outlets everywhere, except for the smallest towns. If you're in a rural area, look for shops marked with a sign of a green cross; almost all small drugstores have one of these.

Supermarkets and news agents all usually have a small supply of cold and headache medicines, often behind the cash register. As in the United States, large supermarkets will have a bigger supply.

# ▌HOLIDAYS

The following days are public holidays in Scotland; note that the dates for England and Wales are slightly different. Ne'er Day and a day to recover (January 1–2), Good Friday, May Day (first Monday in May), Spring Bank Holiday (last Monday in May), Summer Bank Holiday (first Monday in August), St. Andrew's Day (November 30, or the following Monday if this falls on a weekend), and Christmas (December 25–26). Note also that Scottish towns and villages set their own local holidays, on five or six Mondays in spring and summer, varying from town to town.

# ▌HOURS OF OPERATION

Banks are open weekdays 9:30 to 3:30, some days to 4:45. Some banks have extended hours on Thursday evening, and a few are open on Saturday morning. Some also close for an hour at lunchtime. The major airports operate 24-hour banking services seven days a week.

Service stations are at regular intervals on motorways and are usually open 24 hours a day, though stations elsewhere usually close from 9 PM to 7 AM; in rural areas many close at 6 PM and Sunday.

Most museums in cities and larger towns are open daily, although some may be closed on Sunday morning. In smaller villages museums are often open when there

are visitors around—even late on summer evenings—but closed in poor weather, when visitors are unlikely; there's often a contact phone number on the door.

Pharmacies (often called "chemists" in Scotland) usually open 9 to 5 or 5:30 Monday through Saturday, though most large towns and cities have either a large supermarket open extended hours, with a pharmacy on the premises, or have a rotation system for pharmacists on call (there will be a note displayed in the pharmacy's window with the number to call). In rural areas doctors often dispense medicines themselves. In an emergency the police should be able to locate a pharmacist.

Usual business hours are Monday through Saturday 9 to 5 or 5:30. Outside the main centers, most shops observe an early closing day (they close at 1 PM) once a week, often Wednesday or Thursday. In small villages many shops also close for lunch. Department stores in large cities and many supermarkets even in smaller towns stay open for late-night shopping (usually until 7:30 or 8) one or more days a week. Apart from some newsstands and small food stores, many shops close Sunday except in larger towns and cities, where main shopping malls may open.

# ▌MAIL

Stamps may be bought from post offices (open weekdays 9 to 5:30, Saturday 9 to noon), from stamp machines outside post offices, and from news dealers' stores and newsstands. Mailboxes, known as post or letter boxes, are painted bright red; large tubular ones are set on the edge of sidewalks, and smaller boxes are set into post-office walls. Allow at least four days for a letter or postcard to reach the United States by air mail. Surface mail service can take up to four or five weeks.

Airmail letters to the United States cost 54p (under 10 grams) or 78p (under 20 grams); postcards cost 54p. Within the United Kingdom first-class letters cost

34p, second-class letters and postcards 23p. The Rail Mail Web site is ⊕*www. royalmail.com.*

If you're uncertain where you'll be staying, you can arrange to have your mail sent to American Express. The service is free to cardholders; all others pay a small fee. You can also collect letters at any post office by addressing them to poste restante at the post office you nominate. In Edinburgh a convenient central office is St. James Centre Post Office, St. James Centre, Edinburgh, EH1 3SR, Scotland.

### SHIPPING PACKAGES
Most department stores and retail outlets can arrange to ship your goods home. You should check your insurance for coverage of possible damage. If you want to ship goods yourself, use one of the overnight postal services, such as Federal Express, DHL, or TNT.

To find the nearest branch providing overnight mail services, contact the following agencies.

**Express Services DHL** ( ☎08701/100300 ⊕www.dhl.co.uk). **FedEx** ( ☎08456/070809 ⊕www.fedex.com). **TNT** ( ☎0800/100600 ⊕www.tnt.com).

## ▌ MEDIA

### NEWSPAPERS & MAGAZINES
Scotland's major newspapers include the *Scotsman*—a conservative sheet that also styles itself as the journal of record—and the moderate Glasgow-based *Herald*, along with the tabloid *Daily Record*. The leader in terms of circulation, if not downright regional Scottish style, is the Aberdeen-based *Press and Journal*. The *Sunday Post*, conservative in bent, is the country's leading Sunday paper; *Scotland on Sunday* competes directly with London's *Sunday Times* for clout north of the border; and the *Sunday Herald*, an offshoot of the *Glasgow Herald*, is another major title. There are also many regional publications in Scotland; the *List*, a twice-

monthly magazine with listings comparable to London's *Time Out*, covers the Glasgow and Edinburgh scenes. Many Scottish newsstands also feature editions of the leading London newspapers, such as the *London Times*, the *Evening Standard*, the *Independent*, and the *Guardian*; the *Sunday Telegraph* usually has the biggest Scotland coverage.

For magazines the selection is smaller and its purview is less sophisticated. *Heritage Scotland*, a publication of the National Trust, covers the historic preservation beat. *Scottish Homes and Interiors* is devoted to home design and style, and the *Scottish Field* covers matters dealing with the countryside. For more regional coverage check out the glossy *Scottish Life*.

### RADIO & TELEVISION
The Scotland offshoot of the British Broadcasting Corporation, BBC Scotland, is based in Glasgow and has a wide variety of Scotland-based TV programming. BBC Scotland usually feeds its programs into the various BBC channels, including BBC1 and BBC2, the latter considered the more eclectic and artsy, with a higher proportion of alternative humor, drama, and documentaries. Channel 3 is used by independent channels, which can change from region to region in Scotland: Grampian, the Borders, and Scottish are three channels that are regional in focus, with Grampian beamed into the north and west of Scotland and Scottish into the southern regions. Originating in England, Channel 4 is a mixture of mainstream and off-the-wall programming, whereas Channel 5 has more sports and films. Satellite TV has brought dozens more channels to Britain including BBC 3 and BBC 4, which show more experimental, cutting-edge shows than BBC 1 and BBC 2.

Radio has seen a similar explosion for every taste, from 24-hour classics on Classic FM (100–102 MHz) to rock (Richard Branson's Virgin at 105.8 MHz). BBC Radio Scotland is a leading radio station, tops for local news and useful as it provides Scottish (rather than English) weather information. Originating from England—and therefore not always received in regions throughout Scotland—the BBC channels include Channel 1 (FM 97.6) for the young and hip; 2 (FM 88) for middle-of-the-roadsters; 3 (FM 90.2) for classics, jazz, and arts; 4 (FM 92.4) for news, current affairs, drama, and documentaries; and 5 Live (MW 693 kHz) for sports and news coverage, with listener phone-ins.

# ▌MONEY

Prices can seem high in Scotland largely because the exchange rate is so unfavorable for other currencies, especially the U.S. dollar. However, travelers do get some breaks: national museums are free, and staying in a B&B or renting a city apartment brings down lodging costs. The chart below gives some ideas of the kinds of prices you can pay for day-to-day life.

| ITEM | AVERAGE COST |
| --- | --- |
| Cup of Coffee | £1.50 |
| Glass of Wine | £2.20 |
| Glass of Beer | £2.20 |
| Sandwich | £2.00 |
| One-Mile Taxi Ride Edinburgh | £2.20 |
| Newspaper | 40p–60p |

Prices throughout this guide are given for adults. Substantially reduced fees are almost always available for children, students, and senior citizens.

▌TIP→ Banks never have every foreign currency on hand, and it may take as long as a week to order. If you're planning to exchange funds before leaving home, don't wait until the last minute.

## ATMS & BANKS

ATMs are available throughout Scotland at banks and numerous other locations such as railway stations, gas stations, and department stores. Three banks with many branches are Lloyds, Halifax, and the Royal Bank of Scotland. PIN numbers have four or fewer digits.

Your own bank will probably charge a fee for using ATMs abroad; the foreign bank you use may also charge a fee. Nevertheless, you'll usually get a better rate of exchange at an ATM than you will at a currency-exchange office or even when changing money in a bank. And extracting funds as you need them is a safer option than carrying around a large amount of cash.

▌TIP→ PIN numbers with more than four digits are not recognized at ATMs in many countries. If yours has five or more, remember to change it before you leave.

**ATM Locations Cirrus** (☎800/424–7787 ⊕www.mastercard.com). **Plus** (☎800/843–7587 ⊕www.visa.com).

## CREDIT CARDS

Throughout this guide, the following abbreviations are used: **AE**, American Express; **DC**, Diners Club; **MC**, MasterCard; and **V**, Visa.

It's a good idea to inform your credit-card company before you travel, especially if you're going abroad and don't travel internationally very often. Otherwise, the credit-card company might put a hold on your card owing to unusual activity—not a good thing halfway through your trip. Record all your credit-card numbers—as well as the phone numbers to call if your cards are lost or stolen—in a safe place, so you're prepared should something go wrong.

If you plan to use your credit card for cash advances, you'll need to apply for a PIN at least two weeks before your trip. Although it's usually cheaper (and safer) to use a credit card abroad for large purchases (so you can cancel payments or be reimbursed if there's a problem), note that some credit-card companies *and* the banks that issue them add substantial percentages to all foreign transactions, whether they're in a foreign currency or not. Check on these fees before leaving home.

■ TIP→ **Before you charge something, ask the merchant whether he or she plans to do a dynamic currency conversion (DCC). In such a transaction the credit-card** *processor* **(shop, restaurant, or hotel, not Visa or MasterCard) converts the currency and charges you in dollars. In most cases you'll pay the merchant a 3% fee for this service in addition to any credit-card company and issuing-bank foreign-transaction surcharges.**

Dynamic currency conversion programs are becoming increasingly widespread. Merchants who participate in them are supposed to ask whether you want to be charged in dollars or the local currency, but they don't always do so. And even if they do offer you a choice, they may well avoid mentioning the additional surcharges. The good news is that you *do* have a choice. And if this practice really gets your goat, you can avoid it entirely thanks to American Express; with its cards, DCC simply isn't an option.

MasterCard and Visa are the most widely accepted credit cards. American Express is accepted at larger department stores and hotels, but Diners Club is not widely accepted in Scotland.

Reporting Lost Cards **American Express** (☎800/528-4800 in U.S., 336/393-1111 collect from abroad ⊕www.americanexpress.com). **Diners Club** (☎800/234-6377 in U.S., 303/799-1504 collect from abroad ⊕www.dinersclub.com). **MasterCard** (☎800/627-8372 in U.S., 636/722-7111 collect from abroad ⊕www.mastercard.com). **Visa** (☎800/847-2911 in U.S., 410/581-9994 collect from abroad ⊕www.visa.com).

## WORST-CASE SCENARIO

All your money and credit cards have just been stolen. In these days of real-time transactions, this isn't a predicament that should destroy your vacation. First, report the theft of the credit cards. Then get any traveler's checks you were carrying replaced. This can usually be done almost immediately, provided that you kept a record of the serial numbers separate from the checks themselves. If you bank at a large international bank like Citibank or HSBC, go to the closest branch; if you know your account number, chances are you can get a new ATM card and withdraw money right away. **Western Union** (☎800/325-6000 ⊕www.westernunion.com) sends money almost anywhere. Have someone back home order a transfer online, over the phone, or at one of the company's offices, which is the cheapest option. The U.S. State Department's **Overseas Citizens Services** (⊕www.travel.state.gov/travel ☎202/501-4444) can wire money to any U.S. consulate or embassy abroad for a fee of $30. Just have someone back home wire money or send a money order or cashier's check to the state department, which will then disburse the funds as soon as the next working day after it receives them.

## CURRENCY & EXCHANGE

Britain's currency is the pound sterling, which is divided into 100 pence (100p). Bills (called notes) are issued in the values of £50, £20, £10, and £5. Coins are issued in the values of £2, £1, 50p, 20p, 10p, 5p, 2p, and 1p. Scottish coins are the same as English ones, but Scottish notes are issued by three banks: the Bank of Scotland, the Royal Bank of Scotland, and the Clydesdale Bank. They have the same face values as English notes, and English notes are interchangeable with them in Scotland.

At this writing, the exchange rate was U.S. $2.03 to the pound. Britain's entry into the European Union's currency—the euro—continues to be debated.

## TRAVELER'S CHECKS

Some consider this the currency of the cave man, and fewer establishments in Scotland accept traveler's checks these days; think about whether you really want to buy them. Both Citibank (under the Visa brand) and American Express issue traveler's checks in the United States, but Amex is better known and more widely accepted; you can also avoid hefty surcharges by cashing Amex checks at Amex offices. Whatever you do, keep track of all the serial numbers in case the checks are lost or stolen. If you plan to use traveler's checks, buy them in pounds.

Contacts **American Express** (☎888/412–6945 in U.S., 801/945–9450 collect outside of U.S. to add value or speak to customer service ⊕www.americanexpress.com).

## ▌RESTROOMS

Most cities, towns, and villages have public restrooms, indicated by signposts to WC, TOILETS, or PUBLIC CONVENIENCES. They vary hugely in cleanliness. You'll often have to pay a small amount (usually 20p) to enter public conveniences; a request for payment usually indicates a high standard of cleanliness. Gas stations, called petrol stations, also usually have

restrooms (to which the above comments also apply). In towns and cities, department stores, hotels, restaurants, and pubs are usually your best bets for at least reasonable standards of hygiene.

Find a Loo **The Bathroom Diaries** (⊕www. thebathroomdiaries.com) is flush with unsanitized info on restrooms the world over—each one located, reviewed, and rated.

## ▌SAFETY

Overall, Scotland is a very safe country to travel in, but be a cautious traveler and keep your cash, passport, credit cards, and tickets close to you or in a hotel safe. Don't agree to carry anything for strangers. It's a good idea to distribute your cash, credit cards, IDs, and other valuables between a deep front pocket, an inside jacket or vest pocket, and a hidden money pouch. Don't reach for the money pouch once you're in public. Otherwise, you need not avoid wearing jewelry or be wary of passing cyclists snatching your purse. Use common sense as your guide.

## ▌SHOPPING

Tartans, tweeds, and woolens may be a Scottish cliché, but nevertheless the selection and quality of these goods make them a must-have for many visitors, whether a complete made-to-measure traditional kilt outfit or a classy designer sweater from Skye. Particular bargains can be found in Scottish cashmere sweaters; look for Johnstons of Elgin and Ballantyne, two high-quality labels.

Food items are another popular purchase: whether shortbread, smoked salmon, boiled sweets, *tablet* (a type of hard fudge), marmalade and raspberry jams, Dundee cake, or black bun, it's far too easy to eat your way around Scotland.

Unique jewelry is available all over Scotland but especially in some of the remote regions where get-away-from-it-all craftspeople have set up shop amid the idyllic scenery.

Scottish antique pottery and table silver make unusual, if sometimes pricey, souvenirs: a Wemyss-ware pig for the mantelpiece, perhaps, or Edinburgh silver candelabra for the dining table. Antiques shops and one- or two-day antiques fairs held in hotels abound all over Scotland. In general, goods are reasonably priced: shops in small communities must deal fairly if they hope for repeat business. Most dealers will drop the price a little if asked, "What's your best price?"

### KEY DESTINATIONS

For designer clothing, Glasgow is the place to start; the Princes Square mall is an especially rich hunting ground. Buchanan and Sauchiehall streets are good places to head for High Street shops like Monsoon and Next, as are Buchanan Galleries and St. Enoch Shopping Centre. However, if you're coming from the United States you may find clothing rather expensive compared with the prices back home for similar items.

For jewelry, Skye Silver, of Glendale on Skye, and Ola Gorrie at the Longship, of Kirkwall, Orkney, sell particularly attractive and unusual designs. Antique Scottish pebble jewelry is another unique style of jewelry; several specialist antique jewelry shops can be found in Edinburgh and Glasgow.

## ▍SIGHTSEEING PASSES

Discounted sightseeing passes are a great way to save money on visits to castles, gardens, and historic houses. Just check what the pass offers against your itinerary to be sure it's worthwhile.

The Scottish Explorer Ticket, available from any staffed Historic Scotland (HS) property and from many tourist information centers, allows visits to HS properties for 3 days in a 5-day period (£19), 7 days in a 14-day period (£27), or 10 days in a 30-day period (£32). The Trust Discovery Ticket, issued by the National Trust for Scotland, is available for 3 days (£12), 7 days (£17), or 14 days (£22) and allows access to all National Trust for Scotland properties. It's available to overseas visitors only and can be purchased from the National Trust for Scotland online and by phone, or at properties and some of the main tourist information centers.

The Great British Heritage Pass grants you access to sights administered by National Trust for Scotland and Historic Scotland as well as numerous other sights throughout Great Britain. A 7-day pass costs £39; 15-day (£52) and 30-day (£70) passes are also available.

**Discount Passes** **Great British Heritage Pass** ( ⊕ www.britishheritagepass.com). **Historic Scotland** ( ☎ 0131/668–8600 ⊕ www.historic-scotland.gov.uk/explorer). **National Trust for Scotland** ( ☎ 0844/493–2100 ⊕ www.nts.org.uk).

## ▍TAXES

An airport departure tax of £40 (£10 for within U.K. and EU countries) per person is payable, and may be subject to more government increases, although it's included in the price of your ticket.

The British sales tax, V.A.T. (Value-Added Tax), is 17.5%. It's almost always included in quoted prices in shops, hotels, and restaurants. The most common exception is at high-end hotels, where prices often exclude V.A.T. Be sure to verify whether the quoted room price includes V.A.T.

Further details on how to get a V.A.T. refund and a list of stores offering tax-free shopping are available from VisitBritain.

When making a purchase, ask for a V.A.T.–refund form and find out whether the merchant gives refunds—not all stores do, nor are they required to. Have the form stamped like any customs form by customs officials when you leave the country or, if you're visiting several European Union countries, when you leave the EU. After you're through passport control, take the form to a refund-service counter for an on-the-spot refund (which is usually the quickest and easiest option), or mail it to the address on the form (or the envelope with it) after you arrive home. You receive the total refund stated on the form, but the processing time can be long, especially if you request a credit-card adjustment.

Global Refund is a Europe-wide service with 225,000 affiliated stores and more than 700 refund counters at major airports and border crossings. Its refund form, called a Tax Free Check, is the most common across the European continent. The service issues refunds in the form of cash, check, or credit-card adjustment.

**V.A.T. Refunds Global Refund** (☎800/566–9828 ⊕www.globalrefund.com). **VisitBritain** (⊕www.visitbritain.com).

# ▌TIME

Great Britain sets its clocks by Greenwich Mean Time, five hours ahead of the U.S. East Coast. British summer time (GMT plus one hour) requires an additional adjustment from about the end of March to the end of October.

# ▌TIPPING

Tipping is done in Scotland as in theUnited States, but at a lower level. Some restaurants and hotels add a service charge of 10% to 15% to the bill. In this case you aren't expected to tip. Always check first. Taxi drivers, hairdressers, and barbers should also get 10% to 15%. You're not expected to tip theater or movie theater ushers, or elevator operators.

| TIPPING GUIDELINES FOR SCOTLAND | |
|---|---|
| Bartender | £1–£5 depending on the size of the round (in the more modern bars). It's common in traditional pubs to buy the bartender a drink as a tip. |
| Bellhop | £1 to £3 per bag |
| Hotel Concierge | £10 or more, if he or she performs a service for you |
| Hotel Doorman | £2–£5 if he helps you get a cab |
| Hotel Maid | £2–£3 a day (either daily or at the end of your stay, in cash) |
| Hotel Room-Service Waiter | £1 to £2 per delivery, even if a service charge has been added |
| Porter at Airport or Train Station | £1 per bag |
| Skycap at Airport | £1 to £2 per bag checked |
| Taxi Driver | 10%–15%, but round up the fare to the next pound amount |
| Tour Guide | 10% of the cost of the tour, but optional |
| Valet Parking Attendant | £2–£3, but only when you get your car |
| Waiter | 10%–15%, with 15% being the norm at high-end restaurants; nothing additional if a service charge is added to the bill |
| Other | Restroom attendants in more expensive restaurants expect some small change or £1. Tip coat-check personnel at least £1–£2 per item checked unless there's a fee, then nothing. |

# INDEX

## PHOTO CREDITS

# OUT OUR WRITERS

**Nick Bruno** has worked as a tour guide, an English–Italian translator, and as a seller of backpacks and breathable base layers to the masses. Based in Dundee, he writes books and features, contributing to a variety of publications; he also takes photographs. His Fodor's territory included the Edinburgh & the Lothians, Fife & Angus, Around the Great Glen, Northern Highlands & the Western Isles, and Orkney & Shetland chapters, as well as A Golfer's Country.

**Shona Main** grew up in Shetland; after moving to the mainland, she spent some informative years working on magazines for teenagers. She had a brief career in law and politics before she turned to writing. Now based in Dundee, she is a social-work lobbyist as well as a freelance contributor to newspapers and books. Her territory for this edition was Edinburgh & the Lothians, Aberdeen & the Northeast, and Orkney & Shetland.

**Fiona G. Parrott** is a California native who fell in love with Scotland in 1999 and made it her home, traveling the length and breadth of the country. A freelance writer, she contributes regularly to various publications on both sides of the Atlantic. She has lived in Glasgow with her husband and, most recently, two young sons, and spent five years teaching at Glasgow and Strathclyde universities. In 2006 she earned a doctorate from Glasgow University for her travel book on South America. Her contributions to this edition include updating the Glasgow, Borders & the Southwest, Central Highlands, Argyll & the Isles, Understanding Scotland, and Essentials chapters. She has also written for Fodor's *Great Britain*.